Lecture Notes in Computer Science

Commenced Publication in 1973
Founding and Former Series Editors:
Gerhard Goos, Juris Hartmanis, and Jan van Leeuwen

Springer
Berlin
Heidelberg
New York
Hong Kong
London
Milan
Paris
Tokyo

Stefano Berardi Mario Coppo
Ferruccio Damiani (Eds.)

Types for Proofs and Programs

International Workshop, TYPES 2003
Torino, Italy, April 30 - May 4, 2003
Revised Selected Papers

Springer

Volume Editors

Stefano Berardi
Mario Coppo
Ferruccio Damiani
Università di Torino, Dipartimento di Informatica
C. Svizzera 185, 10149 Torino, Italy
E-mail: {berardi, coppo, damiani}@di.unito.it

Library of Congress Control Number: 2004106869

CR Subject Classification (1998): F.3.1, F.4.1, D.3.3, I.2.3

ISSN 0302-9743
ISBN 3-540-22164-6 Springer-Verlag Berlin Heidelberg New York

Springer-Verlag is a part of Springer Science+Business Media

springeronline.com

Typesetting: Camera-ready by author, data conversion by PTP-Berlin, Protago-TeX-Production GmbH
Printed on acid-free paper SPIN: 11012856 06/3142 5 4 3 2 1 0

Preface

These proceedings contain a selection of refereed papers presented at or related to the 3rd Annual Workshop of the Types Working Group (Computer-Assisted Reasoning Based on Type Theory, EU IST project 29001), which was held during April 30 to May 4, 2003, in Villa Gualino, Turin, Italy. The workshop was attended by about 100 researchers. Out of 37 submitted papers, 25 were selected after a refereeing process. The final choices were made by the editors.

Two previous workshops of the Types Working Group under EU IST project 29001 were held in 2000 in Durham, UK, and in 2002 in Berg en Dal (close to Nijmegen), The Netherlands. These workshops followed a series of meetings organized in the period 1993–2002 within previous Types projects (ESPRIT BRA 6435 and ESPRIT Working Group 21900). The proceedings of these earlier workshops were also published in the LNCS series, as volumes 806, 996, 1158, 1512, 1657, 2277, and 2646. ESPRIT BRA 6453 was a continuation of ESPRIT Action 3245, Logical Frameworks: Design, Implementation and Experiments. Proceedings for annual meetings under that action were published by Cambridge University Press in the books "Logical Frameworks", and "Logical Environments", edited by G. Huet and G. Plotkin.

We are very grateful to the members of the research group "Semantics and Logics of Computation" of the Computer Science Department of the University of Turin, who helped organize the Types 2003 meeting in Torino. We especially want to thank Daniela Costa and Claudia Goggioli for the secretarial support, Sergio Rabellino for the technical support, and Ugo de' Liguoro for helping out in various ways.

We also acknowledge the support from the Types Project, EU IST 29001, which makes the Types workshops possible.

March 2004

Stefano Berardi
Mario Coppo
Ferruccio Damiani

Referees

We would like to thank the following people for their kind work in reviewing the papers submitted to these proceedings:

Michael Abbott
Peter Aczel
Robin Adams
Yohji Akama
Fabio Alessi
Thorsten Altenkirch
Chris Andersen
Steffen van Bakel
Clemens Ballarin
Franco Barbanera
Gianpaolo Bella
Gianluigi Bellin
Stefano Berardi
Chantal Berline
Yves Bertot
Frédéric Blanqui
Kim Bruce
Iliano Cervesato
Alberto Ciaffaglione
Norman Danner
Ugo de' Liguoro
Fer-Jan de Vries
Pietro Di Gianantonio
Peter Dybjer
Maribel Fernandez
Jean-Christophe Filliatre
Matthew Flatt
Daniel Fridlender
Herman Geuvers
Pola Giannini
Elio Giovannetti
Adam Grabowsky
Hugo Herbelin
Roger Hindley
Daniel Hirkschoff
Marieke Huisman
Pierre Lescanne
Cedric Lhoussaine
Yong Luo
Zhaohui Luo
Simone Martini
James McKinna
Marino Miculan
Christine Paulin-Mohring
Jens Palsberg
Randy Pollak
Francois Pottier
Frédéric Prost
Christophe Raffalli
Aarne Ranta
Eike Ritter
Simona Ronchi
Pino Rosolini
Luca Roversi
Frédéric Ruyer
Ivan Scagnetto
Vincent Simonet
Jan Smith
Sergei Soloviev
Bas Spitters
Dan Synek
Paul Taylor
Tarmo Uustalu
Femke van Raamsdonk
Jen von Plato
Hongwei Xi
Yamagata Yoriyuki

Table of Contents

A Modular Hierarchy of Logical Frameworks 1
Robin Adams

Tailoring Filter Models 17
Fabio Alessi, Franco Barbanera, Mariangiola Dezani-Ciancaglini

Locales and Locale Expressions in Isabelle/Isar 34
Clemens Ballarin

Introduction to PAF!, a Proof Assistant for ML Programs Verification ... 51
Sylvain Baro

A Constructive Proof of Higman's Lemma in Isabelle 66
Stefan Berghofer

A Core Calculus of Higher-Order Mixins and Classes 83
Lorenzo Bettini, Viviana Bono, Silvia Likavec

Type Inference for Nested Self Types 99
Viviana Bono, Jerzy Tiuryn, Paweł Urzyczyn

Inductive Families Need Not Store Their Indices 115
Edwin Brady, Conor McBride, James McKinna

Modules in Coq Are and Will Be Correct 130
Jacek Chrząszcz

Rewriting Calculus with Fixpoints:
Untyped and First-Order Systems 147
Horatiu Cirstea, Luigi Liquori, Benjamin Wack

First-Order Reasoning in the Calculus of Inductive Constructions 162
Pierre Corbineau

Higher-Order Linear Ramified Recurrence 178
Ugo Dal Lago, Simone Martini, Luca Roversi

Confluence and Strong Normalisation
of the Generalised Multiary λ-Calculus 194
José Espírito Santo, Luís Pinto

Wellfounded Trees and Dependent Polynomial Functors 210
Nicola Gambino, Martin Hyland

Classical Proofs, Typed Processes, and Intersection Types 226
Silvia Ghilezan, Pierre Lescanne

"Wave-Style" Geometry of Interaction Models in Rel
Are Graph-Like Lambda-Models 242
Furio Honsell, Marina Lenisa

Coercions in Hindley-Milner Systems 259
Robert Kießling, Zhaohui Luo

Combining Incoherent Coercions for Σ-Types 276
Yong Luo, Zhaohui Luo

Induction and Co-induction in Sequent Calculus 293
Alberto Momigliano, Alwen Tiu

QArith: Coq Formalisation of Lazy Rational Arithmetic 309
Milad Niqui, Yves Bertot

Mobility Types in Coq 324
Furio Honsell, Ivan Scagnetto

Some Algebraic Structures in Lambda-Calculus
with Inductive Types 338
Sergej Soloviev, David Chemouil

A Concurrent Logical Framework: The Propositional Fragment 355
Kevin Watkins, Iliano Cervesato, Frank Pfenning, David Walker

Formal Proof Sketches 378
Freek Wiedijk

Applied Type System 394
Hongwei Xi

Author Index 409

A Modular Hierarchy of Logical Frameworks

Robin Adams

University of Manchester
robin.adams@ma.man.ac.uk

Abstract. We present a method for defining logical frameworks as a collection of features which are defined and behave independently of one another. Each feature is a set of grammar clauses and rules of deduction such that the result of adding the feature to a framework is a conservative extension of the framework itself. We show how several existing logical frameworks can be so built, and how several much weaker frameworks defined in this manner are adequate for expressing a wide variety of object logics.

1 Introduction

Logical frameworks were invented because there were a large number of differing systems of logic, with no common language or environment for their investigation and implementation. However, we now find ourselves in the same situation with the frameworks themselves. There are many systems that are used as logical frameworks, and it is often difficult to compare them or share results between them. It is often much work to discover whether two frameworks can express the same class of object logics, or whether one is stronger or weaker than the other. If we are interested in metavariables, and we compare Pientka and Pfenning's work [1] with Jojgov's [2], it is difficult to see which differences are due to the different handling of metavariables, and which are due to differences in the underlying logical framework.

To redress this situation somewhat, I humbly present the first steps towards a common scheme within which a surprising number of different frameworks can be fitted. We take a modular approach to the design of logical frameworks, defining a framework by specifying a set of *features*, each of which is defined and behaves independently of the others. Together, all the frameworks that can be built from a given set of features form a *modular hierarchy* of logical frameworks.

We may give an informal definition of a feature thus:

> A *feature* F is a set of grammar clauses and rules of deduction such that, for any logical framework L, the result of adding F to L is a conservative extension of L.

(This cannot be made a formal definition, as we do not (yet) have a notion of "any logical framework".)

S. Berardi, M. Coppo, and F. Damiani (Eds.): TYPES 2003, LNCS 3085, pp. 1–16, 2004.

It is not surprising that features exist — one would expect, for example, that adding a definitional mechanism to a typing system should yield a conservative extension. Perhaps more surprising is the fact that such things as lambda-abstraction can be regarded as features. In fact, we shall show how a logical framework can be regarded as being nothing but a set of features. More precisely, we shall define a system that we call the *basic framework* **BF**, and a number of features that can be added to it, and we shall show how a number of existing frameworks can be built by selecting the appropriate features.

We shall also show that most of these features are unnecessary from the theoretical point of view — that is, a much smaller set of features suffices to express a wide variety of object logics. These 'unnecessary' features may well be desirable for implementation, of course.

It may be asked why we insist that our features always yield conservative extensions. This would seem to be severely limiting; in one's experience with typing systems, rarely are extensions conservative. For typing systems in general, this is true. But I would argue that logical frameworks are an exception. The fact that all the features presented here yield conservative extensions is evidence to this effect. And it would seem to be desirable when working with a logical framework — if we add a feature to widen the class of object logics expressible, for example, we still want the old object logics to behave as they did before.

We suggest that, if this work were taken further, it would be possible and desirable to define mechanisms such as metavariables or subtyping as features, and investigate their properties separately from one another and from any specific framework. If we did this for metavariables, for example, we would then know immediately what the properties of ELF with metavariables were, or Martin-Löf's Theory of Types with metavariables, or ...

2 Logical Frameworks

Let us begin by being more precise as to what we mean by a logical framework.

Broadly speaking, logical frameworks can be used in two distinct ways. The first is to define an object logic by means of a *signature*, a series of declarations of constants, equations, etc. The typable terms under that signature should then correspond to the terms, derivations, etc. of the object logic, using contexts to keep track of free variables and undischarged hypotheses. Examples include the Edinburgh Logical Framework [3] and Martin-Löf's Theory of Types [4]. We shall call a framework used in this way a *logic-modelling* framework.

The second is to use the logical framework as a *book-writing* system, as exemplified by the AUTOMATH family of systems [5]. The most important judgement form in such a framework is that which declares a book correct; the other judgement forms are only needed as auxiliaries for deriving this first form of judgement.

These two kinds of system behave in very similar ways. Any system of one kind can be used as a system of the other, by simply reading 'signature' for 'book', or vice versa. This is a striking fact, considering the difference in use. In a system of the first kind, deriving that a signature is valid is just the first step in using an object logic; in a book-writing system, it is the only judgement form of importance. We shall take advantage of this similarity. Our features shall be written with logic-modelling frameworks in mind; it shall turn out that they are equally useful for building book-writing frameworks.

We consider a *logical framework* to consist of:

1. Disjoint, countably infinite sets of *variables* and *constants.*
2. A number of *syntactic classes* of *expressions*, defined in a BNF-style grammar by a set of *constructors*, each of which forms a member of one class from members of other classes, possibly binding variables.
3. Three syntactic classes that are distinguished as being the classes of *signature declarations*, *context declarations* and *judgement bodies.* Each signature declaration is specified to be either a declaration of a particular constant, or of none. Similarly, each context declaration is specified to be either a declaration of a particular variable or of none.

   We now define a *signature* to be a finite sequence of signature declarations, such that no two declarations are of the same constant. The *domain* of the signature Σ, $\mathrm{dom}\,\Sigma$, is then defined to be the sequence consisting of the constants declared in Σ, in order. Similarly, we define a *context* to be a finite sequence of context declarations, no two of the same variable, and we define its domain similarly.

   Finally, we define a *judgement* to be a string of one of two forms: either

   $$\Sigma \text{ sig}$$

   or

   $$\Gamma \vdash_\Sigma J$$

   where Σ is a signature, Γ a context, and J a judgement body.
4. A set of *defined operations and relations* on terms. Typically, these shall include one or more relations of *reducibility* and *convertibility.*
5. The final component of a logical framework is a set of *rules of deduction* which define the set of *derivable* judgements.

2.1 The Basic Framework BF

As is to be expected, **BF** is a very simple system. It allows: the declaration of variable and constant types; the declaration of variables and constants of a previously declared type; and the assertion that a variable or constant has the type with which it was declared, or is itself a type.

The grammar of **BF** is as follows:

Term	$a ::= x \mid c$
Kind	$A ::= \mathbf{Type} \mid \mathrm{El}(a)$
Signature Declaration	$\delta ::= c : A$ of c
Context Declaration	$\gamma ::= x : A$ of x
Judgement Body	$J ::= \text{valid} \mid A \text{ kind} \mid a : A$

The rules of deduction of **BF** are given in Figure 1.

$$\frac{}{\langle\rangle \text{ sig}} \qquad \frac{\vdash_\Sigma A \text{ kind}}{\Sigma, c : A \text{ sig}} \; (c \notin \text{dom}\,\Sigma)$$

$$\frac{\Sigma \text{ sig}}{\vdash_\Sigma \text{valid}} \qquad \frac{\Gamma \vdash_\Sigma A \text{ kind}}{\Gamma, x : A \vdash_\Sigma \text{valid}} \; (x \notin \text{dom}\,\Gamma)$$

$$\frac{\Gamma \vdash_\Sigma \text{valid}}{\Gamma \vdash_\Sigma c : A} \; (c : A \in \Sigma) \qquad \frac{\Gamma \vdash_\Sigma \text{valid}}{\Gamma \vdash_\Sigma x : A} \; (x : A \in \Gamma)$$

$$\frac{\Gamma \vdash_\Sigma \text{valid}}{\Gamma \vdash_\Sigma \mathbf{Type} \text{ kind}} \qquad \frac{\Gamma \vdash_\Sigma a : \mathbf{Type}}{\Gamma \vdash_\Sigma \text{El}(a) \text{ kind}}$$

Fig. 1. The basic framework **BF**

3 Features and the Modular Hierarchy

A *feature* that *depends* on the logical framework L consists of any number of new entities: new syntactic classes, new constructors, new defined operations and relations and new rules of deduction. The new constructors may take arguments from new classes or those of L, bind new variables or those of L, and return expressions in new classes or those of L. In particular, they may create new signature declarations, context declarations and judgement bodies. Likewise, the new defined operations and relations should be defined on both old and new expressions, and the new rules of deduction may use both old and new judgement forms.

A feature may also introduce *redundancies*. A *redundancy* takes an old constructor and declares that it is to be replaced by a certain expression. That is, the constructor is no longer part of the grammar; wherever it appeared in a defined operation or relation or a rule of deduction, its place is to be taken by the given expression.

Now, if L' is any logical framework that extends L, we define the logical framework $L' + F$ in the obvious manner.

It should be noted that these rules of deduction are assumed to automatically extend themselves when future features are added. For example, if a feature contains the rule of deduction

$$\frac{\Gamma \vdash_\Sigma M : A}{\Gamma \vdash_\Sigma M = M : A}$$

and we later introduce a new constructor for terms M, this rule is assumed to hold for the *new* terms M as well as the old.

(Formally defining features in such a way that this is possible requires explicitly defining classes of *meta-expressions* in the manner of [6]. We shall not go into such details here.)

Finally, we define:

Definition 1. *A feature F that depends on the set of features $\{F_1, F_2, \dots\}$ is a feature that depends on the logical framework*

$$\mathbf{BF} + F_1 + F_2 + \cdots .$$

Thus, if F depends on $\{F_1, F_2, \dots\}$, we can add F to any framework in the hierarchy that contains all of F_1, F_2, ... Note that we do not stipulate in this definition whether the set $\{F_1, F_2, \dots\}$ is finite or infinite.

3.1 Parametrization

The first, and most important, of our features are those which allow the declaration of variables and constants with *parameters.* This mechanism is taken as fundamental by the systems of the AUTOMATH [5] family as well as PAL$^+$ [9], but can be seen as a subsystem of almost all logical frameworks. Parametrization provides a common core, above which the different forms of abstraction (λ-abstraction with typed or untyped domains, and with β- or $\beta\eta$-conversion, as well as PAL$^+$-style abstraction by let-definition) can be built as conservative extensions.

We define a series of features: **SPar** (1), **SPar** (2), **SPar** (3), ... , and also **LPar** (1), **LPar** (2), **LPar** (3), ... These extend one another in the manner shown in Figure 2.

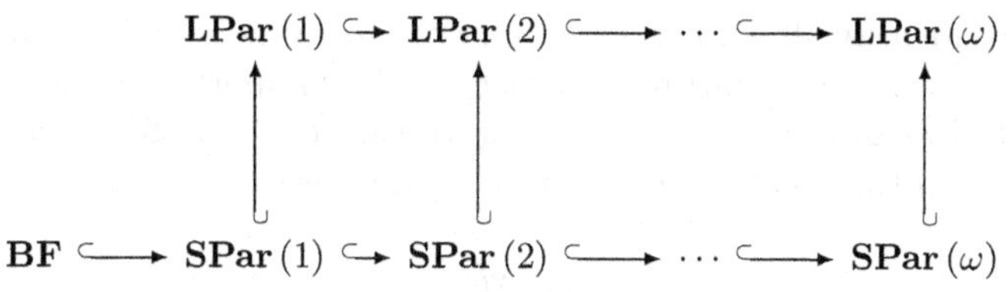

Fig. 2. The initial fragment of the modular hierarchy

BF already allows the declaration of constants in kinds: $c_1 : A$.

LPar (1) allows the declaration of constants in *first-order kinds*: $c_2 : (x_1 : A_1, \dots, x_n : A_n)A$. This declaration indicates that c is a constant that takes *parameters* x_1 of kind A_1, ... , x_n of kind A_n, and returns a term $c_2[x_1, \dots, x_n]$ of kind A.

LPar (2) allows the parameters themselves to have parameters: $c_3 : (x_1 : (x_{11} : A_{11}, \dots, x_{1k_1} : A_{1k_1})A_1, \dots, x_n : (x_{n1} : A_{n1}, \dots, x_{nk_n} : A_{nk_n})A_n)A$. **LPar** (3) allows these second-order parameters to have parameters, and so on. Similarly for declaration of variables.

We also define the feature **LPar** (ω) to be the union of all these features, allowing any level of parametrization.

The sequence of features **SPar** (n) is similar; the only difference is that, in **SPar** (n), every parameter must be in a *small* kind; that is, each A_i, A_{ij}, ... above must be of the form $\mathrm{El}(a)$; it cannot be **Type**. (In **SPar** (n), A itself, the rightmost kind, can be **Type** in the declaration of a constant, but not in a declaration of a variable.)

The full details of these features are as follows:

Parameters in Small Kinds, SPar (n)

Grammar Before we can introduce the new grammar constructors, we need to make a few definitions.

We define an m-th order *pure context* by recursion on m as follows. An m-th order pure context is a string of the form

$$(x_1 : (\Delta_1)\,\mathrm{El}(a_1), \ldots, x_k : (\Delta_k)\,\mathrm{El}(a_k))$$

where each x_i is a variable, all distinct, Δ_i a pure context of order $< m$, and a_i a term. Its *domain* is $(x_1, \ldots, x_k)$.

We define an *abstraction* to be a string of the form

$$[\boldsymbol{x}]M$$

where $\boldsymbol{x}$ is a sequence of distinct variables, and M a term. We take each member of $\boldsymbol{x}$ to be bound within M in this abstraction, and we define free and bound variables and identify all our expressions up to α-conversion in the usual manner. We write $\hat{}M, \hat{}N, \ldots$ for arbitrary abstractions. It is important to note that these are *not* first-class objects of every framework that contains **SPar** (n).

Now, we add the following clause to the grammar:

$$z[\hat{}\boldsymbol{M}]$$

is a term, where z is a variable or constant, and $\hat{}\boldsymbol{M}$ a sequence of abstractions.. This clause subsumes the grammar of **BF**, for $x()$ and $c()$ are terms when x is a **0**-ary variable and c a **0**-ary constant.

We also allow declarations of the form

$$c : (\Delta)A$$

in the signature, where c is a constant, Δ a pure context of order $\leq n$, and A a kind; and those of the form

$$x : (\Delta)\,\mathrm{El}(a)$$

in the context, where x is a variable, Δ a pure context of order $\leq n$, and a a term. Again, these subsume those of **BF**.

Defined Operations We define the operation of *instantiation* as follows. This operation takes the place of substitution; we cannot substitute for a variable of kind $(\Delta)A$, as we have no first-class objects in such a kind — indeed, we have no such kind yet. But it is possible define a term

$$\{\hat{}M_1/x_1, \ldots, \hat{}M_m/x_m\}M$$

where M is a term, and, for $i = 1, \ldots, m$, $\hat{}M_i \equiv [\boldsymbol{y_i}]M_i$ is an abstraction, and x_i a variable, in such a way that first-class abstractions are never needed. They can, later, be added as a conservative extension. It may aid the understanding of the definition of instantiation to note that, once abstractions are added,

$$\{\hat{}M_1/x_1, \ldots, \hat{}M_m/x_m\} \text{ is the normal form of } [\hat{}M_1/x_1, \ldots, \hat{}M_m/x_m]$$

The definition is as follows:

$$\{\hat{}\boldsymbol{M}/\boldsymbol{x}\}z(\hat{}\boldsymbol{N}) \equiv z(\{\hat{}\boldsymbol{M}/\boldsymbol{x}\}\hat{}\boldsymbol{N})$$
$$\text{(if } z \text{ is a constant or a variable not in } \boldsymbol{x}\text{)}$$
$$\{\hat{}\boldsymbol{M}/\boldsymbol{x}\}x_i(\hat{}\boldsymbol{N}) \equiv \{\{\hat{}\boldsymbol{M}/\boldsymbol{x}\}\hat{}\boldsymbol{N}/\boldsymbol{y_i}\}M_i$$

We also need a defined judgement form. If $\hat{}\boldsymbol{M}$ is an abstraction sequence, and Δ a pure context, we define a set of judgements

$$\Gamma \Vdash_\Sigma \hat{}\boldsymbol{M} :: \Delta$$

(read: under signature Σ and context Γ, $\hat{}\boldsymbol{M}$ *satisfies* Δ). The definition is as follows. Let

$$\Delta \equiv x_1 : (\Delta_1)\,\mathrm{El}(a_1), \ldots, x_m : (\Delta_m)\,\mathrm{El}(a_m)$$

and let

$$\hat{}M_i \equiv [\boldsymbol{y_i}]M_i\,.$$

We take $\Gamma \Vdash_\Sigma \hat{}\boldsymbol{M} :: \Delta$ to be defined only when $\boldsymbol{y_i} \equiv \Delta_i$ for all i.

$$\Gamma \Vdash_\Sigma \hat{}\boldsymbol{M} :: \Delta$$

is the following set of judgements:

$$\Gamma, \Delta_1 \vdash_\Sigma M_1 : \mathrm{El}(a_1)$$
$$\Gamma, \{\hat{}M_1/x_1\}\Delta_2 \vdash_\Sigma M_2 : \mathrm{El}(\{\hat{}M_1/x_1\}a_2)$$
$$\Gamma, \{\hat{}M_1/x_1, \hat{}M_2/x_2\}\Delta_3 \vdash_\Sigma M_3 : \mathrm{El}(\{\hat{}M_1/x_1, \hat{}M_2/x_2\}a_3)$$
$$\vdots$$
$$\Gamma, \{\hat{}M_1/x_1, \ldots, \hat{}M_{m-1}/x_{m-1}\}\Delta_m \vdash_\Sigma M_m : \mathrm{El}(\{\hat{}M_1/x_1, \ldots, \hat{}M_{m-1}/x_{m-1}\}a_m)$$

In the case $m = 0$, we take $\Gamma \Vdash_\Sigma \hat{}\boldsymbol{M} :: \Delta$ (i.e. $\Gamma \Vdash_\Sigma \langle\rangle :: \langle\rangle$) to be the single judgement

$$\Gamma \vdash_\Sigma \text{valid}\,.$$

Rules of Deduction The rules of deduction in **SPar** (n) are as follows:

$$\frac{\Delta \vdash_{\Sigma} \text{valid}}{\Sigma, c : (\Delta)\mathbf{Type} \text{ sig}} (c \notin \operatorname{dom} \Sigma) \qquad \frac{\Delta \vdash_{\Sigma} a : \mathbf{Type}}{\Sigma, c : (\Delta) \operatorname{El}(a) \text{ sig}} (c \notin \operatorname{dom} \Sigma)$$

$$\frac{\Gamma, \Delta \vdash_{\Sigma} a : \mathbf{Type}}{\Gamma, x : (\Delta) \operatorname{El}(a) \vdash_{\Sigma} \text{valid}} (x \notin \operatorname{dom} \Gamma)$$

$$\frac{\Gamma \Vdash_{\Sigma} \hat{}\boldsymbol{M} :: \Delta}{\Gamma \vdash_{\Sigma} c[\hat{}\boldsymbol{M}] : \{\hat{}\boldsymbol{M} / \operatorname{dom} \Delta\} A} (c : (\Delta)A \in \Sigma)$$

$$\frac{\Gamma \Vdash_{\Sigma} \hat{}\boldsymbol{M} :: \Delta}{\Gamma \vdash_{\Sigma} x[\hat{}\boldsymbol{M}] : \operatorname{El}(\{\hat{}\boldsymbol{M} / \operatorname{dom} \Delta\} a)} (x : (\Delta) \operatorname{El}(a) \in \Gamma)$$

Finally, **SPar** (ω) is defined to be the union of all the features **SPar** (n).

Parameters in Large Kinds, LPar (n) The features **LPar** (n) and **LPar** (ω) are defined in exactly the same manner as **SPar** (n) and **SPar** (ω), with only two differences. The first is the definition of pure context, which now allows **Type** to appear:

An *m-th order pure context* is a string of the form

$$(x_1 : (\Delta_1)A_1, \dots, x_k : (\Delta_k)A_k)$$

where each x_i is a variable, all distinct, Δ_i is a pure context of order $< m$, and A_i is either **Type** or $\operatorname{El}(a_i)$ for some term a_i.

The second is that large kinds are permitted in context declarations as well as signature declarations; that is, we allow declarations of the form $x : (\Delta)A$ in the context, where x is a variable, Δ a pure context of appropriate order, and A either **Type** or $\operatorname{El}(a)$ for some term a.

3.2 Lambda Abstraction

We can now, if we wish, build in traditional λ-abstraction. It should be noted that this does not change the class of object theories that can be expressed by the framework.

We can make these abstractions typed or untyped (i.e. explicitly include the domain or not), and we can choose to use β or $\beta\eta$-conversion. These two choices lead to four features that can be added to a framework. We shall denote them $\lambda^{\mathrm{t}}_{\beta}$, $\lambda^{\mathrm{ut}}_{\beta}$, $\lambda^{\mathrm{t}}_{\beta\eta}$, $\lambda^{\mathrm{ut}}_{\beta\eta}$. We shall give here the details of $\lambda^{\mathrm{t}}_{\beta}$; the others are very similar.

We shall describe here a feature $\lambda^{\mathrm{t}}_{\beta}$ to be built on top of **BF** + **LPar** (ω). It would be easy to change the details to give a feature that could be added to **BF** + **LPar** (n), **BF** + **SPar** (n), or **BF** + **SPar** (ω).

We add the following clauses to the grammar:

$$\begin{array}{ll} \text{Term} & M ::= \cdots \mid [x:A]M \mid M[M] \\ \text{Kind} & A ::= \cdots \mid (x:A)A \end{array}$$

There are two redundancies in the feature $\lambda^{\mathrm{t}}_{\beta}$. The first: let c be a constant, where Let

$$c : (x_1 : (\Delta_1)A_1, \ldots, x_m : (\Delta_m)A_m)A$$

be in the signature, where

$$\Delta_i \equiv (x_{i1} : (\Delta_{i1})A_{i1}, \ldots, x_{ik_i} : (\Delta_{ik_i})A_{ik_i})A_i \,.$$

Then we identify the term

$$c[[\boldsymbol{x_1}]M_1, \ldots, [\boldsymbol{x_m}]M_m]$$

with the base term

$$\begin{array}{l} c[[x_{11} : (\Delta_{11})A_{11}] \cdots [x_{1k_1} : (\Delta_{1k_1})A_{1k_1}]M_1] \cdots \\ \quad [[x_{m1} : (\Delta_{m1})A_{m1}] \cdots [x_{mk_m} : (\Delta_{mk_m})A_{mk_m}]M_m] \end{array}$$

The second is a similar redundancy for terms beginning with a variable.

We define the relations of β-reduction, β-conversion, etc. on our classes of terms in the usual manner, based on the contraction

$$([x : (\Delta)A]M)[N] \rightsquigarrow_{\beta} [N/x]M \,.$$

The rules of deduction in $\lambda^{\mathrm{t}}_{\beta}$ are now:

$$\frac{\Gamma, x : A \vdash_{\Sigma} B \text{ kind}}{\Gamma \vdash_{\Sigma} (x : A)B \text{ kind}}$$

$$\frac{\vdash_{\Sigma} A \text{ kind}}{\Sigma, c : A \text{ sig}}\,(c \notin \operatorname{dom} \Sigma) \qquad \frac{\Gamma \vdash_{\Sigma} A \text{ kind}}{\Gamma, x : A \vdash_{\Sigma} \text{valid}}\,(x \notin \operatorname{dom} \Gamma)$$

$$\frac{\Gamma, x : A \vdash_{\Sigma} M : B}{\Gamma \vdash_{\Sigma} [x : A]M : (x : A)B} \qquad \frac{\Gamma \vdash_{\Sigma} M : (x : A)B \quad \Gamma \vdash_{\Sigma} N : A}{\Gamma \vdash_{\Sigma} M[N] : [N/x]B}$$

$$\frac{\Gamma \vdash_{\Sigma} M : A \quad \Gamma \vdash_{\Sigma} B \text{ kind}}{\Gamma \vdash_{\Sigma} M : B}\,(A =_{\beta} B)$$

3.3 Other Features

We present a summary of other features in Figures 3 and 4. Each of these features depends on **SPar** (ω). It would be easy enough to write a version dependent on **SPar** (n) for some finite n.

Global Definition of Constants, **cdef** Depends on **SPar** (ω).

$$\text{Signature Declaration } \gamma ::= \cdots \mid c^{\alpha}[\Delta^{\alpha}] := M : A$$

If $c[\Delta] := M : A$ is in the signature, the following is a reduction rule:

$$c[\hat{}\mathbf{N}] \rightsquigarrow_{\delta_c} \{\hat{}\mathbf{N}/\operatorname{dom}\Delta\}$$

$$\frac{\Delta \vdash_{\Sigma} M : A}{\Sigma, c[\Delta] := M : A \text{ sig}} (c \notin \operatorname{dom}\Sigma) \qquad \frac{\Gamma \vdash_{\Sigma} M : A \quad \Gamma \vdash_{\Sigma} B \text{ kind}}{\Gamma \vdash_{\Sigma} M : B} (\Gamma \vdash_{\Sigma} A =_{\delta_c} B)$$

$$\frac{\Gamma \Vdash_{\Sigma} \hat{}\mathbf{N} :: \Delta}{\Gamma \vdash_{\Sigma} c[\hat{}\mathbf{N}] : \{\hat{}\mathbf{N}/\operatorname{dom}\Delta\}A} (c[\Delta] := M : A \in \Sigma)$$

Global Definition of Variables, **vdef** Depends on **SPar** (ω).

$$\text{Context Declaration } \delta ::= \cdots \mid x^{\alpha}[\Delta^{\alpha}] := M : A$$

If $x^{\alpha}[\Delta^{\alpha}] := M^{\beta} : A^{\beta}$ is in the context, the following is a reduction rule:

$$x[\hat{}\mathbf{N}] \rightsquigarrow_{\delta_v} \{\hat{}\mathbf{N}/\operatorname{dom}\Delta\}M$$

$$\frac{\Gamma, \Delta \vdash_{\Sigma} M : A}{\Gamma, x[\Delta] := M : A \vdash_{\Sigma} \text{valid}} (x \notin \operatorname{dom}\Gamma) \qquad \frac{\Gamma \vdash_{\Sigma} M : A \quad \Gamma \vdash_{\Sigma} B \text{ kind}}{\Gamma \vdash_{\Sigma} M : B} (\Gamma \vdash_{\Sigma} a =_{\delta_v} b)$$

$$\frac{\Gamma \Vdash_{\Sigma} \hat{}\mathbf{N} :: \Delta}{\Gamma \vdash_{\Sigma} x[\hat{}\mathbf{N}] : \{\hat{}\mathbf{N}/\operatorname{dom}\Delta\}A} (x[\Delta] := M : A \in \Gamma)$$

Local Definitions, **let** Depends on **vdef**.

$$\begin{array}{ll} \text{Term} & M ::= \cdots \mid \text{let}\, x^{\alpha}[\Delta^{\alpha}] := M : A \,\text{in}\, M \\ \text{Kind} & A ::= \cdots \mid \text{let}\, x^{\alpha}[\Delta^{\alpha}] := M : A \,\text{in}\, A \end{array}$$

$$\begin{array}{l} \text{let}\, v[\Delta] = M : A \,\text{in}\, N \rightsquigarrow_{\delta} \{[\operatorname{dom}\Delta]M/v\}N \\ \text{let}\, v[\Delta] = M : A \,\text{in}\, K \rightsquigarrow_{\delta} \{[\operatorname{dom}\Delta]M/v\}K \end{array}$$

$$\frac{\Gamma, v[\Delta] = M : A \vdash_{\Sigma} K \text{ kind}}{\Gamma \vdash_{\Sigma} \text{let}\, v[\Delta] = M : A \,\text{in}\, K \text{ kind}} \qquad \frac{\Gamma \vdash_{\Sigma} M : A \quad \Gamma \vdash_{\Sigma} B \text{ kind}}{\Gamma \vdash_{\Sigma} M : B} (A =_{\delta} B)$$

$$\frac{\Gamma, v[\Delta] = M : A \vdash_{\Sigma} N : K}{\Gamma \vdash_{\Sigma} \text{let}\, v[\Delta] = M : A \,\text{in}\, N : \text{let}\, v[\Delta] = M : A \,\text{in}\, K}$$

Fig. 3. Miscellaneous features

Judgemental Equality, **eq** Depends on **SPar** (ω).

$$\begin{array}{ll} \text{Judgement body} & J ::= \cdots \mid M = M : A \mid A = A \\ \text{Signature declaration} & \delta ::= \cdots \mid (\Delta)(M = M : A) \end{array}$$

$$\frac{\Gamma \vdash_\Sigma M : A \quad \Gamma \vdash_\Sigma N : A}{\Gamma \vdash_\Sigma M = N : A}\ (M = N) \qquad \frac{\Gamma \vdash_\Sigma A \text{ kind} \quad \Gamma \vdash_\Sigma B \text{ kind}}{\Gamma \vdash_\Sigma A = B}$$

$$\frac{\Delta \vdash_\Sigma M : A \quad \Delta \vdash_\Sigma N : A}{\Sigma, (\Delta)(M = N : A) \text{ sig}}$$

$$\frac{\Gamma \Vdash_\Sigma \hat{}\boldsymbol{P} :: \Delta}{\Gamma \vdash_\Sigma \{\hat{}\boldsymbol{P}/ \operatorname{dom} \Delta\}M = \{\hat{}\boldsymbol{P}/ \operatorname{dom} \Delta\}N : \{\hat{}\boldsymbol{P}/ \operatorname{dom} \Delta\}A}\ ((\Delta)(M = N : A) \in \Sigma)$$

$$\frac{\Gamma \vdash_\Sigma M = N : A}{\Gamma \vdash_\Sigma N = M : A} \qquad \frac{\Gamma \vdash_\Sigma M = N : A \quad \Gamma \vdash_\Sigma N = P : A}{\Gamma \vdash_\Sigma M = P : A}$$

$$\frac{\Gamma \vdash_\Sigma A = B}{\Gamma \vdash_\Sigma B = A} \qquad \frac{\Gamma \vdash_\Sigma A = B \quad \Gamma \vdash_\Sigma B = C}{\Gamma \vdash_\Sigma A = C}$$

$$\frac{\Gamma \vdash_\Sigma M : A \quad \Gamma \vdash_\Sigma A = B}{\Gamma \vdash_\Sigma M : B} \qquad \frac{\Gamma \vdash_\Sigma M = N : A \quad \Gamma \vdash_\Sigma A = B}{\Gamma \vdash_\Sigma M = N : B}$$

Fig. 4. Miscellaneous features

3.4 Conservativity Results

The guiding principle behind the modular hierarchy is that the features are defined, and behave, independently of one another. The formal result that corresponds to this principle is:

Theorem 1. *If L is a logical framework in the hierarchy, and F a feature such that every feature on which F depends is present in L, then $L + F$ is a conservative extension of L.*

This theorem can be proven for the finitely many features we have presented in this paper. We prove that, if J is a judgement of L derivable in $L + F$, then J is derivable in L, by direct induction on the derivation of J in $L + F$. The only non-trivial cases are the conversion rules; these require the Church-Rosser property to be proven for the set of typable terms. This is never too demanding;

even the case of $\beta\eta$-conversion can be handled using, for example, the techniques of [7], because the frameworks, as type systems, are very simple: there is a single predicative universe and no reflection.

4 Existing Logical Frameworks

We show here how several existing logical frameworks are equivalent to systems that are built out of the features we have introduced. As well as the frameworks we have already mentioned, we deal with Luo's frameworks LF [8].

$$\begin{aligned}
\text{PAL} &= \mathbf{BF} + \mathbf{LPar}\,(1) + \mathbf{cdef} \\
\text{AUT-68} &\simeq \mathbf{BF} + \mathbf{SPar}\,(\omega) + \lambda^{\mathtt{t}}_{\beta} + \mathbf{LPar}\,(1) + \mathbf{cdef} \\
\text{AUT-QE} &\simeq \mathbf{BF} + \mathbf{LPar}\,(\omega) + \lambda^{\mathtt{t}}_{\beta} + \mathbf{cdef} \\
\text{ELF} &= \mathbf{BF} + \mathbf{SPar}\,(\omega) + \lambda^{\mathtt{t}}_{\beta} \\
\text{Martin-Löf's Theory of Types} &= \mathbf{BF} + \mathbf{LPar}\,(\omega) + \lambda^{\mathtt{ut}}_{\beta\eta} + \mathbf{eq} \\
\text{LF} &= \mathbf{BF} + \mathbf{LPar}\,(\omega) + \lambda^{\mathtt{t}}_{\beta\eta} + \mathbf{eq}
\end{aligned}$$

(Note: in the second line, the version of $\lambda^{\mathtt{t}}_{\beta}$ included is built on top of $\mathbf{SPar}\,(\omega)$ only, not $\mathbf{LPar}\,(1)$. $AUT-68$ allows the declaration of constants with first-order parameters, but does not allow such lambda-abstractions to be formed.)

The notion of equivalence with which we are working is the possiblity of defining a translations between the members of the syntactic classes of the two frameworks, such that the translate of each rule of deduction of one is admissible in the other, and which are inverses of one another up to the relevant notion of convertibility within each framework.

For the lines in which we have used an equality sign, such translations can be given; the correspondence between the existing framework and the one produced by the hierarchy is fairly close. For the first two 'AUT-' frameworks, the correspondence is not nearly as neat. There is a correspondence between the hierarchy framework and a *variant* of the AUTOMATH framework. This variant removes the distinction between, for example, the constant defined by

$$(\mathbf{0}, x, -, A), (x, c, \mathtt{PN}, B)$$

(defining c with *parameter* $x : A$ inside the kind B) and that defined by

$$(\mathbf{0}, c, \mathtt{PN}, [x : A]B)$$

(defining c with no parameters inside the kind $[x : A]B$). It also replaces AUTOMATH's system of declaring variables with a more orthodox system of contexts.

It is possible to make the correspondence in these two cases better; and it is also possible to tighten the other four, so that the translations are inverses up to identity (that is, α-conversion), not just convertibility. However, doing so requires a large number of features to be defined, with hair-splitting distinctions being made between them. It is not at all clear that the advantages are worth this cost.

To build PAL$^+$ in the hierarchy, there are two possibilities. Firstly, we could write a feature that introduces classes of α-ary terms and kinds for every arity α, in a similar manner to $\lambda^{\mathrm{t}}_{\beta}$, but the only such terms are the α-ary variables and constants. Then we could build on top of this a features similar to **vdef** and **let**, but allowing global and local definitions of any arity term and kind. Putting these three features on top of $\mathbf{BF} + \mathbf{LPar}\,(\omega) + \mathbf{eq}$ yields a framework equivalent to PAL$^+$.

Alternatively, we could build features similar to **vdef** and **let** on top of $\mathbf{BF}{+}\mathbf{LPar}\,(\omega){+}\mathbf{eq}{+}\lambda^{\mathrm{t}}_{\beta\eta}$, including a redundancy that identifies $[x_1 : A_1] \cdots [x_n : A_n]M$ with $\mathrm{let}\, v[x_1 : A_1, \ldots , x_n : A_n] = M : A \,\mathrm{in}\, v$, where A is an inferred kind for M.

5 Use of Frameworks

Note that all the existing frameworks we have considered (with the notable exception of PAL) use either $\mathbf{SPar}\,(\omega)$ or $\mathbf{LPar}\,(\omega)$. This is natural if one is approaching frameworks from the point of view of the lambda calculus; these are the easiest features to define as (say) PTSs. However, it is overkill. For:

Theorem 2.
- *The grammar of propositional logic, and Hilbert-style rules of inference, are representable in* $\mathbf{BF} + \mathbf{SPar}\,(1)$.
- *The grammar of predicate logic, and natural deduction-style rules of inference, are representable in* $\mathbf{BF} + \mathbf{SPar}\,(2)$.
- *Martin-Löf's Theory of Sets is representable in* $\mathbf{BF} + \mathbf{LPar}\,(2) + \mathbf{eq}$.

We only have space here to partially justify a few of these claims. We shall show how to build an arbitrary first-order theory in $\mathbf{BF} + \mathbf{SPar}\,(2)$, and how W-types are built within $\mathbf{BF} + \mathbf{LPar}\,(2) + \mathbf{eq}$.

For a first-order theory in $\mathbf{BF} + \mathbf{SPar}\,(2)$, the signature consists of:

$$\begin{aligned}
\mathrm{term} &: \mathbf{Type} \\
F &: (x_1 : \mathrm{El}(\mathrm{term}),\ \ldots,\ x_n : \mathrm{El}(\mathrm{term}))\,\mathrm{El}(\mathrm{term}) \\
&\quad \text{for each } n\text{-ary function symbol } F \text{ in the language} \\
\mathrm{prop} &: \mathbf{Type} \\
P &: (x_1 : \mathrm{El}(\mathrm{term}),\ \ldots,\ x_n : \mathrm{El}(\mathrm{term}))\,\mathrm{El}(\mathrm{prop}) \\
&\quad \text{for each } n\text{-ary predicate symbol } P \text{ in the language} \\
\rightarrow &: (x : \mathrm{El}(\mathrm{prop}),\ y : \mathrm{El}(\mathrm{prop}))\,\mathrm{El}(\mathrm{prop})
\end{aligned}$$

$$
\begin{aligned}
\forall &: (p : (x : \mathrm{El}(\mathrm{term}))\,\mathrm{El}(\mathrm{prop}))\,\mathrm{El}(\mathrm{prop}) \\
\mathrm{Prf} &: (x : \mathrm{El}(\mathrm{prop}))\mathbf{Type} \\
\to I &: (p, q : \mathrm{El}(\mathrm{prop}),\ H : (x : \mathrm{El}(\mathrm{Prf}[p]))\,\mathrm{El}(\mathrm{Prf}[q]))\,\mathrm{El}(\mathrm{Prf}[\to [p, q]]) \\
\to E &: (p, q : \mathrm{El}(\mathrm{prop}),\ H_1 : \mathrm{El}(\mathrm{Prf}[\to [p, q]]),\ H_2 : \mathrm{El}(\mathrm{Prf}[p]))\,\mathrm{El}(\mathrm{Prf}[q]) \\
\forall I &: (p : (x : \mathrm{El}(\mathrm{term}))\,\mathrm{El}(\mathrm{prop}),\ H : (x : \mathrm{El}(\mathrm{term}))\,\mathrm{El}(\mathrm{Prf}[p[x]]))\,\mathrm{El}(\mathrm{Prf}[\forall[p]]) \\
\forall E &: (p : (x : \mathrm{El}(\mathrm{term}))\,\mathrm{El}(\mathrm{prop}),\ t : \mathrm{El}(\mathrm{term}),\ H : \mathrm{El}(\mathrm{Prf}[\forall[p]]))\,\mathrm{El}(\mathrm{Prf}[p[t]])
\end{aligned}
$$

Theorem 3. *1. There is a bijection ρ between the terms with free variables among $x_1, \ldots, x_n$ in the first-order language, and the terms M such that*

$$x_1 : \mathrm{El}(\mathrm{term}), \ldots, x_n : \mathrm{El}(\mathrm{term}) \vdash_\Sigma M : \mathrm{El}(\mathrm{term})$$

2. There is a bijection σ between the formulas with free variables among x_1, …, x_n in the first-order language, and the terms M such that

$$x_1 : \mathrm{El}(\mathrm{term}), \ldots, x_n : \mathrm{El}(\mathrm{term}) \vdash_\Sigma M : \mathrm{El}(\mathrm{prop})$$

3. Let ϕ, ψ_1, …, ψ_m be formulas with free variables among $x_1, \ldots, x_n$. Then ϕ is provable from hypothese ψ_1, …, ψ_m iff there is a term M such that

$$
\begin{aligned}
x_1 : \mathrm{El}(\mathrm{term}), \ldots, x_n : \mathrm{El}(\mathrm{term}), y_1 : \mathrm{El}(\mathrm{Prf}[\sigma(\psi_1)]), \ldots, y_m : \mathrm{El}(\mathrm{Prf}[\sigma(\psi_m)]) \\
\vdash_\Sigma M : \mathrm{El}(\mathrm{Prf}[\sigma(\phi)])
\end{aligned}
$$

Notice that the correspondance between the entities of the object logic and the terms of the logical framework is a bijection up to *identity* (that is, α-conversion), not up to convertibility; indeed, in a framework whose only features are **SPar** (n) and **LPar** (n), there is no such thing as convertibility. This theorem is much easier to prove than most adequacy theorems, because the correspondence between the framework and the object logic is so much closer than in a traditional logical framework.

We now show how to build W-types within **BF** + **LPar** (2) + **eq**. In the following, we shall suppress instances of El, and use η-contractions; e.g. we write $W[A, B]$ for $W[A, [x : A]B[x]]$.

$$
\begin{aligned}
W &: (A : \mathbf{Type},\ B : (A)\mathbf{Type})\mathbf{Type}, \\
\sup &: (A : \mathbf{Type},\ B : (A)\mathbf{Type},\ a : A,\ b : (B[a])W[A, B])W[A, B] \\
E_W &: (A : \mathbf{Type},\ B : (A)\mathbf{Type},\ C : (W[A, B])\mathbf{Type}, \\
&\qquad f : (x : A,\ y : (B[x])W[A, B], \\
&\qquad g : (v : B[x])C[y[v]])C[\sup[A, B, x, y]], \\
&\qquad z : W[A, B])C[z],
\end{aligned}
$$

$$
\begin{aligned}
&(A : \mathbf{Type},\ B : (A)\mathbf{Type},\ C : (W[A, B])\mathbf{Type}, \\
&f : (x : A,\ y : (B[x])W[A, B],\ g : (v : B[x])C[y[v]])C[\sup[A, B, x, y]], \\
&a : A,\ b : (B[a])W[A, B]) \\
&\quad E_W[A, B, C, f, g, \sup[A, B, a, b]] = f[a, b, [v : B[x]]E_W[A, B, C, f, g, y[v]]] \\
&\quad : C[\sup[A, B, a, b]]
\end{aligned}
$$

6 Conclusion

We have given a modular method for defining logical frameworks, and shown that it captures, up to a reasonable notion of equivalence, several existing logical frameworks. It has revealed common subsystems between these frameworks that may not otherwise have been found — it is doubtful, for example, that one would have discovered the fact that there is a system $\mathbf{BF} + \mathbf{SPar}(\omega)$ which can be conservatively embedded in both ELF and Martin-Löf's Theory of Types without this work. It has revealed much weaker frameworks than we are accustomed to using, that may prove advantageous for theoretical work, such as proving adequacy theorems. And, finally, it may yet provide a method for defining features in a generic manner such that they can be added to any logical framework, and their properties studied independently of any framework.

Future and Related Work

The only work of a similar nature of which I am aware is the Tinkertype system [10]. There are striking similarities between the two systems. However, I believe this work is different in character. Tinkertype's features cannot be defined separately, and do not behave independently; they certainly do not always yield conservative extensions. While this would not be a desideratum for type systems in general, as with which Tinkertype deals, I believe it is important for logical frameworks.

In the future, as well as the obvious matters of defining more features, capturing more aspects of logical frameworks, and exploring the properties of features independently of one another, it would be interesting to see if we could lay down general conditions C_1, C_2, ... on features, and prove results such as:

> Any feature with conditions C_1, C_2, ... yields a conservative extension of any framework composed solely of features that satisfy conditions C_1, C_2, ...

It would also be interesting to see if we could prove generalised adequacy results using the hierarchy, and give general definitions of semantics for an object theory and prove generalised soundness and completeness results.

References

1. Pientka, B., Pfenning, F.: Optimizing higher-order pattern unification (2003)
2. Jojgov, G.I.: Holes with binding power. In: Types for Proofs and Programs: International Workshop, TYPES 2002, Berg en Dal, The Netherlands, April 24-28, 2002. Selected Papers. Volume 2646 of LNCS., Springer-Verlag Heidelberg (2003) 162 - 181
3. Harper, R., Honsell, F., Plotkin, G.: A framework for defining logics. In: Proceedings 2nd Annual IEEE Symp. on Logic in Computer Science, LICS'87, Ithaca, NY, USA, 22–25 June 1987, New York, IEEE Computer Society Press (1987) 194–204

4. Nordström, B., Petersson, K., Smith, J.: Programming in Martin-Löf's Type Theory. an Introduction. Oxford University Press (1990)
5. Nederpelt, R.P., Geuvers, J.H., Vrijer, R.C.D., eds.: Selected Papers on AUTOMATH. Number 133 in Studies in Logic and the Foundations of Mathematics. North-Holland (1994)
6. Klop, J.W., van Oostrom, V., van Raamsdonk, F.: Combinatory reduction systems: introduction and survey. Theoretical Computer Science **121** (1993) 279–308
7. Ghani, N.: Eta-expansions in dependent type theory — the calculus of constructions. In de Groote, P., Hindley, J.R., eds.: Proceedings of the Third International Conference on Typed Lambda Calculus and Applications (TLCA'97), Nancy, France, Springer-Verlag LNCS 1210 (1997) 164–180
8. Luo, Z.: Computation and Reasoning: A Type Theory for Computer Science. Number 11 in International Series of Monographs on Computer Science. Oxford University Press (1994)
9. Luo, Z.: PAL$^+$: a lambda-free logical framework. Journal of Functional Programming **13** (2003) 317–338
10. Levin, M.Y., Pierce, B.C.: Tinkertype: A language for playing with formal systems. Technical report (2000)

Tailoring Filter Models

Fabio Alessi[1], Franco Barbanera[2]*, and Mariangiola Dezani-Ciancaglini[3]**

[1] Dipartimento di Matematica e Informatica, Via delle Scienze, 206 33100 Udine (Italy)
alessi@dimi.uniud.it

[2] Dipartimento di Matematica e Informatica, Viale A.Doria, 6 95125 Catania (Italy)
barba@dmi.unict.it

[3] Dipartimento di Informatica, Corso Svizzera, 125 10149 Torino (Italy)
dezani@di.unito.it

Abstract. Conditions on type preorders are provided in order to characterize the induced filter models for the λ-calculus and some of its restrictions. Besides, two examples are given of filter models in which not all the continuous functions are representable.

1 Introduction

The semantics of the λ-calculus can be looked at from several points of view. A possible one considers a model as an abstract way of handling and dealing with the syntax. This is the point of view of those investigations looking for extensions of the λ-calculus such that the intended semantical domain turns out to be fully abstract w.r.t. the calculus.

From another point of view, instead, the semantics is seen mainly as a tool to confirm one's "syntactic intuitions" and to prove properties of the calculus. According to this latter viewpoint, "semantically oriented" extensions of a calculus are not always commendable. The focus is on the calculus: the model has to fit as tight as possible the calculus, not vice versa. This is indeed the point of view of the present paper, and, in general, the one of an investigation we are carrying on, started in a companion paper [3]. In such a research we try to devise a general setting and uniform tools to "tailor" models closely fitting as many as possible aspects of the computational paradigm embodied by the λ-calculus.

One of the most natural framework for such an investigation is the typing discipline with *Intersection Types*. Intersection type assignment systems allow to characterize many of the most important *denotational* (as well as *operational*) properties of λ-terms. In particular it is possible to describe, in a *natural* and *finitary* way, many semantic domains for the λ-calculus. Such finitary descriptions allow not only to analyze pre-existing models, but also to modify them, sometimes "tailoring" them according to one's needs (see [6,10,14,18,17,22,5,12] and the references there.)

Finitary characterizations of models for the λ-calculus, the so called *filter models*, can be obtained by simply introducing specific constants, typing rules and type preorders

* Partially supported by MURST project NAPOLI.

** Partially supported by EU within the FET - Global Computing initiative, project DART ST-2001-33477, and by MURST Cofin'02 project McTati. The funding bodies are not responsible for any use that might be made of the results presented here.

S. Berardi, M. Coppo, and F. Damiani (Eds.): TYPES 2003, LNCS 3085, pp. 17–33, 2004.

in a basic intersection type assignment system. An element of a particular domain, representing the denotational meaning of a term M, comes then out to correspond to the set of types that can be inferred for M.
In [3] we have characterized those intersection type assignment systems aiming, in perspective, at providing finitary descriptions of filter models validating in a precise way the notions of β and η reduction and expansion for the whole λ-calculus, as well as some of their restrictions, like β_v [21], β-**I** [11] and β-**KN** [17].

The present paper keeps on the same direction by proving a number of characterization results for filter λ-structures induced by type preorders.
Since any type preorder can induce a particular filter λ-structure, it is possible to "tailor" particular models by providing suitable conditions on the inducing type preorders. Our first "tailoring" result characterizes those type preorders inducing λ-structures in which relevant sets of functions can be represented. A second result characterizes λ-structures which are models of the whole λ-calculus. In a third result we characterize those filter λ-structures which are also models of the aforementioned restricted λ-calculi: the call-by-value λ-calculus, the λ**I**-calculus, the λ**KN**-calculus. The result is also extended to the extensional models.

A further "tailoring" result of the present paper concerns the possibility of "trimming" something that is usually overabundant in filter models: the set of the representable functions. Such a task is not a trivial one in the intersection filters setting. In fact in any filter model introduced in the literature, but the one in [8], any continuous function is representable. Our contribution to this task is the construction of type preorders inducing filter models of the whole λ-calculus in which not all continuous functions are representable. The proofs of this property will profit from the characterization results of the paper.

We shall assume the reader to be acquainted with the main concepts concerning the λ-calculus and its models. The paper will be structured as follows: in Section 2 we recall the notions of intersection type language, type preorder and type assignment system, while the definitions of filter λ-structure and filter model will be recalled in Section 3. The four characterization results will form the subject of Section 4. In Section 5 we shall define two particular preorders in whose induced filter models only a proper subset of the continuous functions is representable.

2 Intersection Types Languages and Type Assignments

Intersection types, the building blocks for the filter models, are syntactical objects built by closing a given set $\mathbb{C}$ of *type atoms* (constants) under the *function type* constructor $\rightarrow$ and the *intersection type* constructor $\cap$.

Definition 1 (Intersection type language). *The* intersection type language *over* $\mathbb{C}$, *denoted by* $\mathbb{T} = \mathbb{T}(\mathbb{C})$ *is defined by the following abstract syntax:*

$$\mathbb{T} = \mathbb{C} \mid \mathbb{T}\rightarrow\mathbb{T} \mid \mathbb{T} \cap \mathbb{T}.$$

Much of the expressive power of intersection type languages comes from the fact that they are endowed with a *preorder relation*, $\leq$, which induces, on the set of types, the structure of a meet semi-lattice with respect to $\cap$.

Definition 2 (Intersection type preorder). *An* intersection type preorder *is a pair* $(\mathbb{C}, \leq)$ *where* $\mathbb{C}$ *is a set of type constants and* $\leq$ *is a binary relation over* $\mathbb{T} = \mathbb{T}(\mathbb{C})$ *satisfying the following set of axioms and rules:*

$$(\textit{refl})\ A \leq A \qquad (\textit{idem})\ A \leq A \cap A$$

$$(\textit{incl}_L)\ A \cap B \leq A \qquad (\textit{incl}_R)\ A \cap B \leq B$$

$$(\textit{mon})\ \frac{A \leq A' \quad B \leq B'}{A \cap B \leq A' \cap B'} \qquad (\textit{trans})\ \frac{A \leq B \quad B \leq C}{A \leq C}$$

$$(\Omega)\ \textit{if}\ \Omega \in \mathbb{C} \quad A \leq \Omega \qquad (\nu)\ \textit{if}\ \nu \in \mathbb{C} \quad A \to B \leq \nu$$

NOTATION. - Σ will be short for $(\mathbb{C}, \leq)$.
- $A \sim B$ will be short for $A \leq B \leq A$.
- Since $\cap$ is commutative and associative (modulo $\sim$), we shall write $\bigcap_{i \leq n} A_i$ for $A_1 \cap \ldots \cap A_n$. Similarly we shall write $\cap_{i \in I} A_i$, where I denotes always a finite set. Moreover we make the convention that $\cap_{i \in \emptyset} A_i$ is Ω when $\Omega \in \mathbb{C}$.
- We shall denote by $\leq_\nabla$ the type preorder generated by a recursive set ∇ of axioms and rules of the shape $A \leq B$ (where ∇ it is said to generate $\leq$ if $A \leq B$ holds if and only if it can be derived from the axioms and rules of ∇ together with those in Definition 2). The constants in ∇ will be denoted by $\mathbb{C}^\nabla$.
- When we consider an intersection type preorder of the form $(\mathbb{C}^\nabla, \leq_\nabla)$, we shall write $\mathbb{T}^\nabla$ and Σ^∇ for $\mathbb{T}(\mathbb{C}^\nabla)$ and $(\mathbb{C}^\nabla, _\nabla)$, respectively.
- $A_\nabla B$ will be short for $A_\nabla B_\nabla A$.
- We write "the type preorder Σ validates ∇" to mean that all axioms and rules of ∇ are admissible.[1]

Figure 1 lists a few special purpose axioms and rules which have been considered in the literature. Their meaning can be grasped if we consider types to denote subsets of a domain of discourse and we look at $\to$ as the function space constructor in the light of Curry-Scott semantics, see [23].

$(\Omega\text{-}\eta)$	$\Omega \leq \Omega \to \Omega$	$(\to\text{-}\cap)$	$(A \to B) \cap (A \to C) \leq A \to B \cap C$
$(\Omega\text{-}\textit{lazy})$	$A \to B \leq \Omega \to \Omega$	(η)	$\dfrac{A' \leq A \quad B \leq B'}{A \to B \leq A' \to B'}$

Fig. 1. Possible Axioms and Rules concerning $\leq$.

We can introduce now four significant intersection type preorders which have been extensively considered in the literature. The order is logical, rather than historical, and the references define the corresponding filter models: [9], [14], [1], [6]. A richer list of type preorders can be found in [3]. These preorders are of the form $\Sigma^\nabla = (\mathbb{C}^\nabla, \leq_\nabla)$, with various different names ∇, picked for mnemonic reasons. In Figure 2 we list their sets of constants $\mathbb{C}^\nabla$ and their sets ∇ of extra axioms and rules taken from Figure 1. Here $\mathbb{C}_\infty$ is an infinite set of fresh atoms (i.e. different from Ω, ν).

[1] Recall that a rule is *admissible* in a system if, for each instance of the rule, if its premises are derivable in the system then so is its conclusion.

$\mathbb{C}^{\mathcal{CDV}} = \mathbb{C}_\infty$	$\mathcal{CDV} = \{(\to\text{-}\cap), (\eta)\}$
$\mathbb{C}^{\mathcal{EHR}} = \{\nu\}$	$\mathcal{EHR} = \mathcal{CDV} \cup \{(\nu)\}$
$\mathbb{C}^{\mathcal{AO}} = \{\Omega\}$	$\mathcal{AO} = \mathcal{CDV} \cup \{(\Omega), (\Omega\text{-}lazy)\}$
$\mathbb{C}^{\mathcal{BCD}} = \{\Omega\} \cup \mathbb{C}_\infty$	$\mathcal{BCD} = \mathcal{CDV} \cup \{(\Omega), (\Omega\text{-}\eta)\}$

Fig. 2. Particular Atoms, Axioms and Rules.

2.1 Particular Classes of Type Preorders

In this subsection we introduce important classes of type preorders. The first two are the classes of *natural* type preorders and of *strict natural* type preorders. These are *disjoint* classes, whose relevance lies in their allowing various characterizations in terms of approximable mappings and λ-structures.

Definition 3 ((Strict) Natural type preorders).
Let $\Sigma = (\mathbb{C}, \leq)$ be a type preorder.
(i) Σ *is* strict natural *if $\Omega \notin \mathbb{C}$ and it validates $\mathcal{CDV}$ as defined in Figure 2.*
(ii) Σ *is* natural *if $\Omega \in \mathbb{C}$ and it validates $\mathcal{AO}$ as defined in Figure 2.*

Naturality for type preorders has a strong semantic flavour. If we look at intersection as representing join and at arrow types as representing functions, then rule $(\to\text{-}\cap)$ reflects the join property of step functions with the same antecedent ($(d \Rightarrow e) \sqcup (d \Rightarrow e') \sqsupseteq d \Rightarrow (e \sqcup e')$), rule (η) reflects the order relation between step functions ($d' \sqsubseteq d$ and $e \sqsubseteq e'$ imply $d \Rightarrow e \sqsubseteq d' \Rightarrow e'$), and rule ($\Omega$-*lazy*) reflects the fact that $\bot \Rightarrow \bot$ is the bottom function.

Among the type preorders of Figure 2, $\mathcal{CDV}$, $\mathcal{EHR}$ are strict natural, and $\mathcal{AO}$, $\mathcal{BCD}$ are natural.

Notice that by the implicit assumption that axiom $(\nu) \in \Sigma$ whenever $\nu \in \mathbb{C}^\Sigma$ (Definition 2) a strict natural type theory containing the constant ν validates $\mathcal{EHR}$.

We introduce two other interesting classes of preorders playing a crucial role in the characterization results of Section 4.

Definition 4 (Beta and eta preorders).
Let $\Sigma = (\mathbb{C}, \leq)$ be a type preorder and $\mathbb{T} = \mathbb{T}(\mathbb{C})$.
(i) Σ *is* beta *iff for all $I, A_i, B_i, C, D \in \mathbb{T}$:*

$$\bigcap_{i \in I}(A_i \to B_i) \leq C \to D \implies \bigcap_{i \in J} B_i \leq D \text{ where } J = \{i \in I \mid C \leq A_i\}.$$

(ii) Σ *is* eta *iff for all $\psi \in \mathbb{C}$ at least one of the following conditions hold:*
1) $\nu \leq \psi$;
2) there exist $I, A_i, B_i \in \mathbb{T}$ such that $\bigcap_{i \in I}(A_i \to B_i) \leq \psi$ and $B_i \sim \Omega$ for all $i \in I$;
3) there exist non empty families of types $\{A_i, B_i\}_{i \in I}$, $\{D_{i,j}, E_{i,j}\}_{j \in J_i}$ in $\mathbb{T}$ such that

$$\bigcap_{i \in I}(A_i \to B_i) \leq \psi \leq \bigcap_{i \in I}(\bigcap_{j \in J_i}(D_{i,j} \to E_{i,j})) \;\&$$
$$\forall i \in I.\ A_i \leq \bigcap_{j \in J_i} D_{i,j} \;\&\; \bigcap_{j \in J_i} E_{i,j} \leq B_i.$$

The condition for a natural type theory of being beta reflects the criterion used to establish if a sups of step functions is greater than a step function (see [15]).

When $\Sigma = \Sigma^{\nabla}$ it is usually possible to prove the conditions defined above by induction on the derivation of judgments. For the type preorders of Figure 2 we get that they are all beta and $\mathcal{EHR}$, $\mathcal{AO}$ are eta.

2.2 Intersection Type Assignments

We introduce now the notion of *intersection type assignment system*. First we need a few preliminary definitions. Let *Var* denote the set of term variables.

Definition 5 (Type assignment system).

(i) *A* basis *over $\mathbb{C}$ is a set of statements of the shape $x{:}B$, where the* subjects x *are in Var, the* predicates B *are in $\mathbb{T}(\mathbb{C})$, and all subjects are distinct variables.*

(ii) *An* intersection-type assignment system *relative to $\Sigma = (\mathbb{C}, \leq)$, denoted by $\lambda\cap^{\Sigma}$, is a formal system for deriving judgments of the form $\Gamma \vdash^{\Sigma} M : A$, where the* subject M *is an untyped λ-term, the* predicate A *is in $\mathbb{T}(\mathbb{C})$, and Γ is a basis over $\mathbb{C}$.*

NOTATION. We shall write:

- $x{\in}\Gamma$ as short for $(x : A){\in}\Gamma$ for some A;
- $\Gamma, x{:}A$ as short for $\Gamma \cup \{x{:}A\}$, proviso $x{\notin}\Gamma$.

We use $\uplus$ to denote the union between bases defined by:

$$\begin{aligned}\Gamma_1 \uplus \Gamma_2 = &\{(x{:}\tau) \mid (x{:}\tau){\in}\Gamma_1 \& x{\notin}\Gamma_2\} \cup \\ &\{(x{:}\tau) \mid (x{:}\tau){\in}\Gamma_2 \& x{\notin}\Gamma_1\} \cup \\ &\{(x{:}\tau_1 \cap \tau_2) \mid (x{:}\tau_1){\in}\Gamma_1 \& (x{:}\tau_2){\in}\Gamma_2\}\end{aligned}$$

A term M is said to be *typable* in $\lambda\cap^{\Sigma}$, for a given basis Γ, if there is a type $A{\in}\mathbb{T}(\mathbb{C})$ such that the judgment $\Gamma \vdash^{\Sigma} M : A$ is derivable.

Various type assignment systems can be defined, each of them parametrized w.r.t a particular Σ=($\mathbb{C}$, $\leq$). The simplest system is given in the following definition.

Definition 6 (Basic type assignment system).
Given a type preorder Σ, the axioms and rules of the basic type assignment system, *denoted by $\lambda\cap^{\Sigma}_{\mathcal{B}}$, for deriving judgments $\Gamma \vdash^{\Sigma}_{\mathcal{B}} M : A$, are the following:*

$$(\mathrm{Ax}) \quad \Gamma \vdash^{\Sigma}_{\mathcal{B}} x{:}A \quad \text{if } (x{:}A){\in}\Gamma$$

$$(\to\mathrm{I})\ \frac{\Gamma, x{:}A \vdash^{\Sigma}_{\mathcal{B}} M : B}{\Gamma \vdash^{\Sigma}_{\mathcal{B}} \lambda x.M : A{\to}B} \qquad (\to\mathrm{E})\ \frac{\Gamma \vdash^{\Sigma}_{\mathcal{B}} M : A \to B \quad \Gamma \vdash^{\Sigma}_{\mathcal{B}} N : A}{\Gamma \vdash^{\Sigma}_{\mathcal{B}} MN : B}$$

$$(\cap\mathrm{I})\ \frac{\Gamma \vdash^{\Sigma}_{\mathcal{B}} M : A \quad \Gamma \vdash^{\Sigma}_{\mathcal{B}} M : B}{\Gamma \vdash^{\Sigma}_{\mathcal{B}} M : A \cap B} \qquad (\leq)\ \frac{\Gamma \vdash^{\Sigma}_{\mathcal{B}} M : A \quad A \leq B}{\Gamma \vdash^{\Sigma}_{\mathcal{B}} M : B}$$

If $\Omega{\in}\mathbb{C}$, a natural choice is to set Ω as the universal type of all λ-terms. This amounts to modify the basic type assignment system by adding a suitable axiom for Ω.

Definition 7 **(Ω-type assignment system).**
*Given a type preorder $\Sigma = (\mathbb{C}, \leq)$ with $\Omega \in \mathbb{C}$, the axioms and rules of the Ω-*type assignment system *(denoted $\lambda\cap^{\Sigma}_{\Omega}$), for deriving judgments of the form $\Gamma \vdash^{\Sigma}_{\Omega} M : A$, are those of the basic one, plus the further axiom*

$$(Ax\text{-}\Omega)\ \Gamma \vdash^{\Sigma}_{\Omega} M : \Omega.$$

Analogously to the case of Ω, when $\nu \in \mathbb{C}$, it is natural to consider ν as the universal type for abstractions, hence modifying the basic system by the addition of a special axiom for ν.

Definition 8 **(ν-type assignment system).**
*Given a type preorder $\Sigma = (\mathbb{C}, \leq)$ with $\nu \in \mathbb{C}$, the axioms and rules of the ν-*type assignment system *(denoted $\lambda\cap^{\Sigma}_{\nu}$), for deriving judgements of the form $\Gamma \vdash^{\Sigma}_{\nu} M : A$, are those of the basic one, plus the further axiom*

$$(Ax\text{-}\nu)\ \ \Gamma \vdash^{\Sigma}_{\nu} \lambda x.M : \nu.$$

For simplicity we assume the symbols Ω and ν to be reserved for the universal type constants respectively used in the systems $\lambda\cap^{\Sigma}_{\Omega}$ and $\lambda\cap^{\Sigma}_{\nu}$, i.e. we forbid $\Omega \in \mathbb{C}$ or $\nu \in \mathbb{C}$ when we deal with $\lambda\cap^{\Sigma}_{\mathcal{B}}$.

NOTATION. - $\lambda\cap^{\Sigma}$ will range over $\lambda\cap^{\Sigma}_{\mathcal{B}}$, $\lambda\cap^{\Sigma}_{\Omega}$ and $\lambda\cap^{\Sigma}_{\nu}$. More precisely we assume that $\lambda\cap^{\Sigma}$ stands for $\lambda\cap^{\Sigma}_{\Omega}$ whenever $\Omega \in \mathbb{C}$, for $\lambda\cap^{\Sigma}_{\nu}$ whenever $\nu \in \mathbb{C}$, and for $\lambda\cap^{\Sigma}_{\mathcal{B}}$ otherwise. Similarly for $\vdash^{\Sigma}$.
- When $\Sigma = \Sigma^{\nabla}$ we shall denote $\lambda\cap^{\Sigma}$ and $\vdash^{\Sigma}$ by $\lambda\cap^{\nabla}$ and $\vdash_{\nabla}$, respectively.

It is easy to prove that the following rules are admissible in $\lambda\cap^{\Sigma}$.

$$(\text{W})\ \frac{\Gamma \vdash^{\Sigma} M : A \quad x \notin \Gamma}{\Gamma, x{:}B \vdash^{\Sigma} M : A} \qquad (\text{C})\ \frac{\Gamma, x{:}B \vdash^{\Sigma} M : A \quad \Gamma \vdash^{\Sigma} N : B}{\Gamma \vdash^{\Sigma} M[x := N] : A}$$

$$(\text{S})\ \frac{\Gamma, x{:}B \vdash^{\Sigma} M : A \quad x \notin \text{FV}(M)}{\Gamma \vdash^{\Sigma} M : A} \qquad (\leq\text{L})\ \frac{\Gamma, x{:}B \vdash^{\Sigma} M : A \quad C \leq B}{\Gamma, x{:}C \vdash^{\Sigma} M : A}$$

As usual a generation lemma is handy: its proof can be found in [4].

Lemma 1 **(Generation lemma).**
Let $\Sigma = (\mathbb{C}, \leq)$ be a type preorder and $\mathbb{T} = \mathbb{T}(\mathbb{C})$.
(i) *Assume $A \not\sim \Omega$. Then $\Gamma \vdash^{\Sigma} x : A$ iff $(x{:}B) \in \Gamma$ and $B \leq A$ for some $B \in \mathbb{T}$.*
(ii) *Assume $A \not\sim \Omega$. Then $\Gamma \vdash^{\Sigma} MN : A$ iff $\Gamma \vdash^{\Sigma} M : B_i \to C_i$, $\Gamma \vdash^{\Sigma} N : B_i$, and $\bigcap_{i \in I} C_i \leq A$ for some I and $B_i, C_i \in \mathbb{T}$.*
(iii) *Assume $\nu \not\leq A$. Then $\Gamma \vdash^{\Sigma} \lambda x.M : A$ iff $\Gamma, x{:}B_i \vdash^{\Sigma} M : C_i$, and $\bigcap_{i \in I}(B_i \to C_i) \leq A$ for some I and $B_i, C_i \in \mathbb{T}$.*

3 Filter λ-Structures and (Restricted) Filter Models

It is possible to use intersection types for building models for λ-calculus and some of its restrictions. Let us first recall the general notion of restricted λ-calculus.

Definition 9 (Restricted λ-calculus). *Let* $\mathbb{R} \subseteq \{\langle(\lambda x.M)N, M[x := N]\rangle \mid M, N \in \Lambda\}$. *The* restricted λ-calculus $\lambda_{\mathbb{R}}$ *is the calculus obtained from the standard λ-calculus by restricting the β-rule to the redexes in* $\mathbb{R}$ *(called β-*$\mathbb{R}$*-redexes).*

Next definition of (*restricted*) model is a generalization of the classical notion of model for the untyped λ-calculus of Hindley-Longo (see [16]).

Definition 10 ((Restricted) models). *A* model for the (restricted) λ-calculus $\lambda_{\mathbb{R}}$ consists of a triple $\langle \mathcal{D}, \cdot, [\![\ ]\!]^{\mathcal{D}} \rangle$ such that $\mathcal{D}$ is a set, $\cdot : \mathcal{D} \times \mathcal{D} \to \mathcal{D}$, $Env : Var \to \mathcal{V}$ for some $\mathcal{V} \subseteq \mathcal{D}$ and the interpretation function $[\![\ ]\!]^{\mathcal{D}} : \Lambda \times Env \to \mathcal{D}$ satisfies:

(i) $[\![x]\!]^{\mathcal{D}}_{\rho} = \rho(x)$;
(ii) $[\![MN]\!]^{\mathcal{D}}_{\rho} = [\![M]\!]^{\mathcal{D}}_{\rho} \cdot [\![N]\!]^{\mathcal{D}}_{\rho}$;
(iii) $[\![\lambda x.M]\!]^{\mathcal{D}}_{\rho} \cdot [\![N]\!]^{\mathcal{D}}_{\rho} = [\![M]\!]^{\mathcal{D}}_{\rho[x:=[\![N]\!]^{\mathcal{D}}_{\rho}]}$ *for* $\langle(\lambda x.M)N, M[x := N]\rangle \in \mathbb{R}$;
(iv) *If* $\rho(x) = \rho'(x)$ *for all* $x \in \mathrm{FV}(M)$, *then* $[\![M]\!]^{\mathcal{D}}_{\rho} = [\![M]\!]^{\mathcal{D}}_{\rho'}$;
(v) *If* $y \notin \mathrm{FV}(M)$, *then* $[\![\lambda x.M]\!]^{\mathcal{D}}_{\rho} = [\![\lambda y.M[x := y]]\!]^{\mathcal{D}}_{\rho}$;
(vi) *If* $\forall d \in \mathcal{D}.[\![M]\!]^{\mathcal{D}}_{\rho[x:=d]} = [\![N]\!]^{\mathcal{D}}_{\rho[x:=d]}$, *then* $[\![\lambda x.M]\!]^{\mathcal{D}}_{\rho} = [\![\lambda x.N]\!]^{\mathcal{D}}_{\rho}$.

$\langle \mathcal{D}, \cdot, [\![\ ]\!]^{\mathcal{D}} \rangle$ *is* extensional *if moreover*

$$[\![\lambda x.Mx]\!]^{\mathcal{D}}_{\rho} = [\![M]\!]^{\mathcal{D}}_{\rho}.$$

We can devise semantics domains out of intersection types by means of an appropriate notion of filter over a type preorder. This is a particular case of filter over a generic ⊤-meet semi-lattice (see [19]).

Definition 11 (Σ-filters). *Let* $\Sigma = (\mathbb{C}, \leq)$ *be a type preorder and* $\mathbb{T} = \mathbb{T}(\mathbb{C})$. *A Σ-filter (or a filter over* $\mathbb{T}$*) is a set* $X \subseteq \mathbb{T}$ *such that*

(i) *if* $\Omega \in \mathbb{C}$ *then* $\Omega \in X$;
(ii) *if* $A \leq B$ *and* $A \in X$, *then* $B \in X$;
(iii) *if* $A, B \in X$, *then* $A \cap B \in X$.

$\mathcal{F}^{\Sigma}$ *denotes the set of Σ-filters.*

NOTATION. Given $X \subseteq \mathbb{T}$, $\uparrow X$ denotes the Σ-filter generated by X. For $A \in \mathbb{T}$, we write $\uparrow A$ instead of $\uparrow \{A\}$.

It is possible to turn the space of filters into an applicative structure in which to interpret λ-terms. Assuming the Stone duality viewpoint, the interpretation of terms coincides with the sets of types which are deducible for them.

Definition 12 (Filter structures).

(i) *Application* $\_ \cdot \_ : \mathcal{F}^{\Sigma} \times \mathcal{F}^{\Sigma} \to \mathcal{F}^{\Sigma}$ *is defined as*

$$X \cdot Y = \uparrow \{B \mid \exists A \in Y. A \to B \in X\}.$$

(ii) *For any λ-term* M *and environment* $\rho : Var \to \mathcal{F}^{\Sigma} \setminus \{\emptyset\}$,

$$[\![M]\!]^{\Sigma}_{\rho} = \{A \mid \exists \Gamma \models \rho.\ \Gamma \vdash^{\Sigma} M : A\},$$

where $\Gamma \models \rho$ *if and only if* $(x : B) \in \Gamma$ *implies* $B \in \rho(x)$.

(iii) *A* filter λ-structure *is a triple* $\langle \mathcal{F}^{\Sigma}, \cdot, [\![\ ]\!]^{\Sigma} \rangle$.

By rules (Ω), ($\leq$) and ($\cap$I) the interpretations of all λ-terms are filters.

Thanks to the following theorem, it is sufficient that clause (iii) of Definition 10 holds in order a filter λ-structure $\langle \mathcal{F}^{\Sigma}, \cdot, [\![\ ]\!]^{\Sigma} \rangle$ be also a model for the restricted λ-calculus $\lambda_{\mathbb{R}}$ (called *filter model for* $\lambda_{\mathbb{R}}$).

Theorem 1. *For all type preorders Σ the interpretation function $[\![\ ]\!]^{\Sigma}$ satisfies conditions (i), (ii), (iv), (v), (vi) of Definition 10.*

PROOF. We only consider the interesting cases.

(ii) Let $A \in [\![MN]\!]^{\Sigma}_{\rho}$. The case $A \sim \Omega$ is trivial. Otherwise there exists $\Gamma \models \rho$ such that $\Gamma \vdash^{\Sigma} MN : A$. By Lemma 1(ii) there exist I and $B_i, C_i \in \mathbb{T}$ such that for all $i \in I$, $\Gamma \vdash^{\Sigma} M : B_i \to C_i$, $\Gamma \vdash^{\Sigma} N : B_i$, and $\bigcap_{i \in I} C_i \leq A$. From the first two judgments above, we get $B_i \in [\![N]\!]^{\Sigma}_{\rho}$ and $B_i \to C_i \in [\![M]\!]^{\Sigma}_{\rho}$. By definition of application it follows $A \in [\![M]\!]^{\Sigma}_{\rho} \cdot [\![N]\!]^{\Sigma}_{\rho}$.
Let now $A \in [\![M]\!]^{\Sigma}_{\rho} \cdot [\![N]\!]^{\Sigma}_{\rho}$. Then there exist I, $B_i, C_i \in \mathbb{T}$ such that $\bigcap_{i \in I} C_i \leq A$ and for any $i \in I$, $B_i \to C_i \in [\![M]\!]^{\Sigma}_{\rho}$ and $B_i \in [\![N]\!]^{\Sigma}_{\rho}$, hence there exist two bases over $\mathbb{C}$, Γ_i and Γ'_i, such that $\Gamma_i \models \rho$, $\Gamma'_i \models \rho$, and moreover $\Gamma_i \vdash^{\Sigma} M : B_i \to C_i$, $\Gamma'_i \vdash^{\Sigma} N : B_i$. Consider the basis $\Gamma^* = \uplus_{i \in I}(\Gamma_i \uplus \Gamma'_i)$. We have $\Gamma^* \models \rho$, $\Gamma^* \vdash^{\Sigma} M : B_i \to C_i$ and $\Gamma^* \vdash^{\Sigma} N : B_i$. From the last two judgments, by applying ($\to$E), we deduce $\Gamma^* \vdash^{\Sigma} MN : C_i$, which implies, by ($\cap$I) and ($\leq$), $\Gamma^* \vdash^{\Sigma} MN : A$, hence $A \in [\![MN]\!]^{\Sigma}_{\rho}$.

(vi) Suppose that the premise holds and $A \in [\![\lambda x.M]\!]^{\Sigma}_{\rho}$. The case $\nu \leq A$ is trivial. Otherwise there is $\Gamma \models \rho$ such that $\Gamma \vdash^{\Sigma} \lambda x.M : A$. Since $x \notin \mathrm{FV}(\lambda x.M)$ by rule (S) we can assume $x \notin \Gamma$. By Lemma 1(iii) there exist I and $B_i, C_i \in \mathbb{T}$ such that, for each $i \in I$, $\Gamma, x : B_i \vdash^{\Sigma} M : C_i$, and $\bigcap_{i \in I}(B_i \to C_i) \leq A$. By the premise, we get, for each $i \in I$, $\Gamma, x : B_i \vdash^{\Sigma} N : C_i$, hence by ($\to$I) and ($\leq$) we get $\Gamma \vdash^{\Sigma} \lambda x.N : A$, which implies $[\![\lambda x.M]\!]^{\Sigma}_{\rho} \subseteq [\![\lambda x.N]\!]^{\Sigma}_{\rho}$. Similarly one proves $[\![\lambda x.N]\!]^{\Sigma}_{\rho} \subseteq [\![\lambda x.M]\!]^{\Sigma}_{\rho}$.

Corollary 1 ((Restricted) filter models). *A filter λ-structure $\langle \mathcal{F}^{\Sigma}, \cdot, [\![\ ]\!]^{\Sigma} \rangle$ is a* filter model *for the restricted λ-calculus $\lambda_{\mathbb{R}}$ iff for any redex $(\lambda x.M)N \in \mathbb{R}$, environment ρ,*

$$[\![(\lambda x.M)N]\!]^{\Sigma}_{\rho} = [\![M]\!]^{\Sigma}_{\rho[x:=[\![N]\!]^{\Sigma}_{\rho}]}\text{, that is,}$$

$$(\natural) \quad \exists \Gamma \models \rho.\ \Gamma \vdash^{\Sigma} (\lambda x.M)N : A \ \Leftrightarrow\ \exists \Gamma' \models \rho.\ \Gamma' \vdash^{\Sigma} M[x := N] : A.$$

4 Four Characterization Results

The first two characterization results we give concern natural type preorders. We begin studying the representability of interesting classes of (strict) Scott continuous functions. These characterizations generalise those given in [8].

Definition 13 (Representable functions). *Given a type preorder Σ, a function $f : \mathcal{F}^{\Sigma} \to \mathcal{F}^{\Sigma}$ is said to be* representable *in Σ if it is representable in the induced filter λ-structure $\langle \mathcal{F}^{\Sigma}, \cdot, [\![\ ]\!]^{\Sigma} \rangle$, that is there exists $X \in \mathcal{F}^{\Sigma}$ such that for any $Y \in \mathcal{F}^{\Sigma}$, $X \cdot Y = f(Y)$.*

Next lemma is useful for characterizing the sets of representable functions.

Lemma 2. *Let $\Sigma = (\mathbb{C}, \leq)$ be a natural type preorder and $f : \mathcal{F}^\Sigma \to \mathcal{F}^\Sigma$ be a continuous function. Then f is representable iff for all I and $A_i, B_i, C, D \in \mathbb{T}(\mathbb{C})$, with $D \not\sim \Omega$, it holds*

$$(\flat) \quad (\forall i \in I. B_i \in f(\uparrow A_i)) \; \& \; \bigcap_{i\in I}(A_i \to B_i) \leq C \to D \;\; \Rightarrow \;\; D \in f(\uparrow C).$$

Proof. ($\Leftarrow$) Let $X_f = \uparrow \{A \to B \mid B \in f(\uparrow A)\}$ We prove that for any $C \in \mathbb{T}(\mathbb{C})$ we have $f(\uparrow C) = X_f \cdot \uparrow C$.

$$\begin{aligned}
X \cdot \uparrow C &= \uparrow \{D \mid \exists C' \geq C. C' \to D \in X\} && \text{by definition of application}\\
&= \uparrow \{D \mid C \to D \in X\} && \text{by } (\eta)\\
&= \{D \mid C \to D \in X\} && \text{by } (\to\text{-}\cap)\\
&= \{D \mid \exists I, A_i, B_i. (\forall i \in I. B_i \in f(\uparrow A_i) \&\\
&\qquad \textstyle\bigcap_{i\in I}(A_i \to B_i) \leq C \to D\} && \text{by definition of } X_f\\
&= \{D \mid D \in f(\uparrow C)\} && \text{by } (\flat)\\
&= f(\uparrow C).
\end{aligned}$$

($\Rightarrow$) Suppose by contradiction that there exist I, A_i, B_i, C, D (with $D \not\sim \Omega$), such that $\bigcap_{i\in I}(A_i \to B_i) \leq C \to D$, and for any $i \in I$, $B_i \in f(\uparrow A_i)$, but $D \notin f(\uparrow C)$. If X is any filter candidate to represent f, then, for any $i \in I$, $B_i \in X \cdot \uparrow A_i$, which implies, by easy computations, $A_i \to B_i \in X$, for any $i \in I$. Since $\bigcap_{i\in I}(A_i \to B_i) \leq C \to D$, it follows $C \to D \in X$, hence $D \in X \cdot \uparrow C$, making it impossible that X represents f.

Theorem 2 (Characterization of sets of representable functions).

(i) *The set of functions representable in a strict natural preorder $\Sigma = (\mathbb{C}, \leq)$ contains:*

1) the step function $\bot \Rightarrow \bot$;

2) the strict step functions iff $A {\to} B \leq C {\to} D$ imply $C \leq A, B \leq D$ for all $A, B, C, D \in \mathbb{T}(\mathbb{C})$;

3) the strict continuous functions iff Σ is a beta preorder.

(ii) *The set of functions representable in a natural preorder $\Sigma = (\mathbb{C}, \leq)$ contains:*

1) the step function $\bot \Rightarrow \bot$ iff $A {\to} B \sim \Omega$ implies $B \sim \Omega$;

2) the constant functions iff $\Omega {\to} B \leq C {\to} D$ implies $B \leq D$ for all B, C, D in $\mathbb{T}(\mathbb{C})$;

3) the step functions iff $A {\to} B \leq C {\to} D$ and $D \not\sim \Omega$ imply $C \leq A, B \leq D$ for all $A, B, C, D \in \mathbb{T}(\mathbb{C})$;

4) the continuous functions iff Σ is a beta preorder.

Proof. (sketch) For each point above, the theses follow applying condition ($\flat$) of Lemma 2 to the class of functions involved, taking into account that:

- $D \in (\uparrow A \Rightarrow \uparrow B)(\uparrow C)$ iff $C \leq A$ and $B \leq D$;
- $B \in f(\uparrow A)$ iff $\uparrow A \Rightarrow \uparrow B \sqsubseteq f$;

where $\uparrow A \Rightarrow \uparrow B$ is the step function from $\uparrow A$ to $\uparrow B$, f is a continuous function and $\sqsubseteq$ is the point-wise ordering.

All the type theories of Figure 2 are beta. Moreover, the type preorders $\mathcal{AO}, \mathcal{BCD}$ ($\mathcal{CDV}, \mathcal{EHR}$) are (strict) natural and therefore, by Theorem 2(ii4), in all the filter λ-structures induced by such preorders all (strict) continuous functions are representable.

Our second characterization result on natural type preorders consists in giving a criterion for selecting those type preorders whose induced filter λ-structures are indeed filter models of the whole λ-calculus. To do that we use a result of [20], in which an applicative structure is showed to be a model provided that it contains the combinators **K**, **S** and ε. Thus, a condition for having a filter model can be obtained by simply forcing the existence of such combinators.

Theorem 3 (Characterization of model-inducing preorders).
Let $\Sigma = (\mathbb{C}, \leq)$ *be a natural type preorder. The filter* λ*-structure* $\langle \mathcal{F}^{\Sigma}, \cdot, [\![\ ]\!]^{\Sigma} \rangle$ *is a filter model of the whole* λ*-calculus iff the following three conditions are fulfilled.*

(i) *(existence of* **K***)*
$\forall C, D, E\ \exists I, A_i, B_i . \bigcap_{i \in I}(A_i \to B_i \to A_i) \leq C \to D \to E \Leftrightarrow$
$C \leq E$;

(ii) *(existence of* **S***)*
$\forall D, E, F, G\ \exists I, A_i, B_i, C_i . \bigcap_{i \in I}((A_i \to B_i \to C_i) \to (A_i \to B_i) \to A_i \to C_i)$
$\leq D \to E \to F \to G \Leftrightarrow$
$\exists H . E \leq F \to H$ *and* $D \leq F \to H \to G$;

(iii) *(existence of* ε*)*
$\forall C, D\ \exists I, A_i, B_i . \bigcap_{i \in I}((A_i \to B_i) \to A_i \to B_i) \leq C \to D \Leftrightarrow$
$\exists J, E_j, F_j . C \leq \bigcap_{j \in J}(E_j \to F_j) \leq D$.

The filter λ*-structure* $\langle \mathcal{F}^{\Sigma}, \cdot, [\![\ ]\!]^{\Sigma} \rangle$ *is an extensional model if the third condition above is replaced by:*
(iii′) $\forall A\ \exists I, A_i, B_i . A \sim \bigcap_{i \in I}(A_i \to B_i)$.

These conditions are obtained by considering the application of combinators to filters. Similarly, one could characterize the representability of an arbitrary combinator of the shape $\lambda x_1 \ldots x_n$.C, where C is a combination of variable (that is, it does not contain any λ-abstraction).

Our third result characterizes those type preorders inducing filter models for the main restricted λ-calculi studied in the literature, namely the λ**I**-calculus [11], the λ**K**N-calculus [17] and the call-by-value λ-calculus [21]. The redexes of these calculi are defined as follows.

Definition 14 (Restricted redexes). *([21,11,17])*

(i) *A redex* $(\lambda x.M)N$ *is a* β_v-redex *if* N *is a variable or an abstraction.*

(ii) *A redex* $(\lambda x.M)N$ *is a* β-**I**-redex *if* $x \in \mathrm{FV}(M)$.

(iii) *A redex* $(\lambda x.M)N$ *is a* β-**K**N-redex *if it is a* β-**I**-*redex or* N *is either a variable or a closed strongly normalising term.*

Before characterizing (restricted) filter models we need a technical result on typing properties of strongly normalizing terms: for a proof see [13].

Proposition 1 (Characterization of strongly normalizing terms). *A λ-term M is strongly normalizing iff for any type preorder $\Sigma = (\mathbb{C}, \leq)$ there exists $A \in \mathbb{T}(\mathbb{C})$ and a basis Γ over $\mathbb{C}$ such that $\Gamma \vdash^{\Sigma} M : A$.*

Let $\Sigma = (\mathbb{C}, \leq)$ be a type preorder: we say that a basis Γ^* over $\mathbb{C}$ is a $\langle \Sigma, \Gamma, M \rangle$-basis iff the subjects of Γ^* are the variables which occur free in M and are not subjects of Γ, i.e. $\{x \in \Gamma^*\} = \{x \in \mathrm{FV}(M) \mid x \notin \Gamma\}$.

Theorem 4 (Characterizations of (restricted) filter models). *Let $\Sigma = (\mathbb{C}, \leq)$ be a type preorder and $\Im(\Sigma, M, x)$*[2] *be short for:*

$$\forall \Gamma \textit{basis over } \mathbb{C}\ \forall \Gamma^* \langle \Sigma, \Gamma, M \rangle\textit{-basis}\ \ \forall A, B \in \mathbb{T}(\mathbb{C}).$$
$$\Gamma \vdash^{\Sigma} \lambda x.M : B \to A \ \Rightarrow\ \Gamma^*, \Gamma, x{:}B \vdash^{\Sigma} M : A.$$

The filter λ-structure $\langle \mathcal{F}^{\Sigma}, \cdot, [\![\ ]\!]^{\Sigma} \rangle$:
- (i) *is a model of the call-by-value λ-calculus iff for any M, x, ρ:*
  1) $[\![\lambda x.M]\!]^{\Sigma}_{\rho} \neq \emptyset$ and
  2) $\Im(\Sigma, M, x)$ holds;
- (ii) *is a model of the λ**I**-calculus iff for any M, x, N, ρ such that $x \in \mathrm{FV}(M)$:*
  1) $[\![M[x := N]]\!]^{\Sigma}_{\rho} \neq \emptyset$ implies $[\![N]\!]^{\Sigma}_{\rho} \neq \emptyset$ and
  2) $\Im(\Sigma, M, x)$ holds;
- (iii) *is a model of the λ**KN**-calculus iff it is a model of the λ**I**-calculus;*
- (iv) *is a model of the whole λ-calculus iff for any M, ρ:*
  1) $[\![M]\!]^{\Sigma}_{\rho} \neq \emptyset$ and
  2) $\Im(\Sigma, M, x)$ holds.

PROOF. We prove with details point (i) and give hints for the other points.

($\Rightarrow$) Let $\langle \mathcal{F}^{\Sigma}, \cdot, [\![\ ]\!]^{\Sigma} \rangle$ be a model of the call-by-value calculus. Assume by contradiction that $[\![\lambda x.M_0]\!]^{\Sigma}_{\rho_0} = \emptyset$ for some M_0, x, ρ_0: this implies $[\![(\lambda zy.y)(\lambda x.M_0)]\!]^{\Sigma}_{\rho_0} = [\![\lambda zy.y]\!]^{\Sigma}_{\rho_0} \cdot [\![\lambda x.M_0]\!]^{\Sigma}_{\rho_0} = \emptyset$. Since $(\lambda zy.y)(\lambda x.M_0)$ is a β_v-redex which reduces to $\lambda y.y$ and $A \to A \in [\![\lambda y.y]\!]^{\Sigma}_{\rho}$ for all ρ this contradicts ($\Leftarrow$) of condition ($\natural$) in Corollary 1. Now we prove that $\Im(\Sigma, M, x)$ holds for any M, x. Let $\Gamma \vdash^{\Sigma} \lambda x.M : B \to A$. Then $\Gamma' \vdash^{\Sigma} (\lambda x.M)x : A$, where $\Gamma' = \Gamma, x{:}B$. Let ρ be an environment such that $\rho(y) = \uparrow C$ if $y{:}C \in \Gamma'$. It is easy to check that $\Gamma' \models \rho$. Since $(\lambda x.M)x$ is a β_v-redex, condition ($\natural$) of Corollary 1 holds, hence there exists a basis Γ'' such that $\Gamma'' \models \rho$ and moreover $\Gamma'' \vdash^{\Sigma} M : A$. By definition of $\models$, we have that for any variable y, if $y{:}D \in \Gamma''$ and $y{:}C \in \Gamma'$ then $C \leq D$. Applying rules (S) and ($\leq$ L) we obtain $\Gamma^*, \Gamma, x{:}B \vdash^{\Sigma} M : A$ where $\Gamma^* = \{z : E \in \Gamma'' \mid z \in \mathrm{FV}(M) \,\&\, z \notin \Gamma\}$ is a $\langle \Sigma, \Gamma, M \rangle$-basis. Notice that the predicates in Γ^* must vary according to the environment ρ, and that ρ by construction can assign arbitrary filters to the subjects of Γ^*. The proof of ($\Rightarrow$) is so complete.

($\Leftarrow$) First we show ($\Rightarrow$) of condition ($\natural$) in Corollary 1. From $\Gamma \vdash^{\Sigma} (\lambda x.M)N : A$ by Lemma 1(ii) and $\Im(\Sigma, M, x)$ we get $\Gamma^*, \Gamma, x : B_i \vdash^{\Sigma} M : C_i$, $\Gamma \vdash^{\Sigma} N : B_i$, and $\bigcap_{i \in I} C_i \leq A$ for all $\langle \Sigma, \Gamma, M \rangle$-basis Γ^* and for some I, $B_i, C_i \in \mathbb{T}$. Then $\Gamma^*, \Gamma \vdash M[x := N] : C_i$ follows by rules (C) and (W), and so $\Gamma^*, \Gamma \vdash^{\Sigma} M[x := N] : A$ using rules ($\cap$I) and ($\leq$). We conclude observing that we can choose Γ^* such that $\Gamma^* \models \rho$.

[2] Notice that $\langle \Sigma, \Gamma, M \rangle$-bases in $\Im(\Sigma, M, x)$ are useful only for $\lambda\cap^{\Sigma}_{v}$, since $\lambda\cap^{\Sigma}_{\mathcal{B}}$ and $\lambda\cap^{\Sigma}_{\Omega}$ enjoy the sub-formula property.

As to ($\Leftarrow$) of ($\natural$) let D be a deduction of $\Gamma \vdash M[x := N] : A$ and $\Gamma_i \vdash N : B_i$ for $i{\in}I$ be all the statements in D whose subject is N. Without loss of generality we can assume that x does not occur in Γ.
If I is non-empty, notice that $\Gamma \subseteq \Gamma_i$ but $\Gamma \upharpoonright \mathrm{FV}(N) = \Gamma_i \upharpoonright \mathrm{FV}(N)$ (by $\Gamma \upharpoonright \mathcal{X}$ we denote $\{x : A{\in}\Gamma \mid x{\in}\mathcal{X}\}$). So using rules (S) and ($\cap$I), we have that $\Gamma \vdash N : \bigcap_{i\in I} B_i$. Moreover, one can easily see, by induction on M, that $\Gamma, x : \bigcap_{i\in I} B_i \vdash M : A$. Thus, by rule ($\to$I), we have $\Gamma \vdash \lambda x.M : \bigcap_{i\in I} B_i {\to} A$. Hence, by ($\to$E) we can conclude $\Gamma \vdash (\lambda x.M)N : A$.
If I is empty, we get from D a derivation of $\Gamma \vdash M : A$ by replacing each N by x. Two cases have to be considered:

- if N is a variable, say x, then by Definition 12(ii) $\rho(x) \neq \emptyset$;
- if N is an abstraction, then $[\![N]\!]^{\Sigma}_{\rho} \neq \emptyset$ by hypothesis.

In both cases there is a basis $\Gamma' \models \rho$, such that $\Gamma' \vdash^{\Sigma}_{\nu} N : B$ for some type B. By rule (W) we get $\Gamma, x : B \vdash M : A$ and we can conclude $\Gamma \uplus \{x : B\} \uplus \Gamma' \vdash (\lambda x.M)N : A$.

As to the proofs of the other points, proceed as in the previous case taking into account for point (iii) that if N is a closed strongly normalizing term, by Proposition 1 it is typable in all intersection type systems from the empty basis.

Notice that $\Omega{\in}\mathbb{C}$ or $\nu{\in}\mathbb{C}$ implies condition (i1) of Theorem 4, $\Omega{\in}\mathbb{C}$ or $\nu{\notin}\mathbb{C}$ implies condition (ii1) of Theorem 4 and $\Omega{\in}\mathbb{C}$ implies condition (iv1) of Theorem 4.

The characterization of filter models can be extended to encompass extensionality. To this aim it is useful to know when typing is invariant under η-expansion and η-reduction. Let

$$(\eta\text{-}exp)\ \frac{M \to_\eta N \quad \Gamma \vdash N : A}{\Gamma \vdash M : A} \qquad (\eta\text{-}red)\ \frac{M \to_\eta N \quad \Gamma \vdash M : A}{\Gamma \vdash N : A}$$

Next proposition corresponds to Theorem 4.5 of [3].

Proposition 2 (Characterization of subject η-reduction/expansion).
(i) *Rule (η-exp) is admissible in $\lambda\cap^{\Sigma}$ iff Σ is eta;*
(ii) *Rule (η-red) is admissible in $\lambda\cap^{\Sigma}_{\mathcal{B}}$ iff Σ validates $\mathcal{CDV}$, in $\lambda\cap^{\Sigma}_{\Omega}$ iff Σ validates $\mathcal{CDV} \cup \{(\Omega\text{-}\eta)\}$, and it is never admissible in $\lambda\cap^{\Sigma}_{\nu}$.*

Theorem 5 (Characterization of extensional (restricted) filter models).
Let $\Sigma = (\mathbb{C}, \leq)$ be a type preorder. The filter λ-structure $\langle \mathcal{F}^{\Sigma}, \cdot, [\![\ ]\!]^{\Sigma} \rangle$ is a extensional filter model of the restricted λ-calculus $\lambda_{\mathbb{R}}$ iff it is a model of $\lambda_{\mathbb{R}}$, Σ is an eta type preorder which validates $\mathcal{CDV}$, and moreover if $\Omega{\in}\mathbb{C}$ then Σ validates axiom (Ω-η), if $\nu{\in}\mathbb{C}$ then $\nu{\in}[\![M]\!]^{\Sigma}_{\rho}$ for all M, ρ.
PROOF. ($\Rightarrow$) Let $\varphi{\in}\mathbb{C}$ be a constant that does not satisfy all the conditions in Definition 4(ii). One can show that $\varphi{\notin}[\![\lambda y.xy]\!]^{\Sigma}_{\rho[x:=\uparrow\varphi]}$: this implies that Σ must be eta.
We have $A \to B{\cap}C{\in}[\![\lambda y.xy]\!]^{\Sigma}_{\rho[x:=\uparrow(A\to B)\cap(A\to C)]}$ for all A, B, C, but $A \to B{\cap}C{\in} \uparrow (A \to B) \cap (A \to C)$ only if Σ validates axiom ($\to$-$\cap$). Similarly one can show that Σ must validate axiom (η) and axiom (Ω-η) when $\Omega{\in}\mathbb{C}$. Lastly if $\nu{\in}\mathbb{C}$ then $\nu{\in}[\![\lambda x.Mx]\!]^{\Sigma}_{\rho}$ for all M, ρ by axiom (Ax-ν) implies $\nu{\in}[\![M]\!]^{\Sigma}_{\rho}$ for all M, ρ.
($\Leftarrow$) follows from Proposition 2, but the case $\nu{\in}\mathbb{C}$, in which ν is harmless being contained in the interpretations of all terms.

Using the previous theorems we get: $\langle \mathcal{F}^{\nabla}, \cdot, [\![\;]\!]^{\nabla} \rangle$ with $\nabla \in \{\mathcal{CDV}\}$ is a model of the λ**I**-calculus, with
$nabla = \mathcal{EHR}$ is a model of the call-by-value λ-calculus, with $\nabla \in \{\mathcal{AO}, \mathcal{BCD}\}$ is a model of the whole λ-calculus.

5 Trimmed Filter Models

In this section we provide actual examples of filter models of the whole λ-calculus where not all continuous functions are representable. In particular we devise two type preorders which are natural but not beta. This implies, by Theorem 2(ii4), that some continuous function cannot be represented in the filter λ-structures induced by such preorders. For the first model we acknowledge the adaptation of an idea in [8].

Definition 15 (Trimmed models). *A (strict) filter model will be called* trimmed *if not all the (strict) continuous functions are representable in it.*

The Type Preorder $\Sigma^{\diamondsuit}$

Definition 16 ($\Sigma^{\diamondsuit}$). *Let* $\mathbb{C}^{\diamondsuit} = \{\Omega, \diamondsuit, \heartsuit\}$. *The type preorder* $\Sigma^{\diamondsuit}$ *is the preorder induced by the set of rules* $\diamondsuit = \mathcal{BCD} \cup \{(\diamondsuit\text{-}\heartsuit)\}$, *where*

$$(\diamondsuit\text{-}\heartsuit)\; A \leq A[\diamondsuit := \heartsuit].$$

In order to show that $\Sigma^{\diamondsuit}$ induces a trimmed filter model we need a few technical results.

Lemma 3. (i) $A \leq_{\diamondsuit} B$ *implies* $A[\diamondsuit := \heartsuit] \leq_{\diamondsuit} B[\diamondsuit := \heartsuit]$;
(ii) $\Gamma \vdash^{\diamondsuit} M : A$ *implies* $\Gamma[\diamondsuit := \heartsuit] \vdash^{\diamondsuit} M : A[\diamondsuit := \heartsuit]$;
(iii) $\Gamma, \Gamma' \vdash^{\diamondsuit} M : A$ *implies* $\Gamma, \Gamma'[\diamondsuit := \heartsuit] \vdash^{\diamondsuit} M : A[\diamondsuit := \heartsuit]$;
(iv) $\forall i{\in}I.\; \Gamma, x : A_i \vdash^{\diamondsuit} M : B_i$ *and* $\bigcap_{i\in I}(A_i \to B_i) \leq_{\diamondsuit} \bigcap_{j\in J}(C_j \to D_j)$ *imply* $\forall j{\in}J.\; \Gamma, x : C_j \vdash^{\diamondsuit} M : D_j$.

Proof. (i) By induction on the definition of $\leq_{\diamondsuit}$.
(ii) By induction on derivations using (i) for rule ($\leq_{\diamondsuit}$).
(iii) From (ii) and the admissible rule ($\leq_{\diamondsuit}$L), taking into account that if $(x : B){\in}\Gamma$, then $(x : B[\diamondsuit := \heartsuit]){\in}\Gamma[\diamondsuit := \heartsuit]$ and $B \leq_{\diamondsuit} B[\diamondsuit := \heartsuit]$.
(iv) We shall denote by ψ, ξ (possibly with indexes) elements of $\mathbb{C}^{\diamondsuit}$.We show by induction on the definition of $\leq_{\diamondsuit}$ that

$$(\bigcap_{i\in I}(A_i \to B_i)) \cap (\bigcap_{h\in H} \psi_h) \leq_{\diamondsuit} (\bigcap_{j\in J}(C_j \to D_j)) \cap (\bigcap_{k\in K} \xi_k)$$

and $\forall i{\in}I.\; \Gamma, x : A_i \vdash^{\diamondsuit} M : B_i$ imply $\forall j{\in}J.\; \Gamma, x : C_j \vdash^{\diamondsuit} M : D_j$.

The only interesting case is when the applied rule is ($\diamondsuit$-$\heartsuit$), i.e. we have

$$\bigcap_{i\in I}(A_i \to B_i) \cap (\bigcap_{h\in H} \psi_h) \leq_{\diamondsuit} (\bigcap_{i\in I}(A_i \to B_i) \cap (\bigcap_{h\in H} \psi_h))[\diamondsuit := \heartsuit].$$

By hypothesis $\Gamma, x : A_i \vdash^{\diamondsuit} M : B_i$, so we are done by (iii).

Theorem 6. *The natural type preorder $\Sigma^{\diamondsuit}$ is not beta, but $\langle \mathcal{F}^{\diamondsuit}, \cdot, [\![\ ]\!]^{\diamondsuit} \rangle$ is a filter model of the whole λ-calculus.*

PROOF. A counter-example to the condition of Definition 4(i) is $\diamondsuit \rightarrow \diamondsuit \leq_{\diamondsuit} \heartsuit \rightarrow \heartsuit$, since $\heartsuit \not\leq_{\diamondsuit} \diamondsuit$.
To show that $\langle \mathcal{F}^{\diamondsuit}, \cdot, [\![\ ]\!]^{\diamondsuit} \rangle$ is a model of the whole λ-calculus, it suffices, by Theorem 4(iv), to verify that $\Im(\Sigma^{\diamondsuit}, M, x)$ holds for any M, x. By Lemma 1(iii) $\Gamma \vdash^{\diamondsuit} \lambda x.M : A \rightarrow B$ implies $\Gamma, x : C_i \vdash^{\diamondsuit} M : D_i$ for some I, C_i, D_i such that $\bigcap_{i \in I}(C_i \rightarrow D_i) \leq_{\diamondsuit} A \rightarrow B$. So, we are done by Lemma 3(iv).

The step function $\uparrow \diamondsuit \Rightarrow \uparrow \diamondsuit$ is an instance of non-representable function in $\mathcal{F}^{\diamondsuit}$.

The Type Preorder $\Sigma^{\spadesuit}$

Definition 17 (The mapping p). *Let $\mathbb{C}^{\spadesuit} = \{\Omega, \spadesuit, \clubsuit\}$ The mapping $\mathsf{p} : \mathbb{T}^{\spadesuit} \rightarrow \mathbb{T}^{\spadesuit}$ is inductively defined as follows:*

$$\begin{array}{l} \mathsf{p}(\Omega) = \Omega; \quad \mathsf{p}(\spadesuit) = \Omega; \quad \mathsf{p}(\clubsuit) = \clubsuit; \\ \mathsf{p}(A \rightarrow B) = A \rightarrow \mathsf{p}(B); \\ \mathsf{p}(A \cap B) = \mathsf{p}(A) \cap \mathsf{p}(B). \end{array}$$

Definition 18 ($\Sigma^{\spadesuit}$). *$\Sigma^{\spadesuit}$ is the type preorder induced by the set of rules $\spadesuit = \mathcal{BCD} \cup \{(\spadesuit\text{-}\clubsuit), (\spadesuit\text{-}\clubsuit\text{-}\rightarrow)\}$ where:*

$$\begin{array}{ll} (\spadesuit\text{-}\clubsuit) & A \leq \mathsf{p}(A); \\ (\spadesuit\text{-}\clubsuit\text{-}\rightarrow) & A \rightarrow B \leq \mathsf{p}(A) \rightarrow \mathsf{p}(B). \end{array}$$

Given a basis Γ, let $\mathsf{p}(\Gamma)$ be the basis obtained by substituting any judgment $x{:}A$ of Γ by $x{:}\mathsf{p}(A)$.

We show that $\Sigma^{\spadesuit}$ induces a trimmed filter model. As in the case of $\Sigma^{\diamondsuit}$, we prove some technical results in order to show that $\Im(\Sigma^{\spadesuit}, M, x))$ holds for any M, x.

Lemma 4. (i) *The mapping p is idempotent, i.e. $\mathsf{p}(\mathsf{p}(A)) = \mathsf{p}(A)$.*
(ii) *$A \rightarrow \mathsf{p}(B) \sim_{\spadesuit} \mathsf{p}(A) \rightarrow \mathsf{p}(B)$;*
(iii) *$A \leq_{\spadesuit} B$ implies $\mathsf{p}(A) \leq_{\spadesuit} \mathsf{p}(B)$;*
(iv) *$\Gamma \vdash^{\spadesuit} M : A$ implies $\mathsf{p}(\Gamma) \vdash^{\spadesuit} M : \mathsf{p}(A)$;*
(v) *$\Gamma, \Gamma' \vdash^{\spadesuit} M : A$ implies $\Gamma, \mathsf{p}(\Gamma') \vdash^{\spadesuit} M : \mathsf{p}(A)$;*
(vi) *$\forall i \in I.\ \Gamma, x : A_i \vdash^{\spadesuit} M : B_i$ and $\bigcap_{i \in I}(A_i \rightarrow B_i) \leq_{\spadesuit} \bigcap_{j \in J}(C_j \rightarrow D_j)$ imply $\forall j \in J.\ \Gamma, x : C_j \vdash^{\spadesuit} M : D_j$.*

PROOF. (i) Easy.

(ii) We get $\mathsf{p}(A) \rightarrow \mathsf{p}(B) \leq_{\spadesuit} A \rightarrow \mathsf{p}(B)$ by axiom $(\spadesuit\text{-}\clubsuit)$ and rule (η). Moreover $A \rightarrow \mathsf{p}(B) \leq_{\spadesuit} \mathsf{p}(A) \rightarrow \mathsf{p}(\mathsf{p}(B)) = \mathsf{p}(A) \rightarrow \mathsf{p}(B)$ by axiom $(\spadesuit\text{-}\clubsuit\text{-}\rightarrow)$ and (i).

(iii) By induction on the definition of $\leq_{\spadesuit}$ using (i) and (ii).

(iv) By induction on derivations using (iii) for rule $(\leq_{\spadesuit})$. We give the details just for rule $(\rightarrow \text{E})$. Suppose $M \equiv NL$ and $\Gamma \vdash^{\spadesuit} N : B \rightarrow A$, $\Gamma \vdash^{\spadesuit} L : B$. Then, by induction,

$\mathsf{p}(\Gamma) \vdash^{\spadesuit} N : \mathsf{p}(B \to A)$, $\mathsf{p}(\Gamma) \vdash^{\spadesuit} L : \mathsf{p}(B)$. Since $\mathsf{p}(B \to A) = B \to \mathsf{p}(A)$, by (ii) we get $\mathsf{p}(\Gamma) \vdash^{\spadesuit} NL : \mathsf{p}(A)$.

(v) From (iv) and the admissible rule ($\leq_{\spadesuit}$ L), taking into account that if $(x : B) \in \Gamma$, then $(x : \mathsf{p}(B)) \in \mathsf{p}(\Gamma)$ and $B \leq_{\spadesuit} \mathsf{p}(B)$.

(vi) We shall denote by ψ, ξ (possibly with indexes) elements of $\mathbb{C}^{\spadesuit}$.We show by induction on the definition of $\leq_{\spadesuit}$ that

$$(\bigcap_{i \in I}(A_i \to B_i)) \cap (\bigcap_{h \in H} \psi_h) \leq_{\spadesuit} (\bigcap_{j \in J}(C_j \to D_j)) \cap (\bigcap_{k \in K} \xi_k)$$

$$\text{and } \forall i \in I.\ \Gamma, x : A_i \vdash^{\spadesuit} M : B_i \text{ imply } \forall j \in J.\ \Gamma, x : C_j \vdash^{\spadesuit} M : D_j.$$

The only interesting case is when the applied rules are ($\spadesuit$-$\clubsuit$) or ($\spadesuit$-$\clubsuit$-$\to$), i.e. we have $A \to B \leq_{\spadesuit} \mathsf{p}(A \to B) = A \to \mathsf{p}(B)$ or $A \to B \leq_{\spadesuit} \mathsf{p}(A) \to \mathsf{p}(B)$. By hypothesis $\Gamma, x{:}A \vdash^{\spadesuit} M : B$, so we are done by (v).

Theorem 7. *The natural type preorder $\Sigma^{\spadesuit}$ is not beta, but $\langle \mathcal{F}^{\spadesuit}, \cdot, [\![\ ]\!]^{\spadesuit} \rangle$ is a filter model of the whole λ-calculus.*

Proof. As in the proof of Theorem 6, Lemma 4(vi) allows to prove that for any M, x, $\Im(\Sigma^{\spadesuit}, M, x)$ holds, hence we can apply Theorem 4(iv) in order to conclude that $\langle \mathcal{F}^{\spadesuit}, \cdot, [\![\ ]\!]^{\spadesuit} \rangle$ is a model. On the other hand $\spadesuit$ is not a beta theory. For instance, $\varphi \to \omega \leq_{\spadesuit} \Omega \to \omega$, but $\Omega \not\leq_{\spadesuit} \varphi$.

The step function $\uparrow \spadesuit \Rightarrow \uparrow \clubsuit$ is an example of function not representable in $\mathcal{F}^{\spadesuit}$.

Actually $\mathcal{F}^{\spadesuit}$ is the inverse limit solution of the domain equation $\mathcal{D} \simeq [\mathcal{D} \to \mathcal{D}]$ computed in the category of *p-lattices* (see [2]), whose objects are ω-algebraic lattices $\mathcal{D}$ endowed with a finitary additive projection $\delta : \mathcal{D} \to \mathcal{D}$ and whose morphisms $f : (\mathcal{D}, \delta) \to (\mathcal{D}', \delta')$ are continuous functions such that $\delta' \circ f \sqsubseteq f \circ \delta$.

6 Conclusions

When stepping into the world of λ-calculus semantics, intersection type systems turn out to be a useful "vehicle" to move around, since they provide a finitary way to describe and analyse particular classes of models. By simply adding a single constant or condition on a type preorder, a different semantical domain is characterized. One is then naturally induced to expect that intersection types will provide, in the long run, a sort of tailor shop in which particular domains can be tailored for any specific need. As a matter of fact, the possibility of pacing along this direction has been shown to be real also in [3].

In the present paper we have made a step forward in this direction. Filter λ-structures induced by intersection type preorders have been shown to provide models for the whole λ-calculus and for a number of relevant "restricted" λ-calculi when particular conditions on the type preorders are fulfilled. Even more, our proposed conditions provide precise characterizations for intersection type-induced models.

When a model is produced, the second step is almost always to make it precisely fit the calculus, by "trimming" it and eliminating the exceeding parts. We have shown in the present paper that in the framework of intersection-induced models for the λ-calculus such a trimming is indeed possible, by providing two examples of filter models in which not all the continuous functions are representable.

Much to do is left about model "tailoring", like trying to see if many conditions on type preorders implicitly expressed in terms of generation properties of type assignment can be made explicit on the type preorders itself. Besides it would be interesting to check whether also the webbed models [7] allow for "tailoring operations".

Acknowledgments. The authors are grateful to Furio Honsell, Henk Barendregt and Wil Dekkers for enlightening discussions on the subject of the present paper. We wish also to thank the anonymous referees who pointed us interesting directions for further research and whose comments and suggestions have been very helpful to improve the presentation of the paper.

References

1. Samson Abramsky and C.-H. Luke Ong. Full abstraction in the lazy lambda calculus. *Inform. and Comput.*, 105(2):159–267, 1993.
2. Fabio Alessi. The category *p*-sfp. Internal Report n. 27/96/RR, Dipartimento di Matematica e Informatica, University of Udine, 1996.
3. Fabio Alessi, Franco Barbanera, and Mariangiola Dezani-Ciancaglini. Intersection types and computational rules. In Ruy de Queiroz, Elaine Pimentel, and Lucilia Figueiredo, editors, *WoLLIC'03*, volume 84 of *El. Notes in Theoret. Comput. Sci.* Elsevier, 2003.
4. Fabio Alessi, Mariangiola Dezani-Ciancaglini, and Furio Honsell. A complete characterization of complete intersection-type preorders. *ACM Trans. on Comput. Logic*, 4(1):120–147, 2003.
5. Fabio Alessi, Mariangiola Dezani-Ciancaglini, and Stefania Lusin. Intersection types and domain operators. *Theoret. Comput. Sci.*, 2004. to appear.
6. Henk Barendregt, Mario Coppo, and Mariangiola Dezani-Ciancaglini. A filter lambda model and the completeness of type assignment. *J. Symbolic Logic*, 48(4):931–940 (1984), 1983.
7. Chantal Berline. From computation to foundations via functions and application: The λ-calculus and its webbed models. *Theoret. Comput. Sci.*, 249:81–161, 2000.
8. Mario Coppo, Mariangiola Dezani-Ciancaglini, Furio Honsell, and Giuseppe Longo. Extended type structures and filter lambda models. In Gabriele Lolli, Giuseppe Longo, and Anna Lisa Marcja, editors, *Logic colloquium '82*, pages 241–262. North-Holland, Amsterdam, 1984.
9. Mario Coppo, Mariangiola Dezani-Ciancaglini, and Betti Venneri. Functional characters of solvable terms. *Z. Math. Logik Grundlag. Math.*, 27(1):45–58, 1981.
10. Mario Coppo, Mariangiola Dezani-Ciancaglini, and Maddalena Zacchi. Type theories, normal forms, and D_∞-lambda-models. *Inform. and Comput.*, 72(2):85–116, 1987.
11. Haskell B. Curry and Robert Feys. *Combinatory Logic*, volume I of *Studies in Logic and the Foundations of Mathematics*. North-Holland, Amsterdam, 1958.
12. Mariangiola Dezani-Ciancaglini, Silvia Ghilezan, and Silvia Likavec. Behavioural inverse limit models. *Theoret. Comput. Sci.*, 2004. to appear.
13. Mariangiola Dezani-Ciancaglini, Furio Honsell, and Yoko Motohama. Compositional characterization of λ-terms using intersection types. *Theoret. Comput. Sci.*, 2004. to appear.
14. Lavinia Egidi, Furio Honsell, and Simona Ronchi Della Rocca. Operational, denotational and logical descriptions: a case study. *Fund. Inform.*, 16(2):149–169, 1992.

15. Gerhard K. Gierz, Karl Heinrich Hofmann, Klaus Keimel, Jimmie D. Lawson, Michael W. Mislove, and Dana S. Scott. *A Compendium of Continuous Lattices*. Springer-Verlag, Berlin, 1980.
16. Roger Hindley and Giuseppe Longo. Lambda-calculus models and extensionality. *Z. Math. Logik Grundlag. Math.*, 26(4):289–310, 1980.
17. Furio Honsell and Marina Lenisa. Semantical analysis of perpetual strategies in λ-calculus. *Theoret. Comput. Sci.*, 212(1-2):183–209, 1999.
18. Furio Honsell and Simona Ronchi Della Rocca. An approximation theorem for topological lambda models and the topological incompleteness of lambda calculus. *J. Comput. System Sci.*, 45(1):49–75, 1992.
19. Peter T. Johnstone. *Stone spaces*. Cambridge University Press, Cambridge, 1986. Reprint of the 1982 edition.
20. Albert R. Meyer. What is a model of the lambda calculus? *Inform. and Control*, 52(1):87–122, 1982.
21. Gordon D. Plotkin. Call-by-name, call-by-value and the λ-calculus. *Theoret. Comput. Sci.*, 1(2):125–159, 1975.
22. Gordon D. Plotkin. Set-theoretical and other elementary models of the λ-calculus. *Theoret. Comput. Sci.*, 121(1-2):351–409, 1993.
23. Dana S. Scott. Open problem. In Corrado Böhm, editor, *Lambda Calculus and Computer Science Theory*, volume 37 of *Lecture Notes in Computer Science*, page 369. Springer-Verlag, Berlin, 1975.

Locales and Locale Expressions in Isabelle/Isar

Clemens Ballarin

Fakultät für Informatik
Technische Universität München
85748 Garching, Germany
ballarin@in.tum.de

Abstract. Locales provide a module system for the Isabelle proof assistant. Recently, locales have been ported to the new Isar format for structured proofs. At the same time, they have been extended by locale expressions, a language for composing locale specifications, and by structures, which provide syntax for algebraic structures. The present paper presents both and is suitable as a tutorial to locales in Isar, because it covers both basics and recent extensions, and contains many examples.

1 Overview

Locales are an extension of the Isabelle proof assistant. They provide support for modular reasoning. Locales were initially developed by Kammüller [4] to support reasoning in abstract algebra, but are applied also in other domains — for example, bytecode verification [5]. Kammüller's original design, implemented in Isabelle99, provides, in addition to means for declaring locales, a set of ML functions that were used along with ML tactics in a proof. In the meantime, the input format for proof in Isabelle has changed and users write proof scripts in ML only rarely if at all. Two new proof styles are available, and can be used interchangeably: linear proof scripts that closely resemble ML tactics, and the structured Isar proof language by Wenzel [8]. Subsequently, Wenzel re-implemented locales for the new proof format. The implementation, available with Isabelle2003, constitutes a complete re-design and exploits that both Isar and locales are based on the notion of context, and thus locales are seen as a natural extension of Isar. Nevertheless, locales can also be used with proof scripts: their use does not require a deep understanding of the structured Isar proof style.

At the same time, Wenzel considerably extended locales. The most important addition are locale expressions, which allow to combine locales more freely. Previously only linear inheritance was possible. Now locales support multiple inheritance through a normalisation algorithm. New are also structures, which provide special syntax for locale parameters that represent algebraic structures.

Unfortunately, Wenzel provided only an implementation but hardly any documentation. Besides providing documentation, the present paper is a high-level

S. Berardi, M. Coppo, and F. Damiani (Eds.): TYPES 2003, LNCS 3085, pp. 34–50, 2004.

description of locales, and in particular locale expressions. It is meant as a first step towards the semantics of locales, and also as a base for comparing locales with module concepts in other provers. It also constitutes the base for future extensions of locales in Isabelle. The description was derived mainly by experimenting with locales and partially also by inspecting the code.

The main contribution of the author of the present paper is the abstract description of Wenzel's version of locales, and in particular of the normalisation algorithm for locale expressions (see Section 4.2). Contributions to the implementation are confined to bug fixes and to provisions that enable the use of locales with linear proof scripts.

Concepts are introduced along with examples, so that the text can be used as tutorial. It is assumed that the reader is somewhat familiar with Isabelle proof scripts. Examples have been phrased as structured Isar proofs. However, in order to understand the key concepts, including locales expressions and their normalisation, detailed knowledge of Isabelle is not necessary.

2 Locales: Beyond Proof Contexts

In tactic-based provers the application of a sequence of proof tactics leads to a proof state. This state is usually hard to predict from looking at the tactic script, unless one replays the proof step-by-step. The structured proof language Isar is different. It is additionally based on *proof contexts*, which are directly visible in Isar scripts, and since tactic sequences tend to be short, this commonly leads to clearer proof scripts.

Goals are stated with the **theorem** command. This is followed by a proof. When discharging a goal requires an elaborate argument (rather than the application of a single tactic) a new context may be entered (**proof**). Inside the context, variables may be fixed (**fix**), assumptions made (**assume**) and intermediate goals stated (**have**) and proved. The assumptions must be dischargeable by premises of the surrounding goal, and once this goal has been proved (**show**) the proof context can be closed (**qed**). Contexts inherit from surrounding contexts, but it is not possible to export from them (with exception of the proved goal); they "disappear" after the closing **qed**. Facts may have attributes — for example, identifying them as default to the simplifier or classical reasoner.

Locales extend proof contexts in various ways:

- Locales are usually *named*. This makes them persistent.
- Fixed variables may have *syntax*.
- It is possible to *add* and *export* facts.
- Locales can be combined and modified with *locale expressions*.

The Locales facility extends the Isar language: it provides new ways of stating and managing facts, but it does not modify the language for proofs. Its purpose is to support writing modular proofs.

3 Simple Locales

3.1 Syntax and Terminology

The grammar of Isar is extended by commands for locales as shown in Figure 1. A key concept, introduced by Wenzel, is that locales are (internally) lists of *context elements*. There are four kinds, identified by the keywords **fixes**, **assumes**, **defines** and **notes**.

attr-name	::= *name* | *attribute* | *name attribute*
locale-expr	::= *locale-expr1* ("+" *locale-expr1*)*
locale-expr1	::= (*qualified-name* | "(" *locale-expr* ")") (*name* | "_")*
fixes	::= *name* ["::" *type*] ["(" **structure** ")" | *mixfix*]
assumes	::= [*attr-name* ":"] *proposition*
defines	::= [*attr-name* ":"] *proposition*
notes	::= [*attr-name* "="] (*qualified-name* [*attribute*])+
element	::= **fixes** *fixes* (**and** *fixes*)*
	| **assumes** *assumes* (**and** *assumes*)*
	| **defines** *defines* (**and** *defines*)*
	| **notes** *notes* (**and** *notes*)*
	| **includes** *locale-expr*
locale	::= *element*+
	| *locale-expr* ["+" *element*+]
in-target	::= "(" **in** *qualified-name* ")"
theorem	::= (**theorem** | **lemma** | **corollary**) [*in-target*] [*attr-name*]
theory-level	::= ...
	| **locale** *name* ["=" *locale*]
	| (**theorems** | **lemmas**)
	[*in-target*] [*attr-name* "="] (*qualified-name* [*attribute*])+
	| **declare** [*in-target*] (*qualified-name* [*attribute*])+
	| *theorem proposition proof*
	| *theorem element** **shows** *proposition proof*
	| **print_locale** *locale*
	| **print_locales**

Fig. 1. Locales extend the grammar of Isar.

At the theory level — that is, at the outer syntactic level of an Isabelle input file — **locale** declares a named locale. Other kinds of locales, locale expressions and unnamed locales, will be introduced later. When declaring a named locale, it is possible to *import* another named locale, or indeed several ones by importing a locale expression. The second part of the declaration, also optional, consists of a number of context element declarations. Here, a fifth kind, **includes**, is available.

A number of Isar commands have an additional, optional *target* argument, which always refers to a named locale. These commands are **theorem** (together with

lemma and **corollary**), **theorems** (and **lemmas**), and **declare**. The effect of specifying a target is that these commands focus on the specified locale, not the surrounding theory. Commands that are used to prove new theorems will add them not to the theory, but to the locale. Similarly, **declare** modifies attributes of theorems that belong to the specified target. Additionally, for **theorem** (and related commands), theorems stored in the target can be used in the associated proof scripts.

The Locales package permits a *long goals format* for propositions stated with **theorem** (and friends). While normally a goal is just a formula, a long goal is a list of context elements, followed by the keyword **shows**, followed by the formula. Roughly speaking, the context elements are (additional) premises. For an example, see Section 4.4. The list of context elements in a long goal is also called *unnamed locale.*

Finally, there are two commands to inspect locales when working in interactive mode: **print_locales** prints the names of all targets visible in the current theory, **print_locale** outputs the elements of a named locale or locale expression.

The following presentation will use notation of Isabelle's meta logic, hence a few sentences to explain this. The logical primitives are universal quantification ($\bigwedge$), entailment ($\Longrightarrow$) and equality ($\equiv$). Variables (not bound variables) are sometimes preceded by a question mark. The logic is typed. Type variables are denoted by `'a`, `'b` etc., and $\Rightarrow$ is the function type. Double brackets $[\![$ and $]\!]$ are used to abbreviate nested entailment.

3.2 Parameters, Assumptions, and Facts

From a logical point of view a *context* is a formula schema of the form

$$\bigwedge x_1 \ldots x_n.\ [\![\ C_1;\ \ldots\ ;C_m\ ]\!] \Longrightarrow \ldots$$

The variables $x_1, \ldots, x_n$ are called *parameters*, the premises $C_1, \ldots, C_n$ *assumptions.* A formula F holds in this context if

(1) $$\bigwedge x_1 \ldots x_n.\ [\![\ C_1;\ \ldots\ ;C_m\ ]\!] \Longrightarrow F$$

is valid. The formula is called a *fact* of the context.

A locale allows fixing the parameters $x_1, \ldots, x_n$ and making the assumptions $C_1, \ldots, C_m$. This implicitly builds the context in which the formula F can be established. Parameters of a locale correspond to the context element **fixes**, and assumptions may be declared with **assumes**. Using these context elements one can define the specification of semigroups.

```
locale semi =
  fixes prod :: "['a, 'a] ⇒ 'a" (infixl "·" 70)
  assumes assoc: "(x · y) · z = x · (y · z)"
```

The parameter `prod` has a syntax annotation allowing the infix "·" in the assumption of associativity. Parameters may have arbitrary mixfix syntax, like constants. In the example, the type of `prod` is specified explicitly. This is not necessary. If no type is specified, a most general type is inferred simultaneously for all parameters, taking into account all assumptions (and type specifications of parameters, if present).[1]

Free variables in assumptions are implicitly universally quantified, unless they are parameters. Hence the context defined by the locale `semi` is

$$\bigwedge \texttt{prod}.\ [\![\ \bigwedge \texttt{x y z. prod (prod x y) z = prod x (prod y z)}\ ]\!] \Longrightarrow \ldots$$

The locale can be extended to commutative semigroups.

```
locale comm_semi = semi +
  assumes comm: "x · y = y · x"
```

This locale *imports* all elements of `semi`. The latter locale is called the import of `comm_semi`. The definition adds commutativity, hence its context is

$$\bigwedge \texttt{prod}.\ [\![\bigwedge \texttt{x y z. prod (prod x y) z = prod x (prod y z)};\ \bigwedge \texttt{x y. prod x y = prod y x}\ ]\!] \Longrightarrow \ldots$$

One may now derive facts — for example, left-commutativity — in the context of `comm_semi` by specifying this locale as target, and by referring to the names of the assumptions `assoc` and `comm` in the proof.

```
theorem (in comm_semi) lcomm:
  "x · (y · z) = y · (x · z)"
proof -
  have "x · (y · z) = (x · y) · z" by (simp add: assoc)
  also have "... = (y · x) · z" by (simp add: comm)
  also have "... = y · (x · z)" by (simp add: assoc)
  finally show ?thesis .
qed
```

In this equational Isar proof, "..." refers to the right hand side of the preceding equation. After the proof is finished, the fact `lcomm` is added to the locale `comm_semi`. This is done by adding a **notes** element to the internal representation of the locale, as explained the next section.

3.3 Locale Predicates and the Internal Representation of Locales

In mathematical texts, often arbitrary but fixed objects with certain properties are considered — for instance, an arbitrary but fixed group G — with the purpose of establishing facts valid for any group. These facts are subsequently used on other objects that also have these properties.

Locales permit the same style of reasoning. Exporting a fact F generalises the fixed parameters and leads to a (valid) formula of the form of equation (1).

[1] Type inference also takes into account definitions and import, as introduced later.

If a locale has many assumptions (possibly accumulated through a number of imports) this formula can become large and un-handy. Therefore, Wenzel introduced predicates that abbreviate the assumptions of locales. These predicates are not confined to the locale but are visible in the surrounding theory.

The definition of the locale `semi` generates the *locale predicate* `semi` over the type of the parameter `prod`, hence the predicate's type is `(['a, 'a] ⇒ 'a) ⇒ bool`. Its definition is

```
semi_def:
    semi ?prod ≡ ∀x y z. ?prod (?prod x y) z = ?prod x (?prod y z).
```

In the case where the locale has no import, the generated predicate abbreviates all assumptions and is over the parameters that occur in these assumptions.

The situation is more complicated when a locale extends another locale, as is the case for `comm_semi`. Two predicates are defined. The predicate `comm_semi_axioms` corresponds to the new assumptions and is called *delta predicate*, the locale predicate `comm_semi` captures the content of all the locale, including the import. If a locale has neither assumptions nor import, no predicate is defined. If a locale has import but no assumptions, only the locale predicate is defined.

The Locales package generates a number of theorems for locale and delta predicates. All predicates have a definition and an introduction rule. Locale predicates that are defined in terms of other predicates (which is the case if and only if the locale has import) also have a number of elimination rules (called *axioms*). All generated theorems for the predicates of the locales `semi` and `comm_semi` are shown in Figures 2 and 3, respectively.

Theorems generated for the predicate `semi`.

```
semi_def: semi ?prod ≡ ∀x y z. ?prod (?prod x y) z = ?prod x (?prod y z)

semi.intro:
   (⋀x y z. ?prod (?prod x y) z = ?prod x (?prod y z)) ⟹ semi ?prod
```

Fig. 2. Theorems for the locale predicate `semi`.

Note that the theorems generated by a locale definition may be inspected immediately after the definition in the Proof General interface [1] of Isabelle through the menu item "Isabelle/Isar>Show me ... >Theorems".

Locale and delta predicates are used also in the internal representation of locales as list of context elements. While all **fixes** in a declaration generate internal **fixes**, all assumptions of one locale declaration contribute to one internal

Theorems generated for the predicate `comm_semi_axioms`.

```
comm_semi_axioms_def:
        comm_semi_axioms ?prod ≡ ∀x y. ?prod x y = ?prod y x
comm_semi_axioms.intro:
        (⋀x y. ?prod x y = ?prod y x) ⟹ comm_semi_axioms ?prod
```

Theorems generated for the predicate `comm_semi`.

```
comm_semi_def:   comm_semi ?prod ≡ semi ?prod ∧ comm_semi_axioms ?prod
comm_semi.intro: ⟦semi ?prod; comm_semi_axioms ?prod⟧ ⟹ comm_semi ?prod
comm_semi.axioms:
                 comm_semi ?prod ⟹ semi ?prod
              comm_semi ?prod ⟹ comm_semi_axioms ?prod
```

Fig. 3. Theorems for the predicates `comm_semi_axioms` and `comm_semi`.

assumes element. The internal representation of `semi` is

fixes prod :: `"['a, 'a] ⇒ 'a"`(**infixl**"·"70)
assumes `"semi prod"`
notes assoc : `"?x · ?y · ?z = ?x · (?y · ?z)"`

and the internal representation of `"comm_semi"` is

(2)
fixes prod :: `"['a, 'a] ⇒ 'a"` (**infixl** "·" 70)
assumes `"semi prod"`
notes assoc : `"?x · ?y · ?z = ?x · (?y · ?z)"`
assumes `"comm_semi_axioms prod"`
notes comm : `"?x · ?y = ?y · ?x"`
notes lcomm : `"?x · (?y · ?z) = ?y · (?x · ?z)"`

The **notes** elements store facts the locales. The facts `assoc` and `comm` were added during the declaration of the locales. They stem from assumptions, which are trivially facts. The fact `lcomm` was added later, after finishing the proof in the respective **theorem** command above.

By using **notes** in a declaration, facts can be added to a locale directly. Of course, these must be theorems. Typical use of this feature includes adding theorems that are not usually used as a default rewrite rules by the simplifier to the simpset of the locale by a **notes** element with the attribute `[simp]`. This way it is also possible to add specialised versions of theorems to a locale by instantiating locale parameters for unknowns or locale assumptions for premises.

3.4 Definitions

Definitions were available in Kammüller's version of Locales, and they are in Wenzel's. The context element **defines** adds a definition of the form `p` $x_1 \ldots x_n$ $\equiv$ `t` as an assumption, where `p` is a parameter of the locale (possibly an imported parameter), and `t` a term that may contain the x_i. The parameter may neither occur in a previous **assumes** or **defines** element, nor on the right hand side of the definition. Hence recursion is not allowed. The parameter may, however, occur in subsequent **assumes** and on the right hand side of subsequent **defines**. We call `p` *defined parameter.*

```
locale semi2 = semi +
  fixes rprod (infixl "⊙" 70)
  defines rprod_def: "rprod x y ≡ y · x "
```

This locale extends `semi` by a second binary operation "⊙" that is like "·" but with reversed arguments. The definition of the locale generates the predicate `semi2`, which is equivalent to `semi`, but no `semi2_axioms`. The difference between **assumes** and **defines** lies in the way parameters are treated on export.

3.5 Export

A fact is exported out of a locale by generalising over the parameters and adding assumptions as premises. For brevity of the exported theorems, locale predicates are used. Exported facts are referenced by writing qualified names consisting of locale name and fact name — for example,

```
semi.assoc:
    semi ?prod ⟹ ?prod (?prod ?x ?y) ?z = ?prod ?x (?prod ?y ?z).
```

Defined parameters receive special treatment. Instead of adding a premise for the definition, the definition is unfolded in the exported theorem. In order to illustrate this we prove that the reverse operation "⊙" defined in the locale `semi2` is also associative.

```
theorem (in semi2) r_assoc: "(x ⊙ y) ⊙ z = x ⊙ (y ⊙ z)"
  by (simp only: rprod_def assoc)
```

The exported fact is

```
semi2.r_assoc:
    semi2 ?prod ⟹ ?prod ?z (?prod ?y ?x) = ?prod (?prod ?z ?y) ?x.
```

The defined parameter is not present but is replaced by its definition. Note that the definition itself is not exported, hence there is no `semi2.rprod_def`.[2]

[2] The definition could alternatively be exported using a let-construct if there was one in Isabelle's meta-logic. Let is usually defined in object-logics.

4 Locale Expressions

Locale expressions provide a simple language for combining locales. They are an effective means of building complex specifications from simple ones. Locale expressions are the main innovation of the version of Locales discussed here. Locale expressions are also reason for introducing locale predicates.

4.1 Rename and Merge

The grammar of locale expressions is part of the grammar in Figure 1. Locale names are locale expressions, and further expressions are obtained by *rename* and *merge*.

Rename. The locale expression $e\, q_1 \ldots q_n$ denotes the locale of e where parameters, in the order in which they are fixed, are renamed to q_1 to q_n. The expression is only well-formed if n does not exceed the number of parameters of e. Underscores denote parameters that are not renamed. Parameters whose names are effectively changed lose mixfix syntax, and there is currently no way to re-equip them with such.

Merge. The locale expression $e_1 + e_2$ denotes the locale obtained by merging the locales of e_1 and e_2. This locale contains the context elements of e_1, followed by the context elements of e_2.
In actual fact, the semantics of the merge operation is more complicated. If e_1 and e_2 are expressions containing the same name, followed by identical parameter lists, then the merge of both will contain the elements of those locales only once. Details are explained in Section 4.2 below.
The merge operation is associative but not commutative. The latter is because parameters of e_1 appear before parameters of e_2 in the composite expression.

Rename can be used if a different parameter name seems more appropriate — for example, when moving from groups to rings, a parameter `G` representing the group could be changed to `R`. Besides of this stylistic use, renaming is important in combination with merge. Both operations are used in the following specification of semigroup homomorphisms.

```
locale semi_hom = comm_semi sum + comm_semi +
  fixes hom
  assumes hom: "hom (sum x y) = hom x · hom y"
```

This locale defines a context with three parameters `sum`, `prod` and `hom`. Only the second parameter has mixfix syntax. The first two are associative operations, the first of type `['a, 'a] ⇒ 'a`, the second of type `['b, 'b] ⇒ 'b`.

How are facts that are imported via a locale expression identified? Facts are always introduced in a named locale (either in the locale's declaration, or by using the locale as target in **theorem**), and their names are qualified by the parameter names of this locale. Hence the full name of associativity in `semi` is `prod.assoc`. Renaming parameters of a target also renames the qualifier of facts. Hence, associativity of `sum` is `sum.assoc`. Several parameters are separated by underscores in qualifiers. For example, the full name of the fact `hom` in the locale `semi_hom` is `sum_prod_hom.hom`.

The following example is quite artificial, it illustrates the use of facts, though.

```
theorem (in semi_hom) "hom x · (hom y · hom z) = hom (sum x (sum y z))"
proof -
  have "hom x · (hom y · hom z) = hom y · (hom x · hom z)"
    by (simp add: prod.lcomm)
  also have "... = hom (sum y (sum x z))" by (simp add: hom)
  also have "... = hom (sum x (sum y z))" by (simp add: sum.lcomm)
  finally show ?thesis .
qed
```

Importing via a locale expression imports all facts of the imported locales, hence both `sum.lcomm` and `prod.lcomm` are available in `hom_semi`. The import is dynamic — that is, whenever facts are added to a locale, they automatically become available in subsequent **theorem** commands that use the locale as a target, or a locale importing the locale.

4.2 Normal Forms

Locale expressions are interpreted in a two-step process. First, an expression is normalised, then it is converted to a list of context elements.

Normal forms are based on **locale** declarations. These consist of an import section followed by a list of context elements. Let $\mathcal{I}(l)$ denote the locale expression imported by locale l. If l has no import then $\mathcal{I}(l) = \varepsilon$. Likewise, let $\mathcal{F}(l)$ denote the list of context elements, also called the *context fragment* of l. Note that $\mathcal{F}(l)$ contains only those context elements that are stated in the declaration of l, not imported ones.

Example 1. Consider the locales `semi` and `comm_semi`. We have $\mathcal{I}(\texttt{semi}) = \varepsilon$ and $\mathcal{I}(\texttt{comm\_semi}) = \texttt{semi}$, and the context fragments are

$$\mathcal{F}(\texttt{semi}) = \begin{bmatrix} \textbf{fixes} & \texttt{prod} :: \texttt{"['a, 'a]} \Rightarrow \texttt{'a"}\ (\textbf{infixl}\ \texttt{"·"}\ 70) \\ \textbf{assumes} & \texttt{"semi prod"} \\ \textbf{notes} & \texttt{assoc} : \texttt{"?x · ?y · ?z = ?x · (?y · ?z)"} \end{bmatrix},$$

$$\mathcal{F}(\texttt{comm\_semi}) = \begin{bmatrix} \textbf{assumes} & \texttt{"comm\_semi\_axioms prod"} \\ \textbf{notes} & \texttt{comm} : \texttt{"?x · ?y = ?y · ?x"} \\ \textbf{notes} & \texttt{lcomm} : \texttt{"?x · (?y · ?z) = ?y · (?x · ?z)"} \end{bmatrix}.$$

Let $\pi_0(\mathcal{F}(l))$ denote the list of parameters defined in the **fixes** elements of $\mathcal{F}(l)$ in the order of their occurrence. The list of parameters of a locale expression $\pi(e)$ is defined as follows:

$$\pi(l) = \pi(\mathcal{I}(l)) \,\overline{@}\, \pi_0(\mathcal{F}(l)), \text{ for named locale } l.$$
$$\pi(e\, q_1 \ldots q_n) = [q_1, \ldots, q_n, p_{n+1}, \ldots, p_m], \text{ where } \pi(e) = [p_1, \ldots, p_m].$$
$$\pi(e_1 + e_2) = \pi(e_1) \,\overline{@}\, \pi(e_2)$$

The operation $\overline{@}$ concatenates two lists but omits elements from the second list that are also present in the first list. It is not possible to rename more parameters than there are present in an expression — that is, $n \leq m$ — otherwise the renaming is illegal. If $q_i = \_$ then the ith entry of the resulting list is p_i.

In the normalisation phase, imports of named locales are unfolded, and renames and merges are recursively propagated to the imported locale expressions. The result is a list of locale names, each with a full list of parameters, where locale names occurring with the same parameter list twice are removed. Let $\mathcal{N}$ denote normalisation. It is defined by these equations:

$$\mathcal{N}(l) = \mathcal{N}(\mathcal{I}(l)) \,\overline{@}\, [l\ \pi(l)], \text{ for named locale } l.$$
$$\mathcal{N}(e\, q_1 \ldots q_n) = \mathcal{N}(e)\ [q_1 \ldots q_n / \pi(e)]$$
$$\mathcal{N}(e_1 + e_2) = \mathcal{N}(e_1) \,\overline{@}\, \mathcal{N}(e_2)$$

Normalisation yields a list of *identifiers*. An identifier consists of a locale name and a (possibly empty) list of parameters.

In the second phase, the list of identifiers $\mathcal{N}(e)$ is converted to a list of context elements $\mathcal{C}(e)$ by converting each identifier to a list of context elements, and flattening the obtained list. Conversion of the identifier $l\, q_1 \ldots q_n$ yields the list of context elements $\mathcal{F}(l)$, but with the following modifications:

- Rename the parameter in the ith **fixes** element of $\mathcal{F}(l)$ to q_i, $i = 1, \ldots, n$. If the parameter name is actually changed then delete the syntax annotation. Renaming a parameter may also change its type.
- Perform the same renamings on all occurrences of parameters (fixed variables) in **assumes**, **defines** and **notes** elements.
- Qualify names of facts by $q_1\_\ldots\_q_n$.

The locale expression is *well-formed* if it contains no illegal renamings and the following conditions on $\mathcal{C}(e)$ hold, otherwise the expression is rejected:

- Parameters in **fixes** are distinct;
- Free variables in **assumes** and **defines** occur in preceding **fixes**;[3]
- Parameters defined in **defines** must neither occur in preceding **assumes** nor **defines**.

[3] This restriction is relaxed for contexts obtained with **includes**, see Section 4.4.

4.3 Examples

Example 2. We obtain the context fragment $\mathcal{C}(\texttt{comm\_semi})$ of the locale `comm_semi`. First, the parameters are computed.

$$\pi(\texttt{semi}) = [\texttt{prod}]$$
$$\pi(\texttt{comm\_semi}) = \pi(\texttt{semi}) \overline{@} [] = [\texttt{prod}]$$

Next, the normal form of the locale expression `comm_semi` is obtained.

$$\mathcal{N}(\texttt{semi}) = [\texttt{semiprod}]$$
$$\mathcal{N}(\texttt{comm\_semi}) = \mathcal{N}(\texttt{semi}) \overline{@} [\texttt{comm\_semi prod}] = [\texttt{semi prod}, \texttt{comm\_semi prod}]$$

Converting this to a list of context elements leads to the list (2) shown in Section 3.3, but with fact names qualified by `prod` — for example, `prod.assoc`. Qualification was omitted to keep the presentation simple. Isabelle's scoping rules identify the most recent fact with qualified name $x.a$ when a fact with name a is requested.

Example 3. The locale expression `comm_semi sum` involves renaming. Computing parameters yields $\pi(\texttt{comm\_semi sum}) = [\texttt{sum}]$, the normal form is

$$\mathcal{N}(\texttt{comm\_semi sum}) = \mathcal{N}(\texttt{comm\_semi})[\texttt{sum}/\texttt{prod}] = [\texttt{semi sum}, \texttt{comm\_semi sum}]$$

and the list of context elements

fixes sum :: "['a, 'a] ⇒ 'a"
assumes "semi sum"
notes sum.assoc : "sum (sum ?x ?y) ?z = sum ?x (sum ?y ?z)"
assumes "comm_semi_axioms sum"
notes sum.comm : "sum ?x ?y = sum ?y ?x"
notes sum.lcomm : "sum ?x (sum ?y ?z) = sum ?y (sum ?x ?z)"

Example 4. The context defined by the locale `semi_hom` involves merging two copies of `comm_semi`. We obtain parameter list and normal form:

$$\begin{aligned}
\pi(\texttt{semi_hom}) &= \pi(\texttt{comm_semi sum} + \texttt{comm_semi}) \overline{@} [\texttt{hom}] \\
&= (\pi(\texttt{comm_semi sum}) \overline{@} \pi(\texttt{comm_semi})) \overline{@} [\texttt{hom}] \\
&= ([\texttt{sum}] \overline{@} [\texttt{prod}]) \overline{@} [\texttt{hom}] = [\texttt{sum}, \texttt{prod}, \texttt{hom}] \\
\mathcal{N}(\texttt{semi_hom}) &= \mathcal{N}(\texttt{comm_semi sum} + \texttt{comm_semi}) \overline{@} \\
&\quad [\texttt{semi_hom sum prod hom}] \\
&= (\mathcal{N}(\texttt{comm_semi sum}) \overline{@} \mathcal{N}(\texttt{comm_semi})) \overline{@} \\
&\quad [\texttt{semi_hom sum prod hom}] \\
&= ([\texttt{semi sum}, \texttt{comm_semi sum}] \overline{@} [\texttt{semi prod}, \texttt{comm_semi prod}]) \overline{@} \\
&\quad [\texttt{semi_hom sum prod hom}] \\
&= [\texttt{semi sum}, \texttt{comm_semi sum}, \texttt{semi prod}, \texttt{comm_semi prod}, \\
&\quad \texttt{semi_hom sum prod hom}].
\end{aligned}$$

Hence $\mathcal{C}$(semi_hom), shown below, is again well-formed.

```
fixes    sum :: "['a, 'a] ⇒ 'a"
assumes  "semi sum"
notes    sum.assoc : "sum (sum ?x ?y) ?z = sum ?x (sum ?y ?z)"
assumes  "comm_semi_axioms sum"
notes    sum.comm : "sum ?x ?y = sum ?y ?x"
notes    sum.lcomm : "sum ?x (sum ?y ?z) = sum ?y (sum ?x ?z)"
fixes    prod :: "['b, 'b] ⇒ 'b" (infixl "·" 70)
assumes  "semi prod"
notes    prod.assoc : "?x · ?y · ?z = ?x · (?y · ?z)"
assumes  "comm_semi_axioms prod"
notes    prod.comm : "?x · ?y = ?y · ?x"
notes    prod.lcomm : "?x · (?y · ?z) = ?y · (?x · ?z)"
fixes    hom :: "'a ⇒ 'b"
assumes  "semi_hom_axioms sum"
notes    sum_prod_hom.hom : hom (sum x y) = hom x · hom y
```

Example 5. In this example, a locale expression leading to a list of context elements that is not well-defined is encountered, and it is illustrated how normalisation deals with multiple inheritance. Consider the specification of monads (in the algebraic sense) and monoids.

```
locale monad =
  fixes prod :: "['a, 'a] ⇒ 'a" (infixl "·" 70) and one :: 'a ("1" 100)
  assumes l_one: "1 · x = x" and r_one: "x · 1 = x"
```

Monoids are both semigroups and monads and one would want to specify them as locale expression semi + monad. Unfortunately, this expression is not well-formed. Its normal form

$$\mathcal{N}(\texttt{monad}) = [\texttt{monad prod}]$$

$$\mathcal{N}(\texttt{semi} + \texttt{monad}) = \mathcal{N}(\texttt{semi})\ \overline{@}\ \mathcal{N}(\texttt{monad}) = [\texttt{semi prod}, \texttt{monad prod}]$$

leads to a list containing the context element

fixes prod :: "['a, 'a] ⇒ 'a" (**infixl** "·" 70)

twice and thus violating the first criterion of well-formedness. To avoid this problem, one can introduce a new locale magma with the sole purpose of fixing the parameter and defining its syntax. The specifications of semigroup and monad are changed so that they import magma.

```
locale magma = fixes prod (infixl "·" 70)

locale semi' = magma + assumes assoc: "(x · y) · z = x · (y · z)"
locale monad' = magma + fixes one ("1" 100)
  assumes l_one: "1 · x = x" and r_one: "x · 1 = x"
```

Normalisation now yields

$$\begin{aligned}\mathcal{N}(\texttt{semi' + monad'}) &= \mathcal{N}(\texttt{semi'})\ \overline{@}\ \mathcal{N}(\texttt{monad'})\\ &= (\mathcal{N}(\texttt{magma})\ \overline{@}\ [\texttt{semi' prod}])\ \overline{@}\ (\mathcal{N}(\texttt{magma})\ \overline{@}\ [\texttt{monad' prod}])\\ &= [\texttt{magma prod}, \texttt{semi' prod}]\ \overline{@}\ [\texttt{magma prod}, \texttt{monad' prod}])\\ &= [\texttt{magma prod}, \texttt{semi' prod}, \texttt{monad' prod}]\end{aligned}$$

where the second occurrence of `magma prod` is eliminated. The reader is encouraged to check, using the **print_locale** command, that the list of context elements generated from this is indeed well-formed.

It follows that importing parameters is more flexible than fixing them using a context element. The Locale package provides the predefined locale `var` that can be used to import parameters if no particular mixfix syntax is required. Its definitions is

locale *var* = **fixes** `x_`

The use of the internal variable `x_` enforces that the parameter is renamed before being used, because internal variables may not occur in the input syntax.

4.4 Includes

The context element **includes** takes a locale expression e as argument. It can occur at any point in a locale declaration, and it adds $\mathcal{C}(e)$ to the current context.

If **includes** e appears as context element in the declaration of a named locale l, the included context is only visible in subsequent context elements, but it is not propagated to l. That is, if l is later used as a target, context elements from $\mathcal{C}(e)$ are not added to the context. Although it is conceivable that this mechanism could be used to add only selected facts from e to l (with **notes** elements following **includes** e), currently no useful applications of this are known.

The more common use of **includes** e is in long goals, where it adds, like a target, locale context to the proof context. Unlike with targets, the proved theorem is not stored in the locale. Instead, it is exported immediately.

```
theorem lcomm2:
  includes comm_semi shows "x · (y · z) = y · (x · z)"
proof -
  have "x · (y · z) = (x · y) · z" by (simp add: assoc)
  also have "... = (y · x) · z" by (simp add: comm)
  also have "... = y · (x · z)" by (simp add: assoc)
  finally show ?thesis .
qed
```

This proof is identical to the proof of `lcomm`. The use of **includes** provides the same context and facts as when using `comm_semi` as target. On the other hand, lcomm2 is not added as a fact to the locale comm_semi, but is directly visible in the theory. The theorem is

```
comm_semi ?prod ⟹ ?prod ?x (?prod ?y ?z) = ?prod ?y (?prod ?x ?z).
```

Note that it is possible to combine a target and (several) **includes** in a goal statement, thus using contexts of several locales but storing the theorem in only one of them.

5 Structures

The specifications of semigroups and monoids that served as examples in previous sections modelled each operation of an algebraic structure as a single parameter. This is rather inconvenient for structures with many operations, and also unnatural. In accordance to mathematical texts, one would rather fix two groups instead of two sets of operations.

The approach taken in Isabelle is to encode algebraic structures with suitable types (in Isabelle/HOL usually records). An issue to be addressed by locales is syntax for algebraic structures. This is the purpose of the **(structure)** annotation in **fixes**, introduced by Wenzel. We illustrate this, independently of record types, with a different formalisation of semigroups.

Let 'a semi_type be a not further specified type that represents semigroups over the carrier type 'a. Let s_op be an operation that maps an object of 'a semi_type to a binary operation.

```
typedecl 'a semi_type
consts s_op :: "['a semi_type, 'a, 'a] ⇒ 'a" (infixl "⋆ı" 70)
```

Although s_op is a ternary operation, it is declared infix. The syntax annotation contains the token ı (\<index>), which refers to the first argument. This syntax is only effective in the context of a locale, and only if the first argument is a *structural* parameter — that is, a parameter with annotation **(structure)**. The token has the effect of replacing the parameter with a subscripted number, the index of the structural parameter in the locale. This replacement takes place both for printing and parsing. Subscripted 1 for the first structural parameter may be omitted, as in this specification of semigroups with structures:

```
locale comm_semi' =
  fixes G :: "'a semi_type" (structure)
  assumes assoc: "(x ⋆ y) ⋆ z = x ⋆ (y ⋆ z)" and comm: "x ⋆ y = y ⋆ x"
```

Here x ⋆ y is equivalent to x $\star_1$ y and abbreviates s_op G x y. A specification of homomorphisms requires a second structural parameter.

```
locale semi'_hom = comm_semi' + comm_semi' H +
  fixes hom
  assumes hom: "hom (x ⋆ y) = hom x ⋆₂ hom y"
```

The parameter H is defined in the second **fixes** element of $\mathcal{C}$(semi'_comm). Hence $\star_2$ abbreviates s_op H x y. The same construction can be done with records instead of an *ad-hoc* type. In general, the ith structural parameter is addressed by index i. Only the index 1 may be omitted.

```
record 'a semi = prod :: "['a, 'a] ⇒ 'a" (infixl "·ı" 70)
```

This declares the types `'a semi` and `('a, 'b) semi_scheme`. The latter is an extensible record, where the second type argument is the type of the extension field. For details on records, see [7] Chapter 8.3.

```
locale semi_w_records = struct G +
  assumes assoc: "(x · y) · z = x · (y · z)"
```

The type `('a, 'b) semi_scheme` is inferred for the parameter `G`. Using subtyping on records, the specification can be extended to groups easily.

```
record 'a group = "'a semi" +
  one :: "'a" ("1ı" 100)
  inv :: "'a ⇒ 'a" ("invı _" [81] 80)
locale group_w_records = semi_w_records +
  assumes l_one: "1 · x = x" and l_inv: "inv x · x = 1"
```

Finally, the predefined locale

locale *struct* = **fixes** `S_` (**structure**).

is analogous to `var`. More examples on the use of structures, including groups, rings and polynomials can be found in the Isabelle distribution in the session HOL-Algebra.

6 Conclusions and Outlook

Locales provide simple means of modular reasoning. They allow to abbreviate frequently occurring context statements and maintain facts valid in these contexts. Importantly, using structures, they allow syntax to be effective only in certain contexts, and thus to mimic common practice in mathematics, where notation is chosen very flexibly. This is also known as literate formalisation [2]. Locale expressions allow to duplicate and merge specifications. This is a necessity, for example, when reasoning about homomorphisms. Normalisation makes it possible to deal with diamond-shaped inheritance structures, and generally with directed acyclic graphs. The combination of locales with record types in higher-order logic provides an effective means for specifying algebraic structures: locale import and record subtyping provide independent hierarchies for specifications and structure elements. Rich examples for this can be found in the Isabelle distribution in the session HOL-Algebra.

Primary reason for writing this report was to provide a better understanding of locales in Isar. Wenzel provided hardly any documentation, with the exception of [9]. The present report should make it easier for users of Isabelle to take advantage of locales.

The report is also a base for future extensions. These include improved syntax for structures. Identifying them by numbers seems not natural and can be confusing if more than two structures are involved — for example, when reasoning about universal properties — and numbering them by order of occurrence seems arbitrary. Another desirable feature is *instantiation*. One may, in the course of a theory development, construct objects that fulfil the specification of a locale. These objects are possibly defined in the context of another locale. Instantiation should make it simple to specialise abstract facts for the object under consideration and to use the specified facts.

A detailed comparison of locales with module systems in type theory has not been undertaken yet, but could be beneficial. For example, a module system for Coq has recently been presented by Chrzaszcz [3]. While the latter usually constitute extensions of the calculus, locales are a rather thin layer that does not change Isabelle's meta logic. Locales mainly manage specifications and facts. Functors, like the constructor for polynomial rings, remain objects of the logic.

Acknowledgement. Lawrence C. Paulson and Norbert Schirmer made useful comments on a draft of this paper.

References

1. David Aspinall. Proof general: A generic tool for proof development. In Susanne Graf and Michael I. Schwartzbach, editors, *TACAS 2000*, number 1785 in LNCS, pages 38–42. Springer, 2000.
2. Anthony Bailey. *The machine-checked literate formalisation of algebra in type theory*. PhD thesis, University of Manchester, January 1998.
3. Jacek Chrzaszcz. Implementing modules in the Coq system. In David Basin and Burkhart Wolff, editors, *TPHOLs 2003*, number 2758 in LNCS, pages 270–286. Springer, 2003.
4. Florian Kammüller. Modular reasoning in Isabelle. In David McAllester, editor, *CADE 17*, number 1831 in LNCS, pages 99–114. Springer, 2000.
5. Gerwin Klein. *Verified Java Bytecode Verification*. PhD thesis, Institut für Informatik, Technische Universität München, 2003.
6. Tobias Nipkow. Structured proofs in Isar/HOL. In H. Geuvers and F. Wiedijk, editors, *TYPES 2002*, number 2646 in LNCS, pages 259–278. Springer, 2003.
7. Tobias Nipkow, Lawrence C. Paulson, and Markus Wenzel. *Isabelle/HOL: A Proof Assistant for Higher-Order Logic*. Number 2283 in LNCS. Springer, 2002.
8. Markus Wenzel. *Isabelle/Isar — a versatile environment for human-readable formal proof documents*. PhD thesis, Technische Universität München, 2002. Electronically published as http://tumb1.biblio.tu-muenchen.de/publ/diss/in/2002/wenzel.html.
9. Markus Wenzel. Using locales in Isabelle/Isar. Part of the Isabelle2003 distribution, file src/HOL/ex/Locales.thy. Distribution of Isabelle available at http://isabelle.in.tum.de, 2002.
10. Markus Wenzel. The Isabelle/Isar reference manual. Part of the Isabelle2003 distribution, available at http://isabelle.in.tum.de, 2003.

Introduction to PAF!, a Proof Assistant for ML Programs Verification

Sylvain Baro

PPS – CNRS UMR 7126
Université Denis Diderot
Case 7014
2, Place Jussieu
75251 PARIS Cedex 05

Abstract. We present here a proof assistant dedicated to the proof of ML programs. This document is oriented from a user's point of view. We introduce the system progressively, describing its features as they become useful, and justifying our choices all along.
Our system intends to provide a usual predicate calculus to express and prove properties of functional ML terms including higher order functions with polymorphic types. To achieve this goal, functional expressions are embedded in the logic as first class terms, with their usual syntax and evaluation rules.

The purpose of this paper is to introduce the reader to PAF!, a proof assistant dedicated to the verification of properties of programs written in the functional core of the ML language. More precisely, we will put emphasis on the main features of our system: the convenience and expressive power of our logic to write programs and their specifications; and the innovative design of our interactive *proof assistant*, which allows a high level of interactivity and which simplifies the integration of new tactics into the system.

These two aspects represent our contribution to both the fields of program verification and interactive theorem proving.

Our system is formalised so as to allow formulas to express and prove properties of ML terms. It has two levels: a programming language and a logical language. The programming language is a strictly functional ML which includes: algebraic datatypes, functions defined by pattern matching, recursion and polymorphism. Furthermore, it allows definition of partial functions. The logical language combines a multisorted classical predicate calculus, whose sorts are the ML datatypes and whose first class terms are ML terms, with a dedicated proof language.

Like in ACL2 or nqthm [9,3], in PAF! formulas assert properties of programs, but we chose not to encode logic in the programming language. In a sense, we are closer to PVS [14] which mixes an extended lambda-calculus with higher order predicate calculus, but our term language has both the syntax and the evaluation rules of ML programs. Like PVS, our system allows to handle partial functions, but without using subtyping. As in Type Theory [13], we have

S. Berardi, M. Coppo, and F. Damiani (Eds.): TYPES 2003, LNCS 3085, pp. 51–65, 2004.

inductive datatypes available, but not dependent ones (except for type polymorphism), and datatypes can not embed any logical content. As opposed to Type Theory, proofs do not need to lead to programs, hence we do not need to remain within a constructive framework.

In the world of design and implementation of proof assistants in general, we think our approach to be novel. We are guided by the concern of being able to offer the user "full page" edition capabilities for the development of theories (programs and their intended properties) and proofs. This lead us to conceive the architecture of our system like a dialogue between a *proof engine* in charge of the logical part (in particular, of the validity of each stage of the proof) and a (graphical) user interface, handling edition. Both communicates in a *client – server* fashion through a dedicated proof engine protocol [11]. This aspect of our work was carried out in collaboration with the working group MathOS of the laboratory PPS.

Stress was also put on the extension capabilities of our system. We tried to ease as much as possible the writing of new tactics, without jeopardising the correctness of the system. We use an original architecture, mixing object oriented programming and functional programming (made possible by the use of *Objective Caml*). This architecture satisfies *De Bruijn's criterion* which requires that a proof assistant should be able to generate a *proof object* in a simpler formalism, amenable to double-checking. The current version of the proof engine, including tactics, consists of more than 15000 *Objective Caml* lines of code.

We are convinced that program certification tools should be usable by programmers, and not only by computer scientists: programs should be written as usual. We think that, when we intend to write a certified piece of software, it is sensible to use a restriction of the programming language, but we must stay in the same formalism. This lead us to the *credo* that guided all the design of our proof assistant: WYSIWIP, for "What You See Is What You Prove": in our system, what the user appears to prove is *actually* what he proves. There is no encoding in a hidden logical framework, which would lead him to prove things which seems (to him) unrelated to his problem, urging him to make the effort to understand the underneath part of the system.

The first section shows how to write programs in our framework. Section 2 discusses the issue of program termination. Section 3 and 4 present the specification language and the proof language. The last part of this paper (Section 5 and 6) presents the graphical user interface and key details of the implementation of the system. We conclude with a short comparison with other systems.

Simple examples are used throughout this paper to illustrate our discourse. The interested reader might find more complicated ones in [1].

1 ML Functional Core

1.1 Language

In the following, we use examples to introduce the reader to our system. Commands and answers of the system are given nearly *verbatim*. The real syntax, which is very close, depends of the user interface. Either it is the *toplevel* interface, and the commands are embedded in simple *Objective Caml* function calls (for example, the tactic `Intro` is called with `p "Intro" ;;`). Or it is the graphical user interface, and the commands are typed directly in the placeholders (boxes) or through the use of buttons and menus.

A beginner's example. Assume that `Nil` and `Cons` are the two constructors of polymorphic lists. The definition of the append function may be written as follows:

```
let rec append l1 l2 =
   match l1 with
      Nil         -> l2
    | Cons(x,l1) -> Cons(x,(append l1 l2))
```

This is the recursive definition of a function using pattern matching facilities. From this definition, knowing the types of `Nil` and `Cons`, the system infers the expected ML type for `append`: `(['a] list -> (['a] list -> ['a] list))`.

From the formal point of view, the ML type assigned to `append` is a *sort*. This is a syntactical property of the definition and does not means that `append` will map any pair of lists to a list (*i.e.* is total). The totality of a function can be asserted apart from the definition itself: the system provides a special command for this, which will be discussed in section 2.

This distinction between, let's say, "syntactical" and "logical" types allows one to define partial functions using *partial pattern matching*, as in:

```
let head x = match x with Cons(x,l) -> x
```

This function is typed by the system as `['a] list -> 'a`, despite it is a partial function. Defining partial functions is allowed in our system, using non exhaustive pattern matching, because we use more than a mere *case* operator.

Datatypes. Let us now define a new datatype for binary trees:

```
type ['a] tree = Leaf of 'a | Node of ['a] tree * ['a] tree
```

This definition introduces a new polymorphic sort `['a] tree` and two constructor symbols `Leaf` and `Node` together with their respective sorts `'a -> ['a] tree` and `(['a] tree * ['a] tree) -> ['a] tree`. At the logical level, the sort assignments for constructors are interpreted as *introduction rules* for the corresponding inductive type and a second order formula is generated, which corresponds to the elimination rule of this type (its structural induction principle). This view is close to the ones in [12,10,16].

Using our new data structure, one can define a traversal function which maps a tree to a list of its labels:

```
let rec toList t =
 match t with
```

```
    Leaf(x) -> Cons(x,Nil)
  | Node(Leaf(x),t2) -> Cons(x,(toList t2))
  | Node(Node(t1,t2),t3) -> (toList Node(t1,Node(t2,t3)))
```

The function toList has type `['a] tree -> ['a] list`.

1.2 Reduction, Evaluation, and Equal

We set the semantics of our programming language with its *reduction rules* which describe the way how terms reduce to values. Our reduction rules are given by the natural semantics of ML ([4]), which is a weak call-by-value reduction.

However, there is a difference between evaluation in a programming language scope and evaluation in a logical scope: in the latter one, we might find logical variables in terms. For instance the pattern matching expression `(match Leaf(t) with Leaf(x) -> t1 | z -> t2)` evaluates to t1[t/x] while `(match x with Leaf(x) -> t1 | z -> t2)` does not evaluate: it is considered as a weak normal form. The only case where a head formal variable does not stop the reduction of a pattern matching expression has the form `(match x with z -> u | ...)` which evaluates to u[x/z].

Reduction is built-in and is axiomatised as a relation between terms. But when reasoning about programs, one may need to check *equality* between terms. The only predefined equality provided is the built-in equality at the programming level: the polymorphic operator = of ML. Its semantics is given by the following:

- `C(t1) = C(t2)` evaluates to the boolean ML value `true` if `C` is a constructor symbol and `t1 = t2` evaluates to `true`;
- `C1(t1) = C2(t2)` evaluates to `false` if `C1` and `C2` are distinct constructors;
- `t = t` evaluates to `true`, even if `t` is a variable.
- All the other equational terms are considered as being in normal form. This is in particular the case for `x = y` where `x` and `y` are variables.

2 To Be Total (Or Not to Be Total)

An often needed property of functions involved in a program development is termination. In our system, among others, termination can be established by proving that the function is totally defined on its intended type. In this section what it means in our framework to be "totally defined on the intended type". The presentation of the construction of the proofs is delayed until Section 4.

A First Example. Let us consider again the append function. The user prompts the system for proving its totality by the following command:

```
Total append
```

Then the system urges the user to prove the following:

```
|-
(Forall 'a: type (Forall x: ['a] list (Forall y: ['a] list
              ((append x y): ['a] list)))
```

How should we read this formula ? Syntactically, it consists in three bound universal quantifiers and ends with the type assignment `((append x y):['a] list)`. First, we must distinguish between two kinds of use of universal bindings: `Forall 'a: type` on one side and the two `Forall x:['a] list`, `Forall y: ['a] list` on the other side.

The `Forall 'a: type` binding introduces `'a` as a *type parameter* which can be used in the subformula. The quantification is needed to make sure that the `'a` in the two following bindings are the same type parameter.

But despite the use of the `Forall` keyword, `Forall 'a: type` is not a genuine logical quantifier (we are definitively not in Type Theory). It is merely a syntactical construct to mark that only ML types expressions may be substituted to the parameter `'a`. So neither formulas nor terms can be substituted here, which excludes dependent types.

The `Forall x: ['a] list` binding may be read as the usual syntactical shortcut for bound quantification. From the logical point of view, a formula as `(Forall x:tau F)` where `tau` is an ML type expression and `F` a formula is expended to `(Forall x (tau:x) -> F)` where `->` is the propositional implication.

The explanation we gave for the second kind of bound quantifier leads us to make precise the meaning of what we write as the type assignments: `x:['a] list` or `((append x y):['a] list)`. Formally, it is a schematic atomic formula where `:['a] list` is the predicate symbol and `x` and `(append x y)` are the arguments. The intended semantics of such a predicate is that its argument has sort `['a] list` (for the ML type discipline) and that it *terminates*. In other words, `((append x y): ['a] list)` means that `(append x y)` will evaluate to a list. The formal setting of this use of type assignment is given in [2][1] and is called *strong typing*.

To end the commentary about this first example, let us mention that, whenever a `Forall x:['a] list` quantifier is instantiated with some term `t`, it is required to prove that `t: ['a] list` holds. But having proved the totality of all functions allows the proof engine to prove automatically most of these statements of termination. For example if the user needs to prove that a term t terminates, and t contains a call to `append`, but no fixpoints, neither partial pattern matching, and the totality of `append` has been previously proved, then the statement will be proved automatically using type inference. This allows the user to ignore nearly all the typing proofs that are commonly needed in most theorem provers.

Higher Order Functions. Let us define now the higher order function `map`:

```
let rec map f l =
  match l with
    Nil -> Nil
  | Cons(x,xs) -> Cons((f x), (map f xs))
```

[1] We apologise that its English version is not yet available...

The command `Total map` will produce the following proof obligation:

```
|-
(Forall 'a : type (Forall 'b : type (Forall f: 'a -> 'b
   (Forall l: ['a] list ((map f l): ['b] list)))))
```

The novelty here is the type restriction `f:'a -> 'b`, which entails that `map` will be total as long as it is applied to functions that are themselves total. It is thus not allowed to apply `map` to the partial `head` function.

Partial terms do not deserve a particular treatment: if one wants to prove, say `Odd(predecessor 0)` (where the predecessor is partially defined and weakly typed `nat -> nat`), we are stuck because `(predecessor 0)` cannot be reduced.

3 Specification Language

It is now time to express more intentional properties on the defined functions. PAF! uses a usual vernacular language which comes with function and type definitions. We have already met the `Total` command, we also use the commands `Declare`, `Definition`, `Axiom` and `Theorem`.

Predicates. Let us begin with a simple example: the predicate `Mem(x,l)` which expresses membership of `x` to the list `l`.

We first introduce the *predicate symbol* `Mem` together with its sort:

```
Declare Mem : ('a * ['a] list) -> Prop
```

where `Prop` denotes the sort of logical propositions. We forbid the sort `Prop` on the left hand side of a sort arrow. Thus we do not have full higher order logic but only the fragment needed to assert about (possibly higher order) functions.

The intended meaning of the `Mem` predicate may be given by the two axioms:

```
Axiom MemB  :
 (Forall 'a: type
  (Forall x: 'a (Forall l: ['a] list Mem(x,Cons(x,l)))))


Axiom MemRec  :
 (Forall 'a: type (Forall x: 'a (Forall y: 'a (Forall l: ['a] list
  ( Mem(x,l) -> Mem(x,Cons(y,l)) )))))
```

Now, if `memL` is the ML boolean function testing the list membership, one can state the following lemma to prove the correctness of `memL` w.r.t. its logical specification given by the `Mem` relation with its two axioms:

```
Theorem :
  (Forall 'a: type (Forall x: 'a (Forall l: ['a] list
   (`(memL x l) -> Mem(x,l)))))
```

Notice that in the above formula, the backquote character in the premise `` `(memL x l) `` is a built-in predicate of sort `bool -> Prop` which maps ML boolean values to logical truth values. We have two rules for this predicate: (1) `` `(true) `` is always true; (2) under the hypothesis `` `(false) ``, anything is true.

Equations. A second use of this "boolean promotion" is to set equations. For instance, from the append definition, one can prove that:

```
Theorem append_assoc:
 (Forall 'a : type
   (Forall x: ['a] list (Forall y: ['a] list (Forall z: ['a] list
     `((append (append x y) z) = (append x (append y z)))))))
```

Of course, equations may be guarded as in:

```
Theorem mem_not_eq:
  (Forall 'a:type (Forall x:'a (Forall y:'a (Forall l:['a] list
     Not(Mem(x,l)) -> `((mem x Cons(y,l)) = (x=y))))))
```

This is why equality is not necessarily required at the logical level of our framework. Indeed, for ML program verification, one mainly wants to set equations between ML values and this is obtained by combining the ML built-in equality function with the backquote predicate.

A last example. Let us end the presentation of the specification language with an example about the `toList` function defined in section 1. The aim is to express the correctness of this function by something like: *x belongs to the computed list (toList t) iff it belongs to t.*

Let us first define membership in trees:

```
let rec memT x t =
 match t with
  Leaf(y) -> (x = y)
| Node(t1,t2) -> (or (memT x t1) (memT x t2))

Total memT
```

We may now state that values in the tree will be in the list obtained by applying `toList`.

```
Theorem memL_memT :
(Forall 'a : type (Forall x : 'a  (Forall t : ['a] tree
   `( (memL x (toList t)) = (memT x t) ) )))
```

4 Proofs

The interaction with the proof assistant is rather standard: the proof engine gives a sequent (a *proof goal*) to the user, who answers by typing in a proof command together with its arguments (a *tactic*). Then, the proof engine applies the given tactic to the aimed goal and asks again the user to prove the possible subgoals until no more remain. With the command line interface, the proof is seen as a *script*, as in most proof assistants, but in our graphical interface, the tree structure is kept, allowing the user to prove the goals in any order, and to leave holes in the proof, to be filled later on.

The current implementation of PAF! does not provide a lot of sophisticated tactics but the user may already find: (1) Tactics allowing purely logical reasoning, including most of the natural deduction rules and left rules of the sequent calculus (to ease the reasoning on hypothesis); (2) tactics allowing the use of hypothesis, axioms, theorems and equations. Note that, in the interactive process of building proofs, a theorem can be used before its proof has been achieved; (3) tactics for opening functions definitions, using reduction relation and *strong typing*, since we are concerned by programming features; (4) higher level tactic with more or less automation for structural induction, since we are concerned by programs over inductive datatypes.

These tactics are built on top of a set of primitive rules based on Free Deduction (see [17]) to which we add dedicated rules to handle the ML terms reduction and the strong typing. One of the most useful rule allows us to substitute a term u for a term t in a formula whenever t reduces to u.

Example 1. We first prove the associativity of `append` using the induction tactic. We assume that `append` has been proved total. In answer to the command

```
Theorem assoc_append :
 (Forall 'a : type
  (Forall l1:['a] list (Forall l2:['a] list (Forall l3:['a] list
  '((append (append l1 l2) l3)) = (append l1 (append l2 l3))))))
```

the proof engine prompts the user with the corresponding sequent:

```
|-
(Forall 'a:type
 (Forall l1:['a] list (Forall l2:['a] list (Forall l3:['a] list
  '(((append (append l1 l2) l3)=(append l1 (append l2 l3)))))))
```

Then the user simply enters:

```
ByInduction
```

and the proof engine answers that everything is `Proved`.

One should not be too much enthusiastic about the level of automation of the `ByInduction` tactic. It succeeds here because the proof of associativity of append involves only one induction, one function, constructors and very simple rewriting (or reduction). Note that without parameter the tactic `ByInduction` tries the induction on the first universally bound term variable in the formula.

When it fails to automatically solve its given goal, the `ByInduction` tactic gives the hand back to the user with as many subgoals as required by the structural induction.

Example 2. Let us prove the totality of `toList`, met in Section 1. The goal is:

```
|-
(Forall 'a:type (Forall t:['a] tree ((toList t):['a] list)))
```

Using `ByInduction` on this goal will produce the two subgoals corresponding to the two structural induction cases for our binary trees.

The first subgoal, corresponding to the `Leaf` constructor, is

```
|-
(Forall x15:'a ((toList Leaf(x15)):['a] list))
```

It is solved by our simple `Auto` tactic.

The second subgoal, corresponding to the `Node` constructor, is

```
|-
(Forall x16:['a] tree (Forall x17:['a] tree
  (((toList x16):['a] list) -> (((toList x17):['a] list)
     -> ((toList Node(x16,x17)):['a] list)))))
```

To solve it, some preliminary work is needed. Let us give the sequence of tactics without displaying the intermediate subgoals:

```
Intron 3
Generalize x17
Generalize x16
```

That lead us to the subgoal:

```
[H3 : ((toList x16):['a] list)]
H2 : (x17:['a] tree)
H1 : (x16:['a] tree)
|-
(Forall x16:['a] tree (Forall x17:['a] tree
  (((toList x17):['a] list)
     -> ((toList Node(x16,x17)):['a] list))))
```

The first tactic call (`Intron 3`) introduces 3 premisses of the formula in the hypothesis part of the sequent (above the sign `|-`). It corresponds to the logical introduction rules of natural deduction. The two latter ones correspond to the elimination rule of the universal quantifier, we use them to get the right induction formula. Note that the strong typing proof obligations due to bound quantifier elimination have been automatically solved. This proof is completed by one more use of the `ByInduction` tactic.

Example 3. The last example illustrates what remains to be done in order to improve automation on really trivial proofs. We prove totality of the `memL` function, met in Section 3. The goal to prove is:

```
|-
(Forall 'a:type
   (Forall x:'a (Forall l:['a] list ((memL x l):bool))))
```

We proceed by induction on `l`:

```
ByInduction l
```

The `Nil` case is solved by `Auto`, thus we omit it. The second subgoal is:

```
|-
(Forall x15:'a (Forall x16:['a] list
 ((Forall x:'a ((memL x x16):bool))
   -> (Forall x:'a ((memL x Cons(x15,x16)):bool)))))
```

Remark that, since we have given an argument to the `ByInduction` tactic, it builds the induction formula keeping the `Forall x:'a` binding. Here the tactics fails to prove automatically the subgoals. We thus need to proceed by hand.

First, we introduce the hypothesis with the tactic:

```
Intros
```

and get

```
[H6 : (x:'a)]
H5 : (Forall x:'a ((memL x x16):bool))
H4 : (x16:['a] list)
H3 : (x15:'a)
|-
((memL x Cons(x15,x16)):bool)
```

Let us open the definition of `memL` and evaluates the resulting term.

```
OpenAndEval memL
```

Our goal is now

```
[H6 : (x:'a)]
H5 : (Forall x:'a ((memL x x16):bool))
H4 : (x16:['a] list)
H3 : (x15:'a)
|-
((or (x=x15) (memL x x16)):bool)
```

We now have to use the fact that the boolean function `or` is total and to apply the theorem `or_total`, previously generated by `Total or`:

```
Apply or_total
```

Then we get as a last subgoal:

```
[H6 : (x:'a)]
H5 : (Forall x:'a ((memL x x16):bool))
H4 : (x16:['a] list)
H3 : (x15:'a)
|-
((memL x x16):bool)
```

This subgoal is solved by `Auto` (using induction hypothesis). The strong typing statement `(x=x15):bool` has been solve by `Apply` and is not even displayed to the user, which illustrates what have been told in Section 2.

5 Interfaces

For the moment, two interfaces are usable with PAF!. The first one (of lower level) is a command line interface, which is in fact an *Objective Caml toplevel* extended with functions which allow us to insert new vernacular and proof commands, as well as simple functions for managing the proof.

The second interface (still under heavy development), which unleash the full dynamic power of our proof engine, is a graphical user interface written in Python/Tkinter by Yves Legrandgérard. This interface allows us to insert vernacular commands (*let*, *type*, definitions, declarations, axioms or theorems) at any point in the session, thus allowing full page edition. Proofs may also be edited full page, the interface being aware of their tree-like nature. The user may ignore a proof, or build only part of it, leaving some holes in, or delete parts of it. Goals may be fulfilled in whatever order suits to the user.

This interface is not a simple emulation of full page edition through the use of command line together with *undo*, but communicates with the proof engine through a dedicated Proof Engine Protocol [11,1] over TCP. This protocol is synchronous: the interface issues a request then waits for the answer of the proof engine. On the other hand, the state of the interface is different of the state of the proof engine. Requests are only sent when the user asks for it, and only validated elements (vernacular or proof steps) are known by the proof engine. For example the user may invalidate a particular element, then a request is issued to the proof engine, which suppresses it, if allowed. But the interface keeps this element in an invalidated state until the user either deletes it, or modifies then revalidates it.

Figure 1 shows an example where the user forgot to define a function and had to come back at the beginning to insert it. Some commands have already been issued and accepted by the prover, and proofs have been left apart (and fold) by the user. The colors of the boxes and of the vertical thin lines change following the status of the box: validated, invalidated or false (the reader should take it for truth, since some information gets lost through the use of the printer).

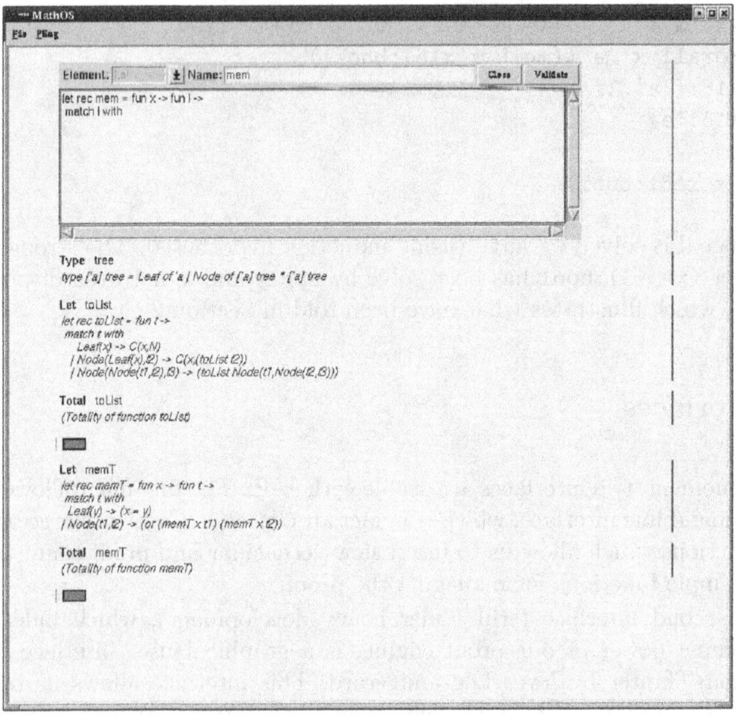

Fig. 1. Inserting a new definition above

6 Implementation

We already mentioned some features of our system: dynamic capabilities, the ability to be extended and the satisfaction of *De Bruijn's criterion*. All this features required to use an innovative architecture for the proof engine. We give here hints on how this was achieved. More details may be found in [1].

6.1 Dynamic . . .

In order to be able to insert or suppress *session elements* (vernacular commands) or *proof elements* in a dynamic fashion (as seen in Section 5), we can not use a simple architecture with one context maintaining the state after the last issued command. We need to use distributed contexts: contexts need to be embedded into each session and into each proof element, and to be linked back to the previous context following the lexical scope of the session: a session elements knows everything which has been declared in other session elements higher in the session, similarly, a proof element knows everything which is in the upper part of the proof, and everything which comes before the theorem it proves.

Inserting and deleting is then just a matter of linking and unlinking contexts, while checking and updating a dependency tree.

6.2 ... Easy to Extend ...

The future of a proof assistant lies in its evolution capability. We wanted ours to be as easy to extend as possible. Of course, writing a heavy automatic decision procedure will always be tricky, but simple (compositional) tactics have to be easy to add, and the cost of writing complex tactics must not be due to the complexity of the system. To achieve this purpose, we made good use of the object oriented features of *Objective Caml*.

Inheritance provides an easy way to force all tactics to follow a given template. In our system, tactics have to inherit the abstract class `proofTac` hence they have to implement two methods: `generate` and `refineFun` (kept abstract in `proofTac`). The `generate` method is responsible for checking if the tactic applies and for the construction of its premisses, while `refineFun` is used to enforce reliability (more is told in Section 6.3).

A tactic may be written, either by calling other more primitive tactics, including the basic rules, or from scratch, through direct manipulation on the sequent and on the formulas through an API. Inheritance allows to design families of tactics, *e.g.* all tactics inheriting `simplTac` try to solve all subgoals before submitting them to the user, without requiring further modification of the tactic.

Composition of tactics allows us to write new ones in a progressive way. For example `Intro`, which does one introduction step, is written using direct manipulations on the sequent (but could have been written using left rules of free deduction), `Intros` simply iterates `Intro` until failure, and `Auto` tries to apply `Intros`, among other high level tactics.

Beside these tactics, one find a set of primitive rules which are not intended to be user friendly, but rather to provide basic "bricks" to build tactics.

On top of this, there is a mechanism of dynamic loading for tactics, which may be compiled (or even downloaded !) and used in PAF! without restarting it.

6.3 ... and Reliable

Although it is nice to be able to write new tactics, it is even nicer if they do not jeopardise the reliability of the system: one may write a tactic, that always "prove" its goal (`GivenToTheStudentAsAnExercise`), but do we want this to be possible ? The solution we adopted is to build afterward an *atomic proof*, which contains only primitive rules, out of the proof actually built by the user.

As in Milner's LCF [7], tactics are written in two parts, one to build the subgoals (`generate`) and one to ensure safety (`refineFun`). `refineFun` takes as an argument the primitive proof corresponding to each premise of the tactic, then has to send back a primitive proof of its conclusion. As for `generate`, it might be built either from scratch or using more primitive tactics to refine the proof progressively. It might as well reuse part of the work made by `generate`. At the end of the process, we get the *atomic proof* represented using an algebraic datatype, which is proof-checked by a specific function.

This method is very convenient, because it allows us to use different algorithms for building of proof and for checking it. The building part must be fast, because it is interactive, so we may use decision procedures which are not able to build the atomic proof. But because checking is made at the end, it will not bother the user if it is not instantaneous to build the atomic proof.

7 Comparison with (a Few) Other Systems

It is interesting to compare our system with others used in program verification.

Our approach is different than Coq's [18], even used with the `Program` tactic [15]. Coq uses program extraction in the Calculus of Construction (which allows only total functions), the program is therefore embedded into the proof, while in our system, it is written as it is. The use of `Program` or Why [6] surely allows the user to write an annotated program, and to verify it, but it is done through encodings into the Calculus of Constructions, which is in contradiction with our WYSIWYP dogma. Another distinction is that we use genuine pattern matching and not a *case* nor a guarded fixpoint operator as in Coq.

Agda [5] is rather different than our system (except on the interface side, Alfa providing full page edition for Agda [8]). One might see Agda as a "super ML with dependent types" where the user writes the program together with the proof in Type Theory. In our system, proofs are distinct from programs. It is legal to write non terminating functions in Agda, and termination may be checked using an external criterion.

We are close to PVS, in spite of some key differences. PVS proves properties on terms of an extended lambda-calculus, as we do, but we chose to stick to a well known programming language. To handle partial functions, PVS proposes subtyping. So all functions are total, but with much control over their domain through the use of a comprehension scheme over types. Our types are simpler, but we allow partial functions. Besides, PVS does not satisfy *De Bruijn's criterion.*

The system we are the closest of is ACL2 [9]. The goals of this system are ours: prove properties directly on the programs, in a functional programming language. ACL2 authors chose LISP, while we chose ML. The big difference between ACL2 and PAF! is the way proofs are built. When a theorem is stated, ACL2 tries to prove it using a very efficient automatic decision procedure. If this fails, the usual way is to state other lemmas before, until all the proofs succeed. In PAF!, we wanted the proofs to be interactively built by the user. We may add that ACL2 does not handle partial functions, nor satisfies *De Bruijn's criterion.*

We are not far from algebraic specification methods: the user of the system defines an algebra using ML datatypes. He is then able to state the intended properties, using equations, to write the program, and finally to prove that it satisfies the intended properties.

8 Conclusion

PAF! is presently usable, but is not yet in a release state. In spite of this, and from the experience we had using it, we have the feeling that our bet is on the good track: What You See is actually What You Prove, the development of new tactics is quite straightforward, and the user interface is promising.

Further work should include extensions of the system in order to handle more features of ML languages (exceptions, etc.). Automation has also to be worked out, as there are currently no complex decision procedures.

Finally, we think that this work opens interesting perspectives in the field of program verification, and that our architecture has a future in the world of proof assistants.

Acknowledgements. The author would like to thank Yves Legrandgérard, for writing the graphical user interface of the system, and Chantal Berline, for correcting most of the mistakes in this paper (remaining ones were added by the author afterward).

References

1. S. Baro. Conception et implémentation d'un système d'aide à la spécification et à la preuve de programmes ML. PhD Université Denis Diderot, 2003.
2. S. Baro and P. Manoury. Un système X. Raisonner formellement sur les programmes ML. Journées Francophones des Langages Applicatifs. INRIA, 2003.
3. R. Boyer and J Strother Moore. *A Computational Logic.* Academic Press, 1979.
4. Dominique Clément, Joëlle Despeyroux, Thierry Despeyroux, and Gilles Kahn. A Simple Applicative Language: Mini-ML. In *Proceedings of ACM Symposium on LISP and Functional Programming*, 1986.
5. Catarina Coquand. *Agda*, 2000. `http://www.cs.chalmers.se/ catarina/agda/`.
6. J.-C. Filliâtre. Why: a multi-language multi-prover verification tool. Submitted to FME 2003, March 2003.
7. Michael J. Gordon, Robin Milner, and Christopher P. Wadsworth. Edinburgh LCF: A mechanised logic of computation. volume 78 of *LNCS*. Springer-Verlag, 1979.
8. Thomas Hallgren. *Alfa*, 2001. `http://www.cs.chalmers.se/ hallgren/Alfa/`.
9. Matt Kaufmann and J Strother Moore. A Precise Description of the ACL2 Logic. Technical report, Computational Logic, Inc., 1997.
10. Jean-Louis Krivine. *Lambda-Calculus, Types and Models.* Ellis and Horwood, 1993.
11. Yves Legrandgérard. Proof Engine Protocol, version 2 specification. manuscript.
12. Daniel Leivant. Reasoning about functional programs and complexity classes associated with type discipline. *Foundations of Computer Science*, 1983.
13. Per Martin-Löf. *Intuitionistic Type Theory.* Studies in Proof Theory. Bibliopolis, 1984.
14. S. Owre, N. Shankar, J. M. Rushby, and D. W. J. Stringer-Calvert. *PVS System Guide.* SRI International, `http://pvs.csl.sri.com`, v2.4 edition, 2001.
15. Catherine Parent. Developing certified programs in the system Coq - the Program tactic. In *Types for Proofs and Programs*, volume 806 of *LNCS*, 1993.
16. Michel Parigot. Recursive programming with proofs. *Theoretical Computer Science*, pages 335–356, 1992.
17. Michel Parigot. Church-Rosser property in classical free deduction. In G. Huet and G. Plotkin, editors, *Logical Environments.* 1993.
18. LogiCal Project The Coq Development Team. *The Coq Proof Assistant Reference Manual.* INRIA, 1999-2001. v7.2 `http://coq.inria.fr`.

A Constructive Proof of Higman's Lemma in Isabelle

Stefan Berghofer*

Technische Universität München
Institut für Informatik, Boltzmannstraße 3, 85748 Garching, Germany
http://www.in.tum.de/ berghofe/

Abstract. Higman's lemma, a specific instance of Kruskal's theorem, is an interesting result from the area of combinatorics, which has often been used as a test case for theorem provers. We present a constructive proof of Higman's lemma in the theorem prover Isabelle, based on a paper proof by Coquand and Fridlender. Making use of Isabelle's newly-introduced infrastructure for program extraction, we show how a program can automatically be extracted from this proof, and analyze its computational behaviour.

1 Introduction

Higman's lemma [8] is an interesting problem from the field of combinatorics. It can be considered as a specific instance of Kruskal's famous tree theorem, which is useful for proving the termination of term rewriting systems using so-called *simplification orders*. Higman's lemma states that every infinite sequence of words $(w_i)_{0 \leq i < \omega}$ contains two words w_i and w_j with $i < j$ such that w_i can be *embedded* into w_j. A sequence with this property is also called *good*, otherwise *bad*. Although a quite elegant *classical* proof of this statement has been given by Nash-Williams [12] using a so-called *minimal bad sequence argument*, there has been a growing interest in obtaining *constructive* proofs of Higman's lemma recently. This is due to the additional informative content inherent in constructive proofs. For example, a termination proof of a string rewrite system based on a constructive proof of Higman's lemma could be used to obtain upper bounds on the length of reduction sequences.

The first formalization of Higman's lemma using a theorem prover was done by Murthy [10] in the Nuprl system [5]. Murthy first formalized Nash-Williams' classical proof, then translated it into a constructive proof using a *double negation translation* followed by Friedman's *A-translation* and finally extracted a program from the resulting proof. Unfortunately, although correct in principle, the program obtained in this way was so huge that it was both incomprehensible and impossible to execute within a reasonable amount of time even on the fastest computing equipment available. This rather disappointing experience prompted

* Supported by DFG Graduiertenkolleg *Logic in Computer Science*, and IST project 29001 *TYPES*

S. Berardi, M. Coppo, and F. Damiani (Eds.): TYPES 2003, LNCS 3085, pp. 66–82, 2004.

several scientists to think about direct formalizations of constructive proofs of Higman's lemma, notably Murthy and Russell [11], as well as Fridlender [7], who formalized Higman's lemma using the ALF proof editor [9] based on Martin-Löf's type theory. Fridlender's paper also gives a detailed account of the history of Higman's lemma. Murthy's classical proof was also reconsidered by Herbelin, who formalized an A-translated version of it in the Coq [2] system. Seisenberger's thesis [14,15] contains an excellent overview of various different formalizations of Higman's lemma, most of which have been carried out with the Minlog [3] proof assistant.

A particularly elegant and short constructive proof, based entirely on inductive definitions, has been suggested by Coquand and Fridlender [6]. The rest of this paper is dedicated to a formalization of this proof in the theorem prover Isabelle. To improve on previous formalizations, the central parts of the proof are formulated using the *Isar* language for human-readable proofs due to Wenzel [17]. Moreover, thanks to the design of Isabelle's program extraction framework [4], we are also able to derive a correctness statement for the extracted program *inside* the logic. This is in contrast to most other implementations of program extraction, whose correctness if often only justified by meta-theoretic arguments on paper. Finally, to make the rather abstract exposition given by Coquand and Fridlender more easily accessible, we also present an intuitive graphical description of the computational behaviour of the extracted programs.

The rest of the paper is structured as follows: In §2, we give some basic definitions concerning sequences of words. §3 is concerned with assigning computational content to proofs involving inductive datatypes and predicates, which play a central role in the formalization. §4 describes the actual formalization in Isabelle, and §5 is devoted to an analysis of the program extracted from the proof. A conclusion is given in §6.

2 Basic Definitions

We start with a few basic definitions. Words are modelled as lists of letters from the two letter alphabet[1]

datatype *letter* = *A* | *B*
types *word* = *letter list*

The empty list is denoted by [], and x # xs is infix notation for *Cons* x xs. We use $[x_1, \ldots, x_n]$ to abbreviate x_1 # ... # []. The embedding relation on words is defined inductively as follows:

consts *emb* :: (*word* × *word*) *set*
inductive *emb*
intros
  emb0: [] $\trianglelefteq$ *bs*

[1] It is worth noting that the extension of the proof to an arbitrary finite alphabet is not at all trivial. For details, see Seisenberger's PhD. thesis [15].

$emb1$: $as \trianglelefteq bs \Longrightarrow as \trianglelefteq b \# bs$
$emb2$: $as \trianglelefteq bs \Longrightarrow a \# as \trianglelefteq a \# bs$

Intuitively, a word *as* can be embedded into a word *bs*, if we can obtain *as* by deleting letters from *bs*. For example, $[A, A] \trianglelefteq [B, A, B, A]$. In order to formalize the notion of a good sequence, it is useful to define the set $L\ v$ of all lists of words containing a word which can be embedded into v:

consts L :: *word* ⇒ *word list set*
inductive $L\ v$
intros
$L0$: $w \trianglelefteq v \Longrightarrow w \# ws \in L\ v$
$L1$: $ws \in L\ v \Longrightarrow w \# ws \in L\ v$

A list of words is *good* if its tail is either *good* or contains a word which can be embedded into the word occurring at the head position of the list:

consts *good* :: *word list set*
inductive *good*
intros
$good0$: $ws \in L\ w \Longrightarrow w \# ws \in good$
$good1$: $ws \in good \Longrightarrow w \# ws \in good$

In contrast to Coquand [6], who defines *Cons* such that it appends elements to the right of the list, we use the usual definition of *Cons*, which appends elements to the left. Therefore, the predicates on lists of words defined in this section, such as the *good* predicate introduced above work "in the opposite direction", e.g. $[[A, A], [A, B], [B]] \in good$, since $[B] \trianglelefteq [A, B]$. In order to express the fact that every infinite sequence is good, we define a predicate *bar* as follows:

consts *bar* :: *word list set*
inductive *bar*
intros
$bar1$: $ws \in good \Longrightarrow ws \in bar$
$bar2$: $(\bigwedge w.\ w \# ws \in bar) \Longrightarrow ws \in bar$

Intuitively, $ws \in bar$ means that either the list of words ws is already *good*, or successively adding words will turn it into a good list. Consequently, $[] \in bar$ means that every infinite sequence $(w_i)_{0 \leq i < \omega}$ must be good, i.e. have a prefix $w_0\ \ldots\ w_n$ with $[w_n,\ \ldots,\ w_0] \in good$, since by successively adding words $w_0,\ w_1,\ \ldots$ to the empty list, we must eventually arrive at a list which is good. Note that the above definition of *bar* is closely related to Brouwer's more general principle of *bar induction* [16, Chapter 4, §8]. Like the accessible part of a relation, the definition of *bar* embodies a kind of well-foundedness principle.

3 Computational Content of Inductive Datatypes and Predicates

The main proof principles used in the proof of Higman's lemma are induction on datatypes and induction on the derivation of inductive predicates (or sets). In order to extract a program from this proof, it is therefore important to investigate which programs correspond to these proof principles.

3.1 Motivation

For *inductive datatypes*, things are rather straightforward: A proof by *induction* on a datatype gives rise to a program defined by *recursion* on the very same datatype. The concept of an *inductive predicate* is quite similar to that of an inductive datatype[2]: While a datatype is characterized by a list of *constructors* together with their types, an inductive predicate is characterized by a list of *introduction rules*. Consequently, the program extracted from a proof by induction on the derivation of an inductive predicate should be a recursive function, too, where the recursion runs over a datatype which encodes the derivation. This datatype can be derived from the introduction rules in a canonical way. Each introduction rule φ corresponds to a constructor of type $\mathsf{tyof}\ \varphi$, where tyof is a *type extraction* function mapping a logical formula to the type of the program extracted from its proof. For the fragment of Isabelle comprising implication ($\Longrightarrow$) and universal quantification ($\bigwedge$), which is used to express the introduction rules, tyof is defined by

$$\begin{array}{lcl} \mathsf{tyof}\ (\bigwedge x :: \alpha.\ \varphi) & \equiv & \alpha \Rightarrow \mathsf{tyof}\ \varphi \\ \mathsf{tyof}\ (\psi \Longrightarrow \varphi) & \equiv & \mathsf{tyof}\ \psi \Rightarrow \mathsf{tyof}\ \varphi \\ \mathsf{tyof}\ (P\ \bar{t}) & \equiv & \alpha_P \end{array}$$

where φ and ψ are *computationally relevant* formulae, and P is a computationally relevant predicate variable. Every such predicate variable P is uniquely associated with a type variable α_P. For a full definition of tyof, the interested reader is referred to [4]. For an inductive predicate such as *bar*, we set $\mathsf{tyof}\ (ws \in bar) \equiv barT$, where $barT$ is a new datatype to be defined inductively. The correspondence between proof rules for inductive predicates and programs, which we have sketched above, is illustrated in Fig. 1. Intuitively, the datatype $barT$ representing the computational content of $ws \in bar$ is an infinitely branching tree from which one can read off words that, when appended to the sequence of words ws, turn it into a *good* sequence. The branches of this tree are labelled with words. For each appended word w, one moves one step closer to the leaves of the tree, following the branch labelled with w. When a leaf, i.e. the constructor *bar1* is reached, the resulting sequence of words must be *good*. An example for such a tree is shown in Fig. 2.

In order to reason about the correctness of programs extracted from proofs involving the *bar* predicate, we need to describe under what conditions an element of $barT$ properly represents a derivation of a formula $ws \in bar$. This connection

[2] It should be noted that this insight is the essence of expressive *type theories* based on inductive types such as the *Calculus of Inductive Constructions* [13], where these two concepts actually coincide due to the identification of propositions and types. However, this is not the case for Isabelle/HOL, which treats propositions and types as different concepts.

Proof	**Program**
induction on datatype $\mathit{list\text{-}induct} : P\ [] \Longrightarrow$ $(\bigwedge x\ xs.\ P\ xs \Longrightarrow P\ (x\ \#\ xs)) \Longrightarrow P\ ys$	recursion on datatype $\mathit{list\text{-}rec} : \alpha\ \mathit{list} \Rightarrow \alpha_P \Rightarrow$ $(\alpha \Rightarrow \alpha\ \mathit{list} \Rightarrow \alpha_P \Rightarrow \alpha_P) \Rightarrow \alpha_P$
inductive predicate introduction rules **inductive** *bar* $\mathit{bar1} : \bigwedge ws.\ ws \in \mathit{good} \Longrightarrow ws \in \mathit{bar}$ $\mathit{bar2} : \bigwedge ws.\ (\bigwedge w.\ w\ \#\ ws \in \mathit{bar}) \Longrightarrow$ $ws \in \mathit{bar}$ induction on derivation $\mathit{bar\text{-}induct} : vs \in \mathit{bar} \Longrightarrow$ $(\bigwedge ws.\ ws \in \mathit{good} \Longrightarrow P\ ws) \Longrightarrow$ $(\bigwedge ws.\ (\bigwedge w.\ w\ \#\ ws \in \mathit{bar}) \Longrightarrow$ $(\bigwedge w.\ P\ (w\ \#\ ws)) \Longrightarrow P\ ws) \Longrightarrow$ $P\ vs$	inductive datatype constructors **datatype** $\mathit{barT} =$ $\mathit{bar1}\ (\mathit{word\ list})$ $\mid \mathit{bar2}\ (\mathit{word\ list})\ (\mathit{word} \Rightarrow \mathit{barT})$ recursion on datatype $\mathit{barT\text{-}rec} : \mathit{barT} \Rightarrow$ $(\mathit{word\ list} \Rightarrow \alpha_P) \Rightarrow$ $(\mathit{word\ list} \Rightarrow (\mathit{word} \Rightarrow \mathit{barT}) \Rightarrow$ $(\mathit{word} \Rightarrow \alpha_P) \Rightarrow \alpha_P) \Rightarrow$ α_P

Fig. 1. Computational content of inductive datatypes and predicates

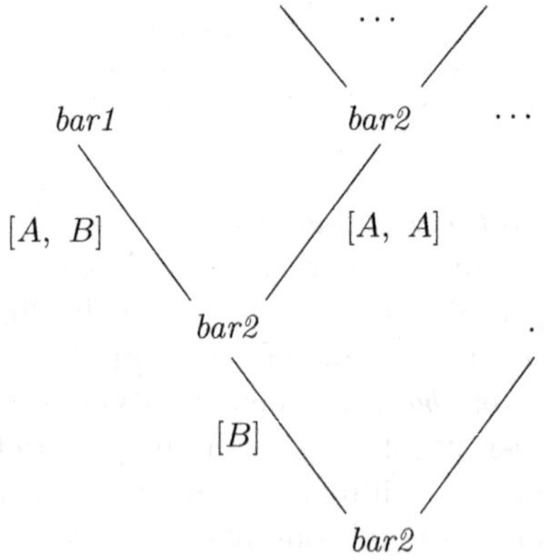

Fig. 2. Computational content of *bar*

between datatypes (or programs) and formulae can be captured by the concept of *modified realizability* due to Kleene and Kreisel. We write realizes $p\ \varphi$ to mean that "program p *realizes* formula φ" or, more intuitively, "p *satisfies* specification φ". For the $\Longrightarrow/\bigwedge$-fragment of Isabelle, realizes is defined by the equations

$$\begin{array}{lcl} \mathsf{realizes}\ p\ (\bigwedge x.\ \varphi) & \equiv & \bigwedge x.\ \mathsf{realizes}\ (p\ x)\ \varphi \\ \mathsf{realizes}\ p\ (\psi \Longrightarrow \varphi) & \equiv & \bigwedge q.\ \mathsf{realizes}\ q\ \psi \Longrightarrow \mathsf{realizes}\ (p\ q)\ \varphi \\ \mathsf{realizes}\ p\ (P\ \bar{t}) & \equiv & P^R\ p\ \bar{t} \end{array}$$

where again φ and ψ are computationally relevant formulae, and P is a computationally relevant predicate variable. Each predicate variable P with n arguments is uniquely associated with a predicate variable P^R with $n+1$ arguments. For the inductive predicate *bar*, we set **realizes** b $(ws \in bar) \equiv (b,\ ws) \in barR$, where *barR* is a new inductive predicate characterized by the introduction rules

$$ws \in good \Longrightarrow (bar1\ ws,\ ws) \in barR$$
$$(\bigwedge w.\ (f\ w,\ w \ \#\ ws) \in barR) \Longrightarrow (bar2\ ws\ f,\ ws) \in barR$$

which express that the constructors of the datatype *barT* realize the introduction rules of the predicate *bar* in the above sense. As a consequence, this means that if $(bar2\ ws\ f_0,\ ws) \in barR$ and

$$f_0\ w_0 = bar2\ (w_0 \ \#\ ws)\ f_1, \quad f_1\ w_1 = bar2\ (w_1 \ \#\ w_0 \ \#\ ws)\ f_2, \quad \ldots,$$
$$f_{n-1}\ w_{n-1} = bar2\ (w_{n-1} \ \#\ \cdots \ \#\ w_0 \ \#\ ws)\ f_n,$$
$$f_n\ w_n = bar1\ (w_n \ \#\ \cdots \ \#\ w_0 \ \#\ ws)$$

then $(w_n \ \#\ \cdots \ \#\ w_0 \ \#\ ws) \in good$. Note that this need not necessarily be the shortest possible *good* sequence. The induction principle for the *bar* predicate, which is shown in Fig. 1, is realized by the recursion combinator

$$barT\text{-}rec\ f\ g\ (bar1\ list) = f\ list$$
$$barT\text{-}rec\ f\ g\ (bar2\ list\ fun) = g\ list\ fun\ (\lambda x.\ barT\text{-}rec\ f\ g\ (fun\ x))$$

The corresponding correctness theorem for this realizer is

$$\begin{array}{l}(b,\ vs) \in barR \Longrightarrow \\ (\bigwedge ws.\ ws \in good \Longrightarrow P^R\ (f\ ws)\ ws) \Longrightarrow \\ (\bigwedge ws\ x.\ (\bigwedge w.\ (x\ w,\ w \ \#\ ws) \in barR) \Longrightarrow \\ \qquad (\bigwedge xa.\ (\bigwedge w.\ P^R\ (xa\ w)\ (w \ \#\ ws)) \Longrightarrow P^R\ (g\ ws\ x\ xa)\ ws)) \Longrightarrow \\ P^R\ (barT\text{-}rec\ f\ g\ b)\ vs\end{array}$$

which is easily proved by induction on the derivation of *barR*.

3.2 General Scheme

We will now generalize what we have just explained by an example. Consider the general definition of an inductive set (or predicate) S

inductive S

$$\begin{array}{l}I_1 : \bigwedge \overline{x_1} :: \overline{\tau_1}.\ \varphi_1^1 \Longrightarrow \cdots \Longrightarrow \varphi_1^{s_1} \Longrightarrow (\bigwedge \overline{z_1^1} :: \overline{\sigma_1^1}.\ \overline{\psi_1^1} \Longrightarrow \overline{t_1^1} \in S) \Longrightarrow \cdots \Longrightarrow \\ \quad (\bigwedge \overline{z_1^{r_1}} :: \overline{\sigma_1^{r_1}}.\ \overline{\psi_1^{r_1}} \Longrightarrow \overline{t_1^{r_1}} \in S) \Longrightarrow \overline{u_1} \in S \\ \vdots \\ I_n : \bigwedge \overline{x_n} :: \overline{\tau_n}.\ \varphi_n^1 \Longrightarrow \cdots \Longrightarrow \varphi_n^{s_n} \Longrightarrow (\bigwedge \overline{z_n^1} :: \overline{\sigma_n^1}.\ \overline{\psi_n^1} \Longrightarrow \overline{t_n^1} \in S) \Longrightarrow \cdots \Longrightarrow \\ \quad (\bigwedge \overline{z_n^{r_n}} :: \overline{\sigma_n^{r_n}}.\ \overline{\psi_n^{r_n}} \Longrightarrow \overline{t_n^{r_n}} \in S) \Longrightarrow \overline{u_n} \in S\end{array}$$

where φ_i^j are *non-recursive* premises (also called *side conditions*), i.e. do not contain S. The *recursive* premises have the form

$$\bigwedge \overline{z_i^j} :: \overline{\sigma_i^j}.\ \overline{\psi_i^j} \Longrightarrow \overline{u_i} \in S$$

where S does not occur in $\overline{\psi_i^j}$, i.e. the occurrence of the recursive set is only *strictly positive*.

Induction The rule for induction on the derivation of S has the form

$$\mathcal{I}_1 \Longrightarrow \cdots \Longrightarrow \mathcal{I}_n \Longrightarrow \overline{x} \in S \Longrightarrow P\ \overline{x}$$

where

$$\begin{array}{rcl}\mathcal{I}_i & = & \bigwedge \overline{x_i}.\ \varphi_i^1 \Longrightarrow \cdots \Longrightarrow \varphi_i^{s_i} \Longrightarrow \\ & & (\bigwedge \overline{z_i^1 :: \sigma_i^1}.\ \overline{\psi_i^1} \Longrightarrow \overline{t_i^1} \in S) \Longrightarrow \cdots \Longrightarrow (\bigwedge \overline{z_i^{r_i} :: \sigma_i^{r_i}}.\ \overline{\psi_i^{r_i}} \Longrightarrow \overline{t_i^{r_i}} \in S) \Longrightarrow \\ & & (\bigwedge \overline{z_i^1 :: \sigma_i^1}.\ \overline{\psi_i^1} \Longrightarrow P\ \overline{t_i^1}) \Longrightarrow \cdots \Longrightarrow (\bigwedge \overline{z_i^{r_i} :: \sigma_i^{r_i}}.\ \overline{\psi_i^{r_i}} \Longrightarrow P\ \overline{t_i^{r_i}}) \Longrightarrow P\ \overline{u_i}\end{array}$$

Computational content of derivations The datatype S^T representing the computational content of the derivation of S is defined by

$$\begin{array}{l}\textbf{datatype}\ S^T\ = \\ \quad I_1\ \overline{\tau_1}\ (\mathsf{tyof}\ \varphi_n^1) \cdots (\mathsf{tyof}\ \varphi_1^{s_1})\ (\overline{\sigma_1^1} \Rightarrow \mathsf{tyof}\ \overline{\psi_1^1} \Rightarrow S^T) \cdots (\overline{\sigma_1^{r_1}} \Rightarrow \mathsf{tyof}\ \overline{\psi_1^{r_1}} \Rightarrow S^T) \\ \mid \cdots \\ \mid I_n\ \overline{\tau_n}\ (\mathsf{tyof}\ \varphi_n^1) \cdots (\mathsf{tyof}\ \varphi_n^{s_n})\ (\overline{\sigma_n^1} \Rightarrow \mathsf{tyof}\ \overline{\psi_n^1} \Rightarrow S^T) \cdots (\overline{\sigma_n^{r_n}} \Rightarrow \mathsf{tyof}\ \overline{\psi_n^{r_n}} \Rightarrow S^T)\end{array}$$

Realizability predicate The predicate S^R, which establishes a connection between elements of the datatype S^T and propositions of the form $\overline{x} \in S$ is defined inductively by the introduction rules

$$\begin{array}{l}I_i^R = \bigwedge \overline{x_i}\ p_i^1 \ldots p_i^{s_i}\ \overline{f_i^1 \ldots f_i^{r_i}}.\ (\mathsf{realizes}\ p_i^1\ \varphi_i^1) \Longrightarrow \cdots \Longrightarrow (\mathsf{realizes}\ p_i^{s_i}\ \varphi_i^{s_i}) \Longrightarrow \\ \quad (\bigwedge \overline{z_i^1}\ \overline{q_i^1}.\ \mathsf{realizes}\ \overline{q_i^1}\ \overline{\psi_i^1} \Longrightarrow (f_i^1\ \overline{z_i^1}\ \overline{q_i^1},\ \overline{t_i^1}) \in S^R) \Longrightarrow \cdots \Longrightarrow \\ \quad (\bigwedge \overline{z_i^{r_i}}\ \overline{q_i^{r_i}}.\ \mathsf{realizes}\ \overline{q_i^{r_i}}\ \overline{\psi_i^{r_i}} \Longrightarrow (f_i^{r_i}\ \overline{z_i^{r_i}}\ \overline{q_i^{r_i}},\ \overline{t_i^{r_i}}) \in S^R) \Longrightarrow \\ \quad\ (I_i\ \overline{x_i}\ p_i^1 \ldots p_i^{s_i}\ f_i^1 \ldots f_i^{r_i},\ \overline{u_i}) \in S^R\end{array}$$

Computational content of induction principle The above rule for induction on the derivation of the set S is realized by the recursion combinator S^T-*rec* for the datatype S^T, which is characterized by the equations

$$\begin{array}{l}S^T\text{-}rec\ g_1 \cdots g_n\ (I_i\ p_i^1 \cdots p_i^{s_i}\ \overline{f_i^1 \cdots f_i^{r_i}}) = g_i\ \overline{p_i^1 \cdots p_i^{s_i}}\ \overline{f_i^1 \cdots f_i^{r_i}} \\ \quad (\lambda \overline{z_i^1}\ \overline{q_i^1}.\ S^T\text{-}rec\ g_1 \cdots g_n\ (f_i^1\ \overline{z_i^1}\ \overline{q_i^1})) \ \cdots\ (\lambda \overline{z_i^{r_i}}\ \overline{q_i^{r_i}}.\ S^T\text{-}rec\ g_1 \cdots g_n\ (f_i^{r_i}\ \overline{z_i^{r_i}}\ \overline{q_i^{r_i}}))\end{array}$$

The fact that this recursion combinator correctly realizes the principle of induction on the derivation d can be expressed by

$$(d,\ \overline{x}) \in S^R \Longrightarrow \mathcal{R}_1 \Longrightarrow \cdots \Longrightarrow \mathcal{R}_n \Longrightarrow P^R\ (S^T\text{-}rec\ g_1 \cdots g_n\ d)\ \overline{x}$$

where

$$\begin{array}{l}\mathcal{R}_i = \bigwedge \overline{x_i}\ p_i^1 \ldots p_i^{s_i}\ \overline{f_i^1 \ldots f_i^{r_i}}.\ (\mathsf{realizes}\ p_i^1\ \varphi_i^1) \Longrightarrow \cdots \Longrightarrow (\mathsf{realizes}\ p_i^{s_i}\ \varphi_i^{s_i}) \Longrightarrow \\ \quad (\bigwedge \overline{z_i^1}\ \overline{q_i^1}.\ \mathsf{realizes}\ \overline{q_i^1}\ \overline{\psi_i^1} \Longrightarrow (f_i^1\ \overline{z_i^1}\ \overline{q_i^1},\ \overline{t_i^1}) \in S^R) \Longrightarrow \cdots \Longrightarrow \\ \quad (\bigwedge \overline{z_i^{r_i}}\ \overline{q_i^{r_i}}.\ \mathsf{realizes}\ \overline{q_i^{r_i}}\ \overline{\psi_i^{r_i}} \Longrightarrow (f_i^{r_i}\ \overline{z_i^{r_i}}\ \overline{q_i^{r_i}},\ \overline{t_i^{r_i}}) \in S^R) \Longrightarrow \\ \quad (\bigwedge \overline{z_i^1}\ \overline{q_i^1}.\ \mathsf{realizes}\ \overline{q_i^1}\ \overline{\psi_i^1} \Longrightarrow P^R\ (f_i^1\ \overline{z_i^1}\ \overline{q_i^1})\ \overline{t_i^1}) \Longrightarrow \cdots \Longrightarrow \\ \quad (\bigwedge \overline{z_i^{r_i}}\ \overline{q_i^{r_i}}.\ \mathsf{realizes}\ \overline{q_i^{r_i}}\ \overline{\psi_i^{r_i}} \Longrightarrow P^R\ (f_i^{r_i}\ \overline{z_i^{r_i}}\ \overline{q_i^{r_i}})\ \overline{t_i^{r_i}}) \Longrightarrow \\ \quad\ P^R\ (g_i\ \overline{x_i}\ p_i^1 \ldots p_i^{s_i}\ f_i^1 \ldots f_i^{r_i})\ \overline{u_i}\end{array}$$

and P^R is a new predicate variable uniquely associated with the predicate variable P in the above induction rule for S. This correctness statement for S^T-*rec* can be proved by induction on the derivation of $(d,\ \overline{x}) \in S^R$.

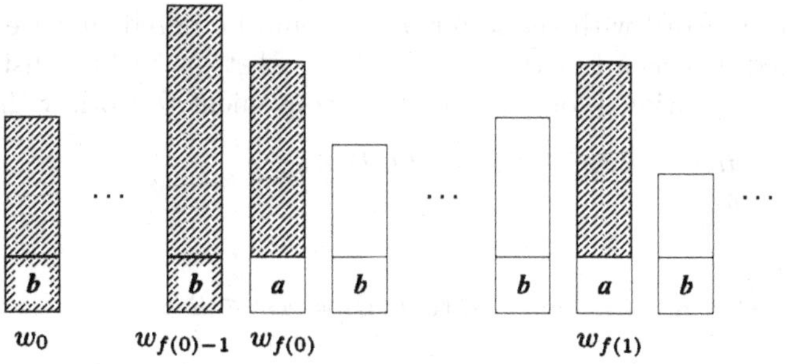

Fig. 3. Minimal bad sequence argument

4 Formalizing Higman's Lemma

Before explaining the actual proof, we will briefly sketch the main idea of Nash-Williams' classical proof[3], since Coquand's proof can be considered as a constructive version of it. In order to show that every infinite sequence is good, we assume there is a bad sequence and use this to derive a contradiction. If there is a bad sequence, we may also construct a bad sequence $(w_i)_{0 \leq i < \omega}$ which is minimal wrt. word length[4]. Since any infinite sequence containing the empty word is necessarily good, each w_i must have the form $a_i \# v_i$. We can find a strictly monotone function f and a letter $a \in \{A, B\}$ such that $a_{f(i)} = a$ for all i. Now consider the sequence $(v_{f(i)})_{0 \leq i < \omega}$. If this sequence was bad, we could construct the sequence

$$s = w_0 \ \ldots \ w_{f(0)-1} \ v_{f(0)} \ v_{f(1)} \ \ldots$$

Because the length of $v_{f(0)}$ is smaller than the length of $w_{f(0)}$, and $(w_i)_{0 \leq i < \omega}$ is minimal, this sequence must be good. For this to be possible, there must be i and j with $i < f(0)$ and $w_i \trianglelefteq v_{f(j)}$, because both $(w_i)_{0 \leq i < \omega}$ and $(v_{f(i)})_{0 \leq i < \omega}$ are bad. However, since $v_{f(j)} \trianglelefteq w_{f(j)}$, this implies that $w_i \trianglelefteq w_{f(j)}$, which contradicts the assumption that $(w_i)_{0 \leq i < \omega}$ is bad. Hence $(v_{f(i)})_{0 \leq i < \omega}$ must be good, which means that there are i and j with $i < j$ and $v_{f(i)} \trianglelefteq v_{f(j)}$, which implies that $a \# v_{f(i)} \trianglelefteq a \# v_{f(j)}$ and therefore $w_{f(i)} \trianglelefteq w_{f(j)}$, which again contradicts the assumption that $(w_i)_{0 \leq i < \omega}$ is bad.

To capture the idea underlying the construction of the sequence s shown above, we introduce a relation T, where $(vs,\ ws) \in T\ a$ means that vs is obtained from ws by first copying the prefix of words starting with the letter b, where $a \neq b$, and then appending the tails of words starting with a. This construction principle is illustrated in Fig. 3, where the shaded parts correspond to the sequence s above. In order to define T, we also introduce an auxiliary relation R, where $(vs,\ ws) \in R\ a$ means that ws can be obtained from vs by

[3] A more general version of this proof for Kruskal's theorem can e.g. be found in the textbook by Baader and Nipkow [1].

[4] A sequence $(w_i)_{0 \leq i < \omega}$ is *smaller* than a sequence $(v_i)_{0 \leq i < \omega}$ wrt. word length, iff there is a k such that $w_j = v_j$ for all $j < k$ and $length(w_k) < length(v_k)$.

prefixing each word with the letter *a*. It should be noted that we could as well have defined *T a* as a function which, given a list *ws*, yields a list *vs*. However, we found the relational formulation more convenient to work with.

consts $R :: letter \Rightarrow (word\ list \times word\ list)\ set$
inductive $R\ a$
intros
  $R0$: $([], []) \in R\ a$
  $R1$: $(vs, ws) \in R\ a \Longrightarrow (w \# vs, (a \# w) \# ws) \in R\ a$

consts $T :: letter \Rightarrow (word\ list \times word\ list)\ set$
inductive $T\ a$
intros
  $T0$: $a \neq b \Longrightarrow (vs, ws) \in R\ b \Longrightarrow (w \# ws, (a \# w) \# ws) \in T\ a$
  $T1$: $(vs, ws) \in T\ a \Longrightarrow (v \# vs, (a \# v) \# ws) \in T\ a$
  $T2$: $a \neq b \Longrightarrow (vs, ws) \in T\ a \Longrightarrow (vs, (b \# w) \# ws) \in T\ a$

The proof of Higman's lemma is divided into several parts, namely *prop1*, *prop2* and *prop3*. From the computational point of view, these theorems can be thought of as functions transforming trees. Theorem *prop1* states that each sequence ending with the empty word satisfies predicate *bar*, since it can trivially be extended to a *good* sequence by appending any word. This easily follows from the introduction rules for *bar*:

theorem *prop1*: $([] \# ws) \in bar$ **by** *rules*

The intuition behind *prop2*, which is shown in Fig. 4, is a bit harder to grasp. Given two trees encoding proofs of $xs \in bar$ and $ys \in bar$, we produce a new tree encoding a proof of $zs \in bar$ by *interleaving* the two input trees. In order to demonstrate that $zs \in bar$, we need to show that, given a sequence of words, we can detect if appending this sequence to *zs* yields a *good* sequence. This is done by inspecting each word in the sequence to be appended. If the word has the form $a \# w$, we move one step ahead in the tree witnessing $xs \in bar$, whereas we move one step ahead in the tree witnessing $ys \in bar$ if it has the form $b \# w$. Whenever we reach a leaf in one of these trees, we can be sure that, due to the additional constraints on *xs*, *ys* and *zs*, we have turned *zs* into a good sequence. If the word to be appended is just the empty word [], we know by *prop1* that any following word will make the sequence good. The proof of *prop2* is by double induction on the derivation of $xs \in bar$ and $ys \in bar$ (yielding the induction hypotheses *I* and *I'*), followed by a case analysis on the word *w* to be appended to the sequence *zs*.

Theorem *prop3* states that we can turn a proof of $xs \in bar$ into a proof of $zs \in bar$, where *zs* is the list obtained by prefixing each word in the (nonempty) list *xs* with the letter *a*. The proof together with its corresponding tree is shown in Fig. 5. Note that the subtrees of this tree (reachable via edges labelled with words *w*) are interleavings of other trees formed using *prop2*. In order to prove $zs \in bar$, we again consider all possible words *w* to be appended to *zs*. There are essentially two different cases which may occur:

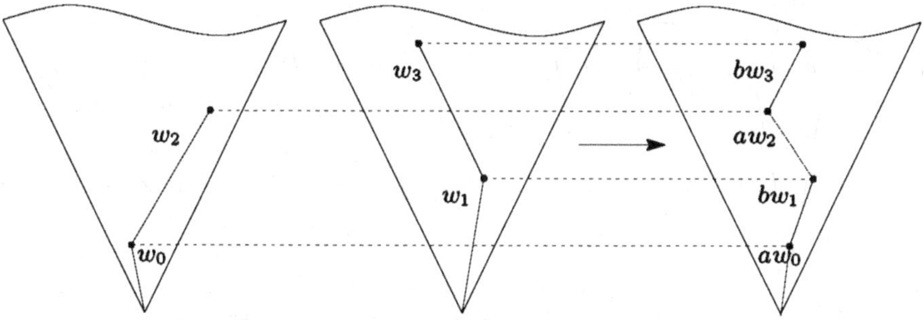


```
theorem prop2:
  assumes ab: a ≠ b and bar: xs ∈ bar
  shows ⋀ys zs. ys ∈ bar ⟹ (xs, zs) ∈ T a ⟹ (ys, zs) ∈ T b ⟹ zs ∈ bar
  using bar
proof induct
  fix xs zs assume xs ∈ good and (xs, zs) ∈ T a
  show zs ∈ bar by (rule bar1) (rule lemma3)
next
  fix xs ys assume I: ⋀w ys zs. ys ∈ bar ⟹ (w # xs, zs) ∈ T a ⟹
    (ys, zs) ∈ T b ⟹ zs ∈ bar
  assume ys ∈ bar thus ⋀zs. (xs, zs) ∈ T a ⟹ (ys, zs) ∈ T b ⟹ zs ∈ bar
  proof induct
    fix ys zs assume ys ∈ good and (ys, zs) ∈ T b
    show zs ∈ bar by (rule bar1) (rule lemma3)
  next
    fix ys zs assume I': ⋀w zs. (xs, zs) ∈ T a ⟹ (w # ys, zs) ∈ T b ⟹ zs ∈ bar
    and ys: ⋀w. w # ys ∈ bar and Ta: (xs, zs) ∈ T a and Tb: (ys, zs) ∈ T b
    show zs ∈ bar
    proof (rule bar2)
      fix w show w # zs ∈ bar
      proof (cases w)
        case Nil thus ?thesis by simp (rule prop1)
      next
        case (Cons c cs) from letter-eq-dec show ?thesis
        proof
          assume ca: c = a
          from ab have (a # cs) # zs ∈ bar by (rules intro: I ys Ta Tb)
          thus ?thesis by (simp add: Cons ca)
        next
          assume c ≠ a with ab have cb: c = b by (rule letter-neq)
          from ab have (b # cs) # zs ∈ bar by (rules intro: I' Ta Tb)
          thus ?thesis by (simp add: Cons cb)
        qed
      qed
    qed
  qed
qed
```

Fig. 4. Proposition 2

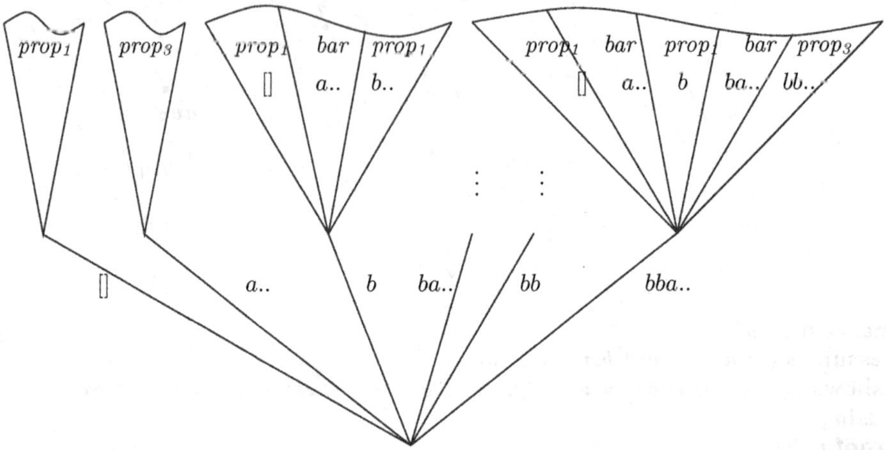


```
theorem prop3:
  assumes bar: xs ∈ bar
  shows ⋀zs. xs ≠ [] ⟹ (xs, zs) ∈ R a ⟹ zs ∈ bar using bar
proof induct
  fix xs zs assume xs ∈ good and (xs, zs) ∈ R a
  show zs ∈ bar by (rule bar1) (rule lemma2)
next
  fix xs zs
  assume I: ⋀w zs. w # xs ≠ [] ⟹ (w # xs, zs) ∈ R a ⟹ zs ∈ bar
  and xsb: ⋀w. w # xs ∈ bar and xsn: xs ≠ [] and R: (xs, zs) ∈ R a
  show zs ∈ bar
  proof (rule bar2)
    fix w
    show w # zs ∈ bar
    proof (induct w)
      case Nil
      show ?case by (rule prop1)
    next
      case (Cons c cs)
      from letter-eq-dec show ?case
      proof
        assume c = a
        thus ?thesis by (rules intro: I [simplified] R)
      next
        from R xsn have T: (xs, zs) ∈ T a by (rule lemma4)
        assume c ≠ a
        thus ?thesis by (rules intro: prop2 Cons xsb xsn R T)
      qed
    qed
  qed
qed
```

Fig. 5. Proposition 3

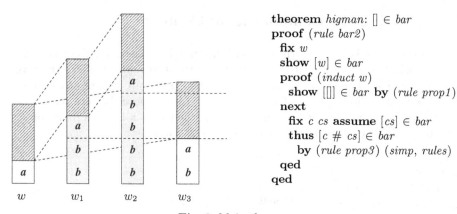

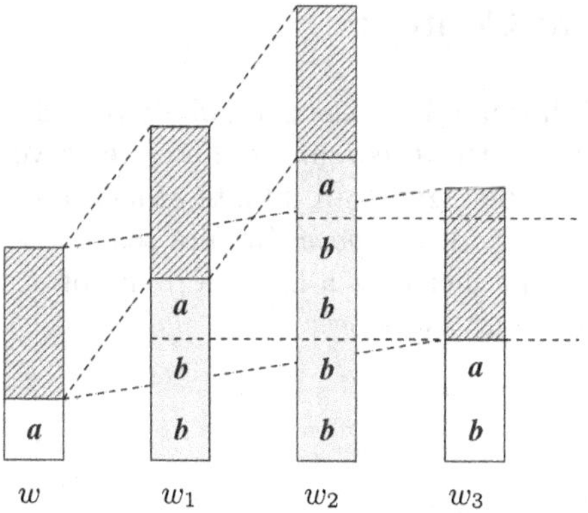


```
theorem higman: [] ∈ bar
proof (rule bar2)
  fix w
  show [w] ∈ bar
  proof (induct w)
    show [[]] ∈ bar by (rule prop1)
  next
    fix c cs assume [cs] ∈ bar
    thus [c # cs] ∈ bar
      by (rule prop3) (simp, rules)
  qed
qed
```

Fig. 6. Main theorem

1. If w consists only of b's, i.e. $w = b^n$ for $0 \leq n$, appending words of the form $b^n..$ or b^m with $m < n$ to the sequence $w \# zs$ will lead to a *good* sequence due to *prop1*, whereas appending words of the form $b^m a..$ with $m < n$ will lead to a *good* sequence due to the fact that $xs \in bar$. The subtrees named *bar* in Fig. 5 correspond to witnesses of this fact.
2. Similarly, if w contains the letter a, i.e. $w = b^n a..$ with $0 \leq n$, appending words of the form $b^n..$ to the sequence $w \# zs$ can be shown to lead to a *good* sequence by appealing to the induction hypothesis. Computationally, this corresponds to a recursive call in the function producing the tree, which is why the corresponding subtrees in Fig. 5 are named *prop3*. Appending words of the form b^m or $b^m a..$ with $m < n$ can be shown to lead to a good sequence by exactly the same argument as in case 1.

The proof of *prop3* is by induction on the derivation of $xs \in bar$, followed by an induction on the word w combined with a case analysis on letters.

We can now put together the pieces and prove the main theorem. In order to prove that $[] \in bar$, it suffices to show that $[w] \in bar$ for any word w. This can be proved by induction on w. If w is empty, the claim follows by *prop1*. Otherwise, if $w = c \# cs$, we have $[cs] \in bar$ by induction hypothesis, which we can turn into a proof of $[c \# cs] \in bar$ using *prop3*. It should be noted that structural induction on lists can be viewed as the constructive counterpart of the minimality argument used in Nash-Williams' classical proof.

The proof, together with a diagram illustrating the intuition behind it, is shown in Fig. 6. The shaded parts of the drawing correspond to sequences for which we already know that they are *good* due to the induction hypothesis $[cs] \in bar$. Processing the word w_1 in Fig. 6 corresponds to following the branch labelled with *bba..* in Fig. 5. Processing the word w_2 in Fig. 6, which starts with at least as many b's as the preceeding word w_1, corresponds to a step in the part of the rightmost subtree in Fig. 5, which was produced by a recursive call to *prop3*. In contrast, processing the word w_3, which starts with fewer b's than w_1, corresponds to a step in the part of the rightmost subtree labelled with *bar*.

5 Analyzing the Computational Content

The computational content of the theorem shown in Fig. 6 is an infinitely branching tree, which is a bit difficult to inspect. Using this theorem, we therefore prove an additional statement yielding a program that, given an infinite sequence of words, returns a finite prefix of this sequence which is *good*. Infinite sequences are encoded as functions of type $nat \Rightarrow \alpha$. The fact that a list is a prefix of an infinite sequence can be characterized recursively as follows:

consts *is-prefix* :: *'a list* ⇒ (*nat* ⇒ *'a*) ⇒ *bool*
primrec
  is-prefix [] *f* = *True*
  is-prefix (*x* # *xs*) *f* = (*x* = *f* (*length xs*) ∧ *is-prefix xs f*)

We now prove that an infinite sequence f of words has a good prefix *vs*, provided there is a prefix *ws* with *ws* ∈ *bar*. The proof is by induction on the derivation of *ws* ∈ *bar*. If the derivation tree is a leaf, this means that the current prefix is already good and we simply return it, otherwise we move ahead one step in the tree and continue the search recursively, i.e. apply the induction hypothesis.

theorem *good-prefix-lemma*:
  assumes *bar*: *ws* ∈ *bar*
  shows *is-prefix ws f* ⟹ ∃ *vs*. *is-prefix vs f* ∧ *vs* ∈ *good* **using** *bar*
proof *induct*
  case *bar1*
  thus *?case* **by** *rules*
next
  case (*bar2 ws*)
  have *is-prefix* (*f* (*length ws*) # *ws*) *f* **by** *simp*
  thus *?case* **by** (*rules intro*: *bar2*)
qed

The fact that any infinite sequence has a good prefix can now be obtained as a corollary of this theorem using *higman*:

theorem *good-prefix*: ∃ *vs*. *is-prefix vs f* ∧ *vs* ∈ *good*
  using *higman*
  by (*rule good-prefix-lemma*) *simp+*

As has already been noted, the function extracted from theorem *good-prefix* need not necessarily find the *shortest* good prefix. As an example, consider the following three functions representing sequences of words:

i	0	1	2	3	4	...
$f_1(i)$	$[A, A]$	$[B]$	$[A, B]$	$[]$	$[]$	...
$f_2(i)$	$[A, A]$	$[B]$	$[B, A]$	$[]$	$[]$	...
$f_3(i)$	$[A, A]$	$[B]$	$[A, B, A]$	$[]$	$[]$	...

When applied to f_1, *good-prefix* returns the good prefix $[[], [], [A, B], [B], [A, A]]$, which is certainly not the shortest one. The reason for this should become clear

```
letter-eq-dec ≡
λx xa.
   case x of A ⇒ case xa of A ⇒ Left | B ⇒ Right
   | B ⇒ case xa of A ⇒ Right | B ⇒ Left

prop1 ≡ λx. bar2 ([] # x) (λw. bar1 (w # [] # x))

prop2 ≡
λx xa xb xc H Ha.
   barT-rec (λws x xa H. bar1 xa)
    (λws xb r xc xd H.
        barT-rec (λws x. bar1 x)
         (λws xb ra xc.
             bar2 xc
              (λw. case w of [] ⇒ prop1 xc
                    | a # list ⇒
                        case letter-eq-dec a x of
                        Left ⇒ r list ws ((x # list) # xc) (bar2 ws xb)
                        | Right ⇒ ra list ((xa # list) # xc)))
         H xd)
    H xb xc Ha

prop3 ≡
λx xa H.
   barT-rec (λws. bar1)
    (λws x r xb.
        bar2 xb
         (list-rec (prop1 xb)
           (λa list H.
               case letter-eq-dec a xa of Left ⇒ r list ((xa # list) # xb)
               | Right ⇒ prop2 a xa ws ((a # list) # xb) H (bar2 ws x))))
    H x

higman ≡ bar2 [] (list-rec (prop1 []) (λa list. prop3 [a # list] a))

good-prefix-lemma ≡ λx. barT-rec (λws. ws) (λws xa r. r (x (length ws)))

good-prefix ≡ λx. good-prefix-lemma x higman
```

Fig. 7. Program extracted from the proof of Higman's lemma

when looking at Fig. 6: In order for the algorithm to recognize that the word $[B]$ can be embedded into some subsequent word, this word has to start with at least one B. However, since the following word starts with an A, the algorithm does not recognize that $[B]$ can be embedded into it. In contrast, when applied to f_2 and f_3, *good-prefix* returns the shortest good prefixes $[[B, A], [B], [A, A]]$ and $[[A, B, A], [B], [A, A]]$, as expected. In the case of f_2, the algorithm recognizes that $[B]$ can be embedded into $[B, A]$, since the latter starts with as many B's as the former. In the case of f_3, the algorithm recognizes that $[A]$ can be embedded into [B, A], and hence, due to lemma *prop3*, also recognizes that [A, A] can be embedded into [A, B, A].

The Isabelle/HOL functions extracted from the proof of theorem *good-prefix* are shown in Fig. 7. The corresponding ML code, together with auxiliary functions, is given in Appendix A. The correctness theorem for *good-prefix* is

$$\mathit{is\text{-}prefix}\ (\mathit{good\text{-}prefix}\ f)\ f\ \wedge\ \mathit{good\text{-}prefix}\ f\ \in\ \mathit{good}$$

whereas for *higman*, it is simply $(\mathit{higman}, [])\in \mathit{barR}$. The correctness theorems for *prop2* and *prop3* are

$$\begin{array}{l} a \neq b \Longrightarrow \\ (\bigwedge x.\ (x,\ xs) \in \mathit{barR} \Longrightarrow \\ \qquad (\bigwedge xa.\ (xa,\ ys) \in \mathit{barR} \Longrightarrow \\ \qquad\qquad (xs,\ zs) \in T\ a \Longrightarrow (ys,\ zs) \in T\ b \Longrightarrow (\mathit{prop2}\ a\ b\ ys\ zs\ x\ xa,\ zs) \in \mathit{barR})) \end{array}$$

and

$$\bigwedge x.\ (x,\ xs) \in \mathit{barR} \Longrightarrow xs \neq [] \Longrightarrow (xs,\ zs) \in R\ a \Longrightarrow (\mathit{prop3}\ zs\ a\ x,\ zs) \in \mathit{barR}$$

Note that of the inductive predicates defined in this section, only *bar* has a computational content. If we were not just interested in a *good* prefix, but also in the exact positions of the two words which can be embedded into each other, we would also have to assign the predicate *good* a computational content.

6 Conclusion

By formalizing Higman's lemma, we have demonstrated that Isabelle's program extraction module is capable of handling realistic examples. The formalization is rather compact and consists of only 280 lines of Isabelle definitions and proof scripts. The automatically extracted program turns out to be quite readable. Its ML version is about 70 lines in length (including auxiliary functions), and performs reasonably well on medium-size sequences. For example, a sequence of 350 words with an average length of 20 letters can be processed in 1.44 seconds on a Pentium III with 1 GHz.

Acknowledgements. I would like to sincerely thank Monika Seisenberger for suggesting this case study and for her help in doing the formalization. Thanks are also due to Tobias Nipkow and Tjark Weber for reading draft versions of this paper and suggesting numerous improvements.

References

[1] F. Baader and T. Nipkow. *Term Rewriting and All That.* Cambridge University Press, 1998.
[2] B. Barras et al. The Coq proof assistant reference manual – version 7.2. Technical Report 0255, INRIA, February 2002.

[3] H. Benl, U. Berger, H. Schwichtenberg, M. Seisenberger, and W. Zuber. Proof theory at work: Program development in the Minlog system. In W. Bibel and P. Schmitt, editors, *Automated Deduction – A Basis for Applications*, volume II: Systems and Implementation Techniques of *Applied Logic Series*, pages 41–71. Kluwer Academic Publishers, Dordrecht, 1998.

[4] S. Berghofer. Program Extraction in simply-typed Higher Order Logic. In H. Geuvers and F. Wiedijk, editors, *Types for Proofs and Programs (TYPES 2002)*, volume 2646 of *Lecture Notes in Computer Science*. Springer-Verlag, 2003.

[5] R. L. Constable et al. *Implementing Mathematics with the Nuprl Proof Development System*. Prentice-Hall, NJ, 1986.

[6] T. Coquand and D. Fridlender. A proof of Higman's lemma by structural induction. Unpublished draft, available at `http://www.math.chalmers.se/ frito/Papers/open.ps.gz`, November 1993.

[7] D. Fridlender. Higman's lemma in type theory. In E. Giménez and C. Paulin-Mohring, editors, *Types for Proofs and Programs, International Workshop TYPES'96*, volume 1512 of *Lecture Notes in Computer Science*, pages 112–133. Springer-Verlag, 1998.

[8] G. Higman. Ordering by divisibility in abstract algebras. *Proceedings of the London Mathematical Society*, 3(2):326–336, 1952.

[9] L. Magnusson. *The Implementation of ALF—a Proof Editor Based on Martin-Löf's Monomorphic Type Theory with Explicit Substitution*. Phd thesis, Dept. of Computing Science, Chalmers Univ. of Technology and Univ. of Göteborg, 1994.

[10] C. Murthy. *Extracting Constructive Content from Classical Proofs*. PhD thesis, Cornell University, 1990.

[11] C. R. Murthy and J. R. Russell. A constructive proof of Higman's lemma. In J. C. Mitchell, editor, *Proceedings of the 5th Annual IEEE Symposium on Logic in Computer Science*, pages 257–269, Philadelphia, PA, June 1990. IEEE Computer Society Press.

[12] C. Nash-Williams. On well-quasi-ordering finite trees. *Proceedings of the Cambridge Philosophical Society*, 59(4):833–835, 1963.

[13] C. Paulin-Mohring. Inductive Definitions in the System Coq - Rules and Properties. In M. Bezem and J.-F. Groote, editors, *Proceedings of the conference Typed Lambda Calculi and Applications*, number 664 in Lecture Notes in Computer Science, 1993. LIP research report 92-49.

[14] M. Seisenberger. Konstruktive Aspekte von Higmans Lemma. Master's thesis, Fakultät für Mathematik, Ludwig-Maximilians-Universität München, 1998.

[15] M. Seisenberger. *On the Constructive Content of Proofs*. PhD thesis, Fakultät für Mathematik, Ludwig-Maximilians-Universität München, 2003.

[16] A. S. Troelstra and D. van Dalen. *Constructivism in Mathematics, Volume 1*, volume 121 of *Studies in Logic and the Foundations of Mathematics*. North-Holland, Amsterdam, 1988.

[17] M. Wenzel. *Isabelle/Isar — a versatile environment for human-readable formal proof documents*. PhD thesis, Institut für Informatik, TU München, 2002. `http://tumb1.biblio.tu-muenchen.de/publ/diss/in/2002/wenzel.html`.

A ML Code Generated from Proof of Higman's Lemma

```
datatype letter = A | B;

datatype nat = id0 | Suc of nat;

datatype barT = bar1 of letter list list
  | bar2 of letter list list * (letter list -> barT);

fun barT_rec f1 f2 (bar1 list) = f1 list
  | barT_rec f1 f2 (bar2 (list, funa)) = f2 list funa (fn x => barT_rec f1 f2 (funa x));

fun op__43_def0 id0 n = n
  | op__43_def0 (Suc m) n = op__43_def0 m (Suc n);

fun size_def3 [] = id0
  | size_def3 (a :: list) = op__43_def0 (size_def3 list) (Suc id0);

fun good_prefix_lemma x =
  (fn H => barT_rec (fn ws => ws) (fn ws => fn xa => fn r => r (x (size_def3 ws))) H);

fun list_rec f1 f2 [] = f1
  | list_rec f1 f2 (a :: list) = f2 a list (list_rec f1 f2 list);

datatype sumbool = Left | Right;

fun letter_eq_dec x =
  (fn xa =>
    (case x of A => (case xa of A => Left | B => Right)
      | B => (case xa of A => Right | B => Left)));

fun prop1 x = bar2 (([] :: x), (fn w => bar1 (w :: ([] :: x))));

fun prop2 x =
  (fn xa => fn xb => fn xc => fn H => fn Ha =>
    barT_rec (fn ws => fn x => fn xa => fn H => bar1 xa)
      (fn ws => fn xb => fn r => fn xc => fn xd => fn H =>
        barT_rec (fn ws => fn x => bar1 x)
          (fn ws => fn xb => fn ra => fn xc =>
            bar2 (xc, (fn w =>
                        (case w of [] => prop1 xc
                          | (xd :: xe) =>
                              (case letter_eq_dec xd x of
                                Left => r xe ws ((x :: xe) :: xc) (bar2 (ws, xb))
                                | Right => ra xe ((xa :: xe) :: xc))))))
          H xd)
      H xb xc Ha);

fun prop3 x =
  (fn xa => fn H =>
    barT_rec (fn ws => fn x => bar1 x)
      (fn ws => fn x => fn r => fn xb =>
        bar2 (xb, (fn w =>
                    list_rec (prop1 xb)
                      (fn a => fn list => fn H =>
                        (case letter_eq_dec a xa of Left => r list ((xa :: list) :: xb)
                          | Right => prop2 a xa ws ((a :: list) :: xb) H (bar2 (ws, x))))
                      w)))
      H x);

val higman : barT =
  bar2 ([], (fn w =>
              list_rec (prop1 [])
                (fn a => fn list => fn H => prop3 ((a :: list) :: []) a H) w));

fun good_prefix x = good_prefix_lemma x higman;
```

A Core Calculus of Higher-Order Mixins and Classes*

Lorenzo Bettini[1], Viviana Bono[2], and Silvia Likavec[2]

[1] Dipartimento di Sistemi ed Informatica, Università di Firenze, Via Lombroso 6/17, 50134 Firenze, Italy, bettini@dsi.unifi.it

[2] Dipartimento di Informatica, Università di Torino, C.so Svizzera 185, 10149 Torino, Italy, {bono,likavec}@di.unito.it

Abstract. This work presents an object-oriented calculus based on *higher-order* mixin construction via *mixin composition*, where some software engineering requirements are modelled in a formal setting allowing to prove the absence of *message-not-understood* run-time errors. Mixin composition is shown to be a valuable language feature enabling a cleaner object-oriented design and development. In what we believe being quite a general framework, we give directions for designing a programming language equipped with higher-order mixins, although our study is not based on any already existing object-oriented language.

1 Introduction

Recently, mixins are undergoing a renaissance (see, for example, [1,7,8]), due to their flexible nature of "incomplete" classes prone to be completed according to the programmer's needs. Mixins [14,19] are (sub)class definitions parameterized over a superclass and were introduced as an alternative to some forms of multiple inheritance [13,22]. A mixin could be seen as a function that, given one class as an argument, produces another class, by adding or overriding certain sets of methods. The same mixin can be used to produce a variety of classes with the same functionality and behavior, since they all have the same sets of methods added and/or redefined. Also, the same mixin can sometimes be applied to the same class more than once, thus enabling incremental changes in the subclasses. The superclass definition is not needed at the time of writing the mixin definition. This minimizes the dependencies between superclass and its subclasses, as well as between class implementors and end-users, thus improving modularity. The uniform extension and modification of classes is instead absent from the classical class-based languages. In this work we extend the core calculus of classes and mixins of [10] with *higher-order* mixins. A mixin can: (*i*) be applied to a class to create a fully-fledged subclass; or (and this is the novelty with respect to [10]) (*ii*) be *composed* with another mixin to obtain yet another mixin with more functionalities. In Section 2.1 we present some

* This work has been partially supported by EU within the FET - Global Computing initiative, project MIKADO IST-2001-32222 and project DART IST-2001-33477, and by MIUR projects NAPOLI and PROTOCOLLO. The funding bodies are not responsible for any use that might be made of the results presented here.

S. Berardi, M. Coppo, and F. Damiani (Eds.): TYPES 2003, LNCS 3085, pp. 83–98, 2004.

uses of mixin inheritance and, in particular, we show that mixin composition enables a cleaner modular object-oriented design.

This paper presents a framework for the construction of composite mixins, and therefore of sophisticated class hierarchies, while keeping the good features of the original core calculus of [10]. In particular, we retain *structural subtyping*. As in most popular object-oriented languages, objects in our calculus can only be created by instantiating a class. We use structural subtyping to remove the dependency of object users on class implementation. Each object has an *object type*, which lists the names and types of methods and fields but does *not* include information about the class from which the object was instantiated. Therefore, objects created from unrelated classes can be substituted for each other if their types satisfy the subtyping relation. Structural subtyping was a deliberate design decision already in [11,10,24], motivated by the desire to minimize code dependencies between object users and class implementors. A different approach would be to follow Java or C++, in which an object's type is related to the class from which it was instantiated, and subtyping relations apply only to objects instantiated from the same class hierarchy (*nominal subtyping*). Subtyping is defined on object types only, not on class and mixin types, to avoid the well-known inheritance-subtyping conflicts (for an account on the subject, see for instance [15]). As a consequence of the absence of subtyping on classes, a higher-order mixin is more than a function that consumes and produces classes, since such a function cannot accept a class with extra methods as an argument. Moreover, the type system would have to express that the result of the "mixin-function" has at least the methods of the argument, and such general extensions to the type system look unnecessarily complex for the model's more specific purpose.

Our design decisions are strongly based on the choices that were made in [10]. Class hierarchies in a well-designed object-oriented program must not be fragile: if a superclass implementation changes but the specification remains intact, the implementors of the subclasses should not have to rewrite subclass implementations. This is only possible if object creation is modular. In particular, a subclass implementation should not be responsible for initializing inherited fields when a new object is created, since some of the inherited fields may be private and thus invisible to the subclass. Also, the definitions of inherited fields may change when the class hierarchy changes, making the subclass implementation invalid. Unlike many theoretical calculi for object-oriented languages, our calculus directly supports modular object construction. The mixin implementor only writes the local constructor for his own mixin. Mixin applications and compositions are reduced to generator functions that call all constructors in the inheritance chain in the correct order, producing a fully initialized object (see Section 3). Unlike some approaches to encapsulation in object calculi such as existential types, the levels of encapsulation describe *visibility*, and not merely *accessibility*. For example, even the names of private items are invisible outside the class in which they are defined. This seems to be a better approach since *no* information about data representation is revealed, not even the number and names of fields. One of the benefits of using visibility-based encapsulation is that no conflicts arise if both the superclass and the subclass declare a private field with the same name. Among other advantages, this allows the same mixin to be applied twice (see the example in Section 2.1). To ensure that mixin inheritance can be statically type checked, the calculus employs constrained parameterization. From each mixin definition

$$
\begin{array}{ll}
e ::= \mathit{const} \mid x \mid \lambda x.e \mid e_1\, e_2 \mid \mathit{fix} & v ::= \mathit{const} \mid x \mid \lambda x.e \mid \mathit{fix} \mid \mathsf{ref} \mid\, ! \\
\quad \mid \mathsf{ref} \mid\, ! \mid := \mid \{x_i = e_i\}^{i \in I} \mid e.x & \quad \mid := \mid := v \mid \{x_i = v_i\}^{i \in I} \\
\quad \mid \mathsf{H}\ h.e \mid \mathsf{classval}\langle v_g, \mathcal{M}\rangle \mid \mathsf{new}\ e & \quad \mid \mathsf{classval}\langle v_g, \mathcal{M}\rangle \\
\quad \mid \mathsf{mixin} & \quad \mid \mathsf{mixinval}\langle v_m, \mathit{New}, \mathit{Redef}, \mathit{Expect}\rangle \\
\qquad \mathsf{method}\ m_j = v_{m_j};\ ^{(j \in \mathit{New})} & \\
\qquad \mathsf{redefine}\ m_k = v_{m_k};\ ^{(k \in \mathit{Redef})} & \\
\qquad \mathsf{expect}\ m_i;\ ^{(i \in \mathit{Expect})} & \\
\qquad \mathsf{constructor}\ v_c; & \\
\quad\ \ \mathsf{end} & \\
\quad \mid \mathsf{mixinval}\langle v_m, \mathit{New}, \mathit{Redef}, \mathit{Expect}\rangle & \\
\quad \mid e_1 \diamond e_2 \mid e_1 \bullet e_2 &
\end{array}
$$

Fig. 1. Syntax of the core calculus: expressions and values.

the type system infers a constraint specifying to which classes the mixin can be applied so that the resulting subclass is type-safe. The constraint includes both *positive* (which methods the class must contain) and *negative* (which methods the class must not contain) information. New and redefined methods are distinguished in the mixin implementation: from the implementor's viewpoint, a new method may have arbitrary behavior, while the behavior of a redefined method must be "compatible" with that of the old method it replaces. Having this distinction in the syntax of our calculus helps mixin implementors avoid unintentional redefinitions of superclass methods and facilitates generation of the constraint for mixin's superclasses and for mixins that participate in mixin composition (see Section 4). A marginal difference with respect to the original mixin calculus [10] is that we do not treat *protected* methods, being an orthogonal issue to higher-order mixins. Nevertheless, protected methods could be easily accounted for via (structural) subtyping as in the original calculus.

2 Syntax of the Calculus

The starting point for our calculus is the core calculus of classes and mixins of Bono et al. [10] that, in turn, is based on *Reference ML* of Wright and Felleisen [25]. To this imperative calculus of records and functions, we add constructs for manipulating classes and mixins. The class and mixin related expressions are: classval, mixin, mixinval, $\diamond$ (mixin application), $\bullet$ (mixin composition) and new. The novelties with respect to [10] are mixinval and $\bullet$ (mixin composition) to deal with *higher-order* mixins.

Expressions and values are given in Figure 1. Most of them are standard, the only constructs that might need some explanation are the following:

- ref, !, $:=$ are operators[1] for defining a reference to a value, for de-referencing a reference, and for assigning a new value to a reference, respectively.
- $\{x_i = e_i\}^{i \in I}$ is a record and $e.x$ is the record selection operation (note that this corresponds to method selection in our calculus).
- h is a set of pairs $h ::= \{\langle x, v\rangle^*\}$ where x is a variable and v is a value (first components of the pairs are all distinct). We have a concept of a *heap*, represented

[1] Introducing ref, !, $:=$ as operators rather than standard forms such as ref$e$, !e, $:=e_1 e_2$, simplifies the definition of evaluation contexts and proofs of properties. As noted in [25], this is just a syntactic convenience, as is the curried version of $:=$.

by h in the expression $\mathsf{H}h.e$, used for evaluating imperative side effects. In the expression $\mathsf{H}\langle x_1, v_1\rangle \ldots \langle x_n, v_n\rangle.e$, H binds variables $x_1, \ldots x_n$ in $v_1, \ldots, v_n$ and in e.

- new e uses generator v_g of the class value to which e evaluates to create a function that returns a new object, as described in Section 3.
- classval$\langle v_g, \mathcal{M}\rangle$ is a *class value*, and it is the result of mixin application. It is a pair, containing the function v_g, that is the generator for the class used to generate its instance objects, and the set $\mathcal{M}$ of the indices of all the methods defined in the class. In our calculus method names are of the shape m_i, where i ranges over an index set, and are univocally identified by their index, i.e., $m_i = m_j$ if and only if $i = j$.
- mixin
  method $m_j = v_{m_j}$; $^{(j \in New)}$
  redefine $m_k = v_{m_k}$; $^{(k \in Redef)}$
  expect m_i; $^{(i \in Expect)}$
  constructor v_c;
  end
  is a *mixin* expression, and it states the methods that are new, redefined, and expected in the mixin (names of which have to be all distinct). More precisely, $m_j = v_{m_j}$ are definitions of the new methods, $m_k = v_{m_k}$ are method redefinitions that will replace the methods with the same name in the superclass, and m_i are method (names) that the superclass is expected to implement. Each method body v_{m_j} (respectively, v_{m_k}) is a function of the private *field* and of *self*, which will be bound to the newly created object at instantiation time. In method redefinitions, v_{m_k} is also a function of *next*, which will be bound to the corresponding old method from the superclass. The v_c value in the constructor clause is a function that returns a record of two components: the fieldinit value is used to initialize the private field; the superinit value is passed as an argument to the superclass constructor. When evaluating a mixin, v_c is used to build the generator as described in Section 3.
- mixinval$\langle v_m, New, Redef, Expect\rangle$ is a *mixin value*, and it is the result of a mixin evaluation. It is a tuple, containing one function and three sets of indices. The function v_m is the (partial) generator for the corresponding mixin. The sets *New*, *Redef*, and *Expect* contain the names of all methods defined in the mixin (new, redefined, and expected).
- $e_1 \diamond e_2$ denotes the application of mixin value e_1 to class value e_2. Given the (super)class value e_2 as an "argument" to e_1, it produces a new (sub)class value.
- $e_1 \bullet e_2$ is a composition of two mixin values e_1 and e_2. It produces a new mixin value taking components from both e_1 and e_2. The resulting mixin can be applied to class values to produce new classes, as well as composed with other mixin values to produce new composite mixins.

As in [10], we define the root of the class hierarchy, class *Object*, as a predefined class value: *Object* $\triangleq$ classval$\langle\, \lambda_.\lambda_.\{\}, [\;]\,\rangle$. The root class is necessary so that all other classes can be treated uniformly and it is the only class value that is not obtained as a result of mixin application. The calculus can then be simplified by assuming that any user-defined class that does not need a superclass is obtained by applying a mixin containing all of the class method definitions to *Object*. For the sake of clarity, in the following examples we will avoid the explicit mixin application to *Object*.

2.1 An Example of Mixin Inheritance

In this section, we present a simple example that shows how mixins can be implemented and used in our calculus and explain some of the uses of mixin application and mixin composition. For readability, the example uses functions with multiple arguments even though they are not formalized explicitly in the calculus.

In the following, we give the definitions of `Encrypted` mixin and `Compress` mixin that implement encryption and compression functionality on top of any stream class, respectively. Note that the class to which the mixin is applied may have more methods than expected by the mixin. For example, `Encrypted` can be applied to `Socket` ◇ *Object*, even though `Socket` ◇ *Object* has other methods besides *read* and *write*. The mixin `Random` allows random access to any stream class, thus we can build a random access file class with the mixin application `Random` ◇ `FileStream`.

```
let FileStream = mixin
  method write = ...
  method read = ...
 end in

let Socket = mixin
  method write = ...
  method read = ...
  method IPaddress = ...
 end in

let Random = mixin
  method lseek = ...
  expect write;
  expect read;
 end in

let Encrypted =
 mixin
  redefine write = λkey. λself. λnext. λdata. next (encrypt(data, key));
  redefine read = λkey. λself. λnext. λ_. decrypt(next (), key);
  constructor λ(key, arg). {fieldinit=key, superinit=arg};
 end in
let Compress =
 mixin
  redefine write = λlevel. λself. λnext. λdata. next (compress(data, level));
  redefine read = λlevel. λself. λnext. λ_. uncompress(next (), level);
  constructor λ(level, arg). {fieldinit=level, superinit=arg};
 end in ...
```

From the definition of `Encrypted`, the type system infers the types of the methods that the mixin wants to redefine. These are the constraints that must be satisfied by any class to which `Encrypted` is applied. The class must contain *write* and *read* methods whose types must be supertypes of those given to *write* and *read*, respectively, in the definition of `Encrypted`. In `Random` such methods are declared as *expected* and they are used within the method *lseek*. Once again the type system infers their types according to how they are used in *lseek*.

To create an encrypted stream class, one must apply the `Encrypted` mixin to an existing stream class. For example, `Encrypted` ◇ `FileStream` is an encrypted file class. The power of mixins can be seen when we apply `Encrypted` to a family of different streams. For example, we can construct `Encrypted` ◇ `Socket`, which is a class that encrypts data communicated over a network. In addition to single inheritance, we can express many uses of multiple inheritance by applying more than one mixin to a class. For example, `PGPSign` ◇ `UUEncode` ◇ `Encrypted` ◇ `Compress` ◇ `FileStream` produces a class of files that are compressed, then encrypted, then uuencoded, then signed. In addition, mixins can be used for forms of inheritance that are not possible in most single and multiple inheritance-based systems. In the above example, the result of applying `Encrypted` to a stream satisfies the constraint required by `Encrypted` itself, therefore, we can apply `Encrypted` more than once: `Encrypted` $\diamond$ `Encrypted` $\diamond$ `FileStream` is a class of files that are encrypted twice. In our calculus, class private fields do not conflict even if they have the same name, so each application of `Encrypted` can have its own encryption key.

Mixin composition further enhances the (re)usability of classes and mixins and enables better modular programming design, by exploiting software composition at a higher level. For example, the programmer is able to build a customized library of reusable mixins starting from existing mixins: one can create the new mixin `2Encrypt` = `Encrypted` $\bullet$ `Encrypted`, instead of always applying the mixin `Encrypted` twice to every stream class in her program. This also enables consistency: if in the future the definition of the mixin `2Encrypt` must be extended, e.g., by also exploiting UU encoding, then by changing only the definition of `2Encrypt`, with an additional mixin composition, it is guaranteed that all the functions that used `2Encrypt` will use the new version. Moreover, construction of mixins can be delegated to different parts of the program (thus exploiting modular programming), and the resulting mixins can then be assembled in order to build a class. For instance, the following code delegates the construction of mixins for encryption and compression to two functions, and then assembles the returned mixins for later use:

$$\begin{array}{l}\mathsf{let}\ m_1 = \text{build\_compression}()\ \ \mathsf{in}\ \mathsf{let}\ m_2 = \text{build\_encryption}()\ \ \mathsf{in}\\ \quad \mathsf{let}\ m = m_1 \bullet m_2\ \ \mathsf{in}\ (\mathsf{new}(m \diamond \text{FileStream})).\text{write}(\texttt{"foo"})\end{array}$$

The function `build_compression` returns a specific mixin according to user's requests: it can return a simple `Compress` mixin, or a more elaborate `UUEncode` $\bullet$ `Compress` mixin. Similarly, `build_encryption`, instead of simply returning a mixin `Encrypted`, returns the composition `PGPSign` $\bullet$ `Encrypted`. All these enhanced modular composition functionalities, supported by mixin composition, would not be directly provided by simple mixin application.

Finally, let us observe that streams are implemented usually via the design pattern *decorator* [21] (for instance, in Java), and this requires additional manual programming. Instead, with mixins (and in particular with mixin composition), streams can be programmed directly exploiting language features. This is just one of the examples of the additional expressiveness provided by mixin composition.

3 Operational Semantics

The operational semantics of the original calculus [10] is very close to an implementation, and we follow the same approach. Our operational semantics is a set of rewriting rules including the standard rules for a lambda calculus with stores (in our case the Reference ML [25]), and some rules that evaluate the object-oriented related forms to records and functions, following the "objects-as-records" technique and Cook's "class-as-generator-of-objects" principle. This operational semantics can be seen also as something extremely close to a denotational description for objects, classes, and mixins, and this "identification" of implementation and semantical denotation is, according to us, a good by-product of our approach.

$$\begin{array}{llrl}
const\ v \to \delta(const, v) & (\delta) & \mathsf{ref} v \to \mathsf{H}\langle x, v\rangle.x & (\text{ref}) \\
\quad \text{if } \delta(const, v) & \text{is defined} & \mathsf{H}\langle x, v\rangle h.R[!x] \to \mathsf{H}\langle x, v\rangle h.R[v] & (\text{deref}) \\
(\lambda x.e)\ v \to [v/x]\ e & (\beta_v) & \mathsf{H}\langle x, v\rangle h.R[:=xv'] \to \mathsf{H}\langle x, v'\rangle h.R[v'] & (\text{assign}) \\
\mathit{fix}\ (\lambda x.e) \to [\mathit{fix}(\lambda x.e)/x]e & (\text{fix}) & R[\mathsf{H}\ h.e] \to \mathsf{H}\ h.R[e],\ R \neq [\,] & (\text{lift}) \\
\{\ldots, x = v, \ldots\}.x \to v & (\text{select}) & \mathsf{H}\ h.\mathsf{H}\ h'.e \to \mathsf{H}\ h\ h'.e & (\text{merge})
\end{array}$$

$$\begin{pmatrix} \mathsf{mixin} \\ \mathsf{method}\ m_j = v_{m_j}; \\ \mathsf{redefine}\ m_k = v_{m_k}; \\ \mathsf{expect}\ m_i; \\ \mathsf{constructor}\ c; \\ \mathsf{end} \end{pmatrix}^{\substack{j \in New \\ k \in Redef \\ i \in Expect}} \to \mathsf{mixinval}\langle Gen_m, New, Redef, Expect\rangle \qquad (\text{mixval})$$

$$\begin{array}{l}
Gen_m \triangleq \lambda x. \\
\quad \mathsf{let}\ t = c(x)\ \ \mathsf{in} \\
\quad\quad \left\{ \begin{array}{l} \mathsf{gen} = \lambda self. \\ \left\{ \begin{array}{ll} m_j = \lambda y.v_{m_j}\ t.\mathsf{fieldinit}\ self\ y & ^{j \in New} \\ m_k = \lambda y.v_{m_k}\ t.\mathsf{fieldinit}\ self\ y & ^{k \in Redef} \end{array} \right\}, \\ \mathsf{superinit} = t.\mathsf{superinit} \end{array} \right\}
\end{array}$$

$$\mathsf{mixinval}\langle Gen_m, New, Redef, Expect\rangle \diamond \mathsf{classval}\langle g, \mathcal{M}\rangle \to \mathsf{classval}\langle Gen, New \cup \mathcal{M}\rangle \qquad (\text{mixapp})$$

$$\begin{array}{l}
Gen \triangleq \lambda x.\lambda self. \\
\quad \mathsf{let}\ mixinrec = Gen_m(x)\ \ \mathsf{in} \\
\quad \mathsf{let}\ mixingen = mixinrec.\mathsf{gen}\ \ \mathsf{in} \\
\quad \mathsf{let}\ supergen = g(mixinrec.\mathsf{superinit})\ \ \mathsf{in} \\
\quad\quad \left\{ \begin{array}{ll} m_j = \lambda y.(mixingen\ self).m_j\ y & ^{j \in New} \\ m_k = \lambda y.(mixingen\ self).m_k\ (supergen\ self).m_k\ y & ^{k \in Redef} \\ m_i = \lambda y.(supergen\ self).m_i\ y & ^{i \in \mathcal{M} - Redef} \end{array} \right\}
\end{array}$$

Fig. 2. Reduction rules

$$\begin{array}{rl}
R ::= & [\,] \mid R\,e \mid v\,R \mid R.x \mid \mathsf{new}\ R \mid R \diamond \mathsf{e} \mid v \diamond R \mid R \bullet \mathsf{e} \mid v \bullet R \\
& \mid \{m_1 = v_1, \ldots, m_{i-1} = v_{i-1}, m_i = R, m_{i+1} = e_{i+1}, \ldots, m_n = e_n\}^{1 \leq i \leq n}
\end{array}$$

Fig. 3. Reduction contexts

The operational semantics extends the one of the core calculus of classes and mixins, [10], and therefore exploits the *Reference ML* of Wright and Felleisen treatment of side-effects [25]. We give the reduction rules in Figures 2 and 4. To abstract from a precise set of constants, we only assume the existence of a partial function $\delta : Const \times ClosedVal \rightharpoonup ClosedVal$ that interprets the application of functional constants to closed values and yields closed values. In Figure 2, R are the *reduction contexts* [23,17,18]. Reduction contexts are necessary to provide a minimal relative linear order among the creation, dereferencing and updating of heap locations, since side effects need to be evaluated in a deterministic order. Their definition can be found in Figure 3. We assume the reader is familiar with the treatment of imperative side-effects via reduction contexts and we refer to [25,10] for a description of the related rules.

(*new*) rule is responsible for instantiating new objects from class definitions. The resulting function can be thought of as the composition of two functions: $\mathit{fix} \circ g$. First, the generator g is applied to an argument v, thus creating a function from *self* to a record of methods. Afterwards, the fixed-point operator *fix* is applied to bind *self* in method bodies and create a recursive record (following [16]). The resulting record is a fully formed object that could be returned to the user.

Rule (*mixval*) turns a mixin expression into a mixin *value*. A mixin value consists of a mixin generator Gen_m and of the sets of mixin method names (new, redefined, and expected; we recall that names are identified with their indices, as said in Section 2). Gen_m is a sort of a compiled (equivalent) version of the mixin expression. Given the parameter for the mixin constructor c, Gen_m returns a record containing a (partial) object generator gen, and the argument superinit for the (future) superclass constructor. We recall that c is a function of one argument which returns a record of two components: one is the initialization expression for the method field (fieldinit), the other is the superclass generator's argument (superinit). The object generator gen binds the private field of the methods defined (*New*) and redefined (*Redef*) by the mixin to fieldinit (recall that method bodies take parameters for *field*, for *self*, and, if the method is a redefinition, also for *next*, which will be bound to the corresponding superclass method). The returned object generator is partial because it comes from a mixin, i.e., the expected methods and the *next* for each redefined method will be provided by a superclass or by other mixins (in fact, note that *next* is not yet bound in m_k's bodies). Notice that all the other mixin operations, i.e., mixin application and mixin composition, are performed on mixin values. In the original calculus of [10], mixin values are created and "blended" directly at mixin-application time with a (super)class value to obtain a (sub)class value. Here mixin values are made explicit to deal smoothly with mixin composition. For all the methods, the method bodies are wrapped inside $\lambda y. \cdots y$ to delay evaluation in our call-by-value calculus.

Rule (*mixapp*) evaluates the application of a mixin value to a class value, performing mixin-based inheritance. A mixin value mixinval$\langle Gen_m, New, Redef, Expect\rangle$ is applied to a class value classval$\langle g, \mathcal{M}\rangle$ which plays the role of the superclass, where g is the object generator of the superclass and $\mathcal{M}$ is the set of all method names defined in the superclass. The resulting class value is classval$\langle Gen, New \cup \mathcal{M}\rangle$, where *Gen* is the generator function for the subclass, and $New \cup \mathcal{M}$ lists all its method names. Using a class generator delays full inheritance resolution until object instantiation time when *self* becomes available. The generator *Gen* takes a single argument x, which is used by the mixin generator, and returns a function from *self* to a record of methods. When the fixed-point operator is applied to the function returned by the generator, it produces a recursive record of methods representing a new object (see rule (*new*)). *Gen* first calls $Gen_m(x)$ to compute the mixin object generator *mixingen*, a function from *self* to a record of mixin methods, and the parameter *mixingen*.superinit to be passed to the superclass generator g, that, in turn, returns a function *supergen* from *self* to a record of superclass methods. *Gen* results to be a function of *self* that returns a record containing *all* the methods — from both the mixin and the superclass. All methods of the superclass that are not redefined by the mixin, m_i where $i \in \mathcal{M} - Redef$, are *inherited* by the subclass: they are taken intact from the superclass's "object" (*supergen self*). These methods m_i include all the methods that are expected by the mixin (this is ensured by the type system, see Section 4). Methods m_j defined by the mixin are taken intact from the mixin's "object" (*mixingen self*). As for *redefined* methods m_k, *next* is bound to (*supergen self*)$.m_k$ in *Gen*. Notice that, at this stage, all methods have already received

$$\begin{array}{l}\mathsf{mixinval}\langle g_1, New_1, Redef_1, Expect_1\rangle \bullet \mathsf{mixinval}\langle g_2, New_2, Redef_2, Expect_2\rangle \rightarrow \\ \qquad \mathsf{mixinval}\langle Gen, New_1 \cup New_2, (Redef_1 \cup Redef_2) - New_2, \\ \qquad\quad (Expect_1 - (New_2 \cup Redef_2)) \cup (Expect_2 - Redef_1)\rangle\end{array}$$

$$\begin{array}{l}Gen \triangleq \lambda x. \\ \quad \mathsf{let}\ leftrec = g_1(x)\ \ \mathsf{in} \\ \quad \mathsf{let}\ rightrec = g_2(leftrec.\mathsf{superinit})\ \ \mathsf{in} \\ \quad \mathsf{let}\ leftgen = leftrec.\mathsf{gen}\ \ \mathsf{in} \\ \quad \mathsf{let}\ rightgen = rightrec.\mathsf{gen}\ \ \mathsf{in} \\ \qquad \left\{\begin{array}{l}\mathsf{gen} = \lambda self. \\ \left\{\begin{array}{ll} m_{j_1} = \lambda y.(leftgen\ self).m_{j_1}\ y & {}^{j_1 \in New_1} \\ m_{j_2} = \lambda y.(rightgen\ self).m_{j_2}\ y & {}^{j_2 \in New_2 - Redef_1} \\ m_{j_3} = \lambda y.(leftgen\ self).m_{j_3}\ (rightgen\ self).m_{j_3}\ y & {}^{j_3 \in Redef_1 \cap New_2} \\ m_{k_1} = \lambda y.(leftgen\ self).m_{k_1}\ y & {}^{k_1 \in Redef_1 - (New_2 \cup Redef_2)} \\ m_{k_2} = \lambda next.(leftgen\ self).m_{k_2}\ ((rightgen\ self).m_{k_2}\ next) & {}^{k_2 \in Redef_1 \cap Redef_2} \\ m_{k_3} = \lambda y.(rightgen\ self).m_{k_3}\ y & {}^{k_3 \in Redef_2 - Redef_1} \end{array}\right\}, \\ \mathsf{superinit} = rightrec.\mathsf{superinit} \end{array}\right\}\end{array}$$

Fig. 4. Reduction rule (mixcomp) for mixin composition

a binding for the private field. The variable *self* is passed all along in all method forms, in such a way that the host object will be bound appropriately at object creation time.

Rule (*mixcomp*) (Fig. 4) composes two mixins to produce a new mixin. The two mixins may partially complete each others' definitions, providing (some of) the missing components. Let us denote the mixin composition by $e_1 \bullet e_2$ and the resulting mixin by e. When composing two mixins, it is necessary to determine which sets of new/redefined/expected methods the new mixin e will have. Our design decision is as follows: the mixin e_2 acts as a "superclass" for e_1 (mirroring mixin application order), and, in particular, some of e_1 methods may override some of e_2 methods. Therefore, all the new methods of the mixin e_1 (New_1) are inserted in the resulting mixin e, while only the new methods of e_2 that are not redefined by e_1 ($j_2 \in New_2 - Redef_1$) become part of the new mixin. Notice that the type rule for mixin composition (*mixin comp*) (Figure 6) must check that no name clashes between new methods of e_1 and any method of e_2 take place. This decision is in line with a good object-oriented design principle of not confusing method redefinitions and name clashes. Therefore, an error is signaled at compile time and not at runtime. As far as redefined methods are concerned, the situation is more complex: the methods specified as redefining in e_1 can override some new methods of e_2, some redefining methods of e_2, and (even if only virtually) some of the expected methods of e_2.

- If a method m_{j_3} in e_1 redefines a method defined in e_2 ($j_3 \in Redef_1 \cap New_2$), then the overriding is completed and m_{j_3} becomes a new method in the resulting mixin e, after binding its *next* to e_2's implementation of m_{j_3};
- If e_1 redefines a method m_{k_2} that, in turn, is redefined by e_2 ($k_2 \in Redef_1 \cap Redef_2$), then this method is still a redefined method in e. Since e_1 "overrides" e_2, therefore m_{k_2}'s implementation of e_1 redefines that of e_2, the *next* in the implementation of e_1 is bound to the implementation of e_2, and the *next* in the implementation of e_2 is not bound, since it will be bound during future mixin composition or mixin application.

This means that the redefinition of a method m_{k_2} by means of e_2 is delayed (while e_1 has already performed its "internal" redefinition of m_{k_2} over e_2);
- If e_1 redefines a method that is expected in e_2, then this method will become a redefined method in e, so it will not appear among the expected methods of e, but it will be a method that e is willing to redefine.

Apart from the above examined methods, method redefinitions that are still present as method redefinitions in the resulting mixin e are: (*i*) the redefining ones from e_2 that are not redefined by e_1 ($k_3 \in \mathit{Redef}_2 - \mathit{Redef}_1$); (*ii*) the ones from e_1 that are not defined in e_2 and hence not "overriding" anything yet ($k_1 \in \mathit{Redef}_1 - (\mathit{New}_2 \cup \mathit{Redef}_2)$).

Finally, new and redefined methods from e_2 can provide some of the definitions that the mixin e_1 expects; in that case, such methods expected by e_1 do not appear anymore in the expected method set of e.

The generator of the new mixin is a combination of the generators of e_1 and e_2. Since e_1 is considered to be the "subclass", the parameter x is passed to g_1, and g_2 receives as a parameter the superinit returned by $g_1(x)$; the superinit field of the record returned by the generator of the new mixin is set to $g_2(g_1(x).\mathsf{superinit}).\mathsf{superinit}$. This strategy for building the new mixin generator corresponds to serializing the call of the two constructors similarly to what happens in standard object-oriented languages. Notice that this is consistent with the type $\mathsf{mixin}\langle\gamma_{b_2}, \gamma_{d_1}, \Sigma_{new}, \Sigma_{red}, \Sigma_{exp}, \Sigma_{old}\rangle$ assigned to the new mixin by the type rule (*mixin comp*) (Figure 6).

4 Type System

In addition to functional, record, and reference types of *Reference ML* type system, our type system has class-types and mixin-types.

The types in our system are the following:

$$\tau ::= \iota \mid \tau_1 \rightarrow \tau_2 \mid \tau\ \mathsf{ref} \mid \{m_i : \tau_{m_i}\}^{i \in I} \mid \mathsf{class}\langle\tau, \Sigma_b\rangle \mid \mathsf{mixin}\langle\tau_1, \tau_2, \Sigma_{new}, \Sigma_{red}, \Sigma_{exp}, \Sigma_{old}\rangle$$

where ι is a constant type, $\rightarrow$ is the functional type operator, τ ref is the type of locations containing a value of type τ. The other type forms are described below.

Σ (possibly with a subscript) denotes a record type of the form $\{m_i : \tau_{m_i}\}^{i \in I}$. The set of indexes I (where $I \subseteq \mathbb{N}$) is often omitted when it is not relevant. A record type can be viewed as a set of pairs *label:type* where labels are pairwise disjoint (Σ_1 and Σ_2 are considered *equal*, denoted by $\Sigma_1 = \Sigma_2$, if they differ only in the order of their elements). Notations and operations on sets are easily extended to record types as in the following definitions:

- if $m_i : \tau_{m_i} \in \Sigma$ we say that the *subject* m_i *occurs* in Σ (with type τ_{m_i}). $\mathit{Subj}(\Sigma)$ denotes the set of all subjects occurring in Σ;
- $\Sigma_1 \cup \Sigma_2$ is the standard set union (used only on Σ_1 and Σ_2 such that $\mathit{Subj}(\Sigma_1) \cap \mathit{Subj}(\Sigma_2) = \emptyset$, in order to guarantee that $\Sigma_1 \cup \Sigma_2$ is a record type);
- $\Sigma_1 - \Sigma_2$ is the standard set difference;
- $\Sigma_1 / \Sigma_2 = \{m_i : \tau_{m_i} \mid m_i : \tau_{m_i} \in \Sigma_1 \wedge m_i \text{ occurs in } \Sigma_2\}$.

The definitions of typing environments Γ and of typing judgments are standard. Our type system supports *structural subtyping* (<: relation) along with a subsumption rule (*sub*). The subtyping rules are shown in Appendix A. Since subtyping on references is unsound and we wish to keep subtyping and inheritance completely separate, we have only the basic subtyping rules for function and record types. Subtyping only exists at the object level, and is not supported for class or mixin types (as explained in the introduction).

In the class type $\text{class}\langle\gamma, \Sigma_b\rangle$, γ is the type of the generator's argument and $\Sigma_b = \{m_i : \tau_{m_i}\}$ is a record type representing *self*.

In the mixin type $\text{mixin}\langle\gamma_b, \gamma_d, \Sigma_{new}, \Sigma_{red}, \Sigma_{exp}, \Sigma_{old}\rangle$

- γ_b is the expected argument type of the superclass generator,
- γ_d is the exact argument type of the mixin generator,
- $\Sigma_{new} = \{m_j : \tau^{\downarrow}_{m_j}\}$ are the exact types of the new methods introduced by the mixin,
- $\Sigma_{red} = \{m_k : \tau^{\downarrow}_{m_k}\}$ are the exact types of the methods redefined by the mixin,
- $\Sigma_{exp} = \{m_i : \tau^{\uparrow}_{m_i}\}$ are the types of the methods that are neither defined nor redefined by the mixin, but expected to be supported by a superclass which the mixin will be applied to, or by another mixin which the mixin will be composed with,
- $\Sigma_{old} = \{m_k : \tau^{\uparrow}_{m_k}\}$ are the types assumed for the old bodies of the methods redefined by the mixin.

We report in Figure 5 the typing rules regarding classes and mixins (the rest of the typing rules are given in Appendix A). Some of them are syntactic variations of those presented in [10] and we refer the reader to that paper for comments about such rules. We only comment upon the rules related to mixin forms. The rules (*mixin*) and (*mixin val*) assign the same type to their respective expressions, although deduced in a different way. In the rule (*mixin*) the side condition $Subj(\Sigma_{new}) \cap Subj(\Sigma_{red}) \cap Subj(\Sigma_{exp}) = \emptyset$ ensures that the names of new, redefined, and expected methods are all distinct. In the rule (*mixin app*), Σ_b contains the type signatures of all methods supported by the superclass to which the mixin is applied, and Σ_b / Σ_{red} are the superclass methods redefined by the mixin (the superclass may have more methods than those required by the mixin constraints). The premises of the rule (*mixin app*) are the following:

i) $\Sigma_b <: (\Sigma_{exp} \cup \Sigma_{old})$ requires the actual types of the superclass methods to be subtypes of those expected by the mixin.

ii) $\Sigma_{red} <: \Sigma_b / \Sigma_{red}$ requires that the types of the actual implementations of methods in the superclass (which may belong to a subtype of the Σ_{old}, from the above constraint) are supertypes of the ones redefined in the mixin. Thus, the types of the methods redefined by the mixin (Σ_{red}) will be subtypes of the superclass methods with the same name.

iii) $Subj(\Sigma_b) \cap Subj(\Sigma_{new}) = \emptyset$ guarantees that no name clash will take place during the mixin application.

Intuitively, the above constraints insure that all the actual method bodies of the newly created subclass are at least as "good" as expected. The resulting class, of type $\text{class}\langle\gamma_d, \Sigma_d\rangle$, contains the signatures of all the methods forming the new class, created as the result of mixin application. Σ_{red} and Σ_{new} are methods defined by the mixin, whereas $\Sigma_b - (\Sigma_b / \Sigma_{red})$ are the methods inherited directly from the superclass. Let us observe that, for any well typed mixin, $Subj(\Sigma_{red}) = Subj(\Sigma_{old})$, therefore for any record type Σ, $\Sigma / \Sigma_{red} = \Sigma / \Sigma_{old}$.

Now we concentrate on the main topic of the paper, the rule for mixin composition (*mixin comp*) given in Figure 6. Since e_2 acts as the "superclass" of e_1, e_1 will pass the argument of type γ_{b_1} to the constructor of the superclass e_2, that expects an argument of

$$\frac{\Gamma \vdash g:\gamma \to \{m_i:\tau_{m_i}\}^{i\in\mathcal{M}} \to \{m_i:\tau_{m_i}\}^{i\in\mathcal{M}}}{\Gamma \vdash \mathsf{classval}\langle g,\mathcal{M}\rangle : \mathsf{class}\langle \gamma, \{m_i:\tau_{m_i}\}^{i\in\mathcal{M}}\rangle}\ (class\ val) \qquad \frac{\Gamma \vdash e:\mathsf{class}\langle \gamma,\{m_i:\tau_{m_i}\}\rangle}{\Gamma \vdash \mathsf{new}\ e:\gamma \to \{m_i:\tau_{m_i}\}}\ (instantiate)$$

$$\frac{\begin{array}{lll}(\mathsf{New}) & \text{For } j\in New\text{:} & \Gamma \vdash v_{m_j}:\eta \to \Sigma \to \tau^{\downarrow}_{m_j}\\ (\mathsf{Redef}) & \text{For } k\in Redef\text{:} & \Gamma \vdash v_{m_k}:\eta \to \Sigma \to \tau^{\uparrow}_{m_k} \to \tau^{\downarrow}_{m_k}\\ (\mathsf{Constr}) & & \Gamma \vdash c:\gamma_d \to \{\text{fieldinit}:\eta, \text{superinit}:\gamma_b\}\\ & & Subj(\Sigma_{new})\cap Subj(\Sigma_{red})\cap Subj(\Sigma_{exp}) = \emptyset \end{array}}{\Gamma \vdash \begin{pmatrix}\mathsf{mixin}\\ \ \mathsf{method}\ m_j = v_{m_j};\\ \ \mathsf{redefine}\ m_k = v_{m_k};\\ \ \mathsf{expect}\ m_i;\\ \ \mathsf{constructor}\ c;\\ \mathsf{end}\end{pmatrix}^{\substack{j\in New\\ k\in Redef\\ i\in Expect}} : \mathsf{mixin}\langle \gamma_b,\gamma_d,\Sigma_{new},\Sigma_{red},\Sigma_{exp},\Sigma_{old}\rangle}\ (mixin)$$

$$\frac{\Gamma \vdash g:\gamma_d \to \{\mathsf{gen}:\Sigma \to \{m_j:\tau^{\downarrow}_{m_j}, m_k:\tau^{\uparrow}_{m_k} \to \tau^{\downarrow}_{m_k}\}^{j\in New,k\in Redef}, \mathsf{superinit}:\gamma_b\}}{\Gamma \vdash \mathsf{mixinval}\langle g, New, Redef, Expect\rangle : \mathsf{mixin}\langle \gamma_b,\gamma_d,\Sigma_{new},\Sigma_{red},\Sigma_{exp},\Sigma_{old}\rangle}\ (mixin\ val)$$

$$\begin{array}{ll} & \Sigma = \Sigma_{new}\cup\Sigma_{red}\cup\Sigma_{exp}\\ \text{where} & \Sigma_{new} = \{m_j:\tau^{\downarrow}_{m_j}\},\ \Sigma_{red} = \{m_k:\tau^{\downarrow}_{m_k}\},\ \Sigma_{exp} = \{m_i:\tau^{\downarrow}_{m_i}\},\ \Sigma_{old} = \{m_k:\tau^{\uparrow}_{m_k}\}\\ & \tau^{\downarrow}_{m_i} \text{ and } \tau^{\uparrow}_{m_k} \text{ are inferred from method bodies and } i\in Expect \end{array}$$

$$\frac{\begin{array}{l}\Gamma \vdash e_1:\mathsf{mixin}\langle \gamma_b,\gamma_d,\Sigma_{new},\Sigma_{red},\Sigma_{exp},\Sigma_{old}\rangle\\ \Gamma \vdash e_2:\mathsf{class}\langle \gamma_c,\Sigma_b\rangle\\ \Gamma \vdash \gamma_b <: \gamma_c\\ \Gamma \vdash \Sigma_b <: (\Sigma_{exp}\cup\Sigma_{old})\\ \Gamma \vdash \Sigma_{red} <: \Sigma_b/\Sigma_{red}\\ Subj(\Sigma_b)\cap Subj(\Sigma_{new}) = \emptyset\end{array}}{\Gamma \vdash e_1 \diamond e_2 : \mathsf{class}\langle \gamma_d,\Sigma_d\rangle}\ (mixin\ app)$$

$$\text{where} \quad \Sigma_d = \Sigma_{new}\cup\Sigma_{red}\cup(\Sigma_b - \Sigma_b/\Sigma_{red})$$

Fig. 5. Typing rules for class and mixin-related forms

type γ_{d_2} for its constructor. Therefore, we require that $\gamma_{b_1} <: \gamma_{d_2}$ (condition (c_1)). The mixin e_1 is allowed to redefine methods: defined by e_2, expected by e_2, or redefined by e_2. In all cases we must check that the redefinition (and the expectation about the old method in the superclass) is type safe (conditions (c_2), (c_3) and (c_4)). If e_1 redefines a method m_k that is in turn redefined by e_2, then we will put the redefined type of m_k from e_1 in Σ_{red} and the old one from e_2 in Σ_{old}. This is consistent with the view that the new mixin will contain m_k with the body from e_1 (with its *next* bound to e_2's implementation, while in m_k's body from e_2 *next* remains still unbound, as the method m_k can be further redefined, see Section 3). If e_1 redefines, instead, an expected method of e_2, that method will not appear in Σ_{exp}, but the redefined type and the old type, as inferred from e_1, will appear in Σ_{red} and Σ_{old}, respectively. Conditions (c_5) and (c_6) check whether e_2 can provide methods (either defined or redefined) that are expected by e_1. If such a method is provided, then it will not appear in Σ_{exp}. In case both e_1

$$\frac{\begin{array}{l} \Gamma \vdash e_1 : \mathsf{mixin}\langle \gamma_{b_1}, \gamma_{d_1}, \Sigma^1_{new}, \Sigma^1_{red}, \Sigma^1_{exp}, \Sigma^1_{old} \rangle \\ \Gamma \vdash e_2 : \mathsf{mixin}\langle \gamma_{b_2}, \gamma_{d_2}, \Sigma^2_{new}, \Sigma^2_{red}, \Sigma^2_{exp}, \Sigma^2_{old} \rangle \\ (c_1)\ \Gamma \vdash \gamma_{b_1} <: \gamma_{d_2} \\ (c_2)\ \Gamma \vdash \tau^{\downarrow}_{m_{k_1}} <: \tau'^{\downarrow}_{m_{j_2}} <: \tau^{\uparrow}_{m_{k_1}} \quad \text{if } k_1 = j_2 \\ (c_3)\ \Gamma \vdash \tau^{\downarrow}_{m_{k_1}} <: \tau'^{\downarrow}_{m_{k_2}} <: \tau^{\uparrow}_{m_{k_1}} \quad \text{if } k_1 = k_2 \\ (c_4)\ \Gamma \vdash \tau^{\downarrow}_{m_{k_1}} <: \tau'^{\uparrow}_{m_{i_2}} <: \tau^{\uparrow}_{m_{k_1}} \quad \text{if } k_1 = i_2 \\ (c_5)\ \Gamma \vdash \tau'^{\downarrow}_{m_{j_2}} <: \tau^{\uparrow}_{m_{i_1}} \quad \text{if } i_1 = j_2 \\ (c_6)\ \Gamma \vdash \tau'^{\downarrow}_{m_{k_2}} <: \tau^{\uparrow}_{m_{i_1}} \quad \text{if } i_1 = k_2 \\ (c_7)\ \Gamma \vdash \tau'^{\uparrow}_{m_{i_2}} <: \tau^{\uparrow}_{m_{i_1}} \vee \Gamma \vdash \tau^{\uparrow}_{m_{i_1}} <: \tau'^{\uparrow}_{m_{i_2}} \quad \text{if } i_1 = i_2 \\ (c_8)\ Subj(\Sigma^1_{new}) \cap (Subj(\Sigma^2_{new}) \cup Subj(\Sigma^2_{red}) \cup Subj(\Sigma^2_{exp})) = \emptyset \end{array}}{\Gamma \vdash e_1 \bullet e_2 : \mathsf{mixin}\langle \gamma_{b_2}, \gamma_{d_1}, \Sigma_{new}, \Sigma_{red}, \Sigma_{exp}, \Sigma_{old} \rangle} \ (\textit{mixin comp})$$

where $\begin{array}{l} \Sigma^1_{new} = \{m_{j_1} : \tau^{\downarrow}_{m_{j_1}}\}, \Sigma^2_{new} = \{m_{j_2} : \tau'^{\downarrow}_{m_{j_2}}\}, \Sigma^1_{red} = \{m_{k_1} : \tau^{\downarrow}_{m_{k_1}}\}, \Sigma^2_{red} = \{m_{k_2} : \tau'^{\downarrow}_{m_{k_2}}\} \\ \Sigma^1_{exp} = \{m_{i_1} : \tau^{\uparrow}_{m_{i_1}}\}, \Sigma^2_{exp} = \{m_{i_2} : \tau'^{\uparrow}_{m_{i_2}}\}, \Sigma^1_{old} = \{m_{k_1} : \tau^{\uparrow}_{m_{k_1}}\}, \Sigma^2_{old} = \{m_{k_2} : \tau'^{\uparrow}_{m_{k_2}}\} \end{array}$

$$\begin{array}{l} \Sigma_{new} = \Sigma^1_{new} \cup (\Sigma^2_{new} - \Sigma^2_{new}/\Sigma^1_{red}) \cup \Sigma^1_{red}/\Sigma^2_{new} \\ \Sigma_{red} = (\Sigma^1_{red} - \Sigma^1_{red}/\Sigma^2_{new}) \cup (\Sigma^2_{red} - \Sigma^2_{red}/\Sigma^1_{red}) \\ \Sigma_{old} = (\Sigma^1_{old} - (\Sigma^1_{old}/\Sigma^2_{new} \cup \Sigma^1_{old}/\Sigma^2_{old})) \cup \Sigma^2_{old} \\ \Sigma_{exp} = (\Sigma^1_{exp} - (\Sigma^1_{exp}/\Sigma^2_{new} \cup \Sigma^1_{exp}/\Sigma^2_{red} \cup \Sigma^1_{exp}/\Sigma^2_{exp})) \cup (\Sigma^2_{exp} - (\Sigma^2_{exp}/\Sigma^1_{red} \cup \Sigma^2_{exp}/\Sigma^1_{exp})) \cup \Sigma_{min} \\ \Sigma_{min} = \{m_i : \min\{\tau^{\uparrow}_{m_i}, \tau'^{\uparrow}_{m_i}\} \mid m_i : \tau^{\uparrow}_{m_i} \in \Sigma^1_{exp}, m_i : \tau'^{\uparrow}_{m_i} \in \Sigma^2_{exp}\} \end{array}$$

Fig. 6. Typing rule for mixin composition

and e_2 expect the same method, the types with which such method is expected must be comparable (condition (c_7)); the method will then appear in Σ_{exp} with the smaller type. Finally, condition (c_8) checks that no name clash occurs among methods defined by e_1 and those defined/redefined/expected by e_2. This decision is in line with a good object-oriented design principle of not confusing method redefinitions and name clashes.

Our system is proved sound, in the sense that "every well-typed program cannot go wrong", which implies the absence of *message-not-understood* runtime errors. We consider *programs*, which are closed terms, and we introduce *faulty programs*, which are a way to approximate the concept of reaching a "stuck state" during the evaluation; for example, a program "reaches a stuck state" if a method call is attempted on an expression that does not evaluate to an object. We prove that if the evaluation for a program p does not diverge, then either p returns a value, or p reduces to a faulty program. We then show that faulty programs are not typable, and, via a subject reduction property, we establish that if a program is typable, then it evaluates to a value, under the condition that the program does not diverge.

Lemma 1 (Subject Reduction). *If $\Gamma \vdash e : \tau$ and e evaluates to e', then $\Gamma \vdash e' : \tau$.*

Theorem 1 (Soundness). *Let p be a program: if $\varepsilon \vdash p : \tau$ then either the evaluation for p diverges, or p evaluates to a value v and $\varepsilon \vdash v : \tau$ (ε stands for the empty typing environment).*

The metatheory for the present system, and in particular the subject reduction property, are extensions of the ones in [9] (Chapter 9). The formal definitions and properties

were analyzed in detail, and can be found at:
`http://www.dsi.unifi.it/ bettini/high-proofs.pdf`.

5 Conclusions

This paper presents a calculus supporting class hierarchies creation via mixin application (already present in [10]) and mixin composition. Our goal was to design a clean and general form of mixin composition without committing ourselves to an already existing language. We chose to extend the calculus [10] because: (*i*) it is an easy-to-extend framework; (*ii*) its operational semantics is close both to an implementation and to a denotational model. Therefore, being able to produce something towards a denotational model for mixins is, in our opinion, a good by-product; (*iii*) it allowed us to choose *structural subtyping* (as opposed to *nominal subtyping* of C++ and Java), since, according to Bracha et al., [5], "When subtyping is structural, mixins do not introduce any new issues with respect to subtyping." Moreover, structural subtyping has the advantage of being independent from the class hierarchy.

In the literature, there are many proposals that deal with mixins. We mention here some of them, the most interesting with respect to our calculus. Bracha and Cook extend Modula-3 with mixins in [14] (this is one of the seminal papers on mixins). The novelty is in seeing object types as mixins, which either explicitly state the modifications to the superclass, or are obtained as a result of mixin composition. The left-hand mixin has a "priority" and the composition is not explicitly written in order to ensure upward compatibility with the existing language. Instead, we think that making the composition explicit (as it is in our calculus) makes the programmer aware of how software components are composed, thus providing more control over the behavior of the program.

Flatt et al. [20] extend a subset of sequential Java called ClassicJava with mixins and call it MixedJava. Mixins use their *inheritance interface* to specify how the inherited methods are extended and/or overridden. Existing mixins can be combined in order to produce new composite mixins. As in our calculus, the left-hand mixin has the "precedence" over the right-hand mixin. Composition is well-defined only if the right-hand mixin implements the left-hand mixin inheritance interface (i.e., the right-hand mixin is required to provide all the methods expected by the left-hand one). In this respect, our approach is more oriented to code composition, in that the new composite mixin is still allowed to have expected methods not yet resolved. The duplication of method names in MixedJava is resolved at run-time with the run-time context information provided by the current *view* of the object (represented as a chain of mixins).

Ancona and Zucca [2,3,4] give a formal model for mixin modules. A mixin is a function from input to output components, and they characterize axiomatically the operators for composing mixins in order to obtain higher-order mixins. They also present a variety of method renaming forms, to deal with different typologies of name collisions. In [1] they present Jam, an extension of Java supporting mixins, but not mixin composition, where name collision is treated essentially as "accidental override".

Our approach is different from the ones of MixedJava and Jam in some respects. Besides not being a Java-like calculus, which allows us to use structural subtyping, our calculus has a more modular class constructor. Moreover, method names collisions are resolved statically by the type system. If this approach may look more restrictive than the ones of MixedJava and Jam, we preferred it because it forces the programmer to be aware of collisions and to resolve them, while automatic handling of such ambiguities may lead to unexpected behavior at run-time.

Boudol [12] extends *Reference* ML [25] with records and *let rec* operator. This enriched ML leads to a theoretically solid treatment of mixins, which are seen as class transformers. The principal difference between the two calculi seems to be in the way references to fields are created. In our calculus these are created at class creation time, when mixin application is evaluated, whereas in the calculus of Boudol they are created at class instantiation time, i.e., when an object is created.

A future research direction is an extension of this calculus where not only classes can be instantiated but also mixins, obtaining a form of *incomplete objects*, to be completed in an object-based fashion. A first version of the incomplete objects is given in [6]. Moreover, higher-order mixins seem to be a natural feature to be added to MoMi [7], a coordination language where object-oriented mobile code is exchanged among the nodes of a network.

Acknowledgment. We would like to thank the anonymous referees for their comments and suggestions, which helped us in giving a better focus to the paper and in improving the overall presentation.

References

1. D. Ancona, G. Lagorio, and E. Zucca. Jam—Designing a Java extension with mixins. *ACM Transactions on Programming Languages and Systems*, 25(5):641–712, 2003.
2. D. Ancona and E. Zucca. A theory of mixin modules: Basic and derived operators. *MSCS*, 8(4):401–446, 1998.
3. D. Ancona and E. Zucca. True modules for Java-like languages. In *Proc. of ECOOP 2001*, volume 2072 of *LNCS*, pages 354–380. Springer-Verlag, 2001.
4. D. Ancona and E. Zucca. A theory of mixin modules: Algebraic laws and reduction semantics. *Mathematical Structures in Computer Science*, 12(6):701–737, 2002.
5. L. Bak, G. Bracha, S. Grarup, R. Griesemer, D. Griswold, and U. Hölzle. Mixins in Strongtalk. In *Proc. of Inheritance Workshop at ECOOP 2002*, 2002.
6. L. Bettini, V. Bono, and S. Likavec. A Core Calculus of Mixin-Based Incomplete Objects. In *Proc. of FOOL 11*, 2004.
7. L. Bettini, V. Bono, and B. Venneri. Coordinating Mobile Object-Oriented Code. In *Proc. of Coordination Models and Languages*, volume 2315 of *LNCS*, pages 56–71. Springer, 2002.
8. L. Bettini, V. Bono, and B. Venneri. Subtyping Mobile Classes and Mixins. In *Proc. of Int. Workshops on Foundations of Object-Oriented Languages, FOOL 10*, 2003.
9. V. Bono. *Type Systems for the Object Oriented Paradigm.* PhD thesis, Univ. di Torino, 1999.
10. V. Bono, A. Patel, and V. Shmatikov. A core calculus of classes and mixins. In *Proc. ECOOP '99*, volume 1628 of *LNCS*, pages 43–66. Springer-Verlag, 1999.
11. V. Bono, A. Patel, V. Shmatikov, and J. C. Mitchell. A core calculus of classes and objects. In *Proc. of the 15th Conference on the Mathematical Foundations of Programming Semantics (MFPS '99)*, volume 220 of *ENTCS*. Elsevier, 1999.
12. G. Boudol. The recursive record semantics of objects revised. In *Proc. ESOP '01*, volume 2028 of *LNCS*, pages 269–283. Springer-Verlag, 2001.
13. N. Boyen, C. Lucas, and P. Steyaert. Generalized mixin-based inheritance to support multiple inheritance. Technical Report vub-prog-tr-94-12, Vrije Universiteit Brussel, 1994.

14. G. Bracha and W. Cook. Mixin-based inheritance. In *Proc. of OOPSLA/ECOOP*, pages 303–311, 1990.
15. K. Bruce. *Foundations of Object-Oriented Languages – Types and Semantics*. The MIT Press, 2002.
16. W. R. Cook. *A Denotational Semantics of Inheritance*. PhD thesis, Brown University, 1989.
17. E. Crank and M. Felleisen. Parameter-passing and the lambda calculus. In *Proc. POPL '91*, pages 233–244, 1991.
18. M. Felleisen and R. Hieb. The revised report on the syntactic theories of sequential control and state. *Theoretical Computer Science*, 103(2):235–271, 1992.
19. M. Flatt, S. Krishnamurthi, and M. Felleisen. Classes and mixins. In *Proc. of POPL '98*, pages 171–183, 1998.
20. M. Flatt, S. Krishnamurthi, and M. Felleisen. A Programmer's Reduction Semantics for Classes and Mixins. In *Formal Syntax and Semantics of Java*, volume 1523 of *LNCS*, pages 241–269, 1999.
21. E. Gamma, R. Helm, R. Johnson, and J. Vlissides. *Design Patterns: Elements of Reusable Object-Oriented Software*. Addison-Wesley, 1995.
22. M. V. Limberghen and T. Mens. Encapsulation and composition as orthogonal operators on mixins: a solution to multiple inheritance problems. *Object Oriented Systems*, 3(1), 1996.
23. I. Mason and C. Talcott. Programming, transforming, and proving with function abstractions and memories. In *Proc. ICALP '89*, volume 372 of *LNCS*, pages 574–588. Springer-Verlag, 1989.
24. A. Patel. *Obstacl: a language with objects, subtyping, and classes*. PhD thesis, Stanford University, 2001.
25. A. Wright and M. Felleisen. A syntactic approach to type soundness. *Information and Computation*, 115(1):38–94, 1994.

A Subtyping Rules and Other Typing Rules

$$\frac{}{\Gamma, \iota_1 <: \iota_2 \vdash \iota_1 <: \iota_2}\ (<:\ proj) \qquad \frac{}{\Gamma \vdash \tau <: \tau}\ (refl) \qquad \frac{\Gamma \vdash \tau_1 <: \tau_2 \quad \Gamma \vdash \tau_2 <: \tau_3}{\Gamma \vdash \tau_1 <: \tau_3}\ (trans)$$

$$\frac{\Gamma \vdash \tau' <: \tau \quad \Gamma \vdash \sigma <: \sigma'}{\Gamma \vdash \tau \to \sigma <: \tau' \to \sigma'}\ (arrow) \qquad \frac{\Gamma \vdash \tau_i <: \sigma_i \quad i \in I \quad I \subseteq J}{\Gamma \vdash \{m_i : \tau_i\}^{i \in I} <: \{m_j : \sigma_j\}^{j \in J}}\ (<:\ record)$$

$$\frac{typeof(const) = \tau}{\Gamma \vdash const : \tau}\ (const) \qquad \frac{}{\Gamma, x : \tau \vdash x : \tau}\ (proj) \qquad \frac{\Gamma, x : \tau \vdash e : \sigma}{\Gamma \vdash \lambda x.e : \tau \to \sigma}\ (\lambda) \qquad \frac{}{\Gamma \vdash\ ! : \tau\ \mathsf{ref} \to \tau}\ (!)$$

$$\frac{\Gamma \vdash e_1 : \tau \to \sigma \quad \Gamma \vdash e_2 : \tau}{\Gamma \vdash e_1\ e_2 : \sigma}\ (app) \qquad \frac{}{\Gamma \vdash fix : (\sigma \to \sigma) \to \sigma}\ (fix) \qquad \frac{\Gamma \vdash e : \{x : \sigma\}}{\Gamma \vdash e.x : \sigma}\ (lookup)$$

$$\frac{\Gamma \vdash e : \tau \quad \Gamma \vdash \tau <: \sigma}{\Gamma \vdash e : \sigma}\ (sub) \qquad \frac{\Gamma \vdash e_i : \tau_i}{\Gamma \vdash \{x_i = e_i\}^{i \in I} : \{x_i : \tau_i\}}\ (record) \qquad \frac{}{\Gamma \vdash \mathsf{ref} : \tau \to \tau\ \mathsf{ref}}\ (ref)$$

$$\frac{}{\Gamma \vdash := \ : \tau\ \mathsf{ref} \to \tau \to \tau}\ (:=) \qquad \frac{\Gamma' = \Gamma, x_1 : \tau_1\ \mathsf{ref}, \ldots, x_n : \tau_n\ \mathsf{ref} \quad \Gamma' \vdash v_i : \tau_i \quad \Gamma' \vdash e : \tau}{\Gamma \vdash H\langle x_1, v_1 \rangle \ldots \langle x_n, v_n \rangle.e : \tau}\ (heap)$$

Type Inference for Nested Self Types*

Viviana Bono[1]**, Jerzy Tiuryn[2], and Paweł Urzyczyn[2]***

[1] Università di Torino, Dipartimento di Informatica, c. Svizzera 185, 10149 Torino, Italy
bono@di.unito.it

[2] Uniwersytet Warszawski, Instytut Informatyki, Banacha 2, 02-097 Warszawa, Poland
{tiuryn,urzy}@mimuw.edu.pl

Abstract. We address the issue of the decidability of the type inference problem for a type system of an object-oriented calculus with general selftypes. The fragment considered in the present paper is obtained by restricting the set of operators to method invocation only. The resulting system, despite its syntactical simplicity, is sufficiently complicated to merit the study of the intricate constraints emerging in the process of type reconstruction, and it can be considered as the core system with respect to typability for extensions with other operators. The main result of the paper is the decidability of type reconstruction, together with a certain form of a principal type property.

1 Introduction

Object-oriented programming languages enjoy an ever growing popularity, as they are a tool for designing maintainable and expandable code, and are also suited for developing mobile code and web applications. Imposing a type discipline on programs ensures safety (i.e., the absence of message-not-understood run-time errors), yet this type discipline must be flexible enough in order not to restrain reusability. Polymorphic type systems are one answer to this double requirement; see for example [6,13]. Among the many features that can be included in such systems, there is the use of *selftype*.

The concept of *self* (sometimes called *this*) is of paramount importance in object-oriented languages. Self is a special variable that allows reference to the object executing the current method, and hence access to its fields and invocation of the sibling methods. This concept, while being a very convenient feature, influences substantially the problem of static typing for object-oriented languages. Self types have been a subject of foundational studies, both in the object-based and in the class-based setting (see, for example, [1,8,11]). The work done in the past has highlighted the importance of typing self in a careful way.

The gain of introducing an appropriate type for self is evident when a form of inheritance is present, whether a class-based one (via class hierarchies), or an object-based one (via method addition/override). In fact, an appropriate type for self would allow

* Research work conducted within the framework of Types WG Project IST-1999-29001.

** This work has been partially supported by EU within the FET - Global Computing initiative, project DART IST-2001-33477, and by MIUR project NAPOLI. The funding bodies are not responsible for any use that might be made of the results presented here.

*** Partly supported by KBN Grant 7 T11C 028 20.

S. Berardi, M. Coppo, and F. Damiani (Eds.): TYPES 2003, LNCS 3085, pp. 99–114, 2004.

the automatic specialization of those inherited/overriden methods that either return the host object, and/or have some parameters of the same type as the host object (*binary* methods). This specialization (also known as *MyType* specialization) can be seen as an alternative to *typecasts*, which are explicit declarations made by the programmer on the expected actual type of the method result according to the type of the object the method is invoked upon. Typecasts are unsafe—the programmer must be "sure" about the actual type of the returned object, since little or even no static checking is performed on typecasts, as we observe, for example, in Java or in C++. Moreover typecasts certainly do not improve readability of code, with a negative impact on the debugging phase. As hinted above, an alternative to typecasts is the introduction of *selftype*, with the meaning "the type of the current object", i.e., "the type of self", to annotate appropriately binary methods and methods that return the host object. Some type systems including selftype are presented in [1,8,11].

In this paper we consider the problem of *type inference* (also called *typability*) in presence of general (arbitrarily nested) selftypes in an object-based setting. Very little is known about type inference with selftypes. To the best of our knowledge, only Palsberg and Jim addressed this subject. In [16], they study the type inference problem for one of the Abadi-Cardelli systems [1] extended with the notion of selftype. In [15], Palsberg presents an algorithm for Abadi-Cardelli's four first-order systems (without any form of selftype), proving that the type inference problem for all four systems is P-complete[1]. The work [16] can be seen as an application of the techniques developed in [15], and it contains a proof that the type-inference problem for an Abadi-Cardelli system with recursive types and width subtyping extended with a simple form of selftype is NP-complete.

The Palsberg-Jim "tiny drop of selftype", as the authors themselves point out, consists of: (*i*) the use of the keyword *selftype*, instead of a bound variable, to stand for the selftype in object types; (*ii*) the restriction that each occurence of selftype "comes with its context", i.e., in their type system *selftype* can appear as a component of an object type only, never in isolation. These two choices imply the following consequences: (*i*) it is not possible to refer to the selftype of enclosing outer objects (i.e., there are no *nested* selftypes); (*ii*) it is not possible to override those methods that return the object itself (i.e., of type selftype).

Of the above two restrictions, the first one seems to be essential. It implies that the access to two or more different *selftype*'s, i.e., two or more different environments, is impossible. Indeed, the "tiny drop of selftype" of Palsberg and Jim can be encoded in a system without selftype (see [9]), meaning that it is a rather weak form of selftype.

We plan, therefore, to analyze the decidability of type inference for a type system that relaxes the above limitations. The system under study is based on the calculus presented in [3] (we will call it C from now on). The calculus C is an untyped version of the calculus introduced in [5], in order to analyze throughout a functional encoding the type system of [4] (hereafter BB), which is, in turn, a simplification of the Lambda Calculus of Objects (hereafter LCO) of Fisher, Honsell, Mitchell [11]. The calculus LCO is a functional object-based calculus enriched with object primitives. Operations allowed on objects are *method addition*, *method override*, and *method invocation* (also

[1] In [12] this result is improved.

called *send*). Method bodies are functions; in particular, self is modelled using a lambda-abstracted variable. In LCO: (*i*) it is possible to refer to the selves of the enclosing objects; (*ii*) override is as general as possible. Selftype is rendered by using the *row-variables* of [14] to characterize types of methods as type-schemes (i.e., types polymorphic in these variables), and to enforce correct instantiation of the schemes as methods are inherited. The type system of C we base our paper on inherits some of the fundamental ideas from the original system in the modelling of selftype. The main difference is avoiding the use of row-variables to model selftype, but exploiting instead Bruce's *matching* [7] and implicit match-bounded quantification over type variables, as studied in the BB calculus of [4]. The designers of LCO conjectured that type inference for LCO was undecidable, but nobody has proven that yet. We focus on the same type inference problem for C, which has a simpler (yet as expressive as) type system than LCO.

Due to the generality of system C, we decided to tackle the related type inference problem in steps. First of all, we discarded the method addition operation. Method addition does not add much to the inherent difficulty of the problem of type inference, because it is performed on objects but it is forbidden on selves[2]. Second, we also discard method override, because method invocation turns out to create a surprisingly non-trivial problem by itself. The possibility of referring to nested selves of enclosing outer objects creates "reference loops" which are difficult to untangle.

It might seem natural to identify objects with recursive records, and hence to identify their types with recursive types, but this is misleading. In fact: (*i*) such choice is not adequate already in our setting with method invocation only, because of the generality of our selves (see the examples in Section 2); (*ii*) generally, this solution does not work in an enlarged setting with method override and/or addition because the meaning of self changes as operations on the host object are performed (see [1], Section 6.7.2).

We make a number of simplifications in our syntax. For instance we consider objects with exactly two methods, and put a "constant" □ as a *place-holder* wherever we mean "an irrelevant subexpression". These simplifications do not influence the essence of the problem, and make it easier to isolate the basic issue: type assignment in presence of multiple selves. The place-holder is just there to hide whatever does not influence typing itself. The presence of two fields only rules out the so-called *message-not-understood* run-time errors, as sends are limited to those two components. Even though catching statically such errors is a primary task of type systems for object-oriented languages, the task of testing a sort of "well-formedness" of objects is essential as well, and this is what our typability algorithm does.

The paper is organized as follows. Section 2 introduces the most basic syntactic categories, terms and types, and explains the motivation of our type assignment. In Section 3, we elaborate the syntactic notions used in the paper. Section 4 presents a type assignment system. In Section 5, we introduce the main tool in establishing a sort of "principal type scheme" property and the confluence property of a certain system of reductions. The principal technical part of the paper is Section 6. It is devoted to an algorithm which transforms a given term into a "type scheme", or reports a failure. Two classes of redexes are introduced: reducible and cyclic. Among the reducible redexes

[2] There are calculi that deal with *self-inflicted* method addition such as [10], but they go beyond the goal of this paper, which is about classical object-based calculi.

there are redexes which we call inconsistent. They are the only source of a possible untypability of a term in our setting. Section 6.4 contains the main technical properties of the reduction system: confluence and termination (Theorem 1), and recovery of typings (Theorem 2). Section 7 contains the main result of the paper, Theorem 3. It states that there is a type scheme assigned to every (and only) typable term such that all the instantiations of this scheme give correct typings of the term. This principal type scheme can be effectively obtained if and only if the term is typable. Therefore the typability problem is decidable. Section 8 gives an informal account on how to deal with method addition and message-not-understood run-time errors.

Due to space limitations, we have omitted from this presentation all proofs and many auxiliary definitions which are not essential for understanding the main results of the paper. The details can be found in the full version of the paper in: `http://www.di.unito.it/~bono/Manuscripts`.

2 Terms and Types

Assume an infinite set of variables (selves), with the notation $s, t, \ldots$ A *term* is either a variable, or a *place-holder* indicated with $\Box$, or:

- an *object*, i.e., an expression of the form $\mathbf{pro}\ s\langle\, M_1, M_2\,\rangle$, where M_1 and M_2 are terms, or:
- a *send*, i.e., an expression of the form $M \Leftarrow i$, where M is a term and $i \in \{1, 2\}$.

The operator $\mathbf{pro}\ s$ binds the self s. Alpha conversion is assumed. The notation $FV(M)$ and $M[N/s]$ is used accordingly (with $\Box[N/s] = \Box$).

The intended meaning of "$\mathbf{pro}\ s\langle\, M_1, M_2\,\rangle$" is an object with two methods M_1 and M_2, which may refer to the whole object via the self variable s. In the notation of [1] this would be written as $\langle\, \varsigma s.M_1, \varsigma s.M_2\,\rangle$. The meaning of "$M \Leftarrow i$" is to extract the i-th method from the object M, and the operational semantics is given by the following reduction rule: $\mathbf{pro}\ s\langle\, M_1, M_2\,\rangle \Leftarrow i \quad \leadsto \quad M_i[\mathbf{pro}\ s\langle\, M_1, M_2\,\rangle/s]$.

The place-holder $\Box$ may be seen as a representation of a piece of code (i.e., a subexpression) which is irrelevant with respect to typing. Our objective is to study the structure of self-references occurring in object expressions, by means of a mathematical abstraction. For the purpose of the analysis of our abstract model, anything that does not contain self-references is considered irrelevant and thus can be represented by a $\Box$. Clearly, a message sent to an irrelevant target is irrelevant too, so we do not find anything wrong in postulating the reduction $\Box \Leftarrow i \leadsto \Box$, which expresses exactly the idea of ignoring the "contents"of $\Box$. On the other hand, the expression $s \Leftarrow i$ has some meaning, but it cannot be evaluated until we substitute an actual object for s.

We want to assign types to expressions of our language. The basic idea is that a type assigned to $\mathbf{pro}\ s\langle\, M_1, M_2\,\rangle$ should be essentially a product of types assigned to M_1 and M_2. Thus, we would like to assert something like $\mathbf{pro}\ s\langle\, 3, 5\,\rangle : \langle\langle\, int, int\,\rangle\rangle$, provided we know that $3, 5 : int$.

In general, the type of a pure object (an expression without sends) should correspond to the shape of the object. If an object refers to a self s, the natural choice is to use a type variable t, corresponding to the self s and assert $\mathbf{pro}\ s\langle\, s, 5\,\rangle : \delta t\,\langle\langle\, t, int\,\rangle\rangle$, where the

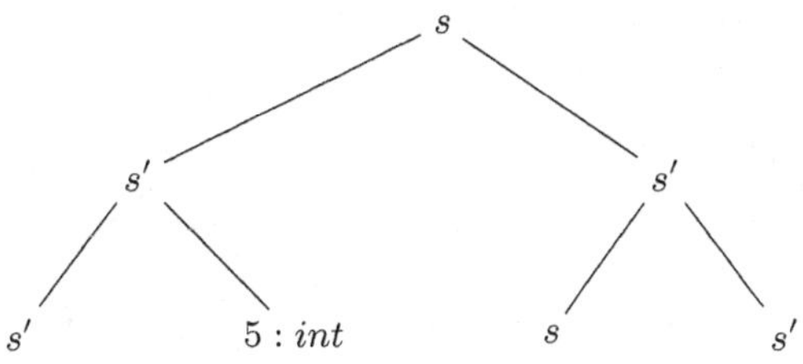

Fig. 1. The structure of a term w.r.t. selves

operator δt binds t within $\langle\langle \dots \rangle\rangle$. This can be extended to more complex pure objects, e.g., $\mathbf{pro}\ s\langle\, \mathbf{pro}\ s'\langle\, s', 5\,\rangle, \mathbf{pro}\ s'\langle\, s, s'\,\rangle\,\rangle$ is of type $\delta t\, \langle\langle\, \delta t'\langle\langle\, t', int\,\rangle\rangle, \delta t'\langle\langle\, t, t'\,\rangle\rangle\,\rangle\rangle$. We can simply identify a pure object with its own type. Indeed, the only difference between the term and the type in the last example is where the constant 5 occurs. All the rest is just syntactic sugar. The essential part, which is the structure of the self-references, is the same, up to renaming, in the term and in the type, and can be drawn as the tree in Fig. 1. This justifies our definition of a type as a term not containing $\Leftarrow$. An assignment of such a type τ to an expression M containing occurrences of $\Leftarrow$ means: M is as good as a pure object of type τ. Moreover, as said above, we do not really care about the place-holder and its types, because the place-holder represents an irrelevant subexpression with respect to typing, therefore we assume $\Box : \Box$ for the place-holder $\Box$.

Our type assignment should enjoy the subject reduction property, i.e., we want $M' : \tau$, whenever $M \rightsquigarrow M'$ and $M : \tau$. This requirement determines what the type assignment rules should be. First of all, observe that $M : \mathbf{pro}\ s\langle\, \tau_1, \tau_2\,\rangle$ should imply that $M \Leftarrow i$ is of type $\tau_i[s := \mathbf{pro}\ s\langle\, \tau_1, \tau_2\,\rangle]$. It is less obvious which type should be assigned to a send of the form $s \Leftarrow i$. Clearly, our identification of an object and its type requires a uniform principle $s : s$. That is, self is of type self. The type of $s \Leftarrow i$ should depend on the context in which the expression occurs. Consider as an example the term $M = \mathbf{pro}\ s\langle\, \mathbf{pro}\ t\langle\, \Box, s \Leftarrow 1\,\rangle, \Box\,\rangle$, depicted as the (A) tree in Fig. 2. It may be tempting to assert $s \Leftarrow 1 : t$, because $s \Leftarrow 1$ certainly points to the root of the object identified by the self t. This amounts to understanding an object type $\mathbf{pro}\ t\langle \dots \rangle$ as a recursive type $\mu t\langle \dots \rangle$, that may freely be replaced by $\langle \dots \rangle[\mu t\langle \dots \rangle / t]$. That, however, would be wrong: consider the expression $M \Leftarrow 1$. We have: $M{\Leftarrow}1 \rightsquigarrow \mathbf{pro}\ t\langle\, \Box, M{\Leftarrow}1\,\rangle \rightsquigarrow \mathbf{pro}\ t\langle\, \Box, \mathbf{pro}\ t\langle\, \Box, M{\Leftarrow}1\,\rangle\,\rangle \rightsquigarrow \cdots$. From this reduction sequence we can see that no finite object type can be assigned to M, as the expression develops into an infinite tree. Thus, M should not be typed at all.

Note that the idea of a recursive type $\mu t\langle\, \Box, t\,\rangle$ is not adequate here, which can be best seen if we modify M to $M' = \mathbf{pro}\ s\langle\, \mathbf{pro}\ t\langle\, t, s \Leftarrow 1\,\rangle, \Box\,\rangle$. While M' expands to an infinite tree in reduction, it is not a full binary tree! Another reason why we do not want to use recursive types is that we want to distinguish between $\mathbf{pro}\ s\langle\, 4, \mathbf{pro}\ s\langle\, 2, s\,\rangle\,\rangle$ and $\mathbf{pro}\ s\langle\, 2, s\,\rangle$.

The problem we encountered in the above example does not occur, if we consider the term $N = \mathbf{pro}\ s\langle\, \mathbf{pro}\ t\langle\, \Box, s \Leftarrow 1 \Leftarrow 1\,\rangle, \Box\,\rangle$. The picture is now represented as the (B) tree in Fig. 2, and the type of $s \Leftarrow 1 \Leftarrow 1$ in this context should undoubtedly be $\Box$.

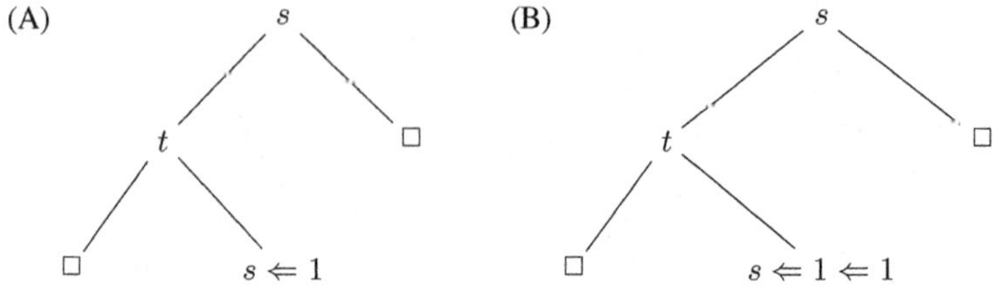

Fig. 2. Terms as trees.

So what is the type of $s \Leftarrow 1$? Now we see it must be $\mathbf{pro}\ t\langle\, \Box, \Box\, \rangle$. But how can we derive it? For this we need to know the type of N from an *environment* that assigns to s the type of the object that s points to. (It is not a type of s as we always have $s : s$.) We arrive at the following rule

$$\frac{t : \mathbf{pro}\ t\langle\, \tau_1, \tau_2\, \rangle \vdash M : t}{t : \mathbf{pro}\ t\langle\, \tau_1, \tau_2\, \rangle \vdash M \Leftarrow i : \tau_i}.$$

Thus to derive the type for N we must first guess it, put it into an environment in which we derive types of the components of N, and finally we apply the following rule for typing objects

$$\frac{s : \mathbf{pro}\ s\langle\, \tau_1, \tau_2\, \rangle \vdash N_1 : \tau_1, \quad s : \mathbf{pro}\ s\langle\, \tau_1, \tau_2\, \rangle \vdash N_2 : \tau_2}{\vdash \mathbf{pro}\ s\langle\, N_1, N_2\, \rangle : \mathbf{pro}\ s\langle\, \tau_1, \tau_2\, \rangle}$$

to eliminate the initial guess from the environment. The need of guessing the final type of a complex expression, before type-checking begins, makes it difficult to apply any structural approach to type inference. The problem becomes even more involved in the presence of an interaction between "external" sends to an object expression and "internal" sends occurring within that expression.

2.1 The Roadmap of Notions

We conclude this informal introduction with a brief description of several syntactic categories used in the course of the proof of the main decidability result. We use the following subsets of the set of all terms, ordered as follows:

types $\subseteq$ *quasi types* $\subseteq$ *stripped terms* $\subseteq$ *terms.*

Stripped terms are terms in which all applications of the send operator $\Leftarrow$ are 'stripped down' to leaves, i.e., $\Leftarrow$ occurs only in the context $s \Leftarrow \Pi$, where s is a self and $\Pi \in \{1,2\}^*$ is a non-empty path. Moreover, if an occurrence of $s \Leftarrow \Pi$ is bound, then the binding $\mathbf{pro}$ is the outermost $\mathbf{pro}$ of the term. The main technical part of the algorithm which decides typability is concerned with stripped terms. The strategy of the algorithm consists in rewriting a given stripped term, trying to eliminate bound occurrences of $s \Leftarrow \Pi$. In this way we arrive at the next syntactic category of terms: quasi types. A stripped term without bound occurrences of $s \Leftarrow \Pi$ (with $\Pi \neq \varepsilon$) is called a quasi type. Hence a quasi type is a term in which all applications of the send operator are 'stripped down' to the leaves and every such an occurrence is free, i.e., no

pro binds a self s which is in the context $s \Leftarrow \Pi$, with $\Pi \neq \varepsilon$. Quasi types behave in several respects similar to types: a quasi type is always typable and moreover its type is uniquely determined by the environment. Finally the smallest syntactic category, types, consists of terms in which no send operator occurs.

Since we are interested in a form of principal typing, we have to allow metavariables which range over types. In this way we obtain a class of meta schemes — these are just like ordinary terms, except that they may contain metavariables. Again, meta schemes are stratified syntactically in a similar way to that described above. Thus we have:

quasi type schemes $\subseteq$ *stripped schemes* $\subseteq$ *meta schemes.*

Quasi type schemes are produced by the algorithm of the paper for each typable term, and only for such terms (see Theorem 3), which is the main result of this paper.

3 Technical Background

If $\Pi \in \{1,2\}^+$, then we define $M \Leftarrow \Pi$ by induction: $M \Leftarrow \Pi i := M \Leftarrow \Pi \Leftarrow i$. Occasionally, we use the notation $M \Leftarrow \Pi$, even if Π can be empty, identifying $M \Leftarrow \varepsilon$ with M. We call every send of the form $s \Leftarrow \Pi$, where $\Pi \neq \varepsilon$, an *atomic send*. A *top send* in an object $M = \mathbf{pro}\ s.\langle M_1, M_2 \rangle$ is an atomic send $s \Leftarrow \Pi$ bound by the top **pro** s in M. The length of Π is the *length* of the send $s \Leftarrow \Pi$. We say that an atomic send $s \Leftarrow \Pi$ is *free* in M if $s \in FV(M)$.

If a term does not contain non-atomic sends, it is often convenient to think of it as a labelled binary tree. Internal nodes are labelled by selves and leaves are labelled by the place-holder, selves or sends. Nodes are identified with paths leading to them. For a string $\Gamma \in \{1,2\}^*$ and a term M, if Γ leads in M to a node we will say that Γ is *contained* in M and write $\Gamma \in M$. For $\Gamma \in M$ we can also refer to a label of Γ meaning the label of the node to which Γ leads in M.

A *type* is a term not containing $\Leftarrow$. In particular an *object type* is a type which is also an object. A *quasi type* is a term in which all sends are atomic and free. A *stripped term* is a term of the form $\mathbf{pro}\ s.\langle M_1, M_2 \rangle$, where M_1 and M_2 are quasi types. Thus in a stripped term all bound sends are top sends.

A *self declaration* is a pair of the form $s : \tau$, where τ is an object type. An *environment* E is a sequence of self declarations, such that no declaration in E involves a (free) variable declared later on in E. More precisely, the definition of an environment, its *domain* $\mathrm{Dom}(E)$, and the set $FV(E)$ of *free selves* of E is stated inductively as follows.

- The empty sequence $\emptyset$ is an environment, and $\mathrm{Dom}(\emptyset) = \emptyset = FV(\emptyset)$.
- If E is an environment, s is a self such that $s \notin FV(E)$, and τ is a type, then $E' = E, s : \tau$ is an environment, with $\mathrm{Dom}(E') = \mathrm{Dom}(E) \cup \{s\}$ and $FV(E') = FV(E) \cup FV(\tau)$.

We will use the convention that if $s : \tau$ is a declaration, then τ is of the form $\tau = \mathbf{pro}\ s.\langle \tau_1, \tau_2 \rangle$. For $s \in \mathrm{Dom}(E)$, we write $E(s) = \tau$ if τ is the type which is assigned to s by the rightmost declaration for s in E.

3.1 Formal Field Selection

Given a quasi type T and $\Pi \in \{1,2\}^*$, we define a quasi type $T.\Pi$, called a *formal field selection*:

- $T.\varepsilon = T$,
- $\sqcup.\Pi = \Box$,
- $(s \Leftarrow \Gamma).\Pi = s \Leftarrow \Gamma\Pi$, for $\Gamma \in \{1,2\}^*$, in particular $s.\Pi = s \Leftarrow \Pi$,
- if $T = \mathbf{pro}\ s.\langle T_1, T_2 \rangle$, then $T.i\Pi = (T_i[T/s]).\Pi$.

Let us stress that, by the above definition, the notations $s.\Pi$ and $s \Leftarrow \Pi$ are interchangeable.

In the last clause of the above definition the substitution $T_i[T/s]$ is just the ordinary substitution of T for all free occurrences of s in T_i. Notice that in this case no free occurrence of s in T_i is a free send. Otherwise, the result of the substitution is not necessarily a quasi type. That is, quasi types are not closed with respect to ordinary substitutions. The general case of substitution of quasi types is dealt with in the full version of the paper.

3.2 Evaluation of Stripped Terms in an Environment

Given a stripped term M, we define a stripped term $(M)_E$, called the *value* of M in the environment E, as follows.

- $(s)_E = s$,
- $(\Box)_E = \Box$,
- $(s \Leftarrow i\Pi)_E = (\tau_i.\Pi)_E$, whenever $E(s) = \mathbf{pro}\ s.\langle \tau_1, \tau_2 \rangle$,
- $(s \Leftarrow i\Pi)_E = s \Leftarrow i\Pi$, if $s \notin \mathrm{Dom}(E)$,
- $(\mathbf{pro}\ s.\langle M_1, M_2 \rangle)_E = \mathbf{pro}\ s\langle (M_1)_E, (M_2)_E \rangle$, where $s \notin FV(E) \cup s \notin \mathrm{Dom}(E)$.

Note that the above definition is correct, i.e., that the induction is well-founded.

Lemma 1. *Let T be a quasi type and let $\Pi \in \{1,2\}^*$. Then for every environment E, we have $((T)_E.\Pi)_E = (T.\Pi)_E$. In particular, $((s \Leftarrow \Gamma)_E.\Pi)_E = (s \Leftarrow \Gamma\Pi)_E$.*

4 Type Assignment

A *type judgement* takes the form $E \vdash M : \tau$, where E is a type environment, M is a term and τ is a type. The rules are listed below. In (obj) we use the abbreviations $\tau = \mathbf{pro}\ s\langle \tau_1, \tau_2 \rangle$ and $M = \mathbf{pro}\ s\langle M_1, M_2 \rangle$.

$$\textbf{(const)}\quad \frac{}{E \vdash \Box : \Box} \qquad\qquad \textbf{(var)}\quad \frac{}{E \vdash s : s}$$

$$\textbf{(obj)}\quad \frac{E, s:\tau \vdash M_1 : \tau_1, \quad E, s:\tau \vdash M_2 : \tau_2}{E \vdash M : \tau}$$

$$\textbf{(send)}\quad \frac{E \vdash M : \tau}{E \vdash M \Leftarrow i : (\tau.i)_E} \qquad \text{(if } (\tau.i)_E \text{ is a type)}$$

First of all, observe that the understanding of $E \vdash M : \tau$ is nonstandard. The environment E does *not* provide types of free variables, as usual, but only "type bindings" used exclusively for typing sends. The type assigned to a free variable is always the variable itself. In particular, one does not need to assume free variables of M to be in the domain of E, provide that there is no (direct or indirect) send involving these variables. For instance we have $\vdash s : s$, but to type $\mathbf{pro}\ s\langle\, s, t\,\rangle \Leftarrow 21$ we need a type binding for t. Furthermore, notice that the type of the place-holder $\Box$ is the place-holder itself, and this reflects our idea that the place-holder stands for ignored sub-expressions. Below we illustrate the features of the system with some examples.

Example 1. Not every term is typable. Consider the following stripped term $M = \mathbf{pro}\ s\langle\, \mathbf{pro}\ t\langle\, s \Leftarrow 1, \Box\,\rangle, \Box\,\rangle$; we show that M is indeed untypable[3]. Assume that $\vdash M : \tau$, for some type τ. It follows that τ must be of the form $\tau = \mathbf{pro}\ s.\langle\, \tau_1, \tau_2\,\rangle$ and that we must have a derivation of $s : \tau \vdash \mathbf{pro}\ t\langle\, s \Leftarrow 1, \Box\,\rangle : \tau_1$. Now, again τ_1 must be of the form $\tau_1 = \mathbf{pro}\ t\langle\, \tau_{11}, \tau_{12}\,\rangle$ and we must have a derivation $s : \tau, t : \tau_1 \vdash s \Leftarrow 1 : \tau_{11}$. Thus $\tau_{11} = (\tau_1)_E = \tau_1$, where $E = \{s : \tau, t : \tau_1\}$. This yields a contradiction.

Observe that the type of a term is not uniquely determined by the term and the environment (see the Example 2). However, it can be shown that the resulting type of a quasi type is uniquely determined by the environment.

Example 2. Consider now a stripped term $M = \mathbf{pro}\ s\langle\, s \Leftarrow 12, s \Leftarrow 112\,\rangle$. The reader will easily check that the following typings are derivable in the system.

$$\vdash M : \mathbf{pro}\ s\langle\, \Box, \Box\,\rangle \tag{1}$$

$$\vdash M : \mathbf{pro}\ s\langle\, \mathbf{pro}\ t\langle\, \mathbf{pro}\ x\langle\, y, z\,\rangle, t\,\rangle, z\,\rangle \tag{2}$$

$$\vdash M : \mathbf{pro}\ s\langle\, \mathbf{pro}\ t\langle\, \mathbf{pro}\ x\langle\, y, s\,\rangle, t\,\rangle, s\,\rangle \tag{3}$$

$$x : \mathbf{pro}\ x\langle\, y, z\,\rangle \vdash M : \mathbf{pro}\ s\langle\, \mathbf{pro}\ t\langle\, x, t\,\rangle, z\,\rangle \tag{4}$$

$$t : \mathbf{pro}\ t\langle\, \mathbf{pro}\ x\langle\, y, z\,\rangle, t\,\rangle \vdash M : \mathbf{pro}\ s\langle\, t, z\,\rangle \tag{5}$$

$$x : \mathbf{pro}\ x\langle\, y, z\,\rangle,\ t : \mathbf{pro}\ t\langle\, x, t\,\rangle \vdash M : \mathbf{pro}\ s\langle\, t, z\,\rangle \tag{6}$$

Types assigned to M in (1) and (2) are clearly of completely different nature. Also the types in (2) and (3) are different due to the different structure of the bindings. Environments in (4)–(6) are used to type atomic sends of M.

We remark on passing that the above type assignment system has the *subject reduction property* (for details see the full version of the paper).

The reader familiar with [4] will notice that our type bindings are directly inspired by the idea of "matching types". A direct comparison between the present system and C of [3] is possible: our syntax of terms is different to that of C, but if we forget about the syntax of terms, a closer look reveals that our rule (obj) corresponds to (two applications of) rule (Val Method Addition) of C, and rule (send) is essentially the same as C's rule (Val Select).

[3] Compare this to the example of Fig. 2 (A) discussed in Section 2.

5 Meta Schemes

We introduce the meta schemes and their instantiations in order to state the principal quasi type theorem. First we introduce a new category of variables, called *metavariables*. For each path $\Delta \in \{1,2\}^*$ we have a countable supply of metavariables α^Δ (possibly with subscripts, when necessary). Each α^Δ can be instantiated with a type which has to satisfy a certain property to be stated later. Metavariables play the same role as selves, except they cannot be bound by **pro**. In particular, the send operation is applicable to a metavariable.

We start with *meta schemes*, $\mathcal{T}$. They are built according to the following grammar

$$\mathcal{T} ::= \Box \mid s \Leftarrow \Pi \mid \alpha^\Delta \Leftarrow \Pi \mid \mathbf{pro}\ s.\langle\, \mathcal{T}_1, \mathcal{T}_2\,\rangle,$$

where Δ and Π range over $\{1,2\}^*$. We identify $s \Leftarrow \varepsilon$ with s and $\alpha^\Delta \Leftarrow \varepsilon$ with α^Δ. Expressions of the form $\alpha^\Delta \Leftarrow \Pi$, where $\Pi \neq \varepsilon$, will be called *meta sends*. Let $TV(\mathcal{T})$ denote the set of all metavariables which occur in $\mathcal{T}$ and let $FS(\mathcal{T})$ denote the set of all sends $s \Leftarrow \Pi$ which occur free in $\mathcal{T}$ (i.e., s is free in $\mathcal{T}$).

A meta scheme in which all sends are free is called a *quasi type scheme*. Observe that a quasi type scheme without metavariables is a quasi type. A *stripped scheme* is a meta scheme in which bindings of sends occur only at the top, i.e., $\mathcal{T}$ is a stripped scheme if it is of the form: $\Box$, $s \Leftarrow \Pi, \alpha^\Delta \Leftarrow \Pi$, or $\mathbf{pro}\ s.\langle\, \mathcal{T}_1, \mathcal{T}_2\,\rangle$, where $\mathcal{T}_1$ and $\mathcal{T}_2$ are quasi type schemes. So, a stripped scheme without metavariables is a stripped term.

Most of the definitions which are applicable to terms are also applicable to meta schemes. For example, the definition of formal field selection can be extended to quasi type schemes by adding the clause for metavariables: $(\alpha^\Delta \Leftarrow \Gamma).\Pi = \alpha^\Delta \Leftarrow \Gamma\Pi$.

An *instantiation* of a meta scheme $\mathcal{T}$ is a pair (E, S), where E is an environment and S is a substitution which assigns to every metavariable $\alpha^\Delta \in TV(\mathcal{T})$ a type ρ such that $(\rho.\Delta)_E = \rho$.

For a substitution S which assigns types to metavariables in $TV(\mathcal{T})$, by $\mathcal{T}\{S\}$ we denote the term obtained by substituting types for metavariables in $\mathcal{T}$. The definition of $\mathcal{T}\{S\}$ is by straightforward induction, the only nontrivial clause being $(\alpha^\Delta \Leftarrow \Pi)\{S\} = S(\alpha^\Delta).\Pi$. Of course, we perform α-conversion, when necessary, in order to avoid send capture. Clearly when $\mathcal{T}$ is a quasi type scheme then $\mathcal{T}\{S\}$ is a quasi type; similarly for stripped schemes.

For a stripped scheme $\mathcal{T}$, the *value* of $\mathcal{T}$ in an instantiation (E, S) for $\mathcal{T}$ is the stripped term $(\mathcal{T}\{S\})_E$.

Meta schemes $\mathcal{T}_1$ and $\mathcal{T}_2$ are said to be *equivalent* if:

- for every instantiation (E, S) of $\mathcal{T}_1$ there is a substitution S' such that (E, S') is an instantiation of $\mathcal{T}_2$ and $(\mathcal{T}_1\{S\})_E = (\mathcal{T}_2\{S'\})_E$; and
- for every instantiation (E, S) of $\mathcal{T}_2$ there is a substitution S' such that (E, S') is an instantiation of $\mathcal{T}_1$ and $(\mathcal{T}_1\{S'\})_E = (\mathcal{T}_2\{S\})_E$.

A meta scheme $\mathcal{T}$ is said to be *typable* if there is an instantiation (E, S) of $\mathcal{T}$ and a type τ such that $E \vdash \mathcal{T}\{S\} : \tau$ is derivable.

6 The Rewrite System

The aim of this section is to give rewrite rules for transforming a given stripped scheme into a quasi type scheme. The transformation is going to be a partial function, i.e., for some stripped schemes there will be no corresponding quasi type scheme. We will describe two kinds of redexes: reducible and cyclic. First we need an auxiliary definition with which we can define the redexes.

6.1 The Projection and Remainder Functions

For a stripped scheme $\mathcal{T}$ we define a pair of functions: a *projection function* $p_{\mathcal{T}} : \{1,2\}^* \to \mathcal{T}$ and a *remainder function* $r_{\mathcal{T}} : \{1,2\}^* \to \{1,2\}^*$. Intuitively $p_{\mathcal{T}}(\Pi)$ is a node of $\mathcal{T}$ which is obtained by travelling in $\mathcal{T}$ along Π, subject to the following conditions. If Π is contained in $\mathcal{T}$ then we terminate at Π. Otherwise we apply the following rules for passing through a leaf Γ:

- if Γ is labelled by a self t which is bound at node Δ, then the next step starts at node Δ;
- if Γ is labelled by the place-holder, then we return to this node in the next step (and thus in all following steps);
- if Γ is labelled by a free send, a meta send, or a top send, then we terminate at this node, i.e., no next step is possible.

Then $r_{\mathcal{T}}(\Pi)$ is what remains of Π upon the termination of the navigation through $\mathcal{T}$. The formal definition now follows.

Case A: $(\Pi \in \mathcal{T})$

$$p_{\mathcal{T}}(\Pi) = \Pi \text{ and } r_{\mathcal{T}}(\Pi) = \varepsilon$$

Case B: ($\Pi_1\Pi_2 \in \mathcal{T}$ is a leaf labelled t, Π_1 is labelled t, and $\Pi_2 \neq \varepsilon$ and $\Delta \neq \varepsilon$)

$$p_{\mathcal{T}}(\Pi_1\Pi_2\Delta) = p_{\mathcal{T}}(\Pi_1\Delta) \text{ and } r_{\mathcal{T}}(\Pi_1\Pi_2\Delta) = r_{\mathcal{T}}(\Pi_1\Delta)$$

Case C: ($\Delta \neq \varepsilon$ and $\Pi \in \mathcal{T}$ is a leaf labelled by one of the following: a free send, a top send, a meta send)

$$p_{\mathcal{T}}(\Pi\Delta) = \Pi \text{ and } r_{\mathcal{T}}(\Pi\Delta) = \Delta$$

Case D: ($\Delta \neq \varepsilon$ and $\Pi \in \mathcal{T}$ is a leaf labelled by the place-holder)

$$p_{\mathcal{T}}(\Pi\Delta) = \Pi \text{ and } r_{\mathcal{T}}(\Pi\Delta) = \varepsilon$$

6.2 Reducible Top Sends

A top send $s \Leftarrow \Pi$ is said to be *reducible* if $p_{\mathcal{T}}(\Pi)$ is not an occurrence of a top send.

Among reducible top sends are those which we call inconsistent. A top send $s \Leftarrow \Pi$ is said to be *inconsistent* if $p_{\mathcal{T}}(\Pi) = i\Delta$, for some i and Δ, and $s \Leftarrow \Pi$ occurs in $\mathcal{T}_i.\Delta$. A reducible send which is not inconsistent is called *consistent*.

Lemma 2. *If a stripped scheme contains an inconsistent top send, then it is not typable.*

Let $s \Leftarrow \Pi$ be a reducible top send in $\mathcal{T}$, and let $p_{\mathcal{T}}(\Pi) = i\Delta$ and $r_{\mathcal{T}}(\Pi) = \xi$. Reduction of $s \Leftarrow \Pi$ consists in replacing every occurrence of $s \Leftarrow \Pi$ in $\mathcal{T}$ by $\mathcal{T}_i.\Delta\xi$. It follows that $\Delta \in \mathcal{T}_i$ and that we have the following two possibilities:

1. Δ is an internal node of $\mathcal{T}_i$. Then $\xi = \varepsilon$.
2. Δ is a leaf in $\mathcal{T}_i$. Then the label of this leaf is one of the following:
   2a. A free send in $\mathcal{T}$;
   2b. A meta send;
   2c. The place-holder.

In each case ((1) or (2)) it follows that the subtree $\mathcal{T}_i.\Delta\xi$ does not contain new top sends, i.e., there may be new occurrences of top sends after the reduction, but the set of all different top sends after the reduction is not larger than before. In fact, when the reducible top send is not inconsistent, the number of top sends after the reduction decreases by one.

The intuitions behind the previous concepts are: (*i*) an inconsistent reducible top send addresses a subtree of the tree representing the term in question which contains the top send itself, meaning that the top send's type should contain itself properly (see the first example in Section 2); (*ii*) a consistent reducible top send is one for which we can mimic the evaluation process, by substituting it with the subtree it addresses. This way we make a step towards a send-free term, which will correspond to the quasi type scheme.

6.3 Cyclic Top Sends

Let $S_{\mathcal{T}}$ be the set of all occurrences of top sends in $\mathcal{T}$. The projection and remainder functions give rise to two mappings $\widehat{p}_{\mathcal{T}} : S_{\mathcal{T}} \to \mathcal{T}$ and $\widehat{r}_{\mathcal{T}} : S_{\mathcal{T}} \to \{1,2\}^*$. For any $\Gamma \in S_{\mathcal{T}}$, if the label of Γ is $s \Leftarrow \Pi$, then $\widehat{p}_{\mathcal{T}}(\Gamma) = p_{\mathcal{T}}(\Pi)$ and $\widehat{r}_{\mathcal{T}}(\Gamma) = r_{\mathcal{T}}(\Pi)$. A top send $s \Leftarrow \Pi$ is said to be *cyclic* if for one of its occurrences $\Gamma \in S_{\mathcal{T}}$ we have $\widehat{p}^k_{\mathcal{T}}(\Gamma) = \Gamma$ for some $k \geq 1$. It follows that the occurrence Γ is unique. We call it a *cyclic occurrence* of $s \Leftarrow \Pi$. The least k satisfying $\widehat{p}^k_{\mathcal{T}}(\Gamma) = \Gamma$ will be called the *period* of $s \Leftarrow \Pi$. The word $\widehat{r}_{\mathcal{T}}(\widehat{p}^{k-1}_{\mathcal{T}}(\Gamma)) \cdots \widehat{r}_{\mathcal{T}}(\widehat{p}_{\mathcal{T}}(\Gamma))\widehat{r}_{\mathcal{T}}(\Gamma)$, where Γ is the cyclic occurrence and k is the period of $s \Leftarrow \Pi$, will be called the *cyclic coefficient* of the cyclic send $s \Leftarrow \Pi$.

Let $s \Leftarrow \Pi$ be a cyclic top send in $\mathcal{T}$ and let Δ be its cyclic coefficient. Reduction of $s \Leftarrow \Pi$ consists in replacing every occurrence of $s \Leftarrow \Pi$ in $\mathcal{T}$ by α^{Δ}, where α^{Δ} is a fresh metavariable not occurring in $\mathcal{T}$.

It follows that sends which label the nodes $\widehat{p}_{\mathcal{T}}(\Gamma), \ldots, \widehat{p}^{k-1}_{\mathcal{T}}(\Gamma)$ are also cyclic in $\mathcal{T}$. After the reduction the send labelling the node $\widehat{p}^{k-1}_{\mathcal{T}}(\Gamma)$ becomes reducible, while the other sends are not subject to immediate reduction in the new scheme.

The intuition behind a cyclic send is that it represents an infinite computation (infinite computations are universally accepted in object-oriented calculi; see typical examples in [1,11]). Essentially, a cyclic send refers to itself within a certain number of computation steps, which is the period.

6.4 Confluence and Termination

The main properties of the above rewrite system are collected in the next two results.

Theorem 1. *Let $\mathcal{T}$ be a stripped scheme.*

1. **(Termination)** *Let n be the number of top sends in $\mathcal{T}$. After n steps of reduction we either arrive at a quasi type scheme, or else we must have earlier detected an inconsistent reducible send.*
2. **(Confluence)** *Let $\mathcal{T}'$ and $\mathcal{T}''$ be two quasi type schemes obtained from $\mathcal{T}$ by a sequence of reductions. Then $\mathcal{T}'$ and $\mathcal{T}''$ are equivalent.*

Theorem 2. *Let $\mathcal{T}$ be a stripped scheme. The following are equivalent.*

1. *$\mathcal{T}$ is typable.*
2. *There exists a sequence of reductions which transforms $\mathcal{T}$ into a quasi type scheme.*
3. *Every sequence of reductions transforms $\mathcal{T}$ into a quasi type scheme.*

Moreover, if $\mathcal{T}^{\#}$ is a quasi type scheme obtained from $\mathcal{T}$ by a sequence of reductions and (E, S) is any instantiation of $\mathcal{T}^{\#}$ such that $(\mathcal{T}^{\#}\{S\})_E$ is a type, say τ, then the judgement $E \vdash \mathcal{T}\{S\} : \tau$ is derivable.

It follows from Theorem 1 that every stripped scheme has at most one normal form $\mathcal{T}^{\#}$, up to scheme equivalence.

Example 3. $M = \mathbf{pro}\ s\langle\, \mathbf{pro}\ t\langle\, \Box, s \Leftarrow 1\,\rangle, \Box\,\rangle$: M is a stripped term, and the top send $s \Leftarrow 1$ is reducible and inconsistent, because $p_M(1) = 1$ and $s \Leftarrow 1$ occurs in the sub-tree M_1 (following the definition of Section 6.2). Thus M is not typable by Lemma 2.

Example 4. $M = \mathbf{pro}\ s\langle\, s \Leftarrow 1, \Box\,\rangle$: M is a stripped term, and the top send $s \Leftarrow 1$ is cyclic. Let $\Gamma = 1$ be the "address" of the top send $s \Leftarrow 1$ (this is correct since such top send is the "1-branch" of the "tree" M) and $\Pi = 1$ (being $s \Leftarrow 1$). Following the definitions of Section 6.3, we calculate $\widehat{p}_M(1) = p_M(1) = 1$ (i.e., the period is 1) and $\widehat{r}_M(\Gamma) = r_M(1) = \varepsilon$ (i.e., the cyclic coefficient is empty). Then we get $\mathbf{pro}\ s\langle\, \alpha, \Box\,\rangle$. By assigning to α a type ρ such that $\rho = \rho$ (the top send is cyclic, and the type assigned to α takes this into account), we have that this term is typable with any type for the first component, the simplest being $\mathbf{pro}\ s\langle\, \Box, \Box\,\rangle$ and $\mathbf{pro}\ s\langle\, s, \Box\,\rangle$.

Example 5. $M = \mathbf{pro}\ s\langle\, s \Leftarrow 12, s \Leftarrow 112\,\rangle$: M is a stripped term, and the top send $s \Leftarrow 12$ is cyclic. We calculate, for $\Gamma = 1$, $\widehat{p}_M(1) = p_M(12) = 1$ (i.e., the period is 1), and $\widehat{r}_M(1) = r_M(12) = 2$ (i.e., the cyclic coefficient is 2), therefore we obtain the quasi-type schema $\mathbf{pro}\ s\langle\, \alpha^2, s \Leftarrow 112\,\rangle$. Now $s \Leftarrow 112$ becomes reducible and we get $\mathbf{pro}\ s\langle\, \alpha^2, \alpha^2 \Leftarrow 12\,\rangle$ by calculating $p_M(112) = 1$ and $r_M(112) = 12$ (following the definitions of Section 6.2), and then by substituting $s \Leftarrow 112$ with $M_1.12 = \alpha^2 \Leftarrow 12$. By assigning to α^2 a type ρ such that $(\rho.2) = \rho$, we can get $M : \mathbf{pro}\ s\langle\, \Box, \Box\,\rangle$, $M : \mathbf{pro}\ s\langle\, \mathbf{pro}\ t\langle\, \mathbf{pro}\ x\langle\, y, z\,\rangle, t\,\rangle z\,\rangle$, etc.

Example 6. $M = \mathbf{pro}\ s\langle\, \mathbf{pro}\ t\langle\, s \Leftarrow 121, s \Leftarrow 221\,\rangle, \mathbf{pro}\ t\langle\, s \Leftarrow 1, s \Leftarrow 122\,\rangle\,\rangle$: M is a stripped term. The top sends $s \Leftarrow 221$ and $s \Leftarrow 122$ form a cycle: we can solve the cycle by starting from the former or from the latter. For example, we start from $s \Leftarrow 221$. We calculate $\widehat{p}_M(12) = p_M(221) = 22$ and $\widehat{p}^2_M(22) = p_M(122) = 12$ (being 22 the "address" of $s \Leftarrow 122$), so the period is 2. We also calculate $\widehat{r}_M(12) = r_M(221) = 1$ and $\widehat{r}^2_M(12) = r_M(122) = 2$, so the cyclic coefficient is 21. Then M rewrites into

$$M' = \mathbf{pro}\ s\langle\, \mathbf{pro}\ t\langle\, s \Leftarrow 121, \alpha^{21}\,\rangle, \mathbf{pro}\ t\langle\, s \Leftarrow 1, s \Leftarrow 122\,\rangle\,\rangle.$$

Now we consider the top send $s \Leftarrow 122$ that become reducible (with $p_M(122) = 12$ and $r_M(122) = 2$), and we substitute it with $M'_1.22$, that is, M' rewrites into $M'' = \mathbf{pro}\ s\langle\, \mathbf{pro}\ t\langle\, s \Leftarrow 121, \alpha^{21}\,\rangle, \mathbf{pro}\ t\langle\, s \Leftarrow 1, \alpha^{21} \Leftarrow 2\,\rangle\,\rangle$. With two more rewriting steps, one for $s \Leftarrow 1$ and $s \Leftarrow 121$, both reducible, we rewrite M'' into $M''' = \mathbf{pro}\ s\langle\, \mathbf{pro}\ t\langle\, s \Leftarrow 121, \alpha^{21}\,\rangle, \mathbf{pro}\ t\langle\, \mathbf{pro}\ t\langle\, s \Leftarrow 121, \alpha^{21}\,\rangle, \alpha^{21} \Leftarrow 2\,\rangle\,\rangle$ and $M^{iv} = \mathbf{pro}\ s\langle\, \mathbf{pro}\ t\langle\, \alpha^{21} \Leftarrow 1, \alpha^{21}\,\rangle, \mathbf{pro}\ t\langle\, \mathbf{pro}\ t\langle\, \alpha^{21} \Leftarrow 1, \alpha^{21}\,\rangle, \alpha^{21} \Leftarrow 2\,\rangle\,\rangle$, proving that M is typable.

If we start from $s \Leftarrow 122$ to solve the cycle, we would substitute α^{12} at the "address" 22 as the first "rewrite" step, instead following the above solution we substituted α^{21} at the "address" 12.

7 Main Result

We define a partial map which assigns to a term M a quasi type scheme $\mathcal{T}_M$, called a *principal quasi type scheme* of M. The partial map is defined by induction on M.

- $\mathcal{T}_c = c$
- $\mathcal{T}_s = s$
- $\mathcal{T}_{\mathbf{pro}\ s.\langle M_1, M_2\rangle} = (\mathbf{pro}\ s\langle\, \mathcal{T}_{M_1}, \mathcal{T}_{M_2}\,\rangle)^{\#}$
- $\mathcal{T}_{M \Leftarrow i} = \mathcal{T}_M.i.$

The above recurrence equations must be understood in such a way that the left hand side is defined if and only if the right hand side is defined. Note that the above definition is correct, i.e., that the induction is well-founded. The intuition is that, by induction, $\mathcal{T}_{M_1}, \mathcal{T}_{M_2}$ are quasi type schemes, therefore $(\mathbf{pro}\ s\langle\, \mathcal{T}_{M_1}, \mathcal{T}_{M_2}\,\rangle)^{\#}$ is a stripped type scheme.

The main result of this paper is the following theorem.

Theorem 3. (Principal quasi type theorem)

1. *M is typable iff $\mathcal{T}_M$ is defined.*
2. *If $\mathcal{T}_M$ is defined, then for every instantiation (E, S) of $\mathcal{T}_M$ such that $(\mathcal{T}_M\{S\})_E$ is a type we have $E \vdash M : (\mathcal{T}_M\{S\})_E$.*
3. *The partial mapping $M \mapsto \mathcal{T}_M$ is computable. Therefore the problem of typability is decidable.*

8 Extensions

We have solved the type reconstruction problem for a system containing only the send operator to highlight the essential mathematical content of the problem itself. However, the approach can be extended to deal with the method addition operator $\longleftarrow\!\!\!+$ of the C calculus [3], and with *message-not-understood* run-time errors, without changing the mathematical core of our solution.

Method addition. We must consider objects with an indefinite number of components. Then, since method addition is permitted only on proper objects, it is enough to extend the notion of "principal quasi type scheme" $\mathcal{T}_M$, in order to check that the (quasi) type of the object receiving the addition is a **pro** $\langle \dots \rangle$ (quasi) type and that it does not contain the method to be added, together with checking that the method body is typable.

Message-not-understood. By allowing objects with more than two components and method addition, the send operator becomes general: method invocation is allowed on proper objects (external send) and on selves (self-inflicted send). In the external case, the right-hand side of the equation $\mathcal{T}_{M \Leftarrow i} = \mathcal{T}_M.i$ of the principal quasi type scheme would be satisfied (and $\mathcal{T}_{M \Leftarrow i}$ would be typable) if $\mathcal{T}_M$ were a quasi type scheme of the form **pro** $\langle \dots \rangle$ containing an i component, and the resulting quasi type scheme would be as in the two-method situation. A more difficult case is when the send is self-inflicted, i.e., if M is a self s: this case must be solved directly during the global process of going from the stripped term containing $M \Leftarrow i$ to its quasi type scheme, because we need to check if the subtree rooted at s has an i branch. In order to do so, for every top send $s \Leftarrow \Pi$ we must check that the branching described by Π exists in the subtree rooted at s.

9 Conclusion and Future Work

We have shown that decidable type reconstruction is possible for languages with nested selftype references. We believe that our result can be the core for typability of richer systems.

Our result raises a number of further questions. Future work will include a detailed comparison, from the point of view of the typability, of our type system with the Palsberg-Jim system [16], restricted to our calculus, and with some of the Abadi-Cardelli systems [1] (in particular the first-order one, to begin with, and the ones with selftypes).

Obviously, one wants to expand the analysis to the case of object languages with a more reasonable choice of operators. Adding method addition must be still formalized, but we conjecture that is nothing more than careful bookwork. Dealing with *message-not-understood* appears to be more delicate, because it implies an extension of the algorithm as hinted above. However, it does not change the techniques we use to detect and solve "loops", which are the central part of our solution. Override is, instead, an open question at the moment. Thus far it can be only shown that adding method override makes the problem PTIME-hard. Intuitively, override, by substituting method bodies, may change the interrelationships among the cyclic top sends, inducing complex equational constraints — a very special case of second-order unification. It appears that self-inflicted overrides (i.e., overrides on selves inside method bodies) are the main issue. Nevertheless, also external overrides introduce some difficulties. To type a method override on an object, we would need to compare the (quasi) type of the overriden (old) method body with the (quasi) type of the overridding (new) one. Then the override is typable only if the two are "equal", but we still do not have a complete notion of principality, therefore we are not able to decide on equality among (quasi) types [4].

Even for our simple language, there are still issues to be investigated. The naive algorithm, involving the construction of $\mathcal{T}_M$, is obviously not feasible, as it involves nested substitutions. Although we believe the problem is solvable in polynomial time, a workable implementation is still to be developed, and does not seem to be trivial.

Acknowledgement. The authors would like to thank the anonymous referees for their advice on how to improve the paper.

References

1. M. Abadi and L. Cardelli. *A Theory of Objects*. Monographs in Computer Science. Springer-Verlag, 1996.
2. Baader, F., Nipkow, T., *Term Rewriting and All That*, Cambridge University Press, 1998.
3. V. Bono. Extensible Objects: a Tutorial. In *Global Computing*, LNCS 2874, pages 57–87. Springer-Verlag, 2003.
4. V. Bono and M. Bugliesi. Matching for the Lambda Calculus of Objects. *Theoretical Computer Science*, 212(1–2):101–140, 1999.
5. V. Bono, M. Bugliesi, and S. Crafa. Typed Interpretations of Extensible Objects. ACM Transactions on Computational Logic, 3(4):562–603, 2002.
6. G. Bracha, M. Odersky, D. Stoutamire and P. Wadler. Making the future safe for the past: Adding genericity to the Java programming language. In *Proc. of OOPSLA'98, SIGPLAN Notices*, 33(10):183–200, 1998.
7. K.B. Bruce. A paradigmatic object-oriented programming language: Design, static typing and semantics. *Journal of Functional Programming*, 4(2):127–206, 1994.
8. K.B. Bruce. *Foundations of Object-Oriented Languages–Types and Semantics*. The MIT Press, 2002.
9. Michele Bugliesi and Santiago Pericas. Depth subtyping and type inference for object calculi. *Information and Computation*, 177(1):2–27, 2002.
10. P. Di Gianantonio, F. Honsell, and L. Liquori. A Lambda Calculus of Objects with Self-inflicted Extension. In *Proc. of ACM-SIGPLAN OOPSLA*, pages 166–178. ACM Press, 1998.
11. K. Fisher, F. Honsell, and J.C. Mitchell. A lambda calculus of objects and method specialization. *Nordic Journal of Computing*, 1(1):3–37, 1994.
12. F. Henglein. Breaking through the n^3 barrier: Faster object type inference. *Theory and Practice of Object Systems (TAPOS)*, 5(1):57–72, 1999.
13. A.V. Hense. *Polymorphic Type Inference for Object-Oriented Programming Languages*. Pirrot Verlag, 1994.
14. J. C. Mitchell. Toward a typed foundation for method specialization and inheritance. In *Proc. of ACM Symp. POPL*, pages 109–124. ACM Press, 1990.
15. J. Palsberg. Efficient inference of object types. *Information and Computation*, 123(2):198–209, 1995.
16. J. Palsberg and T. Jim. Type inference with simple selftypes is NP-complete. *Nordic Journal of Computing*, 4(3):259–286, 1997.

[4] The equality between the type of the old body and of the overriding one is a typical requirement in object-oriented type systems when no subtyping is present.

Inductive Families Need Not Store Their Indices

Edwin Brady[1], Conor McBride[1], and James McKinna[2]

[1] Department of Computer Science, University of Durham
{e.c.brady,c.t.mcbride}@durham.ac.uk
[2] School of Computer Science, University of St. Andrews
james.mckinna@st-andrews.ac.uk

Abstract. We consider the problem of efficient representation of dependently typed data. In particular, we consider a language TT based on Dybjer's notion of **inductive families** [10] and reanalyse their general form with a view to optimising the storage associated with their use. We introduce an execution language, ExTT, which allows the commenting out of computationally irrelevant subterms and show how to use properties of elimination rules to elide constructor arguments and tags in ExTT. We further show how some types can be collapsed entirely at run-time. Several examples are given, including a representation of the simply typed λ-calculus for which our analysis yields an 80% reduction in run-time storage requirements.

1 Introduction

Dependent type theory provides programmers with more than an integrated logic for reasoning about program correctness. It allows more precise types for programs and data in the first place, strengthening the typechecker's language of guarantees. We have richer function types $\forall x : S.\ T$ which adapt their return types to each argument; we also have richer data structures which do not just contain but *explain* data, exposing and enforcing their properties.

Moreover, we may reasonably expect more static detail about programs and data to yield better optimised dynamic behaviour. We need neither test what is guaranteed nor store what is determined by typechecking. Pollack's implicit syntax [23] already supports the omission of much redundant information from concrete syntax for similar reasons.

This paper idenitifies some space optimisations which significantly reduce the storage overheads associated with **inductive families** in the sense of [10]. These are data-indexed collections of mutually recursive datatypes, $\mathsf{D}\,\boldsymbol{x}$, available in systems such as those underlying LEGO [15], COQ [8], ALF [17] and also the language we use here — EPIGRAM [19]. A common example for illustrative purposes is Vect, the family of list types indexed by element type and length:

$$\underline{\text{data}}\ \frac{A : \star \quad n : \mathbb{N}}{\mathsf{Vect}\,A\,n : \star} \quad \underline{\text{where}}\ \frac{}{\varepsilon : \mathsf{Vect}\,A\,0} \quad \frac{a : A \quad v : \mathsf{Vect}\,A\,k}{a :: v : \mathsf{Vect}\,A\,(\mathsf{s}\,k)}$$

S. Berardi, M. Coppo, and F. Damiani (Eds.): TYPES 2003, LNCS 3085, pp. 115–129, 2004.

1.1 Programming with Inductive Families

Function types over inductive families can use specific indices to require and ensure properties of inputs and outputs — e.g., compatibility of length.

$$\underline{\text{let}}\ \frac{u, v\ :\ \mathsf{Vect}\,\mathbb{N}\,n}{\mathbf{vAdd}\ u\ v\ :\ \mathsf{Vect}\,\mathbb{N}\,n} \quad \begin{array}{llll} \mathbf{vAdd} & \varepsilon & \varepsilon & \mapsto \varepsilon \\ \mathbf{vAdd} & (x :: u) & (y :: v) & \mapsto (x + y) :: \mathbf{vAdd}\ u\ v \end{array}$$

The precise type prevents some bogus choices of output — we can only return ε on the first line, only a :: on the second. The input possibilities become narrower too — adding $(x :: u)$ to ε, or vice versa, is not even an issue.

By the same token, the potential for optimisation is clear. Once we know whether the first argument is ε or $(x :: u)$, we can *presuppose* the form of the second argument — we can ignore it in the ε case; in the :: case, we can safely project out y and v without checking the constructor tag. Moreover, if we inspect n, implicitly passed to **vAdd**, we need never check **Vect** constructor tags at all.

We impose invariants on inductive families to improve reliability, but this paper seeks to exploit them for performance. Such optimisations are not available in conventional functional languages — there is no way that inspecting one argument can justify presuppositions about another. If we want to write vector addition using ordinary lists, we must not only consider how to handle length mismatch in our code, we must also effectively test for it at run-time.

1.2 Underlying Type Theory

Following [19], EPIGRAM programs elaborate to well typed terms in a type theory TT, based on Luo's UTT [14] with inductive families [10] and equality as in [18]. Here is its syntax:

$$\begin{array}{llll} t ::= \star_i & \text{(type of types)} & \mid x & \text{(variable)} \\ \quad\mid \forall x\!:\!t.\ t & \text{(function space)} & \mid \mathsf{D} & \text{(inductive family)} \\ \quad\mid \lambda x\!:\!t.\ t & \text{(abstraction)} & \mid \mathsf{c} & \text{(constructor)} \\ \quad\mid t\ t & \text{(application)} & \mid \mathsf{D\text{-}E} & \text{(elimination operator)} \end{array}$$

As usual, we may abbreviate the function space $\forall x\!:\!S.\ T$ by $S \to T$ if x is not free in T. There is an infinite hierarchy of predicative universes, $\star_i : \star_{i+1}$. We leave universe levels to the machine, as in [11].

Computation is by **β-reduction** for λ-abstractions and **ι-reduction** for elimination operators. A data declaration typically elaborates to declarations of a family $\mathsf{D} : \forall \boldsymbol{i}\!:\!\boldsymbol{I}.\ \star$, constructors c, and an elimination operator **D-E** equipped with ι-rules. We write $s \mapsto t$ if s β- or ι-reduces to t. In the usual way, every well typed TT term t computes to a **weak head-normal form** WHNF(t).

A typical constructor has a type like this:[1]

$$\mathsf{c} : \forall \boldsymbol{a}\!:\!\boldsymbol{A}.\ \mathsf{D}\ \boldsymbol{r}_1 \to \ldots \to \mathsf{D}\ \boldsymbol{r}_j \to \mathsf{D}\ \boldsymbol{s}$$

[1] To ease presentation, we keep the non-recursive arguments $\boldsymbol{a}$ to the front and permit only first-order recursive arguments — neither restriction is crucial to this work.

For example, elaborating our Vect example, we acquire $\mathsf{Vect} : \forall A\!:\!\star.\ \forall n\!:\!\mathbb{N}.\ \star$, and constructors:

$$\varepsilon : \forall A\!:\!\star.\ \mathsf{Vect}\ A\ 0$$
$$:: : \forall A\!:\!\star.\ \forall k\!:\!\mathbb{N}.\ \forall a\!:\!A.\ \forall v\!:\!\mathsf{Vect}\ A\ k.\ \mathsf{Vect}\ A\ (\mathsf{s}k)$$

Note that the variables left schematic in the <u>data</u> declaration have become explicitly quantified arguments. In naïve implementations these take up space — every $\mathsf{Vect}\,A\,n$ stores the sequence $0, \ldots, n-1$, and n references to A. Even with perfect sharing, this is quite an overhead — the space implications for families with more complex invariants are quite drastic if this problem is left unchecked.

Basically, the elimination operator, $\mathsf{D}\text{-}\mathbf{E}$ has a type of this form:

$$\begin{array}{ll}
\forall \boldsymbol{i}\!:\!\boldsymbol{I}.\ \forall x\!:\!\mathsf{D}\ \boldsymbol{i}. & \text{(indices, target)} \\
\forall P\!:\!\forall \boldsymbol{i}\!:\!\boldsymbol{I}.\ \mathsf{D}\ \boldsymbol{i} \to \star. & \text{(motive)} \\
\left.\begin{array}{l}
\forall m_{\mathsf{c}} : \forall \boldsymbol{a}\!:\!\boldsymbol{A}.\ \forall y_1\!:\!\mathsf{D}\ \boldsymbol{r}_1.\ \ldots\quad \forall y_j\!:\!\mathsf{D}\ \boldsymbol{r}_j. \\
\qquad\qquad P\ \boldsymbol{r}_1\ y_1 \to \ldots \to P\ \boldsymbol{r}_j\ y_j \to P\ \boldsymbol{s}\ (\mathsf{c}\ \boldsymbol{a}\ \boldsymbol{y}). \\
\ldots
\end{array}\right\} & \text{(methods)} \\
P\ \boldsymbol{i}\ x &
\end{array}$$

The **target**, with given **indices**, explains what to eliminate; the **motive** explains what is to be achieved by the elimination; the **methods** explain how to achieve the motive for each canonical form the target can take, given appropriate inductive hypotheses. The associated ι-rules for definitional equality have this form:

$$\Gamma \vdash \mathsf{D}\text{-}\mathbf{E}\ \boldsymbol{s}\ (\mathsf{c}\ \boldsymbol{a}\ \boldsymbol{y})\ P\ \boldsymbol{m}\ =\ m_{\mathsf{c}}\ \boldsymbol{a}\ \boldsymbol{y}\ (\mathsf{D}\text{-}\mathbf{E}\ \boldsymbol{r}_1\ y_1\ P\ \boldsymbol{m})\ \ldots\ (\mathsf{D}\text{-}\mathbf{E}\ \boldsymbol{r}_j\ y_j\ P\ \boldsymbol{m})$$

When indices are used uniformly, such as the element type of Vect, we adapt the basic $\mathsf{D}\text{-}\mathbf{E}$ slightly, abstracting these parameters once for all. This yields:

$$\begin{array}{rl}
\mathsf{Vect}\text{-}\mathbf{E} : & \forall A\!:\!\star.\ \forall n\!:\!\mathbb{N}.\ \forall v\!:\!\mathsf{Vect}\ A\ n. \\
& \forall P\!:\!\forall n\!:\!\mathbb{N}.\ \forall v\!:\!\mathsf{Vect}\ A\ k.\ \star\,. \\
& \forall m_{\varepsilon}\!:\!P\ 0\ (\varepsilon\ A). \\
& \forall m_{::}\!:\!\forall k\!:\!\mathbb{N}.\ \forall a\!:\!A.\ \forall v\!:\!\mathsf{Vect}\ A\ k.\ (P\ k\ v) \to P\ (\mathsf{s}k)\ (::\ A\ k\ a\ v). \\
& P\ n\ v
\end{array}$$

$$\begin{array}{lcl}
\mathsf{Vect}\text{-}\mathbf{E}\ A\ \ 0\qquad\ (\varepsilon\ A)\quad\ \ P\ m_{\varepsilon}\ m_{::} & = & m_{\varepsilon} \\
\mathsf{Vect}\text{-}\mathbf{E}\ A\ (\mathsf{s}\ k)\ (::\ A\ k\ a\ v)\ P\ m_{\varepsilon}\ m_{::} & = & m_{::}\ k\ a\ v\ (\mathsf{Vect}\text{-}\mathbf{E}\ A\ k\ v\ P\ m_{\varepsilon}\ m_{::})
\end{array}$$

Implementing $\mathsf{Vect}\text{-}\mathbf{E}$ appears to require non-linear matching — there are repeated arguments in both patterns, suggesting a run-time conversion check. In fact this is not needed — the repeated arguments coincide in any *well typed* application of $\mathsf{Vect}\text{-}\mathbf{E}$. We do not need to recheck the duplicate A or k in the patterns $(\varepsilon\ A)$ or $(::\ A\ k\ a\ v)$. So why store them?

In this paper we show how to streamline the implementation of ι-rules so that unnecessary testing is avoided. We introduce extensions to the TT syntax for marking parts of terms to be ignored or removed. So equipped, we consider which constructor arguments can be ignored, and then play a similar game with constructor tags. Finally, we show how to eliminate some structures entirely and make a larger example smaller — the simply typed λ-calculus.

1.3 Related Work

Correctness preserving program transformations [9,22] provide a basis for many optimisations in simply typed functional languages. In this paper we use substitution transformations to mark unused terms for deletion in a similar manner to Berardi's pruning of simply typed λ-terms [4]. Program transformation techniques have also been applied to type theory; Magaud and Bertot [16] show an approach to changing data representation by transforming the constructors and elimination rule of a family and use this technique to change from unary natural numbers to a more efficient binary representation.

The COQ program extraction tool [21,13] attempts to remove purely logical parts of proofs in order to produce executable programs. Our approach differs in that we do not separate the predicative and impredicative type universes but attempt to remove *all* terms which are unused.

Callaghan and Luo [7] use the well-typedness of elimination rules to avoid checking of repeated arguments, a technique which we apply and extend in this paper. Xi's DML [25] also uses dependent types for optimisation, eliminating dead code [26] and array bounds checking [27].

2 Implementing Reduction Rules for Datatypes

The elimination operator $\mathsf{D}\text{-}\mathbf{E}$ is the only means TT provides for inspecting data in the inductive family D. If we optimise $\mathsf{D}\text{-}\mathbf{E}$'s reduction behaviour, we optimise the programs which elaborate in terms of it. Moreover, if any data in the representation of D's elements is not needed by $\mathsf{D}\text{-}\mathbf{E}$, then it is *never* needed at run-time. Let us look more closely at how ι-rules are implemented.

2.1 Pattern Syntax and Its Semantics

We implement ι-rules $\mathsf{D}\text{-}\mathbf{E}\ \boldsymbol{t}_i = e_i$ by pattern matching, marking with $[\cdot]$ those parts of patterns p which *well typed* terms are *presupposed* to match. Unmarking these parts gives back a term, $|p|$.

$$
\begin{array}{llll}
p ::= x & \text{(pattern variable)} & \mid [t] & \text{(presupposed term)} \\
\quad \mid \mathsf{c}\ \boldsymbol{p} & \text{(constructor pattern)} & \mid [\mathsf{c}]\ \boldsymbol{p} & \text{(presupposed-constructor pattern)}
\end{array}
$$

For each ι-law, as above, we write a **ι-scheme**, $\mathsf{D}\text{-}\mathbf{E}\ \boldsymbol{p}_i \mapsto e_i$ with $|\boldsymbol{p}_i| = \boldsymbol{t}_i$ and e_i a term over $\boldsymbol{p}_i$'s **pattern variables**. The ι-schemes are then compiled into an efficient case-expression [2]. However, our pattern syntax will facilitate the discussion without delving into those details.

The partial function MATCH tries to compute a **matching substitution** for a pattern and term (MATCHES lifts MATCH to sequences in the obvious way):

$$
\begin{array}{ll}
\text{MATCH}(\ x\ , t) \Longrightarrow (t/x) & \\
\text{MATCH}(\ \mathsf{c}\ \boldsymbol{p}\ , t) \Longrightarrow \text{MATCHES}(\boldsymbol{p}, \boldsymbol{t}) & \underline{\text{if}}\ \text{WHNF}(t) \Longrightarrow \mathsf{c}'\ \boldsymbol{t}\ \underline{\text{and}}\ \mathsf{c} = \mathsf{c}' \\
\text{MATCH}(\ [t']\ , t) \Longrightarrow \text{ID} & \\
\text{MATCH}([\mathsf{c}]\ \boldsymbol{p}, t) \Longrightarrow \text{MATCHES}(\boldsymbol{p}, \boldsymbol{t}) & \underline{\text{if}}\ \text{WHNF}(t) \Longrightarrow \mathsf{c}'\ \boldsymbol{t} \\
\text{MATCHES}(\ \cdot\ ,\ \cdot\ ) \Longrightarrow \text{ID} & \\
\text{MATCHES}(p\ \boldsymbol{p}, t\ \boldsymbol{t}) \Longrightarrow \text{MATCH}(p, t) \circ \text{MATCHES}(\boldsymbol{p}, \boldsymbol{t}) &
\end{array}
$$

The first two lines of MATCH test constructors and bind pattern variables as usual in implementations of pattern matching from [20] onwards. The remaining two lines, however, presuppose the successful outcome of testing. To justify these presuppositions, we shall require that each ι-scheme is **Γ-respectful** of well typed instances, i.e.

if $\Gamma \vdash \mathsf{D\text{-}\mathbf{E}}\,\boldsymbol{t} : T$ and $\text{MATCHES}(\boldsymbol{p}_i, \boldsymbol{t}) \Longrightarrow \sigma$ then $\Gamma \vdash \mathsf{D\text{-}\mathbf{E}}\sigma|\boldsymbol{p}_i| = \mathsf{D\text{-}\mathbf{E}}\,\boldsymbol{t} : T$

A set of ι-schemes, $\mathsf{D\text{-}\mathbf{E}}\,\boldsymbol{p}_i \mapsto e_i$ is **Γ-well-defined** if, for any $\Gamma \vdash \mathsf{D\text{-}\mathbf{E}}\,\boldsymbol{t} : T$ of the right arity, with a constructor-headed target, we have $\text{MATCHES}(\boldsymbol{p}_i, \boldsymbol{t}) \Longrightarrow \sigma$ for exactly one i. This yields ι-reduction $\mathsf{D\text{-}\mathbf{E}}\,\boldsymbol{t} \mapsto \sigma e_i$. A set of ι-schemes which is Γ-respectful and Γ-well-defined for all Γ is said to **implement** the corresponding ι-rules.

2.2 Standard Implementation

Theorem. For $\mathsf{D} : \forall \boldsymbol{i}{:}\boldsymbol{I}.\,\star$, with typical $\mathsf{c} : \forall \boldsymbol{a}{:}\boldsymbol{A}.\,\mathsf{D}\,\boldsymbol{r}_1 \to \ldots \to \mathsf{D}\,\boldsymbol{r}_j \to \mathsf{D}\,\boldsymbol{s}$, this typical ι-scheme implements the ι-rules (the **standard** implementation):

$$\mathsf{D\text{-}\mathbf{E}}\,[\boldsymbol{s}]\,(\mathsf{c}\,\boldsymbol{a}\,\boldsymbol{y})\,P\,\boldsymbol{m} \mapsto m_{\mathsf{c}}\,\boldsymbol{a}\,\boldsymbol{y}\,(\mathsf{D\text{-}\mathbf{E}}\,\boldsymbol{r}_1\,y_1\,P\,\boldsymbol{m})\,\ldots\,(\mathsf{D\text{-}\mathbf{E}}\,\boldsymbol{r}_j\,y_j\,P\,\boldsymbol{m})$$

Proof. For any Γ, if $\Gamma \vdash \mathsf{D\text{-}\mathbf{E}}\,\boldsymbol{s}'\,(\mathsf{c}\,\boldsymbol{a}'\,\boldsymbol{y}')\,P'\,\boldsymbol{m}' : T$ then

$$\text{MATCHES}([\boldsymbol{s}]\,(\mathsf{c}\,\boldsymbol{a}\,\boldsymbol{y})\,P\,\boldsymbol{m},\ \boldsymbol{s}'\,(\mathsf{c}\,\boldsymbol{a}'\,\boldsymbol{y}')\,P'\,\boldsymbol{m}') \Longrightarrow \sigma$$

but matching the other ι-schemes fails, so these schemes are Γ-well-defined. Moreover, σ is $(\boldsymbol{a}'/\boldsymbol{a};\ \boldsymbol{y}'/\boldsymbol{y};\ P'/P;\ \boldsymbol{m}'/\boldsymbol{m})$. Typechecking, $\mathsf{c}\,\boldsymbol{a}'\,\boldsymbol{y}' : \mathsf{D}\,(\boldsymbol{a}'/\boldsymbol{a};\ \boldsymbol{y}'/\boldsymbol{y})\boldsymbol{s} = \mathsf{D}\,\sigma\boldsymbol{s}$. Hence $\sigma\boldsymbol{s} = \boldsymbol{s}'$ as $\mathsf{D\text{-}\mathbf{E}}\,\boldsymbol{s}'\,(\mathsf{c}\,\boldsymbol{a}'\,\boldsymbol{y}')$ is well-typed. Hence our typical scheme is Γ-respectful. □

The standard implementation comments out the *indices* — just as well, because there is no guarantee that they generally take the constructor form which explicit matching requires. For example, Vect-**E** has standard implementation

$$\begin{array}{llll} \mathsf{Vect\text{-}\mathbf{E}}\,[A]\ [0] & (\varepsilon\,A) & P\,m_\varepsilon\,m_{::} \mapsto & m_\varepsilon \\ \mathsf{Vect\text{-}\mathbf{E}}\,[A]\ [\mathsf{s}\,k] & (::\,A\,k\,a\,v) & P\,m_\varepsilon\,m_{::} \mapsto & m_{::}\,k\,a\,v\,(\mathsf{Vect\text{-}\mathbf{E}}\,A\,k\,v\,P\,m_\varepsilon\,m_{::}) \end{array}$$

2.3 Alternative Implementations

Where the indices of a constructor's return type do happen to resemble constructor or variable patterns, we are free to consider alternative implementations of the corresponding ι-schemes. We may certainly comment out a pattern variable from the target if we can recover it by matching an index. For example, this is also an implementation of Vect-**E**:

$$\begin{array}{llll} \mathsf{Vect\text{-}\mathbf{E}}\,A\ 0 & (\varepsilon\,[A]) & P\,m_\varepsilon\,m_{::} \mapsto & m_\varepsilon \\ \mathsf{Vect\text{-}\mathbf{E}}\,A\,(\mathsf{s}\,k) & (::\,[A]\,[k]\,a\,v) & P\,m_\varepsilon\,m_{::} \mapsto & m_{::}\,k\,a\,v\,(\mathsf{Vect\text{-}\mathbf{E}}\,A\,k\,v\,P\,m_\varepsilon\,m_{::}) \end{array}$$

But we can do better than that. There is no need to check the constructor tags on *both* the length and the target — one check will do. We may take either

$$(\dagger)\ \textsf{Vect-}\mathbf{E}\ A\ \ [0]\qquad (\varepsilon\,[A])\qquad P\ m_\varepsilon\ m_{::} \mapsto m_\varepsilon$$
$$\textsf{Vect-}\mathbf{E}\ A\ ([\textsf{s}]\ k)\ (::\,[A]\,[k]\ a\ v)\ P\ m_\varepsilon\ m_{::} \mapsto m_{::}\ k\ a\ v\ (\textsf{Vect-}\mathbf{E}\ A\ k\ v\ P\ m_\varepsilon\ m_{::})$$

or, instead, privileging index length over vector contents

$$(\ddagger)\ \textsf{Vect-}\mathbf{E}\ A\ \ \textsf{0}\qquad ([\varepsilon]\,[A])\qquad P\ m_\varepsilon\ m_{::} \mapsto m_\varepsilon$$
$$\textsf{Vect-}\mathbf{E}\ A\ (\textsf{s}\ k)\ ([::]\,[A]\,[k]\ a\ v)\ P\ m_\varepsilon\ m_{::} \mapsto m_{::}\ k\ a\ v\ (\textsf{Vect-}\mathbf{E}\ A\ k\ v\ P\ m_\varepsilon\ m_{::})$$

In the sequel, we show how to choose good alternative implementations for elimination operators by systematically exploiting the presence of constructor symbols in indices. This leads naturally to space optimisations, where we do not merely comment out unnecessary data from patterns — we delete them entirely from the representation of datatypes.

2.4 ExTT — an Execution Language for TT with Deleted Terms

We introduce ExTT, an execution language for terms in TT. ExTT extends TT's syntax with **deleted** terms and patterns $\{t\}$, and also with deleted constructor patterns $\{\textsf{c}\}\ \boldsymbol{p}$ corresponding to untagged tuples $\{\textsf{c}\}\ \boldsymbol{t}$. We extend the operational semantics thus:

$$\text{MATCH}(\{t\}, \{t'\}) \Longrightarrow \text{ID}$$
$$\text{MATCH}(\{\textsf{c}\}\ \boldsymbol{p}, t) \Longrightarrow \text{MATCHES}(\boldsymbol{p}, \boldsymbol{t})\ \ \underline{\text{if}}\ \text{WHNF}(t) \Longrightarrow (\{\textsf{c}'\}\ \boldsymbol{t})$$

We are careful to distinguish $(\{\textsf{c}\}\ \{t\})$, which is represented by the empty tuple, from $\{\textsf{c}\ t\}$, which is deleted altogether. The actual evaluation of terms in ExTT can be by any standard method, such as normalisation by evaluation [1, 5], compilation to G machine code [12] or program extraction [13].

The unmarking operation $|\cdot|$ takes both patterns and terms in ExTT back to terms in TT by stripping out both $[\cdot]$ and $\{\}$ marks. Terms in ExTT arise only by optimisations from well typed TT terms hence ExTT needs no typing rules provided that these optimisations are safe.

We specify an **optimisation** by giving a substitution $[\![\cdot]\!]$ from TT identifiers to ExTT terms, ID by default, together with the optimised ExTT ι-schemes. For ι-rules $\Gamma \vdash \textsf{D-}\mathbf{E}\ \boldsymbol{t}_i = e_i$, these have form $\textsf{D-}\mathbf{E}\ \boldsymbol{p}_i \mapsto d_i$, where $|\boldsymbol{p}_i| = \boldsymbol{t}_i$, $|d_i| = e_i$ and every undeleted free variable in d_i is a pattern variable in $\boldsymbol{p}_i$. For all Γ, these schemes must be Γ-well-defined in the obvious way, and Γ-respectful in that

$$\text{if } \Gamma \vdash \textsf{D-}\mathbf{E}\ \boldsymbol{t} : T \text{ and MATCHES}(\boldsymbol{p}_i, [\![\boldsymbol{t}]\!]) \Longrightarrow \sigma$$
$$\text{then there exists a substitution } \tau \text{ such that } \Gamma \vdash \tau\,|\sigma(\textsf{D-}\mathbf{E}\ \boldsymbol{p}_i)| = \textsf{D-}\mathbf{E}\ \boldsymbol{t} : T$$

The rôle of τ is to instantiate the variables free in e_i, but deleted in d_i—these are not needed when executing ExTT terms, hence they need not be matched.

In the following sections, we establish several such optimisations.

3 Eliding Redundant Constructor Arguments

Recall the alternative implementation of Vect-**E** († above) which matches A and k in the indices rather than the target. When can we do this, in general?

Whenever $\mathsf{c}\ \boldsymbol{a},\ \mathsf{c}\ \boldsymbol{b}\ :\ \mathsf{D}\ \boldsymbol{s}$ implies $a_i = b_i$, we say that the ith argument of c is **forceable**. eg., the A argument to ε is forceable since if $\varepsilon\ a,\ \varepsilon\ b\ :\ \mathsf{Vect}\ A\ 0$ then clearly $a = b = A$. For ::, A and k are forceable in the same way.

Constructor arguments which have been commented out owing to their repetition in a ι-scheme are forceable. This is to be expected; such repeated arguments arise from the patterns describing constructor indices.

Consider a typical constructor, fully applied to variables, $\mathsf{c}\ \boldsymbol{a}\ \boldsymbol{y}\ :\ \mathsf{D}\ \boldsymbol{s}$. If we express $\boldsymbol{s}$ as $|\boldsymbol{p}|$ for any patterns $\boldsymbol{p}$, then any a_i appearing as a pattern variable in $\boldsymbol{p}$ is forceable, by injectivity of constructors. We call these arguments **concretely forceable** since they can be retrieved in constant time by pattern matching on the indices.

To express $\boldsymbol{s}$ as $|\boldsymbol{p}|$, we write a program to extract from a term a linear pattern with its variable set:

$$
\begin{array}{l}
\textsc{pat}\ (\ V,\ x\ ) \Longrightarrow (x \cup V, x)\ \underline{\text{if}}\ x \notin V \\
\textsc{pat}\ (\ V, \mathsf{c}\ \boldsymbol{t}) \Longrightarrow (V', \textsc{lazy}(\mathsf{c}, \boldsymbol{p}))\ \underline{\text{if}}\ \textsc{pats}\ (V, \boldsymbol{t}) \Longrightarrow (V', \boldsymbol{p}) \\
\textsc{pat}\ (\ V,\ t\ ) \Longrightarrow (V, [t]) \\
\textsc{pats}(\ V,\ \cdot\ ) \Longrightarrow (V, \cdot) \\
\textsc{pats}(\ V, t\ \boldsymbol{t}) \Longrightarrow (V'', p\ \boldsymbol{p}) \\
\qquad\qquad\qquad \underline{\text{if}}\ \textsc{pat}\ (V, t) \Longrightarrow (V', p)\ \underline{\text{and}}\ \textsc{pats}\ (V', \boldsymbol{t}) \Longrightarrow (V'', \boldsymbol{p}) \\
\textsc{lazy}(\ \mathsf{c}, [\boldsymbol{p}]) \Longrightarrow [\mathsf{c}\ \boldsymbol{p}] \\
\textsc{lazy}(\ \mathsf{c},\ \boldsymbol{p}\ ) \Longrightarrow [\mathsf{c}]\ \boldsymbol{p}\ \ \underline{\text{otherwise}}
\end{array}
$$

For our typical constructor c, we can extract the patterns which D-$\mathbf{E}$ will match by $\textsc{pats}\,(\emptyset, \boldsymbol{s}) \Longrightarrow (V, \boldsymbol{p})$. If an argument $a_i \in V$ then a_i is concretely forceable. It is instantiated by matching $\boldsymbol{p}$, hence we may presuppose it when we match the target, yielding the same result. Hence, we may then choose the alternative implementation:

$$
\mathsf{D}\text{-}\mathbf{E}\ \boldsymbol{p}\ (\mathsf{c}\ \boldsymbol{a}^{[V]}\ \boldsymbol{y})\ P\ \boldsymbol{m}\ \mapsto\ m_{\mathsf{c}} \cdots \qquad \begin{array}{l}\underline{\text{where}}\ a^{[V]} \Longrightarrow [a]\ \underline{\text{if}}\ a \in V \\ \qquad\quad\ a^{[V]} \Longrightarrow a\ \ \underline{\text{otherwise}}\end{array}
$$

Theorem. The following is an optimisation (**forcing**):

$$
\begin{array}{l}
\text{for } \mathsf{c}\ :\ \forall \boldsymbol{a}\!:\!\boldsymbol{A}.\, \mathsf{D}\ \boldsymbol{r}_1 \to \ldots \to \mathsf{D}\ \boldsymbol{r}_j \to \mathsf{D}\ \boldsymbol{s} \qquad \underline{\text{where}}\ \textsc{pats}\,(\emptyset, \boldsymbol{s}) \Longrightarrow (V, \boldsymbol{p}) \\
\text{take } [\![\mathsf{c}]\!] \ \Longrightarrow\ \lambda \boldsymbol{a}; \boldsymbol{y}.\, \mathsf{c}\ \boldsymbol{a}^{\{V\}}\ \boldsymbol{y} \\
\qquad \mathsf{D}\text{-}\mathbf{E}\ \boldsymbol{p}\ (\mathsf{c}\ \boldsymbol{a}^{\{V\}}\ \boldsymbol{y})\ P\ \boldsymbol{m}\ \mapsto\ m_{\mathsf{c}}\ \boldsymbol{a}\ \boldsymbol{y}\ (\mathsf{D}\text{-}\mathbf{E}\ \boldsymbol{r}_1\ y_1\ P\ \boldsymbol{m})\ \ldots\ (\mathsf{D}\text{-}\mathbf{E}\ \boldsymbol{r}_j\ y_j\ P\ \boldsymbol{m}) \\
\qquad \underline{\text{where}}\ a^{\{V\}} \Longrightarrow \{a\}\ \ \underline{\text{if}}\ a \in V \\
\qquad\qquad\quad\ a^{\{V\}} \Longrightarrow a\ \ \underline{\text{otherwise}}
\end{array}
$$

Proof. Clearly, $|\boldsymbol{p}| = \boldsymbol{s}$ and $\left|\mathsf{c}\ \boldsymbol{a}^{\{V\}}\ \boldsymbol{y}\right| = \mathsf{c}\,\boldsymbol{a}\,\boldsymbol{y}$, so if $\Gamma \vdash \mathsf{D}\text{-}\mathbf{E}\,\boldsymbol{s}'(\mathsf{c}\,\boldsymbol{a}'\,\boldsymbol{y}')P'\boldsymbol{m}'\ :\ T$ then, as before, $\boldsymbol{s}' = (\boldsymbol{a}'/\boldsymbol{a};\ \boldsymbol{y}'\boldsymbol{y})\boldsymbol{s}$. Now,

$$
\begin{array}{l}
\textsc{matches}(\boldsymbol{p}, (\boldsymbol{a}'/\boldsymbol{a};\ \boldsymbol{y}'/\boldsymbol{y})\boldsymbol{s}) \Longrightarrow (a_i'/a_i\ \ \underline{\text{if}}\ a_i \in V) \\
\textsc{matches}(\mathsf{c}\ \boldsymbol{a}^{\{V\}}\ \boldsymbol{y}, \mathsf{c}\ \boldsymbol{a}'\ \boldsymbol{y}') \Longrightarrow (a_i'/a_i\ \ \underline{\text{if}}\ a_i \notin V;\ \boldsymbol{y}'/\boldsymbol{y})
\end{array}
$$

Hence any matching substitution σ for the left-hand side satisfies

$$
\textsc{id}\left|\sigma(\mathsf{D}\text{-}\mathbf{E}\ \boldsymbol{p}\ (\mathsf{c}\ \boldsymbol{a}^{\{V\}}\ \boldsymbol{y})\ P\ \boldsymbol{m})\right| = \mathsf{D}\text{-}\mathbf{E}\ \boldsymbol{s}'\ (\mathsf{c}\ \boldsymbol{a}'\ \boldsymbol{y}')\ P'\ \boldsymbol{m}'
$$

So these schemes are Γ-respectful. They are clearly Γ-well-defined, as they discriminate on the target's constructor. □

For our Vect example, forcing is given by:

$$[\![\varepsilon]\!] \Longrightarrow \lambda A.\ \varepsilon\ \{A\}$$
$$[\![::]\!] \Longrightarrow \lambda A; k; a; v.\ ::\ \{A\}\ \{k\}\ a\ v$$

$$\begin{array}{lllll} \mathsf{Vect}\text{-}\mathbf{E}\ A & [0] & (\varepsilon\ \{A\}) & P\ m_\varepsilon\ m_{::} & \mapsto\ m_\varepsilon \\ \mathsf{Vect}\text{-}\mathbf{E}\ A & ([\mathsf{s}]\ k) & (::\ \{A\}\ \{k\}\ a\ v) & P\ m_\varepsilon\ m_{::} & \mapsto\ m_{::}\ k\ a\ v\ (\mathsf{Vect}\text{-}\mathbf{E}\ A\ k\ v\ P\ m_\varepsilon\ m_{::}) \end{array}$$

In the implementation the deleted arguments really are removed from the now fully applied constructors. This is safe because these terms are only decomposed by Vect-**E** which does not expect the deleted arguments.

4 Eliding Redundant Constructor Tags

Recall the second alternative implementation of Vect-**E** (‡) where case selection is by analysis of the length index rather than the target itself.

For which types can we do case selection on an argument other than the target?

If $\mathsf{c}\ \boldsymbol{a}, \mathsf{c}'\ \boldsymbol{b}\ :\ \mathsf{D}\ \boldsymbol{s}$ implies $\mathsf{c} = \mathsf{c}'$, we say that the family D is **detaggable.** Vect is detaggable because the length index determines whether the constructor is ε (if the length index is 0) or :: (if the length index is $\mathsf{s}k$).

For any set of ι-schemes, if the index patterns are already mutually exclusive, we can decide which scheme applies without checking the target's constructor tag. The following program checks if two patterns are guaranteed to match disjoint sets of terms:

$$\begin{array}{ll} \text{DISJOINT}(\ \mathsf{c}\,\boldsymbol{p}\ ,\ \mathsf{c}'\ \boldsymbol{q}\ ) \Longrightarrow \mathsf{true}\ \underline{\text{if}}\ \mathsf{c} \neq \mathsf{c}' \\ \text{DISJOINT}(\ \mathsf{c}\,\boldsymbol{p}\ ,\ \mathsf{c}\,\boldsymbol{q}\ ) \Longrightarrow \exists i.\text{DISJOINT}(p_i, q_i) \\ \text{DISJOINT}(\ [\mathsf{c}]\ \boldsymbol{p}, [\mathsf{c}]\ \boldsymbol{q}) \Longrightarrow \exists i.\text{DISJOINT}(p_i, q_i) \\ \text{DISJOINT}(\ \ p\ \ ,\ \ q\ \ ) \Longrightarrow \mathsf{false}\ \underline{\text{otherwise}} \end{array}$$

Of course if we are to match on the indices then we must actually examine their constructors, so the previous lazy definition of PATS is not sufficient. We compute the patterns we need for this optimisation with EPATS — the same as PATS but with LAZY replaced by EAGER:

$$\text{EAGER}(\ \mathsf{c}, \boldsymbol{p}) \Longrightarrow \mathsf{c}\ \boldsymbol{p}$$

Given a family D with constructors $\mathsf{c}_i\ :\ \forall \boldsymbol{x} : \boldsymbol{X}_i.\mathsf{D}\,\boldsymbol{s}_i$ where $\text{EPATS}(\emptyset, \boldsymbol{s}_i) \Longrightarrow (V_i, \boldsymbol{p}_i)$, we say D is **concretely detaggable** if

$$\forall\, i \neq j.\ \exists k.\ \text{DISJOINT}(p_{ik}, p_{jk}) \Longrightarrow \mathsf{true}$$

Theorem. We may optimise (**detag**) such a concretely detaggable D thus:

$$[\![\mathsf{c}_i]\!]\ \Longrightarrow\ \lambda \boldsymbol{x}.\ \{\mathsf{c}_i\}\ \boldsymbol{x}^{\{V\}}$$
$$\mathsf{D}\text{-}\mathbf{E}\ \boldsymbol{p}_i\ (\{\mathsf{c}_i\}\ \boldsymbol{x}^{\{V\}})\ P\ \boldsymbol{m}\ \mapsto\ e_i$$

Proof. These schemes are Γ-respectful for all Γ by the same argument as for forcing—the switch to eager patterns does not affect the set of variables matched from the indices, nor the success of matching well-typed values. Deleting the constructor in the target can only improve the possibility of a match, but the disjointness condition directly ensures that the schemes remain Γ-well-defined. □

For our Vect example, detagging is given by:

$$[\![\varepsilon]\!] \Longrightarrow \lambda A.\ \{\varepsilon\}\ \{A\}$$
$$[\![::]\!] \Longrightarrow \lambda A; k; a; v.\ \{::\}\ \{A\}\ \{k\}\ a\ v$$

$$\mathsf{Vect}\text{-}\mathbf{E}\ A\ \ 0\ \ \ \ (\{\varepsilon\}\ \{A\})\ \ \ P\ m_\varepsilon\ m_{::} \mapsto m_\varepsilon$$
$$\mathsf{Vect}\text{-}\mathbf{E}\ A\ (\mathsf{s}\ k)(\{::\}\ \{A\}\ \{k\}\ a\ v)\ P\ m_\varepsilon\ m_{::} \mapsto m_{::}\ k\ a\ v\ (\mathsf{Vect}\text{-}\mathbf{E}\ A\ k\ v\ P\ m_\varepsilon\ m_{::})$$

We achieve this space optimisation at the cost of using eager rather than lazy patterns. The number of constructor tests required increases by a constant (possibly zero!) factor and indices may sometimes be computed where they would previously be ignored. Clearly a real implementation would minimise the number of eager patterns required to make the distinction. An analysis of this space/time trade-off is beyond the scope of this paper, but for Vect it seems likely to be worthwhile since we have swapped one constructor test for another.

5 Run-Time Optimisation

In our Vect-**E** example, we have already deleted both ε and its argument. We might be tempted to go a step further, and comment out that entire target.

$$\mathsf{Vect}\text{-}\mathbf{E}\ A\ 0\ [\{\varepsilon\}\ \{A\}]\ P\ m_\varepsilon\ m_{::} \mapsto m_\varepsilon$$

However, this ι-scheme is not respectful and breaks subject reduction thus:

$$\ldots; x : \mathsf{Vect}\ A\ 0 \vdash \mathsf{Vect}\text{-}\mathbf{E}\ A\ 0\ x\ P\ m_\varepsilon\ m_{::} : P\ 0\ x$$
$$\mapsto m_\varepsilon : P\ 0\ \varepsilon$$

The pattern $(\{\varepsilon\}\ \{A\})$ may not test tags or extract arguments, but it still only matches targets whose weak head-normal forms are constructor applications. The optimisations we have seen thus far are safe to use in any context, and we need to reduce under binders when performing the equality checks which ensure that EPIGRAM programs elaborate to well typed terms.

However, at run-time, we can employ a much more restricted notion of computation, reducing only in the *empty* context, $\mathcal{E}$. In this scenario, we can exploit the **adequacy** property of TT — if $\mathcal{E} \vdash t : \mathsf{D}\ \boldsymbol{s}$ then $\mathrm{WHNF}(t)$ is $\mathsf{c}\ \boldsymbol{t}$ for some $\boldsymbol{t}$ — to gain further optimisations, not available in a general context.

In effect, we may employ weaker criteria for alternative implementations of elimination operators in run-time execution. We say that a **run-time optimisation** is given by a substitution and ι-schemes in ExTT as before, except that these schemes need only be $\mathcal{E}$-respectful and $\mathcal{E}$-well-defined.

The adequacy property tells us that the target will always match a constructor pattern at run-time, hence we may safely presuppose a pattern from which no information is gained, as suggested above. Moreover, by applying this observation inductively, we can sometimes extract another, more drastic optimisation from the guarantee of adequacy at run-time.

6 Collapsing Content-Free Families at Run-Time

Consider the less than or equal relation, declared and elaborated as follows:

$$\underline{\text{data}} \quad \frac{x, y \ : \ \mathbb{N}}{x \leq y \ : \ \star} \quad \underline{\text{where}} \quad \frac{}{\mathsf{leO} \ : \ 0 \leq y} \quad \frac{p \ : \ x \leq y}{\mathsf{leS}\ p \ : \ \mathsf{s}x \leq \mathsf{s}y}$$

$$\begin{array}{l} \leq \ : \ \mathbb{N} \to \mathbb{N} \to \star \\ \mathsf{leO} \ : \ \forall y{:}\mathbb{N}.\ \leq 0\ y \\ \mathsf{leS} \ : \ \forall x, y{:}\mathbb{N}.\ \leq x\ y \to \ \leq (\mathsf{s}x)\ (\mathsf{s}y) \end{array}$$

The $\leq$ family describes a property of its indices and stores no other data. It is not surprising therefore to find that much of its content can be deleted. Forcing and detagging yield:

$$\begin{array}{l} [\![\mathsf{leO}]\!] \implies \lambda y.\ (\{\!\!\{\mathsf{leO}\}\!\!\}\ \{\!\!\{y\}\!\!\}) \\ [\![\mathsf{leS}]\!] \implies \lambda x; y; p.\ (\{\!\!\{\mathsf{leS}\}\!\!\}\ \{\!\!\{x\}\!\!\}\ \{\!\!\{y\}\!\!\}\ p) \\ \leq\text{-}\mathbf{E}\ 0 \quad\quad y \quad\quad (\{\!\!\{\mathsf{leO}\}\!\!\}\ \{\!\!\{y\}\!\!\}) \quad P\ m_{\mathsf{leO}}\ m_{\mathsf{leS}} \ \mapsto\ m_{\mathsf{leO}}\ y \\ \leq\text{-}\mathbf{E}\ (\mathsf{s}x)\ (\mathsf{s}y)\ (\{\!\!\{\mathsf{leS}\}\!\!\}\ \{\!\!\{x\}\!\!\}\ \{\!\!\{y\}\!\!\}\ p)\ P\ m_{\mathsf{leO}}\ m_{\mathsf{leS}} \\ \quad\quad\quad\quad \mapsto\ m_{\mathsf{leS}}\ x\ y\ p\ (\leq\text{-}\mathbf{E}\ x\ y\ p\ P\ m_{\mathsf{leO}}\ m_{\mathsf{leS}}) \end{array}$$

Now we are left with only one undeleted argument, the recursive p in leS. This argument serves two purposes — firstly it is the target of the recursive call and secondly it is passed to the method m_{leS}. We might think that p can also be elided — ultimately it can only by examined by $\leq$-**E** which, by induction, can be shown never to examine it. In a partial evaluation setting, however, where we may reduce under binders, we must at least check that the target is canonical for reduction to be possible. If not, we run the risk of reducing a proof of something which cannot be constructed, such as $5 \leq 4$!

At run-time, on the other hand, we never need to check that p is canonical because the adequacy property tells us that it must be. Hence, at run-time, we no longer need to store the recursive argument — the entire family collapses:

$$\begin{array}{l} [\![\mathsf{leO}]\!] \implies \lambda y.\ (\{\!\!\{\mathsf{leO}\ y\}\!\!\}) \\ [\![\mathsf{leS}]\!] \implies \lambda x; y; p.\ (\{\!\!\{\mathsf{leS}\ x\ y\ p\}\!\!\}) \\ [\![\leq\text{-}\mathbf{E}]\!] \implies \lambda x; y; p; P; m_{\mathsf{leO}}; m_{\mathsf{leS}}.\ \leq\text{-}\mathbf{E}\ x\ y\ \{\!\!\{p\}\!\!\}\ P\ m_{\mathsf{leO}}\ m_{\mathsf{leS}} \end{array}$$

For which families can we do this run-time optimisation? If $a, b \ : \ \mathsf{D}\ s$ implies $a = b$ we say that the family D is **collapsible.** $\leq$ is collapsible because any value in $x \leq y$ is determined entirely by the indices x and y.

$$\begin{array}{l} \leq\text{-}\mathbf{E}\ 0 \quad\quad y \quad\quad \{\!\!\{\mathsf{leO}\ y\}\!\!\} \quad P\ m_{\mathsf{leO}}\ m_{\mathsf{leS}} \ \mapsto\ m_{\mathsf{leO}}\ y \\ \leq\text{-}\mathbf{E}\ (\mathsf{s}x)\ (\mathsf{s}y)\ \{\!\!\{\mathsf{leS}\ x\ y\ p\}\!\!\}\ P\ m_{\mathsf{leO}}\ m_{\mathsf{leS}} \\ \quad\quad\quad\quad \mapsto\ m_{\mathsf{leS}}\ x\ y\ (\{\!\!\{p\}\!\!\})\ (\leq\text{-}\mathbf{E}\ x\ y\ \{\!\!\{p\}\!\!\}\ P\ m_{\mathsf{leO}}\ m_{\mathsf{leS}}) \end{array}$$

We say a family is **concretely collapsible** if it is detaggable and for each constructor $\mathsf{c} : \forall \boldsymbol{a} : \boldsymbol{A}.\ \mathsf{D}\ \boldsymbol{r}_1 \to \ldots \to \mathsf{D}\ \boldsymbol{r}_j \to \mathsf{D}\ \boldsymbol{s}$, $\text{EPATS}\ (\emptyset, \boldsymbol{s}) \Longrightarrow (\boldsymbol{a}, \boldsymbol{p})$. That is, the constructor tag and all the non-recursive arguments are *cheaply* recoverable from the indices.

Theorem. We may optimise a concretely collapsible family *at run-time*:

$$\begin{aligned}
&\mathsf{D\text{-}E}\ \boldsymbol{p}\ \{\mathsf{c}\ \boldsymbol{a}\ \boldsymbol{y}\}\ P\ \boldsymbol{m} \\
&\qquad \mapsto m_{\mathsf{c}}\ \boldsymbol{a}\ (\{y_1\})\ \ldots\ (\{y_n\})\ (\mathsf{D\text{-}E}\ \boldsymbol{r}_1\ \{y_1\}\ P\ \boldsymbol{m})\ \ldots\ (\mathsf{D\text{-}E}\ \boldsymbol{r}_n\ \{y_n\}\ P\ \boldsymbol{m}) \\
&[\![\mathsf{c}]\!] \Longrightarrow \lambda \boldsymbol{a}; \boldsymbol{y}.\ (\{\mathsf{c}\ \boldsymbol{a}\ \boldsymbol{y}\}) \\
&[\![\mathsf{D\text{-}E}]\!] \Longrightarrow \lambda \boldsymbol{i}; x; p; \boldsymbol{m}.\ \mathsf{D\text{-}E}\ \boldsymbol{i}\ \{x\}\ P\ \boldsymbol{m}
\end{aligned}$$

Proof. These schemes are $\mathcal{E}$-well-defined by the same argument as for detagging. They are $\mathcal{E}$-respectful because the only possible left-hand sides have the form $\mathcal{E} \vdash \mathsf{D\text{-}E}\ \boldsymbol{s}'\ (\mathsf{c}\ \boldsymbol{a}'\ \boldsymbol{y}')\ P'\ \boldsymbol{m}'$, hence, by disjointness, the only possible match, even with the target deleted, is with the scheme for c, with matching substitution $\sigma = (\boldsymbol{a}'/\boldsymbol{a};\ P'/P;\ \boldsymbol{m}'/\boldsymbol{m})$, binding all the undeleted free variables on the right-hand side because $\text{EPATS}\ (\emptyset, \boldsymbol{s}) \Longrightarrow (\boldsymbol{a}, \boldsymbol{p})$. Taking $\tau = (\boldsymbol{y}'/\boldsymbol{y})$, we see that

$$\mathcal{E} \vdash \tau\, |\sigma(\mathsf{D\text{-}E}\ \boldsymbol{p}\ \{\mathsf{c}\ \boldsymbol{a}\ \boldsymbol{y}\}\ P\ \boldsymbol{m})| = \mathsf{D\text{-}E}\ \boldsymbol{s}'\ (\mathsf{c}\ \boldsymbol{a}'\ \boldsymbol{y}')\ P'\ \boldsymbol{m}'$$

hence these schemes are $\mathcal{E}$-respectful. □

7 Examples

7.1 The Finite Sets

The finite sets, indexed over a natural number n, are a family of types with n elements. Effectively, they are a representation of bounded numbers and are declared as follows:

$$\underline{\text{data}}\quad \frac{n : \mathbb{N}}{\mathsf{Fin}\ n : \star} \quad \underline{\text{where}} \quad \frac{}{\mathsf{f0} : \mathsf{Fin}\ \mathsf{s}n} \quad \frac{i : \mathsf{Fin}\ n}{\mathsf{fs}\ i : \mathsf{Fin}\ \mathsf{s}n}$$

The forcing optimisation elides the indices from the elaborated constructors:

$$\begin{aligned}
&[\![\mathsf{f0}]\!] \Longrightarrow \lambda n.\ \mathsf{f0}\ \{n\} \\
&[\![\mathsf{fs}]\!] \Longrightarrow \lambda n; i.\ \mathsf{fs}\ \{n\}\ i
\end{aligned}$$

After stripping the forceable arguments, the shape of the resulting type matches that of $\mathbb{N}$ — that is, the base constructor takes no arguments and the step constructor takes a single recursive argument. In principle, any optimisations which apply to $\mathbb{N}$ such as Magaud and Bertot's binary representation [16] should also apply to Fin. We hope to recover Xi's efficient treatment of bounded numbers in this way [27] and perhaps extend it to other forms of validation.

7.2 Comparison of Natural Numbers

The Compare family from [19] represents the result of comparing two numbers, storing which is the greater and by how much:

$$\underline{\text{data}}\quad \frac{m, n \,:\, \mathbb{N}}{\mathsf{Compare}\ m\ n \,:\, \star} \quad \underline{\text{where}}\quad \frac{}{\mathsf{lt}\ y \,:\, \mathsf{Compare}\ x\ (x + (\mathsf{s}\ y))}$$

$$\frac{}{\mathsf{eq} \,:\, \mathsf{Compare}\ x\ x}$$

$$\frac{}{\mathsf{gt}\ x \,:\, \mathsf{Compare}\ (y + (\mathsf{s}\ x))\ y}$$

Compare is an example of a family which is collapsible, but not concretely collapsible. Clearly there is only one possible element of Compare m n for each m and n, and given this element we can extract their difference in constant time. If we were to collapse Compare we would replace this simple inspection by the recomputation of the difference each time the same value was used. We restrict concretely collapsible families to those where the recomputation of values is cheap. Nonetheless, by forcing, Compare need only store which index is larger and by how much:

$$\begin{aligned} [\![\mathsf{lt}]\!] &\Longrightarrow \lambda x; y.\ \mathsf{lt}\ \{x\}\ y \\ [\![\mathsf{eq}]\!] &\Longrightarrow \lambda x.\ \mathsf{eq}\ \{x\} \\ [\![\mathsf{gt}]\!] &\Longrightarrow \lambda x; y.\ \mathsf{gt}\ x\ \{y\} \end{aligned}$$

7.3 Accessibility Predicates

In [6], Bove and Capretta use special-purpose accessibility predicates to prove termination of general recursive functions. For example, **quicksort** terminates on the nil, and it terminates on cons x xs if it terminates on **filter** $(<\ x)\ xs$ and **filter** $(\geq\ x)\ xs$. This is expressed by the qsAcc predicate below:

$$\underline{\text{data}}\quad \frac{l \,:\, \mathsf{List}\ \mathbb{N}}{\mathsf{qsAcc}\ l \,:\, \star}$$

$$\underline{\text{where}}\quad \frac{}{\mathsf{qsNil} \,:\, \mathsf{qsAcc}\ \mathsf{nil}}$$

$$\frac{qsl \,:\, \mathsf{qsAcc}\ (\mathbf{filter}\ (<\ x)\ xs) \qquad qsr \,:\, \mathsf{qsAcc}\ (\mathbf{filter}\ (\geq\ x)\ xs)}{\mathsf{qsCons}\ qsl\ qsr \,:\, \mathsf{qsAcc}\ (\mathsf{cons}\ x\ xs)}$$

quicksort itself is defined by induction over qsAcc, so a naïve implementation would need to store the proofs. However, qsAcc is concretely collapsible:

$$\begin{aligned} [\![\mathsf{qsNil}]\!] &\Longrightarrow \{\mathsf{qsNil}\} \\ [\![\mathsf{qsCons}]\!] &\Longrightarrow \lambda x; xs; qsl; qsr.\ \{\mathsf{qsCons}\ x\ xs\ qsl\ qsr\} \end{aligned}$$

Collapsing replaces computation over qsAcc by computation over its indices, restoring the intended operational semantics of the original program! These accessibility predicates are concretely collapsible because their indices are constructed from the constructor patterns of programs.

7.4 The Simply Typed λ-Calculus

We define the simply typed λ-calculus in a similar fashion to [19], making extensive use of inductive families to specify invariants on the data structures. We begin with STy, representing simple monomorphic types:

$$\underline{\text{data}}\quad \frac{}{\mathsf{STy} : \star} \quad \underline{\text{where}} \quad \frac{}{\iota : \mathsf{STy}} \quad \frac{s, t : \mathsf{STy}}{s \Rightarrow t : \mathsf{STy}}$$

We represent contexts by Vects of types, Ctx = Vect STy. The explicit length allows a safe de Bruijn representation of variables, via the Fin family, hence our untyped terms, Expr, are at least well scoped—the length is forceable for each constructor:

$$\underline{\text{data}}\quad \frac{n : \mathbb{N}}{\mathsf{Expr}\; n : \star}$$

$$\underline{\text{where}}\quad \frac{i : \mathsf{Fin}\; n}{\mathsf{eVar}\; i : \mathsf{Expr}\; n} \quad \frac{S : \mathsf{STy} \quad t : \mathsf{Expr}\; \mathsf{s}n}{\mathsf{eLam}\; S\; t : \mathsf{Expr}\; n} \quad \frac{f, s : \mathsf{Expr}\; n}{\mathsf{eApp}\; f\; s : \mathsf{Expr}\; n}$$

The Var relation gives types to variables. Var $G\, i\, T$ states that the ith member of the context G has type T. Clearly Var is concretely collapsible.

$$\underline{\text{data}}\quad \frac{G : \mathsf{Ctx}\; n \quad i : \mathsf{Fin}\; n \quad T : \mathsf{STy}}{\mathsf{Var}\; G\; i\; T : \star}$$

$$\underline{\text{where}}\quad \frac{}{\mathsf{stop} : \mathsf{Var}\; (S{::}G)\; \mathsf{f0}\; S} \quad \frac{v : \mathsf{Var}\; G\; i\; T}{\mathsf{pop}\; v : \mathsf{Var}\; (S{::}G)\; (\mathsf{fs}\; i)\; T}$$

Finally, we have the well typed terms, indexed over contexts, the original raw terms and types. This gives us a particularly safe representation — no typechecker can return the wrong well typed term. This indexing also enables us to synchronise terms safely with value environments during evaluation in the style of Augustsson and Carlsson [3].

$$\underline{\text{data}}\quad \frac{G : \mathsf{Ctx}\; n \quad e : \mathsf{Expr}\; n \quad T : \mathsf{STy}}{\mathsf{Term}\; G\; e\; T : \star}$$

$$\underline{\text{where}}\quad \frac{v : \mathsf{Var}\; G\; i\; T}{\mathsf{var}\; v : \mathsf{Term}\; G\; (\mathsf{eVar}\; i)\; T} \quad \frac{b : \mathsf{Term}\; (S{::}G)\; e\; T}{\mathsf{lam}\; b : \mathsf{Term}\; G\; (\mathsf{eLam}\; S\; e)\; (S \Rightarrow T)}$$

$$\frac{f : \mathsf{Term}\; G\; fe\; (S \Rightarrow T) \quad a : \mathsf{Term}\; G\; ae\; S}{\mathsf{app}\; f\; a : \mathsf{Term}\; G\; (\mathsf{eApp}\; fe\; ae)\; T}$$

Term seems to involve a horrifying amount of duplication. Fortunately, many of the arguments are forceable and thanks to the indexing over raw terms, Term is detaggable. After optimisation, this is all that remains:

$$\begin{aligned}
[\![\mathsf{var}]\!] &\Longrightarrow \lambda n; G; i; T; v.\ \{\mathsf{var}\}\ \{n\}\ \{G\}\ \{i\}\ \{T\}\ \{v\}\\
[\![\mathsf{lam}]\!] &\Longrightarrow \lambda n; G; S; e; T; b.\ \{\mathsf{lam}\}\ \{n\}\ \{G\}\ \{S\}\ \{e\}\ \{T\}\ b\\
[\![\mathsf{app}]\!] &\Longrightarrow \lambda n; G; fe; S; T; f; ae; a.\ \{\mathsf{app}\}\ \{n\}\ \{G\}\ \{fe\}\ S\ \{T\}\ f\ \{ae\}\ a
\end{aligned}$$

The only non-recursive arguments which survive are the domain types of applications. Typechecking thus consists of ensuring that these can be determined.

8 Conclusions and Further Work

The ideas presented here have been tested in a prototype implementation. Execution in this system is by extraction to a Haskell coding of ExTT values without the deleted subterms. We have used the GHC profiling tools [24] to assess the space usage of programs.

Our experiments show a significant reduction in space requirements over a naïve implementation particularly where there is extensive indexing. For vector operations, a 10-20% saving in memory usage is typical (depending on the length of the vector), but for the typechecker, a saving of over 80% has been observed.

Although remarkably straightforward, these optimisations only present themselves when one takes dependently typed programming seriously. The forcing optimisation largely overcomes the space penalty of adopting dependent types, but detagging derives new dynamic benefit from previously unavailable static information. Collapsing, too, has significant consequences, deleting accessibility arguments and all the equational reasoning from run-time code, not because we deem them to be proof-irrelevant, but because they actually are.

We suspect that these optimisations are the first of many. For example, as we erase forceable indices, it is worth identifying operations which affect nothing else, such as **weaken** : $\mathsf{Fin}\ n \rightarrow \mathsf{Fin}\ (\mathsf{s}n)$, which embeds a value in a higher indexed set — this is effectively the identity function. This optimisation applies wherever functions exist only to manage invariants.

We might also consider the low level implementation of high level types, such as the natural numbers. By replacing $\mathbb{N}$-**E** with an appropriate elimination rule for unbounded binary numbers [16] we can achieve a significant speed-up. Any other data structure with the same shape *after optimisation*, eg. Fin, can be treated similarly. In a practical implementation, such optimisations are essential for comparable performance to its conventional counterparts.

Optimisation of a new language with a new type system naturally presents new problems and new opportunities. While we can never hope to produce a completely optimal program in all cases, this research leads us to believe that the presence of much more static information can only give us greater scope for optimisation in both time and space.

References

1. Thorsten Altenkirch, Martin Hofmann, and Thomas Streicher. Categorical reconstruction of a reduction free normalization proof, 1996.
2. Lennart Augustsson. Compiling pattern matching. In Jean-Pierre Jouannaud, editor, *Functional Programming Languages and Computer Architecture*, pages 368–381. Springer-Verlag, September 1985.
3. Lennart Augustsson and Magnus Carlsson. An exercise in dependent types: A well-typed interpreter. `http://www.cs.chalmers.se/ augustss/cayenne/`, 1999.
4. Stefano Berardi. Pruning simply typed lambda terms. *Journal of Logic and Computation*, 6(5):663–681, 1996.

5. U. Berger and H. Schwichtenberg. An inverse of the evaluation functional for typed λ-calculus. In R. Vemuri, editor, *Proceedings of the Sixth Annual IEEE Symposium on Logic in Computer Science*, pages 203–211. IEEE Computer Society Press, 1991.
6. Ana Bove and Venanzio Capretta. Modelling general recursion in type theory, September 2002.
7. Paul Callaghan and Zhaohui Luo. Implementation techniques for inductive types in plastic. In Bengt Nordström Thierry Coquand, Peter Dybjer and Jan Smith, editors, *Types for Proofs and Programs*, volume 1956 of *LNCS*, pages 94–113. Springer-Verlag, 1999.
8. Coq Development Team. The Coq proof assistant — reference manual, 2001.
9. André Luís de Medeiros Santos. *Compilation By Transformation In Non-Strict Functional Languages*. PhD thesis, University of Glasgow, 1995.
10. Peter Dybjer. Inductive families. *Formal Aspects Of Computing*, 6:440–465, 1994.
11. Robert Harper and Randy Pollack. Type checking with universes. *Theoretical Computer Science*, 89(1):107–136, 1991.
12. Thomas Johnsson. Efficient compilation of lazy evaluation, 1984.
13. Pierre Letouzey. A new extraction for Coq. In Herman Geuvers and Freek Wiedijk, editors, *Types for proofs and programs*, volume 2646 of *LNCS*. Springer-Verlag, 2002.
14. Zhaohui Luo. *Computation and Reasoning – A Type Theory for Computer Science*. International Series of Monographs on Computer Science. OUP, 1994.
15. Zhaohui Luo and Robert Pollack. LEGO proof development system: User's manual. Technical report, LFCS, University of Edinburgh, 1992.
16. Nicolas Magaud and Yves Bertot. Changing data structures in type theory: A study of natural numbers. volume 2277 of *LNCS*, pages 181–196. Springer-Verlag, 2000.
17. Lena Magnusson. *The implementation of ALF – A Proof Editor based on Martin-Löf's Monomorphic Type Theory with Explicit Substitutions*. PhD thesis, Chalmers University of Technology, Göteborg, 1994.
18. Conor McBride. *Dependently Typed Functional Programs and their proofs*. PhD thesis, University of Edinburgh, May 2000.
19. Conor McBride and James McKinna. The view from the left. *Journal of Functional Programming*, 14(1), 2004.
20. Fred McBride. *Computer Aided Manipulation of Symbols*. PhD thesis, Queen's University of Belfast, 1970.
21. Christine Paulin-Mohring. *Extraction de programmes dans le Calcul des Constructions*. PhD thesis, Paris 7, 1989.
22. Simon L. Peyton Jones and André L. M. Santos. A transformation-based optimiser for Haskell. *Science of Computer Programming*, 32:3–47, 1998.
23. Randy Pollack. Implicit syntax. Technical report, LFCS, University of Edinburgh, 1992.
24. Patrick M. Sansom and Simon L. Peyton Jones. Time and space profiling for non-strict, higher order functional languages, 1995.
25. Hongwei Xi. *Dependent Types in Practical Programming*. PhD thesis, Department of Mathematical Sciences, Carnegie Mellon University, December 1998.
26. Hongwei Xi. Dead code elimination through dependent types, 1999.
27. Hongwei Xi and Frank Pfenning. Eliminating array bound checking through dependent types, 1998.

Modules in Coq Are and Will Be Correct

Jacek Chrząszcz

Institute of Informatics, Warsaw University
ul. Banacha 2, 02-097 Warszawa, Poland
chrzaszcz@mimuw.edu.pl

Abstract. The paper presents the system of named modules implemented in Coq version 7.4 and shows that this extension is conservative. It is also shown that the implemented module system is ready for the future planned extension of Coq with definitions of functions by means of rewrite rules. More precisely, the impact of the module system on the acceptance criterion for rewrite rules is carefully studied, leading to the formulation of four closure properties that have to be satisfied by the acceptance criterion in order to validate the conservativity proof. It turns out that syntactic termination criteria such as Higher Order Recursive Path Ordering or the General Schema can be adapted to satisfy these closure properties.

1 Introduction

Computer aided theorem proving has become an important part of modern theoretical computer science. Various proof assistants gain more and more popularity and industrial size problems begin to be addressed. To become applicable in the industry, such systems must provide ways to structure large developments and a high degree of automation.

In this paper, we concentrate on the Coq proof assistant [5], a system that is based on the so-called Curry-Howard isomorphism, relating logical formulas to types and their proofs to terms inhabiting these types. The logical formalism implemented in Coq is an extension of the calculus of constructions of Coquand and Huet [7] with inductive types [8] and a predicative hierarchy of universes [14]. Coq is actively developed for more than 10 years now and is used both for fomalizing mathematics (for example the fundamental theorem of algebra) and for program verification (data structures, telecommunication protocols, Javacard platform etc.)

In order to address the large development issues, proof developments in Coq may be divided into files and an ML-style module system has recently been implemented [3]. The latter allows clear modelisation of parametrized theories and certified data structures and their convenient instantiation, therefore encouraging proof reuse.

The automation issues are being addressed by various tactics, but the main show-stopper is the treatment of equations. Even though equational reasoning is so common in mathematics it is still quite difficult to use it in Coq, especially

S. Berardi, M. Coppo, and F. Damiani (Eds.): TYPES 2003, LNCS 3085, pp. 130–146, 2004.

compared to its competitors such as Isabelle [16] or PVS [15]. For that reason the inclusion of an efficient term rewriting engine is also planned for Coq.

In order to make rewriting as efficient as possible it is desirable to include it in the internal conversion relation of Coq. In this way, arbitrarily long reduction sequences would result in very small proof-terms. The other possibility of using rewriting based on the Leibniz equality is much more space- and time-consuming, as each rewriting step generates a fragment of the proof-term proportional to the size of the original goal.

Since the logical correctness of Coq depends on good metatheoretical properties of conversion, like confluence and strong normalization of reduction rules, we have to preserve these properties when extending conversion with user-defined rewrite rules. Since these properties of term rewriting systems are undecidable in general, the research in this area concentrates on incomplete acceptance criteria that guarantee termination and confluence and are flexible enough to accept most rewriting systems already known to be terminating and confluent [1,18].

The goal of this paper is to prove that the modular extension of Coq is conservative and that it will remain so after rewriting is added to Coq. We study the impact of the module system on acceptance criteria for rewrite rules and formulate closure properties that have to be satisfied by the criteria in order to make the conservativity proof work. The closure properties turn out to be compatible with syntactic acceptance criteria available in the literature.

In the type theory setting ML-style modules were first introduced in 1992 in the LF logical framework [12]. Later Courant [9,10] proposed a module calculus suitable for pure type systems, an example of which is the calculus of constructions and many other known type theories. In the calculus of Courant modules are second-class anonymous objects, reductions on modules have subject reduction and termination properties and therefore the modular extension of a given pure type system is conservative.[1] Thanks to the consequent use of module interfaces, Courant's module calculus allows smooth composition of libraries, separate checking of dependent parts of large proof developments and guarantees correctness of proofs upon a conservative upgrade of their components.

Unfortunately, given currently available acceptance criteria, definitions by rewriting cannot be integrated in the calculus of anonymous modules. Indeed, reductions on modules would impose very strong closure properties on acceptance criteria, such as closure by arbitrary substitutions, which does not hold for any of the available acceptance criteria.

The module system implemented in Coq is therefore a syntactic restriction of the calculus of Courant, allowing to use existing acceptance criteria for rewrite rules, without sacrificing good properties of the module system mentioned above. The proof of conservativity is changed accordingly: instead of relying on arbitrary reductions on anonymous modules we chose a particular reduction strategy preserving syntactic constraints, trying to make closure properties imposed on acceptance criteria as weak as possible.

[1] Courant also writes that his proof would still be valid if anonymous inductive types were added to the pure type system.

We start our presentation by formalizing pure type systems with generative definitions, a compromise between anonymous inductive types and global rewriting systems. On one hand, in theoretical papers inductive types are usually treated as anonymous entities [8,20], even though in Coq they are implemented as named. On the other hand, rewriting is usually given in a form of one global rewriting system which is treated as a parameter of typing rules. This approach is of course incompatible with interactive proof assistant, where users are used to construct their proofs and definitions gradually. However, known syntactic acceptance criteria are modular and allow to extend the global set of rewrite rules by entering one accepted rewriting system after another.

In our formalism, definitions by rewriting and inductive definitions are entered in the global environment, and they can be accessed in terms through the names assigned to them by the environment.

Next, this formalism is extended with a system of named modules and the generative definitions now become part of modules and module interfaces. We show, that a potential proof of `False` in the calculus with modules can be transformed into a proof of `False` in the calculus without modules. The closure properties on acceptance criteria for definitions by rewriting result from the analysis of this transformation. We conclude the paper by an argument that these properties are satisfiable.

2 Pure Type Systems with Generative Definitions

We present here a formalization of a pure type system with generative inductive definitions and generative definitions by rewriting, which is quite close to the way these elements are and will be implemented in Coq. The formalism is built upon a set of PTS sorts $\mathcal{S}$, a binary relation $\mathcal{A}$ and a ternary relation $\mathcal{R}$ over $\mathcal{S}$ governing the typing rules **(Term/Ax)** and **(Term/Prod)** respectively (Fig. 4). The syntactic class of pseudoterms is defined as follows:

$$e, t ::= v \mid \mathrm{s} \mid (e_1\ e_2) \mid \lambda v{:}t.\, e \mid \Pi v{:}t_1.\, t_2$$

The difference between e and t is only intuitive, to help the reader distinguish between a role of a term e and a type t, but both these letters denote elements of the syntactic class of pseudoterms. A pseudoterm can be a variable, a sort from $\mathcal{S}$, an application, an abstraction or a product.

Inductive definitions and definitions by rewriting are stored in the environment and used in terms only through names assigned to them by the environment. Therefore an environment is a sequence of declarations, each of them being a constant definition $v : t := e$, a variable declaration $v : t$, an inductive definition $\mathsf{IndDef}(E^I := E^C)$, where E^C and E^I are environments of (possibly mutually defined) inductive types and their constructors, or a definition by rewriting $\mathsf{RewDef}(E^\Gamma, R)$, where E^Γ is an environment of (possibly mutually defined) function symbols and R is a set of rewrite rules defining them. Environments E^I, E^C in inductive definitions and E^Γ in definitions by rewriting contain only variable declarations. We assume that names of all declarations in environments are pairwise disjoint.

Definition 1. *A* pure type system with generative definitions *is defined by the typing rules in Fig. 1, 2, 3 and 4. The relation* $\approx$ *used in the rule* **(Term/Conv)** *is the congruence generated by the sum of beta, delta and rewrite reductions.*

As in [2,19] elimination of inductive types is supposed to be expressed by rewriting.

The rules for correctness of definitions contain side-conditions. The side conditions $\mathsf{POS}_E(E^I := E^C)$ stands for a positivity condition on inductive definitions as given for example in [8,20]. The condition $\mathsf{ACC}_E(E^\Gamma, R)$ stands for an acceptance condition as given for example in [2,19]. Both conditions are meant to assure the decidability of type-checking in any correct environment.

Consider the following sequence of declarations in the Coq-like syntax:[2]

```
Inductive  nat : Set  :=  O : nat | S : nat → nat.
Symbol plus : nat → nat → nat
  Rules
    plus O y    ⟶  y
    plus (S x) y ⟶ S (plus x y)
    plus x (plus y z) ⟶ plus (plus x y) z
    plus x O    ⟶  x
    plus x (S y) ⟶ S (plus x y).
Definition two : nat := plus (S O) (S O).
Parameter n : nat.
```

It can be interpreted as an environment E consisting of the inductive definition of natural numbers, symmetric definition by rewriting of addition, the definition of the constant two and the declaration of a variable n of type *nat*. Assuming that the definition of natural numbers satisfies the condition $\mathsf{POS}()$ and the definition of addition satisfies the condition $\mathsf{ACC}()$, we can derive the judgment $E \vdash \mathtt{ok}$ using the rules in Fig. 1.

The definition of logical consistency for a calculus with generative definitions has to be more involved that the usual requirement that `False` is not inhabited in the empty environment. Indeed, the latter formulation does not account for generative definitions at all. Therefore we define logical consistency by the requirement that `False` is not inhabited in any *closed* environment, i.e. an environment without variable declarations and where all functions are total.

The requirement that functions defined by rewriting are total could very well be included in the condition $\mathsf{ACC}()$. However, we decided to assume the existence of a separate condition on definitions by rewriting, called $\mathsf{COMP}_E(E^\Gamma, R)$ for *completeness*, that is satisfied only if all functions from E^Γ are total, i.e. completely defined by R in the environment E.

The separation between $\mathsf{ACC}()$ and $\mathsf{COMP}()$ is motivated by the idea of working with abstract function symbols, equipped with some rewrite rules not defining them completely. For example if *plus* were declared using only the third rule from the system give above, we could develop a theory of an associative

[2] The syntax of the definition by rewriting is inspired by the experimental "Rewriting" branch of Coq developed by Blanqui. For the sake of clarity we omit certain details, like the environment of rule variables.

$$\frac{}{\epsilon \vdash \mathsf{ok}}$$

$$\frac{E \vdash \mathsf{ok} \quad E \vdash t : \mathrm{s}}{E; v : t \vdash \mathsf{ok}} \qquad \frac{E \vdash \mathsf{ok} \quad E \vdash t : \mathrm{s} \quad E \vdash e : t}{E; v : t := e \vdash \mathsf{ok}}$$

$$\frac{E \vdash \mathsf{ok} \quad E \vdash \mathsf{IndDef}(E^I := E^C) : \mathsf{correct}}{E; \mathsf{IndDef}(E^I := E^C) \vdash \mathsf{ok}} \qquad \frac{E \vdash \mathsf{ok} \quad E \vdash \mathsf{RewDef}(E^\Gamma, R) : \mathsf{correct}}{E; \mathsf{RewDef}(E^\Gamma, R) \vdash \mathsf{ok}}$$

Fig. 1. Environment correctness

Let $E^I = v_1^I : t_1^I \dots v_k^I : t_k^I$ and $E^C = v_1^C : t_1^C \dots v_n^C : t_n^C$

$$\frac{E \vdash t_j^I : \mathrm{s}_j \text{ for } j = 1 \dots k \qquad E; E^I \vdash t_i^C : \mathrm{s}_i' \text{ for } i = 1 \dots n}{E \vdash \mathsf{IndDef}(E^I := E^C) : \mathsf{correct}} \text{ if } \mathsf{POS}_E(E^I := E^C)$$

Let $E^\Gamma = v_1 : t_1 \dots v_n : t_n$ and $R = \{E_i : e_i^L \longrightarrow e_i^R : \hat{t}_i\}_{i=1\dots m}$, where $E_i = v_1^i : t_1^i; \dots ; v_{n_i}^i : t_{n_i}^i$

$$\frac{E \vdash t_k : \mathrm{s}_k \quad \text{for } k = 1 \dots n \qquad \left.\begin{matrix} E; E_i \vdash \mathsf{ok} & E; E^\Gamma; E_i \vdash \hat{t}_i : \hat{s}_i \\ E; E^\Gamma; E_i \vdash e_i^L : \hat{t}_i & E; E^\Gamma; E_i \vdash e_i^R : \hat{t}_i \end{matrix}\right\} \text{for } i = 1 \dots m}{E \vdash \mathsf{RewDef}(E^\Gamma, R) : \mathsf{correct}} \text{ if } \mathsf{ACC}_E(E^\Gamma, R)$$

Fig. 2. Correctness of definitions

$$\frac{E_1; v : t; E_2 \vdash \mathsf{ok}}{E_1; v : t; E_2 \vdash v : t} \qquad \frac{E_1; v : t := e; E_2 \vdash \mathsf{ok}}{E_1; v : t := e; E_2 \vdash v : t} \qquad \frac{E_1; v : t := e; E_2 \vdash \mathsf{ok}}{E_1; v : t := e; E_2 \vdash v \longrightarrow_\delta e}$$

$$\frac{E \vdash \mathsf{ok}}{E \vdash v_i^I : t_i^I} \qquad \frac{E \vdash \mathsf{ok}}{E \vdash v_i^C : t_i^C} \qquad \text{where } \begin{cases} E = E_1; \mathsf{IndDef}(E^I := E^C); E_2 \\ E^I = v_1^I : t_1^I \dots v_n^I : t_n^I \\ E^C = v_1^C : t_1^C \dots v_n^C : t_n^C \end{cases}$$

$$\frac{E \vdash \mathsf{ok}}{E \vdash v_i : t_i} \qquad \frac{E \vdash \mathsf{ok} \quad \delta : E_i \to E}{E \vdash e_i^L \delta \longrightarrow_R e_i^R \delta} \qquad \text{where } \begin{cases} E = E_1; \mathsf{RewDef}(E^\Gamma, R); E_2 \\ E^\Gamma = v_1 : t_1 \dots v_n : t_n \\ R = \{E_i : e_i^L \longrightarrow e_i^R : \hat{t}_i\}_{i=1\dots m} \end{cases}$$

The notation $\delta : E_i \to E$ means $E \vdash v\delta : t\delta$ for all $v : t \in E_i$

Fig. 3. Enviroment lookup

(Term/Prod)
$$\frac{E \vdash t_1 : \mathrm{s}_1 \quad E; v : t_1 \vdash t_2 : \mathrm{s}_2}{E \vdash \Pi v{:}t_1.\, t_2 : \mathrm{s}_3}$$
where $(\mathrm{s}_1, \mathrm{s}_2, \mathrm{s}_3) \in \mathcal{R}$

(Term/Abs)
$$\frac{E; v : t_1 \vdash e : t_2 \quad E \vdash \Pi v{:}t_1.\, t_2 : \mathrm{s}}{E \vdash \lambda v{:}t_1.\, e : \Pi v{:}t_1.\, t_2}$$

(Term/Ax)
$$\frac{E \vdash \mathsf{ok}}{E \vdash \mathrm{s}_1 : \mathrm{s}_2}$$
where $(\mathrm{s}_1, \mathrm{s}_2) \in \mathcal{A}$

(Term/App)
$$\frac{E \vdash e : \Pi v{:}t_1.\, t_2 \quad E \vdash e' : t_1}{E \vdash e\, e' : t_2\{v \mapsto e'\}}$$

(Term/Conv)
$$\frac{E \vdash e : t \quad E \vdash t' : \mathrm{s} \quad E \vdash t \approx t'}{E \vdash e : t'}$$

Fig. 4. PTS rules

function over natural numbers. The usefulness of abstract functions equipped with rewrite rules will become clearer after the introduction of modules, because they will allow us to instantiate abstract elements with concrete ones.

Definition 2. *A correct environment E is* closed *if it contains no variable declarations and if all definitions by rewriting are complete, i.e. every time E can be split into $E_1; \mathsf{RewDef}(E^\Gamma, R); E_2$ the condition $\mathsf{COMP}_{E_1}(E^\Gamma, R)$ is satisfied.*

Definition 3. *A pure type system with generative definitions is* logically consistent *if* `False` *is not inhabited in any closed environment.*

Summarizing, conditions $\mathsf{ACC}()$ and $\mathsf{POS}()$ are supposed to guarantee that typing in every correct environment is decidable and $\mathsf{COMP}()$ is supposed to guarantee that `False` is not provable in any closed environment.

The problem of consistency for the calculus of constructions with rewriting has not been very well studied yet. The only condition that we know that guarantees consistency is given in [2]. Please see the discussion of this question at the end of Sect. 5.

3 Calculus of Named Modules

In this section we define a calculus built on top of a pure type system, containing inductive definitions, definitions by rewriting and a system of named modules. The latter is an adaptation of an ML-style module system with the following usual features:

Structures bundle together related definitions and lemmas. They correspond to records.

Signatures – module types of structures – play the role of interfaces. They correspond to record types with manifest fields [13,11].

Functors are parametric modules. Their application to modules makes instantiation very convenient. They correspond to dependent functions.

Functor types – module types of functors – correspond to dependent products.

Higher order functors are functors taking parameters which are themselves functors.

Subtyping allows to apply functors to modules with more components. It is monotone for signatures and contravariant in the argument type and covariant in the result type for functor types.

Nested modules – modules can be components of stuctures and signatures.

The reader is invited to consult Sect. 1.5.1 of [4] for simple examples of all these features. Below we present the details of the calculus of named modules. We deliberately ignore the problem of name clashes in nested structures and signatures, referring the reader to [4] again for details.

Access paths	p	$::= v \mid p.v$
Terms	e, t	$::= p \mid s \mid (e_1\ e_2) \mid \lambda v{:}t.\, e \mid \Pi v{:}t_1.\, t_2$
Blocks	B	$::= \overline{p}$ — $\mathsf{Rew}(E^{\Gamma}, R)$ — $\mathsf{Ind}(E^I := E^C)$
Block types	BT	$::= \mathsf{RewSpec}(E^{\Gamma}, R)$ — $\mathsf{IndSpec}(E^I := E^C)$
Rewriting systems	R	$::= E_1 : l_1 \longrightarrow r_1 : t_1 \ldots E_n : l_n \longrightarrow r_n : t_n$
Modules		
	m	$::= p \mid \mathsf{Struct}\ \overline{v}_1 : S_1 := P_1 \ldots \overline{v}_n : S_n := P_n\ \mathsf{End} \mid \mathsf{Functor}[v{:}M]\ m \mid (p_1\ p_2)$
Module types	M	$::= \mathsf{Sig}\ \overline{v}_1 : S_1 \ldots \overline{v}_n : S_n\ \mathsf{End} \mid \mathsf{Funsig}(v{:}M_1)\ M_2$
Implementations	P	$::= e \mid B \mid m$
Specifications	S	$::= \mathsf{Ty}(t) \mid \mathsf{Eq}(e : t) \mid \mathsf{Ty}(BT) \mid \mathsf{Eq}(\overline{p} : BT) \mid \mathsf{Ty}(M) \mid \mathsf{Eq}(p : M)$
Specification sorts	SS	$::=$ `modtype` | `blocktype` | `spec`
Environments	E	$::= \epsilon \mid \overline{v}_1 : S_1 \ldots \overline{v}_n : S_n$

Fig. 5. Syntax

Specifications. In order to avoid giving many sets of similar rules, for example for extracting information from the environment and for extracting information from module signatures, we decided (after Courant) to introduce the auxiliary notion of specifications. They allow to factorize extraction rules into one rule for extracting a specification from the environment, one rule for extracting a specification from a signature and one set of rules to extract information from a specification. Specifications are also used to factorize rules for environment creation, typing rules for structures and subtyping rules for signatures.

There are two kinds of specifications: abstract $\mathsf{Ty}(\Phi)$ and manifest $\mathsf{Eq}(\psi : \Phi)$. Using specifications, a variable declaration is written $v : \mathsf{Ty}(\Phi)$, which means that v has type Φ, and a constant declaration is written $v : \mathsf{Eq}(\psi : \Phi)$, meaning that v is of type Φ and equal to ψ.

This way an environment can be uniformly presented as an assignment of specifications to names. Inductive definitions and definitions by rewriting are also tailored to match this framework, but this will be explained later.

Structures and Signatures. From the point of view of typing, signatures correspond to fragments of correct environments (see the rule **(Sig/Form)** in Fig. 7) and structures correspond to fragments of closed environments.

Like environments, signatures assign specifications to names. Structures assign specifications and implementations to names. The typing rule for structures **(Sig/Struct)** explains the role of these elements: every implementation satisfies its corresponding specification, but implementations are not used to type-check subsequent components.

This gives us a nice way to formally distinguish between lemmas with proofs and definitions of constants. A lemma is represented as a triple $v : \mathsf{Ty}(t) := e$ where v is its name, t its formulation and e its proof, which is not used to type subsequent components. A constant definition is a triple $v : Eq(e : t) := e$, where the equality $v \approx e$ can be deduced from its specification and hence used to type subsequent components. Even though the necessity of duplicating e may look strange, advantages of using specifications are worth it.

Blocks and Block Types. Apart from lemmas and constant definitions, structures can also contain inductive definitions and definitions by rewriting (and also modules themselves). Suppose m is a structure containing the first three definitions given in Sect. 2, i.e. the inductive definition of natural numbers, the function *plus* defined by rewriting and the definition of *two*. If we bind m to a name, say A, we expect to be able to use the elements of m, prefixed by A. In particular $A.O$ and $A.S$ should both be constructors of the inductive type $A.nat$ and the rewrite rule $A.plus\ A.O\ x \longrightarrow x$ should be available in the conversion.

Since we want our module system to allow separate checking of modules, the extraction of information from modules should be based on module types and not on module expressions. Therefore it is necessary to put information about inductive definitions and definitions by rewriting inside signatures. In order to enforce the parallel between structures and closed environments, rewriting in structures should be subject to both $\mathsf{ACC}()$ and $\mathsf{COMP}()$ conditions, and rewriting in signatures — just to $\mathsf{ACC}()$.

This is exactly the case in our system. We decided to split $\mathsf{RewDef}(E^{\Gamma}, R)$ into two constructions $\mathsf{RewSpec}(E^{\Gamma}, R)$ and $\mathsf{Rew}(E^{\Gamma}, R)$, the first being an element of specifications and subject to the condition $\mathsf{ACC}(E^{\Gamma}, R)$, and the latter an implementation and subject to the condition $\mathsf{COMP}(E^{\Gamma}, R)$ (see rules **(RewSpec/Form)** and **(RewSpec/Rew)** in Fig. 10).

The reason why the syntactic class of specifications does not directly contain $\mathsf{RewSpec}(E^{\Gamma}, R)$ comes from considering the operation of module renaming:

```
Module B:=A.
```

After that operation, the module type of B should reflect both the fact that the *plus* component is a symbol defined by rewriting and the fact that it is equal to *A.plus*. Since we want to have the principal types property for module types, we decided to wrap $\mathsf{RewSpec}(E^{\Gamma}, R)$ into specifications $\mathsf{Ty}()$ and $\mathsf{Eq}()$.

Inductive definitions are treated similarly: we also split $\mathsf{IndDef}(E^{I} := E^{C})$ into $\mathsf{IndSpec}(E^{I} := E^{C})$ and $\mathsf{Ind}(E^{I} := E^{C})$, but the rule **(IndSpec/Ind)** for typing $\mathsf{Ind}(E^{I} := E^{C})$, has no additional side-condition compared to the rule **(IndSpec/Form)** from Fig. 9.

Note that inductive definitions and definitions by rewriting both have a potential to mutually define many symbols. Therefore we decided to create a new syntactic class of *blocks*, denoting a possibly mutually defined sequence of terms. There is also a whole typing hierarchy for blocks. Next to terms, types, sorts and term specifications, we introduce blocks, block types, the sort `blocktype` and block specifications. A similar hierarchy is also available for modules: there are module expressions, module types, the sort `modtype` and module specifications.

Note that the rules **(IndSpec/Form)** and **(RewSpec/Form)**, correspond to rules from Fig. 2 and a sequence **(Ty/Form)** or **(Eq/Form)** followed by **(Env/Insert)** corresponds to environment insertion rules from

(Env/Empty)	(Env/Insert)	(Env/Lookup)
$\dfrac{}{\epsilon \vdash \mathsf{ok}}$	$\dfrac{E \vdash \mathsf{ok} \quad E \vdash S : \mathsf{spec}}{E; \overline{v} : S \vdash \mathsf{ok}}$	$\dfrac{E_1; \overline{v} : S; E_2 \vdash \mathsf{ok}}{E_1; \overline{v} : S; E_2 \vdash \overline{v} : S}$

Fig. 6. Environment

Fig. 1. Similarly, a sequence **(Env/Lookup)**, followed by **(Ty/Type)** or **(Eq/Type)** or **(Eq/Comp)**, followed optionally by **(IndSpec/IndType)**, **(IndSpec/Constr)**, **(RewSpec/Fun)** or the rule **(RewSpec/Comp)** correspond to environment lookup rules from Fig. 3.

Calculus of Named Modules. Our calculus contains a module system which is a syntactic restriction of the module calculus of Courant. Indeed, the syntactic class of terms does not contain the general selection operator $m.v$, where m is a module expression, but only its restriction to so-called access paths [13]. The same restriction also appears in module and block manifest specifications and in module application.

Definition 4. *The* Calculus of Named Modules *is defined by the typing rules on Fig. 4,*[3] *6, 7, 8, 9, 10 and 11.*[4] *The relation* $\approx$ *appearing in the premises of the rules* **(Term/Conv)** *and* **(Block/Conv)** *is the congruence defined by beta reduction and rules* **(Eq/Comp)** *and* **(RewSpec/Comp)**.

4 Examples

Now we can show the representation expressed in our formal abstract syntax of the binding `Module A:=`m, where m is the structure mentioned in the previous section:

$$
\begin{array}{l}
A : \mathsf{Ty}(\ldots) := \mathsf{Struct} \\
\qquad \begin{array}{rcl}
nat, O, S & : \mathsf{Ty}(\mathsf{IndSpec}(E^I_{nat} := E^C_{nat})) & := \mathsf{Ind}(E^I_{nat} := E^C_{nat}) \\
plus & : \mathsf{Ty}(\mathsf{RewSpec}(E^\Gamma_{nat}, R_{nat})) & := \mathsf{Rew}(E^\Gamma_{plus}, R_{plus}) \\
two & : \mathsf{Eq}(plus\ (S\ O)\ (S\ O) : nat) & := plus\ (S\ O)\ (S\ O)
\end{array} \\
\mathsf{End}
\end{array}
$$

where $E^I_{nat} = nat : \mathsf{Ty}(\mathtt{Set})$, $E^C_{nat} = O : \mathsf{Ty}(nat); S : \mathsf{Ty}(nat \to nat)$, $E^\Gamma_{plus} = plus : \mathsf{Ty}(nat \to nat \to nat)$ and R_{plus} is the system with 5 rules from Sect. 2. Note that nat (and other names as well) appears three times here: first as a name of a structure component, second as a local binder inside $\mathsf{IndSpec}(E^I_{nat} := E^C_{nat})$ and third as a local binder inside $\mathsf{Ind}(E^I_{nat} := E^C_{nat})$. Again, the duplication here is only needed to make the presentation with specifications possible.

[3] To be 100% formal, in the premises of rules **(Term/Prod)** and **(Term/Abs)** the environment should be written $E; v : \mathsf{Ty}(t_1)$.

[4] The framed rules form a subsystem called *principal*, which is used in Sect. 5.

(Sig/Form)
$$\frac{E;\overline{v}_1 : S_1 \ldots \overline{v}_n : S_n \vdash \mathsf{ok}}{E \vdash \mathsf{Sig}\ \overline{v}_1 : S_1 \ldots \overline{v}_n : S_n\ \mathsf{End} : \mathtt{modtype}}$$

(Sig/Access)
$$\frac{E \vdash p : \mathsf{Sig}\ \overline{v}_1 : S_1 \ldots \overline{v}_n : S_n\ \mathsf{End}}{E \vdash \overline{p.v_k} : S_k\{\overline{v}_i \mapsto \overline{p.v_i}\}_{i=1\ldots k-1}}$$

(Sig/Struct)
$$\frac{E \vdash \mathsf{Sig}\ \overline{v}_1 : S_1 \ldots \overline{v}_n : S_n\ \mathsf{End} : \mathtt{modtype} \qquad E;\overline{v}_1 : S_1 \ldots \overline{v}_{k-1} : S_{k-1} \vdash P_k : S_k \text{ for } k = 1 \ldots n}{E \vdash \mathsf{Struct}\ \overline{v}_1 : S_1 := P_1 \ldots \overline{v}_n : S_n := P_n\ \mathsf{End} : \mathsf{Sig}\ \overline{v}_1 : S_1 \ldots \overline{v}_n : S_n\ \mathsf{End}}$$

(Sig/Sub)
$$\frac{E \vdash \mathsf{Sig}\ \overline{v}_1 : S_1 \ldots \overline{v}_n : S_n\ \mathsf{End} : \mathtt{modtype} \qquad E \vdash \mathsf{Sig}\ \overline{v}'_1 : S'_1 \ldots \overline{v}'_{n'} : S'_{n'}\ \mathsf{End} : \mathtt{modtype} \qquad E;\overline{v}_1 : S_1 \ldots \overline{v}_n : S_n \vdash \overline{v}'_k : S'_k \text{ for } k = 1 \ldots n'}{E \vdash \mathsf{Sig}\ \overline{v}_1 : S_1 \ldots \overline{v}_n : S_n\ \mathsf{End} <: \mathsf{Sig}\ \overline{v}'_1 : S'_1 \ldots \overline{v}'_{n'} : S'_{n'}\ \mathsf{End}}$$

(Funsig/Form)
$$\frac{E \vdash M_1 : \mathtt{modtype} \qquad E; v : \mathsf{Ty}(M_1) \vdash M_2 : \mathtt{modtype}}{E \vdash \mathsf{Funsig}(v{:}M_1)\ M_2 : \mathtt{modtype}}$$

(Funsig/Functor)
$$\frac{E; v : \mathsf{Ty}(M_1) \vdash m : M_2 \qquad E \vdash \mathsf{Funsig}(v{:}M_1)\ M_2 : \mathtt{modtype}}{E \vdash \mathsf{Functor}[v{:}M_1]\ m : \mathsf{Funsig}(v{:}M_1) M_2}$$

(Funsig/Sub)
$$\frac{E \vdash M'_1 <: M_1 \qquad E; v : \mathsf{Ty}(M'_1) \vdash M_2 <: M'_2}{E \vdash \mathsf{Funsig}(v{:}M_1)\ M_2 <: \mathsf{Funsig}(v{:}M'_1)\ M'_2}$$

(Mod/App)
$$\frac{E \vdash p : \mathsf{Funsig}(v : M_1)\ M_2 \qquad E \vdash p' : M_1}{E \vdash p\ p' : M_2\{v \mapsto p'\}}$$

(Subsumption)
$$\frac{E \vdash m : M_1 \qquad E \vdash M_1 <: M_2}{E \vdash m : M_2}$$

(Strengthenning)
$$\frac{E \vdash p : M \qquad E \vdash M : \mathtt{modtype}}{E \vdash p : M/p}$$

$$\begin{aligned}
\mathsf{Sig}\ \overline{v}_1 : S_1 \ldots \overline{v}_n : S_n\ \mathsf{End}/p &= \mathsf{Sig}\ \overline{v}_1 : S_1/\overline{p.v_1}; \ldots ; \overline{v}_n : S_n/\overline{p.v_n}\ \mathsf{End} \\
(\mathsf{Funsig}(v{:}M_1)\ M_2)/p &= \mathsf{Funsig}(v{:}M_1)\ M_2
\end{aligned}$$

$$\begin{aligned}
\mathsf{Ty}(t)/p &= \mathsf{Eq}(p : t) & \mathsf{Eq}(e' : t)/p &= \mathsf{Eq}(e' : t) \\
\mathsf{Ty}(BT)/\overline{p} &= \mathsf{Eq}(\overline{p} : BT) & \mathsf{Eq}(\overline{p}' : BT)/\overline{p} &= \mathsf{Eq}(\overline{p}' : BT) \\
\mathsf{Ty}(M)/p &= \mathsf{Eq}(p : M/p) & \mathsf{Eq}(p' : M)/p &= \mathsf{Eq}(p' : M/p)
\end{aligned}$$

Fig. 7. Modules

Symbols ϕ, Ψ, Ξ are either e, t, s, or $p, M, \mathtt{modtype}$, or $\overline{p}, BT, \mathtt{blocktype}$.

(Ty/Form)
$$\frac{E \vdash \Psi : \Xi}{E \vdash \mathsf{Ty}(\Psi) : \mathsf{spec}}$$

(Ty/Sat)
$$\frac{E \vdash P : \Psi \qquad E \vdash \mathsf{Ty}(\Psi) : \mathsf{spec}}{E \vdash P : \mathsf{Ty}(\Psi)}$$

(Ty/Type)
$$\frac{E \vdash P : \mathsf{Ty}(\Psi)}{E \vdash P : \Psi}$$

(Eq/Form)
$$\frac{E \vdash \phi : \Psi \qquad E \vdash \Psi : \Xi}{E \vdash \mathsf{Eq}(\phi : \Psi) : \mathsf{spec}}$$

(Eq/Sat)
$$\frac{E \vdash P \approx \phi \qquad E \vdash P : \Psi \qquad E \vdash \mathsf{Eq}(\phi : \Psi) : \mathsf{spec}}{E \vdash P : \mathsf{Eq}(\phi : \Psi)}$$

(Eq/Type)
$$\frac{E \vdash P : \mathsf{Eq}(\phi : \Psi)}{E \vdash P : \Psi}$$

(Eq/Comp)
$$\frac{E \vdash P : \mathsf{Eq}(\phi : \Psi)}{E \vdash P \approx \phi}$$

Fig. 8. Specifications

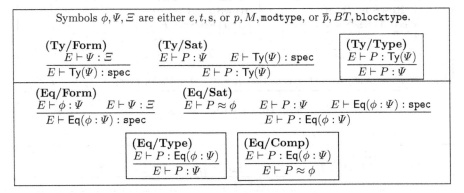

Let $E^I = v_1^I : \mathsf{Ty}(t_1^I) \dots v_k^I : \mathsf{Ty}(t_k^I)$ and $E^C = v_1^C : \mathsf{Ty}(t_1^C) \dots v_n^C : \mathsf{Ty}(t_n^C)$

(IndSpec/Form)

$$\frac{E \vdash t_j^I : \mathrm{s}_j \text{ for } j = 1 \dots k \qquad E; E^I \vdash t_i^C : \mathrm{s}_i' \text{ for } i = 1 \dots n}{E \vdash \mathsf{IndSpec}(E^I := E^C) : \mathtt{blocktype}}$$

if $\mathsf{POS}_E(E^I := E^C)$

(IndSpec/Ind)

$$\frac{E \vdash \mathsf{IndSpec}(E^I := E^C) : \mathtt{blocktype}}{E \vdash \mathsf{Ind}(E^I := E^C) : \mathsf{IndSpec}(E^I := E^C)}$$

(IndSpec/IndType)

$$\frac{E \vdash \overline{p} : \mathsf{IndSpec}(E^I := E^C)}{E \vdash p^j : t_j^I}$$

if $j \in \{1 \dots k\}$

(IndSpec/Constr)

$$\frac{E \vdash \overline{p} : \mathsf{IndSpec}(E^I := E^C)}{E \vdash p^{k+i} : t_i^C\{v_j^I \mapsto p^j\}_{j=1\dots k}}$$

if $i \in \{1 \dots n\}$

Fig. 9. Inductive blocks

Let $E^\Gamma = v_1 : \mathsf{Ty}(t_1) \dots v_n : \mathsf{Ty}(t_n)$ and

$R = \{E_i : e_i^L \longrightarrow e_i^R : \hat{t}_i\}_{i=1\dots m}$, where $E_i = v_1^i : \mathsf{Ty}(t_1^i); \dots ; v_{n_i}^i : \mathsf{Ty}(t_{n_i}^i)$

(RewSpec/Form)

$$\frac{E \vdash t_k : \mathrm{s}_k \quad \text{for } k = 1 \dots n \qquad \left.\begin{array}{ll} E; E_i \vdash \mathsf{ok} & E; E^\Gamma; E_i \vdash \hat{t}_i : \hat{s}_i \\ E; E^\Gamma; E_i \vdash e_i^L : \hat{t}_i & E; E^\Gamma; E_i \vdash e_i^R : \hat{t}_i \end{array}\right\} \text{for } i = 1 \dots m}{E \vdash \mathsf{RewSpec}(E^\Gamma, R) : \mathtt{blocktype}}$$

if $\mathsf{ACC}_E(E^\Gamma, R)$

(RewSpec/Rew)

$$\frac{E \vdash \mathsf{RewSpec}(E^\Gamma, R) : \mathtt{blocktype}}{E \vdash \mathsf{Rew}(E^\Gamma, R) : \mathsf{RewSpec}(E^\Gamma, R)}$$

if $\mathsf{COMP}_E(E^\Gamma, R)$

(RewSpec/Sat)

$$\frac{E \vdash \mathsf{RewSpec}(E^\Gamma, R) : \mathtt{blocktype} \qquad E \vdash p^j : t_j \text{ for } j = 1 \dots n \qquad E; E_i \vdash e_i^L\theta \approx e_i^R\theta \text{ for } i = 1 \dots m}{E \vdash \overline{p} : \mathsf{RewSpec}(E^\Gamma, R)}$$

where $\theta = \{v_j \mapsto p^j\}_{j=1\dots n}$

(RewSpec/Fun)

$$\frac{E \vdash \overline{p} : \mathsf{RewSpec}(E^\Gamma, R)}{E \vdash p^j : t_j}$$

(RewSpec/Comp)

$$\frac{E \vdash \overline{p} : \mathsf{RewSpec}(E^\Gamma, R) \qquad \delta : E_i \to E}{E \vdash e_i^L\theta\delta \approx e_i^R\theta\delta}$$

where $\theta = \{v_j \mapsto p^j\}_{j=1\dots n}$

The notation $\delta : E_i \to E$ means that $E \vdash v\delta : t\delta$ holds for every $v : \mathsf{Ty}(t) \in E_i$.

Fig. 10. Rewriting blocks

(Block/Conv)

$$\frac{E \vdash B : BT \qquad E \vdash BT' : \mathtt{blocktype} \qquad E \vdash BT \approx BT'}{E \vdash B : BT'}$$

Fig. 11. Block conversion

The principal signature of the structure m (omitted in $\mathsf{Ty}(\dots)$ above) can be obtained by removing the implementations (elements after :=) and replacing Struct with Sig. The principal signature of B defined by `Module B:=A` is more interesting. It is obtained by using the **(Strengthening)** rule (Fig. 7):

$$\begin{array}{l}\mathsf{Sig}\\ \quad nat,O,S \;:\; \mathsf{Eq}(A.nat,A.O,A.S : \mathsf{IndSpec}(E^I_{nat} := E^C_{nat}))\\ \quad plus \;:\; \mathsf{Eq}(A.plus : \mathsf{RewSpec}(E^\Gamma_{plus}, R_{plus}))\\ \quad two \;:\; \mathsf{Eq}(plus\ (S\ O)\ (S\ O) : nat)\\ \mathsf{End}\end{array}$$

Note that using **(Sig/Access)** followed by **(Eq/Type)** we can derive the judgment $E \vdash B.nat, B.O, B.S : \mathsf{IndSpec}(E^I_{nat} := E^C_{nat})$, meaning that $B.nat,B.O$, $B.S$ form an inductive family, and using **(Eq/Comp)** instead, we derive the equalities $B.nat \approx A.nat$, $B.O \approx A.O$ and $B.S \approx A.S$.

Module subtyping is governed by **(Sig/Sub)** and **(Funsig/Sub)**, as well as satisfaction rules **(Ty/Sat)**, **(Eq/Sat)** and **(RewSpec/Sat)**. Using the extraction rules followed by the satisfaction rules it is possible to prove the following:

$$\mathsf{Sig}\ nat, O, S : \mathsf{Ty}(\mathsf{IndSpec}(E^I_{nat} := E^C_{nat}))\ \mathsf{End}\ <:\ \mathsf{Sig}\ nat : \mathsf{Ty}(\mathtt{Set})\ \mathsf{End}$$

$$\mathsf{Sig}\ plus : \mathsf{Ty}(\mathsf{RewSpec}(E^\Gamma_{plus}, R_{plus}))\ \mathsf{End}\ <:\ \mathsf{Sig}\ plus : \mathsf{Ty}(nat \to nat \to nat)\ \mathsf{End}$$

Rewrite specifications used in the parameter interface of a functor may ease the development of the functor body. They impose convertibility constraints on the functor arguments. Let us suppose that $P : nat \to \mathtt{Prop}$ is a predicate, and let

$$E^\Gamma_{fg} = f\!:\mathsf{Ty}(nat \to nat);\quad g\!:\mathsf{Ty}(nat \to nat) \qquad R_{fg} = n\!:\mathsf{Ty}(nat) \mid f\ (g\ n) \longrightarrow g\ (f\ n)\ : nat$$

$$E^\Gamma_h = h\!:\mathsf{Ty}(nat \to nat) \qquad R_h = m\!:\mathsf{Ty}(nat) \mid h\ m \longrightarrow S(S\ m)\ : nat$$

Let us now consider a functor F of the following type

$$\begin{array}{l}\mathsf{Funsig}(X : \mathsf{Sig}\ f,g : \mathsf{Ty}(\mathsf{RewSpec}(E^\Gamma_{fg}, R_{fg}))\ \mathsf{End})\\ \quad \mathsf{Sig}\\ \qquad lemma : \mathsf{Eq}(\ \lambda n\!:nat.\ \lambda p\!:P(X.f(X.f(X.g\ n))).\ p\\ \qquad\qquad\qquad : \Pi n\!:nat.\ P(X.f(X.f(X.g\ n))) \to P(X.g(X.f(X.f\ n)))\ )\\ \quad \mathsf{End}\end{array}$$

In the functor result type, correctness of the specification of its single *lemma* component relies on the rewrite rule placed in the functor parameter signature. Now F can be applied to a module path of type

$$\begin{array}{l}\mathsf{Sig}\\ \quad g : \mathsf{Eq}(\ \lambda n\!:nat.\ S\ n\ :\ nat \to nat\ )\\ \quad f : \mathsf{Ty}(\ \mathsf{RewSpec}(E^\Gamma_h, R_h)\ )\\ \mathsf{End}\end{array}$$

In fact, the rule **(RewSpec/Sat)** allows any sequence of function symbols to satisfy $\mathsf{RewSpec}(E^{\Gamma}, R)$ as long as the corresponding conversion can prove equalities of left-hand and right-hand sides of all rules in R. In our example, the structure defines the functions f and g in such a way that both $f(g\,n)$ and $g(f\,n)$ are convertible with $S(S(S\;n))$, and therefore the equation expressed by the rewrite rule in R_{fg} is satisfied.

5 Conservativity

Our calculus of named modules is a conservative extension of the pure type system with generative definitions. This section presents the outline of the proof and a discussion about acceptance criteria for definitions by rewriring.

Closure properties. The calculus of named modules is parametrized by the side-conditions for acceptance of inductive definitions and definitions by rewriting. In order to make these definitions coexist with modules and in particular with module subtyping and functor applications, the acceptance conditions must be closed under some operations on environments. Formally, each side-condition C (POS, ACC and COMP) must satisfy the following closure properties:

$$\mathsf{C}_E(\Omega) \quad \text{implies} \quad \mathsf{C}_{E'}(\Omega') \quad \text{if:}$$

$$\begin{array}{lll}
\text{(C1)}\; E = E_1; \overline{v} : S; E_2 & E' = E_1; E_2\{\overline{v} \mapsto \overline{p}\} & \text{with} \quad E_1 \vdash \overline{p} : S \\
\qquad\; \Omega & \Omega' = \Omega\{\overline{v} \mapsto \overline{p}\}, & \\[1ex]
\text{(C2)}\; E = E_1; E_3 & E' = E_1; E_2; E_3 & \\
\qquad\; \Omega & \Omega' = \Omega & \\[1ex]
\text{(C3)}\; E = E_1; v : \mathsf{Ty}(\mathsf{Sig}\; \overline{v}_1 : S_1 \ldots \overline{v}_n : S_n\; \mathsf{End}); E_2 & & \\
\qquad\; \Omega & E' = E_1; \overline{v}_1 : S_1 \ldots \overline{v}_n : S_n; E_2\{\overline{v.v_i} \mapsto \overline{v}_i\} & \\
 & \Omega' = \Omega\{\overline{v.v_i} \mapsto \overline{v}_i\} & \\[1ex]
\text{(C4)}\; E = E_1; v : \mathsf{Ty}(\mathsf{Funsig}(\hat{v} : M)M'); E_2 & & \\
\qquad\; \Omega & E' = E_1; E_2 & \\
 & \Omega' = \Omega &
\end{array}$$

In all of the above implications it is assumed that both environments E and E' are correct. Moreover in the last two properties, E_2 does not contain modules.

Even though these closure properties look complicated, the first two simply correspond to basic meta-theoretical properties of most type-systems: substitutivity and weakening. It has to be noticed that the condition (C1) is at the same time simpler and harder than usual substitutivity. On one hand, only paths can be substituted which is a crucial simplification for existing syntactic termination criteria for rewriting. On the other hand, the typing judgment $E_1 \vdash \overline{p} : S$ can result from module subtyping or block satisfaction rules, which means that $\overline{p}$ can be more precisely specified than the original variables $\overline{v}$.

The property (C2) simply corresponds to modularity of a given acceptance criterion and is generally needed for effective reloading of previously checked developments. The remaining conditions (C3) and (C4) are used in the conservativity proof presented below.

Conservativity. In a calculus with modules, a proof development can be represented as a structure well-typed in the empty environment. We show that every such structure ending in a proof of `False` can be transformed into a inconsistent closed environment of the underlying pure type system with generative definitions.

Theorem 1. *Every structure well-typed in the empty environment, ending in a component* $v : \mathsf{Ty}(\texttt{False}) := e$ *can be transformed into a closed environment of the underlying pure type system with generative definitions, ending with* $v : \mathsf{Eq}(e' : \texttt{False})$ *for some term* e'.

Proof sketch. Suppose first that the initial structure contains neither sub-modules nor manifest blocks. Then it is trivial to transform it into a closed environment of the underlying pure type system.

Therefore it remains to be shown that any structure can be transformed into one without sub-modules and manifest blocks. Since every manifest block $\overline{v} : \mathsf{Eq}(\overline{v}' : BT) := B$ in a structure without sub-modules can be eliminated by simply substituting $\overline{v}'$ to $\overline{v}$ in the rest of the structure, let us concentrate on sub-modules. The elimination of the latter is done in two phases. First, going from left to right, all module applications in the initial structure are recursively *evaluated* to weak-head normal forms: we replace $p_1\, p_2$ with $m\{v \mapsto p_2\}$ where p_1 is already evaluated to $\mathsf{Functor}[v\!:\!M]m$. Second, sub-modules are eliminated from right to left, by simply removing functors and *flattening* structures.

Below we present the two phases of the conservativity proof in a bit more detailed way and explain the role of closure properties.

Evaluation. While replacing the functor application $p_1\, p_2$ by $m\{v \mapsto p_2\}$, one must make sure that the latter expression is well-typed given that m is well typed in an environment in which p_1 was defined, extended with $v : \mathsf{Ty}(M)$. If m contains definitions by rewriting or inductive definitions, their correctness after the substitution can only be proved if the side-conditions verify closure properties (C1) and (C2). The latter assures that m is still correct in the environment where p_1 is used extended with $v : \mathsf{Ty}(M)$ and (C1) assures that the substitution $\{v \mapsto p_2\}$ can safely be applied.

The other difficulty in the first phase lies in the termination proof. Fortunately our calculus is similar to the calculus of Courant and after solving some technical problems we can use his results to obtain termination.

Flattening. The second phase requires showing that module flattening preserves types. The simple proof by induction on the derivation does not work, so we have to introduce an auxiliary calculus, called principal, consisting of typing rules for terms (Fig. 4) and rules for extracting information from the environment (framed rules in Fig. 6, 7, 8, 9 and 10). We show that term judgments derivable in both calculi in a given correct environment are the same. Since type preservation of flattening in the principal calculus can be proved by simple induction on the derivation, using closure properties (C3) and (C4), we are done. The complete proof can be found in [4]. □

Satisfying closure properties. Let us now fix the base pure type system to be the calculus of constructions. Since inductive types are often theoretically analysed as anonymous entities, all known positivity conditions POS for inductive types obviously satisfy the closure properties.

It turns out also that syntactic order-based termination criteria for object-level rewriting, as defined in [2,19], restricted by the requirement that all function symbols appearing in the left-hand sides of rules of R belong to E^{Γ} and the critical pairs test, also satisfy the above properties and therefore are suitable for ACC. In great simplification both termination criteria [2,19] restrict right-hand sides of rewrite rules to be constructed from local variables, previously defined function symbols, constructors of inductive types and recursive calls with *smaller* arguments. Smaller here means (extended) subterm relation for [2] or a recursive comparison for [19]. The rewriting system defined is Sec. 2 is accepted by both termination criteria and all its critical pairs are joinable.

Due to modularity constraints it seems unlikely to allow foreign function symbols in left-hand sides of rules as in the third rule below:

```
Functor [A : Sig Rewriting plus,mult : nat → nat → nat Rules R End]
Struct
  Rewriting exp : nat → nat → nat
  Rules
    exp x 0 ⟶ S 0
    exp x (S n) ⟶ A.mult x (exp x n)
    exp x (A.plus n m) ⟶ A.mult (exp x n) (exp x m)
End
```

Indeed, even if current rewrite rules R for `plus` and `mult` allow to prove local confluence of the system for `exp`, when some module is substituted to `A`, containing another definition of `plus` and `mult`, the system may stop being confluent.

The status of the condition COMP is the least clear, because little is known about consistency of the calculus of constructions with rewriting. It is believed that *completeness of definitions* techniques of [6] requiring that all constructor instances of a function symbol are reducible, can be extended to the calculus of constructions and proved to guarantee consistency. Such a condition COMP would certainly satisfy the closure properties. Some work in this direction has already been done in [2], but the completeness criterion given in this paper is not modular.

6 Conclusions

We have presented the formalization of a pure type system with generative inductive definitions and definitions by rewriting and showed that its extension with a system of named modules is conservative. The proof allowed us to formulate closure properies which must be satisfied by acceptance criteria for rewrite rules in order to be useful in the calculus with modules.

Since some existing acceptance criteria can already be adapted to satisfy the closure properties, the implementation of a term rewriting engine in Coq is by no means stopped by the modules. Still, finding really flexible acceptance criteria for rewriting is a challenging subject for future work.

Acknowledgment. The author would like to thank the anonymous referee for the extensive comments and suggestions.

References

1. Frédéric Blanqui. Definitions by rewriting in the calculus of constructions. In *Sixteenth Annual IEEE Symposium on Logic in Computer Science*, pages 9–18, Los Alamitos, USA, June 2001. IEEE Comp. Soc. Press.
2. Frédéric Blanqui. Definitions by rewriting in the Calculus of Constructions. *Mathematical Structures in Computer Science*, 2003. To appear.
3. Jacek Chrząszcz. Implementation of modules in the Coq system. In David Basin and Burkhart Wolff, editors, *Proceedings of the Theorem Proving in Higher Order Logics 16th International Conference*, volume 2758 of *LNCS*, pages 270–286, Rome, Italy, September 2003. Springer Verlag.
4. Jacek Chrząszcz. *Modules in Type Theory with Generative Definitions.* PhD thesis, Warsaw Univerity and University of Paris-Sud, Jan 2004. Available from `http://www.mimuw.edu.pl/ chrzaszc/papers`
5. The Coq proof assistant. `http://coq.inria.fr/`.
6. Thierry Coquand. Pattern matching with dependent types. In *Proceedings of the Workshop on Types for Proofs and Programs*, pages 71–83, Båstad, Sweden, 1992.
7. Thierry Coquand and Gérard Huet. The calculus of constructions. *Information and Computation*, 76:95–120, February 1988.
8. Thierry Coquand and Christine Paulin-Mohring. Inductively defined types. In P. Martin-Löf and G. Mints, editors, *Proceedings of Colog'88*, volume 417 of *Lecture Notes in Computer Science*. Springer-Verlag, 1990.
9. Judicaël Courant. A Module Calculus for Pure Type Systems. In *Typed Lambda Calculi and Applications 97*, volume 1210 of *Lecture Notes in Computer Science*, pages 112–128. Springer-Verlag, 1997.
10. Judicaël Courant. *Un calcul de modules pour les systèmes de types purs.* Thèse de doctorat, Ecole Normale Supérieure de Lyon, 1998.
11. Robert Harper and Mark Lillibridge. A type-theoretic approach to higher-order modules with sharing. In POPL'94 [17], pages 123–137.
12. Robert Harper and Frank Pfenning. A module system for a programming language based on the LF logical framework. *Journal of Logic and Computation*, 1(8), 1998.
13. Xavier Leroy. Manifest types, modules, and separate compilation. In POPL'94 [17], pages 109–122.

14. Zhaohui Luo. *An Extended Calculus of Constructions.* PhD thesis, University of Edinburgh, 1990.
15. S. Owre, N. Shankar, J. M. Rushby, and D. W. J. Stringer-Calvert. *PVS Language Reference.* Computer Science Laboratory, SRI International, Menlo Park, CA, September 1999.
16. Lawrence C. Paulson. Isabelle: the next 700 theorem provers. In P. Odifreddi, editor, *Logic and Computer Science.* Academic Press, 1990.
17. *Conference Record of the 21st Symposium on Principles of Programming Languages*, Portland, Oregon, 1994. ACM Press.
18. Daria Walukiewicz-Chrząszcz. Termination of rewriting in the calculus of constructions. *Journal of Functional Programming*, 13(2):339–414, 2003.
19. Daria Walukiewicz-Chrząszcz. *Termination of Rewriting in the Calculus of Constructions.* PhD thesis, Warsaw University and University Paris XI, 2003.
20. Benjamin Werner. *Méta-théorie du Calcul des Constructions Inductives.* PhD thesis, Université Paris 7, 1994.

Rewriting Calculus with Fixpoints: Untyped and First-Order Systems

Horatiu Cirstea, Luigi Liquori, and Benjamin Wack

LORIA & NANCY II & INRIA & NANCY I
54506 Vandoeuvre-lès-Nancy, BP 239 Cedex France
First.Last@loria.fr

Abstract. The rewriting calculus, also called ρ-calculus, is a framework embedding λ-calculus and rewriting capabilities, by allowing abstraction not only on variables but also on patterns. The higher-order mechanisms of the λ-calculus and the pattern matching facilities of the rewriting are then both available at the same level. Many type systems for the λ-calculus can be generalized to the ρ-calculus: in this paper, we study extensively a first-order ρ-calculus *à la* Church, called $\rho^{\mathsf{stk}}_{\rightharpoonup}$. The type system of $\rho^{\mathsf{stk}}_{\rightharpoonup}$ allows one to type (object oriented flavored) fixpoints, leading to an expressive and safe calculus. In particular, using pattern matching, one can encode and typecheck term rewriting systems in a natural and automatic way. Therefore, we can see our framework as a starting point for the theoretical basis of a powerful typed rewriting-based language.

Keywords. Rewriting-calculus, Lambda-calculus, Object-calculus, Pattern Matching, Fixpoints, Type Theory.

1 Introduction

It is not by chance that pattern matching appears as the core mechanism of term rewriting: in fact, the ability to discriminate patterns is present since the beginning of information processing modeling. Pattern matching has also been widely used in functional programming (*e.g.* ML, Haskell, Scheme), logic programming (*e.g.* Prolog), rewrite based programming (*e.g.* Elan [5], Maude [16], script programming (*e.g.* sed, awk). It has been generally considered as a convenient mechanism for expressing complex requirements about the argument of a function, more than a real computation paradigm.

The *Rewriting Calculus*, by unifying λ-calculus and rewriting, makes all the basic ingredients of rewriting explicit objects, in particular the notions of *rule application* and *result*. Pattern matching can therefore be used widely, and a rewrite rule becomes a first-class object, which can be created, manipulated and modified by the calculus itself. We have already shown [8] that the first version of the rewriting calculus can be used as an operational semantics for rewriting based languages and in particular for Elan. For this we have used in the past fixpoint operators inspired from the ones of the λ-calculus and thus untypable in the early version of the simply typed rewriting calculus [7].

Nevertheless, static analysis via a suitable typing system enforces a stronger programming discipline. The main objective of this paper is to present a ρ-calculus *à la* Church ($\rho^{\mathsf{stk}}_{\rightharpoonup}$) featuring first-order types and well-typed self-duplicating terms.

S. Berardi, M. Coppo, and F. Damiani (Eds.): TYPES 2003, LNCS 3085, pp. 147–161, 2004.

In $\rho^{\mathsf{stk}}_{\to}$ (typed) pattern matching is the basic mechanism for programming allowing one to build and typecheck non-normalizing terms: this enables the definition of some interesting *functional recursion operators*. Moreover, the type system of $\rho^{\mathsf{stk}}_{\to}$ is powerful enough to ensure well-typedness of matching equations, *i.e.* the instantiation of formal parameters complies with the typing discipline. Hence, $\rho^{\mathsf{stk}}_{\to}$ represents a good trade-off between the flexibility and the expressiveness of the untyped calculus, and the strictness of a more strongly typed one. This leads us to consider the presented typed system for ρ-calculus as a good candidate for giving the static semantics of a family of rewriting-based languages such as Elan, Maude, *etc.*

One of the particularities of the type system of $\rho^{\mathsf{stk}}_{\to}$ is that it relaxes, using the well-known result of N.P. Mendler [15], the classical property that "well-typed programs normalize". More precisely, non-termination can be type-checked in $\rho^{\mathsf{stk}}_{\to}$ thanks to *ad hoc* patterns; it follows that, roughly speaking, an ML-like let becomes a let rec by abstracting over a suitable algebraic pattern P.

Nevertheless, it is important to remark that when the type discipline is enhanced with dependent types, as it was done recently by the authors [3], all the programs presented in this paper are statically rejected, *i.e.* blocked by the type system. The chosen dependent type theory introduces pattern matching inside types, and matching failures significantly restrict the set of type-checked programs. In fact, the present paper does not fit into the philosophy of [3], where (dependent) type systems were studied especially for logical (proof-oriented) purposes and thus concerned with strong normalization of typable terms.

Plan of the paper. In Section 2, we will describe the syntax and the evaluation rules of the $\rho^{\mathsf{stk}}_{\to}$. We will see how an equivalence on terms handles the undesirable matching failures. Section 3 describes the type system of $\rho^{\mathsf{stk}}_{\to}$. We give some simple type derivations to show how the type system deals with patterns and we state metatheoretical properties of $\rho^{\mathsf{stk}}_{\to}$. In Section 4, we explain how a careful use of the pattern matching capabilities allows us to encode various object calculi and term rewriting systems.

2 The System $\rho^{\mathsf{stk}}_{\to}$

This section presents the basis of $\rho^{\mathsf{stk}}_{\to}$: its syntax, its semantics and some examples showing its expressiveness.

2.1 Syntax

In this paper, we consider the meta-symbols "$\to$" (function- and type-abstraction), "$[\ll]$" (delayed matching constraint), an application operator denoted by concatenation, and "," (structure operator). We assume that the application operator associates to the left, while the other operators associate to the right. The priority of the application is higher than that of "$[\ll]$" which is higher than that of "$\to$" which is, in turn, of higher priority than the ",". The symbol τ ranges over the set $\mathcal{T}y$ of types, the symbol ι ranges over the set $\mathcal{K}y$ of type constants ($\mathcal{K}y \subseteq \mathcal{T}y$), the symbols $A, B, C, \ldots$ range over the set $\mathcal{T}$ of terms, the symbols $X, Y, Z, \ldots$ range over the set $\mathcal{V}$ of variables ($\mathcal{V} \subseteq \mathcal{T}$), the symbols $a, b, c, \ldots, f, g, h$ range over a set $\mathcal{K}$ of term constants ($\mathcal{K} \subseteq \mathcal{T}$). Finally, the symbols P, Q range over the set $\mathcal{P}$ of patterns, ($\mathcal{V} \subseteq \mathcal{P} \subseteq \mathcal{T}$). Sometimes we will use the "overloaded" symbol $\alpha \in \mathcal{V} \cup \mathcal{K}$, and we denote $\overline{A}$ for $A_1 \cdots A_n$, for $n \geq 0$. The syntax is presented in Figure 1. The *types* are as one would expect from a first-order

$\tau \ ::= \ \iota \mid \tau \twoheadrightarrow \tau$		$\mathcal{T}y$ Types
$\Delta \ ::= \ \emptyset \mid \Delta, X{:}\tau \mid \Delta, f{:}\tau$		Contexts
$P \ ::= \ X \mid \mathsf{stk} \mid f\,\overline{P}$	*(variables occur only once in any P)*	$\mathcal{P}$ Patterns
$A \ ::= \ f \mid \mathsf{stk} \mid X \mid P \twoheadrightarrow_\Delta A \mid [P \ll_\Delta A]A \mid A\,A \mid A, A$		$\mathcal{T}$ Terms

Fig. 1. Syntax of $\rho^{\mathsf{stk}}_{\twoheadrightarrow}$

type system, *i.e.* constant-types and arrow-types. The *patterns* are algebraic terms (*i.e.* terms constructed only with variables, constants and application) which can be used as left-hand sides of the rewrite rules; the set of patterns is obviously included in the set of terms. The well-known linearity restriction [17] is needed to keep the small-step semantics confluent. A *rewrite rule* of the form $(P \twoheadrightarrow_\Delta A)$ abstracting over the free variables of P is a first-class citizen of the calculus. The types of the free variables of P are declared in Δ, *i.e.* $\mathsf{Fv}(P) = \mathsf{Dom}(\Delta)$, resulting in a fully annotated calculus *à la* Church. An *application* is implicitly denoted by concatenation. The *delayed matching constraint* $[P \ll_\Delta A]B$ can be seen as the term B with its free variables constrained by the matching between P and A. Again, the context Δ contains the type declarations of all the free variables appearing in the pattern P. A *structure* is a collection of terms that can be seen either as a set of rewrite rules or as a set of results. As we will see in Section 2.3, the symbol stk can be considered as the special constant representing a delayed matching constraint whose matching problem is unsolvable. An alternative approach would be to omit this symbol from the syntax but this has two drawbacks: first, the axioms of the theory presented in Def. 5 would become more complicated; moreover, we would lose the expression of first given in Section 4.2, and thus the proposed encoding of rewriting systems would be no longer possible.

A type judgment (defined in Section 3) stating that a term A has the type τ in a context Γ is written $\Gamma \vdash A : \tau$.

Free Variables and Substitutions. We introduce the notion of free variable and substitution.

Definition 1 (Free variables Fv).

$$\begin{array}{llll}
\mathsf{Fv}(f) \triangleq \emptyset & \mathsf{Fv}(P \twoheadrightarrow_\Delta A) & & \triangleq \mathsf{Fv}(A) \setminus \mathsf{Fv}(P) \\
\mathsf{Fv}(\mathsf{stk}) \triangleq \emptyset & \mathsf{Fv}([P \ll_\Delta A]B) & & \triangleq \mathsf{Fv}((P \twoheadrightarrow_\Delta B)\ A) \\
\mathsf{Fv}(X) \triangleq \{X\} & \mathsf{Fv}(A\,B) \triangleq \mathsf{Fv}(A, B) & & \triangleq \mathsf{Fv}(A) \cup \mathsf{Fv}(B)
\end{array}$$

As usual, we work modulo *α-conversion* and we adopt Barendregt's *"hygiene-convention"* [2], *i.e.* free and bound variables have different names. This allows us to define substitutions quite straightforwardly, since it avoids issues like variable capture.

Definition 2 (Substitutions).
A substitution θ is a mapping from the set of variables to the set of terms. A finite substitution θ has the form $\{A_1/X_1 \ldots A_m/X_m\}$, and its domain $\{X_1, \ldots, X_m\}$ is denoted by $\mathsf{Dom}(\theta)$. The application of a substitution θ to a term A, denoted by $A\theta$, is defined as follows:

$$f\theta \triangleq f \qquad (P \twoheadrightarrow_\Delta A)\theta \triangleq P \twoheadrightarrow_\Delta A\theta$$

$$\mathsf{stk}\theta \triangleq \mathsf{stk} \qquad ([P \ll_\Delta A]B)\theta \triangleq [P \ll_\Delta A\theta]B\theta$$

$$X_i\theta \triangleq \begin{cases} A_i \ \text{if} X_i \in \mathsf{Dom}(\theta) \\ X_i \ \text{otherwise} \end{cases} \qquad (A\,B)\theta \triangleq A\theta\,B\theta \qquad (A, B)\theta \triangleq A\theta, B\theta$$

A substitution θ is well-typed in context *Γ if for any $X \in \mathsf{Dom}(\theta)$ such that $\Gamma \vdash X : \tau$ we have $\Gamma \vdash X\theta : \tau$.*

Matching Equations, Theories. The core mechanism of the rewriting calculus is pattern matching since, as we have already mentioned, when a delayed matching constraint is evaluated the corresponding matching problem should be solved. We define first the classical notions of matching equations and matching solutions.

Definition 3 (Matching).
Given a theory $\mathbb{T}$ (i.e. a set of axioms defining a congruence relation $\stackrel{\mathbb{T}}{=}$):

1. *A matching equation is a problem $\mathsf{T} \triangleq P \prec\!\!\prec_{\mathbb{T}} A$ with P a pattern and A a term.*
2. *A substitution θ is a solution of the matching equation T if:*
   a) $P\theta \stackrel{\mathbb{T}}{=} A$
   b) θ is well-typed in any context Γ in which A and P are typable.
   The set of solutions of T is denoted by $\mathcal{S}ol(\mathsf{T})$.

Different theories and the corresponding pattern matching problems can be formally defined and solved, for example, as explained in [9]. By convention, if the solution of the equation $A \prec\!\!\prec_{\mathbb{T}} B$ is unique, it is denoted by $\theta_{(A \prec\!\prec_{\mathbb{T}} B)}$.

2.2 Operational Semantics of the General Rewriting Calculus, $\rho^{\mathbb{T}}$

By now we have settled all the background necessary to describe in Figure 2 the reduction rules of the general ρ-calculus, called $\rho^{\mathbb{T}}$, parameterized by the theory $\mathbb{T}$. When instantiating $\mathbb{T}$ with concrete theories (*e.g.* theories containing axioms for associativity, associativity-commutativity, *etc*, for a given symbol) different versions of the calculus are obtained. When not essential or clear from the context, we will omit the theory $\mathbb{T}$ in rules and congruences.

Let us quickly explain the top-level rules:

$$(P \twoheadrightarrow_{\Delta} A)\, B \rightarrow_{\rho} [P \ll_{\Delta} B]A$$

$$[P \ll_{\Delta} B]A \rightarrow_{\sigma} A\theta_1, \ldots, A\theta_n \quad \text{with } \{\theta_1, \ldots, \theta_n\} = \mathcal{S}ol(P \prec\!\!\prec_{\mathbb{T}} B)$$

$$(A, B)\, C \rightarrow_{\delta} A\, C, B\, C$$

Fig. 2. Top-level Rules of the General Rewriting Calculus, $\rho^{\mathbb{T}}$

(ρ) this rule "fires" the application of an abstraction to a term, but does not immediately try to solve the associated matching equation.

(σ) this rule is applied if (and only if) the matching equation $P \prec\!\!\prec_{\mathbb{T}} B$ has at least one solution: in this case the matching solutions are computed and applied to the term A. If the matching is not unitary, a structure collecting all the different results is obtained when the rule is applied. If there is no solution, this rule does not apply and thus, the term represents a matching failure. As we will see, further reductions or instantiations are likely to modify B so that the equation has a solution and the rule can be fired.

(δ) this rule distributes structures on the left-hand side of the application. This gives the possibility, for example, to apply in parallel two distinct pattern abstractions A and B to a term C.

We denote by $\mapsto_{\rho\sigma\delta}$ the contextual closure of these rules. Its reflexive and transitive closure is denoted $\mapsto\!\!\!\!\rightarrow_{\rho\sigma\delta}$. The symmetric and transitive closure of $\mapsto\!\!\!\!\rightarrow_{\rho\sigma\delta}$ is denoted $=_{\rho\sigma\delta}$.

2.3 The Fixpoint Rewriting Calculus, $\rho_{\twoheadrightarrow}^{\mathsf{stk}}$

We present a version of the rewriting calculus that handles uniformly matching failures and eliminates them when not significant for the computation. We define the rules for handling this kind of terms and we show how these are integrated in the calculus.

We define first a superposition relation $\sqsubseteq : \mathcal{P} \times \mathcal{T}$ between (patterns and) terms whose aim is to characterize a broad class of matching equations that are *potentially* solvable. If $P \sqsubseteq A$ we say that "*P does potentially superpose with A*" and, by negation, if $P \not\sqsubseteq A$ then "*P surely does not superpose with A*" (*i.e.* independently of subsequent instantiations and reductions).

Definition 4 (Superposition).

1. *The relation $P \sqsubseteq A$ is defined as follows by cases on the structure of P:*

$$f \sqsubseteq f \qquad \mathsf{stk} \sqsubseteq \mathsf{stk} \qquad X \sqsubseteq A \ (\forall A)$$

$$f\,\overline{A} \sqsubseteq B \quad \text{if } (B \equiv f\,\overline{B}) \wedge \overline{A} \sqsubseteq \overline{B}$$

$$P \sqsubseteq A \quad \text{if } A \equiv \begin{cases} X \vee (A_1, A_2) \vee (A_1\, A_2 \wedge A_1 \notin \mathcal{P}) \vee \\ ([Q \ll_{\Delta} A_1]A_2 \wedge Q \sqsubseteq A_1 \wedge P \sqsubseteq A_2) \ (\forall P) \end{cases}$$

2. *If $P \sqsubseteq A$ is not satisfied we write $P \not\sqsubseteq A$.*

Starting from this relation, we define a reduction that eliminates from a ρ-term all the definitive stuck subterms, *i.e.* all the delayed matching constraints whose matching problem is unsolvable independently of subsequent instantiations and reductions.

Definition 5 (Stuck Theory, $\mathbb{T}_{\mathsf{stk}}$).
The relation $\rightharpoonup_{\mathsf{stk}}$ is defined by the following rules:

$$[P \ll_\Delta A]B \rightharpoonup_{\mathsf{stk}} \mathsf{stk} \quad \text{if } P \not\sqsubseteq A \tag{1}$$

$$\mathsf{stk}, A \rightharpoonup_{\mathsf{stk}} A \tag{2}$$

$$A, \mathsf{stk} \rightharpoonup_{\mathsf{stk}} A \tag{3}$$

$$\mathsf{stk}\ A \rightharpoonup_{\mathsf{stk}} \mathsf{stk} \tag{4}$$

We denote by $\mapsto_{\mathsf{stk}}$ the contextual closure of these rules. Its reflexive and transitive closure is denoted by $\mapsto\!\!\!\!\to_{\mathsf{stk}}$. The symmetric and transitive closure of $\mapsto\!\!\!\!\to_{\mathsf{stk}}$ is denoted by $\stackrel{\mathsf{stk}}{=}$. Let $\mathbb{T}_{\mathsf{stk}}$ be the theory associated to the congruence $\stackrel{\mathsf{stk}}{=}$. Matching equations in the theory $\mathbb{T}_{\mathsf{stk}}$ are denoted $P \prec\!\!\prec_{\mathsf{stk}} A$.

As mentioned previously, these rules are used to propagate or eliminate the definitive stuck terms:

- Structures can be seen as collections of results and thus we want to identify all the (matching) failures and eliminate them from these collections; this is done by the first rules $(1-3)$;
- On the other hand, a stk term can be seen as an empty set of results; the rule (4) corresponds then to the (δ) rule dealing with empty structures and thus, to a propagation of the failure.

Lemma 1 (Confluence and Termination of stk-reduction).
The reduction $\mapsto_{\mathsf{stk}}$ is confluent and terminating.

In general, matching modulo the $\mathbb{T}_{\mathsf{stk}}$ theory is obviously infinitary. When restricting to matching equations with an algebraic left-hand side we can still have an infinite number of solutions but a unique representative can be always characterized. Intuitively, in this latter case, the canonic solution of a matching equation is the solution obtained by a syntactic matching algorithm with all the terms reduced in $\mapsto_{\mathsf{stk}}$-normal form. For example, since the solution of the equation $f\ X \prec\!\!\prec_{\mathbb{T}_\emptyset} f\ (a, \mathsf{stk})$ is $\{(a, \mathsf{stk})/X\}$, the solution of $f\ X \prec\!\!\prec_{\mathsf{stk}} f\ (a, \mathsf{stk})$ is $\{a/X\}$, representing a witness for all the solutions with the shape $\{(\mathsf{stk}, \ldots, a, \ldots, \mathsf{stk})/X\}$.

Thus, for the sake of simplicity and in order to keep closer to possible implementations, we define the underlying relation of the calculus:

Definition 6 (Semantics of $\rho^{\mathsf{stk}}_{\rightharpoonup}$).
The underlying relation of $\rho^{\mathsf{stk}}_{\rightharpoonup}$, denoted $\mapsto^{\mathsf{stk}}_{\rho\sigma\delta}$ is defined as the relation $\mapsto_{\mathsf{stk}} \cup \mapsto_{\rho\sigma\delta}$.

For $\mapsto^{\mathsf{stk}}_{\rho\sigma\delta}$, the following holds:

Theorem 1 (Church Rosser for $\rho^{\mathsf{stk}}_{\rightharpoonup}$).
The relation $\mapsto^{\mathsf{stk}}_{\rho\sigma\delta}$ is confluent.

3 The First-Order Type System for $\rho_{\twoheadrightarrow}^{\mathsf{stk}}$

Figure 3 presents the typing rules of $\rho_{\twoheadrightarrow}^{\mathsf{stk}}$, which are directly inspired by the simply typed λ-calculus.

$$\frac{\alpha{:}\tau \in \Gamma \quad \tau \in \mathcal{T}y}{\Gamma \vdash \alpha : \tau}\ (Start) \qquad \frac{\Gamma, \Delta \vdash P : \tau_1 \quad \Gamma, \Delta \vdash A : \tau_2}{\Gamma \vdash P \twoheadrightarrow_{\Delta} A : \tau_1 \twoheadrightarrow \tau_2}\ (Abs)$$

$$\frac{\tau \in \mathcal{T}y}{\Gamma \vdash \mathsf{stk} : \tau}\ (Stuck) \qquad \frac{\Gamma \vdash A : \tau_1 \twoheadrightarrow \tau_2 \quad \Gamma \vdash B : \tau_1}{\Gamma \vdash A\, B : \tau_2}\ (Appl)$$

$$\frac{\Gamma \vdash A : \tau \quad \Gamma \vdash B : \tau}{\Gamma \vdash A, B : \tau}\ (Struct) \qquad \frac{\Gamma, \Delta \vdash P : \tau_1 \quad \Gamma \vdash B : \tau_1 \quad \Gamma, \Delta \vdash A : \tau_2}{\Gamma \vdash [P \ll_{\Delta} B]A : \tau_2}\ (Match)$$

Fig. 3. The Type System for $\rho_{\twoheadrightarrow}^{\mathsf{stk}}$

- $(Start)$: The context determines the type of variables and constants. It cannot contain two declarations for the same variable (or constant);
- (Abs): As mentioned in Section 2.1, $\mathsf{Dom}(\Delta) = \mathsf{Fv}(P)$. For the left-hand side of the arrow-type, we use the type of the pattern P; notice that the (Abs) rule allows one to hide some type informations in a pattern containing applications, *e.g.* τ_2 disappear in the final type of $(f\ X)$ in the judgment $f{:}\tau_2 \twoheadrightarrow \tau_1, X{:}\tau_2 \vdash f\ X : \tau_1$.
- $(Appl)$: We directly exploit the information given in the type of the function, statically checking that the given argument has the expected type τ_1;
- $(Struct)$: This rule states that all the members of a structure have the same type. This is important when considering structures as a collection of results; if a function can return different results, we would at least expect them to have the same type;
- $(Stuck)$: Since stk can appear in any structure, it can have any type;
- $(Match)$: This rule states that the constraint $[P \ll_{\Delta} B]A$ gets the same type as $(P \twoheadrightarrow_{\Delta} A)\ B$. This is sound since $(P \twoheadrightarrow_{\Delta} A)\ B \to_{\rho} [P \ll_{\Delta} B]A$. Once again, $\mathsf{Dom}(\Delta) = \mathsf{Fv}(P)$.

Example 1 (Simple type derivation).
The $(Appl)$ rule is effective for the typing of algebraic terms too. Let $\Gamma \triangleq f{:}\iota \twoheadrightarrow \iota, a{:}\iota$.

$$\frac{\Gamma \vdash f : \iota \twoheadrightarrow \iota \quad \Gamma \vdash a : \iota}{\Gamma \vdash f\ a : \iota}\ (Appl)$$

and, let $\Gamma \triangleq f{:}\tau_1 \twoheadrightarrow \tau_2, g{:}\tau_1 \twoheadrightarrow \iota, a{:}\tau_1$.

$$\frac{\dfrac{\Gamma, X{:}\tau_1 \vdash f\ X : \tau_2 \quad \Gamma, X{:}\tau_1 \vdash g\ X : \iota}{\Gamma \vdash f\ X \twoheadrightarrow_{(X:\tau_1)} g\ X : \tau_2 \twoheadrightarrow \iota}\ (Abs) \qquad \Gamma \vdash f\ a : \tau_2}{\Gamma \vdash (f\ X \twoheadrightarrow_{(X:\tau_1)} g\ X)\ (f\ a) : \iota}\ (Appl)$$

This type system has been designed as a typing discipline for a programming language: its aim is to ensure that the arguments of a function have the same types as the corresponding formal parameters. However, the notion of (well-typed) pattern used here is crucial since it guarantees that the instantiation of the variables of the pattern will be correct with respect to types (*i.e.* the substitutions obtained as result of the matching are well-typed) even if no type-checking is performed in the matching algorithm.

We state in what follows the main properties of the typed calculus.

Lemma 2 (Substitution Lemma).
If $\Gamma, \Delta \vdash A : \tau$, then for any substitution θ well-typed in Γ such that $\mathsf{Dom}(\theta) = \mathsf{Dom}(\Delta)$, *we have $\Gamma \vdash A\theta : \tau$.*

Theorem 2 (Subject Reduction for $\rho_{\rightarrow}^{\mathsf{stk}}$).
If $\Gamma \vdash A : \tau$ and $A \mapsto_{\rho\delta}^{\mathsf{stk}} B$, then $\Gamma \vdash B : \tau$.

Theorem 3 (Type Uniqueness for $\rho_{\rightarrow}^{\mathsf{stk}}$).
If $\Gamma \vdash A : \tau_1$ and $\Gamma \vdash A : \tau_2$, and $\mathsf{stk} \notin A$, *then $\tau_1 \equiv \tau_2$.*

Theorem 4 (Decidability of Typing for $\rho_{\rightarrow}^{\mathsf{stk}}$).
If $\mathsf{stk} \notin A$ *and* $\mathsf{Fv}(A) \subseteq \mathsf{Dom}(\Gamma)$, *then the following problems are decidable:*

1. *Type Reconstruction: for a given Γ, is there a type τ such that $\Gamma \vdash A : \tau$?*
2. *Type Checking: given a context Γ, and a type τ, is it true that $\Gamma \vdash A : \tau$?*

4 Examples and Applications in $\rho_{\rightarrow}^{\mathsf{stk}}$

It has already been shown that the ρ-calculus allows one to faithfully encode first order term rewriting [8] as well as some classical object-calculi [9]. In this section, we show that $\rho_{\rightarrow}^{\mathsf{stk}}$ is sufficiently expressive and flexible for a more concise encoding that does not break the type discipline for these two formalisms. In most of the section, some type decorations of variables and constants are omitted for the sake of readability.

4.1 Encoding Abadi and Cardelli's Object-Calculus

In this section we briefly describe an encoding in the typed $\rho_{\rightarrow}^{\mathsf{stk}}$ of the classical object-calculus $\varsigma\mathcal{O}bj$ [1]. By better exploiting the pattern matching facilities of the $\rho_{\rightarrow}^{\mathsf{stk}}$ we obtain a more concise representation than the one given in previous works for the untyped ρ-calculus. A method is encoded as $(m\ S) \rightarrow \mathcal{T}_m$ [1], where the constant m is the name of the method, the variable S will play the role of the keyword this (containing a copy of the object itself) and $\mathcal{T}_m$ is a term encoding the body of the method. An object obj is

[1] In [9], the original encoding was $m \rightarrow S \rightarrow \mathcal{T}_m$, needing two reduction steps where one is enough with our enhanced encoding.

then a structure filled with methods. The method $meth$ is then called by Kamin's self application [13] which says that $obj.meth \triangleq obj\ (meth\ obj)$:

$$\begin{aligned} obj\ (meth\ obj) &\equiv (\ldots, meth\ S \twoheadrightarrow \mathcal{T}_{meth}, \ldots)\ (meth\ obj) \\ &\mapsto_{\rho\sigma\delta} \ldots, [meth\ S \ll meth\ obj]\mathcal{T}_{meth}, \ldots \\ &\mapsto^{\mathsf{stk}}_{\rho\sigma\delta} \mathcal{T}_{meth}[obj/S] \end{aligned}$$

Observe that the other methods fail because the equation $(m\ S \not\ll meth\ obj)$ has no solution for every $m \not\equiv meth$. The stk terms obtained for each of these method applications can be eliminated from the final result by successive $\mapsto_{\mathsf{stk}}$ steps. The variable S is indeed instantiated with obj in the body of the method, allowing all the usual operations on the keyword this.

As such, the previous example can be typed in the ρ-calculus as follows: lab is the constant type of labels, S has type $lab \twoheadrightarrow \tau$, and τ is the type of $\mathcal{T}_{meth}$. For the sake of simplicity, we suppose obj has just one method triggered by the constant $meth$, with type $(lab \twoheadrightarrow \tau) \twoheadrightarrow lab$.

$$\frac{\Gamma \vdash meth\ S : lab \quad \Gamma \vdash \mathcal{T}_{meth} : \tau}{\Gamma \vdash meth\ S \twoheadrightarrow \mathcal{T}_{meth} : lab \twoheadrightarrow \tau}\ (Abs)$$

Considering the meaning we want for S, it is sound that obj and S have the same type. Then $obj.meth \triangleq obj\ (meth\ obj)$ can be typed as follows (let $\Gamma \triangleq meth{:}(lab \twoheadrightarrow \tau) \twoheadrightarrow lab, \ldots$):

$$\frac{\Gamma \vdash obj : lab \twoheadrightarrow \tau \quad \Gamma \vdash meth\ obj : lab}{\Gamma \vdash obj\ (meth\ obj) : \tau}$$

We end this subsection with an object-oriented version of $\omega\omega$, showing that the divergence of object-oriented programs is somehow built in the self-application. Remember that $S.loop$ denotes the self application $S\ (loop\ S)$.

$$\begin{aligned} \vdash \Omega &\triangleq (loop\ S) \twoheadrightarrow S.loop : lab \twoheadrightarrow \tau \\ \Omega.loop &\equiv (loop\ S \twoheadrightarrow S.loop)\ (loop\ \Omega) \\ &\mapsto\!\!\!\!\twoheadrightarrow_{\rho\sigma\delta} \Omega.loop \\ &\mapsto\!\!\!\!\twoheadrightarrow_{\rho\sigma\delta} \ldots \end{aligned}$$

4.2 Encoding Term Rewriting Systems (TRS)

The correspondence between the ρ-calculus and the TRS is not as straightforward as it may seem. Observe that a ρ-abstraction is consumed by a ρ-reduction, and therefore can operate only locally. For instance, the simple (one-rule) TRS consisting of $f(X) \to X$ reduces $f(f(f(a)))$ to a. In the ρ-calculus, we can have control over the application of this rule:

$$\begin{array}{c} (f\ X \twoheadrightarrow X)\ (f\ (f\ (f\ a))) \mapsto\!\!\!\!\twoheadrightarrow_{\rho\sigma\delta} f\ (f\ a) \\ (f\ Y \twoheadrightarrow Y)\ \big((f\ X \twoheadrightarrow X)\ (f\ (f\ (f\ a)))\big) \mapsto\!\!\!\!\twoheadrightarrow_{\rho\sigma\delta} (f\ Y \twoheadrightarrow Y)\ (f\ (f\ a)) \mapsto\!\!\!\!\twoheadrightarrow_{\rho\sigma\delta} f\ a \end{array}$$

In general, encoding (first and higher order) rewriting systems in the untyped ρ-calculus requires a complex translation mechanism [8,4].

$$
\begin{array}{ll}
 & plus.rec\ \ (add\,\overline{n}\,\overline{m}) \\
\mapsto\!\!\!\to_{\rho\delta} & (add\,0\,Y \twoheadrightarrow Y)\ \ (add\,\overline{n}\,\overline{m}), \\
 & (add\,(suc\,X)\,Y \twoheadrightarrow suc\ (plus.rec\ \ (add\,X\,Y)))\ \ (add\,\overline{n}\,\overline{m}) \\
\mapsto\!\!\!\to_{\rho\delta} & [add\,0\,Y \ll add\,\overline{n}\,\overline{m}]Y, \\
 & suc\,(plus.rec\ \ (add\,\overline{n-1}\,\overline{m})) \\
\mapsto\!\!\!\to_{\mathsf{stk}} & suc\,(plus.rec\ \ (add\,\overline{n-1}\,\overline{m})) \\
\mapsto\!\!\!\to_{\rho\delta} & suc\,\big((add\,0\,Y \twoheadrightarrow Y)\ \ (add\,\overline{n-1}\,\overline{m}), \\
 & \quad (add\,(suc\,X)\,Y \twoheadrightarrow suc\ (plus.rec\ \ (add\,X\,Y)))\ \ (add\,\overline{n-1}\,\overline{m})\big) \\
 & \quad \ldots \\
\mapsto\!\!\!\to_{\rho\delta} & suc\,([add\,0\,Y \ll add\,\overline{n-1}\,\overline{m}]Y, \\
 & \quad suc\,(\cdots suc\,((add\,0\,Y \twoheadrightarrow Y)\ \ (add\,0\,\overline{m}), \\
 & \qquad\qquad (add\,(suc\,X)\,Y \twoheadrightarrow suc\ (plus.rec\ \ (add\,X\,Y)))\ \ (add\,0\,\overline{m})))) \\
\mapsto\!\!\!\to_{\mathsf{stk}} & suc\,(suc\,(\cdots suc\,((add\,0\,Y \twoheadrightarrow Y)\ \ (add\,0\,\overline{m}), \\
 & \qquad\qquad (add\,(suc\,X)\,Y \twoheadrightarrow suc\ (plus.rec\ \ (add\,X\,Y)))\ \ (add\,0\,\overline{m})))) \\
\mapsto\!\!\!\to_{\rho\delta} & suc\,(suc\,(\cdots suc\,([add\,0\,Y \ll add\,0\,\overline{m}]Y, \\
 & \qquad\qquad [add\,(suc\,X)\,Y \ll add\,0\,\overline{m}](suc\ (plus.rec\ \ (add\,X\,Y)))))) \\
\mapsto\!\!\!\to_{\mathsf{stk}} & suc\,(suc\,(\cdots suc\,([add\,0\,Y \ll add\,0\,\overline{m}]Y))) \\
\mapsto\!\!\!\to_{\rho\delta} & suc\,(suc\,(\cdots (suc\,\overline{m}))) \\
\triangleq & \overline{m+n}
\end{array}
$$

Fig. 4. A complete reduction for a ρ-term encoding addition

An (ad-hoc) Object-Oriented Encoding. We can define in the typed $\rho^{\mathsf{stk}}_{\twoheadrightarrow}$ a suitable self-duplicating term that allows us to simulate the *global* behavior of a TRS $\mathcal{R}$. Let us begin with the example of addition, using two constants $rec^{(lab\twoheadrightarrow\iota\twoheadrightarrow\iota)\twoheadrightarrow lab}$ and $add^{\iota\twoheadrightarrow\iota\twoheadrightarrow\iota}$.

Example 2 (Addition).

$$plus \triangleq rec\ S \twoheadrightarrow \begin{pmatrix} add\,0\,Y \twoheadrightarrow Y, \\ add\,(suc\,X)\,Y \twoheadrightarrow suc\ (S.rec\,(add\,X\,Y)) \end{pmatrix}$$

Intuitively, the variable S acts like the meta-variable this in JAVA and thus, the recursive application of the different rules is realized explicitly by using this variable in the right-hand side of the corresponding rules.

This term computes indeed the addition over Peano integers, as illustrated in Fig. 4. The expressions "$\overline{m}$", and "$\overline{m+n}$", and "$\overline{m-n}$" are just aliases for the Peano representations of these numbers as sequences of $suc(\ldots(suc\ 0)\ldots)$). It is worth noticing that all the stuck results are dropped by $\mapsto\!\!\!\to_{\mathsf{stk}}$; the only interesting result is $[add\,0\,Y \ll add\,0\,\overline{m}]Y$. During the reduction, on the left of this term (or terms reducing to it) all the terms get stuck because we try to match 0 against $suc\ \overline{n}$; on the right too because we try to match $suc\,X$ against 0. Notice that if we erase from the term $plus$ all the "administrative" subterms which encode the recursive machinery, we get back a TRS computing addition:

$$
\begin{array}{ll}
add(0,Y) & \to Y \\
add(suc(X),Y) & \to suc\,(add(X,Y))
\end{array}
$$

Observe that, in this rather ad-hoc encoding of $plus$, we have put $S.rec$ only before the symbol add in the right-hand side of the second rule because we know that it is the only position where further rewriting has to be done. In the next paragraph we describe a more general method for encoding a TRS.

An Automated Encoding Using the first Operator. In this paragraph, we show that any convergent and well-typed TRS $\mathcal{R}$ can be mechanically encoded (and typechecked) in $\rho^{\mathsf{stk}}_{\to}$. Recall that a TRS $\mathcal{R}$ is convergent if it is confluent and (strongly) terminating; $\mathcal{R}$ is well-typed if all the rewrite rules can be typechecked with the same type for both sides of the arrow. The encoding is done by wrapping $\mathcal{R}$ into a *typed object-based fixpoint engine* which is a ρ-term that encodes all the rules in $\mathcal{R}$ and applies the translated rules recursively until none of them is applicable. Definition 7 details how this ρ-term is built: the right-hand sides are modified so that the whole system can be re-applied to any of the symbols appearing in the term.

We first define the operator "first" that tries to apply successively n rules $A_1, A_2, \ldots A_n$ to a term B and returns the result of the first rule whose application succeeds (*i.e.* does not reduce to stk). Here we use the constant stk to detect the failure of a given rule and the identity $\mathsf{I} \triangleq Y \to Y$ to yield a successful result:

$$\mathsf{first}(A_1, A_2, \ldots, A_n) \triangleq X \to ((\mathsf{stk} \to A_n\, X, \mathsf{I})\ (\ldots\ (\mathsf{stk} \to A_2\, X, \mathsf{I})\ (A_1 X)))$$

One can check that when we reduce $\mathsf{first}(A, B)\ C$, if $A\ C$ reduces to stk then the final result is the reduct of the term $B\ C$, since the stk produced by $A\ C$ will be discarded by further $\mapsto_{\mathsf{stk}}$ reductions even if it is accepted by the identity. If $A\ C$ reduces to an algebraic term D different of stk, it passes through I and since the matching equation $\mathsf{stk} \ll D$ definitively fails (leading to a stk term), the final result is D. The same behavior is obtained for an arbitrary number of arguments for first. In particular, we will use the term $\mathsf{first}(A_1, \ldots, A_n, \mathsf{I})$, which tries successively the n rules $A_1, \ldots A_n$ on the argument B, and returns B unchanged if every $A_i\ B$ fails.

From a typed point of view, the behavior of first is easy to understand: every A_i can be applied to X, so each must have a type $\tau \to \tau_i$ where $X : \tau$. Moreover, for each i, we apply $(\mathsf{stk} \to A_{i+1}, \mathsf{I})$ to $A_i X$. Here the identity I has type $\tau_i \to \tau_i$. Since all the members of a structure must have the same type, $A_{i+1}X$ has type τ_i too. By trivial induction, all the A_i have the same type, which is the type of $\mathsf{first}(A_1, \ldots, A_n)$. We can informally state this result by $\Gamma \vdash \mathsf{first} : (\tau \to \tau_0) \to \ldots \to (\tau \to \tau_0) \to \tau \to \tau_0$ where Γ is such that $\Gamma \vdash A_i : \tau \to \tau_0$ for each A_i.

In what follows, we denote by $s, t, \ldots$ algebraic terms (in the sense of the grammar $x \mid f(t, \ldots t)$) and a term rewriting system by $\mathcal{R} \triangleq \{t_i \to s_i\}^{i=1..n}$. We write $t \mapsto\!\!\!\twoheadrightarrow_{\mathcal{R}} t'$ when t can be rewritten to the term t' in normal form *w.r.t.* the TRS $\mathcal{R}$.

Definition 7 (Object-based fixpoint engine). *Let $\mathcal{R} = \{t_i \to s_i\}^{i=1..n}$ be an untyped TRS with terms built on a signature $\mathcal{F} = \{a_1, \ldots, a_m\}$; let S be a fresh variable w.r.t. $\mathcal{R}$. The encoding of $\mathcal{R}$ in $\rho^{\mathsf{stk}}_{\to}$ is done as follows:*

- *the terms t_i and s_i are transformed into ρ-terms using the translation $(\!| - |\!)$:*

$$(\!| x |\!) = X$$
$$(\!| f(t_1, \ldots, t_n) |\!) = f\ (\!| t_1 |\!)\ (\!| t_2 |\!) \cdots (\!| t_n |\!)$$

– *the $\rho^{\mathsf{stk}}_{\rightarrow}$-term encoding $\mathcal{R}$ is denoted $(\!|\mathcal{R}|\!)$:*

$$(\!|\mathcal{R}|\!) \triangleq \begin{array}{l} rec(S) \twoheadrightarrow \mathsf{first}\left(\begin{array}{l}(\!| t_1 |\!) \twoheadrightarrow S.rec\,(\!| s_1 |\!),\\ \ldots,\\ (\!| t_n |\!) \twoheadrightarrow S.rec\,(\!| s_n |\!),\\ a_1\,\overline{X} \twoheadrightarrow S.Rec\,(a_1\,\overline{S.rec\,X}),\\ \ldots,\\ a_m\,\overline{X} \twoheadrightarrow S.Rec\,(a_m\,\overline{S.rec\,X})\end{array}\right),\\ Rec(S) \twoheadrightarrow \mathsf{first}\left(\begin{array}{l}(\!| t_1 |\!) \twoheadrightarrow S.rec\,(\!| s_1 |\!),\\ \ldots,\\ (\!| t_n |\!) \twoheadrightarrow S.rec\,(\!| s_n |\!),\\ \mathsf{I}\end{array}\right)\end{array}$$

The result corresponding to the rewriting of an input term t w.r.t. to a TRS $\mathcal{R}$ is computed by the $\rho^{\mathsf{stk}}_{\rightarrow}$-term $(\!|\mathcal{R}|\!).rec\,(\!| t |\!)$.

This encoding enforces an *outermost* strategy: the ρ-term $(\!|\mathcal{R}|\!).rec$ first tries to apply a rule at top level, and if no one succeeds it uses the rules $(a_i\,\overline{S.rec\,X})$, $1 \leq i \leq m$ to propagate the TRS deeper in the term. The second method, called by $S.Rec$, no longer needs to propagate the TRS inside the term because it is used only when the subterms have been totally reduced, thus the only possibly reducible position is the head of the term. Some more subtle combinations of the different rules in the TRS could lead to various interesting strategies like, for example, innermost or call-by-need.

We prove that the encoding is faithful for TRS satisfying confluence and termination, which is often required in rewriting-based languages for (the part of the) rewriting systems that are not guided by a strategy.

Theorem 5 (Soundness and Completeness of the Rewriting Engine).

1. *For any TRS $\mathcal{R}$, and any algebraic input term t, if A is a $\rho^{\mathsf{stk}}_{\rightarrow}$-term in normal form w.r.t. $\mapsto\!\!\!\!\twoheadrightarrow^{\mathsf{stk}}_{\rho\sigma\delta}$ and without matching failures, then:*

$$(\!|\mathcal{R}|\!).rec\,(\!| t |\!) \mapsto\!\!\!\!\twoheadrightarrow^{\mathsf{stk}}_{\rho\sigma\delta} A \;\Rightarrow\; t \mapsto\!\!\!\!\twoheadrightarrow_{\mathcal{R}} t'$$

where $(\!| t' |\!) = A$.

2. *If the TRS $\mathcal{R}$ is* well-typed *and* convergent, *then for any algebraic terms t, t',*

$$t \mapsto\!\!\!\!\twoheadrightarrow_{\mathcal{R}} t' \;\Rightarrow\; (\!|\mathcal{R}|\!).rec\,(\!| t |\!) \mapsto\!\!\!\!\twoheadrightarrow^{\mathsf{stk}}_{\rho\sigma\delta} (\!| t' |\!).$$

Remark 1. These conditions are tight, in the sense that, for most of the non-confluent (or non-terminating) TRS, there is a term t and a reduction path $t \mapsto\!\!\!\!\twoheadrightarrow_{\mathcal{R}} t'$ which can not be mimicked by $(\!|\mathcal{R}|\!).rec\,(\!| t |\!)$. For the non-confluence this can be easily seen: our encoding enforces a particular strategy, so if two reduction paths are possible from a given term, then the engine has to choose one.

Thus, this encoding allows one to use the rewriting calculus in order to represent many well-typed TRS, and at the same time have a control over the correctness of the rules by means of a simple typechecking mechanism.

Example 3 (Computing the length of a list).

$$length \triangleq rec\, S \twoheadrightarrow \mathsf{first}\begin{pmatrix} len\; nil & \twoheadrightarrow 0\,, \\ len\,(cons\; X\; L) & \twoheadrightarrow S.rec\,(suc\,(len\; L))\,, \\ suc\; X & \twoheadrightarrow S.Rec\; suc\,(S.rec\; X) \end{pmatrix},$$

$$Rec\; S \twoheadrightarrow \mathsf{first}\begin{pmatrix} len\; nil & \twoheadrightarrow 0\;, \\ len\,(cons\; X\; L) & \twoheadrightarrow S.rec\,(suc\,(len\; L)), \\ \mathsf{I} & \end{pmatrix}$$

Type-checking all the Encodings. Each of the above encodings can be completed by a type-checking phase. The terms built in $\rho^{\mathsf{stk}}_{\twoheadrightarrow}$ can not be well-typed only if the initial rewriting system cannot be typed correctly.

($plus$) It is easy to check that the naive encoding of $plus$ can be type checked with $\Gamma \vdash plus{:}lab \twoheadrightarrow \iota \twoheadrightarrow \iota$, where $\Gamma \triangleq rec{:}(lab \twoheadrightarrow \iota \twoheadrightarrow \iota) \twoheadrightarrow lab, add{:}\iota \twoheadrightarrow \iota \twoheadrightarrow \iota, suc{:}\iota \twoheadrightarrow \iota, 0{:}\iota$.

($(\!|\mathcal{R}|\!)$) The object-based fixpoint engine has type $lab \twoheadrightarrow \tau \twoheadrightarrow \tau$ where τ is the type of the data manipulated by $\mathcal{R}$. Here rec and Rec both have type $(lab \twoheadrightarrow \tau \twoheadrightarrow \tau) \twoheadrightarrow lab$. There must be a unique type τ for the data manipulated by the TRS: as we said before about first, all the A_i must have a common type $\tau \twoheadrightarrow \tau_0$. Since the identity I (applied if no rule in $\mathcal{R}$ can be used) has a type $\tau \twoheadrightarrow \tau$, all the rules in $\mathcal{R}$ must have the same type for their left and right-hand sides. This condition is not required in term rewriting systems, but it is generally imposed, for safety's sake, in most of the languages based on rewriting (*e.g.* Elan [12], Maude [16]).

($length$) Similarly to $plus$, the term $length$ type-checks with $\Gamma \vdash length : lab \twoheadrightarrow \iota \twoheadrightarrow \iota$, where $\Gamma \triangleq rec{:}(lab \twoheadrightarrow \iota \twoheadrightarrow \iota) \twoheadrightarrow lab, cons{:}\iota \twoheadrightarrow list \twoheadrightarrow list, len{:}list \twoheadrightarrow \iota, nil{:}list$. Notice that the type of the constant rec depends on the type of the data the TRS manipulates: we need in fact a whole class of rec constants (roughly one for each type) in order to write any fixpoint.

5 Conclusions: Related and Future Work

We have studied the expressive power of the simply typed $\rho^{\mathsf{stk}}_{\twoheadrightarrow}$. The defined type system was mainly adapted from the simply typed λ-calculus. The type system deals with all the particularities of the calculus (abstraction over arbitrary patterns, delayed matching constraints, structures of rules and results). The most interesting properties of typed calculi are valid: subject reduction, and type uniqueness, and decidability of typing.

Early versions of the (untyped) rewriting calculus have already been used to describe the implicit (leftmost-innermost) and user defined strategies of Elan [8] but some *ad hoc* operators were added to the basic calculus for this. The $\rho^{\mathsf{stk}}_{\twoheadrightarrow}$ presented here is a simpler formulation of the ρ-calculus essentially based on [11], where no new constructions have to be defined for expressing strategies for quite a large class of rewriting systems. The price to pay for this simplicity is that the encoded rewriting systems we handle are not the most general ones but still the most used ones in practice. The ability to typecheck term rewriting systems and strategies ensures a good trade-off between expressiveness and safety of programs.

Related Work. Some aspects of the relations between rewriting, λ-calculus and types have already been explored. V. van Oostrom has widely studied the confluence of a λ-calculus with patterns [17] but the presented language is untyped. D. Kesner, L. Puel and V. Tannen have proposed a typed pattern calculus [14] which has been designed as a computational interpretation of the Gentzen sequent proofs for the intuitionistic propositional logic. Our encoding of TRS shares some similarities with the one presented by S. Buyn *et al.* [6] that describes an untyped encoding of every strongly separable orthogonal TRS into λ-calculus.

The type system of $\rho_{\rightharpoonup}^{\mathsf{stk}}$ presented in this paper is quite different from the ones recently presented in the literature [10,3] since $\rho_{\rightharpoonup}^{\mathsf{stk}}$ does not use dependent types and thus patterns do not occur in types. In particular, the results about uniqueness, decidability and non-normalization *cannot* be transposed straightforwardly to those (logic-oriented) type systems. Again, the main objective of $\rho_{\rightharpoonup}^{\mathsf{stk}}$ is to set the typed theoretical framework for a programming language featuring sophisticated and user customizable pattern matching facilities.

Some similar ways of producing non-normalization appear in various formalisms. N. P. Mendler [15] has shown that, when introducing recursive definitions in the typed λ-calculus, strong normalization is no longer enforced by typing if the type constructors do not satisfy a *"positiveness condition"*. This kind of condition is still present in the Calculus of Inductive Constructions which is the basis of the Coq proof assistant. The issue appears in programming languages too: for instance, in ML, one can define any recursive function without using the keyword let rec.

Therefore, the type system of $\rho_{\rightharpoonup}^{\mathsf{stk}}$ is suitable for static analysis, *i.e.* it ensures that functions get arguments of the expected type. However, as a wanted feature it does not enforce termination of the typed terms. We have shown the encoding of some interesting terms leading to infinite reductions by the use of the pattern matching features of the calculus. The consequence is that our typing discipline fits for a programming language since we are interested in type consistency and in recursive (potentially non-terminating) programs. Conversely, it is not adapted for defining a *Logical Framework*, since normalization is strongly linked to consistency, and it definitively differs from previous proposals of the authors [10,3].

Acknowledgment. The authors are sincerely grateful to Claude Kirchner for many fruitful discussions and invaluable comments about this work.

References

1. M. Abadi and L. Cardelli. *A Theory of Objects.* Springer Verlag, 1996.
2. H. Barendregt. *Lambda Calculus: its Syntax and Semantics.* North Holland, 1984.
3. G. Barthe, H. Cirstea, C. Kirchner, and L. Liquori. Pure Patterns Type Systems. In *Proc. of POPL*, pages 250–261. The ACM press, 2003.

4. C. Bertolissi, H. Cirstea, and C. Kirchner. Translating Combinatory Reduction Systems into the Rewriting Calculus. In *Proc. of RULE*. ENTCS, 2003.
5. P. Borovansky, C. Kirchner, H. Kirchner, and P.-E. Moreau. ELAN from a rewriting logic point of view. *Theoretical Computer Science*, 2(285):155–185, 2002.
6. S. Byun, J. Kennaway, V. van Oostrom, and F. de Vries. Separability and Translatability of Sequential Term Rewrite Systems into the Lambda Calculus. Technical Report tr-2001-16, University of Leicester, 2001.
7. H. Cirstea and C. Kirchner. The Simply Typed Rewriting Calculus. In *Proc. of WRLA*. ENTCS, 2000.
8. H. Cirstea and C. Kirchner. The rewriting calculus — Part I *and* II. *Logic Journal of the Interest Group in Pure and Applied Logics*, 9(3):427–498, 2001.
9. H. Cirstea, C. Kirchner, and L. Liquori. Matching Power. In *Proc. of RTA*, volume 2051 of *LNCS*, pages 77–92. Springer-Verlag, 2001.
10. H. Cirstea, C. Kirchner, and L. Liquori. The Rho Cube. In *Proc. of FOSSACS*, volume 2030 of *LNCS*, pages 166–180, 2001.
11. H. Cirstea, C. Kirchner, and L. Liquori. Rewriting Calculus with(out) Types. In *Proc. of WRLA*, volume 71 of *ENTCS*, 2002.
12. Équipe Protheo. The Elan Home Page, 2003. `http://elan.loria.fr`.
13. S. N. Kamin. Inheritance in Smalltalk-80: A Denotational Definition. In *Proc. of POPL*, pages 80–87. The ACM press, 1988.
14. D. Kesner, L. Puel, and V. Tannen. A Typed Pattern Calculus. *Information and Computation*, 124(1):32–61, 1996.
15. N. P. Mendler. *Inductive Definition in Type Theory*. PhD thesis, Cornell University, Ithaca, USA, 1987.
16. The Maude Team. The Maude Home Page, 2003. `http://maude.cs.uiuc.edu/`.
17. V. van Oostrom. Lambda Calculus with Patterns. Technical Report IR-228, Faculteit der Wiskunde en Informatica, Vrije Universiteit Amsterdam, 1990.

First-Order Reasoning in the Calculus of Inductive Constructions

Pierre Corbineau

PCRI-LRI(CNRS UMR 8623)-INRIA Futurs
Bât. 490, Université Paris XI
91405 Orsay Cedex, France

Abstract. In this paper we present a contraction-free sequent calculus including inductive definitions for the first-order intuitionistic logic. We show that it is a natural extension to Dyckhoff's *LJT* calculus and we prove the contraction- and cut-elimination properties, thus extending Dyckhoff's result, in order to validate its use as a basis for proof-search procedures. Finally we describe the proof-search strategy used in our implementation as a tactic in the Coq proof assistant [2].

1 Introduction

Most basic intuitionistic predicate calculi using sequents [9,4] include the structural rule of contraction or a left-introduction rule for the arrow in which the principal formula stays in the left premise :

$$\frac{\Gamma, A, A \vdash G}{\Gamma, A \vdash G}\ Contr \qquad \frac{\Gamma, A{\rightarrow}B \vdash A \quad \Gamma, B \vdash G}{\Gamma, A{\rightarrow}B \vdash G}\ L{\rightarrow}$$

Those rules have obvious bad properties if we use them in a bottom-up proof-search procedure since they can lead to loops in the proof-search process if not restricted.

In [5], Roy Dyckhoff described *LJT*, a calculus for the intuitionistic propositional logic without contraction. Instead he put forward that contraction could be shown admissible, i.e. it could be seen as an implicit rule in his system. Furthermore, he split the $L{\rightarrow}$ rule in several subcases depending on the formula being on the left of the arrow, and that way avoided the repetition of the principal formula in the premise.

In [6], together with Sara Negri he gave a direct proof of cut-elimination for this system, and for its extension to first-order quantifiers $\forall$ and $\exists$. Of course this extension did not have any termination property similar to that of *LJT* because of the rules about the universal quantifier.

The propositional part of the *LJT* sequent calculus has been implemented in the Coq proof assistant as a proof-search procedure : the `tauto` [1] tactic [12]. This procedure performs depth-first-search of proofs with optimization of search

[1] in Coq v8.0, tactic names start with lower case letters.

S. Berardi, M. Coppo, and F. Damiani (Eds.): TYPES 2003, LNCS 3085, pp. 162–177, 2004.

using reversibility of rules in the calculus. This tactic is also used as a goal simplification procedure called `intuition`. The approach used was successful so we wanted to extend it to first-order reasoning.

Moreover, two attempts at automating the predicate calculus in Coq were previously made : the first one was the implantation of a decision procedure for the direct predicate calculus [8,1], a decidable restriction of the predicate calculus to its linear fragment, it led to the `linear` tactic [7] which was implemented in early versions of Coq. It has been discontinued since, because this fragment is not powerful enough.

The second attempt has been the port of the `jprover` module [14] from the Nuprl prover [10] to Coq. It is basically made of a classical tableau prover packed with a constraint solver to restrict it to intuitionistic logic. Similarly to `linear` this tactic behaves has a black box constructing a complete proof in one step. But it doesn't handle the case of $\forall x.P[x] \vdash \exists y.P[y]$ where the domain must be inhabited, and it has a very restricted view of logical connectives. Moreover its black-box behavior forbids its use as a goal simplification procedure.

Our purpose was to adapt Dyckhoff's system so that it could be used in a natural way for first-order intuitionistic proof-search in Coq. In order to do that we had to cope with the fact that in Coq only the implication $\rightarrow$ and the universal quantification $\forall$ are primitive constructions — they are two forms of dependent products — whereas standard logical connectives $\wedge,\vee,\bot$ and even the existential quantifier $\exists$ can be defined in terms of inductive definitions.

So we propose here a variant of Dyckhoff's *LJT* calculus where the primitive logical connectives are $\forall,\rightarrow$ and inductive definitions, viewing other connectives as particular cases of inductive definitions, but also allowing many more possible constructions.

In section 2, we first present our inductive definitions and the corresponding notion of first-order formula, and we show how this notion gives a natural extension of Dyckhoff's calculus. Then in section 3 we prove that our calculus enjoys both contraction- and cut-elimination properties. Finally in section 4 we discuss some proof-search strategy issues and present our implementation of a proof-search procedure based on this calculus.

2 A Sequent Calculus with Inductive Formulae

2.1 Introducing Inductive Formulae

In the following text we will use the notations $\overrightarrow{H_i}$, $\overrightarrow{H_i}\rightarrow X$, $\overrightarrow{x}$ and $\forall\overrightarrow{y_i}.X$ as shortcuts for $H_{i,1},\ldots,H_{i,p}$, $H_{i,1}\rightarrow(\ldots\rightarrow(H_{i,p}\rightarrow X))$, $x_1,\ldots,x_p$ and $\forall y_{i,1}\ldots\forall y_{i,p}.X$. Please note that the length of the sequences is always fixed *a priori*, and that the meaning of $\overrightarrow{H_i}$ depends on whether it is or not followed by an arrow. We suppose implication is right-associative and has higher priority than $\forall$. We will also use the $\{\_\}_i$ notation to mean either a sequence of formulae or a (finite) set of premises in a rule, where i ranges over the constructor indices or the hypotheses indices of an inductive formula.

To define our class of formula we start with a signature of first-order constants and predicates of fixed arity. Any term formed by the application of a n-ary predicate to n well-formed terms possibly containing variables will be called *atomic formula*, and the variables occurring in the n terms will be called the free variables of this formula.

Then we define compound formulae and inductive families mutually recursively, so let us begin with the inductive families. An inductive family is a triple $(I, \overrightarrow{X}, \{\mathcal{C}_1 : \tau_1; \mathcal{C}_2 : \tau_2; \ldots\})$ where I is the name of the inductive family, $\overrightarrow{X}$ a possibly empty list of formal parameters having a fixed arity and being either propositional or first-order parameters. $\mathcal{C}_i$ is the name and τ_i the type of the ith constructor, which is itself a formula.

Then we define our formula language inductively as follows: A formula is either an atomic formula or a compound formula. If A and B are formulae then so is $A \rightarrow B$, if $P[x]$ is a formula then so is $\forall x.P[x]$ and if $\overrightarrow{p}$ is a sequence of parameters whose arity and class (formula or term) fit those of the formal parameters of the I family, then $I(\overrightarrow{p})$ is a formula. Implication and universal quantification behave as usual regarding free and bound variables. The free variables in $I(\overrightarrow{p})$ are those in $\overrightarrow{p}$.

A constructor type must be a formula made of a (possibly empty) sequence of universal quantifications and implications and the head of that formula must be $I(\overrightarrow{X})$. The formal parameters must not be bound by the quantifiers. But all other free variables must be universally quantified.

Without loss of generality we will assume that constructor types are in weak prenex form, i.e. all dependent products outermost, thus being of the form $\forall \overrightarrow{y_i}.\overrightarrow{H_i}(\overrightarrow{X}, \overrightarrow{y_i}) \rightarrow I(\overrightarrow{X})$. We will call $\overrightarrow{H_i}$ the logical hypotheses of the constructor and $\overrightarrow{y_i}$ the first-order variables of the constructor.

We suppose that inductive families we consider are neither recursive nor mutually recursive, i.e. the relation defined by the use of an inductive family in the logical hypotheses of another one is well-founded.

Here we give a set of examples of inductive definitions defining standard connectives :

$$(\wedge, (A, B), \{pair : A \rightarrow B \rightarrow A \wedge B\})$$
$$(\vee, (A, B), \{inj_l : A \rightarrow A \vee B;\ inj_r : B \rightarrow A \vee B\})$$
$$(\bot, (), \{\})$$
$$(\top, (), \{triv : \top\})$$
$$(\exists, (H[\_]), \{witness : \forall y.H[y] \rightarrow \exists x.H[x]\})$$

The $\wedge$ and $\vee$ inductive families have two propositional parameters of arity 0, $\top$ and $\bot$ have none, and $\exists$ has one propositional parameter of arity 1.

Given those definitions, the meaning of inductive formulae is that

$$I(\overrightarrow{p}) \Leftrightarrow \bigvee_i (\exists \overrightarrow{y_i}. \bigwedge_j H_{i,j}(\overrightarrow{p}, \overrightarrow{y_i}))$$

But since we use inductive type instead of just defining the connectives as plain identifiers, the elimination principles for the Calculus of Inductive Con-

$$\frac{}{\Gamma, P \vdash P}\ Ax$$

$$\frac{\Gamma, A \vdash B}{\Gamma \vdash A \to B}\ R\to \qquad \frac{\Gamma, P, B \vdash G}{\Gamma, P, P \to B \vdash G}\ La\to$$

$$\frac{\Gamma, A, B \to C \vdash B \quad \Gamma, C \vdash G}{\Gamma, (A \to B) \to C \vdash G}\ L{\to}{\to}$$

$$\frac{\Gamma \vdash A[x]}{\Gamma \vdash \forall x.A[x]}\ R\forall \qquad \frac{\Gamma, \forall x.A[x], A[t] \vdash G}{\Gamma, \forall x.A[x] \vdash G}\ L\forall$$

$$\frac{\Gamma, (\forall x.A[x]) \to B \vdash \forall x.A[x] \quad \Gamma, B \vdash G}{\Gamma, (\forall x.A[x]) \to B \vdash G}\ L\forall{\to}$$

$$\frac{\{\Gamma \vdash H_{i,j}(\overrightarrow{p}, \overrightarrow{t_i})\}_j}{\Gamma \vdash I(\overrightarrow{p})}\ RI_i \qquad \frac{\{\Gamma, \overrightarrow{H_i}(\overrightarrow{p}, \overrightarrow{y_i}) \vdash G\}_i}{\Gamma, I(\overrightarrow{p}) \vdash G}\ LI$$

$$\frac{\Gamma, \{\forall \overrightarrow{y_i}.\overrightarrow{H_i}(\overrightarrow{p}, \overrightarrow{y_i}) \to B\}_i \vdash G}{\Gamma, I(\overrightarrow{p}) \to B \vdash G}\ LI{\to}$$

Fig. 1. The *LJTI* calculus

structions give us primitive left- and right-introduction rules built in the calculus [13], instead of unfolding the definition and dealing with standard connectives.

Let us see somme more exotic examples : many specific predicates may be defined by non-recursive inductive definitions. For example we express that A satisfies the excluded-middle property using:

$$(\text{Dec}, (A), \{istrue : A \to \text{Dec}(A);\ isfalse : (A \to \bot) \to \text{Dec}(A)\})$$

Another example could be to express the Euclidean division of two natural numbers. That is, Eucl_div(a, b) gives both witnesses q,r and proofs of $r < b$ and $a = bq + r$. Eucl_div has two first-order parameters of arity 0 :

$$(\text{Eucl\_div}, (a, b), \{EDintro : \forall q.\forall r.(r < b) \to (a = bq + r) \to \text{Eucl\_div}(a, b)\})$$

2.2 The *LJTI* Sequent Calculus

From now on we will assume that t ranges over first order terms, x, y over first-order variables $A \ldots G$ over arbitrary formulae, P, Q over atomic formulae, x, y over first-order variables, and $\Gamma, \Gamma', \Gamma''$ over multisets of formulae. When we write $P[x]$ we assume that x is not free in $P[y]$ if $x \neq y$, and that any variable free in t is free in $P[t]$ (we allow the use of α-renaming in P).

Using the definition of inductive formula above we define the *LJTI* sequent calculus in figure 1. Please note that using generic inductive definitions we have a smaller number of rules in our system than in *LJT*. Note that in axiom and $La\to$ rules P must be an atomic formula.

In the right introduction rule RI_i, i ranges over the constructor indices, so there is one such rule for each constructor, and in the left introduction rule LI

existential variables $\overrightarrow{y_i}$ must follow the eigenvariable condition, and so must x in the $R\forall$ rule. This means x and $\overrightarrow{y_i}$ must not occur free in the conclusion of those rules (or equivalently they must not occur free in Γ,G or $\overrightarrow{p}$).

For instance, if we try to apply this scheme to $\bot$, we get the following rules :

$$(no\ R\bot\ rule) \qquad \frac{}{\Gamma, \bot \vdash G}\ L\bot \qquad \frac{\Gamma \vdash G}{\Gamma, \bot \rightarrow A \vdash G}\ L\bot\rightarrow$$

You can check that the rules for $\bot$ match those for the standard connectives in [6] except for $L\bot$ which is a special case of weakening that is invertible (see rule (2) and rule (8)). For Eucl_div we would get :

$$\frac{\Gamma \vdash r < b \quad \Gamma \vdash a = bq + r}{\Gamma \vdash \mathrm{Eucl\_div}(a, b)}\ R\mathrm{Eucl\_div} \qquad \frac{\Gamma, r < b, a = bq + r \vdash G}{\Gamma, \mathrm{Eucl\_div}(a, b) \vdash G}\ L\mathrm{Eucl\_div}$$

$$\frac{\Gamma, \forall q.\forall r.(r < b) \rightarrow (a = bq + r) \rightarrow A \vdash G}{\Gamma, \mathrm{Eucl\_div}(a, b) \rightarrow A \vdash G}\ L\mathrm{Eucl\_div}\rightarrow$$

In the LEucl_div rule q and r mustn't be free in Γ or G nor in a or b.

3 Properties of the *LJTI* Calculus

3.1 Inversion Lemmata

We first give a series of lemmata about invertibility of rules, and admissibility of weakening.

We say that a rule is *admissible* in $LJTI$ if for every instance of the premise(s) that are derivable in $LJTI$, we get a derivation of the conclusion in $LJTI$. When there is only one premise in the rule, we say that this rule is *strongly admissible* if the derivation of the conclusion can be made shorter or of equal height than that of the premise, the height being 0 for an axiom and the maximum of the heights of the derivation of the premises plus one otherwise.

Lemma 1. *The following rules are strongly admissible in $LJTI$.*

$$\frac{\Gamma[x] \vdash G[x]}{\Gamma[t] \vdash G[t]} \quad (1) \qquad\qquad \frac{\Gamma \vdash G}{\Gamma, \Gamma' \vdash G}\ W \quad (2)$$

Proof.

rule (1) : by structural induction on the derivation tree, renaming eigenvariables by induction hypothesis.

rule (2) : By structural induction on the derivation tree, using rule (1) to rename eigenvariables where needed.

Lemma 2. *The following rules are strongly admissible in LJTI :*

$$\frac{\Gamma \vdash A \to B}{\Gamma, A \vdash B} \quad (3) \qquad \frac{\Gamma, \forall x. A\,[x] \to B \vdash G}{\Gamma, B \vdash G} \quad (6)$$

$$\frac{\Gamma, P \to B \vdash G}{\Gamma, B \vdash G} \quad (4) \qquad \frac{\Gamma, I(\overrightarrow{p}) \vdash G}{\Gamma, \overrightarrow{H_i}(\overrightarrow{p}, \overrightarrow{t}) \vdash G} \quad (7)$$

$$\frac{\Gamma, (C \to D) \to B \vdash G}{\Gamma, B \vdash G} \quad (5) \qquad \frac{\Gamma, I(\overrightarrow{p}) \to B \vdash G}{\Gamma, \{\forall \overrightarrow{y_i}. \overrightarrow{H_i}(\overrightarrow{p}, \overrightarrow{y_i}) \to B\}_i \vdash G} \quad (8)$$

Proof. By induction on the height of the derivation, using rule (1) to rename eigenvariables and for rule (7).

3.2 Admissibility of Contraction

We first show that the generalized axiom rule is admissible in *LJTI*, and we obtain the admissibility of contraction which allows us to show the admissibility of generic $L\to$ rules used in standard sequent calculi.

To perform induction on formulae, we define a notion of weight which is given below :

$$\mathrm{wt}(P) = 1, P \text{ atomic}$$

$$\mathrm{wt}(A \to B) = 1 + \mathrm{wt}(A) + \mathrm{wt}(B)$$

$$\mathrm{wt}(\forall x. A\,[x]) = 1 + \mathrm{wt}(A\,[x])$$

$$\mathrm{wt}(I(\overrightarrow{p})) = \sum_i \mathrm{wt}(\mathcal{C}_i(\overrightarrow{p}))$$

$$\text{if } \mathcal{C}_i(\overrightarrow{p}) : \forall \overrightarrow{y_i}. \overrightarrow{H_i}(\overrightarrow{p}, \overrightarrow{y_i}) \to I(\overrightarrow{p}) \text{ then}$$

$$\mathrm{wt}(\mathcal{C}_i(\overrightarrow{p})) = (2 \times \mathrm{length}(\overrightarrow{y_i})) + \sum_j 1 + \mathrm{wt}(H_{i,j}(\overrightarrow{p}))$$

This weight is lower than the one in [6] in the case of disjunction, but in fact Dyckhoff's proof is valid even with our weight. The essential fact about this weight is that the rules about inductive formulae that actually have premises, when read upward, replace their principal formula with strictly lighter formulae or remove them.

In our proofs, *Ind* steps mean that we use the induction hypothesis, we use the double bar to distinguish those steps from the others. Admissible rules are labeled by the lemma in which they were introduced.

Lemma 3. *These sequents are provable in LJTI, even if A is not atomic :*

$$\Gamma, A \vdash A \quad (9) \qquad \Gamma, A, A \to B \vdash B \quad (10)$$

Proof. 1. We prove by induction on $\mathrm{wt}(A)$ that for any Γ we have $\Gamma, A \vdash A$, by cases on the shape of A.

- If $A = I(\overrightarrow{p})$ then for all constructors $\mathcal{C}_i$ and logical hypotheses $H_{i,j}$ we have by induction hypothesis $\Gamma, \overrightarrow{H_i}(\overrightarrow{p}, \overrightarrow{y_i}) \vdash H_{i,j}(\overrightarrow{p}, \overrightarrow{y_i})$, so for each i we have $\Gamma, \overrightarrow{H_i}(\overrightarrow{p}, \overrightarrow{y_i}) \vdash I(\overrightarrow{p})$ by RI_i. Since we can choose $\overrightarrow{y_i}$ that do not occur free in Γ nor in $\overrightarrow{p}$ we can use LI to obtain $\Gamma, I(\overrightarrow{p}) \vdash I(\overrightarrow{p})$.
- If $A = I(\overrightarrow{p}) \rightarrow B$, B being an arbitrary formula, for any constructor $\mathcal{C}_k$ and set of formulae Δ we have by induction hypothesis :

$$\Gamma, \Delta, \overrightarrow{H_k}(\overrightarrow{p}, \overrightarrow{z_k}) \rightarrow B \vdash \overrightarrow{H_k}(\overrightarrow{p}, \overrightarrow{z_k}) \rightarrow B$$

Using rule (3) for each $H_{k,j}$ we get :

$$\Gamma, \Delta, \overrightarrow{H_k}(\overrightarrow{p}, \overrightarrow{z_k}) \rightarrow B, \overrightarrow{H_k}(\overrightarrow{p}, \overrightarrow{z_k}) \vdash B$$

Now if we choose $\Delta = \{\forall \overrightarrow{y_i}.\overrightarrow{H_i}(\overrightarrow{p}, \overrightarrow{y_i}) \rightarrow B\}_i, \Delta'$ and Δ' is the sequence of formulae obtained by instantiating one or more of the $\overrightarrow{y_k}$ by the $\overrightarrow{z_k}$ in $\forall \overrightarrow{y_k}.\overrightarrow{H_k}(\overrightarrow{p}, \overrightarrow{y_k}) \rightarrow B$. We can use $L\forall$ for each $z_{k,j}$ with that formula and the formulae in Δ' and we obtain for each constructor $\mathcal{C}_k$:

$$\Gamma, \{\forall \overrightarrow{y_i}.\overrightarrow{H_i}(\overrightarrow{p}, \overrightarrow{y_i}) \rightarrow B\}_i, \overrightarrow{H_k}(\overrightarrow{p}, \overrightarrow{z_k}) \vdash B$$

We can choose the $\overrightarrow{z_k}$ so that they are not free in Γ, $\overrightarrow{p}$ or B and from there we have :

$$\dfrac{\dfrac{\dfrac{\{\Gamma, \{\forall \overrightarrow{y_i}.\overrightarrow{H_i}(\overrightarrow{p}, \overrightarrow{y_i}) \rightarrow B\}_i, \overrightarrow{H_k}(\overrightarrow{p}, \overrightarrow{z_k}) \vdash B\}_k}{\Gamma, \{\forall \overrightarrow{y_i}.\overrightarrow{H_i}(\overrightarrow{p}, \overrightarrow{y_i}) \rightarrow B\}_i, I(\overrightarrow{p}) \vdash B}\ LI}{\Gamma, I(\overrightarrow{p}) \rightarrow B, I(\overrightarrow{p}) \vdash B}\ LI\rightarrow}{\Gamma, I(\overrightarrow{p}) \rightarrow B \vdash I(\overrightarrow{p}) \rightarrow B}\ R\rightarrow$$

- The other cases are handled similarly to [6].

2. We have $\Gamma, A \rightarrow B \vdash A \rightarrow B$ by rule (9), so we get $\Gamma, A, A \rightarrow B \vdash B$ by rule (3).

Lemma 4. *The following rule is admissible in LJTI :*

$$\frac{\Gamma \vdash D \quad \Gamma, B \vdash E}{\Gamma, D \rightarrow B \vdash E} \tag{11}$$

Proof. By induction on the height of the derivation d of the first premise and by cases on its last step.

- If it is by an axiom then D is atomic and $\Gamma = \Gamma', D$. We have :

$$\frac{\Gamma', D, B \vdash E}{\Gamma', D, D \rightarrow B \vdash E}\ La\rightarrow$$

– If it is by RI_i then let $D = I(\overrightarrow{p})$:

$$\dfrac{\dfrac{\dfrac{\dfrac{\dfrac{\{\Gamma \vdash H_{i,j}(\overrightarrow{p}, \overrightarrow{t_i})\}_j \quad \Gamma, B \vdash E}{\Gamma', \overrightarrow{H_i}(\overrightarrow{p}, \overrightarrow{t_i}) \to B \vdash E}\ \text{some } Ind}{\Gamma', \forall \overrightarrow{y_i}.\overrightarrow{H_i}(\overrightarrow{p}, \overrightarrow{y_i}) \to B, \ldots, \overrightarrow{H_i}(\overrightarrow{p}, \overrightarrow{t_i}) \to B \vdash E}\ W}{\Gamma', \forall \overrightarrow{y_i}.\overrightarrow{H_i}(\overrightarrow{p}, \overrightarrow{y_i}) \to B \vdash E}\ \text{some } L\forall}{\Gamma', \{\forall \overrightarrow{y_k}.\overrightarrow{H_k}(\overrightarrow{p}, \overrightarrow{y_k}) \to B\}_k \vdash E}\ W}{\Gamma, I(\overrightarrow{p}) \to B \vdash E}\ LI\to$$

– If it is by LI then $\Gamma = \Gamma', I(\overrightarrow{p})$. We have for every constructor $\mathcal{C}_i$:

$$\dfrac{\Gamma', \overrightarrow{H_i}(\overrightarrow{p}, \overrightarrow{y_i}) \vdash D \quad \begin{array}{c} \Gamma', I(\overrightarrow{p}), B \vdash E \\ \vdots\ \text{rule (7)} \\ \Gamma', \overrightarrow{H_i}(\overrightarrow{p}, \overrightarrow{y_i}), B \vdash E \end{array}}{\Gamma', \overrightarrow{H_i}(\overrightarrow{p}, \overrightarrow{y_i}), D \to B \vdash E}\ Ind$$

If we choose $\overrightarrow{y_i}$ so that they are not free in Γ',$\overrightarrow{p}$,B or E, we use LI and get $\Gamma', I(\overrightarrow{p}), D \to B \vdash E$.

– If it is by $LI\to$ then $\Gamma = \Gamma', I(\overrightarrow{p}) \to C$. We have :

$$\dfrac{\dfrac{\Gamma', \{\forall \overrightarrow{y_i}.\overrightarrow{H_i}(\overrightarrow{p}, \overrightarrow{y_i}) \to C\}_i \vdash D \quad \begin{array}{c} \Gamma', I(\overrightarrow{p}) \to C, B \vdash E \\ \vdots\ \text{rule (8)} \\ \Gamma', \{\forall \overrightarrow{y_i}.\overrightarrow{H_i}(\overrightarrow{p}, \overrightarrow{y_i}) \to C\}_i, B \vdash E \end{array}}{\Gamma', \{\forall \overrightarrow{y_i}.\overrightarrow{H_i}(\overrightarrow{p}, \overrightarrow{y_i}) \to C\}_i, D \to B \vdash E}\ Ind}{\Gamma', I(\overrightarrow{p}) \to C, D \to B \vdash E}\ LI\to$$

– See [6] for the other cases.

Lemma 5. *The following rule is admissible in $LJTI$:*

$$\frac{\Gamma, (C \to D) \to B \vdash E}{\Gamma, C, D \to B, D \to B \vdash E} \tag{12}$$

Proof. The interesting case where $(C \to D) \to B$ is principal is treated similarly to [6], using rule (11) .

Theorem 1. *The* Contraction *rule below is admissible in $LJTI$.*

$$\frac{\Gamma, A, A \vdash G}{\Gamma, A \vdash G}\ Contr$$

Proof. By lexicographic induction on $\mathrm{wt}(A)$ and the height of the derivation of the premise. If A is not principal in the last step deriving the premise, we use the induction hypothesis on the premise(s) of this step and apply the rule on the contracted premise. If A is principal, we do a case analysis on the shape of A.

- If A is an atomic formula P then the last rule is an axiom and $G = P$ so the conclusion is an axiom.
- If $A = I(\overrightarrow{p})$ then we have for each i:

$$\begin{array}{c} \Gamma, I(\overrightarrow{p}), \overrightarrow{H_i}(\overrightarrow{p}, \overrightarrow{y_i}) \vdash G \\ \vdots \text{ rule (7)} \\ \Gamma, \overrightarrow{H_i}(\overrightarrow{p}, \overrightarrow{y_i}), \overrightarrow{H_i}(\overrightarrow{p}, \overrightarrow{y_i}) \vdash G \\ \vdots \text{ some } Ind \\ \Gamma, \overrightarrow{H_i}(\overrightarrow{p}, \overrightarrow{y_i}) \vdash G \end{array}$$

  Since the $\overrightarrow{y_i}$ are not free in Γ or $\overrightarrow{p}$ nor in G, we can use LI to get $\Gamma, I(\overrightarrow{p}) \vdash G$.
- If $A = I(\overrightarrow{p}) \rightarrow C$ then we have :

$$\begin{array}{c} \Gamma, I(\overrightarrow{p}) \rightarrow C, \{\forall \overrightarrow{y_i}. \overrightarrow{H_i}(\overrightarrow{p}, \overrightarrow{y_i}) \rightarrow C\}_i \vdash G \\ \vdots \text{ rule (8)} \\ \Gamma, \{\forall \overrightarrow{y_i}. \overrightarrow{H_i}(\overrightarrow{p}, \overrightarrow{y_i}) \rightarrow C\}_i, \{\forall \overrightarrow{y_i}. \overrightarrow{H_i}(\overrightarrow{p}, \overrightarrow{y_i}) \rightarrow C\}_i \vdash G \\ \vdots \text{ some } Ind \\ \dfrac{\Gamma, \{\forall \overrightarrow{y_i}. \overrightarrow{H_i}(\overrightarrow{p}, \overrightarrow{y_i}) \rightarrow C\}_i \vdash G}{\Gamma, I(\overrightarrow{p}) \rightarrow C \vdash G} LI\rightarrow \end{array}$$

- Otherwise we do as in [6] , using rule (12) when $A = (C \rightarrow D) \rightarrow B$.

Which closes our proof by induction.

Lemma 6. *The following rule is admissible in LJTI :*

$$\frac{\Gamma, A \rightarrow B \vdash A \quad \Gamma, B \vdash G}{\Gamma, A \rightarrow B \vdash G} \tag{13}$$

Proof.

$$\dfrac{\dfrac{\Gamma, A \rightarrow B \vdash A \quad \dfrac{\Gamma, B \vdash G}{\Gamma, A \rightarrow B, B \vdash G} W}{\Gamma, A \rightarrow B, A \rightarrow B \vdash A} \text{rule (11)}}{\Gamma, A \rightarrow B \vdash G} Contr$$

This last lemma shows us that the $LJTI$ calculus is complete with respect to the calculus which could be named LJI where the axiom rule would be the generalized one and all left arrow rules would be replaced by the one from the lemma.

3.3 Cut-Elimination Theorem

The proof outline follows that of [6] except that with our notion of inductive formula there are fewer cases to consider.

Theorem 2. *The* Cut *rule below is admissible in LJTI.*

$$\frac{\Gamma \vdash A \quad \Gamma', A \vdash E}{\Gamma, \Gamma' \vdash E}\, Cut$$

Proof. By lexicographic induction on wt(A) and on the sum of the heights of the derivations of the premises :

If the first premise is an axiom, let $\Gamma = \Gamma'', A$:

$$\frac{\Gamma', A \vdash E}{\Gamma'', \Gamma', A \vdash E}\, W$$

If the second premise is an axiom, either $E \in \Gamma'$ or $A = E$ and the conclusion is an axiom.

Otherwise, neither premise is an axiom.

If A is not principal on the left, by cases on the last step of the left derivation :

- LI : We have

$$\dfrac{\dfrac{\{\Gamma'', \overrightarrow{H_i}(\overrightarrow{p}, \overrightarrow{y_i}) \vdash A\}_i}{\Gamma'', I(\overrightarrow{p}) \vdash A}\, LI \qquad \Gamma', A \vdash E}{\Gamma'', I(\overrightarrow{p}), \Gamma' \vdash E}\, Cut$$

  For each i we use the induction hypothesis :

$$\dfrac{\Gamma'', \overrightarrow{H_i}(\overrightarrow{p}, \overrightarrow{y_i}) \vdash A \quad \Gamma', A \vdash E}{\Gamma'', \overrightarrow{H_i}(\overrightarrow{p}, \overrightarrow{y_i}), \Gamma' \vdash E}\, Cut$$

  After renaming $\overrightarrow{y_i}$ if they occur free in Γ' or E, We use LI and obtain $\Gamma'', I(\overrightarrow{p}), \Gamma' \vdash E$.
- $LI\!\rightarrow$

$$\dfrac{\dfrac{\Gamma'', \{\forall \overrightarrow{y_i}.\overrightarrow{H_i}(\overrightarrow{p}, \overrightarrow{y_i}) \rightarrow C\}_i \vdash A}{\Gamma'', I(\overrightarrow{p}) \rightarrow C \vdash A}\, LI\!\rightarrow \qquad \Gamma', A \vdash E}{\Gamma'', I(\overrightarrow{p}) \rightarrow C, \Gamma' \vdash E}\, Cut$$

  becomes :

$$\dfrac{\dfrac{\Gamma'', \{\forall \overrightarrow{y_i}.\overrightarrow{H_i}(\overrightarrow{p}, \overrightarrow{y_i}) \rightarrow C\}_i \vdash A \quad \Gamma', A \vdash E}{\Gamma'', \{\forall \overrightarrow{y_i}.\overrightarrow{H_i}(\overrightarrow{p}, \overrightarrow{y_i}) \rightarrow C\}_i, \Gamma' \vdash E}\, Cut}{\Gamma'', I(\overrightarrow{p}) \rightarrow C, \Gamma' \vdash E}\, LI\!\rightarrow$$

- other cases are dealt with similarly to [6].

If A is principal on the left and not on the right, by cases on the last step of the right premise derivation :

- RI_i : We have

$$\dfrac{\Gamma \vdash A \quad \dfrac{\{\Gamma', A \vdash H_{i,j}(\overrightarrow{p}, \overrightarrow{t_i})\}_j}{\Gamma', A \vdash I(\overrightarrow{p})} RI_i}{\Gamma, \Gamma' \vdash I(\overrightarrow{p})} Cut$$

For each j we use the induction hypothesis :

$$\dfrac{\Gamma \vdash A \quad \Gamma', A \vdash H_{i,j}(\overrightarrow{p}, \overrightarrow{t_i})}{\Gamma, \Gamma' \vdash H_{i,j}(\overrightarrow{p}, \overrightarrow{t_i})} Cut$$

And we use the RI_i rule to get $\Gamma, \Gamma' \vdash I(\overrightarrow{p})$.

- LI

$$\dfrac{\Gamma \vdash A \quad \dfrac{\{\Gamma'', A, \overrightarrow{H_i}(\overrightarrow{p}, \overrightarrow{y_i}) \vdash E\}_i}{\Gamma'', A, I(\overrightarrow{p}) \vdash E} LI}{\Gamma, \Gamma'', I(\overrightarrow{p}) \vdash E} Cut$$

For each i we use the induction hypothesis :

$$\dfrac{\Gamma \vdash A \quad \Gamma'', A, \overrightarrow{H_i}(\overrightarrow{p}, \overrightarrow{y_i}) \vdash E}{\Gamma, \Gamma'', \overrightarrow{H_i}(\overrightarrow{p}, \overrightarrow{y_i}) \vdash E} Cut$$

After renaming $\overrightarrow{y_i}$ if they occur free in Γ, we use LI to get $\Gamma, \Gamma'', I(\overrightarrow{p}) \vdash E$.

- $LI{\rightarrow}$

$$\dfrac{\Gamma \vdash A \quad \dfrac{\Gamma'', A, \{\forall \overrightarrow{y_i}. \overrightarrow{H_i}(\overrightarrow{p}, \overrightarrow{y_i}) \rightarrow C\}_i \vdash E}{\Gamma'', A, I(\overrightarrow{p}) \rightarrow C \vdash E} LI{\rightarrow}}{\Gamma, \Gamma'', I(\overrightarrow{p}) \rightarrow C \vdash E} Cut$$

becomes :

$$\dfrac{\dfrac{\Gamma \vdash A \quad \Gamma'', A, \{\forall \overrightarrow{y_i}. \overrightarrow{H_i}(\overrightarrow{p}, \overrightarrow{y_i}) \rightarrow C\}_i \vdash E}{\Gamma, \Gamma'', \{\forall \overrightarrow{y_i}. \overrightarrow{H_i}(\overrightarrow{p}, \overrightarrow{y_i}) \rightarrow C\}_i \vdash E} Cut}{\Gamma, \Gamma'', I(\overrightarrow{p}) \rightarrow C \vdash E} LI{\rightarrow}$$

- Otherwise, see [6].

If A is principal in both premises, by cases on the shape of A :

- $A = I(\overrightarrow{p})$

$$\dfrac{\dfrac{\{\Gamma \vdash H_{i,j}(\overrightarrow{p}, \overrightarrow{t_i})\}_j}{\Gamma \vdash I(\overrightarrow{p})} RI_i \quad \dfrac{\{\Gamma', \overrightarrow{H_k}(\overrightarrow{p}, \overrightarrow{y_k}) \vdash E\}_k}{\Gamma', I(\overrightarrow{p}) \vdash E} LI}{\Gamma, \Gamma' \vdash E} Cut$$

becomes :

$$\dfrac{\{\Gamma \vdash H_{i,j}(\overrightarrow{p}, \overrightarrow{t_i})\}_j \quad \begin{array}{c} \Gamma', \overrightarrow{H_i}(\overrightarrow{p}, \overrightarrow{y_i}) \vdash E \\ \vdots \text{ rule (1)} \\ \Gamma', \overrightarrow{H_i}(\overrightarrow{p}, \overrightarrow{t_i}) \vdash E \end{array}}{\Gamma, \Gamma' \vdash E} \text{some } Cut$$

– $A = I(\overrightarrow{p}) \rightarrow B$

$$\dfrac{\dfrac{\Gamma, I(\overrightarrow{p}) \vdash B}{\Gamma \vdash I(\overrightarrow{p}) \rightarrow B}\, R{\rightarrow} \qquad \dfrac{\Gamma', \{\forall \overrightarrow{y_i}. \overrightarrow{H_i}(\overrightarrow{p}, \overrightarrow{y_i}) \rightarrow B\}_i \vdash E}{\Gamma', I(\overrightarrow{p}) \rightarrow B \vdash E}\, LI{\rightarrow}}{\Gamma, \Gamma' \vdash E}\, Cut$$

For each constructor index i we can turn our proof of $\Gamma, I(\overrightarrow{p}) \vdash B$ into a proof of $\Gamma, \overrightarrow{H_i}(\overrightarrow{p}, \overrightarrow{y_i}) \vdash B$ by rule (7), choosing the $\overrightarrow{y_i}$ free in $B, \overrightarrow{p}$ and Γ. Thus we can use $R{\rightarrow}$ and $R\forall$ to obtain $\Gamma \vdash \forall \overrightarrow{y_i}. \overrightarrow{H_i}(\overrightarrow{p}, \overrightarrow{y_i}) \rightarrow B$.
Then for each i, we do a cut on $\forall \overrightarrow{y_i}. \overrightarrow{H_i}(\overrightarrow{p}, \overrightarrow{y_i}) \rightarrow B$ with the second premise $\Gamma', \{\forall \overrightarrow{y_i}. \overrightarrow{H_i}(\overrightarrow{p}, \overrightarrow{y_i}) \rightarrow B\}_i \vdash E$ and we get the sequent $\Gamma, \dots, \Gamma, \Gamma' \vdash E$ which we reduce to $\Gamma, \Gamma' \vdash E$ by making contractions on Γ.
– The other cases are dealt with as in [6]

This closes our proof by induction.

This gives us the cut-elimination property for $LJTI$ by removing the topmost cuts first.

4 Embedding Our Calculus in a Proof-Search Procedure

4.1 Basic Strategy

To perform bottom-up proof-search using our calculus, we use bounded depth-first search, using our bound on non-decreasing rules.

We first notice that we can do without the atomicity condition in Ax and $La{\rightarrow}$ rules, since those generalized rules are admissible : for Ax see rule (9), and for $La{\rightarrow}$ use rule (10), cut and contraction. This can speed up proofs by avoiding the destruction of two opposite occurrences of the same compound formula followed by as many axiom rules as the number of its subformulae.

In order to refine our strategies we separated the inductive families in classes. First we distinguish between first-order inductive whose constructors may have first-order (quantified) variables, and propositional inductive families whose constructors are propositional formulae, and among them we have three classes :

– Those with no constructor are the absurd class (for instance $\bot$)
– Those with one constructor are the conjunctive class ($\wedge$,$\top$,...)
– Those with more than one constructors are the disjunctive class ($\vee$,Dec,...)

Of course the axiom and left-absurdity rules are to be used as soon as possible. Moreover, it is fundamental that we try to apply the generalized $La{\rightarrow}$ rule before trying any $LI{\rightarrow}$ rule in order to shortcut that part of parallel destruction.

This calculus also has a lot of invertible rules which must be used before the non-invertible ones, because there will be no need to backtrack if the proof fails next. Notice that for the conjunctive class, the right introduction rule is invertible. Moreover, some rules like $L\forall{\rightarrow}$ and $L{\rightarrow}{\rightarrow}$ are only partially invertible,

$$\begin{array}{ll}
\mathcal{SF}^+(A) = +A & \mathcal{SF}^-(A) = -A \ (A \text{ atomic}) \\
\mathcal{SF}^+(A \to B) = \mathcal{SF}^-(A) \cup \mathcal{SF}^+(B) & \mathcal{SF}^-(A \to B) = \mathcal{SF}^+(A) \cup \mathcal{SF}^-(B) \\
\mathcal{SF}^+(\forall x.P[x]) = \mathcal{SF}^+(P[?_n]) & \mathcal{SF}^-(\forall x.P[x]) = \mathcal{SF}^-(P[?_n]) \\
\mathcal{SF}^+(I(\overrightarrow{p})) = \bigcup_{i,j} \mathcal{SF}^+(H_{i,j}(\overrightarrow{p}, \overrightarrow{?_{i,k}})) & \mathcal{SF}^-(I(\overrightarrow{p})) = \bigcup_{i,j} \mathcal{SF}^-(H_{i,j}(\overrightarrow{p}, \overrightarrow{?_{i,k}}))
\end{array}$$

(where $?_n$ and $\overrightarrow{?_{i,k}}$ are fresh metavariables)

$$\mathcal{SF}(\Gamma \vdash G) = \mathcal{SF}^+(G) \cup \bigcup_{H \in \Gamma} \mathcal{SF}^-(H)$$

Fig. 2. signed atomic subformulae

so we first try to prove the non-invertible premise and if we succeed there will be no need to backtrack if the second premise fails.

The last point is that some rules generate more than one subgoal to be proved, so we try to delay them as much as possible.

4.2 Instantiation Strategy

When all else fails we try to apply instantiating rules $L\forall$ and RI, with I a first-order inductive. To use those rules some terms t must replace the quantified variable(s). To find these terms, we use a well-known notion of polarity (see for instance [11]) to define the set of signed atomic subformulae $\mathcal{SF}(\Gamma \vdash G)$ of a sequent by induction on the structure of its formulae (see figure 2).

We remark that signed atomic subformulae in premises of rules are also in the conclusion, maybe in a more general form (with some terms replaced with metavariables). This can be seen as a kind of subformula property in our calculus, and in the end we only need pairs of matching subformulae of opposite signs used in axiom or $La\!\to$ rules, and inductive formulae with terminal rules : negative absurdity or positive tautology[2]. We call those particular subformulae trivial subformulae, and they are also necessary in a derivation.

When we want to use a trivial subformula under a quantifier or an inductive definition to prove our sequent, we just need any term t to instantiate our quantified variable, in order to bring that trivial subformula to the top and apply a terminating rule, so we create a goal stating we have a term to instantiate our variable and ask Coq to use `trivial` or `auto` to solve that non-logical goal. We have to use this trick because in Coq, unlike first-order logic, the quantification domain may be empty, and this emptiness is undecidable in general (type inhabitation is what Coq is all about).

Otherwise we try to build matching pairs of atomic subformulae, and that we do by using first-order unification between atomic subformulae of opposite sign, and by looking at the terms associated to the quantified variables in the unifiers, for example, if we have to prove that $\forall x.P[x] \vdash \exists y.P[f(y)]$, we have the

[2] We call tautology any propositional inductive family with a constant constructor

signed atomic subformulae $-P[?_1]$ and $+P[f(?_2)]$. And we have $\{?_1 \mapsto f(?_2)\}$ as a unifier. So we will try to use a term of the form $f(?_2)$ to instantiate $?_1$.

Now, we can get three different kinds of terms to instantiate our variables: ground terms (without metavariables), open terms (containing metavariables but not outermost), or trivial terms (equal to a metavariable).

If we get ground terms we just use them so, turning $\forall x.P[x]$ into $P[t]$.

If we get open terms, we *specialize* our quantified formulae: in our example with $f(?_2)$, we turn $\forall x.P[x]$ in $\forall y.P[f(y)]$. For positive inductive formulae we do the same and we use $\exists$ to quantify over open positions in the term. For instance if we consider the following goal :

$$\Gamma, \forall x.\forall y.y = 2 \times f(y,x) + 1 \vdash \text{Eucl\_div}(a, 2)$$

The unification algorithm will yield $f(a, ?_1)$ for q and 1 for r, and the specialization scheme will give the following goals to try to prove :

$$\Gamma, \forall x.\forall y.y = 2 \times f(y,x) + 1 \vdash \exists x.1 < 2 \wedge a = 2 \times f(a,x) + 1$$

If we get trivial terms, it means that there is a formula of opposite sign that unifies with this one and that this one doesn't need to be specialized, this is the case for example in $\forall x.P[x] \vdash \exists y.P[y]$. In that case, we proceed like we do with trivial subformulae and we get an additional Coq subgoal about domain inhabitation. Having destroyed our quantifier, we can hope the search procedure will finally bring the matching subformula in outermost position.

You can argue that our specialization scheme leads to non-termination, but in fact the calculus itself doesn't terminate so we just place a counter on the use of those rules plus the $L\forall\!\rightarrow$ rule, and we give a bound to our search procedure.

4.3 The `firstorder` Tactic

As announced earlier, this proof-search procedure is available in Coq. Since our experience in maintaining the `tauto/intuition` tactic showed us that a lot of time was spend doing pattern matching on contexts (see [3]) we decided to avoid doing it too often.

So we decided to work at the ML level with a persistent data structure reflecting the logical content of the current subgoal. Since we are keeping track of the head-form of our formulae, we can work *modulo* constant unfolding and $\beta\iota$-reduction at a very low performance cost. The unification algorithm also does some reduction, but it is basically first-order unification since we are not supposed to have any quantified variable at the head of an application.

This implementation choice gave very encouraging results when compared to `tauto`. In some propositional examples `firstorder` solved the goal in less than 1 minute where `tauto` ran overnight without giving a result. For example try

$$(A_0{\leftrightarrow}A_1){\rightarrow}(A_1{\leftrightarrow}A_2), (A_1{\leftrightarrow}A_2){\rightarrow}(A_2{\leftrightarrow}A_0), (A_2{\leftrightarrow}A_0){\rightarrow}(A_0{\leftrightarrow}A_1) \vdash A_0{\leftrightarrow}A_1$$

with a bigger odd number of variables.

The `firstorder` tactic is available in Coq `v8.0` and can be used like `tauto`. A global integer option may be set using the command (`Set Firstorder Depth`

n). This option is the maximum number of non-terminating rules allowed in a branch of the proof, so increasing it may allow your goal to be solved at the cost of a longer search time.

However, in the current state, all propositional inductive definitions are supported but first-order ones are only supported when they have one constructor with only one first-order variable. We are planning to fully support first-order inductive families in the near future.

5 Conclusion and Future Work

We have presented a contraction-free sequent calculus to deal with first-order intuitionistic logic in the Coq proof assistant where most connectives are defined as inductive families. We have shown that this contraction-free calculus enjoys admissibility of contraction and cut-elimination, thus establishing a weak form of subformula property. We have shown how this calculus was implemented as a proof-search tactic in Coq.

Although our inductive formulae do not have more expressivity than standard first-order intuitionistic logic, they give a more uniform reasoning framework. From a more practical point of view they allow users to define their own connectives without having to consider if they would be supported by such or such automatic tactic.

Beside searching for smarter search strategies, there are two directions in which we should extend our work to be able to deal with inductive predicates such as `le` (less than or equal to). One is to try to consider recursive inductive definitions for which our theorems don't apply as such: the weight function is not well-defined and we may lose completeness. The other one is to have inductive predicates whose type in Coq would be an arity instead of a simple sort, but equality is one of those predicates so we couldn't avoid performing some equational reasoning. Indeed, we plan to handle such cases as part of a more general integration of equational reasoning and our proof-search procedure in Coq.

References

1. G. Bellin and J. Ketonen. A decision procedure revisited: Notes on direct logic, linear logic and its implementation. *Theoretical computer science*, 95(1):115–142, 1992.
2. The Coq Development Team (INRIA-LRI-CNRS). The Coq proof assistant reference manual. `http://coq.inria.fr`
3. D. Delahaye. A tactic language for the system Coq. In *Proceedings of Logic for Programming and Automated Reasoning*, volume 1955 of *LNCS/LNAI*, pages 85–95. Springer, 2000.
4. A. G. Dragalin. *Mathematical Intuitionism: Introduction to Proof Theory*, volume 67 of *Translations of Mathematical Monographs*. American Mathematical Society, Providence, Rhode Island, 1987.

5. R. Dyckhoff. Contraction-free sequent calculi for intuitionistic logic. *Journal of Symbolic Logic*, 57(3):795–807, 1992.
6. R. Dyckhoff and S. Negri. Admissibility of structural rules for contraction-free systems of intuitionistic logic. *Journal of Symbolic Logic*, 65:1499–1518, 2000.
7. J.-C. Filliâtre. A decision procedure for direct predicate calculus: study and implementation in the Coq system. Technical Report 96–25, LIP, ENS Lyon, 1995.
8. J.Ketonen and R.Weyhrauch. A decidable fragment of predicate calculus. *Theoretical Computer Science*, 32:297–307, 1984.
9. S. C. Kleene. *Introduction to metamathematics*, volume I of *Bibliotheca Mathematica*. North-Holland, Amsterdam, 1952.
10. C. Kreitz. *The Nuprl Proof Development System, Version 5*, 2002. `http://www.cs.cornell.edu/Info/Projects/NuPrl/`
11. C. Kreitz and J. Otten. Connection-based theorem proving in classical and non-classical logics. *Journal of Universal Computer Science*, 5(3):88–112, 1999.
12. C. Munoz. Démonstration automatique dans la logique propositionnelle intuitionniste. Master's thesis, Université Paris 7, 1994.
13. C. Paulin-Mohring. Inductive definitions in the system Coq: Rules and properties. In M. Bezem and J. F. Groote, editors, *TLCA'93, Utrecht, The Netherlands, 16–18 March 1993*, volume 664 of *LNCS*, pages 328–345, Berlin, 1993. Springer-Verlag.
14. S. Schmitt, L. Lorigo, C. Kreitz, and A. Nogin. Integrating connection-based theorem proving into interactive proof assistants. In R. Gore, A. Leitsch, and T. Nipkow, editors, *IJCAR'01*, volume 2083 of *LNAI*, pages 421–426. Springer, 2001.

Higher-Order Linear Ramified Recurrence*

Ugo Dal Lago[1], Simone Martini[1], and Luca Roversi[2]

[1] Dipartimento di Scienze dell'Informazione, Università di Bologna, Bologna, Italy
{dallago,martini}@cs.unibo.it
[2] Dipartimento di Informatica, Università di Torino, Torino, Italy
roversi@di.unito.it

Abstract. Higher-Order Linear Ramified Recurrence (**HOLRR**) is a linear (affine) λ-calculus — every variable occurs at most once — extended with a recursive scheme on free algebras. Two simple conditions on type derivations enforce both polytime completeness and a strong notion of polytime soundness on typeable terms. Completeness for **PTIME** holds by embedding Leivant's ramified recurrence on words into **HOLRR**. Soundness is established at all types — and not only for first order terms. Type connectives are limited to tensor and linear implication. Moreover, typing rules are given as a simple deductive system.

1 Introduction

The main goal of giving machine-independent characterizations of **PTIME** is to overcome the drawback of conceiving feasible algorithms by thinking directly in terms of low-level machine primitives, like those of Turing machines. The research about this subject has brought forth a wide variety of interesting calculi, that can be classified under two parameters: their originating background, and their expressivity — the ability to naturally express higher-order functions.

Concerning the originating background, proposals range from those which are purely recursion-theoretical to the ones which are purely proof-theoretical.

For example, Bellantoni and Cook's *safe recursion on notation* [3] is of the former kind. Its recursive scheme forbids application of a recursively defined function to the result of a recursive call. The constraint is expressed directly inside the syntax of the recursive schemes, by distinguishing two classes of arguments, namely safe and normal arguments. Another example of a first-order function algebra capturing **PTIME** is Leivant's *ramified recurrence on words* [11,12], which relies on the notion of tier to control the use of arguments in recursive schemes.

On the other side, purely proof-theoretical systems are logical, deductive systems, usually expressed on a graph language, that of proof-nets. Main examples of this class are *light linear logic* (**LLL**, [6]), *light affine logic* (**LAL**, [1,2]), and *soft linear logic* (**SLL**, [10]). Boxes are certain regions inside a proof-net, and a

* All the authors are partially supported by MIUR COFIN 2002 PROTOCOLLO project. The latter is also supported by DART IST-2001-33477 project.

S. Berardi, M. Coppo, and F. Damiani (Eds.): TYPES 2003, LNCS 3085, pp. 178–193, 2004.

box may contain other boxes, in a stratified fashion. The computational core is cut-elimination, whose complexity is controlled by box stratification: the time necessary to normalize a proof-net is a polynomial in the size of the proof, the exponent of the polynomial depending only on the box-nesting depth. This, together with the fact that usual data types can be coded by fixed-depth proofs, implies polytime soundness.

Many interesting systems should be classified in-between these two styles. In these systems, recursion is embedded into typed calculi, and other mechanisms — usually ramification or linearity — are needed to control the computational complexity growth. Typical examples of such systems, here dubbed as type-theoretical, are **HOSLR** [8,9] and **LT** [4,5]. In the two systems mentioned, the syntax of Gödel's system **T** is modified to accommodate safe recursion, but a number of additional constraints, a restricted form of linearity *in primis*, are needed to guarantee polynomial soundness. Generalizations of ramified recurrence to higher-order types are presented in [15,14]. In these systems, however, the lack of any linearity constraint prevents from getting a polytime bound. Indeed, at higher types they show either a poly-space or a Kalmar elementary bound. Another related work is [13], where syntactical restrictions on a simply typed calculus with constants and recursion allow to restrict the space of representable functions to relevant complexity classes.

Results. In this paper, we introduce the system of Higher-Order Linear Ramified Recurrence (**HOLRR**). It is a type theoretical system smoothly blending both recursion and proof-theoretic components.

The proof-theoretical core of the system is a linear affine λ-calculus: any variable can be used at most once. Recursion is embedded in the system as a variable binder, whose syntax is inspired by boxes of linear lambda calculi. The types are generated by the usual multiplicative connectives (tensor and arrow). Base types includes denumerably many copies of several free algebras. There is no need for additional type constructs; in particular, there is no explicit modality.

Our principal aim is to obtain results akin to those of Bellantoni, Niggl and Schwichtenberg's **LT** [4,5], but in a framework with a polynomial bound expressed as a function of specific parameters of the term. Sect. 5 analytically compares the two systems. Here, we stress that: (i) no additional syntactic restriction on terms is needed, besides those induced by typeability; (ii) the degree of the polynomial bounding normalization time of a term M depends only on one parameter of a type derivation for M — its recursion depth.

In particular, we prove a soundness result *à la* **LLL**. Under a given strategy, any term which can be typed satisfying two simple conditions (*word-contextuality* and *ramification*) normalizes in a polynomially bounded time. To be precise, we will prove that, for any (word-contextual and ramified) type derivation π for M, M normalizes in time $O(|M|^h)$, where h depends only on the recursion depth of π. This means that, whenever the recursion depth of type derivations for terms encoding input data is bounded, the defining function is polytime — a similar situation occurring in **LLL** or **LAL**.

Completeness for **PTIME** holds by embedding Leivant's ramified recurrence on words into **HOLRR**.

2 Syntax

A *free algebra* $\mathbb{A}$ is a couple $(\mathcal{C}_{\mathbb{A}}, \mathcal{R}_{\mathbb{A}})$ where $\mathcal{C}_{\mathbb{A}} = \{c_1^{\mathbb{A}}, \ldots, c_{k(\mathbb{A})}^{\mathbb{A}}\}$ is a finite set of *constructors* and $\mathcal{R}_{\mathbb{A}} : \mathcal{C}_{\mathbb{A}} \to \mathbb{N}$ maps every constructor to its *arity*. A free algebra $\mathbb{A} = (\{c_1^{\mathbb{A}}, \ldots, c_{k(\mathbb{A})}^{\mathbb{A}}\}, \mathcal{R}_{\mathbb{A}})$ is a *word algebra* if

- $\mathcal{R}(c_i^{\mathbb{A}}) = 0$ for one (and only one) $i \in \{1, \ldots, k(\mathbb{A})\}$;
- $\mathcal{R}(c_j^{\mathbb{A}}) = 1$ for every $j \neq i$ in $\{1, \ldots, k(\mathbb{A})\}$.

If $\mathbb{A} = (\{c_1^{\mathbb{A}}, \ldots, c_{k(\mathbb{A})}^{\mathbb{A}}\}, \mathcal{R}_{\mathbb{A}})$ is a word algebra, we will assume $c_{k(\mathbb{A})}^{\mathbb{A}}$ to be the distinguished element of $\mathcal{C}_{\mathbb{A}}$ whose arity is 0 and $c_1, \ldots, c_{k(\mathbb{A})-1}$ will denote the elements of $\mathcal{C}_{\mathbb{A}}$ whose arity is 1. $\mathbb{B} = (\{c_1^{\mathbb{B}}, c_2^{\mathbb{B}}, c_3^{\mathbb{B}}\}, \mathcal{R}_{\mathbb{B}})$ is the word algebra of binary strings. $\mathbb{C} = (\{c_1^{\mathbb{C}}, c_2^{\mathbb{C}}\}, \mathcal{R}_{\mathbb{C}})$, where $\mathcal{R}_{\mathbb{C}}(c_1^{\mathbb{C}}) = 2$ and $\mathcal{R}_{\mathbb{C}}(c_2^{\mathbb{C}}) = 0$ is the free algebra of binary trees.

A will be a fixed, finite family $\{\mathbb{A}_1, \ldots, \mathbb{A}_n\}$ of free algebras, where constructor sets $\mathcal{C}_{\mathbb{A}_1}, \ldots, \mathcal{C}_{\mathbb{A}_n}$ are assumed to be pairwise disjoint. We will hereby assume both $\mathbb{B}$ and $\mathbb{C}$ to be in A.

The language $\mathrm{M_A}$ of **HOLRR** *terms* is defined by the following productions:

$$
\begin{aligned}
M ::= {} & x \mid c \mid (M, M) \mid MM \mid \lambda x.M \mid \ \textbf{let}\ (x, x) \Leftarrow M \ \textbf{in}\ M \mid \\
& \{\!\{M, \ldots, M\}\!\}[x/M, \ldots, x/M]\ M \mid \langle\!\langle M, \ldots, M\rangle\!\rangle[x/M, \ldots, x/M]\ M
\end{aligned}
$$

where c ranges over the constructors for the free algebras in A. An occurrence of a term N inside another term M has *recursion degree* n if it is nested into n terms in the form $\langle\!\langle M, \ldots, M\rangle\!\rangle$ inside M. When we write a term as $\overline{M}$, we are implicitly assuming it to be closed (i.e. to contain no free variables).
The language $\mathrm{T_A}$ of **HOLRR** types is defined by the following productions:

$$
A ::= B_{\mathbb{A}}^n \mid A \otimes A \mid A \multimap A
$$

where n ranges over $\mathbb{N}$ and $\mathbb{A}$ ranges over A. Tensor associates to the left, both in types and terms (that is, pairs). $A \in \mathrm{T_A}$, define the *lifting* $\#(A) \in \mathrm{T_A}$ of A:

$$
\begin{aligned}
\#(B_{\mathbb{A}}^n) &= B_{\mathbb{A}}^{n+1} \\
\#(A \square B) &= \#(A) \square \#(B) \text{ with } \square \in \{\otimes, \multimap\}.
\end{aligned}
$$

The *level* $\mathbb{L}(A) \in \mathbb{N}$ of a type A is defined by induction on A:

$$
\begin{aligned}
\mathbb{L}(B_{\mathbb{A}}^n) &= n \\
\mathbb{L}(A \otimes B) = \mathbb{L}(A \multimap B) &= \max\{\mathbb{L}(A), \mathbb{L}(B)\}.
\end{aligned}
$$

The *index set* $\mathbb{I}(A) \subseteq \mathbb{N}$ of A is defined in a similar way:

$$
\begin{aligned}
\mathbb{I}(B_{\mathbb{A}}^n) &= \{n\} \\
\mathbb{I}(A \otimes B) = \mathbb{I}(A \multimap B) &= \mathbb{I}(A) \cup \mathbb{I}(B).
\end{aligned}
$$

The rules in Fig. 1 define the assignment of types in $\mathrm{T_A}$ to terms in $\mathrm{M_A}$. A type derivation π with conclusion $\Gamma \vdash M : A$ will be denoted by $\pi : \Gamma \vdash M : A$. If there is $\pi : \Gamma \vdash M : A$ then we will write $\Gamma \vdash_{\mathbf{H}} M : A$ and mark M as a *typeable* **HOLRR** term. $\mathrm{M}_{\mathrm{A}}^{\mathbf{H}}$ is the set of **HOLRR** typeable terms. A type derivation $\pi : \Gamma \vdash M : A$ is in *standard form* if Γ does not contain variables introduced by rule W.

$$\frac{}{x : A \vdash x : A}\ A \qquad \frac{\Gamma \vdash M : B}{\Gamma, x : A \vdash M : B}\ W$$

$$\frac{\Gamma, x : A \vdash M : B}{\Gamma \vdash \lambda x.M : A \multimap B}\ I_{\multimap} \qquad \frac{\Gamma \vdash M : A \multimap B \quad \Delta \vdash N : A}{\Gamma, \Delta \vdash MN : B}\ E_{\multimap}$$

$$\frac{\Gamma \vdash M : A \quad \Delta \vdash N : B}{\Gamma, \Delta \vdash (M, N) : A \otimes B}\ I_{\otimes} \qquad \frac{\Gamma \vdash M : A \otimes B \quad \Delta, x : A, y : B \vdash N : C}{\Gamma, \Delta \vdash \mathbf{let}(x, y) \Leftarrow M \ \mathbf{in}\ N : C}\ E_{\otimes}$$

$$\frac{n \in \mathbb{N} \quad c \in \mathcal{C}_{\mathbb{A}}}{\vdash c : \underbrace{B_{\mathbb{A}}^n \multimap \ldots \multimap B_{\mathbb{A}}^n}_{\mathcal{R}_{\mathbb{A}}(c)\ times} \multimap B_{\mathbb{A}}^n}\ I_c$$

$$\frac{\begin{array}{c} A \equiv B_{\mathbb{A}}^i \qquad \Gamma \equiv x_1 : B_1, \ldots, x_n : B_n \\ \Gamma \vdash M_{c_i^{\mathbb{A}}} : \underbrace{A \multimap \ldots \multimap A}_{\mathcal{R}_{\mathbb{A}}(c_i^{\mathbb{A}})\ times} \multimap C \qquad \Delta_i \vdash N_i : B_i \qquad \Theta \vdash L : A \end{array}}{\Delta_1, \ldots, \Delta_n, \Theta \vdash \{\!\{M_{c_1} \cdots M_{c_k}\}\!\}[x_1/N_1, \ldots, x_n/N_n]\ L : C}\ E_{\multimap}^C$$

$$\frac{\begin{array}{c} A \equiv B_{\mathbb{A}}^i \qquad \Gamma \equiv x_1 : B_1, \ldots, x_n : B_n \\ \Gamma \vdash M_{c_i^{\mathbb{A}}} : \underbrace{A \multimap \ldots \multimap A}_{\mathcal{R}_{\mathbb{A}}(c_i^{\mathbb{A}})\ times} \multimap \underbrace{C \multimap \ldots \multimap C}_{\mathcal{R}_{\mathbb{A}}(c_i^{\mathbb{A}})\ times} \multimap C \\ \Delta_i \vdash N_i : B_i \qquad \Theta \vdash L : A \end{array}}{\Delta_1, \ldots, \Delta_n, \Theta \vdash \langle\!\langle M_{c_1} \cdots M_{c_k}\rangle\!\rangle[x_1/N_1, \ldots, x_n/N_n]\ L : C}\ E_{\multimap}^R$$

Fig. 1. Type assignment rules

The *recursion depth* $\mathbb{R}(\pi)$ of a **HOLRR** type derivation $\pi : \Gamma \vdash M : A$ is defined by induction on the structure of π. In particular:

- If π is an instance of rules A or I_c, then $\mathbb{R}(\pi) = 0$.
- If the last rule used in π is $E_{\multimap}^R$, then π has the following shape

$$\frac{\pi_1 \quad \ldots \quad \pi_m \quad \Theta \vdash L : B_{\mathbb{A}}^i}{\Delta, \Theta \vdash \langle\!\langle M_1, \ldots, M_n\rangle\!\rangle[x_1/N_1, \ldots, x_m/N_m]\ L : C}$$

and $\mathbb{R}(\pi)$ is $i + \max\{\mathbb{R}(\pi_1), \ldots, \mathbb{R}(\pi_m)\}$.

- In all the other cases, π can be written as follows

$$\frac{\pi_1 \quad \dots \quad \pi_m}{\Gamma \vdash M : A}\ .$$

We will define $\mathbb{R}(\pi)$ as $\max\{\mathbb{R}(\pi_1), \dots, \mathbb{R}(\pi_m)\}$.

Proposition 1. *If $\Gamma \vdash_{\mathbf{H}} M : A$ and $\Delta, x : A \vdash_{\mathbf{H}} N : B$, then $\Gamma, \Delta \vdash_{\mathbf{H}} N\{M/x\} : B$.*

Proof. Induction on the structure of the derivation for $\Delta, x : A \vdash N : B$. □

For every term t of a free algebra $\mathbb{A} \in \mathrm{A}$ and for every natural number n, there is an **HOLRR** type derivation $\pi(t, n) : \vdash t : B^n_{\mathbb{A}}$. This allows to prove:

Proposition 2. *If $x_1 : A_1, \dots, x_n : A_n \vdash_{\mathbf{H}} M : B$, then $x_1 : \#(A_1), \dots, x_n : \#(A_n) \vdash_{\mathbf{H}} M : \#(B)$*

The reduction rule $\to$ on $\mathrm{M_A}$ is given in Fig. 2; $\leadsto$ is the contextual closure of $\to$. $\leadsto^*$ is locally confluent and strongly normalizable, property provable by embedding the calculus into system **T**; so, it is Church-Rosser as well.

Redexes in the form $\langle\!\langle M_{c_1}, \dots, M_{c_k} \rangle\!\rangle [x_1/\overline{N_1}, \dots, x_n/\overline{N_n}]\ t$ are called *recursive redexes*; those in the form $\{\!\{M_{c_1}, \dots, M_{c_k}\}\!\} [x_1/N_1, \dots, x_n/N_n]\ t$ are *conditional redexes*; all the others are called *linear redexes*.

$$(\lambda x.M)N \to M\{N/x\}$$

$$\textbf{let } (x, y) \Leftarrow (M, N) \textbf{ in } L \to L\{M/x, N/y\}$$

$$\begin{array}{l}\langle\!\langle M_{c_1}, \dots, M_{c_k} \rangle\!\rangle [x_1/\overline{N_1}, \dots, x_n/\overline{N_n}]\ c_i(t_1, \dots, t_{\mathcal{R}(c_i)}) \to \\ \quad M_{c_i}\{\overline{N_1}/x_1, \dots, \overline{N_n}/x_n\}\ t_1 \cdots t_{\mathcal{R}(c_i)} \\ \qquad \langle\!\langle M_{c_1}, \dots, M_{c_k} \rangle\!\rangle [x_1/\overline{N_1}, \dots, x_n/\overline{N_n}]\ t_1 \\ \qquad \dots \\ \qquad \langle\!\langle M_{c_1}, \dots, M_{c_k} \rangle\!\rangle [x_1/\overline{N_1}, \dots, x_n/\overline{N_n}]\ t_{\mathcal{R}(c_i)}\end{array}$$

$$\begin{array}{l}\{\!\{M_{c_1}, \dots, M_{c_k}\}\!\} [x_1/N_1, \dots, x_n/N_n]\ c_i(t_1, \dots, t_{\mathcal{R}(c_i)}) \to \\ \qquad M_{c_i}\{N_1/x_1, \dots, N_n/x_n\}\ t_1 \cdots t_{\mathcal{R}(c_i)}\end{array}$$

Fig. 2. Normalization on terms

The following proposition will be useful in the following

Proposition 3. *If $\vdash M : B^n_{\mathbb{A}}$, then the (unique) normal form of M is a free algebra term t. Moreover, t can be obtained from M by successively firing redexes with null recursion degree.*

Proof. By a standard reducibility argument. □

$\mathrm{M}_{\mathbb{A}}^{\mathbf{H}}$ contains terms that cannot be reduced in polynomial time. To enforce this property, we introduce the following two conditions on type derivations:

- a type derivation π is *word-contextual* if every occurrence of B_i in every instance of $E_{\multimap}^{R}$, inside π, has form $B_{\mathbb{W}}^{m}$, $\mathbb{W}$ being a *word* algebra.
- a type derivation π is *ramified* if every instance of $E_{\multimap}^{R}$ inside π satisfies $\mathbb{L}(A) > \mathbb{L}(C)$.

In the following section, we will show that these conditions are both crucial to reach polytime soundness. If $\pi : \Gamma \vdash M : A$, where π is word-contextual and ramified, M is said to be *word-ramified* and we will write $\pi : \Gamma \vdash_{\mathbf{WR}} M : A$. The class of all word-ramified **HOLRR** terms will be denoted as $\mathrm{M}_{\mathbb{A}}^{\mathbf{WR}}$.

3 Polytime Soundness

The goal is to prove polytime soundness for **HOLRR** in the form of

Theorem 1. *There is a sound and complete normalization strategy such that the time required to normalize a term M is $O(|M|^h)$ where h only depends on $\mathbb{R}(\pi)$, $\pi : \Gamma \vdash M : A$ being word-contextual and ramified.*

The reduction strategy we use proceeds by firing the rightmost innermost redex among those with minimum recursion degree, where the firing of a recursive redex corresponds to a complete unfolding, counted as a single step. *Rightmost innermost minimum recursion degree strategy* is the name of such a reduction strategy, and $M \mapsto N$ denotes that M rewrites to N by one of its possible steps.

We will prove Theorem 1 studying normalization by way of interaction graphs, which are graphs corresponding to **HOLRR** type derivations. Notice that we will not use interaction graphs as a virtual machine computing normal forms — they are merely a tool facilitating the study of **HOLRR** dynamics.

Let $\mathrm{L}_{\mathbb{A}}$ be the set

$$\{W, I_{\multimap}, E_{\multimap}, I_{\otimes}, E_{\otimes}, P, C\} \cup \bigcup_{\mathbb{A} \in \mathbb{A}} \bigcup_{c \in \mathcal{C}_{\mathbb{A}}} \{I_c\} \cup \{E_{\multimap}^{C}, E_{\multimap}^{R}, P^{C}, P^{R}\}.$$

Elements of $\mathrm{L}_{\mathbb{A}}$ either are typing rule names or lie in $\{P, C, P^C, P^R\}$ — they are premises (P), conclusions (C) or limit conditionals (P^C) and recursions (P^R).

An *interaction graph* is a quadruple (V, E, α, β) such that

- (V, E) is a directed graph;
- $\alpha : V \to \mathrm{L}_{\mathbb{A}}$
- $\beta : E \to \mathrm{T}_{\mathbb{A}}$

$\mathrm{G}_{\mathbb{A}}$ is the set of all interaction graphs. We will now introduce a class $\mathrm{G}_{\mathbb{A}}^{\mathbf{H}}$ of interaction graphs corresponding to **HOLRR** type derivations. $\mathrm{G}_{\mathbb{A}}^{\mathbf{H}}$ is defined inductively, mimicking the process of type derivation building. First, the interaction graphs in figure 3(a) lie in $\mathrm{G}_{\mathbb{A}}^{\mathbf{H}}$. Moreover, suppose $G_0, \ldots, G_{k(\mathbb{A})+n} \in \mathrm{G}_{\mathbb{A}}^{\mathbf{H}}$ and they have form as in Fig. 3(b); then all the interaction graphs depicted in Fig. 4 lie in $\mathrm{G}_{\mathbb{A}}^{\mathbf{H}}$, provided the constraints listed next to each graph are satisfied.

To every **HOLRR** type derivation $\pi : \Gamma \vdash M : A$ corresponds an interaction graph $\mathcal{G}(\pi) \in \mathrm{G}_{\mathbb{A}}^{\mathbf{H}}$. Moreover, every instance of rules $I_{\multimap}, E_{\multimap}, I_{\otimes}, E_{\otimes}, I_c, E_{\multimap}^{C}, E_{\multimap}^{R}$

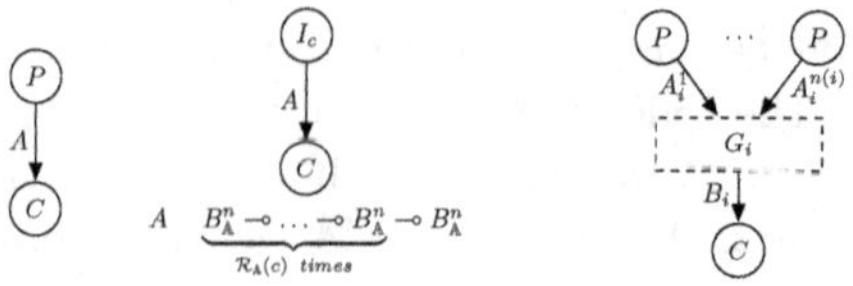

(a) (b)

Fig. 3. Some interaction graphs.

in π corresponds to a vertex in $\mathcal{G}(\pi)$ having the same label. In particular, if v corresponds to an instance $\overline{\vdash c : B^n_{\mathbb{A}} \multimap \ldots \multimap B^n_{\mathbb{A}}}$ of rule I_c, then $\delta(v)$ is the integer n, and, if this occurrence of c has recursion degree m, then $\gamma(v)$ is m.

Lemma 1. *There are two constants $n, m \in \mathbb{Q}$ such that, for every $\pi : \Gamma \vdash M : A$ in standard form, we have $n|M| \leq |V| \leq m|M|$, where $\mathcal{G}(\pi) = (V, E, \alpha, \beta)$.*

Inside a given graph, we call *traps* those subgraphs corresponding to normal form derivations $\pi(t, n) : \vdash t : B^n_{\mathbb{W}}$ (where $\mathbb{W}$ is a word algebra) and ending on the last $E_{\multimap}$ (for instance, Fig. 5 shows the trap corresponding to $\pi(c_1^{\mathbb{B}} c_2^{\mathbb{B}} c_1^{\mathbb{B}} c_3^{\mathbb{B}}, 0)$. We are here interested in certain paths inside interaction graphs: given an interaction graph $G = (V, E, \alpha, \beta)$, an *n-typed path* of G is a sequence $\overline{v} = v_1, \ldots, v_m \in V^+$ such that the two following conditions hold:

- for every $i \in \{1, \ldots, m-1\}$, either $(v_i, v_{i+1}) \in E$ and $n \in \mathbb{I}(\beta(v_i, v_{i+1}))$ or $(v_{i+1}, v_i) \in E$ and $n \in \mathbb{I}(\beta(v_{i+1}, v_i))$, and
- for every $i \in \{1, \ldots, m-1\}$, if v_i is part of a trap, then $v_{i+1}, \ldots, v_m$ must all be part of the same trap.

Intuitively, when a typed path enters a trap, it cannot exit it.

Suppose v is a vertex of G, ϕ is a positive integer and ψ is a nonnegative integer. Then the *weight* $W_{\phi,\psi}(v)$ of v is defined by cases:

$$W_{\phi,\psi}(v) = \begin{cases} 1 & \textit{if } \alpha(v) = I_c \wedge \delta(v) \geq \psi \\ 0 & \textit{if } \alpha(v) \neq I_c \\ \phi^{\gamma(v)(\psi+1)^{\psi-\delta(v)}} & \textit{if } \alpha(v) = I_c \wedge \delta(v) < \psi \end{cases}$$

The weight $W_{\phi,\psi}(\overline{v})$ of a n-typed path $\overline{v} = v_1, \ldots, v_m$ is $\sum_{v \in \{v_1, \ldots, v_m\}} W_{\phi,\psi}(v)$, where every vertex counts once even if it occurs many times in $\overline{v}$. The *n-weight* $W^n_{\phi,\psi}(G)$ of an interaction graph G is just the maximum among $W_{\phi,\psi}(\overline{v})$ over all n-typed paths $\overline{v}$ inside G. The weight of an interaction graph is parametric on ϕ and ψ. The following result, however, holds for every ϕ and ψ.

Lemma 2. *Let $\pi_M : \Gamma \vdash M : A$ and suppose π_M contains a subderivation in the form $\pi(t, n)$. Then $W^n_{\phi,\psi}(\mathcal{G}(\pi_M)) \geq |t|$.*

Remark 1. Basic observations are worth doing to understand the proof of proposition 4 below. The goal is to understand how $W^n_{\phi,\psi}(\mathcal{G}(\pi_N))$ and $W^n_{\phi,\psi}(\mathcal{G}(\pi_M))$

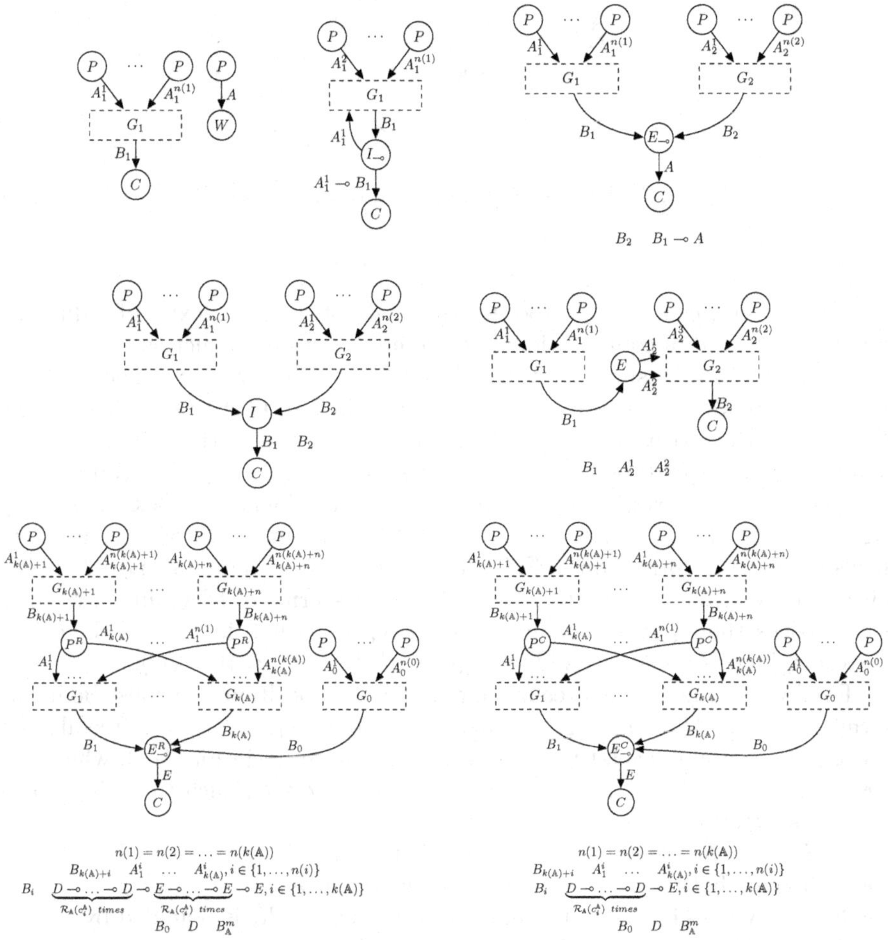

Fig. 4. Inductive cases

relate each other, when $\pi_M : \Gamma \vdash_{\mathbf{WR}} M : A$, and $\pi_N : \Gamma \vdash_{\mathbf{WR}} N : A$, and M rewrites to N.

Rewriting on terms, as in Fig. 2, is matched by certain transformations on the corresponding graphs, described in Fig. 6. The graph transformations take into account the modifications on the graphs, but for the erasure of sub-terms, which is the computational effect of weakening. When describing the modifications on the graphs induced by the firing of a redex, it is always understood that after any transformation as in Fig. 6, one should also perform all those transformations which correspond to the deletion of a sub-term as caused by a substitution for a weakened variable. These transformations can always be written as the one in Fig. 7, where G only depends on the term being deleted. We remark once again

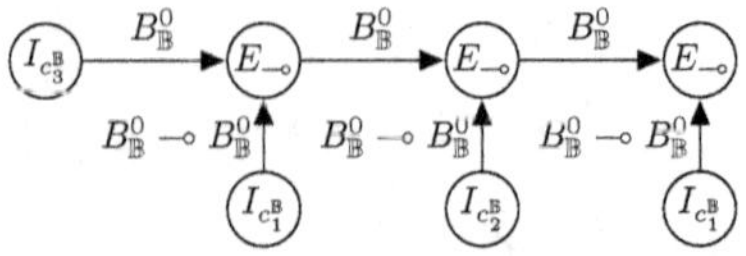

Fig. 5. The trap corresponding to $\pi(c^{\mathbb{B}}_1 c^{\mathbb{B}}_2 c^{\mathbb{B}}_1 c^{\mathbb{B}}_3, 0)$.

that we use graphs as a mere tool for the study of the complexity of reduction, and not as a kind of computational device implementing reduction.

As a first case, assume M yields N by firing a linear redex. Then, $\mathcal{G}(\pi_M)$ transforms to $\mathcal{G}(\pi_N)$ by one between the rules in Fig. 6(a) or Fig. 6(b). Then, $\mathcal{G}(\pi_N)$ has less vertices than $\mathcal{G}(\pi_M)$ and for every n-typed path $\overline{v}$ in $\mathcal{G}(\pi_N)$, there is a corresponding n-typed path $\overline{w}$ in $\mathcal{G}(\pi_M)$, with $W_{\phi,\psi}(\overline{v}) \leq W_{\phi,\psi}(\overline{w})$.

Assume, instead, to fire a conditional redex, namely $\{\!\{M_{c_1}, \ldots, M_{c_k}\}\!\}[x_1/N_1, \ldots, x_m/N_m]\ t$. At the graph level we need to focus on the transformation in Fig. 6(c), where K will contain at most k nodes, all labeled with $E_{\multimap}$, while $t_1, \ldots, t_k$ all are sub-terms of t. Again, $\mathcal{G}(\pi_N)$ has less vertices than $\mathcal{G}(\pi_M)$ and for every n-typed path $\overline{v}$ in $\mathcal{G}(\pi_N)$, there is a corresponding n-typed path $\overline{w}$ in $\mathcal{G}(\pi_M)$, with $W_{\phi,\psi}(\overline{v}) \leq W_{\phi,\psi}(\overline{w})$.

Finally, assume to fire a recursive redex. By proposition 3, it must be in the form $\langle\!\langle M_{c_1}, \ldots, M_{c_k}\rangle\!\rangle[x_1/s_1, \ldots, x_m/s_m]\ t$, where $t, s_1, \ldots, s_m$ are free-algebra terms. At the graph level, the transformation behaves as in Fig. 6(d), where:

- For every $i \in \{1, \ldots, l\}$, there is a constructor $c \in \mathcal{C}_{\mathbb{A}}$ such that $c(t^i_1 \ldots t^i_{k_i})$ is a sub-term of t;
- $K, K_1, \ldots, K_l$ contain nodes v such that $\alpha(v) = E_{\multimap}$;
- $|t|$ bounds both l and the number of vertices in K;
- For every $i \in \{1, \ldots, l\}$, the number of vertices in K_i is bounded by k_i;
- $E_1, \ldots, E_l$ all are in the form $D \multimap \ldots \multimap D$.

If $p \geq n$, then $W^p_{\phi,\psi}(\mathcal{G}(\pi_N)) \leq W^p_{\phi,\psi}(\mathcal{G}(\pi_M))$: for every p-typed path $\overline{v}$ inside $\mathcal{G}(\pi_N)$, there is a corresponding p-typed path $\overline{w}$ inside $\mathcal{G}(\pi_M)$, where $W_{\phi,\psi}(\overline{v}) \leq W_{\phi,\psi}(\overline{w})$. Assume now that $p < n$. Certainly, any p-typed path $\overline{v}$ inside $\mathcal{G}(\pi_N)$ can be mimicked by a p-typed path $\overline{w}$ inside $\mathcal{G}(\pi_M)$ in such a way that a constructor vertex in $\overline{w}$ corresponds to every constructor vertex appearing in $\overline{v}$. This correspondence, however, is not injective. Whenever u is a vertex appearing in $\overline{w}$ and belonging to $G(M_{c_i})$, $\overline{v}$ can contain distinct $u_1, \ldots, u_j$ (where $j \leq l$), all of them being "copies" of u. On the other hand, all the equations $\gamma(u_1) = \ldots = \gamma(u_j) = \gamma(u) - 1$ hold. Notice that, by our definition of a p-typed path, if u belongs to the trap $G(s_i)$, then $\overline{v}$ can only contain *one* copy of u.

The remarks here above lead to the following, crucial, result:

Proposition 4. *There is a function $f : \mathbb{N} \to \mathbb{N}$ such that, for every word-contextual and ramified $\pi_M : \Gamma \vdash M : A$, if $M \mapsto^* N$ and t is a free algebra term appearing in N, then $|t| = O(|M|^{f(\mathbb{R}(\pi_M))})$.*

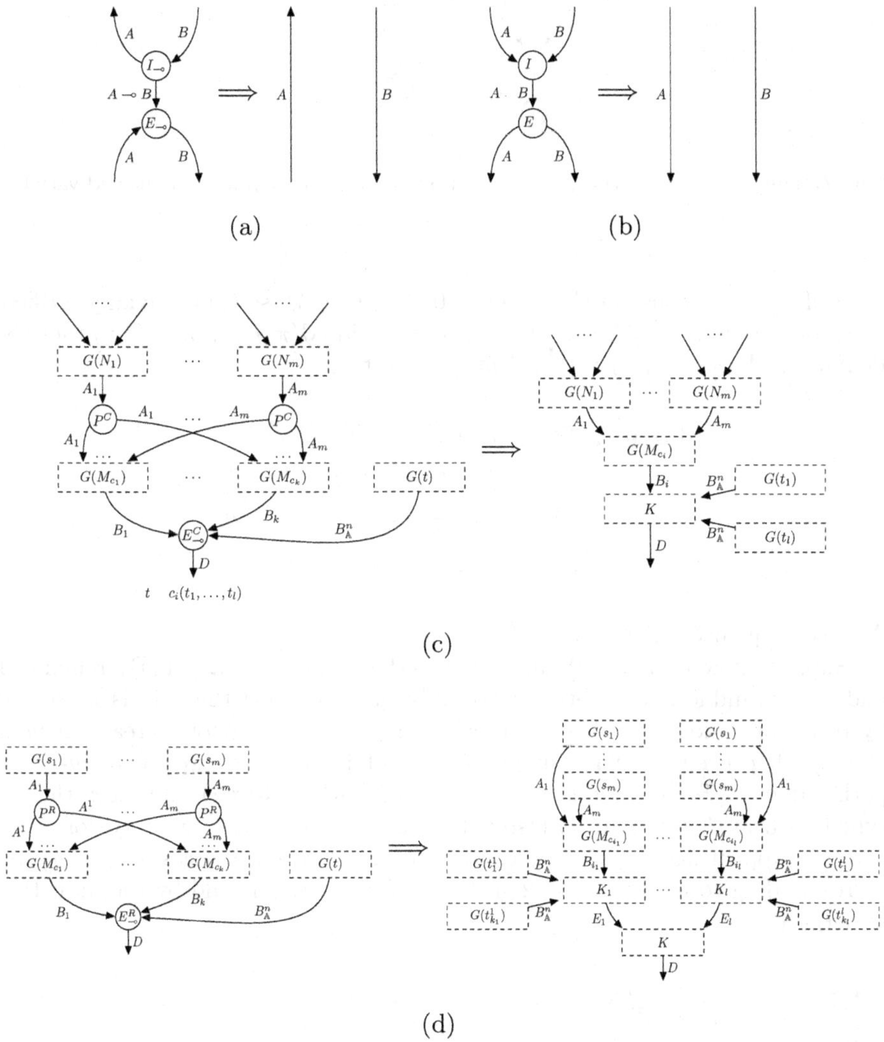

Fig. 6. The graph transformations produced by the firing of a redex.

Proof. Let $\mathcal{G}(\pi_M) = (V, E, \alpha, \beta)$. We will prove that, for every $n, m \in \mathbb{N}$, if $M \mapsto^n N$, then

$$W^m_{|V|,\mathbb{R}(\pi_M)}(\mathcal{G}(\pi_N)) \leq W^m_{|V|,\mathbb{R}(\pi_M)}(\mathcal{G}(\pi_M)) \tag{1}$$

$$W^m_{|V|,\mathbb{R}(\pi_M)}(\mathcal{G}(\pi_M)) \leq \begin{cases} |V| & \text{if } \mathbb{R}(\pi_M) \leq m \\ |V|^{(\mathbb{R}(\pi_M)+1)^{\mathbb{R}(\pi_M)-m+1}} & \text{otherwise} \end{cases} \tag{2}$$

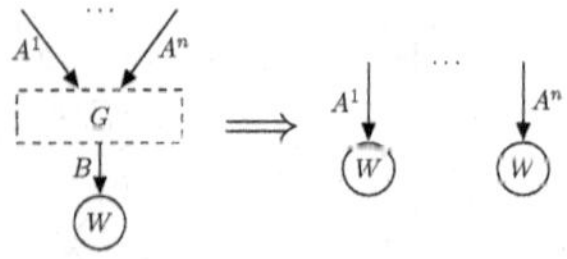

Fig. 7. The graph transformation induced by the substitution for a weakened variable.

First of all, let us consider the case $n = 0$. N equals M, so (1) is trivially verified. Suppose $\overline{v} = v_1, \dots, v_p$ be an m-typed path inside $\mathcal{G}(\pi_M)$. If $m \leq \mathbb{R}(\pi)$ then, by definition, $W_{|V|,\mathbb{R}(\pi_M)}(\overline{v}) \leq |V|$. If $m > \mathbb{R}(\pi)$, then

$$\begin{aligned} W_{|V|,\mathbb{R}(\pi_M)}(\overline{v}) &\leq |V||V|^{\mathbb{R}(\pi_M)(\mathbb{R}(\pi_M)+1)^{\mathbb{R}(\pi_M)-m}} \\ &\leq |V|^{\mathbb{R}(\pi_M)(\mathbb{R}(\pi_M)+1)^{\mathbb{R}(\pi_M)-m}+1} \\ &\leq |V|^{(\mathbb{R}(\pi_M)+1)(\mathbb{R}(\pi_M)+1)^{\mathbb{R}(\pi_M)-m}} \\ &= |V|^{(\mathbb{R}(\pi_M)+1)^{\mathbb{R}(\pi_M)-m+1}} \end{aligned}$$

As a consequence, (2) holds.

Suppose now that $n > 0$ and that the thesis holds for $n-1$. By remarks 1 and by the induction hypothesis, we only have to show that (1) is preserved by recursion unfolding — in other cases, path weights cannot increase. If $m \geq \mathbb{R}(\pi_M)$, then even recursion unfolding do not increase the weight of m-typed paths. If $m < \mathbb{R}(\pi_M)$, let $\overline{w}$ be an m-typed path in $\mathcal{G}(\pi_N)$ and let $\overline{v}$ the m-typed path in $\mathcal{G}(\pi_M)$ that corresponds to $\overline{w}$. As discussed previously, for every vertex u appearing in $\overline{v}$, $\overline{w}$ may contain several distinct vertices $u_1, \dots, u_j$, all corresponding to u. By lemma 2, $j \leq W^{m+1}_{|V|,\mathbb{R}(\pi_M)}(\mathcal{G}(\pi_M))$ and by the induction hypothesis

$$\begin{aligned} \sum_{i=1}^{j} W_{|V|,\mathbb{R}(\pi_M)}(u_j) &= \sum_{i=1}^{j} |V|^{\gamma(u_i)(\mathbb{R}(\pi_M)+1)^{\mathbb{R}(\pi_M)-m}} \\ &= \sum_{i=1}^{j} |V|^{(\gamma(u)-1)(\mathbb{R}(\pi_M)+1)^{\mathbb{R}(\pi_M)-m}} \\ &\leq \left(|V|^{(\mathbb{R}(\pi_M)+1)^{\mathbb{R}(\pi_M)-m}}\right)\left(|V|^{(\gamma(u)-1)(\mathbb{R}(\pi_M)+1)^{\mathbb{R}(\pi_M)-m}}\right) \\ &= |V|^{\gamma(u)(\mathbb{R}(\pi_M)+1)^{\mathbb{R}(\pi_M)-m}} = W_{|V|,\mathbb{R}(\pi_M)}(u). \end{aligned}$$

This, by lemma 1, concludes the proof. □

Proposition 5. *There is a function $g : \mathbb{N} \to \mathbb{N}$ such that, if $\pi_M : \Gamma \vdash M : A$ is word-contextual and ramified, the number of recursive redexes fired during normalization is $O(|M|^{g(\mathbb{R}(\pi_M))})$.*

Proof. A recursive redex with recursion degree m can be copied $O(|M|^{mf(\mathbb{R}(\pi_M))})$ times during normalization, as can be proved from proposition 4 by induction on m. Now, notice that $m \leq \mathbb{R}(\pi_M)$. As a consequence, the function $g(n) = nf(n) + 1$ is a suitable bound. □

Summing up, proposition 4 gives a bound on the size of free algebra terms appearing inside reducts of a given (word-ramified) term M. This is proved by showing that (for every $n \in \mathbb{N}$) the n-weight of the underlying interaction graph does not increase during normalization. This result, by itself, does not prove anything on the complexity of normalization. Proposition 5, however, exploits it by bounding the total number of recursive redexes fired during normalization of M. So, the proof of Theorem 1 can follow. From proposition 5, the number of recursive redexes the normalization fires is $O(|M|^{g(\mathbb{R}(\pi_M))})$, where $g : \mathbb{N} \rightarrow \mathbb{N}$ does not depend on $|M|$. By proposition 4, the time to unfold a recursive redex is itself $O(|M|^{f(\mathbb{R}(\pi_M))})$, where $f : \mathbb{N} \rightarrow \mathbb{N}$ does not depend on $|M|$. Finally, notice that, by firing a linear or conditional redex, the underlying interaction graph shrinks. This concludes the proof.

4 Polytime Completeness

This property holds by representing *predicative sorting* into **HOLRR**. Predicative sorting, introduced below, reformulates *ramified recurrence* (or *predicative recursion*) *on words* [11]; given a word algebra $\mathbb{W}$, predicative recursion is a function algebra generating all, and only, the polynomial functions in the form $f : \mathbb{W}^n \rightarrow \mathbb{W}$. *Predicative sorting* on $\mathbb{W}$ follows:

1. The function $f_{c^{\mathbb{W}}_{k(\mathbb{W})}} : \mathbb{W}^0 \rightarrow \mathbb{W}$ that returns $c^{\mathbb{W}}_{k(\mathbb{W})}$ can be predicatively sorted by $\varepsilon \rightarrow n$, for every $n \in \mathbb{N}$, ε being the empty sequence;
2. For every $i \in \{1, \dots, k(\mathbb{W}) - 1\}$, the function $f_{c^{\mathbb{W}}_i} : \mathbb{W} \rightarrow \mathbb{W}$ defined by $f_{c^{\mathbb{W}}_i}(t) = c^{\mathbb{W}}_i\ t$ can be predicatively sorted by $(n) \rightarrow n$ for every $n \in \mathbb{N}$;
3. For every $n \in \mathbb{N}$ and $1 \leq i \leq n$, the projection $\pi^n_i : \mathbb{W}^n \rightarrow \mathbb{W}$ can be predicatively sorted by $(m_1, \dots, m_n) \rightarrow m$ for every $m, m_1, \dots, m_n \in \mathbb{N}$, with $m_i = m$;
4. If $f : \mathbb{W}^n \rightarrow \mathbb{W}$ can be predicatively sorted by $(m_1, \dots, m_n) \rightarrow m$ and $g_1, \dots, g_n : \mathbb{W}^p \rightarrow \mathbb{W}$ are such that g_i can be predicatively sorted by $(r_1, \dots, r_p) \rightarrow m_i$, then the function $h : \mathbb{W}^p \rightarrow \mathbb{W}$ defined by the equation
$$h(t_1, \dots, t_p) = f(g_1(t_1, \dots, t_p), \dots, g_n(t_1, \dots, t_p)))$$
can be predicatively sorted by $(r_1, \dots, r_p) \rightarrow m$;
5. Suppose for every $i \in \{1, \dots, k(\mathbb{W}) - 1\}$ there is a function $f_i : \mathbb{W}^{n+1} \rightarrow \mathbb{W}$ that can be predicatively sorted by $(l, m_1, \dots, m_n) \rightarrow m$ and that $f_{k(\mathbb{W})} : \mathbb{W}^n \rightarrow \mathbb{W}$ can be predicatively sorted by $(m_1, \dots, m_n) \rightarrow m$. Then the function $h : \mathbb{W}^{1+n} \rightarrow \mathbb{W}$ defined by
$$h(c^{\mathbb{W}}_i\ t, t_1, \dots, t_n) = f_i(t, t_1, \dots, t_n,)$$
$$h(c^{\mathbb{W}}_{k(\mathbb{W})}, t_1, \dots, t_n) = f_{k(\mathbb{W})}(t_1, \dots, t_n).$$

can be predicatively sorted by $(l, m_1, \ldots, m_n) \to m$.

6. Suppose for every $i \in \{1, \ldots, k(\mathbb{W}) - 1\}$ there is a function $f_i : \mathbb{W}^{n+2} \to \mathbb{W}$ that can be predicatively sorted by $(l, m_1, \ldots, m_n, m) \to m$ and that $f_{k(\mathbb{W})} : \mathbb{W}^n \to \mathbb{W}$ can be predicatively sorted by $(m_1, \ldots, m_n) \to m$. Then a function $h : \mathbb{W}^{1+n} \to \mathbb{W}$ can be defined recursively:

$$h(c_i^{\mathbb{W}}\, t, t_1, \ldots, t_n) = f_i(t, t_1, \ldots, t_n, h(t, t_1, \ldots, t_n))$$
$$h(c_{k(\mathbb{W})}^{\mathbb{W}}, t_1, \ldots, t_n) = f_{k(\mathbb{W})}(t_1, \ldots, t_n).$$

If $l > m$, then h can be predicatively sorted by $(l, m_1, \ldots, m_n) \to m$.

By the definition here above, if $f : \mathbb{W}^n \to \mathbb{W}$ can be predicatively sorted, then it is *definable by predicative recursion.*

Remark 2. If f can be predicatively sorted by $(m_1, \ldots, m_n) \to m$ and $m_i < m$, then f is independent from its i-th argument (see [8]). We will suppose that, in rule 3, $m_1, \ldots, m_n \geq m$. This ensures that, if f can be predicatively sorted by $(m_1, \ldots, m_n) \to m$, then $m_1, \ldots, m_n \geq m$, simplifying the proof of completeness, without loss of generality.

Theorem 2 (Completeness). *Assume* $f : \mathbb{W}^n \to \mathbb{W}$ *be predicatively sorted by* $(m_1, \ldots, m_n) \to m$. *There is a closed term* M_f *that represents* f, *whose type can be* $B_{\mathbb{W}}^{l_1} \otimes \cdots \otimes B_{\mathbb{W}}^{l_n} \multimap B_{\mathbb{W}}^{l}$, *where* $l, l_1, \ldots, l_n \in \mathbb{N}$ *and, for every* $i \in \{1, \ldots, n\}$, *either* $m_i = m$ *and* $l_i = l$, *or* $m_i > m$ *and* $l_i > l$.

The proof uses the definition of the terms:

$$\mathbf{Coerc} : B_{\mathbb{W}}^{n} \multimap B_{\mathbb{W}}^{m}$$
$$\mathbf{Duplicate} : B_{\mathbb{W}}^{n} \multimap B_{\mathbb{W}}^{m} \otimes B_{\mathbb{W}}^{l}$$
$$\nabla(M) : B_{\mathbb{W}}^{i_1} \otimes \cdots \otimes B_{\mathbb{W}}^{i_p} \otimes B_{\mathbb{W}}^{n} \multimap B_{\mathbb{W}}^{n}$$

such that:

$$\mathbf{Coerc}(t) \rightsquigarrow^* t$$
$$\mathbf{Duplicate}(t) \rightsquigarrow^* (t, t)$$
$$\nabla(M)(t_1, \ldots, t_p, t) \rightsquigarrow^* M(t_1, \ldots, t_p, t, t)$$

where $t : B_{\mathbb{W}}^{n}$, $t_j : B_{\mathbb{W}}^{i_j}$ $(j \in \{1, \ldots, p\})$, $M : B_{\mathbb{W}}^{i_1} \otimes \cdots \otimes B_{\mathbb{W}}^{i_p} \otimes B_{\mathbb{W}}^{n} \otimes B_{\mathbb{W}}^{n} \multimap B_{\mathbb{W}}^{n}$, $n \in \mathbb{N}$ and $m, l < n$. In particular:

- **Coerc** is $\lambda x.\langle\langle \lambda y.c_1^{\mathbb{W}} y, \ldots, \lambda y.c_{k(A)-1}^{\mathbb{W}} y, c_{k(A)}^{\mathbb{W}} \rangle\rangle\, x$;
- **Duplicate** is $\lambda x.\langle\langle M_1, \ldots, M_{k(\mathbb{W})} \rangle\rangle\, x$, where, for every $i \in \{1, \ldots, k(\mathbb{W}) - 1\}$, M_i is $\lambda y.$ **let** $(z, w) \Leftarrow y$ **in** $(c_i^{\mathbb{W}} z, c_i^{\mathbb{W}} w)$ and $M_{k(\mathbb{W})}$ is $(c_{k(\mathbb{W})}^{\mathbb{W}}, c_{k(\mathbb{W})}^{\mathbb{W}})$;
- $\nabla(M)$ is

  $$\lambda y.\ \mathbf{let}\ (y_1, \ldots, y_n, w) \Leftarrow y\ \mathbf{in}\ \langle\langle L, \ldots, L, P \rangle\rangle [x_1/y_1, \ldots, x_n/y_n, z/w]\ c_1^{\mathbb{W}} c_{k(\mathbb{W})}^{\mathbb{W}}$$

  where $L = \lambda x.\lambda y.M(x_1, \ldots, x_n, z, y)$ and $P = z$.

5 Comparison with Previous Work

There are a number of type systems with the same goal as **HOLRR** [4,5,7,9]. The most similar is certainly **LT**, introduced in [4] and later refined in [5]. **HOLRR** and **LT** are designed from different starting points. **LT** is basically a *restriction* of Gödel system **T**, extending the ideas of safe recursion [3] to the higher-order. **HOLRR**, on the other hand, is obtained by *endowing* linear affine lambda calculus with constants, conditionals and recursions, somehow being inspired by Leivant's ramified recurrence on words.

Linearity is a key ingredient to control the complexity of normalization, in presence of higher-order recursion. The terms of **LT** are not strictly linear: free variables of ground types can appear more than once. On the other side, any variable of **HOLRR** occurs at most once in a typeable term, and recursion preserves this constraint. The strict linearity of **HOLRR** fits precisely with the introduction of linear arrows, when discharging an assumption.

Ramification and safety are other tools to get rid of exponential growth. **LT** models safety by distinguishing among complete and incomplete variables and by using two families of arrows and products, with careful constraints on their interplay. **HOLRR** ramification has the same flavor as in the original work on ramified recurrence on words [11,12], without any major change.

HOLRR accommodates generic free algebras in a uniform way, with just one recursion scheme. **LT** is only about word algebras: the introduction of tree algebras would require to extend the linear discipline to ground variables [9].

In both cases, the system is polytime complete. However, polytime soundness is formulated and proved in two different ways. In **LT**, any term M with free variables $x_1, \dots, x_n$ is equipped with a polynomial $P_M(y_1, \dots, y_n)$ in such a way that the time to normalize $M\{N_1/y_1, \dots, N_n/y_n\}$ is $O(P_M(|N_1|, \dots, |N_n|))$; this result, however, relies on a number of assumptions: all the terms involved must have linear type, $N_1, \dots, N_n$ must all be closed and cannot contain complete free variables of higher type, all free variables of $M\{N_1/y_1, \dots, N_n/y_n\}$ have to be linear and incomplete. This means that there is no evident relation between the structure of M and the degree of P_M. On the contrary, the time needed to compute the normal form of every word-contextual term M of **HOLRR** is $O(|M|^h)$, h only depending on the recursion depth of a type derivation for M. In particular, the recursion depth of any type derivation for any term of any free algebra is null. We claim that our soundness theorem is deeper and more general than the one on **LT**.

6 Relaxing Conditions on Type Derivations

If we drop word-contextuality and ramification, we immediately get outside **PTIME**. For example, if we allow $\mathbb{L}(A)$ to be equal to $\mathbb{L}(C)$ in rule $E^R_{\multimap}$, we can build a term M with $\vdash M : B^0_{\mathbb{B}} \multimap B^0_{\mathbb{B}}$ such that

$$M\ c^{\mathbb{B}}_{i_1} \dots c^{\mathbb{B}}_{i_n} c^{\mathbb{B}}_3 \leadsto^* c^{\mathbb{B}}_{i_1} c^{\mathbb{B}}_{i_1} c^{\mathbb{B}}_{i_2} c^{\mathbb{B}}_{i_2} \dots c^{\mathbb{B}}_{i_n} c^{\mathbb{B}}_{i_n} c^{\mathbb{B}}_3.$$

Iterating M, we easily obtain an exponential behavior. Assume now that, in rule $E^R_{\multimap}$, $B_1, \ldots, B_n$ are arbitrary types, namely that type derivations are not word-contextual. The term $\lambda x.\lambda y.\lambda z.x(yz)$ encoding function composition can be given type $(B^0_{\mathbb{B}} \multimap B^0_{\mathbb{B}}) \multimap (B^0_{\mathbb{B}} \multimap B^0_{\mathbb{B}}) \multimap (B^0_{\mathbb{B}} \multimap B^0_{\mathbb{B}})$; using the obvious generalization of ∇, we obtain a term N with type $(B^0_{\mathbb{B}} \multimap B^0_{\mathbb{B}}) \multimap (B^0_{\mathbb{B}} \multimap B^0_{\mathbb{B}})$ encoding self application. Again, iterating N yields an exponential blow up. The same problem occurs by starting from $c^{\mathbb{C}}_1$ with type $B^0_{\mathbb{C}} \multimap B^0_{\mathbb{C}} \multimap B^0_{\mathbb{C}}$.

7 Conclusions

We provide a higher-order system that embeds, quite naturally, Leivant's ramified recurrence on words.

A final remark about soundness follows. If $\pi_M : \Gamma \vdash M : A$ is a word-contextual ramified derivation, we obtain a bound $O(|M|^{f(\mathbb{R}(\pi_M))})$, for some suitable f. Now, the exponent *does depend* on M. But suppose $\pi_M : \Gamma \vdash M : A \multimap B$ and $\pi_N : \Delta \vdash N : A$ to be word-contextual and ramified. The type derivation $\pi_{MN} : \Gamma, \Delta \vdash MN : B$ is word-contextual and ramified, and $\mathbb{R}(\pi_{MN}) = \max\{\mathbb{R}(\pi_M), \mathbb{R}(\pi_N)\}$. Taking M as a program, the time to compute M on argument N is $O(|MN|^{f(\mathbb{R}(\pi_{MN}))})$ — a polynomial on $|N|$ whenever inputs to M have bounded recursion depth. This includes all the cases where inputs are closed normal forms of a base type. Future work addresses the characterization of higher-order types whose normal forms all have the same recursion depth.

References

1. Andrea Asperti. Light affine logic. In *Proceedings of the 13th IEEE Syposium on Logic in Computer Science*, pages 300–308, 1998.
2. Andrea Asperti and Luca Roversi. Intuitionistic light affine logic. *ACM Transactions on Computational Logic*, 3(1):137–175, 2002.
3. Stephen Bellantoni and Stephen Cook. A new recursion-theoretic characterization of the polytime functions. *Computational Complexity*, 2:97–110, 1992.
4. Stephen Bellantoni, Karl Heinz Niggl, and Helmut Schwichtenberg. Higher type recursion, ramification and polynomial time. *Annals of Pure and Applied Logic*, 104:17–30, 2000.
5. Stephen Bellantoni and Helmut Schwichtenberg. Feasible computation with higher types. Marktoberdorf Summer School Proceedings, 2001.
6. Jean-Yves Girard. Light linear logic. *Information and Computation*, 143(2):175–204, 1998.
7. Martin Hofmann. Linear types and non-size-increasing polynomial time computation. In *Proceedings of the 14th IEEE Syposium on Logic in Computer Science*, pages 464–473, 1999.
8. Martin Hofmann. *Type systems for polynomial-time computation.* Habilitationsschrift, Darmstadt University of Technology, 1999.
9. Martin Hofmann. Safe recursion with higher types and BCK-algebra. *Annals of Pure and Applied Logic*, 104:113–166, 2000.
10. Yves Lafont. Soft linear logic and polynomial time. *Theoretical Computer Science*, To appear.

11. Daniel Leivant. Stratified functional programs and computational complexity. In *Proceedings of 20th ACM Symposium on Principles of Programming Languages*, pages 325–333, 1993.
12. Daniel Leivant. Ramified recurrence and computational complexity I: word recurrence and poly-time. In *Feasible Mathematics II*, pages 320–343. Birkhäuser, 1995.
13. Daniel Leivant. Applicative control and computational complexity. In *Proceedings of 13th International Workshop on Computer Science Logic*, pages 82–95, 1999.
14. Daniel Leivant. Ramified recurrence and computational complexity III: Higher type recurrence and elementary complexity. *Annals of Pure and Applied Logic*, 96:209–229, 1999.
15. Daniel Leivant and Jean-Yves Marion. Ramified recurrence and computational complexity II: Substitution and poly-space. In *Proceedings of 8th International Workshop on Computer Science Logic*, pages 486–500, 1994.

Confluence and Strong Normalisation of the Generalised Multiary λ-Calculus

José Espírito Santo and Luís Pinto*

Departamento de Matemática, Universidade do Minho
4710-057 Braga, Portugal
{jes,luis}@math.uminho.pt

Abstract. In a previous work we introduced the *generalised multiary λ-calculus* $\lambda\mathbf{J}^{\mathbf{m}}$, an extension of the λ-calculus where functions can be applied to lists of arguments (a feature which we call "multiarity") and encompassing "generalised" eliminations of von Plato. In this paper we prove confluence and strong normalisation of the reduction relations of $\lambda\mathbf{J}^{\mathbf{m}}$. Proofs of these results lift corresponding ones obtained by Joachimski and Matthes for the system ΛJ. Such lifting requires the study of how multiarity and some forms of generality can express each other. This study identifies a variant of ΛJ, and another system isomorphic to it, as being the subsystems of $\lambda\mathbf{J}^{\mathbf{m}}$ with, respectively, minimal and maximal use of multiarity. We argue then that $\lambda\mathbf{J}^{\mathbf{m}}$ is the system with the right use of multiarity.

1 Introduction

In [2] we defined the generalised multiary λ-calculus $\lambda\mathbf{J}^{\mathbf{m}}$, an extension of the λ-calculus where application is generalised in two directions: (i) "generality", in the sense of von Plato's generalised eliminations [7]; and (ii) "multiarity", *i.e.* the ability of applying functions to lists of arguments. The original motivation was to extend Schwichtenberg's work on permutative conversions for intuitionistic cut-free sequent calculus [6]. $\lambda\mathbf{J}^{\mathbf{m}}$ comes equipped with a set of permutative conversions for which the permutability theorem holds: two $\lambda\mathbf{J}^{\mathbf{m}}$-terms determine the same λ-term iff they are inter-permutable. We established confluence and strong normalisation of these conversions.

In this paper we study confluence and strong normalisation for the reduction rules of $\lambda\mathbf{J}^{\mathbf{m}}$. Our strategy is to use corresponding properties of the system ΛJ of Joachimski and Matthes [4,5] (the type-theoretic counterpart to von Plato's natural deduction system with generalised eliminations). This is a natural approach because ΛJ may be seen as a notational variant of a subsystem of $\lambda\mathbf{J}^{\mathbf{m}}$ called $\lambda\mathbf{J}$.

We lift the results of ΛJ to $\lambda\mathbf{J}^{\mathbf{m}}$ via a mapping ν whose idea is to express multiarity by means of generality. To fully achieve this we also need another

* Both authors are supported by FCT through the Centro de Matemática da Universidade do Minho, and also by the thematic network APPSEM II; the second author was also supported by the thematic network TYPES.

S. Berardi, M. Coppo, and F. Damiani (Eds.): TYPES 2003, LNCS 3085, pp. 194–209, 2004.

mapping μ, which expresses certain uses of generality by multiarity and which calculates the normal forms for the reduction rule of $\lambda\mathbf{J}^{\mathbf{m}}$ with the same name. It follows that μ and ν are inverse bijections between μ-normal forms and terms of $\lambda\mathbf{J}$. We develop this idea and investigate how these mappings preserve reduction. It turns out that a slight variant of $\lambda\mathbf{J}$ is isomorphic to the subsystem of $\lambda\mathbf{J}^{\mathbf{m}}$ determined by the μ-normal forms.

This emphasis on how multiarity and generality may express each other contrasts with that in [2], where multiarity and generality are studied as independent features of $\lambda\mathbf{J}^{\mathbf{m}}$.

This paper is organised as follows: Section 2 reviews $\lambda\mathbf{J}^{\mathbf{m}}$ and its subsystem $\lambda\mathbf{J}$; Section 3 studies mappings μ and ν and establishes the above mentioned isomorphism; Section 4 proves various results of concluence and strong normalisation; Section 5 concludes.

Notations: Let R be a binary relation over an inductively defined set of expressions. $\rightarrow_R$ denotes the compatible closure of R. $\rightarrow_R^+$ and $\rightarrow_R^*$ denote respectively the transitive; and the reflexive and transitive closure of $\rightarrow_R$. Given relations R and S, we write R, S and RS for $R \cup S$ and $S \circ R$, respectively, whenever convenient.

2 $\lambda\mathbf{J}^{\mathbf{m}}$: The Generalised Multiary λ-Calculus

2.1 Expressions and Typing Rules

Let $\mathbf{V}$ denote a denumerable set of variables and x, y, w, z range over it. In the generalised multiary λ-calculus $\lambda\mathbf{J}^{\mathbf{m}}$ there are two kinds of expressions: terms and lists.

Definition 1. *Terms and lists of* $\lambda\mathbf{J}^{\mathbf{m}}$ *are described in the following grammar:*

$$\begin{array}{ll} (terms\ of\ \lambda\mathbf{J}^{\mathbf{m}})\ t, u, v ::= x \mid \lambda x.t \mid t(u, l, (x)v) \\ (lists\ of\ \lambda\mathbf{J}^{\mathbf{m}}) \qquad\quad l ::= t :: l \mid [] \end{array}$$

The sets of $\lambda\mathbf{J}^{\mathbf{m}}$*-terms and* $\lambda\mathbf{J}^{\mathbf{m}}$*-lists are denoted by* $\mathbf{\Lambda J}^{\mathbf{m}}$ *and* $\mathcal{L}\mathbf{J}^{\mathbf{m}}$ *respectively. A term construction of the form* $t(u, l, (x)v)$ *is called a* generalised multiary application *(*gm-application *for short) and* t *is called its* head. *In terms* $\lambda x.v$ *and* $t(u, l, (x)v)$*, occurrences of* x *in* v *are bound. The list* $[]$ *is called the* empty list *and lists of the form* $t :: l$ *are called* cons-lists. *The notation* $[u_1, \ldots, u_n]$ *abbreviates* $u_1 :: \ldots :: u_n :: []$.

Two definitions that play a special role in the following are:

Definition 2. *A gm-application is called a* cut *if its head is not a variable.*

Definition 3. *A variable x is* main and linear *in a term t if $t = x$ or t is of the form $x(u,l,(y)v)$ where $x \notin u,l,v$. We write* **mla**(x,v) *if v is a gm-application and x is* **m***ain and* **l***inear in v.*

Formulas (= *types*) A, B, C, ... are built up from propositional variables using just $\supset$ (for implication) and *contexts* Γ are finite sets of *variable : formula* pairs, associating at most one formula to each variable.

Sequents of $\lambda\mathbf{J}^{\mathbf{m}}$ are of one of the following two forms

$$\Gamma; - \vdash t : A$$
$$\Gamma; B \vdash l : C,$$

called *term sequents* and *list sequents* respectively. The distinguished position in the LHS of sequents is called the *stoup* and may either be empty (as in term sequents) or hold a formula (the case of list sequents). Read a list sequent $\Gamma; B \vdash l : C$ as "list l leads the formula B to its instance C in context Γ". C is an *instance* of B if B is of the form $B_1 \supset ... \supset B_k \supset C$, for some $k \geq 0$.

Definition 4. *The typing rules of $\lambda\mathbf{J}^{\mathbf{m}}$ are as follows:*

$$\frac{}{x:A,\Gamma; - \vdash x:A}\ Axiom$$

$$\frac{x:A,\Gamma; - \vdash t:B}{\Gamma; - \vdash \lambda x.t : A \supset B}\ Right$$

$$\frac{\Gamma; - \vdash t : A \supset B \quad \Gamma; - \vdash u : A \quad \Gamma; B \vdash l : C \quad x:C,\Gamma; - \vdash v : D}{\Gamma; - \vdash t(u,l,(x)v) : D}\ gm - Elim$$

$$\frac{}{\Gamma; C \vdash [] : C}\ Ax$$

$$\frac{\Gamma; - \vdash u : A \quad \Gamma; B \vdash l : C}{\Gamma; A \supset B \vdash u :: l : C}\ Lft$$

with the proviso that $x : A$ does not belong to Γ in Right *and the proviso that $x : C$ does not belong to Γ in* gm-Elim.

An instance of rule *gm – Elim* is called a *generalised multiary elimination* (or gm-elimination, for short). [2] explains in which sense these typing rules define a sequent calculus which extends with cuts Schwichtenberg's multiary cut-free sequent calculus [6]. It also explains how to interpret $\lambda\mathbf{J}^{\mathbf{m}}$ in Herbelin's $\overline{\lambda}$-calculus [3], where the key ideia is to interpret a gm-application $t(u,l,(x)v)$ as the combination $v\{x := t(u :: l)\}$ of an head-cut and a mid-cut.

2.2 Reduction Rules

Definition 5. *The* reduction rules *for* $\lambda\mathbf{J}^{\mathbf{m}}$ *are as follows:*

$$
\begin{array}{rrl}
(\beta_1) & (\lambda x.t)(u,[],(y)v) & \to \mathbf{s}(\mathbf{s}(u,x,t),y,v) \\
(\beta_2) & (\lambda x.t)(u,v::l,(y)v') & \to \mathbf{s}(u,x,t)(v,l,(y)v') \\
(\pi) & t(u,l,(x)v)(u',l',(y)v') & \to t(u,l,(x)v(u',l',(y)v')) \\
(\mu) & t(u,l,(x)x(u',l',(y)v)) & \to t(u,\mathbf{append}(l,u',l'),(y)v), \quad x \notin u',l',v
\end{array}
$$

where

$$
\begin{array}{rl}
\mathbf{s}(t,x,x) & = t \\
\mathbf{s}(t,x,y) & = y,\ y \neq x \\
\mathbf{s}(t,x,\lambda y.u) & = \lambda y.\mathbf{s}(t,x,u) \\
\mathbf{s}(t,x,u(v,l,(y)v')) & = \mathbf{s}(t,x,u)(\mathbf{s}(t,x,v),\mathbf{s}'(t,x,l),(y)\mathbf{s}(t,x,v'))
\end{array}
$$

$$
\begin{array}{rl}
\mathbf{s}'(t,x,[]) & = [] \\
\mathbf{s}'(t,x,v::l) & = \mathbf{s}(t,x,v)::\mathbf{s}'(t,x,l)
\end{array}
$$

$$
\begin{array}{rl}
\mathbf{append}([],u,l) & = u::l \\
\mathbf{append}(u'::l',u,l) & = u::\mathbf{append}(l',u,l)
\end{array}
$$

A detailed motivation for the reduction rules can be found in [2]. In brief, rules (β_1), (β_2) and (π) perform cut-elimination, *i.e.* they aim at reducing all gm-applications in a term to the form where the head is a variable. Reduction rule (μ) is structural and is used to eliminate gm-applications $t(u,l,(x)v)$ such that $\mathbf{mla}(x,v)$.

Consider the following grammar:

$$
\begin{array}{rl}
t,u,v & ::= x \mid \lambda x.t \mid t'(u,l,(y)v) \\
l & ::= u::l \mid []
\end{array}
$$

The β,π-normal forms are generated by this grammar provided t' is a variable. The μ-normal forms are generated by this grammar provided that in the last production for terms, not $\mathbf{mla}(y,v)$, *i.e.* if v is of the form $y(u',l',(y')v')$, then y must occur either in u', l' or v'. Finally β,π,μ-normal forms are generated by this grammar provided the last production satisfies the two provisos above.

As observed in [2] subject reduction holds for $\to_{\beta,\pi,\mu}$.

2.3 λJ: The Generalised λ-Calculus

We now introduce the cons-free subsystem of $\lambda\mathbf{J}^{\mathbf{m}}$, called $\lambda\mathbf{J}$.

Definition 6. *Terms and lists of* $\lambda\mathbf{J}$ *are as follows:*

$$
\begin{array}{rl}
(\lambda\mathbf{J}-\mathit{terms})\ t,u,v & ::= x \mid \lambda x.t \mid t(u,l,(x)v) \\
(\lambda\mathbf{J}-\mathit{lists})\qquad l & ::= []
\end{array}
$$

$\mathbf{\Lambda J}$ *is used to denote the set of* $\lambda\mathbf{J}$*-terms.*

Since there is only one form of lists in $\lambda\mathbf{J}$, every gm-application in $\lambda\mathbf{J}$ is of the form $t(u,[],(x)v)$, which we call a *generalised application* (or g-application, for short). $\lambda\mathbf{J}$-terms can simply be described as:

$$(\lambda\mathbf{J}-terms)\ t,u,v ::= x \mid \lambda x.t \mid t(u\cdot(x)v) \ ,$$

where $t(u\cdot(x)v)$ is used as an abbreviation to $t(u,[],(x)v)$. This expression can be typed by the derived rule (called *generalised elimination*)

$$\frac{\Gamma;-\vdash t:A\supset B \quad \Gamma;-\vdash u:A \quad x:B,\Gamma;-\vdash v:C}{\Gamma;-\vdash t(u\cdot(x)v):C}\ g-Elim\ , \qquad (1)$$

with proviso $x:B$ does not belong to Γ. Such rule corresponds to an instance of the rule $gm-Elim$ where the penultimate premiss is an instance of Ax.

Definition 7. *The* reduction rules *for* $\lambda\mathbf{J}$ *are as follows:*

$$\begin{array}{rl}(\beta_1) \quad (\lambda x.t)(u\cdot(y)v) & \to \mathbf{s}(\mathbf{s}(u,x,t),y,v)\\ (\pi)\ t(u\cdot(x)v)(u'\cdot(y)v') & \to t(u\cdot(x)v(u'\cdot(y)v'))\end{array}$$

where

$$\begin{array}{rl}\mathbf{s}(t,x,x) &= x\\ \mathbf{s}(t,x,y) &= y,\ y\neq x\\ \mathbf{s}(t,x,\lambda y.u) &= \lambda y.\mathbf{s}(t,x,u)\\ \mathbf{s}(t,x,u(v\cdot(y)v')) &= \mathbf{s}(t,x,u)(\mathbf{s}(t,x,v)\cdot(y)\mathbf{s}(t,x,v'))\end{array}$$

Comparatively to $\lambda\mathbf{J}^{\mathbf{m}}$, $\lambda\mathbf{J}$ drops all rules and clauses involving cons. Since β_2-redexes and μ-*contracta* fall outside $\mathbf{\Lambda J}$ (notice that $\mathbf{append}([],u',l')$ is a cons-list), the rules (β_2) and (μ) are omitted.

The system thus obtained is no more than a notational variant of the ΛJ-calculus of Joachimski and Matthes.

3 Relating Generality and Multiarity

Generality can express multiarity and multiarity is a shorthand for certain forms of generality. In this section this idea is made precise and consequences of it are extracted.

3.1 The Bijection between Terms of λJ and μ-Normal Forms

We start by explaining how to express multiarity in terms of generality. The basic idea is to replace each cons by a g-application that introduces a fresh name. For instance,

$$t(u,[u_1,u_2],(x)v) \rightsquigarrow t(u\cdot(z_1)z_1(u_1\cdot(z_2)z_2(u_2\cdot(x)v))),$$

where z_1 and z_2 are fresh variables. This idea is embodied in the following type-preserving mapping.

Definition 8. *The mapping* ν *is as follows.*

$$\nu : \mathbf{\Lambda J^m} \longrightarrow \mathbf{\Lambda J}$$

$$\begin{aligned}
\nu(x) &= x \\
\nu(\lambda x.t) &= \lambda x.\nu(t) \\
\nu(t(u,l,(x)v)) &= \nu(t)(\nu(u)\cdot(z)\nu'(z,l,x,\nu(v))), \quad z \text{ fresh}
\end{aligned}$$

$$\begin{aligned}
\nu'(z,[],x,v) &= \mathbf{s}(z,x,v) \\
\nu'(z,u::l,x,v) &= z(\nu(u)\cdot(w)\nu'(w,l,x,v)), \quad w \text{ fresh}
\end{aligned}$$

Conversely, in $t(u,l,(x)v)$, if v is a gm-application $x(u',l',(y)v')$ such that $x \notin u',l',v'$, then v may be eliminated with the help of cons. In fact, the former term can be reduced to $t(u, \mathbf{append}(l,u',l'),(y)v')$, where the append operation generates $u'::l'$ and, if l is not empty, a further cons to concatenate l with $u'::l'$. This is precisely reduction rule μ. The following type-preserving mapping reduces the μ-redexes of a term in a innermost-first fashion.

Definition 9. *The mapping* μ *is as follows.*

$$\mu : \mathbf{\Lambda J^m} \longrightarrow \mathbf{\Lambda J^m}$$

$$\begin{aligned}
\mu(x) &= x \\
\mu(\lambda x.t) &= \lambda x.\mu(t) \\
\mu(t(u,l,(x)v)) &= \begin{cases} \mu(t)(\mu(u), \mathbf{append}(\mu'(l),u',l'),(y)v'), \\ \qquad\qquad \text{if } \mu(v) = x(u',l',(y)v') \text{ and } x \notin u',l',v' \\ \\ \mu(t)(\mu(u),\mu'(l),(x)\mu(v)), \quad \text{otherwise} \end{cases}
\end{aligned}$$

$$\begin{aligned}
\mu'([]) &= [] \\
\mu'(u::l) &= \mu(u)::\mu'(l)
\end{aligned}$$

The results that follow show that the restriction of mapping μ to $\mathbf{\Lambda J}$ and the restriction of mapping ν to μ-normal forms are mutual inverses.

Lemma 1. $t \rightarrow_\mu^* \mu(t)$, *for all* $t \in \mathbf{\Lambda J^m}$.

Proof. Proved together with $l \rightarrow_\mu^* \mu'(l)$, for all $l \in \mathcal{L}\mathbf{J^m}$, by simultaneous induction on t and l. □

Lemma 2. *If* $t \rightarrow_\mu t'$, *then (i)* $\mu(t) = \mu(t')$ *and (ii)* $\nu(t) = \nu(t')$, *for all* $t,t' \in \mathbf{\Lambda J^m}$.

Proof. (i) is proved together with $l \rightarrow_\mu l'$ implies $\mu'(l) = \mu'(l')$, for all $l,l' \in \mathcal{L}\mathbf{J^m}$, by simultaneous induction on $t \rightarrow_\mu t'$ and $l \rightarrow_\mu l'$. (ii) is proved together with $l \rightarrow_\mu l'$ implies $\nu'(z,l,x,v) = \nu'(z,l',x,v)$, for all $l,l' \in \mathcal{L}\mathbf{J^m}$ and all $v \in \mathbf{\Lambda J}$, by simultaneous induction on $t \rightarrow_\mu t'$ and $l \rightarrow_\mu l'$. □

Lemma 3. $\mu(t)$ *is* μ*-normal, for all* $t \in \mathbf{\Lambda J^m}$.

Proof. Proved together with $\mu'(l)$ is μ-normal, for all $l \in \mathcal{L}\mathbf{J}^{\mathbf{m}}$, by simultaneous induction on t and l. □

Proposition 1. *(i)* $\rightarrow_\mu$ *is confluent.*
(ii) $\rightarrow_\mu$ *is strongly normalising.*
(iii) $\mu(t)$ *is the unique normal form of* t *w.r.t.* $\rightarrow_\mu$*, for all* $t \in \mathbf{\Lambda J^m}$.

Proof. (i) follows from lemmas 1 and 2. In order to guarantee (ii), observe that each μ-step reduces the number of μ-redexes. (iii) results from the combination of lemmas 1 and 3 and confluence of $\rightarrow_\mu$. □

Lemma 4. $\nu(t) \rightarrow^*_\mu t$*, for all* $t \in \mathbf{\Lambda J^m}$.

Proof. Proved together with $t(u\cdot(z)\nu'(z,l,x,v)) \rightarrow^*_\mu t(u,l,(x)v)$, for all $t,u,v \in \mathbf{\Lambda J}$ and all $l \in \mathcal{L}\mathbf{J}^{\mathbf{m}}$ s.t. $z \notin l, v$, by simultaneous induction on t and l. □

Corollary 1. $t \rightarrow^*_\mu \mu(\nu(t))$*, for all* $t \in \mathbf{\Lambda J^m}$.

Proof. By Lemma 1, it suffices $\mu(\nu(t)) = \mu(t)$. From Lemma 1 (applied twice) and Lemma 4, $\nu(t)$ reduces both to $\mu(\nu(t))$ and $\mu(t)$, which are μ-normal. Thus by confluence, $\mu(\nu(t)) = \mu(t)$. □

Proposition 2. *(i)* $\nu(t) = t$*, for all* $t \in \mathbf{\Lambda J}$.
(ii) $\mu(t) = t$*, for all μ-normal* $t \in \mathbf{\Lambda J^m}$.

Proof. (i) Follows by induction on t. (ii) Since t is μ-normal, Proposition 1 imposes $t = \mu(t)$. □

Proposition 3. *(i)* $\nu(\mu(t)) = t$*, for all* $t \in \mathbf{\Lambda J}$.
(ii) $\mu(\nu(t)) = t$*, for all μ-normal* $t \in \mathbf{\Lambda J^m}$.

Proof. (i) From lemmas 1 and 2 we get $\nu(\mu(t)) = \nu(t)$, which is just t by the proposition above. (ii) Lemmas 1 and 4 imply reduction of $\nu(t)$ to t and $\mu(\nu(t))$ respectively. Thus t and $\mu(\nu(t))$ are two μ-normal forms of $\nu(t)$, which by confluence of $\rightarrow_\mu$ must be equal. □

3.2 Preservation of Reduction by Mappings μ and ν

Preservation of reduction μ is considered in Lemma 2.

Lemma 5. *(i) If* $t \rightarrow_\beta t'$*, then* $\nu(t) \rightarrow_\beta \nu(t')$*, for all* $t, t' \in \mathbf{\Lambda J^m}$.
(ii) If $t \rightarrow_\beta t'$*, then* $\mu(t) \rightarrow_\beta \rightarrow^*_\mu \mu(t')$*, for all* $t, t' \in \mathbf{\Lambda J^m}$.

Proof. (i) is proved together with $l \to_\beta l'$ implies $\nu'(z, l, x, v) \to_\beta \nu'(z, l', x, v)$, for all $l, l' \in \mathcal{L}\mathbf{J^m}$ and all $v \in \mathbf{\Lambda J}$, by simultaneous induction on $t \to_\beta t'$ and $l \to_\beta l'$. (ii) follows from the commutation in $\lambda\mathbf{J^m}$ between $\to_\beta$ and $\to_\mu$: if $t \to_\beta t_1$ and $t \to_\mu t_2$, there exists t_3 such that $t_1 \to_\mu^* t_3$ and $t_2 \to_\beta t_3$. □

In contrast to rule (β), one-to-one preservation of π-steps is problematic: mapping ν needs several steps in $\lambda\mathbf{J}$ to simulate a single step in $\lambda\mathbf{J^m}$ and mapping μ does not even preserve π-steps. These mismatches, between rule (π) and mappings ν and μ, are an obstacle to proving confluence of $\lambda\mathbf{J^m}$ along the lines of the proof of Theorem 5, where we lift confluence of $\lambda\mathbf{J}$. Such proof requires preservation of (π) (as well as (β)) by mapping μ. We illustrate these mismatches with an example.

Let t, u, u_1, u_2, u', v be μ-normal forms in $\lambda\mathbf{J}$, hence invariant both for μ and ν. Consider the following three terms in $\lambda\mathbf{J}$

$$\begin{aligned} t_0 &= t(u\cdot(z_1)z_1(u_1\cdot(z_2)z_2(u_2\cdot(x)x)))(u'\cdot(y)v) \ , \\ t_1 &= t(u\cdot(z_1)z_1(u_1\cdot(z_2)z_2(u_2\cdot(x)x))(u'\cdot(y)v)) \ , \\ t_2 &= t(u\cdot(z_1)z_1(u_1\cdot(z_2)z_2(u_2\cdot(x)x(u'\cdot(y)v)))) \ , \end{aligned}$$

and the corresponding μ-normal forms

$$\begin{aligned} u_0 &= \mu(t_0) = t(u, [u_1, u_2], (x)x)(u'\cdot(y)v) \ , \\ u_1 &= \mu(t_1) = t(u\cdot(z_1)z_1(u_1, [u_2], (x)x)(u'\cdot(y)v)) \ , \\ u_2 &= \mu(t_2) = t(u, [u_1, u_2, u'], (y)v) \ . \end{aligned}$$

Consider also

$$\begin{aligned} v_1 &= t(u\cdot(z_1)z_1(u_1, [u_2], (x)x(u'\cdot(y)v))) \ , \\ v_2 &= t(u, [u_1, u_2], (x)x(u'\cdot(y)v)) \ . \end{aligned}$$

Observe that $\nu(u_0) = t_0$, $\nu(u_1) = t_1$ and $\nu(u_2) = \nu(v_1) = \nu(v_2) = t_2$. Observe also that there are the following reductions among these terms:

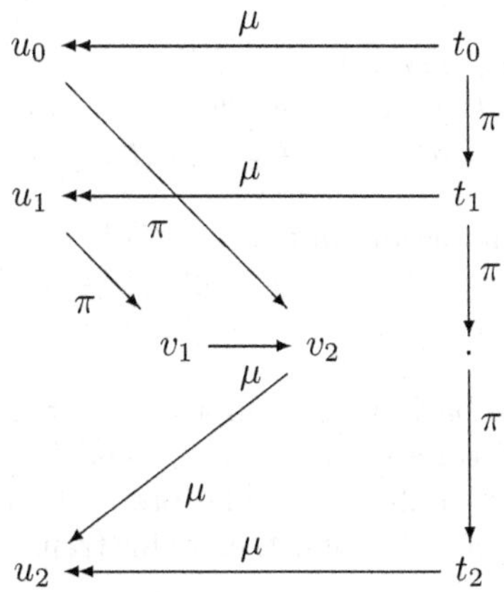

Notice that $u_0 \to_\pi v_2$ whereas $\nu(u_0)$ requires three π-steps to reach $\nu(v_2)$. In general we have the following:

Lemma 6. *If $t \rightarrow_\pi t'$, then $\nu(t) \rightarrow_\pi^+ \nu(t')$, for all $t, t' \in \mathbf{\Lambda J^m}$.*

Proof. Proved together with $l \rightarrow_\pi l'$ implies $\nu'(z, l, x, v) \rightarrow_\pi^+ \nu'(z, l', x, v)$, for all $l, l' \in \mathcal{L}\mathbf{J^m}$ and all $v \in \mathbf{\Lambda J}$, by simultaneous induction on $t \rightarrow_\pi t'$ and $l \rightarrow_\pi l'$. □

Going back to the example, observe that $t_0 \rightarrow_\pi t_1$ but $\mu(t_0)$ does not reduce to $\mu(t_1)$, it π-reduces to v_2. However, making enough π-reductions from t_1, one reaches a term (t_2 in the example) whose μ-normal form (u_2 in the example) is the same as the μ-normal form of v_2. Making enough π-reductions means to perform π-reductions as long as this generates π-redexes which hide μ-redexes. For instance, observe that the head of t_0 is a μ-redex. The reduction $t_0 \rightarrow_\pi t_1$ creates the π-redex $z_1(u_1 \cdot (z_2) z_2 (u_2 \cdot (x) x))(u' \cdot (y) v)$ which hides in t_1 the mentioned μ-redex. Since the reduction of this π-redex causes a descendent of the original μ-redex to reappear, we perform it. Moreover, as another μ-redex becomes hidden, this process continues. We introduce a new reduction rule in $\lambda\mathbf{J}$ to perform such sequences of π-reductions in a single step.

Definition 10. *The rule (π') is the following:*

$$(\pi') \quad t(u \cdot (x) v)(u' \cdot (y) v') \rightarrow t(u \cdot (x) @'(x, v, u', y, v'))$$

where

$$@'(x, t, u, y, v) = \begin{cases} x(u' \cdot (z) @'(z, v', u, y, v)), \\ \qquad\qquad \textit{if } t = x(u' \cdot (z) v') \textit{ and } x \notin u', v' \\ \\ t(u \cdot (y) v), \quad \textit{otherwise} \end{cases}$$

For instance, in the example before $t_1 \rightarrow_{\pi'} t_2$. Observe that $\rightarrow_{\pi'} \subseteq \rightarrow_\pi^+$ and that a term is π'-normal if and only if it is π-normal.

We now see how the situation improved w.r.t. the preservation of π-steps.

Lemma 7. *(i) If $t \rightarrow_\pi t'$, then $\nu(t) \rightarrow_{\pi'} \nu(t')$, for all $t, t' \in \mathbf{\Lambda J^m}$ such that t is μ-normal.*
(ii) If $t \rightarrow_{\pi'} t'$, then $\mu(t) \rightarrow_\pi \rightarrow_\mu^* \mu(t')$, for all $t, t' \in \mathbf{\Lambda J}$.

Proof. (ii) is proved by induction on $t \rightarrow_{\pi'} t'$. (i) is proved together with $l \rightarrow_\pi l'$ implies $\nu'(z, l, x, v) \rightarrow_{\pi'} \nu'(z, l', x, v)$, for all $l, l' \in \mathcal{L}\mathbf{J^m}$ and all $v \in \mathbf{\Lambda J}$, by simultaneous induction on $t \rightarrow_\pi t'$ and $l \rightarrow_\pi l'$. □

Now we turn to some basic results about rule (π'), leading to Corollary 2, which shows how to perform a sequence of (β) and (π) reductions by means of a sequence of (β) and (π') reductions. The proof of confluence of the relation $\rightarrow_{\beta,\pi,\mu}$ on $\lambda\mathbf{J^m}$-terms, given in Section 4, uses this transformation and the lemma above.

The mapping π in the definition below is considered in [4] and produces π-normal forms.

Definition 11. *The mapping π is as follows.*

$$\pi : \mathbf{\Lambda J} \longrightarrow \mathbf{\Lambda J}$$

$$\begin{aligned}\pi(x) &= x\\ \pi(\lambda x.t) &= \lambda x.\pi(t)\\ \pi(t(u\cdot(x)v)) &= @(\pi(t),\pi(u),x,\pi(v))\end{aligned}$$

where

$$@(t,u,x,v) = \begin{cases} t'(u'\cdot(y)@(v',u,x,v)), & \text{if } t = t'(u'\cdot(y)v') \\ t(u\cdot(x)v), & \text{otherwise} \end{cases}$$

[4] observes that (i) $t \to_\pi^* \pi(t)$, for all $t \in \mathbf{\Lambda J}$; (ii) if $t \to_\pi^* t'$ then $\pi(t) = \pi(t')$ for all $t, t' \in \mathbf{\Lambda J}$ (and from these two follows confluence of $\to_\pi$); (iii) $\to_\pi$ is strongly normalising for all terms of $\lambda\mathbf{J}$.

Next lemma establishes that rule (π') suffices to reduce a term to its π-normal form.

Lemma 8. $t \to_{\pi'}^* \pi(t)$, *for all* $t \in \mathbf{\Lambda J}$.

Proof. Because $\to_{\pi'} \subseteq \to_\pi^+$ and $\to_\pi$ is terminating, $\to_{\pi'}$ is also terminating. Let t' be a π'-normal form of t. Since t' is also a π-normal form, $t \to_\pi^* t'$ and $\to_\pi$ is confluent, it follows that $t' = \pi(t)$. Thus $t \to_{\pi'}^* \pi(t)$. □

We establish now a kind of commutation between reduction $\to_\beta$ and mapping π, that uses next lemma.

Lemma 9. $\mathbf{s}(\pi(t), x, \pi(u)) \to_\pi^* \pi(\mathbf{s}(t,x,u))$, *for all* $t, u \in \mathbf{\Lambda J}$.

Proof. The proof is by induction on u. It uses the fact that, for all $t, t_0, u_0, v_0 \in \mathbf{\Lambda J}$, $\mathbf{s}(t,x,@(t_0,u_0,y,v_0)) \to_\pi^* @(\mathbf{s}(t,x,t_0), \mathbf{s}(t,x,u_0), y, \mathbf{s}(t,x,v_0))$, proved by induction on t_0 □

Proposition 4. *If* $t \to_\beta u$, *then* $\pi(t) \to_{\beta,\pi'}^* \pi(u)$, *for all* $t, u \in \mathbf{\Lambda J}$.

Proof. By induction on $t \to_\beta u$. The base case uses the lemma before. □

Corollary 2. *If* $t \to_{\beta,\pi}^* u$, *then* $\pi(t) \to_{\beta,\pi'}^* \pi(u)$, *for all* $t, u \in \mathbf{\Lambda J}$.

Proof. Follows by induction on the number of steps in the reduction sequence. The case corresponding to a β-step uses the proposition before and the case corresponding to a π-step uses invariance of $\to_\pi$ w.r.t. mapping π. □

3.3 Two Isomorphic Subsystems of $\lambda\mathbf{J^m}$

Some of the preservation results obtained above can be put together so that the bijection between μ-normal forms and terms of $\lambda\mathbf{J}$ becomes an isomorphism, provided those two sets of terms are equipped with appropriate reduction relations.

Let $\lambda\mathbf{J}'$ denote the system obtained from $\lambda\mathbf{J}$ replacing rule (π) by rule (π'). Let $\lambda\mathbf{J}^{\mathbf{m}}_{\mu}$ denote the subsystem of μ-normal forms of $\lambda\mathbf{J^m}$ obtained by closing relation $\rightarrow_{\beta,\pi}$ for mapping μ. More precisely, in $\lambda\mathbf{J}^{\mathbf{m}}_{\mu}$ the one step relations $\rightarrow_{\beta_\mu}$ and $\rightarrow_{\pi_\mu}$ are given by:

$$\begin{array}{lll} t \rightarrow_{\beta_\mu} t' & \text{if} \quad t \rightarrow_{\beta} t'' \text{ and } t' = \mu(t''), & \text{for some } t'' \in \lambda\mathbf{J^m}; \\ t \rightarrow_{\pi_\mu} t' & \text{if} \quad t \rightarrow_{\pi} t'' \text{ and } t' = \mu(t''), & \text{for some } t'' \in \lambda\mathbf{J^m}. \end{array}$$

Notice that in $\lambda\mathbf{J}^{\mathbf{m}}_{\mu}$ there is no need for a μ-reduction.

Theorem 1. *(i) $t \rightarrow_{\beta_\mu} t'$ iff $\nu(t) \rightarrow_{\beta} \nu(t')$, for all μ-normal forms t, t'.*
(ii) $t \rightarrow_{\pi_\mu} t'$ iff $\nu(t) \rightarrow_{\pi'} \nu(t')$, for all μ-normal forms t, t'.
(iii) $t \rightarrow_{\beta} t'$ iff $\mu(t) \rightarrow_{\beta_\mu} \mu(t')$, for all $t, t' \in \mathbf{\Lambda J}$.
(iv) $t \rightarrow_{\pi'} t'$ iff $\mu(t) \rightarrow_{\pi_\mu} \mu(t')$, for all $t, t' \in \mathbf{\Lambda J}$.

Proof. We just show the "only if" statements since the "if" statements follow from these and the fact that ν and μ are mutual inverses. (i) follows from lemmas 1, 2 and 5. (ii) follows from lemmas 1, 2 and 7. (iii) and (iv) hold by lemmas 5 and 7 respectively. □

Now confluence and strong normalisation of relation $\rightarrow_{\beta,\pi}$ on $\lambda\mathbf{J}$ are used to obtain corresponding properties for $\lambda\mathbf{J}'$ and thus for its isomorphic system $\lambda\mathbf{J}^{\mathbf{m}}_{\mu}$.

Theorem 2. *$\rightarrow_{\beta,\pi'}$ in $\lambda\mathbf{J}'$ is confluent.*

Proof. Assume $t \rightarrow^*_{\beta,\pi'} t_1$ and $t \rightarrow^*_{\beta,\pi'} t_2$. Then, since $\rightarrow_{\pi'} \subseteq \rightarrow^+_{\pi}$, also $t \rightarrow^*_{\beta,\pi} t_1$ and $t \rightarrow^*_{\beta,\pi} t_2$. Using confluence of $\rightarrow^*_{\beta,\pi}$ for $\lambda\mathbf{J}$, there exists t_3 such that $t_1 \rightarrow^*_{\beta,\pi} t_3$ and $t_2 \rightarrow^*_{\beta,\pi} t_3$. So, using Corollary 2 followed by Lemma 8, one obtains $t_1 \rightarrow^*_{\beta,\pi'} \pi(t_3)$ and $t_2 \rightarrow^*_{\beta,\pi'} \pi(t_3)$. □

Theorem 3. *There is no infinite $\rightarrow_{\beta,\pi'}$-reduction starting at a typable term of $\lambda\mathbf{J}'$.*

Proof. If there was, since $\rightarrow_{\pi'} \subseteq \rightarrow^+_{\pi}$, one could build an infinite sequence of β,π-steps, starting at a typable term of $\lambda\mathbf{J}$, contradicting strong normalisation of $\lambda\mathbf{J}$. □

4 Results of Confluence and Strong Normalisation for $\lambda\mathbf{J}^{\mathbf{m}}$

This section studies confluence and strong normalisation for the notions of reduction in $\lambda\mathbf{J}^{\mathbf{m}}$ resulting from all possible combinations of rules (β), (π) and (μ). The proofs of confluence presented here follow one of two directions: (i) for notions of reduction involving only rules (β) and (π), arguments are simple extensions of those used in [4]; (ii) for notions of reduction including μ, arguments are built in a modular way, using essentially properties of presevation of reduction by mappings μ and ν, together with confluence results for $\lambda\mathbf{J}$. Strong normalisation of $\rightarrow_{\beta,\pi,\mu}$ for all typable terms of $\lambda\mathbf{J}^{\mathbf{m}}$ is obtained from the strong normalisation of $\rightarrow_{\beta,\pi}$ for $\lambda\mathbf{J}$'s typable terms, with the help of results of preservation of reduction by mapping ν. Strong normalisation of typable terms for all the other relations follows, since they are included in $\rightarrow_{\beta,\pi,\mu}$. In fact, for relations not involving rule (β), strong normalisation holds for all terms.

4.1 Confluence

Firstly we tackle confluence of relations $\rightarrow_{\pi}$, $\rightarrow_{\beta}$ and $\rightarrow_{\beta,\pi}$ in $\lambda\mathbf{J}^{\mathbf{m}}$. The following definition extends Definition 11.

Definition 12. *The mapping π is as follows.*

$$\pi : \mathbf{\Lambda J^m} \longrightarrow \mathbf{\Lambda J^m}$$

$$\begin{aligned} \pi(x) &= x \\ \pi(\lambda x.t) &= \lambda x.\pi(t) \\ \pi(t(u,l,(x)v)) &= @(\pi(t),\pi(u),\pi'(l),x,\pi(v)) \end{aligned}$$

$$\begin{aligned} \pi'([]) &= [] \\ \pi'(u::l) &= \pi(u)::\pi'(l) \end{aligned}$$

where

$$@(t,u,l,x,v) = \begin{cases} t'(u',l',(y)@(v',u,l,x,v)), & \textit{if } t = t'(u',l',(y)v') \\ t(u,l,(x)v), & \textit{otherwise} \end{cases}$$

Lemma 10. *$\pi(t)$ is π-normal, for all $t \in \mathbf{\Lambda J^m}$.*

Proof. Proved together with $\pi'(l)$ is π-normal, for all $l \in \mathcal{L}\mathbf{J^m}$, by simultaneous induction on t and l. □

Lemma 11. *$t \rightarrow_{\pi}^{*} \pi(t)$, for all $t \in \mathbf{\Lambda J^m}$.*

Proof. Proved together with $l \rightarrow_{\pi}^{*} \pi'(l)$, for all $l \in \mathcal{L}\mathbf{J^m}$, by simultaneous induction on t and l. □

Lemma 12. *If* $t_1 \to_\pi^* t_2$, *then* $\pi(t_1) = \pi(t_2)$, *for all* $t_1, t_2 \in \mathbf{\Lambda J^m}$.

Proof. Proved together with the fact that $l_1 \to_\pi^* l_2$ implies $\pi'(l_1) = \pi'(l_2)$, for all $l_1, l_2 \in \mathcal{L}\mathbf{J^m}$, by simultaneous induction on $t \to_\pi^* t'$ and $l \to_\pi^* l'$. □

Proposition 5. $\to_\pi^*$ *has the triangle property w.r.t. mapping* π.[1]

Proof. If $t_1 \to_\pi^* t_2$, from the two lemmas above, $t_2 \to_\pi^* \pi(t_2) = \pi(t_1)$. □

Definition 13. *Reduction* $\Rightarrow_\beta$ *is inductively defined on terms of* $\lambda\mathbf{J^m}$ *as follows:*

$$
\begin{array}{l}
x \Rightarrow_\beta x;\\
\lambda x.t \Rightarrow_\beta \lambda x.t' \text{ if } t \Rightarrow_\beta t';\\
t(u, l, (x)v) \Rightarrow_\beta t'(u', l', (x)v') \text{ if } t \Rightarrow_\beta t', u \Rightarrow_\beta u', l \Rightarrow_\beta l', v \Rightarrow_\beta v';\\
(\lambda y.t)(u, [], (x)v) \Rightarrow_\beta \mathbf{s}(\mathbf{s}(u', y, t'), x, v') \text{ if } t \Rightarrow_\beta t', u \Rightarrow_\beta u', v \Rightarrow_\beta v';\\
(\lambda y.t)(u, u_0 :: l, (x)v) \Rightarrow_\beta \mathbf{s}(u', y, t')(u_0', l', (x)v') \text{ if}\\
\qquad\qquad\qquad\qquad t \Rightarrow_\beta t', u \Rightarrow_\beta u', u_0 \Rightarrow_\beta u_0', l \Rightarrow_\beta l', v \Rightarrow_\beta v';\\
[] \Rightarrow_\beta [];\\
u :: l \Rightarrow_\beta u' :: l' \text{ if } u \Rightarrow_\beta u', l \Rightarrow_\beta l'.
\end{array}
$$

Observe that $\Rightarrow_\beta$ is reflexive and $\to_\beta \subseteq \Rightarrow_\beta \subseteq \to_\beta^*$.

Definition 14. *The mapping* β *is as follows.*

$$
\beta : \mathbf{\Lambda J^m} \longrightarrow \mathbf{\Lambda J^m}
$$

$$
\begin{array}{rl}
x^\beta &= x\\
(\lambda x.t)^\beta &= \lambda x.t^\beta\\
t(u, l, (x)v)^\beta &= \begin{cases}
\mathbf{s}(\mathbf{s}(u^\beta, y, t_1^\beta), x, v^\beta), & \\
\qquad\qquad \text{if } t = \lambda y.t_1 \text{ and } l = [] & \\
\mathbf{s}(u^\beta, y, t_1^\beta)(u_1^\beta, l_1^{\beta'}, (x)v^\beta), & \\
\qquad\qquad \text{if } t = \lambda y.t_1 \text{ and } l = u_1 :: l_1 & \\
t^\beta(u^\beta, l^{\beta'}, (x)v^\beta), \quad \text{otherwise} &
\end{cases}
\end{array}
$$

$$
\begin{array}{rl}
[]^{\beta'} &= []\\
(u :: l)^{\beta'} &= u^\beta :: l^{\beta'}
\end{array}
$$

Proposition 6. $\Rightarrow_\beta$ *has the triangle property w.r.t.* β.

Proof. By induction on $\Rightarrow_\beta$. It uses parallelism of $\Rightarrow_\beta$, *i.e.* the fact that if $t \Rightarrow_\beta t'$ and $u \Rightarrow_\beta u'$ then $\mathbf{s}(t, x, u) \Rightarrow_\beta \mathbf{s}(t', x, u')$, as well as simple inversion principles for $\Rightarrow_\beta$. □

Lemma 13. *If* $t \Rightarrow_\beta t_1$ *and* $t \to_\pi t_2$, *then* $t_1 \to_\pi^* t_3$ *and* $t_2 \Rightarrow_\beta t_3$, *for some* $t_3 \in \mathbf{\Lambda J^m}$.

[1] A relation $\to$ has the triangle property w.r.t. a function f if $a \to b$ implies $b \to f(a)$

Proof. Proved together with the fact that if $l \Rightarrow_\beta l_1$ and $l \rightarrow_\pi l_2$, then there exists $l_3 \in \mathcal{L}\mathbf{J}^{\mathbf{m}}$ such that $l_1 \rightarrow_\pi^* l_3$ and $l_2 \Rightarrow_\beta l_3$, for all $l, l_1, l_2 \in \mathcal{L}\mathbf{J}^{\mathbf{m}}$, by simultaneous induction on $t \Rightarrow_\beta t_1$ and $l \Rightarrow_\beta l_1$. This proof uses parallelism of $\rightarrow_\pi^*$. □

Corollary 3. *$\Rightarrow_\beta$ and $\rightarrow_\pi^*$ commute.*

Proof. Follows from the previous lemma by a simple diagram chase. □

Proposition 7. *$\Rightarrow_\beta \rightarrow_\pi^*$ has the triangle property w.r.t. $\pi \circ \beta$.*

Proof. Follows from the triangle properties of $\rightarrow_\pi^*$ and $\Rightarrow_\beta$ w.r.t. π and β, together with commutativity between the two relations. □

Theorem 4. *$\rightarrow_\pi$, $\rightarrow_\beta$ and $\rightarrow_{\beta,\pi}$ are confluent.*

Proof. Confluence of a relation can be obtained from a triangle property, as shown in Lemma 1 of [4]. (Confluence of $\rightarrow_\pi$ can also be obtained immediately from lemmas 11 and 12.) As to confluence of $\rightarrow_{\beta,\pi}$, observe that $\rightarrow_{\beta,\pi}^*$ is confluent and that the reflexive and transitive closure of $\Rightarrow_\beta \rightarrow_\pi^*$ is equal to $\rightarrow_{\beta,\pi}^*$, since $\rightarrow_{\beta,\pi} \subseteq \Rightarrow_\beta \rightarrow_\pi^* \subseteq \rightarrow_{\beta,\pi}^*$. □

Now we consider confluence in the presence of rule μ. The method used before still works when one adjoins rule μ, because: (i) $\rightarrow_{\pi,\mu}^*$ has a triangle property (w.r.t. $\mu \circ \pi$); and (ii) $\rightarrow_\mu^*$ commutes with $\Rightarrow_\beta$. However, in the presence of rule μ, one can lift confluence results of $\lambda\mathbf{J}$.

Theorem 5. *$\rightarrow_{\beta,\pi,\mu}$, $\rightarrow_{\beta,\mu}$ and $\rightarrow_{\pi,\mu}$ are confluent.*

Proof. Let R be relation β (resp. π or $\beta \cup \pi$) and let R' be β (resp. π' or $\beta \cup \pi'$). Assume $t \rightarrow_{R,\mu}^* t_1$ and $t \rightarrow_{R,\mu}^* t_2$. Then, by lemmas 2, 5 and 6 it follows that $\nu(t) \rightarrow_R^* \nu(t_1)$ and $\nu(t) \rightarrow_R^* \nu(t_2)$. Now confluence of R in $\lambda\mathbf{J}$ guarantees the existence of t_3 such that $\nu(t_1) \rightarrow_R^* t_3$ and $\nu(t_2) \rightarrow_R^* t_3$. So, using Lemma 8 and Corollary 2, $\nu(t_1) \rightarrow_{R'}^* \pi(t_3)$ and $\nu(t_2) \rightarrow_{R'}^* \pi(t_3)$, which in turn, by lemmas 5 and 7, implies $\mu(\nu(t_1)) \rightarrow_{R,\mu}^* \mu(\pi(t_3))$ and $\mu(\nu(t_2)) \rightarrow_{R,\mu}^* \mu(\pi(t_3))$. Then, from Corollary 1, it follows $t_1 \rightarrow_\mu^* \mu(\nu(t_1))$ and $t_2 \rightarrow_\mu^* \mu(\nu(t_2))$ and thus t_1 and t_2 have $\mu(\pi(t_3))$ as common reduct. □

4.2 Strong Normalisation

Theorem 6. *There is no infinite $\rightarrow_{\beta,\pi,\mu}$-reduction sequence starting at a typable term of $\lambda\mathbf{J}^{\mathbf{m}}$.*

Proof. Suppose there is such an infinite reduction sequence S. It cannot contain infinitely many β,π-steps. Otherwise, since (i) μ-reduction is invariant under ν (Lemma 2), (ii) each β,π-step in $\lambda\mathbf{J}^{\mathbf{m}}$ originates under ν one or more β,π-steps in $\lambda\mathbf{J}$ (lemmas 5 and 6) and (iii) ν preserves typability, one could build in $\lambda\mathbf{J}$ an infinite sequence of β,π-steps starting at a typable term, contradicting strong normalisation of $\lambda\mathbf{J}$. Therefore beyond a certain point in sequence S there are solely μ-steps, necessarily in infinite number, which is also impossible due to strong normalisation of $\rightarrow_\mu$ (Proposition 1). □

Theorem 7. *There is no infinite* $\to_{\pi,\mu}$*-reduction sequence in* $\lambda\mathbf{J^m}$.

Proof. Similar to the one above showing strong normalisation of $\to_{\beta,\pi,\mu}$. Additionally, one just needs to observe that $\to_\pi$ in $\lambda\mathbf{J}$ is strongly normalising. □

5 Conclusion

This work shows that the reduction relations of $\lambda\mathbf{J^m}$ enjoy strong normalisation of typable terms and confluence. As such $\lambda\mathbf{J^m}$ is a well-behaved extension of the λ-calculus and we intend to explore its potential in functional programming. On the other hand, as shown in [2], $\lambda\mathbf{J^m}$ captures as subsystems, not only the system ΛJ of Joachimski and Matthes, but also the multiary λ-calculus $\lambda\mathcal{P}\mathbf{h}$ [1], as well as a notational variant of λ-calculus. So, we consider $\lambda\mathbf{J^m}$ a useful tool for the computational interpretation of successively stronger fragments of sequent calculus, deserving further study in this direction.

Our investigations of the relationship between generality and multiarity identify two isomorphic subsystems of $\lambda\mathbf{J^m}$: (i) a variant of $\lambda\mathbf{J}$, which is the subsystem with minimal use of multiarity (*i.e.* no use); (ii) the subsystem of μ-normal forms, which is the subsystem with maximal use of multiarity (*i.e.* uses cons for expressing generality whenever possible). Think of $t \in \lambda\mathbf{J}$ and of all its μ-reduction sequences, leading to $\mu(t)$. In a sense, all the terms involved in these reduction sequences are representations of the same term, ranging from the term t with minimal use of multiarity to the term $\mu(t)$ with maximal use of multiarity, going through intermediate terms that do not belong to the subsystems: t and $\mu(t)$ are canonical representations whereas the intermediate terms are a redundancy allowed in $\lambda\mathbf{J^m}$. Thus the two isomorphic subsystems are non-redundant opposite extremes w.r.t. the use of multiarity.

However both subsystems have shortcomings because of this extreme nature. In the former, multiarity is not available as a shorthand. In the latter, it is a simple definition of expressions and reduction that is not available, because unconstrained gm-application, as well as β- and π-reduction, can create μ-redexes, *i.e.* do not preserve maximal multiarity. Although exhibiting some redundancy, $\lambda\mathbf{J^m}$ does not suffer from the drawbacks of these subsystems. Therefore it seems to be the system with the right use of multiarity.

Acknowledgment. Diagram in Subsection 3.2 was produced with Paul Taylor's macros.

References

1. J. Espírito Santo, *An isomorphism between a fragment of sequent calculus and an extension of natural deduction, in: M. Baaz and A. Voronkov (Eds.), Proc. of LPAR'02*, 2002, Springer-Verlag, LNAI vol. **2514**, 354–366.
2. J. Espírito Santo and L. Pinto, *Permutative conversions in intuitionistic multiary sequent calculus with cuts, in: M. Hoffman (Ed.), Proc. of TLCA*, 2003, Springer-Verlag, LNCS vol. **2701**, 286–300.

3. H. Herbelin, *A λ-calculus structure isomorphic to a Gentzen-style sequent calculus structure, in: L. Pacholski and J. Tiuryn (Eds.), Proceedings of CSL'94*, 1995, Springer-Verlag, LNCS vol. **933**, 61–75.
4. F. Joachimski and R. Matthes, *Standardization and confluence for a Lambda Calculus with generalized applications, in: L. Bachmair (Ed.), Proc. of RTA*, 2000, Springer-Verlag, LNCS vol. **1833**, 141–155.
5. F. Joachimski and R. Matthes, *Short proofs of normalisation for the simply typed λ-calculus, permutative conversions and Gödel's* **T**, *Archive for Mathematical Logic*, **42** (2003) 59–87.
6. H. Schwichtenberg, *Termination of permutative conversions in intuitionistic Gentzen calculi*, *Theoretical Computer Science*, **212** (1999) 247–260.
7. J. von Plato, *Natural deduction with general elimination rules*, *Archive for Mathematical Logic*, **40** (2001) 541–567.

Wellfounded Trees and Dependent Polynomial Functors

Nicola Gambino* and Martin Hyland

Department of Pure Mathematics and Mathematical Statistics
University of Cambridge
{N.Gambino,M.Hyland}@dpmms.cam.ac.uk

Abstract. We set out to study the consequences of the assumption of types of wellfounded trees in dependent type theories. We do so by investigating the categorical notion of wellfounded tree introduced in [16]. Our main result shows that wellfounded trees allow us to define initial algebras for a wide class of endofunctors on locally cartesian closed categories.

1 Introduction

Types of wellfounded trees, or $\mathcal{W}$-types, are one of the most important components of Martin-Löf's dependent type theories. First, they allow us to define a wide class of inductive types [5,15]. Secondly, they play an essential role in the interpretation of constructive set theories in dependent type theories [3]. Finally, from the proof-theoretic point of view, they represent the paradigmatic example of a generalised inductive definition and contribute considerably to the proof-theoretic strength of dependent type theories [8].

In [16] a categorical counterpart of the notion of $\mathcal{W}$-type was introduced. In a locally cartesian closed category, $\mathcal{W}$-types are defined as the initial algebras for endofunctors of a special kind, to which we shall refer here as *polynomial functors*. The purpose of this paper is to study polynomial endofunctors and $\mathcal{W}$-types more closely. In particular, we set out to explore some of the consequences of the assumption that a locally cartesian closed category has $\mathcal{W}$-types, i.e. that every polynomial endofunctor has an initial algebra. To explore these consequences we introduce *dependent polynomial functors*, that generalize polynomial functors.

Our main theorem then shows that the assumption of $\mathcal{W}$-types is sufficient to define explicitly initial algebras for dependent polynomial functors. We expect this result to lead to further insight into the interplay between dependent type theory and the theory of inductive definitions. In this paper, we will limit ourselves to giving only two applications of our main theorem. First, we show how the class of polynomial functors is closed under fixpoints. We hasten to point out that related results appeared in [1,2]. One of our original goals was indeed to put those results in a more general context and simplify their proofs.

* EPSRC Postdoctoral Research Fellow in Mathematics.

S. Berardi, M. Coppo, and F. Damiani (Eds.): TYPES 2003, LNCS 3085, pp. 210–225, 2004.

Secondly, we show how polynomial functors have free monads, and these free monads are themselves polynomial. The combination of these two facts leads to further observations concerning the categories of algebras of polynomial endofunctors. These results are relevant for our ongoing research on 2-categorical models of the differential λ-calculus [6].

The interplay between dependent type theories and categories is here exploited twice. On the one hand, category theory provides a mathematically efficient setting to present results that apply not only to the categories arising from the syntax of dependent type theories, but also to the categories providing their models. On the other hand, dependent type theories provide a convenient language to manipulate and describe the objects and the arrows of locally cartesian closed categories via the internal language of such a category [18].

In order to set up the internal language for a locally cartesian closed category with $\mathcal{W}$-types, it is necessary to establish some technical results that ensure a correct interaction between the structural rules of the internal language and the rules for $\mathcal{W}$-types. Although these results are already contained in [16] we give new and simpler proofs of some of them. Once this is achieved, we can freely exploit the internal language to prove the consequences of the assumption of $\mathcal{W}$-types in a category.

2 Polynomial Functors

2.1 Locally Cartesian Closed Categories

We say that a category $\mathcal{C}$ is a *locally cartesian closed category*, or a lccc for short, if for every object I of $\mathcal{C}$ the slice category $\mathcal{C}/I$ is cartesian closed[1]. Note that if $\mathcal{C}$ is a lccc then so are all its slices. For an arrow $f : B \to A$ in a lccc $\mathcal{C}$ we write $\Delta_f : \mathcal{C}/A \to \mathcal{C}/B$ for the associated pullback functor, which can be defined since slice categories have cartesian products. The key fact about locally cartesian closed categories is the following proposition [7].

Proposition 1. *Let $\mathcal{C}$ be a lccc. For any arrow $f : B \to A$ in $\mathcal{C}$, the pullback functor $\Delta_f : \mathcal{C}/A \to \mathcal{C}/B$ has both a left and a right adjoint.*

Given an arrow $f : B \to A$ in a lccc $\mathcal{C}$, we will write $\Sigma_f : \mathcal{C}/B \to \mathcal{C}/A$ and $\Pi_f : \mathcal{C}/B \to \mathcal{C}/A$ for the left and right adjoint to the pullback functor, respectively. We indicate the existing adjunctions as $\Sigma_f \dashv \Delta_f \dashv \Pi_f$.

An abuse of language. For an arrow $f : B \to A$, we write the image of $X \to A$ in $\mathcal{C}/A$ under Δ_f as $\Delta_f(X) \to B$. These arrows fit into the pullback diagram

$$\begin{array}{ccc} \Delta_f X & \longrightarrow & X \\ \downarrow & & \downarrow \\ B & \xrightarrow{\ f\ } & A \end{array}$$

[1] Here and in the following, when we require the existence of some structure in a category, we always mean that this structure is given to us by an explicitly defined operation.

The Beck-Chevalley condition. The Beck-Chevalley condition, which holds in any lccc, expresses categorically that substitution behaves correctly with respect to type-formation rules. More precisely, it asserts that for a pullback diagram of the form

$$\begin{array}{ccc} D & \xrightarrow{k} & B \\ {\scriptstyle g}\downarrow & & \downarrow{\scriptstyle f} \\ C & \xrightarrow{h} & A \end{array}$$

the canonical natural transformations $\Sigma_g \, \Delta_k \Rightarrow \Delta_h \, \Sigma_f$ and $\Delta_h \, \Pi_f \Rightarrow \Pi_g \, \Delta_k$ are isomorphisms.

The axiom of choice. The type-theoretic axiom of choice [15] is expressed by the fact that, for two arrows $g : C \to B$ and $f : B \to A$, the canonical natural transformation $\Sigma_h \, \Pi_p \, \Delta_{\varepsilon_C} \Rightarrow \Pi_f \, \Sigma_g$ is an isomorphism, where

$$\begin{array}{ccc} \Delta_f \Pi_f C & \xrightarrow{p} & \Pi_f C \\ {\scriptstyle q}\downarrow & & \downarrow{\scriptstyle h} \\ B & \xrightarrow{f} & A \end{array}$$

is a pullback diagram and $\varepsilon_C : \Delta_f \; \Pi_f \, C \to C$ is a component of the counit of the adjunction $\Delta_f \dashv \Pi_f$.

2.2 Internal Language

Associated to a lccc $\mathcal{C}$ there is a dependent type theory $\mathsf{Th}(\mathcal{C})$ to which we shall refer as the *internal language* of $\mathcal{C}$. A complete presentation of such a dependent type theory can be found in [9,14,18]. We limit ourselves to recalling only those aspects that are most relevant for the remainder of this work. The standard judgement forms, written here as

$$(B_a \mid a \in A)\,,\ (B_a = B'_a \mid a \in A)\,,\ (b_a \in B_a \mid a \in A)\,,\ (b_a = b'_a \in B_a \mid a \in A),$$

are assumed to have their usual meaning [15]. The dependent type theory $\mathsf{Th}(\mathcal{C})$ has the following primitive forms of type:

$$1\,, \quad Id_A(a, a')\,, \quad \sum_{a \in A} B_a\,, \quad \prod_{a \in A} B_a\,.$$

We refer to these as the unit, identity, dependent sum and dependent product types, respectively. As usual, these primitive forms of type allow us to define the forms of type $A \times B$ and B^A , to which we refer as the product and function types. The dependent type theory $\mathsf{Th}(\mathcal{C})$ has a straightforward interpretation in $\mathcal{C}$ and thus provides a convenient language to define objects and arrows in $\mathcal{C}$.

2.3 Polynomial Functors

Let $\mathcal{C}$ be a lccc. For an object I of $\mathcal{C}$, we write I also for the unique arrow $I \to 1$ into the terminal object 1 of $\mathcal{C}$. Observe this arrow determines functors $\Delta_I : \mathcal{C} \to \mathcal{C}/I$ and $\Sigma_I : \mathcal{C}/I \to \mathcal{C}$. We are now ready to introduce polynomial functors. For an arrow $f : B \to A$ in $\mathcal{C}$, we define a functor $\mathcal{P}_f : \mathcal{C} \to \mathcal{C}$, called the *generalized polynomial functor associated to* f, as the composite

$$\mathcal{C} \xrightarrow{\Delta_B} \mathcal{C}/B \xrightarrow{\Pi_f} \mathcal{C}/A \xrightarrow{\Sigma_A} \mathcal{C} \tag{1}$$

Definition 2. We say that $P : \mathcal{C} \to \mathcal{C}$ is a *generalized polynomial functor* if it is naturally isomorphic to a functor $\mathcal{P}_f : \mathcal{C} \to \mathcal{C}$ defined as $\mathcal{P}_f =_{\text{df}} \Sigma_A \, \Pi_f \, \Delta_B$, for some arrow $f : B \to A$ of $\mathcal{C}$.

Note. To avoid clashes with the existing terminology, we adopted the name generalised polynomial functors. This is in analogy with the distinction between generalised inductive definitions and ordinary ones. Since in this paper we only consider polynomial functors in the generalised sense, we refer to them simply as polynomial functors.

Let us look more closely at the definition of polynomial endofunctors. For an arrow $f : B \to A$, we have the two functors $\Sigma_A : \mathcal{C}/A \to \mathcal{C}$ and $\Delta_B : \mathcal{C} \to \mathcal{C}/B$. The functor Δ_B takes an object X of $\mathcal{C}$ to the left-hand side of the pullback diagram:

$$\begin{array}{ccc} X \times B & \longrightarrow & X \\ \downarrow & & \downarrow{\scriptstyle X} \\ B & \xrightarrow{B} & 1 \end{array}$$

We can therefore write $\Delta_B X = X \times B$. The action of Σ_A is very simple: given an object $Y \to A$ of $\mathcal{C}/A$ we have $\Sigma_A(Y \to A) = Y$. These observations lead to a description of polynomial functors in the internal language, which we shall exploit. The object $f : B \to A$ of $\mathcal{C}/A$ determines the judgement $(B_a \mid a \in A)$ of $\mathsf{Th}(\mathcal{C})$. We can then explicitly define in $\mathsf{Th}(\mathcal{C})$

$$\mathcal{P}_f(X) =_{\text{df}} \sum_{a \in A} X^{B_a} ,$$

for a type X. The interpretation in $\mathcal{C}$ of the right-hand side of the definition is indeed $\mathcal{P}_f(X)$, as defined in (1).

2.4 Basic Properties of Polynomial Functors

Proposition 3. *The composition of two polynomial functors is polynomial.*

Proof. A proof using the internal language is in [2], but it is also possible to give a diagrammatic one. In either case one uses crucially the axiom of choice. □

We now assume that the lccc $\mathcal{C}$ has finite disjoint coproducts. As pullback functors are left adjoints, these finite coproducts are preserved under pullbacks and $\mathcal{C}$ has stable disjoint coproducts. They can be represented in a familiar way in the internal language $\mathsf{Th}(\mathcal{C})$, which now has also the primitive forms of type 0 and $A + B$ called the empty and disjoint sum types, respectively.

The class of polynomial functors is closed under a further operation, that will be very important in the following. To discuss it, let us introduce a family of functors $P_X : \mathcal{C} \to \mathcal{C}$, for X in $\mathcal{C}$, associated to a functor $P : \mathcal{C} \to \mathcal{C}$. First of all, observe that the function mapping (X, Y) into $X + PY$ can be extended to a bifunctor $\mathcal{C} \times \mathcal{C} \to \mathcal{C}$. This determines a functor $\mathcal{C} \to \mathsf{End}(\mathcal{C})$ mapping X into P_X, whose action on Y in $\mathcal{C}$ is defined by letting $P_X(Y) = X + PY$.

Proposition 4. *Let $P : \mathcal{C} \to \mathcal{C}$ be a functor and X be an object of $\mathcal{C}$. If P is polynomial then so is P_X.*

Proof. We give a proof using the internal language. Let $f : B \to A$ and consider the polynomial functor $\mathcal{P}_f$ associated to f. For X and Y in $\mathcal{C}$ we then have

$$X + \mathcal{P}_f(Y) = X + \sum_{a \in A} Y^{B_a} \cong \sum_{z \in X+A} Y^{B_z}$$

where $(B_z \mid z \in X + A)$ is defined so that the judgements $(B_{\iota_1(x)} = 0 \mid x \in X)$ and $(B_{\iota_2(a)} = B_a \mid a \in A)$ are derivable. □

To recall the notions of strength for a functor, let us consider a monoidal category $(\mathcal{C}, \otimes, I, a, l, r)$, where I is the unit object and a, l, r are natural isomorphisms giving the associativity, left and right unit laws and satisfying the monoidal coherence axioms [12]. We can regard a lccc $\mathcal{C}$ as a monoidal category where cartesian product is the tensor, and the terminal object is the unit.

Definition 5. Let $P : \mathcal{C} \to \mathcal{C}$ be a functor. By a *strength* for P we mean a natural transformation σ with components $\sigma_{X,Y} : X \otimes PY \to P(X \otimes Y)$, for X and Y in $\mathcal{C}$, such that for all X, Y, Z in $\mathcal{C}$ the following equations hold:

$$P(l_X) \circ \sigma_{X,I} = l_X\,, \quad P(r_Y) \circ \sigma_{I,Y} = r_Y\,, \quad \sigma_{X,Y \otimes Z} \circ (1_X \otimes \sigma_{Y,Z}) = \sigma_{X \times Y, Z}\,.$$

Proposition 6. *Every polynomial functor has a strength.*

Proof. Let us use the internal language to define the arrow

$$\sigma_{X,Y} : X \times \mathcal{P}_f Y \to \mathcal{P}_f(X \times Y)$$

which gives us one of the components of the required strength σ for a polynomial functor $\mathcal{P}_f$. First, observe that the domain and the codomain of $\sigma_{X,Y}$ can be described in $\mathsf{Th}(\mathcal{C})$ as $X \times \sum_{a \in A} Y^{B_a}$ and $\sum_{a \in A} (X \times Y)^{B_a}$ respectively. We can then define $\sigma_{X,Y}$ by letting $\sigma_{X,Y}(x, a, t) =_{\mathrm{df}} \big(a, (\lambda b \in B_a)(x, t(b))\big)$ for $(x, a, t) \in X \times \sum_{a \in A} Y^{B_a}$. □

3   Change of Base

In the following, we shall be interested in the effect that pullback functors have on algebras for polynomial endofunctors. Let us first recall some basic definitions. Let $P : C \to C$ be an endofunctor on a category C. An *algebra* for P, or a P-algebra, is a diagram of the form $x : PX \to X$ in C. An arrow of P-algebras from $PX \to X$ to $PY \to Y$ is given by a commuting diagram of form

$$
\begin{array}{ccc}
PX & \xrightarrow{\ Pf\ } & PY \\
\downarrow & & \downarrow \\
X & \xrightarrow{\ f\ } & Y
\end{array}
$$

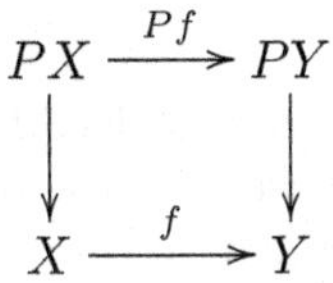

There is then a manifest category P-*alg* of P-algebras and P-algebra arrows. We write $U : P\text{-}alg \to C$. for the obvious forgetful functor.

In the following, we will work in a lccc C. For an arrow $u : I \to J$ in C we will show that the algebras for the polynomial functor $\mathcal{P}_f$ on C/J associated to an arrow f of C/J can be mapped functorially into algebras for the polynomial endofunctor $\mathcal{P}_{\Delta_u(f)}$ on C/I associated to the arrow $\Delta_u(f)$ of C/I. As we will see, this is a purely formal consequence of some observations concerning the 2-category of polynomial functors, that we define below. The treatment is inspired by the formal theory of monads [10,19].

3.1   The 2-Category of Polynomial Functors

Let us define the 2-category Poly. An object of Poly is a pair $(C, \mathcal{P}_f)$ where C is a lccc and $\mathcal{P}_f$ is the polynomial endofunctor on C associated to an arrow $f : B \to A$ in C. A 1-cell with domain $(C, \mathcal{P}_f)$ and codomain $(D, \mathcal{P}_g)$ is given by a pair (F, ϕ) where $F : C \to D$ is a functor and $\phi : \mathcal{P}_g F \Rightarrow F \mathcal{P}_f$, is a natural transformation, usually drawn in a diagram of form

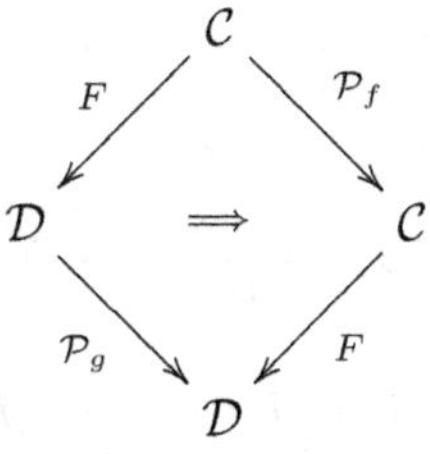

The 2-cells of Poly are defined exactly as the ones in 2-categories of monads [19]. We can now define a 2-functor Alg : Poly $\to$ Cat, but for the purposes of this paper, it is sufficient to give the definition of its action on objects and 1-cells. For an object $(C, \mathcal{P}_f)$ of Poly we define

$$
\mathsf{Alg}(C, \mathcal{P}_f) =_{\mathrm{df}} \mathcal{P}_f\text{-}alg.
$$

Given a 1-cell $(F, \phi) : (\mathcal{C}, \mathcal{P}_f) \to (\mathcal{D}, \mathcal{P}_g)$ in Poly, the functor $\mathsf{Alg}(F, \phi)$ is defined by mapping a $\mathcal{P}_f$-algebra $x : \mathcal{P}_f\, X \to X$ into the the composite

$$\mathcal{P}_g\, F\, X \xrightarrow{\phi_X} F\, \mathcal{P}_f\, X \xrightarrow{Fx} F\, X$$

that is a $\mathcal{P}_g$-algebra.

3.2 Pullback of Algebras

By a *locally cartesian closed functor*, or lccc functor, we mean a functor that preserves the locally cartesian closed structure up to isomorphism. The next proposition is a simple but useful fact.

Proposition 7. *Let $\mathcal{C}$ and $\mathcal{D}$ be lccc's, and let $F : \mathcal{C} \to \mathcal{D}$ be a lccc functor. For any arrow $f : B \to A$ there is a natural isomorphism*

$$\chi_F : \mathcal{P}_{Ff}\, F \Rightarrow F\, \mathcal{P}_f$$

such that the 1-cell $(F, \chi_F) : (\mathcal{C}, \mathcal{P}_f) \to (\mathcal{D}, \mathcal{P}_{Ff})$ determines a commuting diagram of form

$$\begin{CD}
\mathcal{P}_f\text{-}alg @>>> \mathcal{C}\\
@V{\mathsf{Alg}(F,\chi_F)}VV @VVFV\\
\mathcal{P}_{Ff}\text{-}alg @>>> \mathcal{D}
\end{CD}$$

where the horizontal arrows are the forgetful functors.

Proof. For an arrow $f : B \to A$ the required natural isomorphism χ_F is obtained by pasting the three isomorphims in the diagram

$$\begin{CD}
\mathcal{C} @>\Delta_B>> \mathcal{C}/B @>\Pi_f>> \mathcal{C}/A @>\Sigma_A>> \mathcal{C}\\
@VFVV \cong @VV{F/B}V \cong @VV{F/A}V \cong @VVFV\\
\mathcal{D} @>>\Delta_{FB}> \mathcal{D}/FB @>>\Pi_{Ff}> \mathcal{D}/FA @>>\Sigma_{FA}> \mathcal{D}
\end{CD}$$

where for an object I, we write $F/I : \mathcal{C}/I \to \mathcal{D}/FI$ for the obvious functor induced by F. The isomorphisms in the diagram exist since F is a lccc functor. The rest of the proof follows by direct calculation. □

We can apply Proposition 7 to pullback functors, as they are lccc functors [7].

Corollary 8. *Let $\mathcal{C}$ be a lccc. Let I be an object of $\mathcal{C}$. For an arrow $f : B \to A$ in $\mathcal{C}$ there is a natural isomorphism $\chi_{\Delta_I} : \mathcal{P}_g\, \Delta_I \Rightarrow \Delta_I\, \mathcal{P}_f$, where $g =_{\mathrm{df}} \Delta_I f$.*

4 Wellfounded Trees

Definition 9. We say that a lccc $\mathcal{C}$ *has $\mathcal{W}$-types* if for every arrow $f : B \to A$ in $\mathcal{C}$ there is a diagram $\mathcal{P}_f(\mathcal{W}_f) \to \mathcal{W}_f$ which is an initial algebra for $\mathcal{P}_f : \mathcal{C} \to \mathcal{C}$.

Recall that, by a theorem of Lambek, the arrow $\mathcal{P}_f(\mathcal{W}_f) \to \mathcal{W}_f$ is an isomorphism. Once the internal language of a lccc with $\mathcal{W}$-types is set up, we will therefore be allowed to write

$$W \cong \sum_{a \in A} W^{B_a}$$

where $f : B \to A$ and $W =_{\mathrm{df}} \mathcal{W}_f$. The next subsection is devoted to justify the use of the internal language in connection to $\mathcal{W}$-types.

4.1 Pullback of Wellfounded Trees

In [16] it is proved that if $\mathcal{C}$ has $\mathcal{W}$-types then so do all its slices. A proof of this fact can be obtained by defining explicitly initial algebras for polynomial endofunctors on the slice categories. It is also observed there that the pullback functors preserve $\mathcal{W}$-types. Although in [16] it is suggested to prove this second fact using the explicit definition of $\mathcal{W}$-types in slice categories, we give a new and more direct proof of this fact.

Let $\mathcal{C}$ be a lccc and let I be an object in $\mathcal{C}$. Recall from Corollary 8 that there is a natural isomorphism $\chi_{\Delta_I} : \mathcal{P}_g\, \Delta_I \Rightarrow \Delta_I\, \mathcal{P}_f$ where $g =_{\mathrm{df}} \Delta_I(f)$. This natural transformation determines a functor $F_I : \mathcal{P}_f\text{-}alg \to \mathcal{P}_g\text{-}alg$ defined as $F_I =_{\mathrm{df}} \mathsf{Alg}(\Delta_I, \chi_{\Delta_I})$. We now use the inverse to χ_{Δ_I}, given by a natural transformation $\psi : \Delta_I\, \mathcal{P}_f \Rightarrow \mathcal{P}_g\, \Delta_I$, to define a functor $G_I : \mathcal{P}_g\text{-}alg \to \mathcal{P}_f\text{-}alg$ that is right adjoint to F_I. First of all, observe that ψ gives us a natural transformation $\xi : \mathcal{P}_f\, \Pi_I \Rightarrow \Pi_I\, \mathcal{P}_g$ that is defined as the composite

$$\mathcal{P}_f \Pi_I \xRightarrow{\eta\, \mathcal{P}_f\, \Pi_I} \Pi_I\, \Delta_I \mathcal{P}_f\, \Pi_I \xRightarrow{\Pi_I\, \psi\, \Pi_I} \Pi_I\, \mathcal{P}_g \Delta_I\, \Pi_I \xRightarrow{\Pi_I\, \mathcal{P}_g\, \varepsilon} \Pi_I \mathcal{P}_g$$

where η and ε are the unit and the counit of the adjunction $\Delta_I \dashv \Pi_I$, respectively. Hence we have that $(\Pi_I, \xi) : (\mathcal{C}/I, \mathcal{P}_g) \to (\mathcal{C}, \mathcal{P}_f)$ is a 1-cell in Poly and thus we can simply define $G_I =_{\mathrm{df}} \mathsf{Alg}(\Pi_I, \xi)$.

Theorem 10. *Let $\mathcal{C}$ be a lccc and let $f : B \to A$ be an arrow in $\mathcal{C}$. For any object I of $\mathcal{C}$ the adjunction $\Delta_I \dashv \Pi_I$ lifts to an adjunction $F_I \dashv G_I$, i.e. in the diagram*

$$\begin{array}{ccc}
\mathcal{P}_g\text{-}alg & \longrightarrow & \mathcal{C}/I \\
F_I \uparrow \downarrow G_I & & \Delta_I \uparrow \downarrow \Pi_I \\
\mathcal{P}_f\text{-}alg & \longrightarrow & \mathcal{C}
\end{array}$$

where $g =_{\mathrm{df}} \Delta_I(f)$, the inner and outer squares commute.

The functor G_I can be described also in the internal language. Let us consider a $\mathcal{P}_g$-algebra, i.e. an arrow $z : \mathcal{P}_g Z \to Z$ in $\mathcal{C}/I$. This arrow determines the judgement

$$(\ z(i,(a,s)) \in Z_i \mid i \in I\,, (a,s) \in \sum_{a \in A} Z_i{}^{B_a}\ )$$

where $(Z_i \mid i \in I)$ is the judgement associated to the object $Z \to I$ of $\mathcal{C}/I$. We can then derive the judgement

$$(\ (\lambda i \in I)\, z(i,(a,(\lambda b \in B_a)\, t(b,i))) \in \prod_{i \in I} Z_i \mid (a,t) \in \sum_{a \in A} \prod_{i \in I} Z_i{}^{B_a})$$

which gives us a $\mathcal{P}_f$-algebra $\mathcal{P}_f \Pi_I Z \to \Pi_I Z$. This is exactly the image under G_I of the $\mathcal{P}_f$-algebra $\mathcal{P}_g Z \to Z$. A proof of Theorem 10 can then be obtained either reasoning with diagrams or with the internal language. We can now derive a simple proof of the pullback stability for $\mathcal{W}$-types.

Corollary 11 (Pullbacks preserve $\mathcal{W}$-types). *Let $\mathcal{C}$ be a lccc. Let $u : I \to J$ be an arrow in $\mathcal{C}$. For objects $B \to J$ and $A \to J$ in $\mathcal{C}/J$ and an arrow $f : B \to A$ between them, there is an isomorphism $\mathcal{W}_{\Delta_u(f)} \cong \Delta_u \mathcal{W}_f$.*

Proof. Note that without loss of generality we can assume that J is the terminal object of $\mathcal{C}$ and thus consider the pullback functors $\Delta_I : \mathcal{C} \to \mathcal{C}/I$ determined by $I : I \to 1$. But now it suffices to appy Theorem 10 and observe that F_I, defined as $F_I =_{\mathrm{df}} \mathsf{Alg}(\Delta_I, \chi_{\Delta_I})$, preserves initial objects because it is a left adjoint. □

5 Dependent Polynomial Functors

We can now pick up the fruits of the work done in the last section and exploit freely the internal language to prove further consequences of the assumption of the existence of $\mathcal{W}$-types in a lccc. Here we show how $\mathcal{W}$-types can be used to define initial algebras for a class of functors that is wider than the one of polynomial functors. Let $\mathcal{C}$ be a lccc. For a diagram, which we do *not* assume to be commuting, of form

$$\begin{array}{ccc} B & \xrightarrow{\ f\ } & A \\ & {\scriptstyle s}\searrow \quad \swarrow{\scriptstyle r} & \\ & I & \end{array} \qquad (2)$$

we define $\mathcal{D} : \mathcal{C}/I \to \mathcal{C}/I$, called the *dependent polynomial endofunctor* associated to the diagram, as the composite

$$\mathcal{C}/I \xrightarrow{\Delta_s} \mathcal{C}/B \xrightarrow{\Pi_f} \mathcal{C}/A \xrightarrow{\Sigma_r} \mathcal{C}/I$$

We can describe the action of $\mathcal{D}$ on an object $(X_i \mid i \in I)$ of $\mathcal{C}/I$ by letting

$$\mathcal{D}(X_i \mid i \in I) =_{\mathrm{df}} \big(\sum_{a \in A_i} \prod_{b \in B_a} X_{sb} \mid i \in I \big) \tag{3}$$

for an object $(X_i \mid i \in I)$ of $\mathcal{C}/I$. Using this description, we can observe that initial algebras for dependent polynomial functors are categorical counterparts of the so-called *general trees* of Martin-Löf type theory, as described in [17, Chapter 16]. We now give some examples of dependent polynomial functors.

(i) Polynomial functors on slice categories are special examples of dependent polynomial functors. Observe that, if the diagram in (2) commmutes, then the formula in (3) simplifies to

$$\mathcal{D}(X_i \mid i \in I) = \big(\sum_{a \in A_i} X_i^{B_a} \mid i \in I \big) .$$

(ii) Let $f : B \to A$ be an arrow in $\mathcal{C}$ and define $W =_{\mathrm{df}} \mathcal{W}_f$. For our applications, it is useful to observe that, for an arrow $g : C \to B$, the endofunctor $F : \mathcal{C}/W \to \mathcal{C}/W$ defined in the internal language by letting

$$F \Big(X_{(a,t)} \mid (a,t) \in W \Big) =_{\mathrm{df}} \Big(\sum_{b \in B_a} X_{t(b)}^{C_b} \mid (a,t) \in W \Big) ,$$

is a dependent polynomial functor. Indeed, it is naturally isomorphic to the functor associated to the diagram

$$\begin{array}{ccc} \sum_{(a,t) \in W} \sum_{b \in B_a} C_b & \xrightarrow{\;p\;} & \sum_{(a,t) \in W} B_a \\ & {}_{s}\searrow \quad \swarrow_{r} & \\ & W & \end{array}$$

where $p(a,t,b,c) =_{\mathrm{df}} (a,t,b)$, $s(a,t,b,c) =_{\mathrm{df}} t(b)$ and $r(a,t,b) =_{\mathrm{df}} (a,t)$ for $(a,t) \in W$, $b \in B_a$, $c \in C_b$.

(iii) If $\mathcal{C}$ has finite disjoint coproducts, the coproduct of two dependent polynomial functors is still a dependent polynomial functor. For two dependent polynomial functors $\mathcal{D}_1, \mathcal{D}_2$ associated respectively to the two diagrams

$$\begin{array}{ccc} B_1 & \xrightarrow{\;f_1\;} & A_1 \\ & {}_{s_1}\searrow \quad \swarrow_{r_1} & \\ & I & \end{array} \qquad \begin{array}{ccc} B_2 & \xrightarrow{\;f_2\;} & A_2 \\ & {}_{s_2}\searrow \quad \swarrow_{r_2} & \\ & I & \end{array}$$

the functor $\mathcal{D}_1 + \mathcal{D}_2$ is naturally isomorphic to the dependent polynomial functor associated to the diagram

$$\begin{array}{ccc} B_1 + B_2 & \xrightarrow{\;f_1+f_2\;} & A_1 + A_2 \\ & {}_{[s_1,s_2]}\searrow \quad \swarrow_{[r_1,r_2]} & \\ & I & \end{array}$$

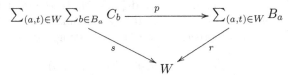

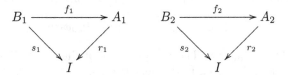

5.1 Initial Algebras

We want to prove our first main result. We assume that the lccc $\mathcal{C}$ has $\mathcal{W}$-types.

Theorem 12. *Every dependent polynomial functor has an initial algebra.*

The proof involves a generalisation of the argument showing that $\mathcal{W}$-types exist in slice categories [16, Proposition 3.8], a result that follows indeed as a corollary of our theorem. We begin by constructing a candidate to be the initial algebra for the dependent polynomial functor defined in (3). Let us consider the $\mathcal{W}$-types $\mathcal{W}_f$ and $\mathcal{W}_{f\times I}$ associated to $f : B \to A$ and $f \times 1_I : B \times I \to A \times I$. The canonical isomorphisms

$$\mathcal{W}_f \cong \sum_{a\in A} \mathcal{W}_f^{B_a}, \qquad \mathcal{W}_{f\times I} \cong I \times \sum_{a\in A} \mathcal{W}_{f\times I}^{B_a}$$

will be treated here as equalities to simplify the presentation. Let us recall that there is an arrow $\rho : \mathcal{W}_f \to A$ defined by letting $\rho(a,t) =_{\mathrm{df}} a$ for $(a,t) \in \mathcal{W}_f$.

The strategy to define the candidate $V \to I$ to be an initial algebra will be as follows. First, we will define V as the object fitting in the equalizer diagram

$$V \xrightarrow{\ \eta\ } \mathcal{W}_f \underset{\xi'}{\overset{\xi}{\rightrightarrows}} \mathcal{W}_{f\times I} \tag{4}$$

determined by appropriate arrows ξ and ξ'. Secondly, the required object of $\mathcal{C}/I$ can then be defined as $r\,\rho\,\eta : V \to I$. It now remains to define the arrows ξ, ξ'. The arrow ξ is defined by recursion on $\mathcal{W}_f$ by letting, for $(a,t) \in \mathcal{W}_f$,

$$\xi(a,t) =_{\mathrm{df}} (ra, a, (\lambda b \in B_a)\, \xi(tb)) .$$

The definition of ξ' is more involved. First, we define $\phi : \mathcal{W}_{f\times I} \times B \to \mathcal{W}_{f\times I}$ by recursion. For $(i,a,t,b) \in \mathcal{W}_{f\times I}$, define

$$\phi(i,a,t,b) =_{\mathrm{df}} \big(sb, a, (\lambda b' \in B_a)\, \phi(t(b'), b')\big) .$$

Then, we define $\psi : \mathcal{W}_{f\times I} \to \mathcal{W}_{f\times I}$ by letting, for $(i,a,t) \in \mathcal{W}_{f\times I}$,

$$\psi(i,a,t) =_{\mathrm{df}} (i, a, t, (\lambda b \in B_a)\phi(tb, b)) .$$

Finally, we fix $\xi' =_{\mathrm{df}} \psi\, \xi$. The key property of the object V that allows us to prove Theorem 12 is stated in the next lemma.

Lemma 13. *For all $(a,t) \in \mathcal{W}_f$, we have $(a,t) \in \sum_{a\in A_i} \prod_{b\in B_a} V_{sb}$ if and only if $(a,t) \in V_i$, where $i =_{\mathrm{df}} ra$.*

Proof. Let $(a,t) \in \mathcal{W}_f$ and define $i =_{\mathrm{df}} ra$. First of all one needs to show that, for all $b \in B_a$

$$\xi(tb) = \phi(\xi(tb), b) \iff sb = \rho(tb) \ \wedge\ \xi(tb) = \psi\, \xi(tb) . \tag{5}$$

This can be proved by unfolding the relevant definitions. We then get

$$\begin{aligned}
(a,t) \in V_i &\iff \xi(a,t) = \xi'(a,t) && \text{by def. of } V \\
&\iff (\forall b \in B_a)\ \xi(tb) = \phi(\xi(tb), b) && \text{by def. of } \xi\,, \xi' \\
&\iff (\forall b \in B_a)\ sb = \rho(tb) \wedge \xi(tb) = \psi\, \xi(tb) && \text{by (5)} \\
&\iff (a,t) \in \textstyle\sum_{a \in A_i} \prod_{b \in B_a} V_{sb} && \text{by def. of } V
\end{aligned}$$

as required. □

Lemma 13 shows that $V \to I$ can be equipped with a structure map, and thus gives us an algebra for the dependent polynomial functor defined in (3). The initiality of this algebra follows from reasoning that is completely analogous to that in [16, Proposition 3.8] and hence is omitted here.

5.2 Applications

We give a first application of Theorem 12. Let us consider two arrows $f : B \to A$ and $g : D \to C$ in a lccc $\mathcal{C}$ with $\mathcal{W}$-types. We can then define a bifunctor $F : \mathcal{C} \times \mathcal{C} \to \mathcal{C}$ whose action on an object (X, Y) is defined by letting

$$F(X,Y) =_{\mathrm{df}} \mathcal{P}_f(X) \times \mathcal{P}_g(Y)\,.$$

For a fixed object X of $\mathcal{C}$, the functor $F^X : \mathcal{C} \to \mathcal{C}$ that maps Y into $F(X,Y)$ can easily be seen to be polynomial. It therefore has an initial algebra, that we denote as

$$F^X(\,\mu Y.F(X,Y)\,) \longrightarrow \mu Y.F(X,Y)$$

The assignment of $\mu Y.F(X,Y)$ to X can then be extended to a functor $\mathcal{C} \to \mathcal{C}$. We refer to these functors as *fixpoint functors.* We can now state our second main result.

Theorem 14. *Fixpoint functors are polynomial.*

Proof. We limit ourselves to sketch the main idea of the argument. Let us actually suppose that the fixpoint functor is polynomial, and let $Q \to P$ be an arrow in $\mathcal{C}$ such that

$$\mu Y.F(X,Y) \cong \sum_{p \in P} X^{Q_p}\,.$$

Direct calculations imply that there must be isomorphisms

$$P \cong A \times \sum_{c \in C} P^{D_c}\,,$$

$$Q_{(a,c,t)} \cong B_a + \sum_{d \in D_c} Q_{t(d)}$$

for $(a, c, t) \in A \times \sum_{c \in C} P^{D_c}$. The first isomorphism certainly holds if we define P as the $\mathcal{W}$-type of the arrow $g \times 1_A : D \times A \to C \times A$ and use Corollary 11. Theorem 12 shows that it is also possible to satisfy the second isomorphism by defining $Q \to P$ as the initial algebra for an appropriate dependent polynomial functor. Recalling the examples of dependent polynomial functors given earlier in this section, it is immediate to observe that the functor $F : \mathcal{C}/P \to \mathcal{C}/P$ defined by letting

$$F(X_{(a,c,t)} \mid (a, c, t) \in P) =_{\mathrm{df}} B_a + \sum_{d \in D_c} X_{t(d)}$$

for $(X_{(a,c,t)} \mid (a, c, t) \in P)$ in $\mathcal{C}/P$, is a dependent polynomial functors, since it is the sum of two such functors. □

6 Free Monads

6.1 Background

We review some facts concerning endofunctors and monads, and some results concerning free monads. More details can be found in [4,11].

Definition 15. Let P be an endofunctor on $\mathcal{C}$. We say that P *has a free monad* if the forgetful functor $U : P\text{-}alg \to \mathcal{C}$ has a left adjoint.

The next proposition shows that the existence of a free monad for an endofunctor is a necessary and sufficient condition for its category of algebras to be isomorphic to a category of algebras for a monad.

Proposition 16. *The forgetful functor $U : P\text{-}alg \to \mathcal{C}$ has a left adjoint if and only if it is monadic over $\mathcal{C}$.*

Proof. The proof is an application of Beck's theorem [13] characterising monadic adjunctions. One should observe that the functor U satisfies all the hypothesis of Beck's theorem except for the existence of a left adjoint. □

When (T, η, μ) is a monad on a category $\mathcal{C}$ we write $T\text{-}Alg$ for the usual category of T-algebras. Note that we follow a suggestion of Peter Freyd in using $P\text{-}alg$ for the algebras of an endofunctor P and $T\text{-}Alg$ for the algebras for a monad T. Again, we write $U : T\text{-}Alg \to \mathcal{C}$ for the forgetful functor. We can then restate Proposition 16 as follows.

Proposition 17. *(T, η, μ) is a free monad for P if and only if there is an equivalence $T\text{-}Alg \to P\text{-}alg$ such that the following diagram commutes*

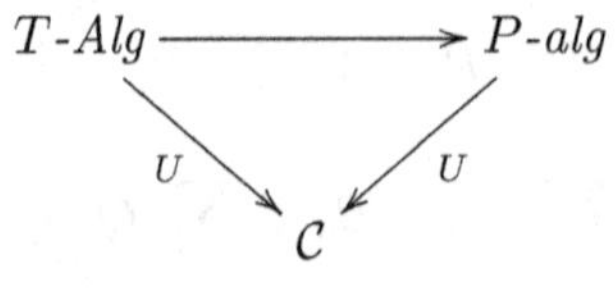

We wish to give a more concrete description of the free monad for an endofunctor on a locally cartesian closed category with coproducts. To do so, we use the family of functors $P_X : \mathcal{C} \to \mathcal{C}$, for X in $\mathcal{C}$, associated to a functor $P : \mathcal{C} \to \mathcal{C}$ and defined in Subsection 2.4. As we did in the discussion leading to Proposition 4, we assume that $\mathcal{C}$ has finite disjoint coproducts.

Proposition 18. *Let P be an endofunctor on $\mathcal{C}$. The following are equivalent:*

(i) the endofunctor P has a free monad;
(ii) the comma category $X \downarrow U$ has an initial object, for all X in $\mathcal{C}$;
(iii) the endofunctor P_X has an initial algebra, for all X in $\mathcal{C}$.

Proof. The equivalence (i) $\Leftrightarrow$ (ii) follows by Definition 15 and by the possibility of determining a left adjoint via initial objects in comma categories [13]. The equivalence (ii) $\Leftrightarrow$ (iii) follows from the isomorphism $X \downarrow U \cong P_X$-*alg*. One could also verify directly the implication (iii) $\Rightarrow$ (i) by defining explicitly the free monad (T, η, μ) for P. The functor T is defined by letting $T(X)$ be the initial algebra for P_X, for X in $\mathcal{C}$. □

We conclude this review by recalling the notion of strenth for a monad and a simple fact about it.

Definition 19. Let (T, η, μ) be a monad on $\mathcal{C}$. By a *strength* for (T, η, μ) we mean a strength σ for the functor T such that, for all X and Y in $\mathcal{C}$, we have

$$\sigma_{X,Y} \circ (1_X \otimes \eta_Y) = \eta_{X \otimes Y}\,, \quad \mu_{X \otimes Y} \circ T(\sigma_{X,Y}) \circ \sigma_{X,TY} = \sigma_{X,Y} \circ (1_X \otimes \mu_Y)\,.$$

Proposition 20. *Let P be an endofunctor on $\mathcal{C}$ and (T, η, μ) be the free monad on P. A strength for the functor P determines a strength for the monad (T, η, μ).*

Proof. The strength can be defined using the explicit description of the free monad given in the proof of Proposition 18. □

6.2 Free Monads for Polynomial Functors

We begin by ensuring the existence of free monads for polynomial functors.

Theorem 21. *If $\mathcal{C}$ is a lccc with finite disjoint coproducts and $\mathcal{W}$-types, then every polynomial endofunctor on $\mathcal{C}$ has a free monad.*

Proof. Let $P : \mathcal{C} \to \mathcal{C}$ be a polynomial functor. If we knew that for every X in $\mathcal{C}$ the functor $P_X : \mathcal{C} \to \mathcal{C}$ had an initial algebra, then we could invoke Proposition 18 and conclude the desired claim. By Proposition 4, however, the functors $P_X : \mathcal{C} \to \mathcal{C}$, for X in $\mathcal{C}$, are polynomial, and therefore they have an initial algebra by the assumption that $\mathcal{C}$ has $\mathcal{W}$-types. □

The next corollary, a consequence of Proposition 16 and Theorem 21, allows us to observe the existence of structure on the categories of algebras for polynomial functors. From now on, we assume that $\mathcal{C}$ is a lccc with finite disjoint coproducts and $\mathcal{W}$-types.

Corollary 22. *For every polynomial functor P on $\mathcal{C}$, the category P-alg is isomorphic to the category T-Alg, where T is free monad on P.*

We can also derive information on free monads for polynomial functors.

Proposition 23. *Free monads for polynomial functors have a strength.*

Proof. The claim is a consequence of Proposition 6 and Proposition 20. □

We conclude the paper with our third and last main result, whose proof is completely analogous to that of Theorem 14.

Theorem 24. *The free monad on a polynomial functor is polynomial.*

Acknowledgements. We thank Peter Aczel, Thorsten Altenkirch, Benno van den Berg, Marcelo Fiore and Erik Palmgren for stimulating discussions.

References

1. Abbott, M.: *Categories of Containers.* Ph.D. thesis, University of Leicester (2003).
2. Abbott, M., Altenkirch, T., Ghani, N.: Categories of Containers. in *Foundations of Software Science and Computation Structures* LNCS 2620, Springer (2003) 23 – 38.
3. Aczel, P.: The Type Theoretic Interpretation of Constructive Set Theory: Inductive Definitions, in: R.B. Barcan Marcus et al. (eds.) *Logic, Methodology and Philosophy of Science, VII,* North-Holland (1986).
4. Barr, M., Wells, C.: *Toposes, triples and theories.* Springer-Verlag (1985).
5. Dybjer, P: Representing inductively defined sets by wellorderings in Martin-Löf's type theory. *Theoretical Computer Science* 176, (1997), 329 – 335.
6. Ehrhard, T., Regnier, L.: The differential lambda-calculus. *Theoretical Computer Science,* 309 (2003) 1 – 41.
7. Freyd, P.: Aspects of topoi. *Bull. Austral. Math. Soc.* 7 (1972) 1 – 76.
8. Griffor, E., Rathjen, M.: The Strength of Some Martin-Löf's Type Theories, *Archiv for Mathematical Logic* 33 (1994) 347 – 385.
9. Hofmann, M.: On the interpretation of type theory in locally cartesian closed categories. In *Computer Science Logic '94.* LNCS 933, Springer (1995) 427 – 441.
10. Kelly, G.M., Street, R.: Review of the elements of 2-categories. *Proc. Sydney Category Theory Seminar 1972/73* LNM 420, Springer (1974) 75 – 103.
11. Kelly, G.M.: A unified treatment of transfinite constructions for free algebras, free monoids, colimit, associated sheaves and so on. *Bull. Austral. Math. Soc.* 22 (1980) 1 – 83.
12. Kelly, G.M.: *Basic Concepts of Enriched Category Theory* Cambridge University Press (1982).
13. Mac Lane, S.: *Categories for the working mathematician.* Springer-Verlag (1998).
14. Maietti, M.E.: *The type theory of categorical universes.* Ph.D. thesis, Università di Padova (1998).
15. Martin-Löf, P. *Intuitionistic Type Theory.* Bibliopolis (1984).
16. Moerdijk, I., Palmgren, E.: Wellfounded trees in categories. *Annals of Pure and Applied Logic* 104 (2000) 189 – 218.

17. Nordström, B., Petersson K., Smith J.: *Programming in Martin-Löf Type Theory.* Oxford University Press (1990).
18. Seely, R.A.G.: Locally cartesian closed categories and type theory. *Math. Proc. Camb. Phil. Soc.* 95 (1984) 33 – 48.
19. Street, R.: The formal theory of monads. *J. of Pure and Appl. Algebra* 2 (1972) 149 – 168.

Classical Proofs, Typed Processes, and Intersection Types
Extended Abstract

Silvia Ghilezan[1]* and Pierre Lescanne[2]

[1] Faculty of Engineering, University of Novi Sad, Novi Sad, Serbia
gsilvia@uns.ns.ac.yu
[2] LIP, École Normale Supérieure de Lyon, Lyon, France
Pierre.Lescanne@ens-lyon.fr

Abstract. Curien and Herbelin provided a Curry and Howard correspondence between classical propositional logic and a computational model called $\overline{\lambda}\mu\widetilde{\mu}$ which is a calculus for interpreting classical sequents. A new terminology for $\overline{\lambda}\mu\widetilde{\mu}$ in terms of pairs of *callers–callees* which we name *capsules* enlightens a natural link between $\overline{\lambda}\mu\widetilde{\mu}$ and process calculi. In this paper we propose an intersection type system $\overline{\lambda}\mu\widetilde{\mu}^{\cap}$ which is an extension of $\overline{\lambda}\mu\widetilde{\mu}$ with intersection types. We prove that all strongly normalizing $\overline{\lambda}\mu\widetilde{\mu}$-terms are typeable in the new system, which was not the case in $\overline{\lambda}\mu\widetilde{\mu}$. Also, we prove that all typeable $\widetilde{\mu}$-free terms are strongly normalizing.

1 Introduction

In this paper we study $\overline{\lambda}\mu\widetilde{\mu}$, a type assignment system designed by Curien and Herbelin [8,12] which gives a computational content to classical logic. It deals with *interactions* and therefore it seems to be well suited as a process language. Our main concerns are the *type-free* $\overline{\lambda}\mu\widetilde{\mu}$*-calculus*, the untyped calculus underlying $\overline{\lambda}\mu\widetilde{\mu}$, as well as the *intersection type system* $\overline{\lambda}\mu\widetilde{\mu}^{\cap}$, which is an extension of $\overline{\lambda}\mu\widetilde{\mu}$ with intersection types. The main components of type-free $\overline{\lambda}\mu\widetilde{\mu}$ are *capsules* in which two entities interact, one named *caller* performs basically one of two actions, it either gets data from another entity named *callee* or asks the callee to be its continuation. A *callee* can ask the caller to take the place of one of its specified internal caller variables. These components are nested with more than one process being active at the moment. Presented this way, (notice that we changed the terminology for a more appealing one) type-free $\overline{\lambda}\mu\widetilde{\mu}$ seems rather application oriented and one may believe that it has been designed by computer scientists or artificial intelligence researchers [18]. But this is not the case. Indeed $\overline{\lambda}\mu\widetilde{\mu}$ has deep and interesting logic properties as it is an interpretation of classical propositional logic for which it offers a Curry-Howard correspondence, i.e., a correspondence between propositions and types, proofs and terms, proof normalization and term reduction.

* Partially supported by grant 1630 "Representation of proofs with applications, classification of structures and infinite combinatorics" (of the Ministry of Science, Technology, and Development of Serbia).

S. Berardi, M. Coppo, and F. Damiani (Eds.): TYPES 2003, LNCS 3085, pp. 226–241, 2004.

The Curry-Howard correspondence [14,20] is one of the main achievements in logic in computer science over the last years. Originally it has been introduced to show the connection between intuitionistic logic and lambda calculus, but several attempts have been made since to include classical logic. A natural deduction approach, $\lambda\mu$-calculus, was proposed by Parigot [15,16] while several sequent calculus proposals have been studied [3,1,8,11]. We have chosen the calculus $\overline{\lambda}\mu\widetilde{\mu}$ of Curien and Herbelin because it has interesting features. In particular, its connection with cut elimination [10] is somewhat direct and its link with process calculi and, why not, with object oriented languages seems promising.

Both $\lambda\mu$ and $\overline{\lambda}\mu\widetilde{\mu}$ are proven to be strongly normalizing [16,12]. Still, there are strongly normalizing terms not typeable in these systems. In this paper we are interested in computations that terminate, more precisely we study the characterization of strongly normalizing type-free $\overline{\lambda}\mu\widetilde{\mu}$-terms by intersection types. In such a system typeable terms are exactly the strongly normalizing terms. This characterization was done first for lambda calculus by Coppo, Dezani, Venneri, Pottinger and Sallé in [5,6,7,17,19]. No attempt has been made so far to extend it to classical logic interpretation. One of the main features of our type system is the exclusive use of introduction rules (left and right) for the intersection. This feature is usual for connectors in sequent calculus, but it is nice to keep it also for intersection operators. The proof of typeability of strongly normalizing $\overline{\lambda}\mu\widetilde{\mu}$-terms relies on a concept of perpetual strategy which has been already used in similar proofs for explicit substitutions [4,9] and which seems particularly well suited in such a system. The proof of strong normalization of typeable $\widetilde{\mu}$-free $\overline{\lambda}\mu\widetilde{\mu}$-terms is based on a very simple and nice definition of reducible sets which is expected to have other applications.

The paper is organized in the following way. Section 2 deals with the type-free $\overline{\lambda}\mu\widetilde{\mu}$-calculus, the untyped syntax underlying $\overline{\lambda}\mu\widetilde{\mu}$-calculus with particular focus on the newly defined perpetual strategies. In Section 3 we define an intersection type system $\overline{\lambda}\mu\widetilde{\mu}^{\cap}$, which is an extension of the type system $\overline{\lambda}\mu\widetilde{\mu}$ of Curien and Herbelin. In Section 4 we prove by means of perpetual strategies that all strongly normalizing $\overline{\lambda}\mu\widetilde{\mu}$-terms are typeable in the new system $\overline{\lambda}\mu\widetilde{\mu}^{\cap}$. In Section 5 we prove the strong normalization of $\widetilde{\mu}$-free terms typeable in $\overline{\lambda}\mu\widetilde{\mu}^{\cap}$ employing the reducibility method.

2 Sequent-Style Untyped $\overline{\lambda}\mu\widetilde{\mu}$-Calculus

2.1 Untyped Syntax

We consider the *type-free* $\overline{\lambda}\mu\widetilde{\mu}$*-calculus*, the sequent style formulation of the untyped calculus underlying $\overline{\lambda}\mu\widetilde{\mu}$ calculus proposed by Curien and Herbelin in [8,12]. We focus on the so called $\overline{\lambda}\mu\widetilde{\mu}$-calculus, which is one of the $\lambda\mu\widetilde{\mu}$-calculi introduced in [8].

Type-free $\overline{\lambda}\mu\widetilde{\mu}$ has three syntactic categories (features), which we call CalleR, CalleE, and Capsules:

$$\begin{array}{lll} \textsf{CalleR} & r ::= x \mid \lambda x.r \mid \mu\alpha.c \\ \textsf{CalleE} & e ::= \alpha \mid r \bullet e \mid \widetilde{\mu}x.c \\ \textsf{Capsules} & c ::= \langle r \parallel e \rangle \end{array}$$

The elements of CalleR, CalleE and Capsules are together referred to as $\overline{\lambda}\mu\widetilde{\mu}$-terms. There are two kinds of variables in this system: the set Var_r is made of Latin variables x, y,... which represent inputs, in particular they are bound by λ-abstractions or $\widetilde{\mu}$-abstractions, and the set Var_e is made of Greek variables α,β,... which represent continuations and which can be bound by μ-abstractions. In a process interpretation, variables can be seen as communication channels, respectively input channels (Var_r) and output channels (Var_e). The core of type-free $\overline{\lambda}\mu\widetilde{\mu}$ is made of capsules $\langle caller \parallel callee\rangle$ where *caller* and *callee* are two components supposed to communicate through a private channel. If the *caller* is of the form $\lambda x.r$ this means that its channel is active and waits for a value from the *callee* which is supposed to be ready to send its first item. If the caller is of the form $\mu\alpha.c$ this means that c expects the callee to be its continuation. If the callee is of the form $\widetilde{\mu}x.c$ this means that c will take the caller to fill its hole named x.

Type-free $\overline{\lambda}\mu\widetilde{\mu}$ has three reductions (evaluation rules) which make the previous interpretation more precise.

$$\begin{array}{lrcl}
(\lambda) & \langle \lambda x.r \parallel r' \bullet e\rangle & \longrightarrow & \langle r[x \leftarrow r'] \parallel e\rangle \\
(\mu) & \langle \mu\alpha.c \parallel e\rangle & \longrightarrow & c[\alpha \leftarrow e] \\
(\widetilde{\mu}) & \langle r \parallel \widetilde{\mu}x.c\rangle & \longrightarrow & c[x \leftarrow r]
\end{array}$$

Example. Let w be $\lambda x.\mu\alpha.\langle x \parallel x \bullet \alpha\rangle$ and d be $\langle w \parallel w \bullet \beta\rangle$. The term d corresponds to the term $(\lambda x.xx)(\lambda x.xx)$ in λ-calculus. We have

$$\begin{array}{rcl}
d & \underset{(\lambda)}{\longrightarrow} & \langle \mu\alpha.\langle w \parallel w \bullet \alpha\rangle \parallel \beta\rangle \\
 & \underset{(\mu)}{\longrightarrow} & \langle w \parallel w \bullet \beta\rangle \quad \equiv \quad d
\end{array}$$

but also

$$\begin{array}{rcl}
d & \underset{(\lambda)}{\longrightarrow} & \langle \mu\alpha.\langle w \parallel w \bullet \alpha\rangle \parallel \beta\rangle \\
 & \underset{(\lambda)}{\longrightarrow} & \langle \mu\alpha.\langle \mu\alpha_1.\langle w \parallel w \bullet \alpha_1\rangle \parallel \alpha\rangle \parallel \beta\rangle \\
 & \underset{(\lambda)}{\longrightarrow} & \langle \mu\alpha.\langle \mu\alpha_1.\langle \mu\alpha_2.\langle w \parallel w \bullet \alpha_2\rangle \parallel \alpha_1\rangle \parallel \alpha\rangle \parallel \beta\rangle \\
 & \underset{(\lambda)}{\longrightarrow} & \ldots
\end{array}$$

Both reductions are infinite.

For all $\overline{\lambda}\mu\widetilde{\mu}$-term r, e, and c, we define two sets of *free variables*, namely $\mathtt{Fv_r}(r)$, $\mathtt{Fv_e}(r)$, $\mathtt{Fv_r}(e)$, $\mathtt{Fv_e}(e)$, $\mathtt{Fv_r}(c)$ and $\mathtt{Fv_e}(c)$ in the following way:

⋆ CalleR

$$\begin{array}{ll}
\mathtt{Fv_r}(x) = \{x\} & \mathtt{Fv_e}(x) = \emptyset \\
\mathtt{Fv_r}(\lambda x.r) = \mathtt{Fv_r}(r) \setminus \{x\} & \mathtt{Fv_e}(\lambda x.r) = \mathtt{Fv_e}(r) \\
\mathtt{Fv_r}(\mu\alpha.c) = \mathtt{Fv_r}(c) & \mathtt{Fv_e}(\mu\alpha.c) = \mathtt{Fv_e}(c) \setminus \{\alpha\}
\end{array}$$

⋆ CalleE

$$\begin{array}{ll}
\mathtt{Fv_r}(\alpha) = \emptyset & \mathtt{Fv_e}(\alpha) = \{\alpha\} \\
\mathtt{Fv_r}(r \bullet e) = \mathtt{Fv_r}(r) \cup \mathtt{Fv_r}(e) & \mathtt{Fv_e}(r \bullet e) = \mathtt{Fv_e}(r) \cup \mathtt{Fv_e}(e) \\
\mathtt{Fv_r}(\widetilde{\mu}x.c) = \mathtt{Fv_r}(c) \setminus \{x\} & \mathtt{Fv_e}(\widetilde{\mu}x.c) = \mathtt{Fv_r}(c)
\end{array}$$

⋆ Capsules
$\mathtt{Fv_r}(\langle r \parallel e \rangle) = \mathtt{Fv_r}(r) \cup \mathtt{Fv_r}(e)$
$\mathtt{Fv_e}(\langle r \parallel e \rangle) = \mathtt{Fv_e}(r) \cup \mathtt{Fv_e}(e)$

In this paper, we use Barendregt convention on variables, also called hygiene. It says that in a statement or an expression, there is no subexpression in which a variable is both free and bounded.

From those reduction rules, one easily deduces that the *normal forms* are generated by the following abstract syntax.

$$r_{nf} ::= x \mid \lambda x.r_{nf} \mid \mu\alpha.c_{nf}$$
$$e_{nf} ::= \alpha \mid r_{nf} \bullet e_{nf} \mid \widetilde{\mu}x.c_{nf}$$
$$c_{nf} ::= \langle x \parallel \alpha \rangle \mid \langle x \parallel r_{nf} \bullet e_{nf} \rangle \mid \langle \lambda x.r_{nf} \parallel \alpha \rangle$$

In what follows we use the predicate nf to characterize the normal forms of type-free $\overline{\lambda}\mu\widetilde{\mu}$, in other words, one has $\mathsf{nf}(M)$ if and only if M is a normal form. We use notations NF_c, NF_r and NF_e for the three sets of normal forms in Capsules, CalleR and CalleE and SN_c, SN_r and SN_e for the three sets of strongly normalizing terms in Capsules, CalleR and CalleE.

Type-free $\overline{\lambda}\mu\widetilde{\mu}$ is not confluent due to the critical pair

$$\langle \mu\alpha.\langle y \parallel \beta \rangle \parallel \widetilde{\mu}x.\langle z \parallel \gamma \rangle \rangle$$

which reduces to two different normal forms $\langle y \parallel \beta \rangle$ and $\langle z \parallel \gamma \rangle$.

2.2 Perpetual Strategies

In this paper we deal with strong normalization. It is well known that reduction preserves strong normalization, namely

$$M \longrightarrow N \quad \Rightarrow \quad (SN(M) \quad \Rightarrow \quad SN(N)).$$

Actually, we would like to get preservation of strong normalization by expansion. For that we define a specific strategy $\leadsto$, the so called *perpetual strategy* [2], which specifies some reductions, in other words,

$$M \leadsto N \quad \Rightarrow \quad M \longrightarrow N$$

and which preserves normalization by expansion namely,

$$M \leadsto N \quad \Rightarrow \quad (SN(N) \quad \Rightarrow \quad SN(M)).$$

It seems that this is better defined by contraposition.

$$M \leadsto N \quad \Rightarrow \quad (\neg SN(M) \quad \Rightarrow \quad \neg SN(N)).$$

This means that if one reduces a non strongly normalizing term M to a term N by the perpetual strategy, then N is still non strongly normalizing. The perpetual strategy

$$
\begin{array}{rll}
\mathsf{perpc}\ \langle \mu\alpha.c \,\|\, \widetilde{\mu}x.c' \rangle = & \mathbf{if}\ c[\alpha \leftarrow \widetilde{\mu}x.c'] \notin SN_c\ \mathbf{then}\ c[\alpha \leftarrow \widetilde{\mu}x.c'] & :: \quad \gamma : \mathsf{Capsules} \\
& \mathbf{else}\ c'[x \leftarrow \mu\alpha.c] & :: \quad \gamma : \mathsf{Capsules} \\
\mathsf{perpc}\ \langle \mu\alpha.c \,\|\, e \rangle = & (\mathbf{assume}\ e \neq \widetilde{\mu}x.c') & \\
& \quad \mathbf{if}\ \alpha \in \mathtt{Fv_e}(c)\ \mathbf{or}\ \mathsf{nf}(e)\ \mathbf{then}\ c[\alpha \leftarrow e] & :: \quad \gamma : \mathsf{Capsules} \\
& \quad \mathbf{else}\ \langle \mu\alpha.c \,\|\, \mathsf{perpe}\ e \rangle & :: \quad \gamma : \mathsf{Capsules} \\
\mathsf{perpc}\ \langle r \,\|\, \widetilde{\mu}x.c \rangle = & (\mathbf{assume}\ r \neq \mu\alpha.c) & \\
& \quad \mathbf{if}\ x \in \mathtt{Fv_r}(c)\ \mathbf{or}\ \mathsf{nf}(r)\ \mathbf{then}\ c[x \leftarrow r] & :: \quad \gamma : \mathsf{Capsules} \\
& \quad \mathbf{else}\ \langle \mathsf{perpr}\ r \,\|\, \widetilde{\mu}x.c \rangle & :: \quad \gamma : \mathsf{Capsules} \\
\mathsf{perpc}\ \langle \lambda x.r \,\|\, r' \bullet e' \rangle = & \mathbf{if}\ x \in \mathtt{Fv_r}(r)\ \mathbf{or}\ \mathsf{nf}(r')\ \mathbf{then}\ \langle r[x \leftarrow r'] \,\|\, e' \rangle & :: \quad \gamma : \mathsf{Capsules} \\
& \mathbf{else}\ \langle \lambda x.r \,\|\, (\mathsf{perpr}\ r') \bullet e' \rangle & :: \quad \gamma : \mathsf{Capsules} \\
\mathsf{perpc}\ \langle y \,\|\, e \rangle = & (\mathbf{assume}\ e \neq \widetilde{\mu}x.c') & \\
& \quad \mathbf{if}\ \mathsf{nf}(e)\ \mathbf{then}\ unit & :: \quad \nu\varphi : \mathsf{Unit} \\
& \quad \mathbf{else}\ \langle y \,\|\, \mathsf{perpe}\ e \rangle & :: \quad \gamma : \mathsf{Capsules} \\
\mathsf{perpc}\ \langle r \,\|\, \beta \rangle = & (\mathbf{assume}\ r \neq \mu\alpha.c) & \\
& \quad \mathbf{if}\ \mathsf{nf}(r)\ \mathbf{then}\ unit & :: \quad \nu\varphi : \mathsf{Unit} \\
& \quad \mathbf{else}\ \langle \mathsf{perpr}\ r \,\|\, \beta \rangle & :: \quad \gamma : \mathsf{Capsules} \\
& & \\
\mathsf{perpr}\ \lambda x.r = & \mathbf{if}\ \mathsf{nf}(r)\ \mathbf{then}\ unit & :: \quad \nu\varphi : \mathsf{Unit} \\
& \mathbf{else}\ \lambda x.(\mathsf{perpr}\ r) & :: \quad \rho : \mathsf{CalleR} \\
\mathsf{perpr}\ \mu\alpha.c = & \mathbf{if}\ \mathsf{nf}(c)\ \mathbf{then}\ unit & :: \quad \nu\varphi : \mathsf{Unit} \\
& \mathbf{else}\ \mu\alpha.(\mathsf{perpc}\ c) & :: \quad \rho : \mathsf{CalleR} \\
\mathsf{perpr}\ x = & unit & :: \quad \nu\varphi : \mathsf{Unit} \\
& & \\
\mathsf{perpe}\ r \bullet e = & \mathbf{if}\ \mathsf{nf}(r)\ \mathbf{and}\ \mathsf{nf}(e)\ \mathbf{then}\ unit & :: \quad \nu\varphi : \mathsf{Unit} \\
& \mathbf{if}\ \mathsf{nf}(r)\ \mathbf{and}\ \neg\mathsf{nf}(e)\ \mathbf{then}\ r \bullet (\mathsf{perpe}\ e) & :: \quad \epsilon : \mathsf{CalleE} \\
& \mathbf{if}\ \neg\mathsf{nf}(r)\ \mathbf{and}\ \neg\mathsf{nf}(e)\ \mathbf{then}\ (\mathsf{perpr}\ r) \bullet e & :: \quad \epsilon : \mathsf{CalleE} \\
\mathsf{perpe}\ \widetilde{\mu}x.c = & \mathbf{if}\ \mathsf{nf}(c)\ \mathbf{then}\ unit & :: \quad \nu\varphi : \mathsf{Unit} \\
& \mathbf{else}\ \widetilde{\mu}x.(\mathsf{perpc}\ c) & :: \quad \epsilon : \mathsf{CalleE} \\
\mathsf{perpe}\ \alpha = & unit & :: \quad \nu\varphi : \mathsf{Unit}
\end{array}
$$

Fig. 1. Definition of the functions perpc, perpr and perpe.

we are going to define is deterministic which means when we write $M \rightsquigarrow N$, then N is uniquely determined by M. Therefore, we can write N as $(\mathsf{perp}\ M)$. Moreover the perpetual strategy reaches normal forms of strongly normalizing terms, namely

$$M \overset{*}{\rightsquigarrow} N \wedge \mathsf{nf}(N) \quad \Leftrightarrow \quad M \twoheadrightarrow N \wedge \mathsf{nf}(N)$$

where $\overset{*}{\rightsquigarrow}$ is the transitive closure of $\rightsquigarrow$. This means that SN can be generated by induction as follows

$$SN = NF \cup \{M \in \mathsf{Term} \mid (\mathsf{perp} M) \in SN\}.$$

In this section, we define by mutual recursion three specific strategies for type-free $\overline{\lambda}\mu\widetilde{\mu}$ in the sets Capsules, CalleR and CalleE, called perpc, perpr and perpe. In order to illustrate the kind of typing suggested by $\overline{\lambda}\mu\widetilde{\mu}$ (see Section 3) we define the functions perpc, perpr and perpe in that style. This means that each function takes a term and returns two kinds of results. Each result is labeled by an identifier written in Greek letters to keep the spirit of $\overline{\lambda}\mu\widetilde{\mu}$. For instance, perpc returns either a value of type Unit labeled by $\nu\varphi$ or a value of type Capsules labeled by γ. Actually $(\mathsf{perpc}\ c)$ returns the value *unit* of type Unit when c is a normal form (the label $\nu\varphi$ reminds nf) and returns a value c' of type Capsules if the perpetual strategy applied on c yields c'. Hence if we write the type à la $\overline{\lambda}\mu\widetilde{\mu}$, we have

$$\begin{array}{l} \mathsf{perpc} :: (c : \mathsf{Capsules} \vdash \nu\varphi : \mathsf{Unit}, \gamma : \mathsf{Capsules}) \\ \mathsf{perpr} :: (r : \mathsf{CalleR} \vdash \nu\varphi : \mathsf{Unit}, \rho : \mathsf{CalleR}) \\ \mathsf{perpe} :: (e : \mathsf{CalleE} \vdash \nu\varphi : \mathsf{Unit}, \epsilon : \mathsf{CalleE}) \end{array}$$

Note that we introduce the type à la $\overline{\lambda}\mu\widetilde{\mu}$ by "::". We define these three functions together in Figure 1.

Lemma 1 (Perpetuality).

- $(\mathsf{perpc}\; c) \in SN_c \quad \Rightarrow \quad c \in SN_c$
- $(\mathsf{perpr}\; r) \in SN_r \quad \Rightarrow \quad r \in SN_r$
- $(\mathsf{perpe}\; e) \in SN_e \quad \Rightarrow \quad e \in SN_e$

Lemma 2. *SN_r, SN_e and SN_c are the least sets such that*
$SN_r = NF_r \cup \{r \in \mathit{CalleR} \mid (\mathit{perpr}\; r) \in SN_r\}$
$SN_e = NF_e \cup \{e \in \mathit{CalleE} \mid (\mathit{perpe}\; e) \in SN_e\}$
$SN_c = NF_c \cup \{c \in \mathit{Capsules} \mid (\mathit{perpc}\; c) \in SN_c\}$

3 The Type Assignment System

Simple types corresponding to classical propositions are

$$A, B ::= p \mid A \to B$$

A *basic r-type assignment* is an expression of the form $x : A$, whereas a *basic e-type assignment* is an expression of the form $\alpha : A$. A set $\{x_1 : A_1, \ldots, x_n : A_n\}$ with

$$\frac{}{\Gamma \mid \alpha : A \vdash \Delta, \alpha : A}\,(e\text{-}ax) \qquad \frac{}{\Gamma, x : A \vdash x : A \mid \Delta}\,(r\text{-}ax)$$

$$\frac{\Gamma \vdash r : A \mid \Delta \quad \Gamma \mid e : B \vdash \Delta}{\Gamma \mid r \bullet e : A \to B \vdash \Delta}\,(\to L) \qquad \frac{\Gamma, x : A \vdash r : B \mid \Delta}{\Gamma \vdash \lambda x.r : A \to B \mid \Delta}\,(\to R)$$

$$\frac{c : (\Gamma, x : A \vdash \Delta)}{\Gamma \mid \widetilde{\mu}x.c : A \vdash \Delta}\,(\widetilde{\mu}) \qquad \frac{c : (\Gamma \vdash \beta : B, \Delta)}{\Gamma \vdash \mu\beta.c : B \mid \Delta}\,(\mu)$$

$$\frac{\Gamma \vdash r : A \mid \Delta \quad \Gamma \mid e : A \vdash \Delta}{\langle r \parallel e \rangle : (\Gamma \vdash \Delta)}\,(cut)$$

Fig. 2. The type system $\overline{\lambda}\mu\widetilde{\mu}$.

distinct r-variables is an r-*context*. A set $\{\alpha_1 : A_1, \ldots, \alpha_m : A_m\}$ with distinct e-variables is an e-*context*. r-contexts are denoted by $\Gamma, \Gamma_1, \ldots$, whereas e-contexts are denoted by $\Delta, \Delta_1, \ldots$.

The typing system $\overline{\lambda}\mu\widetilde{\mu}$ of Curien and Herbelin is based on three typing judgments corresponding to syntactic categories:

$$\begin{array}{c} c : (\Gamma \vdash \Delta) \\ \Gamma \vdash r : A \mid \Delta \\ \Gamma \mid e : A \vdash \Delta. \end{array}$$

The first one is the type of a capsule, the second is the type of a caller and the third is the type of a callee. The rules of the type system $\overline{\lambda}\mu\widetilde{\mu}$ are given in Figure 2.

Example. By the Curry-Howard correspondence simply typed lambda calculus corresponds to intuitionistic logic. It is well-known that classical logic is obtained from intuitionistic logic by adding Peirce's law $((A \to B) \to A) \to A$. According to this, Peirce's law is not inhabited in simply typed lambda calculus, i.e., there is no lambda term of that type. The derivation in Figure 3 shows that there is a $\overline{\lambda}\mu\widetilde{\mu}$-term whose type is Peirce's law. Here we show that Peirce's law is inhabited in $\overline{\lambda}\mu\widetilde{\mu}$, so that the $\overline{\lambda}\mu\widetilde{\mu}$-term $\lambda x.\mu\beta.\langle x \parallel (\lambda y.\mu\gamma.\langle y \parallel \beta\rangle) \bullet \beta\rangle$ is typeable by Peirce's law. Let $\mathcal{A}$ be the typing tree for $x : T \mid (\lambda y.\mu\gamma.\langle y \parallel \beta\rangle) \bullet \beta : T \vdash \beta : A$, where T denotes the formula $(A \to B) \to A$. $\mathcal{A}$ and the tree for typing Peirce's law are given in Figure 3.

Still in $\overline{\lambda}\mu\widetilde{\mu}$ one cannot type all normal forms, e.g., the $\overline{\lambda}\mu\widetilde{\mu}$-term $\lambda x.\mu\alpha.\langle x \parallel x \bullet \alpha\rangle$ (seen in Section 2) which is a normal form and corresponds to the lambda term $\lambda x.xx$ is not typeable in $\overline{\lambda}\mu\widetilde{\mu}$. For this reason we introduce intersection types and corresponding new type assignment rules.

$$\dfrac{\dfrac{\dfrac{\dfrac{x:T,y:A\vdash y:A\mid\beta:B,\alpha:A \qquad x:T,y:A\mid\alpha:A\vdash\alpha:A,\beta:B}{\langle y\parallel\alpha\rangle:(x:T,y:A\vdash\beta:B,\alpha:A)}\,(cut)}{x:T,y:A\vdash\mu\beta.\langle y\parallel\alpha\rangle:B\mid\alpha:A}\,(\mu)}{x:T\vdash\lambda y.\mu\beta.\langle y\parallel\alpha\rangle:A\to B\mid\alpha:A}\,(\to R) \qquad x:T\mid\alpha:A\vdash\alpha:A}{x:T\mid(\lambda y.\mu\beta.\langle y\parallel\alpha\rangle)\bullet\alpha:T\vdash\alpha:A}\,(\to L)$$

The proof tree $\mathcal{A}$

$$\dfrac{\dfrac{\dfrac{x:T\vdash x:T\mid\alpha:A \qquad \mathcal{A}}{\langle x\parallel(\lambda y.\mu\beta.\langle y\parallel\alpha\rangle)\bullet\alpha\rangle:(x:T\vdash\alpha:A)}\,(cut)}{x:T\vdash\mu\alpha.\langle x\parallel(\lambda y.\mu\beta.\langle y\parallel\alpha\rangle)\bullet\alpha\rangle:A\mid}\,(\mu)}{\vdash\lambda x.\mu\alpha.\langle x\parallel(\lambda y.\mu\beta.\langle y\parallel\alpha\rangle)\bullet\alpha\rangle:((A\to B)\to A)\to A\mid}\,(\to R)$$

Fig. 3. The proof tree for Peirce's law

$$\frac{}{\Gamma \mid \alpha : A \vdash \Delta, \alpha : A}\,(e\text{-}ax) \qquad \frac{}{\Gamma, x : A \vdash x : A \mid \Delta}\,(r\text{-}ax)$$

$$\frac{\Gamma \vdash r : A \mid \Delta \quad \Gamma \mid e : B \vdash \Delta'}{\Gamma \mid r \bullet e : A \to B \vdash \Delta \sqcap \Delta'}\,(\to L) \qquad \frac{\Gamma, x : A \vdash r : B \mid \Delta}{\Gamma \vdash \lambda x.r : A \to B \mid \Delta}\,(\to R)$$

$$\frac{c : (\Gamma, x : A \vdash \Delta)}{\Gamma \mid \widetilde{\mu} x.c : A \vdash \Delta}\,(\widetilde{\mu}) \qquad \frac{c : (\Gamma \vdash \beta : B, \Delta)}{\Gamma \vdash \mu\beta.c : B \mid \Delta}\,(\mu)$$

$$\frac{\Gamma \vdash r : A \mid \Delta \quad \Gamma \mid e : A \vdash \Delta'}{\langle r \parallel e \rangle : (\Gamma \vdash \Delta \sqcap \Delta')}\,(cut)$$

$$\frac{\Gamma, x : A \mid e : C \vdash \Delta}{\Gamma, x : A \cap B \mid e : C \vdash \Delta} \quad \frac{\Gamma, x : A \vdash r : C \mid \Delta}{\Gamma, x : A \cap B \vdash r : C \mid \Delta}\,(\cap L_r)$$

$$\frac{\Gamma \vdash r : A \mid \Delta \quad \Gamma \vdash r : B \mid \Delta}{\Gamma \vdash r : A \cap B \mid \Delta}\,(\cap R_r)$$

$$\frac{\Gamma \mid e : A \vdash \Delta \vdash \Delta}{\Gamma \mid e : A \cap B \vdash \Delta}\,(\cap L_e)$$

$$\frac{\Gamma \mid e : C \vdash \Delta, \alpha : A \quad \Gamma \mid e : C \vdash \Delta, \alpha : B}{\Gamma \mid e : C \vdash \Delta, \alpha : A \cap B} \quad \frac{\Gamma \vdash r : C \mid \Delta, \alpha : A \quad \Gamma \vdash r : C \mid \Delta, \alpha : B}{\Gamma \vdash r : C \mid \Delta, \alpha : A \cap B}\,(\cap R_e)$$

Fig. 4. The type system $\overline{\lambda}\mu\widetilde{\mu}^{\cap}$.

Intersection types are generated in the following way:

$$A, B ::= p \mid A \to B \mid A \cap B$$

Intersection of contexts is defined in the following way:

$$\begin{aligned} \Gamma_1 \sqcap \Gamma_2 = {} & \{x : A \mid x : A \in \Gamma_1 \wedge x \notin \Gamma_2\} \cup \\ & \{x : A \mid x : A \in \Gamma_2 \wedge x \notin \Gamma_1\} \cup \\ & \{x : A \cap B \mid x : A \in \Gamma_1 \wedge x : B \in \Gamma_2\} \end{aligned} \qquad \begin{aligned} \Delta_1 \sqcap \Delta_2 = {} & \{\alpha : A \mid \alpha : A \in \Delta_1 \wedge \alpha \notin \Delta_2\} \cup \\ & \{\alpha : A \mid \alpha : A \in \Delta_2 \wedge \alpha \notin \Delta_1\} \cup \\ & \{\alpha : A \cap B \mid \alpha : A \in \Delta_1 \wedge \alpha : B \in \Delta_2\}. \end{aligned}$$

The type system $\overline{\lambda}\mu\widetilde{\mu}^{\cap}$ is obtained by extending $\overline{\lambda}\mu\widetilde{\mu}$ with type assignment rules regarding intersection given in Figure 4.

It is worth noticing that if c is a capsule then the last rule of a tree that types c is always (cut). It was shown by Hindley in [13] that intersection in lambda calculus does not behave as intuitionistic conjunction. In a similar way intersection in $\overline{\lambda}\mu\widetilde{\mu}$ does not behave as classical conjunction.

Example. The above mentioned $\overline{\lambda}\mu\widetilde{\mu}$-term $\mu\alpha.\langle x \parallel x \bullet \alpha\rangle$ which is not typeable in $\overline{\lambda}\mu\widetilde{\mu}$ is typeable in $\overline{\lambda}\mu\widetilde{\mu}^{\cap}$ with the same type $A \cap (A \to B)$ as in lambda calculus with intersection types, i.e., $\mu\alpha.\langle x \parallel x \bullet \alpha\rangle : (A \cap (A \to B)) \to B$.

Still there are $\overline{\lambda}\mu\widetilde{\mu}$-terms that are not typeable in $\overline{\lambda}\mu\widetilde{\mu}^{\cap}$. The term $\langle w \parallel w \bullet \alpha\rangle$, where $w \equiv \lambda x.\mu\beta.\langle x \parallel x \bullet \beta\rangle$, simulates the term $(\lambda x.xx)(\lambda x.xx)$ of the lambda calculus, as noticed above. It cannot be typed in $\overline{\lambda}\mu\widetilde{\mu}^{\cap}$. Roughly speaking, we see that w and $w \bullet \alpha$ should match their types, which leads to match a type, say C, with a type $C \to D$.

Lemma 3 (Context expansion lemma). *Let $\Gamma \subseteq \Gamma'$ and $\Delta \subseteq \Delta'$.*

(i) If $\Gamma \vdash r : A \mid \Delta$, then $\Gamma' \vdash r : A \mid \Delta'$.
(ii) If $\Gamma \mid e : A \vdash \Delta$, then $\Gamma' \mid e : A \vdash \Delta'$.
(iii) If $c : (\Gamma \vdash \Delta)$, then $c : (\Gamma' \vdash \Delta')$.

Lemma 4 (Context restriction lemma).

(i) If $\Gamma \vdash r : A \mid \Delta$, then $\Gamma \upharpoonright \mathtt{Fv_r}(r) \vdash r : A \mid \Delta \upharpoonright \mathtt{Fv_e}(r)$.
(ii) If $\Gamma \mid e : A \vdash \Delta$, then $\Gamma \upharpoonright \mathtt{Fv_r}(e) \mid e : A \vdash \Delta \upharpoonright \mathtt{Fv_e}(e)$.
(iii) If $c : (\Gamma \vdash \Delta)$, then $c : (\Gamma \upharpoonright \mathtt{Fv_r}(c) \vdash \Delta \upharpoonright \mathtt{Fv_e}(c))$.

Lemma 5 (Context intersection lemma).

(i) If $\Gamma \vdash r : A \mid \Delta$, then $\Gamma \sqcap \Gamma' \vdash r : A \mid \Delta$.
(ii) If $\Gamma \mid e : A \vdash \Delta$, then $\Gamma \sqcap \Gamma' \mid e : A \vdash \Delta$.
(iii) If $c : (\Gamma \vdash \Delta)$, then $c : (\Gamma \sqcap \Gamma' \vdash \Delta)$.

Lemma 6 (Typeability lemma).

(i) If $\lambda x.r$ is typeable, then $\Gamma \vdash \lambda x.r : \bigcap_{i\in I} A_i \to B_i \mid \Delta$, for some $\Gamma,\ \Delta,\ A_i,\ B_i$.
(ii) If $r \bullet e$ is typeable, then $\Gamma \mid r \bullet e : \bigcap_{i\in I} A_i \to B_i \vdash \Delta$, for some $\Gamma,\ \Delta,\ A_i,\ B_i$.
(iii) If $\mu\alpha.c$ is typeable, then $\Gamma \vdash \mu\alpha.c : \bigcap_{i\in I} A_i \mid \Delta$, for some $\Gamma,\ \Delta,\ A_i$. If in addition $\alpha \notin \mathtt{Fv_e}(c)$ then $\Gamma \vdash \mu\alpha.c : A \mid \Delta$, for some $\Gamma,\ \Delta$ and any A.
(iv) If $\widetilde{\mu}x.c$ is typeable, then $\Gamma \mid \widetilde{\mu}x.c : \bigcap_{i\in I} A_i \vdash \Delta$, for some $\Gamma,\ \Delta,\ A_i$. If in addition $x \notin \mathtt{Fv_r}(c)$ then $\Gamma \mid \widetilde{\mu}x.c : A \vdash \Delta$, for some $\Gamma,\ \Delta$ and any A.

Lemma 7 (Elimination lemma).

(i) If $\Gamma \vdash \lambda x.r : \bigcap_{i\in I} A_i \to B_i \mid \Delta$, then $\Gamma, x : A_i \vdash r : B_i \mid \Delta$.
(ii) If $\Gamma \mid r \bullet e : \bigcap_{i\in I} A_i \to B_i \vdash \Delta$, then $\Gamma \vdash r : A_i \mid \Delta_1$ and $\Gamma \mid e : B_i \vdash \Delta_2$, for some $i \in \{1,2\}$ and $\Delta_1 \sqcap \Delta_2 = \Delta$.

Lemma 8. *(i) If $r'[x \leftarrow r]$ is typeable, say $\Gamma \vdash r'[x \leftarrow r] : A \mid \Delta$, and $x \in \mathtt{Fv_r}(r')$, then there exists B such that $\Gamma \vdash r : B \mid \Delta$ and $\Gamma, x : B \vdash r' : A \mid \Delta$.*
(ii) If $e[x \leftarrow r]$ is typeable, say $\Gamma \mid e[x \leftarrow r] : A \vdash \Delta$, and $x \in \mathtt{Fv_r}(e)$, then there exists B such that $\Gamma \vdash r : B \mid \Delta$ and $\Gamma, x : B \mid e : A \vdash \Delta$.
(iii) If $c[x \leftarrow r] : (\Gamma \vdash \Delta)$ and $x \in \mathtt{Fv_r}(c)$, then there exists B such that $\Gamma \vdash r : B \mid \Delta$ and $c : (\Gamma, x : B \vdash \Delta)$.

Lemma 9. *(i) If $r[\alpha \leftarrow e]$ is typeable, say $\Gamma \vdash r[\alpha \leftarrow e] : A \mid \Delta$, and $\alpha \in \mathtt{Fv_e}(r)$, then there exists B such that $\Gamma \mid e : B \vdash \Delta$ and $\Gamma \vdash r : A \mid \alpha : B, \Delta$.*
(ii) If $e'[\alpha \leftarrow e]$ is typeable, say $\Gamma \mid e'[\alpha \leftarrow e] : A \vdash \Delta$, and $\alpha \in \mathtt{Fv_e}(e')$, then there exists B such that $\Gamma \mid e : B \vdash \Delta$ and $\Gamma \mid e' : A \vdash \alpha : B, \Delta$.
(iii) If $c[\alpha \leftarrow e] : (\Gamma \vdash \Delta)$ and $\alpha \in \mathtt{Fv_e}(c)$, then there exists B such that $\Gamma \mid e : B \vdash \Delta$ and $c : (\Gamma \vdash \alpha : B, \Delta)$.

4 Typeability of Strongly Normalizing Terms

Proposition 10 (Typeability of normal forms). *Normal forms are typeable in* $\overline{\lambda}\mu\widetilde{\mu}^{\cap}$.

Proof. By induction on the structure of the normal forms c, r and e.

Callers: if the normal form is x , $\lambda x.r_{nf}$ or $\mu\alpha.c_{nf}$, then all three cases are straightforward. Let us consider $\mu\alpha.c_{nf}$. By induction, one may suppose that $c_{nf} : (\Gamma \vdash \alpha : A, \Delta)$, then by (μ), $\Gamma \vdash \mu\alpha.c_{nf} : A \mid \Delta$.

Callees: the proof is again straightforward for normal forms α or $\widetilde{\mu}x.c_{nf}$. Let us consider the normal form $r_{nf} \bullet e_{nf}$, where r_{nf} and e_{nf} are normal forms. By the induction hypothesis there are contexts Γ, Δ, Γ_1, and Δ_1 and types A and B such that $\Gamma \vdash r_{nf} : A \mid \Delta$ and $\Gamma_1 \mid e_{nf} : B \vdash \Delta_1$. By Lemma 5 we get $\Gamma \sqcap \Gamma_1 \vdash r_{nf} : A \mid \Delta$ and $\Gamma \sqcap \Gamma_1 \mid e_{nf} : B \vdash \Delta_1$. Now the application of $(\rightarrow L)$ leads to $\Gamma \sqcap \Gamma_1 \mid r_{nf} \bullet e_{nf} : A \rightarrow B \vdash \Delta \sqcap \Delta_1$.

Capsules: the normal form is $\langle x \parallel \alpha \rangle$, $\langle x \parallel r_{nf} \bullet e_{nf} \rangle$ or $\langle \lambda x.r_{nf} \parallel \alpha \rangle$, where r_{nf} and e_{nf} are normal forms. All three cases follow the same pattern as above. Let us consider $\langle x \parallel r_{nf} \bullet e_{nf} \rangle$. By the induction hypothesis and by Lemma 7 there are contexts Γ and Δ such that $\Gamma \mid r_{nf} \bullet e_{nf} : A \rightarrow B \vdash \Delta$. One can distinguish two cases:

1. If the variable x is a free variable of the callee $r_{nf} \bullet e_{nf}$, which means that it is declared in Γ, say $\Gamma = \Gamma_1, x : C$, then $\Gamma_1, x : (A \rightarrow B) \cap C \mid r_{nf} \bullet e_{nf} : A \rightarrow B \vdash \Delta$ is obtained by $(\cap L_r)$. On the other hand $\Gamma_1, x : (A \rightarrow B) \cap C \vdash x : A \rightarrow B \mid \Delta$ is obtained from $\Gamma_1, x : A \rightarrow B \vdash x : A \rightarrow B \mid \Delta$, again by $(\cap L_r)$. Hence, we get $\langle x \parallel r_{nf} \bullet e_{nf} \rangle : (\Gamma_1, x : (A \rightarrow B) \cap C \vdash \Delta)$.

2. If the variable x is not a free variable of the callee $r_{nf} \bullet e_{nf}$, then without lack of generality, by Context restriction lemma 4 we can suppose that x is not declared in Γ, which means that $\langle x \parallel r_{nf} \bullet e_{nf} \rangle : (\Gamma, x : A \rightarrow B \vdash \Delta)$. □

Proposition 11 (Perpetual subject expansion).

(i) If perpr r *is typeable, then* r *is typeable.*
(ii) If perpe e *is typeable, then* e *is typeable.*
(iii) If $c \in SN_c$ *and for all* c' *such that* $h(c') < h(c)$ *(where* $h(c)$ *is the length of the longest reduction at* c*)* c' *is typeable, then* c *is typeable.*

Proof. We prove the parts simultaneously by induction on the generation of perpr r, perpe e and $h(c)$.

Let us start with case (iii). In most of the cases the typability of perpc c is enough to conclude on the typability of c. The only exception is when $c \equiv \langle \mu\alpha.c'' \parallel \widetilde{\mu}x.c' \rangle$ and perpc $c \equiv c''[\alpha \leftarrow \widetilde{\mu}x.c'] \notin SN_c$, which is avoided by the assumption $c \in SN_c$.

$c \equiv \langle \mu\alpha.c' \parallel e \rangle$ *and* perpc $c \equiv c'[\alpha \leftarrow e]$. If $\alpha \in \mathtt{Fv_e}(c')$ then by Lemma 9, there exists A such that $\Gamma \mid e : A \vdash \Delta$ and $c' : (\Gamma \vdash \alpha : A, \Delta)$. By (μ) $\Gamma \vdash \mu\alpha.c' : A \mid \Delta$, therefore $\langle \mu\alpha.c' \parallel e \rangle : (\Gamma \vdash \Delta)$. If $\alpha \notin \mathtt{Fv_e}(c')$, then $\mathsf{nf}(e)$ hence, e is typeable by Lemma 10 (say $\Gamma_1 \mid e : A \vdash \Delta_1$) , and perpc $c \equiv c'$. Therefore, by Lemma 6 $\mu\alpha.c'$ is typeable by $\Gamma_2 \vdash \mu\alpha.c' : A \mid \Delta_2$. By Context intersection lemma 5, we get $\Gamma_1 \sqcap \Gamma_2 \vdash \mu\alpha.c' : A \mid \Delta_1$ and $\Gamma_1 \sqcap \Gamma_2 \mid e : A \vdash \Delta_2$, hence the result follows by (cut)

$c \equiv \langle \mu\alpha.c' \parallel e\rangle : (\Gamma_1 \sqcap \Gamma_2 \vdash \Delta_1 \sqcap \Delta_2)$. Notice that this case cannot be deduced by the first rule of Figure 1.

$c \equiv \langle \mu\alpha.c' \parallel e\rangle$ *and* perpc $c \equiv \langle \mu\alpha.c' \parallel \text{perpe}\ e\rangle$. Then $\alpha \notin \mathtt{Fv_e}(c')$. Since by induction perpc c is typeable, we can assert that $\mu\alpha.c'$ and perpe e are typeable. By induction e is typeable, say by $\Gamma_2 \mid e : A \vdash \Delta_2$ and because $\alpha \notin \mathtt{Fv_e}(c')$ $\Gamma_1 \vdash \mu\alpha.c' : A \mid \Delta_1$. We have then $\Gamma_1 \sqcap \Gamma_2 \vdash \mu\alpha.c' : A \mid \Delta_1$ and $\Gamma_1 \sqcap \Gamma_2 \mid e : A \vdash \Delta_2$. Therefore $c \equiv \langle \mu\alpha.c' \parallel e\rangle : (\Gamma_1 \sqcap \Gamma_2 \vdash \Delta_1 \sqcap \Delta_2)$.

$c \equiv \langle r \parallel \widetilde{\mu}x.c'\rangle$ *and* perpc $c \equiv c'[x \leftarrow r]$.

- Case $x \in \mathtt{Fv_r}c'$ works as the previous similar case with perpc $c \equiv c'[\alpha \leftarrow e]$ and $\alpha \in \mathtt{Fv_e}(c')$.
- Case $x \notin \mathtt{Fv_r}(c')$ and $\mathsf{nf}(r)$ works as the similar case with perpc $c \equiv c'[\alpha \leftarrow e]$ and $\alpha \notin \mathtt{Fv_e}(c')$ and $\mathsf{nf}(e)$.
- Case $c \equiv \langle \mu\alpha.c'' \parallel \widetilde{\mu}x.c'\rangle$, then $c''[\alpha \leftarrow \widetilde{\mu}x.c'] \in SN_c$. By induction it is typable hence, c'' is typable by $c'' : (\Gamma_1 \vdash \alpha : A, \Delta_1)$. By $(\cap R_e)$ we get $c'' : (\Gamma_1 \vdash \alpha : A \cap B, \Delta_1)$ so $\mu\alpha.c''$ is typable by $\Gamma_1 \vdash \mu\alpha.c'' : A \cap B \mid \Delta_1$. On the other hand, $c'[x \leftarrow \mu\alpha.c']$ is typable by $c' : (\Gamma_2, x : B \vdash \Delta_2)$ hence $c' : (\Gamma_2, x : A \cap B \vdash \Delta_2)$. Therefore, $\widetilde{\mu}x.c'$ is typable by $\Gamma_2 \mid \widetilde{\mu}x.c' : A \cap B \vdash \Delta_2$. Hence $c \equiv \langle r \parallel \widetilde{\mu}x.c'\rangle : (\Gamma_1 \sqcap \Gamma_2, x : B \vdash \Delta_1 \sqcap \Delta_2)$.

$c \equiv \langle r \parallel \widetilde{\mu}x.c'\rangle$ *and* perpc $c \equiv \langle \text{perpr}\ r \parallel \widetilde{\mu}x.c'\rangle$. We can paraphrase the case $c \equiv \langle \mu\alpha.c' \parallel e\rangle$ and perpc $c \equiv \langle \mu\alpha.c' \parallel \text{perpe}\ e\rangle$.

$c \equiv \langle \lambda x.r \parallel r' \bullet e'\rangle$ *and* $x \in \mathtt{Fv_r}(r)$ *or* $\mathsf{nf}(r')$. Assume perpc $c \equiv \langle r[x \leftarrow r'] \parallel e'\rangle : (\Gamma \vdash \Delta)$. Therefore the last rule that types perpc c is (cut). This means that there exists an A such that $\Gamma \vdash r[x \leftarrow r'] : A \mid \Delta_1$ and $\Gamma \mid e' : A \vdash \Delta_2$.

- ⋆ If $x \in \mathtt{Fv_r}(r)$, by Lemma 8 there exists B such that $\Gamma, x : B \vdash r : A \mid \Delta_1$ and $\Gamma \vdash r' : B \mid \Delta_1$. Therefore $\Gamma \vdash \lambda x.r : B \to A \mid \Delta_1$. By $(\to L)$, one gets $\Gamma \mid r' \bullet e' : B \to A \vdash \Delta_1 \sqcap \Delta_2$. By (cut), $\langle \lambda x.r \parallel r' \bullet e'\rangle : (\Gamma \vdash \Delta_1 \sqcap \Delta_2)$.
- ⋆ If $x \notin \mathtt{Fv_r}(r)$ and $\mathsf{nf}(r')$, then $r[x \leftarrow r'] \equiv r$. By assumption $\Gamma \vdash r : A \mid \Delta_1$. From $\mathsf{nf}(r')$ by Proposition 10 follows that r' is typeable, i.e., $\Gamma' \vdash r' : B \mid \Delta'$. By Context intersection lemma and Context expansion lemma, one gets $\Gamma \sqcap \Gamma', x : B \vdash r : A \mid \Delta_1, \Gamma \sqcap \Gamma' \vdash r' : B \mid \Delta'$ and $\Gamma \sqcap \Gamma' \mid e' : A \vdash \Delta_2$. Collecting all these judgments through appropriate rules, one gets $\langle \lambda x.r \parallel r' \bullet e'\rangle : (\Gamma \sqcap \Gamma' \vdash \Delta_1 \sqcap \Delta_2 \sqcap \Delta')$.

$c \equiv \langle \lambda x.r \parallel r' \bullet e'\rangle$ *and* $x \notin \mathtt{Fv_r}(r)$ *and* $\neg\mathsf{nf}(r')$. By assumption perpc $c \equiv \langle \lambda x.r \parallel \text{perpr}(r') \bullet e'\rangle : (\Gamma \vdash \Delta)$. By Typeability lemma there exist A and B such that $\Gamma \vdash \lambda x.r : A \to B \mid \Delta_1$ and $\Gamma \mid \text{perpr}(r') \bullet e' : A \to B \vdash \Delta_2$. Moreover, by Lemma 7 $\Gamma, x : A \vdash r : B \mid \Delta_1, \Gamma \vdash \text{perpr}(r') : A \mid \Delta_2'$ and $\Gamma \vdash e' : B \mid \Delta_2''$. By induction, there exist Γ', Δ' and C such that $\Gamma' \vdash r' : C \mid \Delta'$. According to Context intersection lemma and $(\to L)$ $\Gamma \sqcap \Gamma' \mid r' \bullet e' : C \to B \vdash \Delta' \sqcap \Delta_2''$. Since $x \notin \mathtt{Fv_r}(r)$ then $\Gamma \vdash r : B \mid \Delta_1$ by Context restriction lemma. Therefore, by Context expansion and Context intersection lemma $\Gamma \sqcap \Gamma', x : C \vdash r : B \mid \Delta_1$, hence $\Gamma \sqcap \Gamma' \vdash \lambda x.r : C \to B \mid \Delta_1$. Therefore by (cut) $\langle \lambda x.r \parallel r' \bullet e'\rangle : \Gamma \sqcap \Gamma' \vdash \Delta_1 \sqcap \Delta_2'' \sqcap \Delta'$.

$\boxed{c \equiv \langle x \parallel e \rangle}$ by assumption $\langle x \parallel \mathsf{perpe}\ e \rangle$ is typeable and by induction e is typeable, say $\Gamma \mid e : A \vdash \Delta$. On the other hand $x : A \vdash x : A \mid$. Therefore, $\Gamma \sqcap \{x : A\} \mid e : A \vdash \Delta$ and $\Gamma \sqcap \{x : A\} \vdash x : A \mid \Delta$ hence, $\langle x \parallel e \rangle : (\Gamma \sqcap \{x : A\} \vdash \Delta)$.

Cases $\mathsf{perpr}\ r$ and $\mathsf{perpe}\ e$ are easy and made on the same scheme as $\mathsf{perpc}\ c$. □

Proposition 12. *Strongly normalizing $\overline{\lambda}\mu\widetilde{\mu}$-terms are typeable in $\overline{\lambda}\mu\widetilde{\mu}^{\cap}$.*

Proof. Lemma 2 characterizes strongly normalizing terms as finitely reachable from normal forms by "perpetual expansion". Therefore the result comes from Lemma 10 on *typeablity of normal forms* and Lemma 11 on the *perpetual subjects expansion.* □

5 Strong Normalization of Typeable Terms

In this section, we consider terms that are free of any occurrence of $\widetilde{\mu}$ ($\widetilde{\mu}$-free terms). This way we avoid the difficult problem of having the critical pair between the rules (μ) and $(\widetilde{\mu})$ and consider a confluent subsystem of $\overline{\lambda}\mu\widetilde{\mu}$.

Let $\mathcal{S} \subseteq \mathsf{Capsules}$, $\mathcal{R} \subseteq \mathsf{CalleR}$ and $\mathcal{E} \subseteq \mathsf{CalleE}$. Then we say that $\mathcal{S}$ is $(\mathcal{R}, \mathcal{E})$-*saturated* if the following holds:

1. $(\forall e \in \mathcal{E})\langle x \parallel e \rangle \in \mathcal{S}$;
2. $(\forall r', s_i \in \mathcal{R})\langle r[x \leftarrow r'] \parallel e \rangle \in \mathcal{S} \Rightarrow \langle \lambda x.r \parallel r' \bullet e \rangle \in \mathcal{S}$;
3. $(\forall e, e_j \in \mathcal{E}) c[\alpha \leftarrow e] \in \mathcal{S} \Rightarrow \langle \mu\alpha.c \parallel e \rangle \in \mathcal{S}$;

Lemma 13. *SN_c is (SN_r, SN_e)-saturated.*

Proof. 1. Straightforward, since $\langle x \parallel e \rangle \in SN_c$ whenever $e \in SN_e$.

2. If $\langle r[x \leftarrow r'] \parallel e \rangle \in SN_c$, then in order to conclude $\langle \lambda x.r \parallel r' \bullet e \rangle \in SN_c$ the only problem could rise when $x \notin \mathtt{Fv_r}(r)$, but this is avoided by the assumption $r' \in SN_r$.
3. Similarly. The only problem that could appear here is if $e \equiv \widetilde{\mu}x.c'$. In this case we could not prove that $\langle \mu\alpha.c \parallel \widetilde{\mu}x.c' \rangle \in \mathcal{S}$, since there could be an infinite reduction starting with $c'[x \leftarrow \mu\alpha.c]$. Nevertheless this cannot happen, since we consider $\widetilde{\mu}$-free terms. □

We define two type interpretation:

- ⋆ e-interpretation $[\![A]\!]_e$ - *Callees*:
  1. $[\![p]\!]_e = SN_e$;
  2. $[\![B \cap C]\!]_e = [\![B]\!]_e \cap [\![C]\!]_e$;
  3. $[\![B \to C]\!]_e = Var_e \cup \{r \bullet e \mid r \in [\![B]\!]_r \text{ and } e \in [\![C]\!]_e\}$.
- ⋆ r-interpretation $[\![A]\!]_r$ - *Callers*:
  1. $[\![p]\!]_r = SN_r$;
  2. $r \in [\![A]\!]_r$ if and only if $\langle r \parallel e \rangle \in SN_c$ for all $e \in [\![A]\!]_e$.

Lemma 14. $[\![A]\!]_r \subseteq SN_r$, $[\![A]\!]_e \subseteq SN_e$ *and* $Var_r \subseteq [\![A]\!]_r$.

Proposition 15 (Adequacy). *Let r, e and c be $\widetilde{\mu}$-free terms.*
Callers*:*
$\vec{x_i} : \vec{A_i}, \Gamma \vdash r : A \mid \vec{\alpha_j} : \vec{B_j}, \Delta \quad \Rightarrow \quad (\forall r_i \in [\![A_i]\!]_r)(\forall e_j \in [\![B_j]\!]_e)\; r[\vec{x_i} \leftarrow \vec{r_i}][\vec{\alpha_j} \leftarrow \vec{e_j}] \in [\![A]\!]_r$.
Callees*:*
$\vec{x_i} : \vec{A_i}, \Gamma \mid e : B \vdash \vec{\alpha_j} : \vec{B_j}, \Delta \quad \Rightarrow \quad (\forall r_i \in [\![A_i]\!]_r)(\forall e_j \in [\![B_j]\!]_e)\; e[\vec{x_i} \leftarrow \vec{r_i}][\vec{\alpha_j} \leftarrow \vec{e_j}] \in [\![A]\!]_e$.
Capsules*:*
$c : (\vec{x_i} : \vec{A_i}, \Gamma \vdash \vec{\alpha_j} : \vec{B_j}, \Delta) \quad \Rightarrow \quad (\forall r_i \in [\![A_i]\!]_r)(\forall e_j \in [\![B_j]\!]_e)\; c[\vec{x_i} \leftarrow \vec{r_i}][\vec{\alpha_j} \leftarrow \vec{e_j}] \in SN_c$.

Proof. By induction on the derivation in $\overline{\lambda}\mu\widetilde{\mu}^{\cap}$.

Callers:

Case r is a variable. Then $r \equiv x_i$ or $r \equiv y$, $y : C \in \Gamma$. The case $r \equiv x_i$ is straightforward since $r[\vec{x_i} \leftarrow \vec{r_i}][\vec{\alpha_j} \leftarrow \vec{e_j}] \equiv r_i \in [\![A_i]\!]_r$. If $r \equiv y$ and $y : C \in \Gamma$, then $r[\vec{x_i} \leftarrow \vec{r_i}][\vec{\alpha_j} \leftarrow \vec{e_j}] \equiv y$ and $y \in [\![C]\!]_r$ by Lemma 14.3.

Case $r \equiv \lambda x.s$, the last applied rule is $(\rightarrow R)$. Then $\vec{x_i} : \vec{A_i}, \Gamma \vdash \lambda x.s : C \rightarrow D \mid \vec{\alpha_j} : \vec{B_j}, \Delta$ is obtained from $\vec{x_i} : \vec{A_i}, x : C, \Gamma \vdash s : D \mid \vec{\alpha_j} : \vec{B_j}, \Delta$. First of all, we conclude by induction that $s[\vec{x_i} \leftarrow \vec{r_i}][\vec{\alpha_j} \leftarrow \vec{e_j}] \in [\![D]\!]_r$, hence $s[\vec{x_i} \leftarrow \vec{r_i}][\vec{\alpha_j} \leftarrow \vec{e_j}] \in SN_r$ and also $\lambda x.s[\vec{x_i} \leftarrow \vec{r_i}][\vec{\alpha_j} \leftarrow \vec{e_j}] \in SN_r$. We have two subcases to consider.

1. For every α, obviously $\langle \lambda x.s[\vec{x_i} \leftarrow \vec{r_i}][\vec{\alpha_j} \leftarrow \vec{e_j}] \parallel \alpha \rangle \in SN_r$.

2. By the induction hypothesis, for every $r_i \in [\![A_i]\!]_r$, $r' \in [\![C]\!]_r$ and $e_j \in [\![B_j]\!]_e$, one has $s[\vec{x_i} \leftarrow \vec{r_i}][x \leftarrow r'][\vec{\alpha_j} \leftarrow \vec{e_j}] \in [\![D]\!]_r$. By the definition of $[\![D]\!]_r$ one gets

$$\langle s[\vec{x_i} \leftarrow \vec{r_i}][x \leftarrow r'][\vec{\alpha_j} \leftarrow \vec{e_j}] \parallel e \rangle \in SN_c$$

for all $e \in [\![D]\!]_e$. The set SN_c is (SN_r, SN_e)-saturated as shown in Lemma 13, hence

$$\langle \lambda x.s[\vec{x_i} \leftarrow \vec{r_i}][\vec{\alpha_j} \leftarrow \vec{e_j}] \parallel r' \bullet e \rangle \in SN_c.$$

by case 2. of the definition of saturated sets. It is easy to see that $r' \bullet e \in [\![C \rightarrow D]\!]_e$ since $r' \in [\![C]\!]_r$ and $e \in [\![D]\!]_e$. Also we can notice that in this way we obtained all callees in $[\![C \rightarrow D]\!]_e$ which are of the shape $s \bullet e_1$.

The previous two subcases prove that for all $e \in [\![C \rightarrow D]\!]_e$, one has $\langle \lambda x.s[\vec{x_i} \leftarrow \vec{r_i}][\vec{\alpha_j} \leftarrow \vec{e_j}] \parallel e \rangle \in SN_c$ and we conclude that

$$(\lambda x.s)[\vec{x_i} \leftarrow \vec{r_i}][\vec{\alpha_j} \leftarrow \vec{e_j}] \in [\![C \rightarrow D]\!]_r.$$

Case $r \equiv \mu\alpha.c$, the last rule applied is (μ). From $c : (\vec{x_i} : \vec{A_i}, \Gamma \vdash \alpha : A, \vec{\alpha_j} : \vec{B_j}, \Delta)$, by the induction hypothesis

$$c[\vec{x_i} \leftarrow \vec{r_i}][\alpha \leftarrow e][\vec{\alpha_j} \leftarrow \vec{e_j}] \in SN_c$$

for all $r_i \in [\![A_i]\!]_r$, $e \in [\![A]\!]_e$ and $e_j \in [\![B_j]\!]_e$.

Since SN_c is (SN_r, SN_e)-saturated (case 3. of the definition) one has

$$\langle \mu\alpha.c[\vec{x_i} \leftarrow \vec{r_i}][\vec{\alpha_j} \leftarrow \vec{e_j}] \parallel e \rangle \in SN_c.$$

Let us notice here that $\mu\alpha.c[\vec{x_i} \leftarrow \vec{r_i}][\vec{\alpha_j} \leftarrow \vec{e_j}] \in SN_r$. By definition of $[\![A]\!]_r$ we obtain

$$\mu\alpha.c[\vec{x_i} \leftarrow \vec{r_i}][\vec{\alpha_j} \leftarrow \vec{e_j}] \in [\![A]\!]_r,$$

thus $(\mu\alpha.c)[\vec{x_i} \leftarrow \vec{r_i}][\vec{\alpha_j} \leftarrow \vec{e_j}] \in [\![A]\!]_r$.

The cases $(\cap L_r)$, $(\cap R_r)$ and $(\cap R_e)$ are easy to prove.

Callees:

Case e is a variable. Then $e \equiv \alpha_j$ or $e \equiv \alpha$, $\alpha : C \in \Delta$. The case $e \equiv \alpha_j$ is straightforward since $e[\vec{x_i} \leftarrow \vec{r_i}][\vec{\alpha_j} \leftarrow \vec{e_j}] \equiv e_j \in [\![B_j]\!]_e$. If $e \equiv \alpha$ and $\alpha : C \in \Delta$, then $e[\vec{x_i} \leftarrow \vec{r_i}][\vec{\alpha_j} \leftarrow \vec{e_j}] \equiv \alpha$. Moreover $\alpha \in [\![C]\!]_e$ holds by definition of type e-interpretation.

Case $e \equiv r' \bullet e'$, the last rule applied is $(\rightarrow L)$. Then $\vec{x_i} : \vec{A_i}, \Gamma \mid r' \bullet e' : (C \rightarrow D) \vdash \vec{\alpha_j} : \vec{B_j}, \Delta$ is obtained from $\vec{x_i} : \vec{A_i}, \Gamma \vdash r' : C \mid \vec{\alpha_j} : \vec{B_j}, \Delta$ and $\vec{x_i} : \vec{A_i}, \Gamma \mid e' : D \vdash \vec{\alpha_j} : \vec{B_j}, \Delta$. By the induction hypothesis $r'[\vec{x_i} \leftarrow \vec{r_i}][\vec{\alpha_j} \leftarrow \vec{e_j}] \in [\![C]\!]_r$ and $e'[\vec{x_i} \leftarrow \vec{r_i}][\vec{\alpha_j} \leftarrow \vec{e_j}] \in [\![D]\!]_e$ for all $r_i \in [\![A_i]\!]_r$ and $e_j \in [\![B_j]\!]_e$. According to the definition of $[\![C \rightarrow D]\!]_e$ we get $r'[\vec{x_i} \leftarrow \vec{r_i}][\vec{\alpha_j} \leftarrow \vec{e_j}] \bullet e'[\vec{x_i} \leftarrow \vec{r_i}][\vec{\alpha_j} \leftarrow \vec{e_j}] \in [\![C \rightarrow D]\!]_e$ which leads to $(r' \bullet e')[\vec{x_i} \leftarrow \vec{r_i}][\vec{\alpha_j} \leftarrow \vec{e_j}] \in [\![C \rightarrow D]\!]_e$.

The cases $(\cap L_r)$, $(\cap L_e)$ and $(\cap R_e)$ are easy to prove.

Capsules:

Let $c \equiv \langle r \parallel e \rangle : (\vec{x_i} : \vec{A_i}, \Gamma \vdash \vec{\alpha_j} : \vec{B_j}, \Delta)$. The last rule applied in typing a capsule is (cut) which means that there exist D, D', r and e such that $\vec{x_i} : \vec{A_i}, \Gamma \vdash r : D \mid \vec{\alpha_j} : \vec{B_j}, \Delta$ and $\vec{x_i} : \vec{A_i}, \Gamma \mid e : D' \vdash \vec{\alpha_j} : \vec{B_j}, \Delta$ and $c = \langle r \parallel e \rangle$. By the induction hypothesis $r[\vec{x_i} \leftarrow \vec{r_i}][\vec{\alpha_j} \leftarrow \vec{e_j}] \in [\![D]\!]_r$ and $e[\vec{x_i} \leftarrow \vec{r_i}][\vec{\alpha_j} \leftarrow \vec{e_j}] \in [\![D]\!]_e$ for all $r_i \in [\![A_i]\!]_r$ and $e_j \in [\![B_j]\!]_e$. According to the definition of $[\![D]\!]_r$ we obtain $\langle r[\vec{x_i} \leftarrow \vec{r_i}][\vec{\alpha_j} \leftarrow \vec{e_j}] \parallel e[\vec{x_i} \leftarrow \vec{r_i}][\vec{\alpha_j} \leftarrow \vec{e_j}] \rangle \in SN_c$. Therefore $c[\vec{x_i} \leftarrow \vec{r_i}][\vec{\alpha_j} \leftarrow \vec{e_j}] \in SN_c$. □

Proposition 16. *$\widetilde{\mu}$-free terms typeable in $\overline{\lambda}\mu\widetilde{\mu}^{\cap}$ are strongly normalizing.*

Proof. By taking $[\vec{x_i} \leftarrow \vec{x_i}]$ and $[\vec{\alpha_j} \leftarrow \vec{\alpha_j}]$ one gets: $\Gamma \vdash r : A \mid \Delta \Rightarrow r \in [\![A]\!]_r$, $\Gamma \mid e : A \vdash \Delta \Rightarrow e \in [\![A]\!]_e$ and $c : (\Gamma \vdash \Delta) \Rightarrow c \in SN_c$. Combined with Lemma 14 this gives the result. □

According to Proposition 12 and Proposition 16 we get the equivalence of typeable and strongly normalizing $\widetilde{\mu}$-free terms.

Corollary 17. *$\widetilde{\mu}$-free terms are typeable in $\overline{\lambda}\mu\widetilde{\mu}^{\cap}$ if and only if they are strongly normalizing.*

6 Conclusion

Our method based on a general concept of saturated sets and type interpretation should be easily extended to other kinds of normalization. It can also be used to study filter types for this calculus.

The intersection type system $\overline{\lambda}\mu\widetilde{\mu}^{\cap}$ introduced in this paper completely characterizes all strongly normalizing $\widetilde{\mu}$-free terms. Nevertheless, the method presented in Section 5 fails to prove the strong normalization of all $\overline{\lambda}\mu\widetilde{\mu}$-terms typeable in $\overline{\lambda}\mu\widetilde{\mu}^{\cap}$. Therefore, an open problem that lurks behind this paper is to find a proof-technique for proving the strong normalization of all terms typeable in $\overline{\lambda}\mu\widetilde{\mu}^{\cap}$.

By considering strongly normalizing terms that go beyond those representing classical proofs, we have opened a door to a new process calculus language which has to be explored from the pragmatic as well as from the semantic point of view.

References

1. F. Barbanera and S. Berardi. A symmetric lambda calculus for classical program extraction. *Information and Computation*, 125(2):103–117, 1996.
2. H. P. Barendregt. *The Lambda Calculus: its Syntax and Semantics*. North-Holland, Amsterdam, revised edition, 1984.
3. H. P. Barendregt and S. Ghilezan. Lambda terms for natural deduction, sequent calculus and cut-elimination. *Journal of Functional Programming*, 10(1):121–134, 2000.
4. E. Bonelli. Perpetuality in a named lambda calculus with explicit substitutions. *Mathematical Structures in Computer Science*, 1:47–90, 2001.
5. M. Coppo and M. Dezani-Ciancaglini. A new type-assignment for lambda terms. *Archiv für Mathematische Logik*, 19:139–156, 1978.
6. M. Coppo and M. Dezani-Ciancaglini. An extension of the basic functionality theory for the λ-calculus. *Notre Dame Journal of Formal Logic*, 21(4):685–693, 1980.
7. M. Coppo, M. Dezani-Ciancaglini, and B. Venneri. Principal type schemes and λ-calculus semantics. In J. P. Seldin and J. R. Hindley, editors, *To H. B. Curry: Essays on Combinatory Logic, Lambda Calculus and Formalism*, pages 535–560. Academic Press, London, 1980.
8. P.-L. Curien and H. Herbelin. The duality of computation. In *Proceedings of the 5th ACM SIGPLAN International Conference on Functional Programming (ICFP'00)*, Montreal, Canada, 2000. ACM Press.
9. D. Dougherty and P. Lescanne. Reductions, intersection types, and explicit substitution. In S. Abramsky, editor, *Typed Lambda Calculi and Application, 5th International Conference, TLCA 2001*, volume 2044 of *Lecture Notes in Computer Science*, pages 121–135, Krakow, Poland, 2001. Springer-Verlag.
10. A. D. Dragalin. *Mathematical Intuitionism*, volume 67 of *Translation of Mathematical Monographs*. American Mathematical Society, 1988.
11. H. Herbelin. *Séquents qu'on calcule : de l'interprétation du calcul des séquents comme calcul de λ-termes et comme calcul de stratégies gagnantes*. Thèse d'université, Université Paris 7, Janvier 1995.
12. H. Herbelin. Explicit substitution and reducibility. *Journal of Logic and Computation*, 11(3):431–451, 2001.
13. J. R. Hindley. Coppo–Dezani types do not correspond to propositional logic. *Theoretical Computer Science*, 28(1-2):235–236, 1984.
14. W. A. Howard. The formulas-as-types notion of construction. In J. P. Seldin and J. R. Hindley, editors, *To H.B. Curry: Essays on Combinatory Logic, Lambda Calculus and Formalism*, pages 479–490, London, 1980. Academic Press.
15. M. Parigot. An algorithmic interpretation of classical natural deduction. In *Proc. of Int. Conf. on Logic Programming and Automated Reasoning, LPAR'92*, volume 624 of *Lecture Notes in Computer Science*, pages 190–201. Springer-Verlag, 1992.
16. M. Parigot. Proofs of strong normalisation for second order classical natural deduction. *The Journal of Symbolic Logic*, 62(4):1461–1479, December 1997.

17. G. Pottinger. A type assignment for the strongly normalizable λ-terms. In J. P. Seldin and J. R. Hindley, editors, *To H. B. Curry: Essays on Combinatory Logic, Lambda Calculus and Formalism*, pages 561–577. Academic Press, London, 1980.
18. J. A. Rees. A security kernel based on the lambda calculus. A.I. Memo 1564, Massachusetts Institute of Technology, March 1996.
19. P. Sallé. Une extension de la théorie des types en lambda-calcul. In G. Ausiello and C. Böhm, editors, *Fifth International Conference on Automata, Languages and Programming*, volume 62 of *Lecture Notes in Computer Science*, pages 398–410. Springer-Verlag, 1978.
20. Ph. Wadler. Proofs are programs: 19th century logic and 21st century computing. available as `http://www.research.avayalabs.com/user/wadler/topics/history.html`.

"Wave-Style" Geometry of Interaction Models in Rel Are Graph-Like Lambda-Models*

Furio Honsell[1] and Marina Lenisa[1]

Dipartimento di Matematica e Informatica, Università di Udine,
Via delle Scienze 206, 33100 Udine, ITALY.
tel. +39 0432 558417, fax: +39 0432 558499
{honsell,lenisa}@dimi.uniud.it.

Abstract. We study the connections between *graph models* and *"wave-style" Geometry of Interaction* (GoI) λ-models. The latters arise when Abramsky's GoI axiomatization, which generalizes Girard's original GoI, is applied to a traced monoidal category with the *categorical product* as tensor, using a countable power as the traced strong monoidal functor !. Abramsky hinted that the category *Rel* of sets and relations is the basic setting for traditional denotational "static semantics". However, the category *Rel* together with the cartesian product apparently escapes original Abramsky's axiomatization. Here we show that, by moving to the category *Rel** of *pointed sets* and relations preserving the distinguished point, and by sligthly relaxing Abramsky's GoI axiomatization, we can recover a large class of graph-like models as wave models. Furthermore, we show that the class of untyped λ-theories induced by wave-style GoI models is richer than that induced by game models.

Keywords: (linear) graph model, traced monoidal category, weak linear category, categorical geometry of interaction.

Introduction

Geometry of Interaction and game models have been the most relevant novelties in the last decade in the field of semantic analysis of proof theory and functional languages.

In [1], Abramsky provides a categorical axiomatization/generalization of Girard's *Geometry of Interaction* (GoI) [18], embracing previous axiomatic approaches, such as that based on *dynamic algebras* [16,17] and the one in [4]. This generalization is based on traced monoidal categories, [23], and it consists in building a compact closed category $\mathcal{G}(\mathcal{C})$ (*GoI category*) from a traced symmetric monoidal category $\mathcal{C}$. In [2,3], the construction is extended to exponentials, which, in a general categorical setting, are captured by a strong monoidal functor ! on the traced category $\mathcal{C}$, together with some additional structure. Under these conditions on $\mathcal{C}$, the GoI category $\mathcal{G}(\mathcal{C})$ is a *weak linear category* (WLC),

* Research supported by the MIUR Projects COFIN 2001013518 COMETA and 20022018192_002 PROTOCOLLO, and by the UE Project IST-2000-29001 TYPES.

S. Berardi, M. Coppo, and F. Damiani (Eds.): TYPES 2003, LNCS 3085, pp. 242–258, 2004.

i.e. a weakening of a linear category (see [13]). Moreover, every reflexive object in a WLC gives rise to a *linear combinatory algebra* (LCA).

Following [1,2], there are two main instantiations of the GoI axiomatization. In the "particle-style" GoI, the tensor on the underlying category is a coproduct and the strong monoidal functor is a *countable* copower. Girard's GoI is an instance of this. Composition in the GoI category can be intuitively understood by simulating the flow of a particle around a network. Dually, in the "wave-style" GoI, the tensor is a product and the strong monoidal functor amounts to a *countable* power. Composition in the GoI category is defined now statically and globally. In [1], the category $(Rel, +)$ was suggested as the "basic setting" for particle/*dynamic semantics*, while $(Rel, \times)$ as the "basic setting" for wave/*static semantics*. This is clearly the case of the former, wich underlies many game categories in the style of [5], and contains as subalgebras those fruitfully used in [6,8,7]. On the other hand, the thesis that $(Rel, \times)$ is the basic setting for static semantics is less immediate, also because $(Rel, \times)$ itself apparently escapes the original GoI axiomatization of [3].

The connections between traditional (static) semantics and wave GoI have not received much attention in the literature, apart from the investigations of some special wave-style models in [10,9]. In the present paper and in [20], this connection has been taken seriously, and categories of relations in the wave-style have been explored, *vis-à-vis* graph models.

In this paper, we show that, by moving to the category Rel^* of pointed sets and relations preserving the distinguished point, and by slightly relaxing the GoI axiomatization of [3], we can recover many familiar graph models of λ-calculus. In particular, we show that GoI algebras on $(Rel^*, \times^*)$ are essentially *graph-like models* in the sense of Scott-Plotkin-Engeler, [26,24]. Moreover, we show that the λ-theories modeled in this setting do go beyond sensible and semi-sensible theories. This should be contrasted with the fact that, in [14], it has been shown that game models, i.e. particle-style GoI models, capture only a very limited number of λ-theories, related to Böhm trees and Levy-Longo trees.

The paper consists of three parts.

In the first part (Section 1), we study standard *graph models* (GMs) and *linear graph models* (LGMs) from a purely set-theoretical viewpoint. The latter have been introduced by Abramsky, and they are special cases of LCAs, providing combinatory models for the linear λ-calculus. A natural, but somewhat not immediate fact that we prove is that every GM can be recovered from a LGM via standardisation. An important consequence is that all λ-theories induced by GM's can be captured by LGMs. In the literature many variants of the original notion of GM have been studied (see e.g. [26,24,15]). Here we provide purely set-theoretical presentations of some variants of the original notions of (L)GM, which, as we will see, arise as wave GoI models.

In the second part of the paper (Section 2), we study LGMs from a categorical point of view. In particular, we show that many (*pointed*) LGMs can be captured as special WLCs in the wave-style. Somewhat surprisingly, the original Scott-

Plotkin-Engeler graph model escapes this categorical description, because of the behaviour of the empty relation.

In the third part of the paper (Sections 3 and 4), we study wave GoI algebras. In particular, we introduce a weaker axiomatization of the *GoI situation* of [3], which still ensures that a GoI category is a WLC, and hence it allows to build a GoI algebra. This weaker axiomatization allows us to capture the case of $(Rel^*, \times^*)$. We show that the class of GoI algebras induced by $(Rel^*, \times^*)$ are *pointed* LGMs. Finally, we show that there are wave GoI models realizing non-sensible λ-theories.

Notation. Let $\mathcal{P}$, $\mathcal{P}_f$, $\mathcal{P}_{fne}$ denote the (finite, finite non-empty) powerset. Let $\subseteq$, $\subseteq_f$, $\subseteq_{fne}$ denote (finite, finite non-empty) subset inclusion. Let U, V be objects in a category $\mathcal{C}$. We denote by $\tau : U \lhd V : \tau'$ a retraction of U in V, i.e. $\tau' \circ \tau = id_U$. Let *Pfn* be the category of sets and *partial* functions. Let *Rel* be the category of sets and relations. Relations $f \subseteq A \times B$ will be denoted by $f : A \multimap B$. Let *Rel** be the category of pointed sets $(A, *_A)$ and relations which preserve the distinguished point, i.e. $f : (A, *_A) \multimap (B, *_B)$ iff $(*_A, *_B) \in f$. The sets of finite streams and the set of infinite streams on a set A will be denoted by $A^{<\omega}$ and A^ω, respectively. Streams in A^ω will be denoted by $\boldsymbol{a}, \boldsymbol{b}, \ldots$ The i-th component of a (finite) stream $\boldsymbol{a}$ is denoted by a_i; a^ω denotes the infinite stream whose components are all equal to a.

1 Linear Combinatory Algebras and Graph Models

In this section, first we recall basic facts concerning *linear combinatory algebras* (LCAs) and we introduce the new notion of *linear combinatory λ-model*. Then we focus on a special class of (linear) combinatory λ-models, i.e. *(linear) graph models* ((L)GMs), and we show that every graph model is induced by a linear one. Finally, we present some variants of the original notion of (L)GM, which will be of interest in the sequel, namely *Rel* (L)GMs, *pointed* (L)GMs, *stream-based* (L)GMs, together with their generalizations w.r.t. cardinality.

1.1 Linear Combinatory Algebras, λ-Models and Graph Models

The notion of linear combinatory algebra refines the notion of combinatory algebra, in that it has an extra unary operation ! and a set of combinators, refining Curry's original set of combinators:

Definition 1 (Linear Combinatory Algebra). *A* linear combinatory algebra *(LCA) $\mathcal{A} = (A, \cdot, !)$ is an applicative structure $(A, \cdot)$ with a unary (injective) operation !, and distinguished elements (combinators) $B, C, I, K, W, D, \delta, F$ satisfying the following equations (we associate $\cdot$ to the left and we assume ! to have order of precedence greater than $\cdot$): for all $x, y, z \in A$,*

$$
\begin{array}{ll}
Bxyz = x(yz) & Wx!y = x!y!y \\
Cxyz = (xz)y & D!x = x \\
Ix = x & \delta !x = !!x \\
Kx!y = x & F!x!y = !(xy)
\end{array}
$$

The notion of LCA corresponds to a Hilbert style axiomatization of the $\{!, \multimap\}$-fragment of linear logic. Every LCA induces a standard combinatory algebra (CA), by the combinatory version of Girard's translation of Intuitionistic Linear Logic into Intuitionistic Logic (see [3] for more details), i.e.:

Proposition 1 (Standardisation). *Let $(A, \cdot, !)$ be a LCA. Then $(A, \cdot_s)$, where $x \cdot_s y \triangleq x \cdot !y$, is a CA with combinators B_s, C_s, I_s, K_s, W_s defined by:*

$$C_s \triangleq D' \cdot C \qquad I_s \triangleq D' \cdot I$$
$$B_s \triangleq C \cdot (B \cdot (B \cdot B \cdot B) \cdot (D' \cdot I)) \cdot (C \cdot ((B \cdot B) \cdot F) \cdot \delta)$$
$$K_s \triangleq D' \cdot K \qquad W_s \triangleq D' \cdot W \ ,$$

where $D' \triangleq C(BBI)(BDI)$ is such that, for all x, y, $D'x!y = xy$.

It is well known that λ-models à la Hindley-Longo can be characterized as *combinatory λ-models* (see e.g. [11]):

Definition 2 (Combinatory λ-model). *A CA $\mathcal{A} = (A, \cdot)$ is a* combinatory λ-model *if there exists an extra* selector *combinator ϵ such that, for all $x, y \in A$,*

$$\epsilon xy = xy \quad and \quad (\forall z.\ xz = yz) \Rightarrow \epsilon x = \epsilon y\ .$$

Here we introduce the linear version of the notion of combinatory λ-model:

Definition 3 (Combinatory Linear λ-model). *A LCA $\mathcal{A} = (A, \cdot, !)$ is a* combinatory linear λ-model *if there exist* linear selector ϵ *and* selector *combinator ϵ_s such that, for all $x, y \in A$,*

$$\epsilon xy = xy \quad and \quad (\forall z.\ xz = yz) \Rightarrow \epsilon x = \epsilon y$$
$$\epsilon_s !x!y = x!y \quad and \quad (\forall z.\ x!z = y!z) \Rightarrow \epsilon_s !x = \epsilon_s !y\ .$$

Then we have:

Proposition 2. *Every combinatory linear λ-model gives rise by standardisation to a combinatory λ-model.*

Graph models (GMs) à la Scott-Plotkin-Engeler and Abramsky's *linear graph models* (LGMs) are examples of combinatory (linear) λ-models:

Definition 4 ((Linear) Graph Model). *A* graph model (GM) *$\mathcal{U}$ is an applicative structure $(\mathcal{P}(U), \cdot_\tau)$, where U is a (infinite) set with a retraction in* Pfn[1] *$\tau : \mathcal{P}_f(U) \times U \lhd U$, and the application $\cdot_\tau$ is defined by: for all $x, y \in \mathcal{P}(U)$,*

$$x \cdot_\tau y \triangleq \{a \mid \exists w \subseteq_f y.\ \tau(w, a) \in x\}\ .$$

A linear graph model (LGM) *is a structure $\mathcal{U} = (\mathcal{P}(U), \cdot_{\tau_1}, !_{\tau_2})$, where U is a (infinite) set with retractions in* Pfn *$\tau_1 : U \times U \lhd U$ and $\tau_2 : \mathcal{P}_f(U) \lhd U$, and linear application $\cdot_{\tau_1}$ and $!_{\tau_2}$ are defined by: for all $x, y \in \mathcal{P}(U)$,*

$$x \cdot_{\tau_1} y \triangleq \{a \mid \exists b \in y.\ \tau_1(b, a) \in x\}\ ,$$

$$!_{\tau_2} x \triangleq \{\tau_2(w) \mid w \subseteq_f x\}\ .$$

[1] I.e. an injection.

One can define combinators on (linear) graph models in such a way that:

Proposition 3. *Every (L)GM is a combinatory (linear) λ-model.*

As one expects, given a LGM, by standardisation, we get a GM:

Proposition 4. *Let $\mathcal{U} \triangleq (\mathcal{P}(U), \cdot_{\tau_1}, !_{\tau_2})$ be a LGM with retractions $\tau_1 : U \times U \lhd U$ and $\tau_2 : \mathcal{P}_f(U) \lhd U$. Then by standardisation we get a GM $\mathcal{S}(\mathcal{U}) \triangleq (\mathcal{P}(U), \cdot_\tau)$, where the retraction $\tau : \mathcal{P}_f(U) \times U \lhd U$ is defined by $\tau_1 \circ (\tau_2 \times id_U)$.*

An interesting fact, which has a simple but non trivial proof, is that there exists a (non trivial) dual construction for building a LGM from a GM, for which standardisation is an inverse:

Proposition 5. *For any GM $\mathcal{U}$, there is a LGM $\mathcal{L}(\mathcal{U})$ such that $\mathcal{S}(\mathcal{L}(\mathcal{U})) = \mathcal{U}$.*

Proof. Let $\mathcal{U} \triangleq (\mathcal{P}(U), \cdot_\tau)$ be a GM. For any bijection $\xi : U \to \mathcal{P}_f(U)$ (which exists by cardinality reasons), the retractions $\tau_1 : U \times U \lhd U$, $\tau_1 \triangleq \tau \circ (\xi \times id_U)$, and $\tau_2 : \mathcal{P}_f(U) \lhd U$, $\tau_2 \triangleq \xi^{-1}$ induce a LGM $(\mathcal{P}(U), \cdot_{\tau_1}, !_{\tau_2})$. We take such LGM as $\mathcal{L}(\mathcal{U})$. □

Remarkably, the construction in the proof of Proposition 5 holds for any choice of the bijection ξ. From the point of view of λ-theories, we have the following important consequence:

Corollary 1. *The class of λ-theories induced by GMs coincides with the class of λ-theories induced by GMs obtained from LGMs via standardisation.*

1.2 Rel (Linear) Graph Models

We introduce a class of generalized (L)GMs, where retractions are allowed to be *relations* instead of functions. The constructions in [26] and some weak variants of filter models [12], can be viewed as instances of *Rel* graph models.

Definition 5 (*Rel* (Linear) Graph Model). *A Rel* graph model *is an applicative structure $(\mathcal{P}(U), \cdot_\tau)$, where U is a (infinite) set with a retraction in* Rel *$\tau : \mathcal{P}_f(U) \times U \lhd U$, and the application $\cdot_\tau$ is defined by: for all $x, y \in \mathcal{P}(U)$,*

$$x \cdot_\tau y \triangleq \{a \mid \exists w \subseteq_f y. \exists c \in x.\ ((w, a), c) \in \tau\}\ .$$

A Rel linear graph model *is a structure $\mathcal{U} = (\mathcal{P}(U), \cdot_{\tau_1}, !_{\tau_2})$ where U is a (infinite) set with retractions in* Rel *$\tau_1 : U \times U \lhd U$ and $\tau_2 : \mathcal{P}_f(U) \lhd U$, and linear application $\cdot_{\tau_1}$ and $!_{\tau_2}$ are defined by: for all $x, y \in \mathcal{P}(U)$,*

$$x \cdot_{\tau_1} y \triangleq \{a \mid \exists b \in y. \exists c \in x.\ ((b, a), c) \in \tau_1\}$$

$$!_{\tau_2} x \triangleq \{a \mid \exists w \subseteq_f x.\ (w, a) \in \tau_2\}\ .$$

Proposition 6. Rel *(L)GMs are combinatory (linear) λ-models.*

Proof. We just show how to define selectors. Linear selector: $\epsilon \triangleq \{d \mid \exists a, b, c \in U.\ (((c, c), d) \in \tau_1\ \wedge\ ((a, b), c) \in \tau_1)\}$. Standard selector: $\epsilon_s \triangleq \{b \mid \exists w \subseteq v \subseteq_f U.\ \exists a, c, c' \in U.\ (((\{c\}, c'), b) \in \tau\ \wedge\ ((w, a), c) \in \tau\ \wedge\ ((v, a), c') \in \tau)\}$. □

One can check that Propositions 4–5 extend to *Rel* (L)GMs.

1.3 Pointed Rel (Linear) Graph Models

Pointed *Rel* graph models arise when we carry out the graph model construction in *Rel**. Namely, we fix a special point $* \in U$, and we take as carrier the pointed powerset $(\mathcal{P}^*U, \{*\})$, i.e. the set of all subsets u of U such that $* \in U$, together with point-preserving codings.

Definition 6 (Pointed *Rel* (Linear) Graph Model). *Let U be a (infinite) set with a special point $* \in U$.*
A pointed *Rel* graph model *(pointed graph model, for short) is an applicative structure $(\mathcal{P}^*(U), \cdot_{\tau^*})$, where $\tau^* : \mathcal{P}^*_f(U) \times U \lhd U$ is a retraction in* Rel* *i.e. $((\{*\}, *), *) \in \tau^*$, $\mathcal{P}^*_f(U)$ denotes the set of all finite pointed subsets of U, and the application $\cdot_{\tau^*}$ is defined by: for all $x, y \in \mathcal{P}^*(U)$,*

$$x \cdot_{\tau^*} y \triangleq \{a \mid \exists w \subseteq_{fne} y.\ \exists c \in x.\ ((w, a), c) \in \tau^*\} \ .$$

A pointed *Rel* linear graph model *(pointed linear graph model, for short) is a structure $\mathcal{U} = (\mathcal{P}^*(U), \cdot_{\tau_1^*}, !_{\tau_2^*})$ where $\tau_1^* : U \times U \lhd U$, $\tau_2^* : \mathcal{P}^*_f(U) \lhd U$ are retractions in* Rel*, *i.e. $((*, *), *) \in \tau_1^*$ and $(\{*\}, *) \in \tau_2^*$ and linear application $\cdot_{\tau_1^*}$ and $!_{\tau_2^*}$ are defined by: for all $x, y \in \mathcal{P}^*(U)$,*

$$x \cdot_{\tau_1^*} y \triangleq \{a \mid \exists b \in y.\ \exists c \in x.\ ((b, a), c) \in \tau_1^*\} \ ,$$

$$!_{\tau_2^*} x \triangleq \{a \mid \exists w \subseteq_{fne} x.\ (w, a) \in \tau_2^*\} \ .$$

Proposition 7. *Every pointed (L)GM is a combinatory (linear) λ-model.*

Similar results to those in Propositions 4–5 hold then for pointed (L)GMs.

Remark 1. Notice that, in the spirit of [25], the above constructions of (L)GMs go through even if we consider $\mathcal{P}_{<\kappa}$, for any regular cardinal κ, in place of $\mathcal{P}_f$ (i.e. $\mathcal{P}_{<\omega}$). We call κ-(L)GMs the corresponding (L)GMs induced by such codings.

1.4 Stream-Based (Linear) Graph Models

Interesting variants of graph models are obtained by considering codings on (possibly finite) streams, in place of codings on the powerset. As we will see, these can be actually viewed as special cases of graph models as defined in the previous sections. The interest of stream-based graph models lies in the fact that, as we will see, they arise in the categorical context of weak linear categories and of Geometry of Interaction. Both the standard, *Rel* and pointed graph models considered previously have corresponding stream based variants. Here we give the details only in the case of pointed graph models with finite streams. Similarly one can define (pointed) graph models with streams with finite codomain, or general streams.

Definition 7 (Finite-stream Graph Models). *Let U be a (infinite) set with a special point $* \in U$.*
A finite-stream graph model *is an applicative structure $(\mathcal{P}^*(U), \cdot_{\tau^*})$, where $\tau^* : U^{*<\omega} \times U \lhd U$, $U^{*<\omega}$ is the set of finite streams with at least one occurrence of $*$, and τ^* is a retraction in* Rel* *i.e. $((\langle * \rangle, *), *) \in \tau^*$, and the application $\cdot_{\tau^*}$ is defined by: for all $x, y \in \mathcal{P}^*(U)$,*

$$x \cdot_{\tau^*} y \triangleq \{a \mid \exists \boldsymbol{u}.\ \exists c \in x.\ (\forall i.\ u_i \in y\ \wedge\ ((\boldsymbol{u}, a), c) \in \tau^*)\} .$$

A finite-stream linear graph model *is a structure $\mathcal{U} = (\mathcal{P}^*(U),\ \cdot_{\tau_1^*},\ !_{\tau_2^*})$ where $\tau_1^* : U \times U \lhd U$, $\tau_2^* : U^{*<\omega} \lhd U$ are retractions in* Rel*, *i.e. $((*, *), *) \in \tau_1^*$ and $(\langle * \rangle, *) \in \tau_2^*$ and linear application $\cdot_{\tau_1^*}$ and $!_{\tau_2^*}$ are defined by: for all $x, y \in \mathcal{P}^*(U)$,*

$$x \cdot_{\tau_1^*} y \triangleq \{a \mid \exists b \in y.\ \exists c \in x.\ ((b, a), c) \in \tau_1^*\} ,$$

$$!_{\tau_2^*} x \triangleq \{a \mid \exists \boldsymbol{u}.\ ((\forall i.\ u_i \in x\ \wedge\ (\boldsymbol{u}, a) \in \tau_2^*)\} .$$

Proposition 8. *Every finite-stream (L)GM is a combinatory (linear) λ-model.*

Similar results to those in Propositions 4–5 hold also for finite-stream (L)GMs.

The connection between stream-based (L)GMs and powerset-based (L)GMs is given by the following

Theorem 1. *Every finite-stream (L)GM is isomorphic to a pointed (L)GM.*

Proof. We give the proof for the linear case. Let $(\mathcal{P}^*(U), \cdot_{\tau_1^*}, !_{\tau_2^*})$ be a finite-stream linear graph model. Now we take $\xi : \mathcal{P}_f^* U \multimap U^{*<\omega}$ to be the injective relation defined by $(v, \boldsymbol{a}) \in \xi$ iff, for all i, $a_i \in v$ and for all $b \in v$ there exists i s.t. $a_i = b$. Then $\theta_2^* : \mathcal{P}_f^* U \multimap U$, $\theta_2^* \triangleq \tau_2^* \circ \xi$ is s.t. $!_{\theta_2^*} x = \{a \mid v \subseteq_{fne} x.\ (v, a) \in \theta_2^*\} = !_{\tau_2^*} x$, i.e. the finite-stream LGM $(\mathcal{P}^*(U), \cdot_{\tau_1^*}, !_{\theta_2^*})$ is a pointed LGM with codings τ_1^*, θ_2^*. Notice that the coding θ_2^* in the proof above is forced to be non functional. □

However, notice that the converse of the above theorem fails.

2 Weak Linear Categories and Linear Graph Models

In this section, we discuss Abramsky's axiomatic construction of an LCA from a *weak linear category* (WLC). WLCs are the counterpart for linear combinatory algebras of the notion of linear category for linear λ-models (see [13]). In particular, we show that the category *Rel** with tensor the cartesian product, together with suitable stream-based functors turns out to be a WLC. Moreover, the LCAs arising from the WLC *Rel** capture exactly the classes of stream-based (L)GMs.

We start by recalling Abramsky's notion of WLC and the construction of an LCA from a WLC (for basic categorical definitions see Appendix A).

Definition 8 (Weak Linear Category). *A* weak linear category (WLC) $(\mathcal{C}, \otimes,$
$!)$ *consists of:*

- *a symmetric monoidal closed category* $(\mathcal{C}, \otimes)$;
- *a symmetric monoidal functor* $! : \mathcal{C} \to \mathcal{C}$;
- *the following four monoidal pointwise natural transformations:*

  $der : ! \Rightarrow Id$ (dereliction)
  $\delta : ! \Rightarrow !!$ (comultiplication)
  $con : ! \Rightarrow ! \otimes !$ (contraction)
  $weak : ! \Rightarrow \mathcal{K}_I$ (weakening) ,

  where $\mathcal{K}_I$ *is the constant* I *functor.*

Definition 9. *A* reflexive *object in a WLC* $\mathcal{C}$ *is an object* V *in* $\mathcal{C}$ *with the following retracts:*

$$V \multimap V \lhd V \qquad !V \lhd V \qquad I \lhd V .$$

Theorem 2 ([3]). *Let* $(\mathcal{C}, \otimes, !)$ *be a WLC and* V *be a reflexive object in* $\mathcal{C}$ *with retracts* $\theta_1 : V \multimap V \lhd V : \theta'_1$ *and* $\theta_2 : !V \lhd V : \theta'_2$. *Then* $(\mathcal{C}(I, V), \cdot, !)$ *is a LCA, where* $\cdot$ *and* $!$ *are defined by: for* $f, g \in \mathcal{C}(I, V)$,

$$f \cdot g \triangleq ev \circ ((\theta'_1 \circ f) \otimes g) \circ \phi'_I \qquad !f \triangleq \theta_2 \circ (!f) \circ \phi'_I ,$$

where $\phi'_I : I \to !I$ *is the isomorphism associated to the strong monoidal functor* $!$ *(see Appendix A).*

The category Rel^* is symmetric monoidal closed w.r.t. the product $\times^*$ inherited from Rel. Moreover, $(Rel^*, \times^*)$ together with any of the following symmetric monoidal functors based on streams is a WLC:

Definition 10. *i) Let* $(\ )^{*<\omega} : Rel^* \to Rel^*$ *be the functor defined by:*

- *for any pointed set* $(A, *_A)$, *let* $(A, *_A)^{<\omega} \triangleq (A^{*<\omega}, \langle *_A \rangle)$, *where* $A^{*<\omega}$ *is the set of finite streams with at least one occurrence of* $*_A$;
- *for any* $f : (A, *_A) \twoheadrightarrow (B, *_B)$, *let* $f^{*<\omega} : (A^{*<\omega}, \langle *_A \rangle) \twoheadrightarrow (B^{*<\omega}, \langle *_B \rangle)$ *be defined by* $(\boldsymbol{a}, \boldsymbol{b}) \in f^{*<\omega}$ *iff* $|\boldsymbol{a}| = |\boldsymbol{b}|$ *and* $\forall i.\ (a_i, b_i) \in f$.

ii) Let $(\ )^{*\omega} : Rel^* \to Rel^*$ *be the functor defined by:*

- *for any pointed set* $(A, *_A)$, $(A, *_A)^{*\omega} \triangleq (A^{*\omega}, *^\omega_A)$ *where* $A^{*\omega}$ *is the set of (infinite) streams with at least one occurrence of* $*_A$;
- *for any* $f : (A, *_A) \twoheadrightarrow (B, *_B)$, *let* $f^{*\omega} : (A^{*\omega}, \langle *_A \rangle) \twoheadrightarrow (B^{*\omega}, \langle *_B \rangle)$ *be defined by* $(\boldsymbol{a}, \boldsymbol{b}) \in f^{*\omega}$ *iff* $\forall i.\ (a_i, b_i) \in f$.

iii) Let $(\ )^{*\omega}_f : Rel^* \to Rel^*$ *be the functor defined by:*

- *for any pointed set* $(A, *_A)$, $(A, *_A)^{*\omega}_f \triangleq (A^{*\omega}_f, *^\omega_A)$, *where* $A^{*\omega}_f$ *is the restriction of* $A^{*\omega}$ *to the streams with finite codomain*[2];
- *the definition on arrows is similar to (ii).*

[2] I.e. the set $[\mathbf{N} \to_{fcod} X]$ of functions from $\mathbf{N}$ in X with *finite* codomain.

Proposition 9. *($Rel^*, \times^*$) with one of the functors in Definition 10 is a WLC.*

Proof. The proof of the fact that $(Rel^*, \times^*)$ is symmetric monoidal closed, with right adjoint of $\times^*$ the product $\times^*$ itself, and of the fact that the functors of Definition 10 are monoidal is routine. We just sketch the definition of some natural transformations for $!^* = (\ )^{*\omega}$. Let $con : (\ )^{*\omega} \Rightarrow (\ )^{*\omega} \times (\ )^{*\omega}$, $con_A : (A)^{*\omega} \multimap (A)^{*\omega} \times (A)^{*\omega}$ be defined by $con_A \triangleq \{(a, (a', a'')) \mid a, a', a'' \in A^{*\omega} \ \wedge \ \forall i \geq 0.\ a''_{2i+1} = a_i \ \wedge \ \forall i \geq 1.\ a''_{2i} = a'_i\}$. Let $weak_A : A^{*\omega} \to I$, $weak_A \triangleq \{(a^\omega, *) \mid a \in A\}$. □

Theorem 3. *The class of LCAs generated by reflexive objects in the WLC* $(\mathrm{Rel}^*, \times^*, !^*)$*, where* $!^*$ *is either* $(\ )^{*<\omega}$ *or* $(\ )^{*\omega}_f$ *or* $(\ )^{*\omega}$*, is isomorphic to the class of finite-stream, finite-codomain stream, and stream LGMs, respectively.*

Proof. We consider the case $!^* = (\ )^{*<\omega}$. The other cases can be dealt with similarly. Using Theorem 2, one can easily check that any set U with retracts $\theta_1^* : U \times^* U \lhd U$ and $\theta_2^* : U^{*<\omega} \lhd U$ gives rise to a LCA isomorphic, via $\lambda_U : I \times^* U \to U$, to a finite-stream graph model. And vice versa. □

As a consequence, by Theorem 1, the LCAs generated by reflexive objects in the WLC $(Rel^*, \times^*, !^*)$ are pointed LGMs.

The situation is summarized in Table 1. Notice that, in the case of infinite streams (possibly with finite codomain), the cardinality of U is at least $2^{\aleph_0}$. Moreover, for $! = (\ )^{*\omega}$, we get a pointed ω_1-LGM.

Table 1. Wave graph models on Rel^*.

WLC	UNIVERSAL OBJECT	LCA
$(Rel^*, \times^*, (\ )^{*<\omega})$	$\theta_1^* : U \times U \lhd U,\ \theta_2^* : U^{*<\omega} \lhd U$	$\Rightarrow$ $\exists \xi : \mathcal{P}_f^* U \lhd U^{*<\omega}$ s.t. $(\mathcal{P}^* U, \cdot_{\theta_1^*}, !_{\theta_2^* \circ \xi})$ pointed LGM
$(Rel^*, \times^*, (\ )_f^{*\omega})$	$\theta_1^* : U \times U \lhd U,\ \theta_2^* : U_f^{*\omega} \lhd U$	$\Rightarrow$ $\exists \xi : \mathcal{P}_f^* U \lhd U_f^{*\omega}$ s.t. $(\mathcal{P}^* U, \cdot_{\theta_1^*}, !_{\theta_2^* \circ \xi})$ pointed LGM
$(Rel^*, \times^*, (\ )^{*\omega})$	$\theta_1^* : U \times U \lhd U,\ \theta_2^* : U^{*\omega} \lhd U$	$\Rightarrow$ $\exists \xi : \mathcal{P}_{<\omega_1}^* U \lhd U^{*\omega}$ s.t. $(\mathcal{P}^* U, \cdot_{\theta_1^*}, !_{\theta_2^* \circ \xi})$ pointed ω_1-LGM

Remark 2. Notice that the basic category *Rel* of sets and relations fails to be a WLC, since there is no notion of "empty" stream, and the definition of weakening $weak_A$: $A^\omega \multimap I$, $weak_A \triangleq \{(a^\omega, *) \mid a \in A,\ * \in I\}$ is *not* natural on the *empty* relation. This is the reason why one has to shift to pointed relations.
Moreover, the powerset functor $\mathcal{P}_f$ fails to induce a structure of WLC on *Rel* (and Rel^*). Namely, the "natural" definition of dereliction, i.e. $der_A : \mathcal{P}_f(A) \multimap A$, $der_A \triangleq \{(\{a\}, a) \mid a \in A\}$, is not pointwise natural.

3 The Geometry of Interaction Construction

In this section, we recall the categorical axiomatization of the *Geometry of Interaction* (GoI) developed in [1,2,3]. This is based on traced categories, see [23]. Any traced monoidal category gives rise, by the construction of [1], to a *GoI category.* If moreover the traced category we start from has a strong traced monoidal functor together with suitable retractions, then the GoI category is a WLC, and hence, by Theorem 2, it can generate a (GoI) LCA. This situation, called *GoI situation*, is axiomatized and studied in [3]. However, a GoI situation gives only sufficient conditions for a GoI category to be a WLC. In this section, we introduce the notion of *weak GoI situation* (wGoI situation), in which we give weaker, but still sufficient conditions on the retractions for the GoI category to be a WLC. In the next section, we will see that the notion of wGoI situation captures many graph models introduced in Section 1.

GoI categories arise from traced symmetric monoidal categories by the following construction:

Proposition 10 (GoI Construction, [1]). *Given a traced symmetric monoidal category $\mathcal{C}$, we define a* GoI category $\mathcal{G}(\mathcal{C})$ *by:*

- **Objects***: pairs of objects of $\mathcal{C}$, denoted by (A^+, A^-), where A^+ and A^- are objects of $\mathcal{C}$.*
- **Arrows***: an arrow $f : (A^+, A^-) \to (B^+, B^-)$ in $\mathcal{G}(\mathcal{C})$ is $f : A^+ \otimes B^- \to A^- \otimes B^+$ in $\mathcal{C}$.*
- **Identity***: $id_{(A^+,A^-)} = \sigma_{A^+,A^-}$.*
- **Composition***: it is given by* symmetric feedback. *Given $f : (A^+, A^-) \to (B^+, B^-)$ and $g : (B^+, B^-) \to (C^+, C^-)$, $g \circ f : (A^+, A^-) \to (C^+, C^-)$ is given by: $g \circ f \triangleq Tr^{B^- \otimes B^+}_{A^+ \otimes C^-, A^- \otimes C^+}(\gamma' \circ (f \otimes g) \circ \gamma)$, where $\gamma \triangleq (id_{A^+} \otimes id_{B^-} \otimes \sigma_{C^-,B^+}) \circ (id_{A^+} \otimes \sigma_{C^-,B^-} \otimes id_{B^+})$ and $\gamma' \triangleq (id_{A^-} \otimes id_{C^+} \otimes \sigma_{B^+,B^-}) \circ (id_{A^-} \otimes \sigma_{B^+,C^+} \otimes id_{B^-}) \circ (id_{A^-} \otimes id_{B^+} \otimes \sigma_{B^-,C^+})$.*
- **Tensor***: $(A^+, A^-) \otimes (B^+, B^-) \triangleq (A^+ \otimes B^+, A^- \otimes B^-)$, and, for any $f : (A^+, A^-) \to (B^+, B^-)$ and $g : (C^+, C^-) \to (D^+, D^-)$, $f \otimes g \triangleq (id_{A^-} \otimes \sigma_{B^+,C^-} \otimes id_{D^+}) \circ (f \otimes g) \circ (id_{A^+} \otimes \sigma_{C^+,B^-} \otimes id_{D^-})$.*
- **Unit***: (I, I).*

Then $\mathcal{G}(\mathcal{C})$ is compact closed. Moreover, $F : \mathcal{C} \to \mathcal{G}(\mathcal{C})$ with $F(A) = (A, I)$ and $F(f) = f$ is a full and faithful embedding.

In [3], sufficient conditions are given on the traced monoidal category $\mathcal{C}$ for $\mathcal{G}(\mathcal{C})$ to be a WLC, and hence, by Theorem 2, to give rise to a GoI LCA. We recall this construction:

Definition 11 (GoI Situation, [3]). *A* GoI situation *is a triple $(\mathcal{C}, T, U)$, where:*

- *$\mathcal{C}$ is a traced symmetric monoidal category;*
- *$T : \mathcal{C} \to \mathcal{C}$ is a traced strong symmetric monoidal functor with the following retractions (which are monoidal natural transformations):*
  1. *$e : TT \lhd T : e'$* (Comultiplication)
  2. *$d : Id \lhd T : d'$* (Dereliction)

3. $c : T \otimes T \lhd T : c'$ (Contraction)
4. $w : K_I \lhd T : w'$ (Weakening), *where* K_I *denotes the constant* I *functor.*

– U *is an object of* $\mathcal{C}$*, called a* GoI reflexive object*, with retractions*
1. $\theta_1 : U \otimes U \lhd U : \theta'_1$
2. $I \lhd U$
3. $\theta_2 : TU \lhd U : \theta'_2$.

Theorem 4 ([3]). *Let* $(\mathcal{C}, T, U)$ *be a GoI situation. Then*
i) $(\mathcal{G}(\mathcal{C}), !)$ *is a WLC with* $! : \mathcal{G}(\mathcal{C}) \to \mathcal{G}(\mathcal{C})$ *defined as follows:* $!(A^+, A^-) \triangleq (TA^+, TA^-)$*, and, for* $f : (A^+, A^-) \to (B^+, B^-)$*,* $!f \triangleq TA^+ \otimes TB^- \overset{\simeq}{\to} T(A^+ \otimes B^-) \overset{Tf}{\to} T(A^- \otimes B^+) \overset{\simeq}{\to} TA^- \otimes TB^+$.
ii) $(\mathcal{C}(U, U), \cdot, !)$ *is a LCA, where for any* $f, g \in \mathcal{C}(U, U)$*,* $f \cdot g \triangleq Tr^U_{U,U}((id_U \otimes g) \circ (\theta'_1 \circ f \circ \theta_1))$*, and* $!f \triangleq \theta_2 \circ Tf \circ \theta'_2$.

Definition 12. *We call* GoI LCA*, (or* GoI algebra*), a LCA which comes from a GoI situation.*

As pointed out in [3], particle GoI situations arise when the strong monoidal functor is given by a countable copower. Dually, in the wave case, GoI situations arise when the monoidal functor is given by a countable power. In what follows, we focus on the wave case. An example of wave GoI category is $(\omega\text{-}CPO, \times)$ together with the stream functor $(\ )^\omega$, [3]. However, the basic setting for wave GoI, i.e. $(Rel^*, \times^*)$ (and $(Rel, \times)$) together with the stream functor fail to give rise to a GoI situation. The induced GoI category, however, is still a WLC. In the next definition we introduce the notion of *weak GoI situation*, which captures the basic case of $(Rel^*, \times^*)$. In a weak GoI situation, the naturality condition of the retractions is relaxed, by requiring only *naturality up-to retraction*:

Definition 13 (Weak GoI Situation). *A* weak GoI situation *(wGoI situation) is a triple* $(\mathcal{C}, T, U)$ *where* $\mathcal{C}$ *and* U *satisfy the conditions in Definition 11, and* T *is a traced strong symmetric monoidal functor with retractions which are natural only up-to retraction, i.e.:*

1. $\{e_A : TTA \lhd TA : e'_A\}_A$ (Comultiplication) *is a family of monoidal retractions s.t., for all* $f : A \to B$*,* $e'_B \circ Tf \circ e_A = TTf$*;*
2. $\{d_A : A \lhd TA : d'_A\}_A$ (Dereliction) *is a family of monoidal retractions s.t., for all* $f : A \to B$*,* $d'_B \circ Tf \circ d_A = f$*;*
3. $\{c_A : TA \otimes TA \lhd TA : c'_A\}_A$ (Contraction) *is a family of monoidal retractions s.t., for all* $f : A \to B$*,* $c'_B \circ Tf \circ c_A = Tf \otimes Tf$*;*
4. $\{w_A : I \lhd TA : w'_A\}_A$ (Weakening) *is a family of monoidal retractions s.t., for all* $f : A \to B$*,* $w'_B \circ Tf \circ w_A = id_I$.

It is immediate to see that a GoI situation is in particular a wGoI Situation. Moreover, a direct calculation shows that *der*, δ, *con*, *weak*, as defined in [3] in terms of the retractions on $\mathcal{C}$, are monoidal pointwise natural transformations on $\mathcal{G}(\mathcal{C})$. Therefore:

Theorem 5. *A wGoI situation gives rise to a GoI category which is a WLC.*

The situation is summarized in Figure 1.

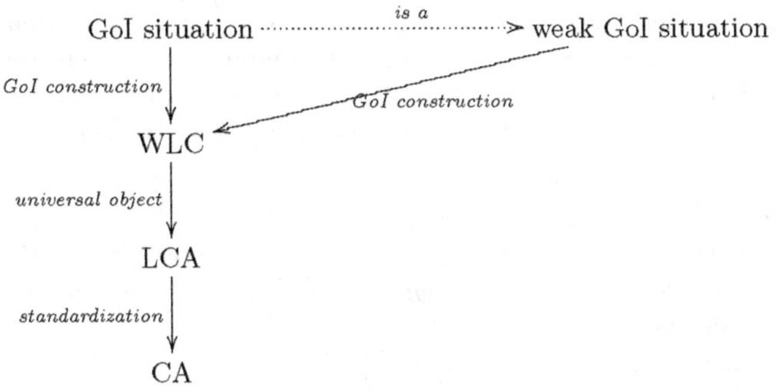

Fig. 1. (Weak) GoI construction.

4 Wave GoI Algebras and Linear Graph Models

In this section, first we show that some pointed linear graph models can be viewed as wave GoI algebras arising from the traced category $(Rel^*, \times^*)$, together with suitable stream functors as monoidal functors. Moreover we show that such wave models can induce λ-theories where not all unsolvables of order 0 are equated.

4.1 GoI Algebras on $(Rel^*, \times^*)$

The category $(Rel^*, \times^*)$ is traced with the trace operator $Tr^U_{A,B}(\ )$ defined by: for $f : A \times U \twoheadrightarrow B \times U$, $Tr^U_{A,B}(f) \triangleq \{(a,b) \mid \exists u.\ (a,u,b,u) \in f\}$.

Both the functor of streams $(\ )^{*\omega}$ and that of streams with finite codomain $(\ )^{*\omega}_f$ induce on $(Rel^*, \times^*)$ a wGoI situation. We focus on $(\ )^{*\omega}_f$.

Proposition 11. *For any GoI reflexive object U in Rel^*, $(Rel^*, \times^*, (\ )^{*\omega}_f, U)$ is a wGoI situation.*

Proof. The functor $(\ )^{*\omega}_f$ is traced strong monoidal with isomorphism $\phi'_I : I \to I^{*\omega}_f$, defined by $\phi'_I(*) = *^\omega$, and natural isomorphism $\phi : (\ )^{*\omega}_f \times (\ )^{*\omega}_f \to (\otimes\ )^{*\omega}_f$ with components $\phi_{A,B} : A^{*\omega}_f \times B^{*\omega}_f \to (A \times B)^{*\omega}_f$ defined by $\phi_{A,B}(\boldsymbol{a}, \boldsymbol{b}) = \boldsymbol{c}$, where $c_i = (a_i, b_i)$. We only sketch the definitions of the monoidal retractions:
- $e_A : (A^{*\omega}_f)^{*\omega}_f \to A^{*\omega}_f$, $e_A \triangleq \xi \circ \chi_A$, where $\chi_A : [\mathbf{N} \to_{fcod} [\mathbf{N} \to_{fcod} A]] \lhd [\mathbf{N} \times \mathbf{N} \to_{fcod} A]$ is a component of the retraction natural in A induced by curryfication, and $\xi \triangleq \lambda f \in [\mathbf{N} \times \mathbf{N} \to_{fcod} A].\lambda n \in \mathbf{N}.f(\epsilon^{-1}(n))$, where $\epsilon : \mathbf{N} \times \mathbf{N} \simeq \mathbf{N}$ is any bijective coding of pairs;
- $c_A : A^{*\omega}_f \times A^{*\omega}_f \to A^{*\omega}_f$, $c_A(\boldsymbol{a}, \boldsymbol{a}') = \boldsymbol{a}''$, where, for all $i \geq 0$, $a''_{2i+1} = a_i$ and, for all $i \geq 1$, $a''_{2i} = a'_i$;
- $d_A : A \to A^{*\omega}_f$, $d_A(a) = a^\omega$, $d'_A : A^{*\omega}_f \to A$, $d'_A(a^\omega) = a$;
- $w_A : I \twoheadrightarrow A^{*\omega}_f$, $w_A \triangleq \{(*, a^\omega) \mid a \in A\}$, $w'_A : A^{*\omega}_f \to I$, $w'_A \triangleq \{(a^\omega, *) \mid a \in A\}$. □

Notice that d in the proof above is natural up-to retraction, but not in the full sense. This justifies the definition of weak GoI situation.

Remark 3. Notice that both the finite powerset functor $\mathcal{P}^*_f$ and the finite stream functor $(\ )^{*<\omega}$ fail to be strong monoidal, and hence they do not give a GoI situation on Rel^*. Moreover, the category $(Rel, \times)$ together with the (infinite) stream functor fails to give a wGoI situation, because weakening (as it is defined in the proof of Proposition 11) does not satisfy the condition of Definition 13 on the empty relation.

Proposition 12. *i) The GoI category $\mathcal{G}(Rel^*, \times^*, (\ )^{*\omega}_f)$ is a WLC.*
ii) Let U be a GoI reflexive object in Rel^*, with retractions $\theta_1^* : U \times^* U \lhd U$, $\theta_2^* : U_f^{*\omega} \lhd U$. Then $(\mathcal{P}^*(U \times U), \cdot_{\theta_1^*}, !_{\theta_2^*})$ is a LCA, where, $\cdot_{\theta_1^*}$ and $!_{\theta_2^*}$ are defined by (using "functional" notation): for all $x, y \in \mathcal{P}(U \times U)$
- $x \cdot_{\theta_1^*} y = \{(a,b) \mid \exists (c,d) \in y.\ (\theta_1^*(a,d), \theta_1^*(b,c)) \in x\}$;
- $!_{\theta_2^*} x = \{(\theta_2^*(\boldsymbol{a}), \theta_2^*(\boldsymbol{b})) \mid \boldsymbol{a}, \boldsymbol{b} \in U_f^{*\omega}\ \wedge\ \forall i.(a_i, b_i) \in x\}$.

A crucial fact for our purposes is that all the GoI algebras of Proposition 12 give rise, for a suitable choice of the coding relations, to finite-codomain stream LGMs, and hence, by suitable analogue of Theorem 1, to pointed LGMs.

Theorem 6. *Let $\mathcal{U} = (\mathcal{P}^*(U \times U), \cdot_{\theta_1^*}, !_{\theta_2^*})$ be a GoI algebra induced by $(Rel^*, \times^*, (\ )_f^{*\omega})$, with $\theta_1^* : U \times U \lhd U$, $\theta_2^* : U_f^{*\omega} \lhd U$. Then $\mathcal{U}$ coincides with the pointed LGM $\mathcal{U}' = (\mathcal{P}^*(U'), \cdot_{\tau_1^*}, !_{\tau_2^*})$, where $U' \triangleq U \times U$, $\tau_1^* : U' \times U' \lhd U'$ and $\tau_2^* : \mathcal{P}_f^*(U') \lhd U'$ are defined by:*

$$\tau_1^* \triangleq \langle \theta_1^* \circ (\pi_1 \circ \pi_2 \times \pi_2 \circ \pi_1), \theta_1^* \circ (\pi_2 \circ \pi_2 \times \pi_1 \circ \pi_1) \rangle \ ,$$

$$\tau_2^* \triangleq (\theta_2^* \times \theta_2^*) \circ \zeta \ ,$$

where $\zeta : \mathcal{P}_f^*(U \times U) \multimap U_f^{*\omega} \times U_f^{*\omega}$ is the injective relation defined by $(u, (\boldsymbol{a}, \boldsymbol{b})) \in \zeta$ iff for all i, $(a_i, b_i) \in u$ and for all $(c,d) \in u$ there exists i such that $a_i = c$ and $b_i = d$.

Proof. Let $x, y \in \mathcal{P}^*(U \times U)$. By Proposition 12, $x \cdot_{\theta_1^*} y = \{(a,b) \mid \exists (c,d) \in y.\ (\theta_1^*(a,d), \theta_1^*(b,c)) \in x\} = \{(a,b) \mid \exists (c,d) \in y.\ \tau_1^*((c,d),(a,b)) \in x\}$, by definition of τ_1^*; i.e. $\cdot_{\theta_1^*}$ is the application on the LGM $\mathcal{U}'$. Moreover, by Proposition 12, $!_{\theta_2^*} x = \{(\theta_2^*(\boldsymbol{a}), \theta_2^*(\boldsymbol{b})) \mid \boldsymbol{a}, \boldsymbol{b} \in U_f^{*\omega}\ \wedge\ \forall i.(a_i, b_i) \in x\} = \{(\theta_2^*(\boldsymbol{a}), \theta_2^*(\boldsymbol{b})) \mid \boldsymbol{a}, \boldsymbol{b} \in U_f^{*\omega}\ \wedge\ \exists u \subseteq_{fne} x.\ \forall i.(a_i, b_i) \in u \wedge \forall (c,d) \in u\ \exists i.(a_i = c \wedge b_i = d)\} = \{(\theta_2^* \times \theta_2^*)(\zeta(u)) \mid u \subseteq_{fne} x\} = \{\tau_2^*(u) \mid u \subseteq_{fne} x\}$, by definition of τ_2^*; i.e. $!_{\theta_2^*}$ is the ! operator on the pointed LGM $\mathcal{U}'$. □

Notice that by considering the GoI construction over $(Rel^*, \times^*)$, we get a class of LGMs which is a subclass of the one obtained in Section 2, where $(Rel^*, \times^*)$ itself is viewed as a WLC.

The broad abstract pattern is given in Figure 2.

4.2 Wave GoI λ-Theories

The class of λ-theories induced by wave models is quite rich, or at least it goes beyond theories where all unsolvable of order 0 are equated in the bottom element, as in models based on games *à la* [5,22] (see [14]). Namely:

Lemma 1. *For any $k \geq 0$, there exists a GoI algebra on $(Rel^*, \times^*, (\ )_f^{*\omega})$ with k* self-singletons *(up-to-$*$) different from $*$, i.e. elements $a \in U$ such that $\theta_1^*(a,a) = a$ and $\theta_2^*(\{a, *\}) = a$.*

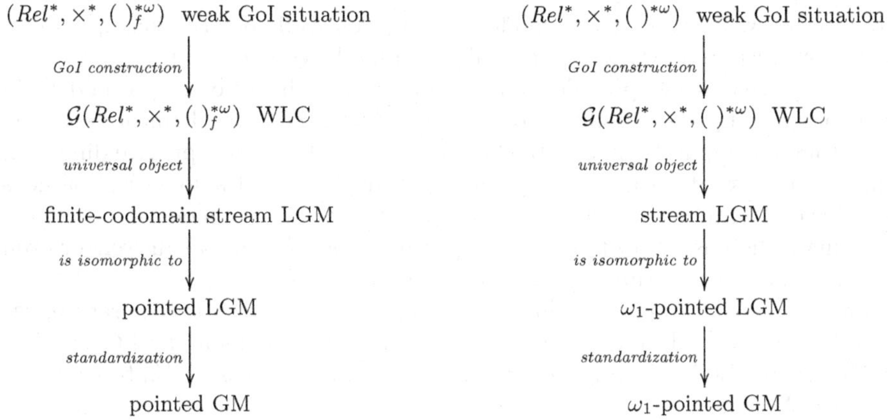

Fig. 2. Wave GoI constructions on *Rel**.

One can easily check that any self-singleton (up-to-$*$) a belongs to the interpretation of a term iff it reduces to a closed λ-term (see [21]). Therefore:

Theorem 7. *There exists a wave model in which* $[\![\lambda x.\Delta\Delta]\!] \neq [\![\lambda x.\Delta\Delta x]\!]$.

5 Conclusions and Future Work

Building on [1,3], we have investigated the connections between graph models and wave GoI models arising in the basic setting of $(Rel^*, \times^*)$. We have shown that such wave models are (pointed) graph models, which yield models of the λ-calculus capturing a rich class of λ-theories. The category $(Rel, \times)$ apparently fails to give a WLC and a wGoI situation, because weakening is not well-behaved on the empty relation.

However, in [20], in order to capture the case of $(Rel, \times)$, a *strict* variant of the GoI situation of [3] has been introduced, giving rise to a *strict* WLC, where only a restricted form of weakening holds. LCAs arising from strict WLCs are themselves strict, i.e. application is strict, and only a restricted form of K combinator is available. These are models for restricted λ-calculi, such as Church's λI-calculus and the $\lambda\beta_{KN}$-calculus of [19].

In summing up, we make a disclaimer. The objective of the paper is not that of characterizing λ-theories arising from graph models or linear graph models, or wave-style graph models. This problem is very difficult, but orthogonal to the one we have addressed. We have shown nonetheless that the class of λ-theories induced by GoI wave-style graph models is richer than that of game models. Our goal in this paper is rather that of showing that the basic intuitions underlying the applicative machinery of graph models can be subsumed in a more general setting, by a suitable relaxation of the categorical axiomatization of GoI provided by Abramsky. Actually, graph models arising from GoI constructions generalize in various intriguing ways the original graph model construction.

The present paper provides new insights in the theory of graph models, in that it opens up the possibility of applying Abramky's paradigm of "splitting the atom of computation" also to this class of models. In the opposite direction, the paper illustrates that the expressive power of the GoI axiomatization goes well-beyond game-like models and subsumes also graph-like models.

Finally, here is a list of intriguing open questions. Definitive answers or even well-motivated conjectures appear to be rather difficult.

- Many classes of graph-like models have been considered in the literature, see [15]. Do they all induce the same λ-theories as the class of standard GMs?
- Can original LGMs and the generalizations of graph models in [15] be captured as wave WLCs?
- Are all the theories of GMs induced by wave GoI algebras? Which theories escape GoI characterizations?
- Are there particle-style λ-algebras alternative to the ones based on game categories, which induce a richer class of λ-theories?
- Finally, an interesting issue to be investigated is that of giving a logical characterization via *intersection types* [12] to the graph models arising from wave GoI constructions. We feel that this will shed more light both on intersection types and on wave models.

References

1. S.Abramsky. Retracing some paths in Process Algebra, *Concur'96*, U. Montanari and V. Sassone eds., 1996, 1–17.
2. S.Abramsky. Interaction, Combinators, and Complexity, lecture notes, Siena (Italy), 1997.
3. S.Abramsky, E.Haghverdi, P.Scott. Geometry of Interaction and Linear Combinatory Algebras, *Math.Struct. in Comp.Science* **12**(5), 2002, 625–665.
4. S.Abramsky, R.Jagadeesan. New foundations for the Geometry of Interaction, *Inf. and Comp.* **111**(1), 1994, 53–119.
5. S.Abramsky, R.Jagadeesan, P.Malacaria. Full Abstraction for PCF, *Inf. and Comp.* **163**, 2000, 409–470.
6. S.Abramsky, M.Lenisa. A Fully-complete PER Model for ML Polymorphic Types, *CSL'00*, LNCS **1862**, 2000, 140–155.
7. S.Abramsky, M.Lenisa. Fully Complete Minimal PER Models for the Simply Typed λ-calculus, *CSL'01*, LNCS **2142**, 2001, 443–457.
8. S.Abramsky, J.Longley. Realizability models based on history-free strategies, draft, 2000.
9. S.Abramsky, P.Mellies. Concurrent Games and Full Completeness, *LICS'99*, 431–442.
10. P.Baillot, V.Danos, T.Ehrard, L.Regnier. *Timeless games*, *CSL'97*, LNCS **1414**, 1997.
11. H.Barendregt. *The Lambda Calculus, its Syntax and Semantics,* North Holland, Amsterdam, 1984.
12. H.Barendregt, M.Coppo, M.Dezani. A filter lambda model and the completeness of type assignment system, *J. Symbolic Logic* **48**, 1983, 931–940.

13. P.Benton, G.Bierman, V. de Paiva, M.Hyland. Term assignment for intuitionistic linear logic, TR **262**, Computer Laboratory, Cambridge, 1992.
14. P.Di Gianantonio, G.Franco, F.Honsell. Game Semantics for Untyped λ-calculus, *TLCA'99*, LNCS **1581**, 1999, 114–128.
15. P.Di Gianantonio, F.Honsell. An abstract notion of application, *TLCA'93*, LNCS **664**, 124–138.
16. V.Danos, L.Regnier. Local and Asynchronous beta-reduction (An analysis of Girard's Execution Formula), *LICS'93*, 296–306.
17. V.Danos, L.Regnier. Proof-nets and the Hilbert space, in J.-Y.Girard et al. eds., *Advances in linear Logic*, London Math. Soc. Series **222**, Cambridge University Press, 307–328.
18. J.-Y.Girard. Geometry of Interaction I: Interpretation of System F, *Logic Colloquium'88*, R.Ferro et al. eds., North Holland, 221–260.
19. F.Honsell, M.Lenisa. Semantical Analysis of Perpetual Strategies in lambda-calculus, *TCS*, **212**, 1999, 183–209.
20. F.Honsell, M.Lenisa. Strict Geometry of Interaction Graph Models, *LPAR'03*, LNAI **2850**, 2003, 403–417.
21. F.Honsell, S.Ronchi Della Rocca. An approximation theorem for topological lambda models and the topological incompleteness of lambda models, *J. Comp. System Sci.* **45**, 1992, 49–75.
22. M.Hyland, L.Ong. On full abstraction for PCF, *Inf. and Comp.* **163**, 2000.
23. A.Joyal, R.Street, D.Verity. Traced monoidal categories, *Math. Proc. Comb. Phil. Soc.* **119**, 1996, 447–468.
24. G.Plotkin. Set-theoretical and other elementary models of the λ-calculus, *Volume in Honour of Corrado Böhm*, M.Dezani et al. eds., Elsevier, 351–410.
25. D.Scott. Some physical issues concerning theories of combinators, *λ-calculus and Computer Science Theory*, LNCS **37**, 346–366.
26. D.Scott. Lambda calculus: some models, some philosophy, *Proc. The Kleene Symp.*, J.Barwise ed., North Holland, Amsterdam, 1980.

A Categorical Definitions

We collect some categorical definitions. For more details (in particular for the definition of *traced category*), we refer to [3,23].

A *monoidal functor* between monoidal categories $\mathcal{C}$ and $\mathcal{D}$ is a triple (F, ϕ, ϕ'_I), where $F : \mathcal{C} \to \mathcal{D}$ is a functor, ϕ is a natural transformation with components $\phi_{A,B} : FA \otimes FB \to F(A \otimes B)$ and $\phi'_I : I \to FI$ is a morphism in $\mathcal{D}$ such that the following diagrams commute

$$\begin{array}{ccc}
FA \otimes (FB \otimes FC) & \xrightarrow{\alpha} & (FA \otimes FB) \otimes FC \\
\downarrow{\scriptstyle id_{FA} \otimes \phi} & & \downarrow{\scriptstyle \phi \otimes id_{FC}} \\
FA \otimes F(B \otimes C) & & F(A \otimes B) \otimes FC \\
\downarrow{\scriptstyle \phi} & & \downarrow{\scriptstyle \phi} \\
F(A \otimes (B \otimes C)) & \xrightarrow{F\alpha} & F((A \otimes B) \otimes C)
\end{array}$$

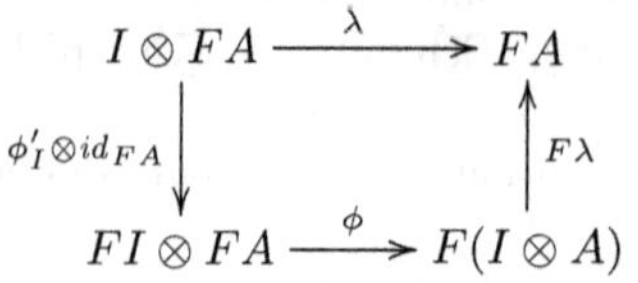

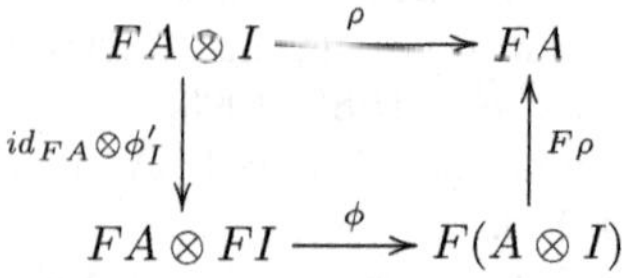

$$
\begin{array}{ccc}
I \otimes FA & \xrightarrow{\ \lambda\ } & FA \\
{\scriptstyle \phi'_I \otimes id_{FA}} \downarrow & & \uparrow {\scriptstyle F\lambda} \\
FI \otimes FA & \xrightarrow{\ \phi\ } & F(I \otimes A)
\end{array}
\qquad
\begin{array}{ccc}
FA \otimes I & \xrightarrow{\ \rho\ } & FA \\
{\scriptstyle id_{FA} \otimes \phi'_I} \downarrow & & \uparrow {\scriptstyle F\rho} \\
FA \otimes FI & \xrightarrow{\ \phi\ } & F(A \otimes I)
\end{array}
$$

A monoidal functor is *strong* when ϕ is a natural isomorphism and ϕ' is an isomorphism.

A monoidal functor $F : \mathcal{C} \to \mathcal{D}$, with $\mathcal{C}$ and $\mathcal{D}$ symmetric monoidal categories, is *symmetric* if the following diagram commutes:

$$
\begin{array}{ccc}
FA \otimes FB & \xrightarrow{\ \phi_{A,B}\ } & F(A \otimes B) \\
{\scriptstyle \sigma_{FA,FB}} \downarrow & & \downarrow {\scriptstyle F\sigma_{A,B}} \\
FB \otimes FA & \xrightarrow{\ \phi_{B,A}\ } & F(B \otimes A)
\end{array}
$$

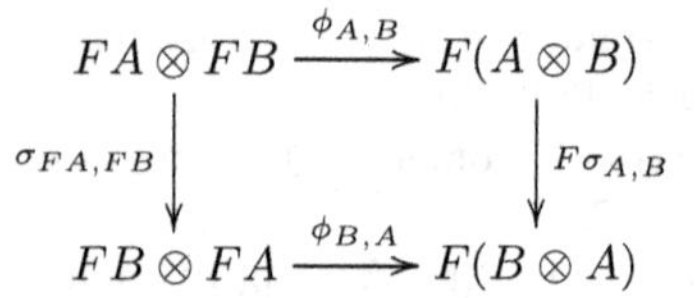

A strong symmetric monoidal functor $F : \mathcal{C} \to \mathcal{D}$ between traced categories is *traced* if, for all $f : A \otimes U \to B \otimes U$, $\mathrm{Tr}^{FU}_{FA,FB}(\phi^{-1}_{B,U} \circ Ff \circ \phi_{A,U}) = F(\mathrm{Tr}^{U}_{A,B}(f))$.

A *monoidal* natural transformation m between monoidal functors (F, ϕ, ϕ'_I) and (G, ψ, ψ'_I) is a natural transformation $m : F \Rightarrow G$ s.t. the following diagrams commute:

$$
\begin{array}{ccc}
FA \otimes FB & \xrightarrow{\ \phi_{A,B}\ } & F(A \otimes B) \\
{\scriptstyle m_A \otimes m_B} \downarrow & & \downarrow {\scriptstyle m_{A \otimes B}} \\
GA \otimes GB & \xrightarrow{\ \psi_{A,B}\ } & G(A \otimes B)
\end{array}
\qquad
\begin{array}{ccc}
I & \xrightarrow{\ \phi'_I\ } & FI \\
{\scriptstyle \psi'_I} \searrow & & \downarrow {\scriptstyle m_I} \\
 & & GI
\end{array}
$$

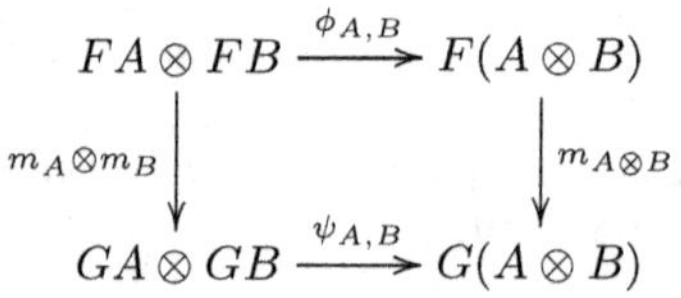

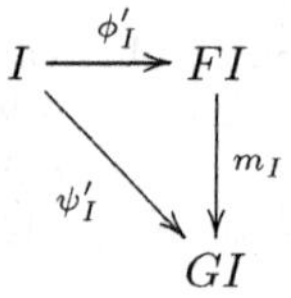

A monoidal *pointwise* natural transformation is a family of maps $m_A : FA \to GA$ s.t. the naturality diagram commutes for morphisms of the form $f : I \to A$, for all object A.

Coercions in Hindley-Milner Systems*

Robert Kießling and Zhaohui Luo

Department of Computer Science, University of Durham

Abstract. Coercive subtyping is a theory of abbreviation for dependent type theories. In this paper, we incorporate the idea of coercive subtyping into the traditional Hindley-Milner type systems in functional programming languages. This results in a typing system with coercions, an extension of the Hindley-Milner type system. A type inference algorithm is developed and shown to be sound and complete with respect to the typing system. A notion of derivational coherence is developed to deal with the problem of ambiguity and the corresponding type inference algorithm is shown to be sound and complete.

1 Introduction

The Hindley-Milner type system (HM system for short) [8] is the standard core of the modern typed functional programming languages. Various extensions to the HM system have been proposed in order to enrich a programming language with new and more powerful features. These include, for example, Haskell's class mechanism [10], which provides convenient overloading facilities among other things.

Coercive subtyping [14] is a theory of abbreviation developed in the setting of dependent type theories, where coercions are regarded as abbreviation mechanisms and directly characterised in the proof system (type theory) extended with coercions. It has been implemented in several proof development systems [1,19,4] and effectively used in proof development (e.g., [1]).

In this paper, we incorporate the idea of coercive subtyping into the traditional HM type system. There are several motivations in studying the possible combination of coercive subtyping and traditional polymorphic typing systems. First, it leads to a novel approach that increases the power of the HM system with new abbreviation mechanisms, which we believe would be useful in various programming activities. Secondly, coercive subtyping provides a clean and simple theory for abbreviation in dependent type theories. Incorporating its ideas into traditional type systems may lead to simple theoretical development and better understanding of the more powerful facilities (e.g., overloading) found useful in programming. Thirdly, not the least important, studying coercions in polymorphic type systems meets with new challenges, partly because type uniqueness simply does not hold in a polymorphic system.

* This work is partly supported by the UK EPSRC grants GR/M75518, GR/R84092 and GR/R72259, the EU TYPES grant 21900 on the TYPES project and by an EPSRC studentship.

S. Berardi, M. Coppo, and F. Damiani (Eds.): TYPES 2003, LNCS 3085, pp. 259–275, 2004.

One of the results of our work is a typing system with coercions, an extension of the HM type system, together with a sound and complete type inference algorithm. Since the HM system is polymorphic, where a term may have more than one type, the introduction of coercions has to be very careful; a naive way to introduce coercions causes problems. For example, one of the decisions we have made is that if a term is already typable in the original HM system, then no coercions will be inserted. This also conforms with the intuition and, in practice, an implementation of the extended system will not alter the meanings of the existing programs.

We shall also study a notion of derivational coherence that is developed to deal with the problem of ambiguity of computational meanings of a term. A term may have different completions – there may be different ways to insert coercions to make a term typable. The notion of derivational coherence captures this and we have developed a sound and complete type inference algorithm for derivationally coherent terms.

We regard the Hindley-Milner system as well-known and refer its introduction for example to [21]. In the remainder of this section, we give a summary of work on coercive subtyping and other related work. In Section 2, we give a brief introduction to our approach by considering several simple examples. The extended typing system with coercions is presented and explained formally in Section 3. In Section 4, the type inference algorithm is presented and proved to be sound and complete. Derivational coherence is introduced in Section 5, where we also give the corresponding algorithm and discuss the proofs of its soundness and completeness. We conclude with some discussions about future work.

1.1 Coercive Subtyping

Coercive subtyping is a framework of abbreviation for dependent type theories [14]. The basic idea is: if there is a coercion c from A to B, then an object of type A may be regarded as an object of type B via c in appropriate contexts. More precisely, a functional operation f with domain B can be applied to any object a of A and the application fa is definitionally equal to $f(ca)$. Intuitively, we can view f as a context which requires an object of B; then the argument a in the context f stands for its image of the coercion, ca. Therefore, the term fa, originally not well-typed, becomes well-typed and "abbreviates" $f(ca)$.

The second author and his colleagues have studied the above simple idea in the Logical Framework (and type theory), resulting in a very powerful theory of abbreviation and inheritance, including parameterised coercions and coercions between parameterised inductive types. In coercive subtyping, the coercion mechanism is directly characterised in the type theory proof-theoretically. Some important meta-theoretic aspects of coercive subtyping such as the results on conservativity, coherence, and transitivity elimination have been studied. They not only justify the adequacy of the theory from the proof-theoretic consideration, but provide the basis for implementation of coercive subtyping. See [1,4, 13,14,20] for details of some of these development and applications of coercive subtyping.

Coercion mechanisms with certain restrictions have been implemented for dependent type theory both in the proof development system Lego [15] and Coq [2], by Bailey [1] and Saïbi [19], respectively. Callaghan of the Computer Assisted Reasoning Group at Durham has implemented Plastic [4], a proof assistant that supports the Logical Framework LF and coercive subtyping with a mixture of simple coercions, parameterised coercions, coercion rules for parameterised inductive types, and dependent coercions.

Remark 1. Incorporating the idea of coercive subtyping to a polymorphic calculus is not straightforward. Coercive subtyping has been developed in dependent type theories with inductive data types, which are rather sophisticated systems. However, most of them (or at least the standard ones) have the property of type uniqueness; that is every well-typed object has a unique type up to computational equality. Compared with the polymorphic calculi such as the HM type system where an object may have more than one type, one may say that dependent type theories are 'simpler'. It is important to bear this in mind when we consider combining coercive subtyping with a polymorphic calculus.

1.2 Modelling Subtyping by Coercions

Various notions of coercion have been studied in the literature, particularly when subtyping systems are considered. In subtyping, we have the subsumption rule, which says that if $a : A$ and $A \leq B$, then $a : B$. This can be modelled by means of coercions (maps from A to B). In [3], this idea was proposed and used to give a coercion-based semantic interpretation of Cardelli and Wegner's system Fun [5]. The idea of coercive subtyping discussed above was influenced by this work.

People have used the term coercion to interpret subtyping simpler settings as well. For example, Mitchell [17,18] considers a system where conceptually a subtype is a subset and thus coercions essentially represent set inclusions. In [6, 12], the term coercion is used to denote a special restricted form of mapping in modelling and explaining subtyping.

Remark 2. Note that, because of the subsumption rule in subtyping, a term obtains more types, while in our setting, a term does not get more types. Rather, in coercive subtyping or the extended HM-system considered in this paper, where there is no subsumption rule, there are more well-typed terms, which are regarded as abbreviations, and typing conflicts are resolved by the insertion of coercions. Furthermore, this is studied in the typing system at the proof-theoretic level.

2 Some Simple Examples

We consider the HM type system extended with coercions. Coercions are regarded as abbreviations; more precisely, if a term is not well-typed in the original HM type system, and after inserting coercions it becomes well-typed, then we regard the term to be well-typed and "abbreviate" the completed term with appropriate coercions inserted.

We shall consider extending the HM type system with two forms of coercions: argument coercions and function coercions. By argument coercions, we mean that the argument of a function is coerced according to the typing requirement; more precisely, the term fa abbreviates $f(ca)$ if $f : \sigma \to \tau$, $a : \sigma_0$, and there is a coercion c from σ_0 to σ. By function coercion, we mean that a term in a function position is coerced into an appropriate function accordingly; more precisely, ka abbreviates $(ck)a$ if $k : \sigma$, $a : \sigma_0$, and there is a coercion from σ to a function type $\sigma_0 \to \tau$.

In the following, we give some simple examples to explain the above basic idea. The first two examples explain argument coercions, while the last example about overloading explains how function coercions work. We assume that the types include integers (Int), floating numbers (Float), booleans (Bool), monads (Tσ, where σ is any type), and a unit type (called Plus).

An Example of Basic Coercions

The simplest example of coercions, as often used in programming languages, is to convert integers to floating point numbers. For example, we can declare

$$\texttt{int2float} : \text{Int} \to \text{Float}$$

as a coercion, either in a context or in a program by using the coercion declaration[1] `cdec int2float` : Int $\to$ Float `in` . Then, assuming 2 : Int and `plusone` : Float $\to$ Float, the term `plusone` 2 is typable and abbreviates its "completion" `plusone` (`int2float` 2), where the coercion `int2float` is inserted. Note that the completion is typable in the original HM system. More formally, we say that the term (or program) `cdec int2float` : Int $\to$ Float `in plusone` 2 has type Float. The function `int2float` here is represented as a constant in the typing system. It could be defined externally (e.g., using system call at runtime).

This coercion is usually handled automatically by programming systems, without a formal explanation. We provide a principled explanation of this in a setting where we can, for example, formally answer coherence questions. Note that we can handle the converse coercion, from floating point numbers to integers using e.g. `floor`, in the same way.

Using Coercions in Monads

Monads are a commonly used vehicle in functional programming to deal with "imperative" features like state, random numbers, partial functions, error handling or input/output. Every Monad consists at least of a unary type constructor (called T here), an injection function (called "return" here) and a lifting function. We refer the reader for example to [22] for a full introduction.

[1] We leave out some type variable annotation; see Sec. 3.2 and 3.3 for more details

Coercions can ease use of monads, by allowing omission of the injection of a value into its "monadified" type (function `return`). T in the types for the examples below can be seen as the error monad. There are two ways to create values of this monadic type: one is a regular, good value ($\texttt{return} : \forall\alpha.\, \alpha \to T\alpha$) and the other is to signal an error or exception ($\texttt{err} : \forall\alpha.\, T\alpha$). We can then define a reciprocal function, from Float to T Float, which captures the division by zero error:

$$\lambda x.\ \texttt{if}\ (\texttt{iszero}\ x)\ \texttt{err}\ (\texttt{return}\ (\texttt{sysdiv}\ 1.0\ x)),$$

where

$$\texttt{if} : \forall\alpha.\texttt{Bool} \to \alpha \to \alpha \to \alpha$$

$$\texttt{iszero} : \text{Float} \to \texttt{Bool}$$

$$\texttt{sysdiv} : \text{Float} \to \text{Float} \to \text{Float}$$

Using the coercion abbreviation mechanism, however, we can leave the `return` implicit by declaring it as a coercion:

$$\begin{array}{l}\texttt{cdec return} : \forall\alpha.\, \alpha \to T\alpha\ \texttt{in} \\ \lambda x.\, \texttt{if}\ (\texttt{iszero}\ x)\ \texttt{err}\ (\texttt{sysdiv}\ 1.0\ x)\end{array}$$

Similar situations occur frequently when a monadic programming style is used, making this a fairly useful abbreviation, both for code clarity and brevity.

Note that, as shown by this example, coercions are not necessarily representing simple inclusion between types (as considered in the setting of subtyping [17]). They are arbitrary functional maps which one wishes to omit, in preference to the abbreviated form. In particular, the intuition that a type that can be coerced into another type can be viewed as set-theoretic inclusion does not apply.

Using Coercions for Overloading

Coercions can be used to represent ad hoc polymorphism, or overloading. For example, assume that we have two functions for addition, one for the integers and the other for the floating point numbers:

$$\texttt{plusi} : \text{Int} \to \text{Int} \to \text{Int}$$

$$\texttt{plusf} : \text{Float} \to \text{Float} \to \text{Float}$$

and we wish to use a single notation `plus` in both cases. This can be done by means of coercions. What we need to do is to consider a (unit) type `Plus` which has element `plus : Plus` and then declare the following two (function) coercions:

$$\texttt{cdec}\ (\lambda x.\texttt{plusi}) : \texttt{Plus} \to (\text{Int} \to \text{Int} \to \text{Int})$$

$$\texttt{cdec}\ (\lambda x.\texttt{plusf}) : \texttt{Plus} \to (\text{Float} \to \text{Float} \to \text{Float})$$

Then, we can use

$$\texttt{plus}\ 1\ 2 \qquad or \qquad \texttt{plus}\ 1.0\ 2.5$$

as intended, as these two terms abbreviate `plusi` 1 2 and `plusf` 1.0 2.5, respectively.

Note that, in this example, the coercions are defined λ-terms rather than just constants. It also shows that coercions are not just the same as a previously defined function. The idea of using unit types for overloading was studied by the second author [14]. See [1] for more applications of this idea.

Remark 3. We considered `Plus` to be a unit type. In fact, there could be multiple elements in `Plus` (i.e. constants of that type), but they are all treated the same.

3 Typing System

3.1 Base Language

Our starting point in this development is an existing programming language, namely a minimal polymorphic programming language with Hindley-Milner type system [8] which we call the **base language**. We assume readers are familiar with the basic ideas. We omit additional elements necessary to make this into a programming language, namely declaration of new types and recursion. This is because we focus on typing, and those features do not affect type checking. They can be added.

The typing judgment in the base language is denoted by

$$\Gamma \vdash_{HM} e : \tau,$$

which can be read as "term e has type τ in context Γ". We are extending the base language with a coercion mechanism, which leads to our system $\vdash$. We shall explain in Section 3.4 how we can recover the HM system from our rules.

3.2 Syntax and Notations

Apart from coercion-specific extensions, we use standard notions of terms, types, type schemes and contexts [8]. The syntactic symbols to be used are as follows.

Type variables
$\alpha, \beta, \gamma, \varrho$

Sets of type variables
$\bar{\alpha}, \bar{\beta}, \bar{\gamma}, \bar{\varrho}$

Types
$\sigma, \tau, \varrho \quad ::= \alpha \mid \sigma \to \sigma$

Type schemes
$\mu \quad ::= \forall \bar{\alpha}.\, \sigma$

(Object language) Variables
x, y, z

Terms
$e, f, g \quad ::= x \mid ee \mid \lambda x.\, e \mid \texttt{let}\ x = e\ \texttt{in}\ e \mid \texttt{cdec}\ c : \forall \bar{\alpha}.\, \sigma \to \sigma\ \texttt{in}\ e$

Contexts
$\Gamma, \Delta \quad ::= \emptyset \mid \Gamma, x : \mu \mid \Gamma, \texttt{cdec}\ c : \forall \bar{\alpha}.\, \sigma \to \tau$

Notations. The following notations will be used in our description of the system.

- FV stands for the set of (object) variables declared in a context: $FV(\emptyset) = \emptyset$, $FV(\Gamma, x : \mu) = FV(\Gamma) \cup \{x\}$ and $FV(\Gamma, \texttt{cdec}\ c : \mu) = FV(\Gamma)$.
- FTV denotes the set of **free type variables** of a context, type, type scheme or term. It is defined as:

$$\begin{array}{llll} FTV(\Gamma, x : \mu) & = FTV(\Gamma) \cup FTV(\mu) & FTV(\emptyset) & = \emptyset \\ FTV(\Gamma, \texttt{cdec}\ c : \mu) & = FTV(\Gamma) \cup FTV(c) \cup FTV(\mu) & & \\ FTV(\sigma \to \tau) & = FTV(\sigma) \cup FTV(\tau) & FTV(\alpha) & = \{\alpha\} \\ FTV(\forall \bar{\alpha}. \sigma) & = FTV(\sigma) \setminus \bar{\alpha} & FTV(x) & = \emptyset \\ FTV(ef) & = FTV(e) \cup FTV(f) & FTV(\lambda x.\, e) & = FTV(e) \\ FTV(\texttt{let}\ x = e\ \texttt{in}\ f) & = FTV(e) \cup FTV(f) & & \\ FTV(\texttt{cdec}\ c : \mu\ \texttt{in}\ e) & = FTV(\mu) \cup FTV(e) \cup FTV(c) & & \end{array}$$

- Let Γ be a context. The coercion-free part of Γ is denoted by $\widehat{\Gamma}$, and defined as $\widehat{\emptyset} = \emptyset$, $\widehat{\Gamma, x : \mu} = \widehat{\Gamma}, x : \mu$ and $\widehat{\Gamma'} = \widehat{\Gamma}$, where Γ' is $\Gamma, \texttt{cdec}\ c : \forall \bar{\alpha}.\ \sigma \to \tau$. Furthermore, we write $\Gamma(x) = \mu$ if $x : \mu$ is an entry of Γ.
- $\forall \emptyset.\, \sigma$ is a special case of $\forall \bar{\alpha}.\, \sigma$, denoting a type scheme with no bound variables. We may omit $\forall \emptyset$ when the context makes it clear we denote a type scheme instead of a type.
- $\sigma \prec_{\bar{\alpha}} \mu$ means that σ is a **generic instance** of μ where all (free) type variables of σ are in $\bar{\alpha}$.

3.3 Judgment Forms and Rules

The rules in fig. 1 define our typing system. The forms of judgments are:

- $\Gamma \vdash^{\bar{\alpha}} e : \tau \Rightarrow e'$. This should be read as "term e has type τ and completion e' in context Γ with free type variables $\bar{\alpha}$. We extend the usual typing judgment for ML-like languages $\Gamma \vdash e : \tau$ by allowing coercion declarations in the context, adding the completion e' and an explicit annotation for the free type variables which may occur in Γ, τ and e.
- Γ $\bar{\alpha}$-**valid**. To capture the notion that a "context Γ is valid with free type variables in $\bar{\alpha}$", we write Γ $\bar{\alpha}$-**valid**. Note that this judgment is useful as we consider coercions in contexts subject to certain restrictions.
- $\Gamma \vdash^{\bar{\alpha}} \sigma \to_c \tau$. This third form of judgment expresses that "coercion c from σ to τ can be derived from context Γ".

We also use the notation $\Gamma \not\vdash_{HM} e : ?$ to express the side condition that e is not typable in the HM system.

Product Types. We can extend the language without affecting the basic results and mechanisms presented. For example some of the examples below will require the use of pairs. We can extend the language to add them to our language in the standard way, using the rules like the following:

$$\textit{PairIn} \quad \frac{\Gamma \vdash^{\bar{\alpha}} e_1 : \tau_1 \Rightarrow e_1' \quad \Gamma \vdash^{\bar{\alpha}} e_2 : \tau_2 \Rightarrow e_2'}{\Gamma \vdash^{\bar{\alpha}} \langle e_1, e_2 \rangle : \tau_1 \times \tau_2 \Rightarrow \langle e_1', e_2' \rangle}$$

CId	$$\dfrac{}{\emptyset\ \bar{\alpha}\textbf{-valid}}$$	
CVar	$$\dfrac{\Gamma\ \bar{\alpha}\textbf{-valid}}{\Gamma, x{:}\mu\ \bar{\alpha}\textbf{-valid}}$$	$x \notin FV(\Gamma)$, $FTV(\mu) \subseteq \bar{\alpha}$
CCoer	$$\dfrac{\Gamma\ \bar{\alpha}\textbf{-valid} \quad \Gamma \vdash^{\bar{\alpha}\cup\bar{\beta}} c_0 : \sigma \to \tau \Rightarrow c}{\Gamma, \mathsf{cdec}\ c : \forall\bar{\beta}.\ \sigma \to \tau\ \bar{\alpha}\textbf{-valid}}$$	$\bar{\alpha} \cap \bar{\beta} = \emptyset$
Id	$$\dfrac{\Gamma\ \bar{\alpha}\textbf{-valid}}{\Gamma \vdash^{\bar{\alpha}} x : \tau \Rightarrow x}$$	$\tau \prec_{\bar{\alpha}} \mu$, $\Gamma(x) = \mu$
Abs	$$\dfrac{\Gamma, x : \forall\emptyset.\sigma \vdash^{\bar{\alpha}} e : \tau \Rightarrow e'}{\Gamma \vdash^{\bar{\alpha}} \lambda x.e : \sigma \to \tau \Rightarrow \lambda x.e'}$$	
App	$$\dfrac{\Gamma \vdash^{\bar{\alpha}} e_1 : \sigma \to \tau \Rightarrow e_1' \quad \Gamma \vdash^{\bar{\alpha}} e_2 : \sigma \Rightarrow e_2'}{\Gamma \vdash^{\bar{\alpha}} e_1 e_2 : \tau \Rightarrow e_1' e_2'}$$	
App$_{ac}$	$$\dfrac{\begin{array}{l}\Gamma \vdash^{\bar{\alpha}} e_1 : \sigma \to \tau \Rightarrow e_1' \quad \Gamma \vdash^{\bar{\alpha}} e_2 : \sigma_0 \Rightarrow e_2' \\ \Gamma \vdash^{\bar{\alpha}} \sigma_0 \to_c \sigma\end{array}}{\Gamma \vdash^{\bar{\alpha}} e_1 e_2 : \tau \Rightarrow e_1'(c e_2')}$$	$\widehat{\Gamma} \not\vdash_{HM} e_1' e_2' : ?$
App$_{fc}$	$$\dfrac{\begin{array}{l}\Gamma \vdash^{\bar{\alpha}} e_1 : \varrho_0 \Rightarrow e_1' \quad \Gamma \vdash^{\bar{\alpha}} e_2 : \sigma \Rightarrow e_2' \\ \Gamma \vdash^{\bar{\alpha}} \varrho_0 \to_c (\sigma \to \tau)\end{array}}{\Gamma \vdash^{\bar{\alpha}} e_1 e_2 : \tau \Rightarrow (c e_1') e_2'}$$	$\widehat{\Gamma} \not\vdash_{HM} e_1' e_2' : ?$
Let	$$\dfrac{\Gamma \vdash^{\bar{\alpha}\cup\bar{\beta}} e_1 : \sigma \Rightarrow e_1' \quad \Gamma, x : \forall\bar{\beta}.\sigma \vdash^{\bar{\alpha}} e_2 : \tau \Rightarrow e_2'}{\Gamma \vdash^{\bar{\alpha}} \mathtt{let}\ x = e_1\ \mathtt{in}\ e_2 : \tau \Rightarrow \mathtt{let}\ x = e_1'\ \mathtt{in}\ e_2'}$$	$\bar{\alpha} \cap \bar{\beta} = \emptyset$
Decl	$$\dfrac{\begin{array}{l}\Gamma \vdash^{\bar{\alpha}\cup\bar{\beta}} c : \sigma \to \tau \Rightarrow c' \\ \Gamma, \mathsf{cdec}\ c' : \forall\bar{\beta}.\ \sigma \to \tau \vdash^{\bar{\alpha}} e : \varrho \Rightarrow e'\end{array}}{\Gamma \vdash^{\bar{\alpha}} \mathsf{cdec}\ c : \forall\bar{\beta}.\sigma \to \tau\ \mathsf{in}\ e : \varrho \Rightarrow e'}$$	$\bar{\alpha} \cap \bar{\beta} = \emptyset$
Lup	$$\dfrac{}{\Gamma, \mathsf{cdec}\ c : \forall\bar{\beta}.\ \sigma_0 \to \tau_0, \Gamma' \vdash^{\bar{\alpha}} \sigma \to_c \tau}$$	$\sigma \to \tau \prec_{\bar{\alpha}} \forall\bar{\beta}.\sigma_0 \to \tau_0$

Fig. 1. Typing Rules

The results and the type checking algorithm can be extended in straight-forward ways.

3.4 Explanations

We give some informal explanations and prove some basic properties of the system presented above.

Completion and Relation to HM. The above system is an extension of the system $\vdash_{HM}$ in the sense that, if we remove rules *App$_{ac}$*, *App$_{fc}$*, *Decl*,

Lup and *CCoer* and the notation of completion, the resulting system is equivalent to Hindley-Milner typing. We say that a program e is **well-typed** if $\emptyset \vdash^{\bar{\alpha}} e : \tau \Rightarrow e'$ for some type τ, completion e', and set of type variables $\bar{\alpha}$.

An addition to the language is **completion**. Informally, we insert all the needed coercion functions in a term e to form its completion e', such that the completed term is typable in the system without the coercion rules App_{ac}, App_{fc} and *CCoer*, i.e. in the base language $\vdash_{HM}$. This is formally captured by lemma 1, which will establish the relationship between our typing judgment $\vdash$ and that of the base language $\vdash_{HM}$. It makes precise why we call e' "completion": because the completion is an expansion of the term e in question, and this completion type checks in the base language.

Definition 1 (Term Expansion). *The notion that a term e_2 expands a term e_1, in symbols $e_1 \leq e_2$, is inductively defined as follows.*

$x \leq x$
$\lambda x.\, e_1 \leq \lambda x.\, e_2$ *if* $e_1 \leq e_2$
$\texttt{let}\ x = e_1\ \texttt{in}\ e_2 \leq \texttt{let}\ x = e_3\ \texttt{in}\ e_4$ *if* $e_1 \leq e_3$ *and* $e_2 \leq e_4$
$e_1 e_2 \leq e_3 e_4$ *if* $e_1 \leq e_3$ *and* $e_2 \leq e_4$
$e_2 e_3 \leq (e_1 e_2) e_3$
$e_1 e_3 \leq e_1 (e_2 e_3)$
$\texttt{cdec}\ c : \forall \bar{\alpha}.\, \sigma \to \tau\ \texttt{in}\ e \leq e$
$e_1 \leq e_3$ *if* $e_1 \leq e_2$ *and* $e_2 \leq e_3$

Lemma 1 (Completion). *If $\Gamma \vdash^{\bar{\alpha}} e : \tau \Rightarrow e'$, then $\Gamma \vdash_{HM} e' : \tau$, and $e \leq e'$.*

Proof Sketch. We prove the following two statements by simultaneous induction on the derivations of $\Gamma \vdash^{\bar{\alpha}} e : \tau \Rightarrow e'$ and Γ $\bar{\alpha}$-**valid**.

- If $\Gamma \vdash^{\bar{\alpha}} e : \tau \Rightarrow e'$, then $\Gamma \vdash_{HM} e' : \tau$ and $e \leq e'$.
- If Γ $\bar{\alpha}$-**valid** and $\Gamma \vdash^{\bar{\alpha}} \sigma \to_c \tau$, then $\Gamma \vdash_{HM} c : \sigma \to \tau$.

Free Type Variables $\bar{\alpha}$. The handling of type variables needs some explanation. The standard notation of typing judgment assumes that the free type variables in Γ can be chosen arbitrarily. On the other hand, we require that all variables must either be bound or chosen from the $\bar{\alpha}$ denoted in the judgment. Formally, the role of the free type variable annotations is captured by the following lemma which has three parts, for each of the judgements.

Lemma 2 (Free type variables).

1. *If $\Gamma \vdash^{\bar{\alpha}} e : \tau \Rightarrow e'$, then $FTV(\Gamma) \subseteq \bar{\alpha}$, $FTV(e) \subseteq \bar{\alpha}$ and $FTV(\tau) \subseteq \bar{\alpha}$.*
2. *If Γ $\bar{\alpha}$-**valid**, then $FTV(\Gamma) \subseteq \bar{\alpha}$.*
3. *If $\Gamma \vdash^{\bar{\alpha}} \sigma \to_c \tau$, then $FTV(\Gamma) \subseteq \bar{\alpha}$, $FTV(\sigma \to \tau) \subseteq \bar{\alpha}$ and $FTV(c) \subseteq \bar{\alpha}$.*

By explicitly denoting all possible free type variables, we no longer require the notion of "generalisation" in the formulation of the *Let* rule, which, in our opinion, clarifies its intention.

Remark 4. Another way of looking at this is that there are no free type variables, but all type variables are bound – some explicitly in type schemes, while all others are bound by the global quantification $\forall\bar{\alpha}$. To our knowledge, this is the first time this reformulation of the *Let* rule is published. It is due to McKinna [16].

In the rule *Abs*, we add x to the context, quantifying over no variables. This means that all type variables in σ are non-generic and cannot be instantiated in the derivation of $e : \tau$. This is in contrast to the *Let* rule which allows generic type variables.

Global and local coercions. Besides assignments of types (more precisely type schemes) to variables, our contexts also contain declarations of (global) coercions, of the form $\texttt{cdec}\ c : \forall\bar{\alpha}.\sigma \to \tau\ \texttt{in}\ e$. The form of coercions is unlimited and can be any expression in the base language, like a constant function between base types or a function between arbitrary types computing the result in a complex way. The coercions declared in a context are well-typed and can be looked up by means of the rule (*Lup*). We have

Lemma 3. *If* $\Gamma \vdash^{\bar{\alpha}} \sigma \to_c \tau$*, then* $\Gamma \vdash^{\bar{\alpha}} c : \sigma \to \tau\ \Rightarrow\ c$.

In fact, we know that any declared coercion is well-typed in the HM system (c.f., Lemma 1).

Besides global coercions, we also allow local coercion declarations in programs, similar to the way `let` works.

Example 1 (Localised Coercions). This example shows the scope of coercion declaration. In $\Delta = \texttt{plusone} : \text{Int} \to \text{Int}, 1 : \text{Int}, 1.0 : \text{Float}, \mathit{plus} : \text{Float} \to \text{Float} \to \text{Float}$, the following program is well-typed.

$$\begin{array}{l}\texttt{plus}\ (\texttt{plusone}\ 1)\\ \qquad (\texttt{cdec}\ \texttt{floor} : \forall\emptyset.\,\text{Float} \to \text{Int}\ \texttt{in}\ \texttt{plusone}\ 1.0)\end{array}$$

However, since the coercion is not available when `plusone` is first used, the following is not typable in Δ:

$$\begin{array}{l}\texttt{plus}\ (\texttt{plusone}\ 1.0)\\ \qquad (\texttt{cdec}\ \texttt{floor} : \forall\emptyset.\,\text{Float} \to \text{Int}\ \texttt{in}\ \texttt{plusone}\ 1.0)\end{array}$$

Rules for argument and function coercions. Let us have a closer look at the special rules App_{ac} and App_{fc} for argument and function coercions, in particular on their side condition. By $\widehat{\Gamma} \not\vdash_{HM} e'_1 e'_2 : ?$ we mean that $e'_1 e'_2$ is not typable in the base language, i.e. there is no type τ such that $\widehat{\Gamma} \vdash_{HM} e'_1 e'_2 : \tau$. We illustrate the necessity of this side condition with an example which shows that otherwise ambiguity arises which would lead to non-unique meaning of certain terms.

Example 2. We assume that A and B are any base types inhabited by the constants $a : A$ and $b_1, b_2 : B$, and we have product types. Using the abbreviations

$$\begin{aligned}&\Gamma{=}\texttt{cdec}\ \lambda\langle x,y\rangle.\,\langle b_1,b_2\rangle : \forall\emptyset.\ A\times A\to B\times B\\ &f{=}\lambda\langle x,y\rangle.\,x\\ &g{=}\lambda\langle x,y\rangle.\,\langle y,x\rangle\end{aligned}$$

we can obviously derive

$$\begin{aligned}&\Gamma\vdash^{\bar\alpha} f : B\times B\to B\ \Rightarrow\ f\\ &\Gamma\vdash^{\bar\alpha} g : A\times A\to A\times A\ \Rightarrow\ g\\ &\Gamma\vdash^{\bar\alpha} g : B\times B\to B\times B\ \Rightarrow\ g\end{aligned}$$

Thus using App_{ac} *without* the side condition $\Gamma \nvdash_{HM} e_1'e_2' : ?$ we could derive the following, where $c = \lambda\langle x,y\rangle.\,\langle b_1,b_2\rangle$:

$$\begin{aligned}&\Gamma\vdash^{\bar\alpha} f(g\langle a,a\rangle) : B\ \Rightarrow\ f(c(g\langle a,a\rangle))\\ &\Gamma\vdash^{\bar\alpha} f(g\langle a,a\rangle) : B\ \Rightarrow\ f(g(c\langle a,a\rangle))\end{aligned}$$

However, $f(c(g\langle a,a\rangle))$ computes to b_1 while $f(g(c\langle a,a\rangle))$ to b_2. This is a very bad situation, since it means that evaluation can no longer be uniquely defined, and thus the term $f(g\langle a,a\rangle)$ no longer has a definite, unique meaning.

The side condition prevents this particular ambiguity, by forbidding the use of App_{ac} and App_{fc} when App can be used. In other words, it gives preference to derivations which does not involve coercions, and a coercion may only be applied if needed since otherwise typing would fail. The side condition is decidable, for example by traditional algorithm $\mathcal{W}$. This side condition does not prevent all forms of ambiguities, however. Section 5 discusses how to deal with them.

The example shows an essential difference to coercive subtyping in Type Theory with its unique and explicit typing, where the type of g would fully determine the type of the coercion function to apply and whether a coercion is needed at all.

The side conditions on rules App_{ac} and App_{fc} have another effect too. In coercive subtyping for Type Theory, the question arises whether identity coercions (i.e. the identity function declared as coercion) are allowed. We do not forbid them, but these side conditions ensure that they will never be used, since an application with an identity coercion can always be typed without it.

Let Expression. One noticeable feature of our typing rules is that there are no coercion-specific rules involving `let`. Corresponding to the rules for application, one might expect to find something like:

$$Let_c\quad \frac{\Gamma\vdash^{\bar\alpha\cup\bar\beta} e_1:\sigma_0\ \Rightarrow\ e_1' \qquad \Gamma, x:\forall\bar\beta.\,\sigma\vdash^{\bar\alpha} e_2:\tau\ \Rightarrow\ e_2' \qquad \Gamma\vdash^{\bar\alpha\cup\bar\beta}\sigma_0\to_c\sigma}{\Gamma\vdash^{\bar\alpha}\texttt{let}\ x=e_1\ \texttt{in}\ e_2:\tau\ \Rightarrow\ \texttt{let}\ x=ce_1'\ \texttt{in}\ e_2'}\quad \bar\alpha\cap\bar\beta=\emptyset$$

With this rule basic soundness conditions still hold, like lemma 1 saying that the completion is well-typed in the base language. Thus it is not obviously wrong to add thus rule. Simple examples show that Let_c is not admissible. Consider (assuming A, B, C and D are any types) $\Gamma = x : A, c : A \to B, \texttt{cdec}\ c : A \to B$. With the new rule we can then derive $\texttt{let}\ y = x\ \texttt{in}\ y : B$, without it we cannot.

Another example shows the complication of the rule Let_c. With $\Gamma = a : A, b : B, c_1 : A \to (C \to D), c_2 : B \to C, \texttt{cdec}\ c_1 : A \to (C \to D), \texttt{cdec}\ c_2 : B \to C$ and assuming the Let_c rule is present, we are able to derive $\Gamma \vdash^{\emptyset} \texttt{let}\ x = a\ \texttt{in}\ xb : D \Rightarrow \texttt{let}\ x = c_1 a\ \texttt{in}\ c_2 b$. Essentially, this amounts to a simultaneous use of functional and argument coercions which is not admissible in our rules.

These examples illustrate that Let_c would allow a more liberal use of coercions. Our intention however is to restrict the situations in which they can occur to allow a formulation of derivational coherence (see section 5). A consequence of a rule like Let_c is that a type checking algorithm (Section 4) would need to search for σ which is not present in the conclusion of the rule; this may cause difficulties.

4 Type Checking Algorithm

The previous section describes our type system which adds coercions to Hindley-Milner type systems. The rules in fig. 1 describe well-typing, but they do not provide a decision procedure to verify well-typedness. This is mainly due to the application rules (App, App_{ac} and App_{fc}), in which the argument type σ cannot be inferred from the typing judgment whose validity is to be verified, and thus there are infinitely many derivation trees to check.

This section provides a different set of rules to resolve this problem (fig. 2).

4.1 Algorithm

In the tradition of algorithm $\mathcal{W}$ [8], the rules in fig. 2 describe typing for most general types. These rules can be read as an algorithm, which we call "algorithm $\mathcal{W}_\mathcal{C}$", to give non-deterministic answers to the question: "Given Γ and e, what are the type and completion of e?". The inputs are context Γ and term e and the outputs substitution S, type τ and completion e'. It is non-deterministic because of the rules $LCdec_1^{\mathcal{W}}$ and $LCdec_2^{\mathcal{W}}$, where multiple coercions c can be found for a given pair of types σ and τ. In Section 5 we will provide a deterministic algorithm together with a characterisation of its modified behaviour.

$\mathcal{W}_\mathcal{C}$ is presented with judgments of the following forms:

- $\Gamma \vdash^{\mathcal{W}} e \rightsquigarrow \langle S, \tau, e' \rangle$, which can be read as "In context Γ, term e type checks to substitution S, type τ and completion e'.
- $\Gamma \rightsquigarrow$ **valid** expresses that "Γ is valid"; in particular, it means that the coercions declared in it are well-typed.
- $\Gamma \vdash_L \sigma \to \tau \rightsquigarrow c$ stands for "in context Γ, the lookup for a coercion from type σ to type τ yields the coercion term c".

$CId^{\mathcal{W}}$
$$\frac{}{\emptyset \rightsquigarrow \textbf{valid}}$$

$CVar^{\mathcal{W}}$
$$\frac{\Gamma \rightsquigarrow \textbf{valid}}{\Gamma, x{:}\mu \rightsquigarrow \textbf{valid}} \quad x \notin FV(\Gamma)$$

$CCoer^{\mathcal{W}}$
$$\frac{\Gamma \rightsquigarrow \textbf{valid} \quad \Gamma \vdash^{\mathcal{W}} c \rightsquigarrow \langle \tau, S, c' \rangle}{\Gamma, \texttt{cdec}\ c : \forall \bar{\beta}.\, \sigma \rightarrow \tau \rightsquigarrow \textbf{valid}}$$

$Id^{\mathcal{W}}$
$$\frac{\Gamma, x : \forall \alpha_1, \ldots, \alpha_n.\, \tau, \Gamma' \rightsquigarrow \textbf{valid}}{\Gamma, x : \forall \alpha_1, \ldots, \alpha_n.\, \tau, \Gamma' \vdash^{\mathcal{W}} x \rightsquigarrow \langle [\beta_i \,/\, \alpha_i]\tau, \emptyset, x \rangle} \quad \beta_i \text{ new}$$

$Abs^{\mathcal{W}}$
$$\frac{\Gamma, x : \forall \emptyset.\, \alpha \vdash^{\mathcal{W}} e \rightsquigarrow \langle \tau, S \circ \{\, \alpha \mapsto \sigma \,\}, e' \rangle}{\Gamma \vdash^{\mathcal{W}} \lambda x.\, e \rightsquigarrow \langle \sigma \rightarrow \tau, S, \lambda x.\, e' \rangle} \quad \alpha \text{ new}$$

$App^{\mathcal{W}}$
$$\frac{\begin{array}{l}\Gamma \vdash^{\mathcal{W}} e_1 \rightsquigarrow \langle S_1, \tau_1, e_1' \rangle \\ S_1\Gamma \vdash^{\mathcal{W}} e_2 \rightsquigarrow \langle S_2, \sigma_2, e_2' \rangle \\ \textit{unify}_{\mathcal{C}}(\Gamma, S_2\tau_1, \tau_2, e_1', e_2') \rightsquigarrow \langle T, e_3' \rangle\end{array}}{\Gamma \vdash^{\mathcal{W}} e_1 e_2 \rightsquigarrow \langle T S_2 \tau_1, T \circ S_2 \circ S_1, e_3' \rangle} \quad \alpha, \beta \text{ new}$$

$Let^{\mathcal{W}}$
$$\frac{\begin{array}{l}\Gamma \vdash^{\mathcal{W}} e_1 \rightsquigarrow \langle \tau_1, S_1, e_1' \rangle \\ S_1\Gamma, x : Gen(\tau_1, S_1\Gamma) \vdash^{\mathcal{W}} e_2 \rightsquigarrow \langle \tau_2, S_2, e_2' \rangle\end{array}}{\begin{array}{l}\Gamma \vdash^{\mathcal{W}} \texttt{let}\ x = e_1\ \texttt{in}\ e_2 \\ \qquad \rightsquigarrow \langle \tau_2, S_2 \circ S_1, \texttt{let}\ x = e_1'\ \texttt{in}\ e_2' \rangle\end{array}}$$

$Decl^{\mathcal{W}}$
$$\frac{\begin{array}{l}\Gamma \vdash^{\mathcal{W}} c \rightsquigarrow \langle \varrho_0, \emptyset, c' \rangle \\ \Gamma, \texttt{cdec}\ c' : \forall \bar{\beta}.\, \sigma \rightarrow \tau \vdash^{\mathcal{W}} e \rightsquigarrow \langle \varrho, S, e' \rangle\end{array}}{\Gamma \vdash^{\mathcal{W}} \texttt{cdec}\ c : \forall \bar{\beta}. \sigma \rightarrow \tau\ \texttt{in}\ e \rightsquigarrow \langle \varrho, S, e' \rangle} \quad \sigma \rightarrow \tau \prec \varrho_0$$

$Unc^{\mathcal{W}}$
$$\frac{\textit{unify}(\beta, \tau) = T}{\textit{unify}_{\mathcal{C}}(\Gamma, \beta \rightarrow \alpha, \tau, e_1, e_2) \rightsquigarrow \langle T, e_1 e_2 \rangle}$$

$Unc^{\mathcal{W}}_{ac}$
$$\frac{\begin{array}{c}\textit{unify}(\beta \rightarrow \tau, \sigma_0 \rightarrow \sigma) = T \\ \Gamma \vdash_L \sigma_0 \rightarrow \sigma \rightsquigarrow c\end{array}}{\textit{unify}_{\mathcal{C}}(\Gamma, \beta \rightarrow \alpha, \tau, e_1, e_2) \rightsquigarrow \langle T, e_1(c e_2) \rangle} \quad \begin{array}{l}\textit{unify}(\beta, \tau) \\ \textit{fails}\end{array}$$

$Unc^{\mathcal{W}}_{fc}$
$$\frac{\begin{array}{c}\textit{unify}(\beta \rightarrow (\tau \rightarrow \tau_1), \sigma_0 \rightarrow \sigma) = T \\ \Gamma \vdash_L \sigma_0 \rightarrow \sigma \rightsquigarrow c\end{array}}{\textit{unify}_{\mathcal{C}}(\Gamma, \beta, \tau, e_1, e_2) \rightsquigarrow \langle T, (c e_1) e_2 \rangle} \quad \begin{array}{l}\textit{unify}(\beta, \tau) \\ \textit{fails}\end{array}$$

$LVar^{\mathcal{W}}$
$$\frac{\Gamma \vdash_L \sigma \rightarrow \tau \rightsquigarrow c}{\Gamma, x : \mu \vdash_L \sigma \rightarrow \tau \rightsquigarrow c}$$

$LCdec^{\mathcal{W}}_1$
$$\frac{\Gamma \vdash_L \sigma \rightarrow \tau \rightsquigarrow c}{\Gamma, \texttt{cdec}\ c_0 : \forall \bar{\beta}.\, \sigma_0 \rightarrow \tau_0 \vdash_L \sigma \rightarrow \tau \rightsquigarrow c}$$

$LCdec^{\mathcal{W}}_2$
$$\frac{}{\Gamma, \texttt{cdec}\ c : \forall \bar{\beta}.\, \sigma \rightarrow \tau \vdash_L \sigma \rightarrow \tau \rightsquigarrow c}$$

Fig. 2. Algorithm $\mathcal{W}_{\mathcal{C}}$

We use the standard notion of first-order unification *unify*. It is easy to see that the traditional algorithm $\mathcal{W}$ can be recovered from the rules in fig. 2 by removing rules $CCoer^{\mathcal{W}}$, $Decl^{\mathcal{W}}$, $Unc^{\mathcal{W}}_{ac}$ and $Unc^{\mathcal{W}}_{fc}$. (In that case $\vdash_{I}$ will not be used either.) Using this observation and soundness and completeness of $\mathcal{W}$, we can see that the condition on c in rule $Decl^{\mathcal{W}}$ is actually the same as in *Decl* in fig. 1.

Note that the side condition of rules App_{ac} and App_{fc} in fig. 1 refers to the separate system of HM typing, while the implementation uses a simple unification test in $Unc^{\mathcal{W}}$ and does not need to refer to a separate type checking algorithm.

4.2 Soundness and Completeness

Algorithm $\mathcal{W}_{\mathcal{C}}$ (fig. 2) is a sound and complete implementation of the typing rules (fig. 1), in the following sense.

Soundness expresses that the computed result type and completion can be derived using the typing rules.

Theorem 1 (Soundness). *Assume that we can derive* $\Gamma \vdash^{\mathcal{W}} e \rightsquigarrow \langle \tau, S, e' \rangle$. *Let* $\bar{\alpha} = FTV(S\Gamma, \tau, e)$. *Then* $S\Gamma \vdash^{\bar{\alpha}} e : \tau \Rightarrow e'$.

Proof Sketch. We can prove this by strengthening it with the additional condition if $\Gamma \rightsquigarrow$ **valid** and $\bar{\alpha} = FTV(\Gamma)$, then Γ $\bar{\alpha}$-**valid**. We then do simultaneous induction on the derivations of $\Gamma \vdash^{\mathcal{W}} e \rightsquigarrow \langle \tau, S, e' \rangle$ and $\Gamma \rightsquigarrow$ **valid**, using much of the structure and lemmas from [7]. Use of $Unc^{\mathcal{W}}$ in $App^{\mathcal{W}}$ by the algorithm corresponds to rule *App*, whereas $Unc^{\mathcal{W}}_{ac}$ and $Unc^{\mathcal{W}}_{fc}$ correspond to App_{ac} and App_{fc}, resp.

Completeness means that for any given completion, every derivable type for a term is an instance of the type computed by the algorithm for the result with this completion.

Theorem 2 (Completeness). *If* $S\Gamma \vdash^{\bar{\alpha}} e : \tau \Rightarrow e'$, *then there are exactly one type* σ *and substitution* T *such that* $\Gamma \vdash^{\mathcal{W}} e \rightsquigarrow \langle \sigma, T, e' \rangle$, *and there is a substitution* U *with* $\tau = U\sigma$ *and* $S\Gamma = UT\Gamma$.

Proof Sketch. The proof uses induction on the derivation of $S\Gamma \vdash^{\bar{\alpha}} e : \tau \Rightarrow e'$. Thus when looking for the right derivations for $\mathcal{W}_{\mathcal{C}}(\Gamma; e)$ to prove the theorem, we already know the completion in the result. This completion resolves possible ambiguities in the choice of rules $Unc^{\mathcal{W}}_{ac}$ or $Unc^{\mathcal{W}}_{fc}$.

5 Resolving Ambiguities

The rules in fig. 2 allow certain ambiguities, that can occur if there is more than one matching coercion during coercion search in $Unc^{\mathcal{W}}$. Assume, for example, that A and B are base types and Γ is $f : \alpha \times \alpha \rightarrow \alpha, a : A,$ `cdec` $c_1 : \forall\emptyset.\ A \rightarrow$

$A \times A$, $\mathsf{cdec}\ c_2 : \forall\emptyset.\ A \to B \times B$. Then we have both $\Gamma \vdash^{\mathcal{W}} fa \leadsto \langle A, \emptyset, f(c_1 a)\rangle$ and $\Gamma \vdash^{\mathcal{W}} fa \leadsto \langle B, \emptyset, f(c_2 a)\rangle$.

Such a situation is not desirable, since it means that the evaluation behaviour is not uniquely defined. This is the **coherence** problem which needs to be addressed for any system of (coercive) subtyping.

We can solve this problem by replacing $unify_C$ in $App^{\mathcal{W}}$ by $unify^1_C$, which succeeds if and only if $unify_C$ returns a unique result:

Definition 2 ($unify^1_C$). *$unify^1_C(\Gamma, \beta, \tau, e) \leadsto \langle T, f\rangle$ if $unify_C(\Gamma, \beta, \tau, e) \leadsto \langle T, f\rangle$ and for all U, g such that $unify^1_C(\Gamma, \beta, \tau, e) \leadsto \langle U, g\rangle$, $U = T$ and $f = g$.*

$unify^1_C$ is effectively decidable since $unify_C$ is decidable and can only return a finite number of results.

We call algorithm $\mathcal{W}^1_C$ the algorithm obtained from $\mathcal{W}_C$ where the $App^{\mathcal{W}}$ case uses $unify^1_C$ instead of $unify_C$, and $\vdash^{\mathcal{W}}_1$ for the corresponding judgment. Algorithm $\mathcal{W}^1_C$ can return at most one result, and is therefore a deterministic algorithm, in contrast to non-deterministic $\mathcal{W}_C$.

These additional side conditions clearly limit the cases in which the algorithm succeeds. This still allows all the examples presented earlier. However the question is how this restricted behaviour can be described in the typing rules. For this, we introduce the notion of "derivational coherence".

Definition 3 (Derivational Coherence). *A term e is **derivationally coherent** over a context Γ if for each subterm f of e and $\Gamma_1 \vdash^{\bar{\alpha}} f : \tau_1 \Rightarrow e'_1$ and $\Gamma_2 \vdash^{\bar{\alpha}} f : \tau_2 \Rightarrow e'_2$ occurring anywhere in any derivation of $\Gamma \vdash^{\bar{\alpha}} e : \tau \Rightarrow e'$ for any τ_1, τ_2, e'_1 and e'_2, the two completions are the same, i.e. $e'_1 = e'_2$.*

Using this notion, we can formulate a soundness and completeness result for $\mathcal{W}^1_C$.

Theorem 3. *For all Γ, e, the following holds. There are τ, S and e' such that $\Gamma \vdash^{\mathcal{W}}_1 e \leadsto \langle \tau, S, e'\rangle$ if and only if e is derivationally coherent over Γ and there are σ, f' and $\bar{\alpha}$ such that $\Gamma \vdash^{\bar{\alpha}} e : \sigma \Rightarrow f'$. In both directions, $e' = f'$ and $\sigma \prec_{\bar{\alpha}} \tau$.*

For the proof we note that the derivation trees for typing derivation and for type checking are isomorphic, and thus we can establish the conditions in which ambiguities occur by an inductive analysis of them, using the previous soundness and completeness results (Theorems 1 and 2).

6 Conclusion

We have presented an extension of the Hindley-Milner polymorphic system with coercions by incorporating the idea from coercive subtyping. The extended typing system can be further enriched with other features such as records whose associated inheritance relation can be represented as coercions. More details of the work, including a prototype implementation of the extended system and the details of the proofs, can be found in the forthcoming thesis of the first author [11].

There are several issues to be further studied. For example, in our rules we have not included "transitivity" as found in general subtyping or coercive subtyping systems. For basic types, adding transitivity of coercions is not a problem; it simply becomes a decidable search problem of the transitive closure of the coercions between basic types, representable as a finite graph [19]. However, when coercions parameterised over type variables are considered, as they are allowed here in general, it is not clear to us that the coercion search with transitivity is decidable.

Coercion rules are another field of further study (e.g., see [14]). The current system would allow to add rules to derive new coercions from the rules already declared, like lifting of coercions over lists. The requirement is that coercion search must be decidable.

As mentioned in the introduction, coercion search for type theory is facilitated considerably by the unique typing property. That is no longer given, however, if metavariables are added. Thus we can look to apply the techniques of this paper to type theory with metavariables.

Coercion mechanisms as discussed in this paper facilitate overloading among other things. Another mechanism for overloading is the class mechanism in Haskell [23,10]. An interesting research topic is to compare these mechanisms formally and consider a possible general framework for abbreviations.

Acknowledgements. We thank Paul Callaghan and James McKinna for discussions and comments on a draft.

References

1. A. Bailey. *The Machine-checked Literate Formalisation of Algebra in Type Theory.* PhD thesis, University of Manchester, 1999.
2. B. Barras et al. *The Coq Proof Assistant Reference Manual (Version 6.3.1).* INRIA-Rocquencourt, 2000.
3. Val Breazu-Tannen, Thierry Coquand, Carl Gunter, and André Ščedrov. Inheritance as implicit coercion. *Information and Computation*, 93:172–221, 1991. Also in the collection [9].
4. P. Callaghan and Z. Luo. An implementation of LF with coercive subtyping and universes. *Journal of Automated Reasoning*, 27(1):3–27, 2001.
5. Luca Cardelli and Peter Wegner. On understanding types, data abstraction and polymorphism. *Computing Surveys*, 17(4):471–522, 1985.
6. G. Chen. *Subtyping, Type Conversion and Transitivity Elimination.* PhD thesis, University of Paris VII, 1998.
7. Luis Damas. *Type Assignment in Programming Languages.* PhD thesis, Laboratory for Foundations of Computer Science, University of Edinburgh, 1985. CST-33-85.
8. Luis Damas and Robin Milner. Principal type-schemes for functional programming languages. In *Ninth Annual Symposium on Principles of Programming Languages (POPL) (Albuquerque, NM)*, pages 207–212. ACM, January 1982.

9. Carl A. Gunter and John C. Mitchell. *Theoretical Aspects of Object-Oriented Programming, Types, Semantics, and Language Design.* Foundations of Computing Series. MIT Press, 1994.
10. Simon Peyton Jones, Mark Jones, and Erik Meijer. Type classes: an exploration of the design space, 1997.
11. Robert Kießling. Coercions in Hindley-Milner systems. forthcoming thesis, 2004.
12. Giuseppe Longo, Kathleen Milsted, and Sergei Soloviev. Coherence and transitivity of subtyping as entailment. *Journal of Logic and Computation*, 10(4):493–526, August 2000.
13. Y. Luo and Z. Luo. Coherence and transitivity in coercive subtyping. *Proc. of the 8th Inter. Conf. on Logic for Programming, Artificial Intelligence and Reasoning (LPAR'01), Havana, Cuba. LNAI 2250*, 2001.
14. Z. Luo. Coercive subtyping. *Journal of Logic and Computation*, 9(1):105–130, 1999.
15. Z. Luo and R. Pollack. LEGO Proof Development System: User's Manual. LFCS Report ECS-LFCS-92-211, Department of Computer Science, University of Edinburgh, 1992.
16. James McKinna. personal communication, 2001.
17. John C. Mitchell. Coercion and type inference. In *Tenth Annual Symposium on Principles of Programming Languages (POPL) (Austin, TX)*, pages 175–185. ACM, January 1983.
18. John C. Mitchell. Type inference with simple subtypes. *Journal of Functional Programming*, 1(2):245–286, July 1991.
19. A. Saïbi. Typing algorithm in type theory with inheritance. *Proc of POPL'97*, 1997.
20. S. Soloviev and Z. Luo. Coercion completion and conservativity in coercive subtyping. *Annals of Pure and Applied Logic*, 113(1-3):297–322, 2002.
21. Simon Thompson. *Type Theory and Functional Programming.* International Computer Science Series. Addison-Wesley, 1991.
22. Philip Wadler. Monads for functional programming. In J. Jeuring and E. Meijer, editors, *Advanced Functional Programming*, volume 925 of *Lecture Notes in Computer Science*, pages 24–52. Springer-Verlag, 1995.
23. Philip Wadler and Stephen Blott. How to make *ad-hoc* polymorhism less *ad-hoc*. In *Proceedings of POPL '89*, pages 60–76. ACM, January 1989.

Combining Incoherent Coercions for Σ-Types

Yong Luo and Zhaohui Luo

Department of Computer Science, University of Durham

Abstract. Coherence is a vital requirement for the correct use of coercive subtyping for abbreviation and other applications. However, some coercions are incoherent, although very useful. A typical example of such is the subtyping rules for Σ-types: the component-wise rules and the rule of the first projection. Both of these groups of rules are often used in practice (and coherent themselves), but they are incoherent when put together directly. In this paper, we study this case for Σ-types by introducing a new subtyping relation and the resulting system enjoys the properties of coherence and admissibility of substitution and transitivity.

1 Introduction

Coercive subtyping for dependent type theories, as studied in [16,17] and implemented in proof assistants such as Lego [19], Coq [3] and Plastic [7], is a powerful abbreviation mechanism and has been used in applications of proof development (*e.g.* [2]). An important requirement of coercion mechanism is that of coherence, that is, coercions between any two types must be computationally equal. This requirement is essential for the consistent use and correct implementation of the mechanism.

A coherence problem. Some coercions cannot be put together directly in a coherent way, although very useful. A typical example of such coercions is those concerning Σ-types (types of dependent pairs). There are at least two sets of natural and useful coercion rules: the component-wise subtyping rules and the rule of the first projection. They are coherent separately (see [13] for the coherence of the former and [2] for the use of the latter), but incoherent when put together directly (see the counter example in section 3 for details). This prevents them from being used together.

Our solution to this coherence problem is basically, in this paper, by introducing a new subtyping relation and giving a new formulation of coercive subtyping, to ensure that there is only one coercion (with respect to computational equality) between any two types (if there is one).

Transitivity. This new formulation not only satisfies coherence requirements but also enjoys other properties, particularly, the admissibility of substitution and transitivity because such properties are important for an implementation of coercive subtyping. Through our investigation, we found out that the property of admissibility of transitivity is actually very hard to come by. In this paper,

S. Berardi, M. Coppo, and F. Damiani (Eds.): TYPES 2003, LNCS 3085, pp. 276–292, 2004.

we shall consider two subtyping relations simultaneously, give new transitivity rules and prove that all of them are admissible.

In section 2, we shall give an overview of coercive subtyping and introduce some concepts such as Well-Defined Coercions and notations to be used later in the paper. In section 3, the coherence problem and its solution will be intuitively explained through a counter example. In section 4, there is a formal presentation of the solution. A new definition of coherence, new rules of substitution and transitivity are also given. Some important properties, coherence and the admissibility of substitution and transitivity, are proved. Discussions are in the last section, where we discuss issues such as decidability and wider applications of the methods developed in this paper.

2 Coercive Subtyping and Well-Defined Coercions

In this section, we give an overview of coercive subtyping, introduce some notations and the concept of well-defined coercions that will be used later in the paper.

2.1 Coercive Subtyping

The basic idea of coercive subtyping, as studied in [17], is that A is a subtype of B if there is a (unique) coercion c from A to B, and therefore, any object of type A may be regarded as object of type B via c, where c is a functional operation from A to B in the type theory.

A coercion plays the role of abbreviation. More precisely, if c is a coercion from K_0 to K, then a functional operation f with domain K can be applied to any object k_0 of K_0 and the application $f(k_0)$ is definitionally equal to $f(c(k_0))$. Intuitively, we can view f as a context which requires an object of K; then the argument k_0 in the context f stands for its image of the coercion, $c(k_0)$. Therefore, one can use $f(k_0)$ as an abbreviation of $f(c(k_0))$.

The above simple idea, when formulated in the logical framework, becomes very powerful. The second author and his colleagues have developed the framework of coercive subtyping that covers variety of subtyping relations including those represented by parameterised coercions and coercions between parameterised inductive types. See [17,2,7,18,8] for details of some of these development and applications of coercive subtyping.

Some important meta-theoretic aspects of coercive subtyping have been studied. In particular, the results on conservativity and on transitivity elimination for subkinding have been proved in [11,21]. The main result of [21] is essentially that coherence of basic subtyping rules does imply conservativity. These results not only justify the adequacy of the theory from the proof-theoretic consideration, but also provide the proof-theoretic basis for implementation of coercive subtyping.

How to prove coherence and admissibility of transitivity at the type level has been studied in [13] recently. In particular, the concept of *Well-defined coercions* has been developed, and the suitable subtyping rules for Π-types and Σ-types have been given as examples to demonstrate these proof techniques.

Coercive subtyping is formally formulated as an extension of (type theories specified in) the logical framework LF[1], whose rules are given in [15]. Types in LF are called kinds. The kind *Type* represents the conceptual universe of types and a kind of form $(x:K)K'$ represents the dependent product with functional operations f as objects (*e.g.*, abstraction $[x:K]k'$) which can be applied to objects of kind K to form application $f(k)$. For every type (an object of kind *Type*), $El(A)$ is the kind of objects of A. LF can be used to specify type theories, such as Martin-Löf's type theory [20] and UTT [15].

As presented in [17], a system with coercive subtyping is an extension of any type theory specified in LF by a set of basic subtyping rules $\mathcal{R}$ whose conclusions are subtyping judgements of the form $\Gamma \vdash A <_c B : Type$. And the subtyping rules in $\mathcal{R}$ are supposed to be coherent.

Notation. We shall use the following notations:

- We sometimes use $M[x]$ to indicate that variable x may occur free in M.
- Context equality: for $\Gamma \equiv x_1 : K_1, ..., x_n : K_n$ and $\Gamma' \equiv x_1 : K_1', ..., x_n : K_n'$, we shall write $\vdash \Gamma = \Gamma'$ for the sequence of judgements $\vdash K_1 = K_1'$, ..., $x_1 : K_1, ..., x_{n-1} : K_{n-1} \vdash K_n = K_n'$.
- Types of non-dependent pairs: if A and B are types, we sometimes write $A \times B$ for $\Sigma(A, [x:A]B)$ where x is not free in B.

2.2 Well-Defined Coercions

Recently, a new concept of Well-defined Coercions (WDC) has been developed in [13]. Suppose there is a set of coercions, which is coherent and have admissibility properties, we prove that, after adding new subtyping rules, the extended system still keeps the coherence and admissibility properties.

Definition 1. (Well-defined coercions) *If $\mathcal{C}$ is a set of subtyping judgements of the form $\Gamma \vdash M <_d M' : Type$ which satisfies the following conditions, we say that $\mathcal{C}$ is a* well-defined set of judgements for coercions, *or briefly called* Well-defined Coercions (WDC)*.*

1. *(Coherence)*
   a) *$\Gamma \vdash A <_c B : Type \in \mathcal{C}$ implies $\Gamma \vdash A : Type$, $\Gamma \vdash B : Type$ and $\Gamma \vdash c : (A)B$.*
   b) *$\Gamma \vdash A <_c A : Type \notin \mathcal{C}$ for any Γ, A, and c.*
   c) *$\Gamma \vdash A <_{c_1} B : Type \in \mathcal{C}$ and $\Gamma \vdash A <_{c_2} B : Type \in \mathcal{C}$ imply $\Gamma \vdash c_1 = c_2 : (A)B$.*
2. *(Congruence) $\Gamma \vdash A <_c B : Type \in \mathcal{C}$, $\Gamma \vdash A = A' : Type$, $\Gamma \vdash B = B' : Type$ and $\Gamma \vdash c = c' : (A)B$ imply $\Gamma \vdash A' <_{c'} B' \in \mathcal{C}$.*
3. *(Transitivity) $\Gamma \vdash A <_{c_1} B : Type \in \mathcal{C}$ and $\Gamma \vdash B <_{c_2} A' : Type \in \mathcal{C}$ imply $\Gamma \vdash A <_{c_2 \circ c_1} A' : Type \in \mathcal{C}$.*

[1] The LF here is different from the Edinburgh Logical Framework [10].

4. *(Substitution)* $\Gamma, x : K, \Gamma' \vdash A <_c B : Type \in \mathcal{C}$ *implies for any* k *such that* $\Gamma \vdash k : K$, $\Gamma, [k/x]\Gamma' \vdash [k/x]A <_{[k/x]c} [k/x]B : Type \in \mathcal{C}$.
5. *(Weakening)* $\Gamma \vdash A <_c B : Type \in \mathcal{C}$, $\Gamma \subseteq \Gamma'$ *and* Γ' *is valid imply* $\Gamma' \vdash A <_c B : Type \in \mathcal{C}$.

In this paper, the set $\mathcal{R}$ of basic coercion rules includes the following rule, where $\mathcal{C}$ is a WDC:

$$(WDCrule) \qquad \frac{\Gamma \vdash A <_c B : Type \in \mathcal{C}}{\Gamma \vdash A <_c B : Type}$$

3 The Basic Subtyping Rules and the Coherence Problem

In this section, we give an example to illustrate the coherence problem of the component-wise subtyping rules for Σ-types and the subtyping rule of its first projection and explain informally the solution through a counter example.

Subtyping rules for Σ-types. As studied in [13], there are three component-wise subtyping rules for Σ-types. One of these rules is the following.

$$(First\,Component\,rule) \quad \frac{\Gamma \vdash A <_c A' : Type \;\; \Gamma \vdash B : (A')Type}{\Gamma \vdash \Sigma(A, B \circ c) <_{d_1} \Sigma(A', B) : Type}$$

where $d_1 = [z : \Sigma(A, B \circ c)]pair(A', B, c(\pi_1(A, B \circ c, z)), \pi_2(A, B \circ c, z))$, which basically means that, for example, $A \times B$ is a subtype of $A' \times B$ if A , A' and B are types and A is a subtype of A'.

The coercion of the first projection is very useful; for example, it is used significantly in Bailey's PhD thesis [2] for formalisation of mathematics. Formally, the subtyping rule is the following:

$$(\pi_1 rule) \qquad \frac{\Gamma \vdash A : Type \;\; \Gamma \vdash B : (A)Type}{\Gamma \vdash \Sigma(A, B) <_{\pi_1(A,B)} A : Type}$$

With this coercion, it is very easy to express some mathematical properties. For example, the type of collection of groups is a subtype of the type of semi-groups (*i.e.* a group is also a semi-group). Any functional operator with the domain of semi-groups can be applied to any group with a coercion.

A counter example. If the subtyping rule $(\pi_1 rule)$ and the component-wise subtyping rules for Σ-types are combined together, we would have the following two derivations.

The first derivation is

$$\frac{\dfrac{\Gamma \vdash A : Type \; \Gamma \vdash B : (A)Type}{\Gamma \vdash \Sigma(A, B) : Type} \qquad \dfrac{\Gamma \vdash B : (A)Type}{\Gamma \vdash B \circ \pi_1(A, B) : (\Sigma(A, B))Type}}{\Gamma \vdash \Sigma(\Sigma(A, B), B \circ \pi_1(A, B)) <_{d_1} \Sigma(A, B) : Type}$$

and the rule $(\pi_1 rule)$ is used in the last step.

The second derivation is

$$\dfrac{(\pi_1 rule)\dfrac{\Gamma \vdash A : Type \;\; \Gamma \vdash B : (A)Type}{\Gamma \vdash \Sigma(A,B) <_{\pi_1(A,B)} A : Type} \quad \Gamma \vdash B : (A)Type}{\Gamma \vdash \Sigma(\Sigma(A,B), B \circ \pi_1(A,B)) <_{d_2} \Sigma(A,B) : Type}$$

and the rule ($\pi_1 rule$) is used in the first step and the First Component rule is used in the last step.

There are two coercions d_1 and d_2 from type $\Sigma(\Sigma(A,B), B \circ \pi_1(A,B))$ to type $\Sigma(A,B)$[2] and we have the following equations

$$d_1(pair(pair(a,b_1),b_2)) = pair(a,b_1)$$
$$d_2(pair(pair(a,b_1),b_2)) = pair(a,b_2)$$

We can see that d_1 and d_2 are neither computationally nor extensionally equal. Hence, the vital requirement of coercive subtyping system, coherence, fails.

Informal explanation of our solution. From the above counter example, we see that the existence of the two derivations makes the system incoherent. To make it coherent, a natural way is to block one of the derivations. The first one cannot be blocked, otherwise we lose the meaning that the first projection (π_1) is regarded as coercion. And hence we can only block the second derivation. More precisely, we must not allow $\Gamma \vdash A <_c A' : Type$ is used as the first promise of the component-wise subtyping rules if it is (directly) derived from $\pi_1 rule$. In other words, a condition of the component-wise subtyping rules is that the first promise is not (directly) derived from $\pi_1 rule$. There are several attempts to satisfy this condition, one of which is to consider a notion of size as a side-condition because A is a sub-term of $\Sigma(A,B)$ in the conclusion of $\pi_1 rule$, and their sizes are intuitively different. However, the well-definedness of size is problematic when we present the whole subtyping system (see discussion section for more details).

In this paper, rather than thinking of any side-conditions, we introduce a new subtyping relation ($\prec$) to represent coercion π_1. This new subtyping relation will never appear in the first premises of the component-wise subtyping rules and hence the unwanted derivations such as the second one in the counter example are blocked.

To make the subtyping system coherent is one thing; to make it also enjoy the property of admissibility of transitivity is another. During our investigation, we experienced that some formulations satisfy the property of coherence, but not the admissibility of transitivity. The formulation in the next section will enjoy all these properties.

---

[2] There are two different coercions from $(A \times B) \times B$ to $A \times B$ if A and B are types.

4 A Formal Presentation

In this section, we shall give a formal presentation of a new subtyping relation and related subtyping rules. The coherence and admissibility of substitution and transitivity will also be proved.

4.1 A New Subtyping Relation

We have seen the problem with the combination of the component-wise subtyping rules and the subtyping rule of the first projection. Now, we introduce a new relation to solve this problem and, consider a new system $T[\mathcal{R}\pi_1]$, which is an extension of coercive subtyping with the judgement form:

- $\Gamma \vdash A \prec_c B : Type$ asserts that type A is a subtype of type B with c.

As we will see later, subtyping relation $<$ and $\prec$ are different. $\prec$ represents the idea that π_1 is regarded as a coercion, but $<$ doesn't.

The coercive definition rules. The main idea of coercive subtyping can informally be represented by the following coercive definition rule (contexts are omitted):

$$\frac{K <_c K' \quad k : K \quad f : (x : K')K''}{f(k) = f(c(k)) : [c(k)/x]K''}$$

The same idea is for the new subtyping relation. A new basic subkinding rule for $\prec$ is the following:

$$\frac{A \prec_c B : Type}{El(A) <_c El(B)}$$

By the coercive definition rule, we have the following derivable rule:

$$\frac{A \prec_c B : Type \quad k : El(A) \quad f : (x : El(B))K}{f(k) = f(c(k)) : [c(k)/x]K}$$

which says that if $A \prec_c B$, any functional operator f with domain B can be applied to any object x of A and, $f(x) = f(c(x))$.

We present the new subtyping system in two stages: first an intermediate system $T[\mathcal{R}\pi_1]_0$ and the definition of coherence, and then the system $T[\mathcal{R}\pi_1]$.

4.2 The System $T[\mathcal{R}\pi_1]_0$ and $T[\mathcal{R}\pi_1]$

Formally, $T[\mathcal{R}\pi_1]_0$ is an extension of type theory T (only) with the following rules:

- A set $\mathcal{R}$ of basic subtyping rules whose conclusions are subtyping judgements of the form $\Gamma \vdash A <_c B : Type$.

- The following congruence rule for subtyping judgements

$$(Cong)\quad \frac{\Gamma \vdash A <_c B : Type \quad \Gamma \vdash A = A' : Type \; \Gamma \vdash B = B' : Type \; \Gamma \vdash c = c' : (A)B}{\Gamma \vdash A' <_{c'} B' : Type}$$

- The new subtyping rules for the first projection in Figure 1, whose conclusions are of the form $\Gamma \vdash A \prec_c B : Type$.

Notation: we shall use $\Gamma \vdash A \propto_c B : Type$ to represent $\Gamma \vdash A <_c B : Type$ or $\Gamma \vdash A \prec_c B : Type$. For example, $\frac{\Gamma \vdash A \propto_c B : Type}{J}$ actually represents two rules $\frac{\Gamma \vdash A <_c B : Type}{J}$ and $\frac{\Gamma \vdash A \prec_c B : Type}{J}$; $\frac{\Gamma \vdash A \propto_c B : Type \quad \Gamma' \vdash A' \propto_{c'} B' : Type}{J}$ actually represents four rules. We shall also say that A is a subtype of B or there is a coercion c from A to B if $\Gamma \vdash A \propto_c B : Type$.

New subtyping rule for the first projection:

$$\frac{\Gamma \vdash A : Type \quad \Gamma \vdash B : (A)Type}{\Gamma \vdash \Sigma(A, B) \prec_{\pi_1(A,B)} A : Type}$$

$$\frac{\Gamma \vdash A \propto_c A' : Type \quad \Gamma \vdash B : (A)Type}{\Gamma \vdash \Sigma(A, B) \prec_{c \circ \pi_1(A,B)} A' : Type}$$

New congruence rule:

$$\frac{\Gamma \vdash A \prec_c B : Type \quad \Gamma \vdash A = A' : Type \; \Gamma \vdash B = B' : Type \; \Gamma \vdash c = c' : (A)B}{\Gamma \vdash A' \prec_{c'} B' : Type}$$

Fig. 1. New subtyping rules for the first projection

Remark 1. We have the following remarks.

- The basic understanding of the new subtyping rules for the first projection is that $\Sigma(A, B)$ is a subtype of A' if $A = A'$ or A is a subtype of A'.
- New substitution and transitivity rules for subtyping relations $<$ and $\prec$ will be given later and, we will prove that all of them are admissible. We do not include them in $T[\mathcal{R}\pi_1]_0$.

New subtyping rules for parameterised inductive types. Now, we give the component-wise subtyping rules for Σ-types and the rules for Π-types in Figure 2 and 3 to demonstrate what the subtyping rules should be for the new subtyping relation.

First Component rule:

$$\frac{\Gamma \vdash A <_c A' : Type \quad \Gamma \vdash B : (A')Type}{\Gamma \vdash \Sigma(A, B \circ c) <_{d_1} \Sigma(A', B) : Type}$$

where $d_1 = [z : \Sigma(A, B \circ c)]pair(A', B, c(\pi_1(A, B \circ c, z)), \pi_2(A, B \circ c, z))$

Second Component rule:

$$\frac{\Gamma \vdash B : (A)Type \quad \Gamma \vdash B' : (A)Type \quad \Gamma, x : A \vdash B(x) \propto_{e[x]} B'(x) : Type}{\Gamma \vdash \Sigma(A, B) <_{d_2} \Sigma(A, B') : Type}$$

where $d_2 = [z : \Sigma(A, B)]pair(A, B', \pi_1(A, B, z), e[\pi_1(A, B, z)](\pi_2(A, B, z)))$

First-Second Component rule:

$$\frac{\begin{array}{c}\Gamma \vdash A <_c A' : Type \quad \Gamma \vdash B : (A)Type \quad \Gamma \vdash B' : (A')Type \\ \Gamma, x : A \vdash B(x) \propto_{e[x]} B'(c(x)) : Type\end{array}}{\Gamma \vdash \Sigma(A, B) <_{d_3} \Sigma(A', B') : Type}$$

where $d_3 = [z : \Sigma(A, B)]pair(A', B', c(\pi_1(A, B, z)), e[\pi_1(A, B, z)](\pi_2(A, B, z)))$

Fig. 2. New component-wise subtyping rules for Σ-types

Domain rule:

$$\frac{\Gamma \vdash A' \propto_c A : Type \quad \Gamma \vdash B : (A)Type}{\Gamma \vdash \Pi(A, B) <_{d_1} \Pi(A', B \circ c) : Type}$$

where $d_1 = [f : \Pi(A, B)]\lambda(A', B \circ c, app(A, B, f) \circ c)$

Codomain rule:

$$\frac{\Gamma \vdash B : (A)Type \quad \Gamma \vdash B' : (A)Type \quad \Gamma, x : A \vdash B(x) \propto_{e[x]} B'(x) : Type}{\Gamma \vdash \Pi(A, B) <_{d_2} \Pi(A, B') : Type}$$

where $d_2 = [f : \Pi(A, B)]\lambda(A, B', [x : A]e[x](app(A, B, f, x)))$

Domain-Codomain rule:

$$\frac{\begin{array}{c}\Gamma \vdash A' \propto_c A : Type \quad \Gamma \vdash B : (A)Type \quad \Gamma \vdash B' : (A')Type \\ \Gamma, x' : A' \vdash B(c(x')) \propto_{e[x']} B'(x') : Type\end{array}}{\Gamma \vdash \Pi(A, B) <_{d_3} \Pi(A', B') : Type}$$

where $d_3 = [f : \Pi(A, B)]\lambda(A', B', [x' : A']e[x'](app(A, B, f, c(x'))))$

Fig. 3. New subtyping rules for Π-types

Remark 2. We have the following remarks.

- In Figure 2 and 3, the conclusions of the rules are always of the form $\Gamma \vdash A <_c B : Type$, no matter the premises are of the form $\Gamma \vdash A <_c B : Type$ or $\Gamma \vdash A \prec_c B : Type$.
- The essence of the new subtyping relation is that, the judgement form $\Gamma \vdash A \prec_c B : Type$ is never used in the premises of the first component of the component-wise subtyping rules in Figure 2. And hence the second derivation of the counter example in section 3 is blocked.
- The basic understanding of the new subtyping rules for Π-types is that $\Pi(A, B)$ is a subtype of $\Pi(A', B')$ if A' is a subtype of A and B is a sub-family of B' (we omit other cases such as: $\Pi(A, B)$ is a subtype of $\Pi(A, B')$ if B is a sub-family of B').
- For the new component-wise subtyping rules for Σ-types, because of the incoherence when π_1 is also regarded as a coercion, we need to have a stricter understanding, that is, $\Sigma(A, B)$ is a subtype of $\Sigma(A', B')$ if A is a subtype of A' and B is a sub-family of B' and the sizes of A and A' are the same ($size$ is defined in the definition 4). In the following section, we will prove that the sizes of A and B are the same if $\Gamma \vdash A <_c B : Type$ and, the size of A is bigger than the size of B if $\Gamma \vdash A \prec_c B : Type$.

The subtyping system we presented here covers all the coercions derived from the component-wise subtyping rules and the subtyping rule for the first projection when they are used separately. Actually, it has more coercions. For example, if A, B and C are different types, we can have a coercion from $A \times (B \times C)$ to $A \times B$ because there is a coercion from $B \times C$ to B. But we can never derive a coercion from $A \times (B \times C)$ to $A \times B$ by the component-wise subtyping rules or the subtyping rule for the first projection separately. What we have excluded are those coercions that need component-wise subtyping rules for Σ-types but the sizes of their first components are different. For example, we don't have a coercion from $(A \times B) \times C$ to $A \times C$ because the sizes of $A \times B$ and A are different although there is a coercion from $A \times B$ to A.

In $T[\mathcal{R}\pi_1]_0$, the subtyping judgements do not contribute to any derivation of a judgement of any other forms in the original type theory T. Therefore, we have the following lemma.

Lemma 1. *$T[\mathcal{R}\pi_1]_0$ is a conservative extension of T.*

Remark 3. As the two subtyping relations $<$ and $\prec$ do contribute to each other, $T[\mathcal{R}\pi_1]_0$ is not a conservative extension of $T[\mathcal{R}]_0$ whose subtyping judgements are only of the form $\Gamma \vdash A <_c B : Type$ (see [17] for details).

Now, we define the most basic requirement for the new subtyping relation in the following.

Definition 2. (Coherence condition of $T[\mathcal{R}\pi_1]_0$) *We say that $T[\mathcal{R}\pi_1]_0$ is coherent if it has the following properties.*

1. $\Gamma \vdash A \propto_c B : Type$ *implies* $\Gamma \vdash A : Type$, $\Gamma \vdash B : Type$, *and* $\Gamma \vdash c : (A)B$.
2. $\Gamma \vdash A \propto_c B : Type$ *implies* $\Gamma \not\vdash A = B : Type$.
3. $\Gamma \vdash A <_c B : Type$ *and* $\Gamma \vdash A <_{c'} B : Type$ *imply* $\Gamma \vdash c = c' : (A)B$.
4. $\Gamma \vdash A \prec_c B : Type$ *and* $\Gamma \vdash A \prec_{c'} B : Type$ *imply* $\Gamma \vdash c = c' : (A)B$.
5. *(Disjointness)* $\Gamma \vdash A <_c B : Type$ *implies* $\Gamma \not\vdash A \prec_{c'} B : Type$ *for any* c', *and vice versa,* $\Gamma \vdash A \prec_c B : Type$ *implies* $\Gamma \not\vdash A <_{c'} B : Type$ *for any* c'.

Remark 4. One may consider a more general coherence condition like, if $\Gamma \vdash A \propto_c B : Type$ and $\Gamma \vdash A \propto_{c'} B : Type$ then $\Gamma \vdash c = c' : (A)B$. This will include the case which both $\Gamma \vdash A <_c B : Type$ and $\Gamma \vdash A \prec_c B : Type$ may happen. However, one of the reasons we need the new subtyping relation ($\prec$) is deliberately to make sure that $\Gamma \vdash A <_c B : Type$ and $\Gamma \vdash A \prec_c B : Type$ may never hold at the same time for any A and B. Disjointness is regarded as a part of coherence condition.

The system $T[\mathcal{R}\pi_1]$. The system $T[\mathcal{R}\pi_1]$ is an extension of $T[\mathcal{R}\pi_1]_0$ with the inference rules in Appendix. Comparing with the original subkinding rules in [17], a new rule is added.

$$(\textit{New Basic Subkinding Rule}) \qquad \frac{\Gamma \vdash A \prec_c B : Type}{\Gamma \vdash El(A) <_c El(B)}$$

There is only one subkinding judgement form $\Gamma \vdash K <_c K'$, although there are two subtyping judgement forms $\Gamma \vdash A <_c B : Type$ and $\Gamma \vdash A \prec_c B : Type$. At the kind level, we are more concerned with the existence of a coercion no matter it is derived from which form at the type level.

Remark 5. The main result of [21] is essentially that coherence of subtyping rules does imply conservativity. In the next section, we shall also prove the coherence of $T[\mathcal{R}\pi_1]_0$. So, $T[\mathcal{R}\pi_1]$ is also expected to be a conservative extension of T.

4.3 Coherence of $T[\mathcal{R}\pi_1]_0$

Now, we prove the coherence of $T[\mathcal{R}\pi_1]_0$, which essentially says that coercions between any two types must be unique. In this paper, the set $\mathcal{R}$ of basic subtyping consists of the rule ($WDCrule$) and the new subtyping rules for Σ-types and Π-types (in Figure 2 and 3) and, the system $T[\mathcal{R}\pi_1]_0$ also includes the congruence rule (*Cong*) and the new subtyping rules in Figure 1. Furthermore, we assume that for any judgement $\Gamma \vdash A <_c B : Type \in \mathcal{C}$, neither A nor B is computationally equal to a Σ-type or Π-type. We also assume that the original type theory T has good properties, in particular the properties of Church-Rosser and Strong Normalisation and the property of context replacement by equal kinds.

We give a definition of $size(A)$ that only counts how many times that π_1 can be applied for an object of type A. In order to define $size$, we define $presize$ first.

Definition 3. ***(presize)*** *Let $\Gamma \vdash M : Type$ be a derivable judgement in $T[\mathcal{R}\pi_1]_0$ and M a normal form (*i.e. *$M \equiv nf(M)$),*

1. *if M is not a Σ-type then $presize(M) =_{df} 0$,*
2. *if $M \equiv \Sigma(A, B)$ then $presize(M) =_{df} presize(A) + 1$.*

Remark 6. For the second case, because M is a normal form, so is A. Therefore *presize* is well-defined.

Definition 4. ***(size)*** *The definition of size in $T[\mathcal{R}\pi_1]_0$: Let $\Gamma \vdash M : Type$ be a derivable judgement in $T[\mathcal{R}\pi_1]_0$, $size(M) =_{df} presize(nf(M))$.*

Remark 7. $T[\mathcal{R}\pi_1]_0$ is a conservative extension of T and every well-typed term in T has its unique normal form. So, the value of $size(M)$ is unique and *size* is well-defined.

Lemma 2. *In $T[\mathcal{R}\pi_1]_0$, if $\Gamma \vdash M_1 = M_2 : Type$ then $size(M_1) = size(M_2)$.*

Proof. $T[\mathcal{R}\pi_1]_0$ is a conservative extension of T and T has properties of Church-Rosser and strong normalisation, *i.e.* $nf(M_1) \equiv nf(M_2)$.

Lemma 3. *Let $\Gamma \vdash M : Type$ be a derivable judgement in $T[\mathcal{R}\pi_1]_0$.*

- *if M is not computationally equal to a Σ-type then $size(M) = 0$ and,*
- *if $\Gamma \vdash M = \Sigma(A, B) : Type$ then $size(M) = size(A) + 1$.*

Proof. By the definition of *size* and Lemma 2.

Lemma 4. *In $T[\mathcal{R}\pi_1]_0$, if $\Gamma \vdash M_1 <_d M_2 : Type$ then $size(M_1) = size(M_2)$.*

Proof. By induction on derivations and Lemma 2 and Lemma 3. Note that $size(M_1) = size(M_2) = 0$ if the last rule of $\Gamma \vdash M_1 <_d M_2 : Type$ is one of the rules for Π-types.

Lemma 5. *In $T[\mathcal{R}\pi_1]_0$, if $\Gamma \vdash M_1 \prec_c M_2 : Type$ then $size(M_1) > size(M_2)$.*

Proof. By induction on derivations and Lemma 2, Lemma 3 and Lemma 4.

The following theorems prove the coherence of $T[\mathcal{R}\pi_1]_0$.

Theorem 1.
- *If $\Gamma \vdash M_1 \propto_c M_2 : Type$ then $\Gamma \vdash M_1 : Type$, $\Gamma \vdash M_2 : Type$ and $\Gamma \vdash c : (M_1)M_2 : Type$.*
- *If $\Gamma \vdash M_1 \propto_c M_2 : Type$ then $\Gamma \not\vdash M_1 = M_2 : Type$.*
- *If $\Gamma \vdash M_1 \prec_c M_2 : Type$ then $\Gamma \not\vdash M_1 <_d M_2 : Type$ for any d. And vice versa, if $\Gamma \vdash M_1 <_c M_2 : Type$, then $\Gamma \not\vdash M_1 \prec_d M_2 : Type$ for any d.*

Proof. By induction on derivations, the definition of WDC, Lemma 4 and Lemma 5.

Theorem 2. *If* $\vdash \Gamma = \Gamma'$ $\Gamma \vdash M_1 = M_1' : Type$ *and* $\Gamma \vdash M_2 = M_2' : Type$ *and*

1. $\Gamma \vdash M_1 <_d M_2 : Type$ *and* $\Gamma' \vdash M_1' <_{d'} M_2' : Type$*, or*
2. $\Gamma \vdash M_1 \prec_d M_2 : Type$ *and* $\Gamma' \vdash M_1' \prec_{d'} M_2' : Type$

then $\Gamma \vdash d = d' : (M_1)M_3$.

Proof. By induction on derivations. A most important arguement in this proof is that, any derivations of $\Gamma \vdash M_1 <_d M_2$ and $\Gamma' \vdash M_1' <_d M_2'$, or $\Gamma \vdash M_1 \prec_d M_2$ and $\Gamma' \vdash M_1' \prec_{d'} M_2'$ must contain sub-derivations whose last rules are the same rule, followed by applications of the congruence rules.

4.4 Admissibility of Substitution and Transitivity

Now, we give the subtyping rules of substitution and transitivity and, prove that these rules are admissible. In an implementation of coercive subtyping, these rules are ignored simply because they cannot be directly implemented. For this reason among others, proving the admissibility of such rules (or their elimination) is always an important task for any subtyping system.

Admissible substitution rules. The substitution rules are as follows, which are what we expect normally.

$$\frac{\Gamma, x : K, \Gamma' \vdash A <_c B : Type \quad \Gamma \vdash k : K}{\Gamma, [k/x]\Gamma' \vdash [k/x]A <_{[k/x]c} [k/x]B : Type}$$

$$\frac{\Gamma, x : K, \Gamma' \vdash A \prec_c B : Type \quad \Gamma \vdash k : K}{\Gamma, [k/x]\Gamma' \vdash [k/x]A \prec_{[k/x]c} [k/x]B : Type}$$

Admissible transitivity rules. We give the following four transitivity rules that are basically saying that if there are coercions c and c' from type A to B and from type B to C, then $c' \circ c$ is a coercion from type A to C.

$$\frac{\Gamma \vdash A <_{c_1} B : Type \quad \Gamma \vdash B <_{c_2} C : Type}{\Gamma \vdash A <_{c_2 \circ c_1} C : Type} \qquad \frac{\Gamma \vdash A \prec_{c_1} B : Type \quad \Gamma \vdash B \prec_{c_2} C : Type}{\Gamma \vdash A \prec_{c_2 \circ c_1} C : Type}$$

$$\frac{\Gamma \vdash A <_{c_1} B : Type \quad \Gamma \vdash B \prec_{c_2} C : Type}{\Gamma \vdash A \prec_{c_2 \circ c_1} C : Type} \qquad \frac{\Gamma \vdash A \prec_{c_1} B : Type \quad \Gamma \vdash B <_{c_2} C : Type}{\Gamma \vdash A \prec_{c_2 \circ c_1} C : Type}$$

Remark 8. The above transitivity rule are sufficient and correct, in the sense that, first, they capture the meaning of transitivity, and second, they enjoy the properties in the lemmas 4 and 5 . Other rules of different combination such as the rule

$$\frac{\Gamma \vdash A <_{c_1} B : Type \quad \Gamma \vdash B <_{c_2} C : Type}{\Gamma \vdash A \prec_{c_2 \circ c_1} C : Type}$$

are not correct and contradictory to the above properties.

Theorem 3. ***(Substitution in*** $T[\mathcal{R}\pi_1]_0$***)*** *If* $\Gamma \vdash k : K$ *and*

1. *if* $\Gamma, x : K, \Gamma' \vdash M_1 <_c M_2 : Type$, *then* $\Gamma, [k/x]\Gamma' \vdash [k/x]M_1 <_{[k/x]c} [k/x]M_2 : Type$, *and*
2. *if* $\Gamma, x : K, \Gamma' \vdash M_1 \prec_c M_2 : Type$, *then* $\Gamma, [k/x]\Gamma' \vdash [k/x]M_1 \prec_{[k/x]c} [k/x]M_2 : Type$.

Proof. By induction on derivations.

In order to prove the admissibility of the transitivity rules, we also need to prove the theorem about weakening.

Theorem 4. ***(Weakening in*** $T[\mathcal{R}\pi_1]_0$***)*** *If* $\Gamma \subseteq \Gamma'$, Γ' *is valid and*

1. *if* $\Gamma \vdash M_1 <_c M_2 : Type$ *then* $\Gamma' \vdash M_1 <_c M_2 : Type$, *and*
2. *if* $\Gamma \vdash M_1 \prec_c M_2 : Type$ *then* $\Gamma' \vdash M_1 \prec_c M_2 : Type$.

Proof. By induction on derivations.

To prove the admissibility of transitivity rules, the usual methods (*e.g.* by induction on derivations) do not seem to work. We develop a new measure (*Depth*) that is an adoption of the measure (*depth*) developed by Chen, Aspinall and Companoni [9]. In the measure *Depth*, the subtyping judgements ($<$ and $\prec$) only count.

Definition 5. *(Depth) Let D be a derivation of a subtyping judgement of the form* $\Gamma \vdash A <_c B : Type$ *or* $\Gamma \vdash A \prec_c B : Type$.

$$D : \qquad \frac{S_1 \;...\; S_n \; T_1 \;...\; T_m}{\Gamma \vdash A \propto_c B : Type}$$

where $\Gamma \vdash A \propto_c B : Type$ *represents* $\Gamma \vdash A <_c B : Type$ *or* $\Gamma \vdash A \prec_c B : Type$, $S_1,...,S_n$ *are derivations of subtyping judgements of the form* $\Gamma \vdash M_1 <_d M_2 : Type$ *or* $\Gamma \vdash M_1 \prec_d M_2 : Type$ *and,* $T_1,..., T_m$ *are derivations of other forms of judgements,*

$$Depth(D) =_{df} 1 + max\{Depth(S_1), ..., Depth(S_n)\}$$

Specially, if $n = 0$ *then* $Depth(D) =_{df} 1$.

The following lemmas show that, from a derivation D of a subtyping judgement J one can always get a derivation D' of the judgement obtained from J by context replacement such that D and D' have the same depth.

Lemma 6. *If* $\vdash \Gamma = \Gamma'$ *and*

1. *if D is a derivation of* $\Gamma \vdash M_1 <_d M_2 : Type$, *then there is a derivation* D' *of* $\Gamma' \vdash M_1 <_d M_2 : Type$ *such that* $Depth(D) = Depth(D')$, *or*
2. *if D is a derivation of* $\Gamma \vdash M_1 \prec_d M_2 : Type$, *then there is a derivation* D' *of* $\Gamma' \vdash M_1 \prec_d M_2 : Type$ *such that* $Depth(D) = Depth(D')$.

Proof. By induction on derivations.

Lemma 7. *If* $\Gamma, x : K, \Gamma' \vdash M_1 <_{c_1} M_2 : Type \in \mathcal{C}$ *and* $\Gamma \vdash c_2 : (K')K$ *then* $\Gamma, y : K', [c_2(y)/x]\Gamma' \vdash [c_2(y)/x]M_1 <_{[c_2(y)/x]c_1} [c_2(y)/x]M_2 : Type \in \mathcal{C}$.

Proof. By the weakening and substitution in the definition of WDC.

Lemma 8. *If* $\Gamma \vdash c_2 : (K')K$ *and,*

1. *if* D *is a derivation of* $\Gamma, x : K, \Gamma' \vdash M_1 <_{c_1} M_2 : Type$, *then there is a derivation* D' *of* $\Gamma, y : K', [c_2(y)/x]\Gamma' \vdash [c_2(y)/x]M_1 <_{[c_2(y)/x]c_1} [c_2(y)/x]M_2 : Type$ *such that* $Depth(D) = Depth(D')$, *or*
2. *if* D *is a derivation of* $\Gamma, x : K, \Gamma' \vdash M_1 <_{c_1} M_2 : Type$, *then there is a derivation* D' *of* $\Gamma, y : K', [c_2(y)/x]\Gamma' \vdash [c_2(y)/x]M_1 <_{[c_2(y)/x]c_1} [c_2(y)/x]M_2 : Type$ *such that* $Depth(D) = Depth(D')$.

Proof. By induction on derivations and Lemma 7. The theorem of weakening and substitution in type theory T and the property of conservativity of $T[\mathcal{R}\pi_1]_0$ over T are also needed in this proof.

Now, we can prove the admissibility of transitivity rules.

Theorem 5. ***(Transitivity in*** $T[\mathcal{R}\pi_1]_0$***)*** *If* $\Gamma \vdash M_2 = M_2' : Type$ *and*

1. *if* $\Gamma \vdash M_1 <_{d_1} M_2 : Type$ *and* $\Gamma \vdash M_2' <_{d_2} M_3 : Type$, *then* $\Gamma \vdash M_1 <_{d_2 \circ d_1} M_3 : Type$, *and*
2. $\Gamma \vdash M_1 \prec_{d_1} M_2 : Type$ *and* $\Gamma \vdash M_2' \prec_{d_2} M_3 : Type$, *then* $\Gamma \vdash M_1 \prec_{d_2 \circ d_1} M_3 : Type$.
3. *if* $\Gamma \vdash M_1 <_{d_1} M_2 : Type$ *and* $\Gamma \vdash M_2' \prec_{d_2} M_3 : Type$, *then* $\Gamma \vdash M_1 \prec_{d_2 \circ d_1} M_3 : Type$, *and*
4. $\Gamma \vdash M_1 \prec_{d_1} M_2 : Type$ *and* $\Gamma \vdash M_2' <_{d_2} M_3 : Type$, *then* $\Gamma \vdash M_1 \prec_{d_2 \circ d_1} M_3 : Type$, *and*

Proof. By induction on $Depth(D) + Depth(D')$, where D is a derivation of $\Gamma \vdash M_1 <_{d_1} M_2 : Type$ or $\Gamma \vdash M_1 \prec_{d_1} M_2 : Type$, D' is a derivation of $\Gamma \vdash M_2' <_{d_2} M_3 : Type$ or $\Gamma \vdash M_2' \prec_{d_2} M_3 : Type$.

5 Discussions

Side conditions.[3] In order to block the unwanted derivations, one may still try to keep the rule $\pi_1 rule$ in section 3 and use side conditions for the First Component rule, without introducing any new subtyping relation. For instance, one of such side conditions for the First Component rule is the following.

$$\frac{\Gamma \vdash A <_c A' : Type \quad \Gamma \vdash B : (A')Type}{\Gamma \vdash \Sigma(A, B \circ c) <_{d_1} \Sigma(A', B) : Type} \quad (size(A) = size(A'))$$

[3] Thanks to an anonymous referee for the comments on this issue.

or

$$\frac{\Gamma \vdash A <_c A' : Type \quad \Gamma \vdash B : (A')Type}{\Gamma \vdash \Sigma(A, B \circ c) <_{d_1} \Sigma(A', B) : Type} \quad (size(A) \not> size(A'))$$

In $T[\mathcal{R}\pi_1]_0$, *size* is well-defined. Similarly, *size* can be defined in $T[\mathcal{R}]_0$ and one can prove its well-definedness (see [17,13] for more details of $T[\mathcal{R}]_0$ and $T[\mathcal{R}]$. Here, $\mathcal{R}$ includes one of the above rules). It is obvious that $T[\mathcal{R}\pi_1]_0$ and $T[\mathcal{R}]_0$ are equivalent in terms of the following lemma.

Lemma 9. *If* $\Gamma \vdash A \propto_c B : Type$ *is derivable in* $T[\mathcal{R}\pi_1]_0$ *then* $\Gamma \vdash A <_c B : Type$ *is derivable in* $T[\mathcal{R}]_0$ *and vice versa.*

However, since the system $T[\mathcal{R}]$ includes the Coercive definition rule and the Coercive application rules in Appendix, A and A' in the side-condition may not be well-typed in the original type theory any more. The way to compute such terms is to insert coercions first and then do usual computation in the original type theory. So the property that inserting coercion is decidable in $T[\mathcal{R}]$ must be proved first in order to argue the well-definedness of *size*. There is a circularity, that is, a property of $T[\mathcal{R}]$ is needed in order to present $T[\mathcal{R}]$ itself.

Algorithm and decidability. Since we proved the coherence and admissibility of substitution and transitivity, the coercion searching for whole system is decidable if it is decidable for $\mathcal{C}$. In other words, there is an algorithm to check whether there exists a coercion between any two types. We omit the details here.

Further study. In this paper, we had a case study about how to combine incoherent coercions. The methods developed here may have a wider application. In general, it is also natural to consider new subtyping relations to block those derivations which make the coercive subtyping system incoherent. The method to introduce new transitivity rules may guide a further study of a system in which there are more than one subtyping relations.

The subtyping rules for parameterised inductive types need further study. For example, we introduce subtyping rules for lists as follows.

$$\frac{\Gamma \vdash A \propto_c B : Type}{\Gamma \vdash List(A) <_d List(B) : Type}$$

where $d = map(A, B, c)$ such that $d(nil(A)) = nil(B)$ and $d(cons(A, a, l)) = cons(B, c(a), d(l))$.

As studied in [14], if we add this rule in the system, the transitivity rules would not be admissible. In a forthcoming paper, we will study new computation rules for parameterised inductive types and such rules will make, for example, $map(B, C, c') \circ map(A, B, c)$ and $map(A, C, c' \circ c)$ computationally equal. And hence the above subtyping rules for lists enjoy the property of admissibility of transitivity.

Related work. The early development of the framework of coercive subtyping is closely related to Aczel's idea in type-checking overloading methods for classes [1] and the work on giving coercion semantics to lambda calculi with subtyping by Breazu-Tannen et al [6]. Barthe and his colleagues have studied constructor subtyping and its possible applications in proof systems [4,5]. A recent logical study of subtyping in system **F** can be found in [12] and Chen has studied the issue of transitivity elimination in that framework [9].

Acknowlegements. We would like to thank the member of the Computer-Assisted Reasoning Group at Durham for discussions and the TYPES03 referees for the comments on the paper.

References

1. P. Aczel. Simple overloading for type theories. Draft, 1994.
2. A. Bailey. *The Machine-checked Literate Formalisation of Algebra in Type Theory.* PhD thesis, University of Manchester, 1998.
3. B. Barras et al. *The Coq Proof Assistant Reference Manual (Version 6.3.1).* INRIA-Rocquencourt, 2000.
4. G. Barthe and M.J. Frade. Constructor subtyping. *Proceedings of ESOP'99, LNCS 1576*, 1999.
5. G. Barthe and F. van Raamsdonk. Constructor subtyping in the calculus of inductive constructions. *Proceedings of FOSSACS'00, LNCS 1784*, 2000.
6. V. Breazu-Tannen, T. Coquand, C. Gunter, and A. Scedrov. Inheritance and explicit coercion. *Information and Computation*, 93, 1991.
7. P. Callaghan and Z. Luo. An implementation of LF with coercive subtyping and universes. *Journal of Automated Reasoning*, 27(1):3–27, 2001.
8. P. C. Callaghan, Z. Luo, and J. Pang. Object languages in a type-theoretic meta-framework. *Workshop of Proof Transformation and Presentation and Proof Complexities (PTP'01)*, 2001.
9. G. Chen. *Subtyping, Type Conversion and Transitivity Elimination.* PhD thesis, University of Paris VII, 1998.
10. R. Harper, F. Honsell, and G. Plotkin. A framework for defining logics. *Proc. 2nd Ann. Symp. on Logic in Computer Science. IEEE*, 1987.
11. A. Jones, Z. Luo, and S. Soloviev. Some proof-theoretic and algorithmic aspects of coercive subtyping. *Types for proofs and programs (eds, E. Gimenez and C. Paulin-Mohring), Proc. of the Inter. Conf. TYPES'96, LNCS 1512*, 1998.
12. G. Longo, K. Milsted, and S. Soloviev. A logic of subtyping. In *Proc. of LICS'95*, 1995.
13. Y. Luo and Z. Luo. Coherence and transitivity in coercive subtyping. In R. Nieuwenhuis and A. Voronkov, editors, *8th International Conference on Logic for Programming, Artificial Intelligence, and Reasoning*, volume 2250 of *LNAI*, pages 249–265. Springer-Verlag, 2001.
14. Y. Luo, Z. Luo, and S. Soloviev. Weak transitivity in coercive subtyping. In H. Geuvers and F. Wiedijk, editors, *Types for Proofs and Programs*, volume 2646 of *LNCS*, pages 220–239. Springer-Verlag, 2002.
15. Z. Luo. *Computation and Reasoning: A Type Theory for Computer Science.* Oxford University Press, 1994.
16. Z. Luo. Coercive subtyping in type theory. *Proc. of CSL'96, the 1996 Annual Conference of the European Association for Computer Science Logic, Utrecht. LNCS 1258*, 1997.
17. Z. Luo. Coercive subtyping. *Journal of Logic and Computation*, 9(1):105–130, 1999.

18. Z. Luo and P. Callaghan. Coercive subtyping and lexical semantics (extended abstract). *LACL'98*, 1998.
19. Z. Luo and R. Pollack. LEGO Proof Development System: User's Manual. LFCS Report ECS-LFCS-92-211, Department of Computer Science, University of Edinburgh, 1992.
20. B. Nordström, K. Petersson, and J. Smith. *Programming in Martin-Löf's Type Theory: An Introduction.* Oxford University Press, 1990.
21. S. Soloviev and Z. Luo. Coercion completion and conservativity in coercive subtyping. Annals of Pure and Applied Logic, 2002.

Appendix

The following are the inference rules for the coercive subkinding extension $T[\mathcal{R}\pi_1]$ (not including the rules for subtyping)

Basic subkinding rule

$$\frac{\Gamma \vdash A <_c B : Type}{\Gamma \vdash El(A) <_c El(B)} \qquad \frac{\Gamma \vdash A \prec_c B : Type}{\Gamma \vdash El(A) <_c El(B)}$$

Coercive application rules

$$\frac{\Gamma \vdash f : (x:K)K' \quad \Gamma \vdash k_0 : K_0 \quad \Gamma \vdash K_0 <_c K}{\Gamma \vdash f(k_0) : [c(k_0)/x]K'}$$

$$\frac{\Gamma \vdash f = f' : (x:K)K' \quad \Gamma \vdash k_0 = k_0' : K_0 \quad \Gamma \vdash K_0 <_c K}{\Gamma \vdash f(k_0) = f'(k_0') : [c(k_0)/x]K'}$$

Coercive definition rule

$$\frac{\Gamma \vdash f : (x:K)K' \quad \Gamma \vdash k_0 : K_0 \quad \Gamma \vdash K_0 <_c K}{\Gamma \vdash f(k_0) = f(c(k_0)) : [c(k_0)/x]K'}$$

Subkinding for dependent product kinds

$$\frac{\Gamma \vdash K_1' = K_1 \quad \Gamma, x' : K_1' \vdash K_2 <_c K_2' \quad \Gamma, x : K_1 \vdash K_2\ kind}{\Gamma \vdash (x:K_1)K_2 <_{[f:(x:K_1)K_2][x':K_1']c(f(x'))} (x':K_1')K_2'}$$

$$\frac{\Gamma \vdash K_1' <_c K_1 \quad \Gamma, x' : K_1' \vdash [c(x')/x]K_2 = K_2' \quad \Gamma, x : K_1 \vdash K_2\ kind}{\Gamma \vdash (x:K_1)K_2 <_{[f:(x:K_1)K_2][x':K_1']f(c(x'))} (x':K_1')K_2'}$$

$$\frac{\Gamma \vdash K_1' <_{c_1} K_1 \quad \Gamma, x' : K_1' \vdash [c_1(x')/x]K_2 <_{c_2} K_2' \quad \Gamma, x : K_1 \vdash K_2\ kind}{\Gamma \vdash (x:K_1)K_2 <_{[f:(x:K_1)K_2][x':K_1']c_2(f(c_1(x')))} (x':K_1')K_2'}$$

Congruence rules for subkinding

$$\frac{\Gamma \vdash K_1 <_c K_2 \quad \Gamma \vdash K_1 = K_1' \quad \Gamma \vdash K_2 = K_2' \quad \Gamma \vdash c = c' : (K)K'}{\Gamma \vdash K_1' <_{c'} K_2'}$$

Transitivity and Substitution rules for subkinding

$$\frac{\Gamma \vdash K <_c K' \quad \Gamma \vdash K' <_{c'} K''}{\Gamma \vdash K <_{c' \circ c} K''} \qquad \frac{\Gamma, x : K, \Gamma' \vdash K_1 <_c K_2 \quad \Gamma \vdash k : K}{\Gamma, [k/x]\Gamma' \vdash [k/x]K_1 <_{[k/x]c} [k/x]K_2}$$

Induction and Co-induction in Sequent Calculus

Alberto Momigliano[1,2] and Alwen Tiu[3,4]

[1] LFCS, University of Edinburgh
[2] DSI, University of Milan
amomigl1@inf.ed.ac.uk
[3] LIX, École polytechnique
[4] Computer Science and Engineering Department, Penn State University
tiu@cse.psu.edu

Abstract. Proof search has been used to specify a wide range of computation systems. In order to build a framework for reasoning about such specifications, we make use of a sequent calculus involving induction and co-induction. These proof principles are based on a proof theoretic notion of definition, following on work by Schroeder-Heister, Girard, and McDowell and Miller. Definitions are essentially stratified logic programs. The left and right rules for defined atoms treat the definitions as defining fixed points. The use of definitions also makes it possible to reason intensionally about syntax, in particular enforcing free equality via unification. The full system thus allows inductive and co-inductive proofs involving higher-order abstract syntax. We extend earlier work by allowing induction and co-induction on general definitions and show that cut-elimination holds for this extension. We present some examples involving lists and simulation in the lazy λ-calculus. Two prototype implementations are available: one via the Hybrid system implemented on top of Isabelle/HOL and the other in the BLinc system implemented on top of λProlog.

1 Introduction

A common approach to specifying computation systems is via deductive systems, e.g., structural operational semantics. Such specifications can be represented as logical theories in a suitably expressive formal logic in which *proof-search* can then be used to model the computation. This use of logic as a specification language is along the line of *logical frameworks* [22]. The representation of the syntax of computation systems inside formal logic can benefit from the use of *higher-order abstract syntax* (HOAS), a high-level and declarative treatment of object-level bound variables and substitution. At the same time, we want to use such a logic in order to reason over the *meta-theoretical* properties of object languages, for example type preservation in operational semantics [15], soundness and completeness of compilation [19] or congruence of bisimulation in transition systems [16]. Typically this involves reasoning by (structural) induction and, when dealing with infinite behaviour, co-induction [5].

The need to support both inductive and co-inductive reasoning and some form of HOAS requires some careful design decisions, since the two are prima facie notoriously incompatible. While any meta-language based on a λ-calculus can be used to specify and possibly perform computations over HOAS encodings, meta-reasoning has traditionally

S. Berardi, M. Coppo, and F. Damiani (Eds.): TYPES 2003, LNCS 3085, pp. 293–308, 2004.

involved (co)inductive specifications both at the level of the syntax and of the judgements as well (which are of course unified at the type-theoretic level). The first provides crucial freeness properties for datatypes constructors, while the second offers principle of case analysis and (co)induction. This is well-known to be problematic, since HOAS specifications lead to non-monotone (co)inductive definitions, which by cardinality and consistency reasons are not permitted in inductive logical frameworks. Moreover, even when HOAS is weakened so as to be made compatible with standard proof assistants [7] such as HOL or Coq, the latter tend to be still too *strong*, in sense of allowing the existence of too many functions and yielding the so called *exotic* terms. This causes a loss of adequacy in HOAS specifications, which is one of the pillar of formal verification. On the other hand, logics such as LF [11] that are weak by design in order to support this style of syntax are not directly endowed with (co)induction principles.

The contribution of this paper lies in the design of a new logic, called Linc (for a logic with λ-terms, induction and co-induction), that carefully adds principles of induction and co-induction to a higher-order intuitionistic logic based on a proof theoretic notion of definition, following on work (among others) by Schroeder-Heister [27], Girard [10] and McDowell and Miller [14]. Definitions are akin to logic programs, but allow to view theories as "closed" or defining fixed points. This alone allows us to perform case analysis. Our approach to formalizing induction and co-induction is via the least and greatest solutions of the fixed point equations specified by the definitions. Such least and greatest solutions are guaranteed to exist by a stratification condition on definitions (which basically ensures monotonicity). The proof rules for induction and co-induction makes use of the notion of *pre-fixed points* and *post-fixed points* respectively. In the inductive case, this corresponds to the induction invariant, while in the co-inductive one to the so-called simulation.

The simply typed language underlying Linc and the notion of definition make it possible to reason *intensionally* about syntax, in particular enforcing *free* equality via

$$\frac{B,B,\Gamma \longrightarrow C}{B,\Gamma \longrightarrow C}\; c\mathcal{L} \qquad \frac{\Gamma \longrightarrow C}{B,\Gamma \longrightarrow C}\; w\mathcal{L} \qquad \frac{}{\bot,\Gamma \longrightarrow B}\; \bot\mathcal{L} \qquad \frac{}{\Gamma \longrightarrow \top}\; \top\mathcal{R}$$

$$\frac{B,\Gamma \longrightarrow D}{B \wedge C,\Gamma \longrightarrow D}\; \wedge\mathcal{L} \qquad \frac{C,\Gamma \longrightarrow D}{B \wedge C,\Gamma \longrightarrow D}\; \wedge\mathcal{L} \qquad \frac{\Gamma \longrightarrow B \quad \Gamma \longrightarrow C}{\Gamma \longrightarrow B \wedge C}\; \wedge\mathcal{R}$$

$$\frac{B,\Gamma \longrightarrow D \quad C,\Gamma \longrightarrow D}{B \vee C,\Gamma \longrightarrow D}\; \vee\mathcal{L} \qquad \frac{\Gamma \longrightarrow B}{\Gamma \longrightarrow B \vee C}\; \vee\mathcal{R} \qquad \frac{\Gamma \longrightarrow C}{\Gamma \longrightarrow B \vee C}\; \vee\mathcal{R}$$

$$\frac{B\,t,\Gamma \longrightarrow C}{\forall x.B\,x,\Gamma \longrightarrow C}\; \forall\mathcal{L} \qquad \frac{\Gamma \longrightarrow B\,y}{\Gamma \longrightarrow \forall x.B\,x}\; \forall\mathcal{R} \qquad \frac{B\,y,\Gamma \longrightarrow C}{\exists x.B\,x,\Gamma \longrightarrow C}\; \exists\mathcal{L} \qquad \frac{\Gamma \longrightarrow B\,t}{\Gamma \longrightarrow \exists x.B\,x}\; \exists\mathcal{R}$$

$$\frac{\Gamma \longrightarrow B \quad C,\Gamma \longrightarrow D}{B \supset C,\Gamma \longrightarrow D}\; \supset\mathcal{L} \qquad \frac{B,\Gamma \longrightarrow C}{\Gamma \longrightarrow B \supset C}\; \supset\mathcal{R}$$

$$\frac{}{C \longrightarrow C}\; init \qquad \frac{\Delta_1 \longrightarrow B_1 \quad \cdots \quad \Delta_n \longrightarrow B_n \quad B_1,\ldots,B_n,\Gamma \longrightarrow C}{\Delta_1,\ldots,\Delta_n,\Gamma \longrightarrow C}\; mc, \text{ where } n > 0$$

Fig. 1. Inference rules for the core Linc

unification, which can be used on first-order terms or higher-order λ-terms. In fact, we can support HOAS encodings of constructors without requiring them to belong to a datatype. In particular we can *prove* the freeness properties of those constructors, namely injectivity, distinctness and case exhaustion. Judgements are encoded as definitions accordingly to their informal semantics, either inductive, co-inductive or regular, i.e. true in every fixed point. Given the stratification condition, we (currently) fall short of the LF-like idea of *Full* HOAS, although, exploiting the equivalence with the completion of a logic program [26], the monotonicity requirement can be weakened beyond the scope of current induction-based proof-assistants.

Linc can be proved to be a conservative extension of $FO\lambda^{\Delta\mathbb{N}}$ [14] and a generalization to the higher-order case of Martin-Löf [13] first-order theory of iterated inductive definitions. Moreover, at the best of our knowledge, it is the first sequent calculus with a cut-elimination theorem for co-inductive definitions. Further, its modular design makes its extension easy, for example in the direction of $FO\lambda^{\nabla}$ [18] or the regular world assumption [28].

The rest of the paper is organized as follows. Section 2 introduces the proof system for the logic Linc. Section 3 shows some examples of using induction and co-induction to prove several properties of list-related predicates and the lazy λ-calculus. Section 4 gives an overview of the cut-elimination procedure, the detailed proof of which is available in [31]. Section 5 surveys the related work and Section 6 concludes this paper.

2 The Logic Linc

The logic Linc shares the core fragment with $FO\lambda^{\Delta\mathbb{N}}$, which is an intuitionistic version of Church's Simple Theory of Types. Formulae in the logic are built from predicate symbols and the usual logical connectives $\bot$, $\top$, $\wedge$, $\vee$, $\supset$, $\forall_\tau$ and $\exists_\tau$. Following Church, formulae will be given type o. The quantification type τ can have higher types, but those are restricted to not contain o. Thus the logic has a first-order proof theory but allows for the encoding of higher-order abstract syntax. The core fragment of the logic is presented in the sequent calculus in Figure 1. A sequent is denoted by $\Gamma \longrightarrow C$ where C is a formula and Γ is a multiset of formulae. Notice that in the presentation of the rule schemes, we make use of HOAS, e.g., in the application $B\,x$ it is implicit that B has no free occurrence of x. In the $\forall\mathcal{R}$ and $\exists\mathcal{L}$ rules, y is an eigenvariable that is not free in the lower sequent of the rule. Whenever we write down a sequent, it is assumed implicitly that the formulae are well-typed and in $\beta\eta$-long normal forms: the type context, i.e., the types of the constants and the eigenvariables used in the sequent, is left implicit as well. The *mc* rule is a generalization of the cut rule that simplifies the presentation of the cut-elimination proof.

2.1 A Proof-Theoretic Notion of Definitions

We extend the core logic in Figure 1 by allowing the introduction of non-logical constants. An atomic formula, i.e., a formula that contains no occurrences of logical constants, can be defined in terms of other logical or non-logical constants. Its left and right rules are, roughly speaking, carried out by replacing the formula corresponding to its definition with the atom itself. A defined atom can thus be seen as a generalized connective, whose behaviour is determined by its defining clauses. The syntax of definition clauses used by McDowell and Miller [14] resembles that of logic programs, that is, a definition clause consists of a head and a body, with the usual pattern matching in the head; for example, the predicate *nat* for natural numbers is written $\{nat\ z \triangleq \top,\ nat\ s\ x \triangleq nat\ x\}$. We adopt here a simpler presentation by putting all pattern matching in the body and combining multiple clauses with the same head in one clause with disjunctive body. Of course, this will require us to have explicit equality as part of our syntax. The corresponding *nat* predicate in our syntax will be written

$$nat\ x \triangleq [x = z] \vee \exists y.[x = s\ y] \wedge nat\ y$$

and corresponds to the notion of *iff-completion* of a logic program.

Definition 1. *A* definition clause *is written* $\forall \bar{x}[p\,\bar{x} \triangleq B\,\bar{x}]$, *where p is a predicate constant. The atomic formula* $p\,\bar{x}$ *is called the* head *of the clause, and the formula* $B\,\bar{x}$ *is called the* body. *The symbol* $\triangleq$ *is used simply to indicate a definition clause: it is not a logical connective. A* definition *is a (perhaps infinite) set of definition clauses. A predicate may occur only at most once in the heads of the clauses of a definition.*

We will generally omit the outer quantifiers in a definition clause to simplify the presentation.

Not all definition clauses are admitted in our logic, e.g., definitions with circular calling through implications (negations) must be avoided as it can lead to inconsistency [25]. The notion of *level* of a formula allows to define a proper stratification on definitions. To each predicate p we associate a natural number $\mathrm{lvl}(p)$, the level of p. The notion of level is extended to formulae and sequents.

Definition 2. *Given a formula B, its* level $\mathrm{lvl}(B)$ *is defined as follows:*

1. $\mathrm{lvl}(p\,\bar{t}) = \mathrm{lvl}(p)$, $\mathrm{lvl}(\bot) = \mathrm{lvl}(\top) = 0$
2. $\mathrm{lvl}(B \wedge C) = \mathrm{lvl}(B \vee C) = \max(\mathrm{lvl}(B), \mathrm{lvl}(C))$
3. $\mathrm{lvl}(B \supset C) = \max(\mathrm{lvl}(B) + 1, \mathrm{lvl}(C))$
4. $\mathrm{lvl}(\forall x.B\,x) = \mathrm{lvl}(\exists x.B\,x) = \mathrm{lvl}(B\,t)$, *for any term t.*

The level of a sequent $\Gamma \longrightarrow C$ *is the level of C. A definition clause* $\forall \bar{x}[p\,\bar{x} \triangleq B\,\bar{x}]$ *is stratified if* $\mathrm{lvl}(B\,\bar{x}) \leq \mathrm{lvl}(p)$. *A definition is stratified if all its definition clauses are stratified.*

An occurrence of a formula A in a formula C is *strictly positive* if that particular occurrence of A is not to the left of any implication in C. The stratification of definitions above implies that for every definition clause all occurrences of the head in the body are strictly positive.

Given a definition clause $p\,\bar{x} \triangleq B\,\bar{x}$, the right and left rules for predicate p are

$$\frac{B\,\bar{t}, \Gamma \longrightarrow C}{p\,\bar{t}, \Gamma \longrightarrow C}\ def\mathcal{L} \qquad \frac{\Gamma \longrightarrow B\,\bar{t}}{\Gamma \longrightarrow p\,\bar{t}}\ def\mathcal{R}$$

The rules for equality predicates makes use of substitutions. We assume the usual definition of capture-avoiding substitutions. We use θ, ρ, δ and σ to denote those and their application is written in post-fix notation, e.g., $t\theta$. The left and right rules for equality are as follows

$$\frac{\{\Gamma\rho \longrightarrow C\rho \mid s\rho =_{\beta\eta} t\rho, \rho \in CSU(s,t)\}}{s = t, \Gamma \longrightarrow C}\ \mathrm{eq}\mathcal{L} \qquad \frac{}{\Gamma \longrightarrow t = t}\ \mathrm{eq}\mathcal{R}$$

The substitution ρ in eq$\mathcal{L}$ is called a *unifier* of s and t. The set $CSU(s,t)$ is a *complete set of unifiers*, i.e., given any unifier θ_1 of s and t, there is a unifier $\theta_2 \in CSU(s,t)$ such that $\theta_1 = \theta_2 \circ \gamma$, for some substitution γ. In the first order case, a set containing just the most general unifier is a complete set of unifiers. In general, however, the complete set of unifiers may contain more than one unifier and therefore we specify a set of sequents as the premise of the eq$\mathcal{L}$ rule, which is to say that each sequent in the set is a premise of the rule. Note that in applying eq$\mathcal{L}$, eigenvariables can be instantiated as a result.

2.2 Induction and Co-induction

A definition $p\,x \triangleq B\,x$ can be seen as a fixed point equation saying that for every term t, $p\,t$ if and only if $B\,t$ holds. Since our notion of definition requires strict positivity of occurrences of p in B, existence of fixed points is always guaranteed. Hence the provability of $p\,t$ means that t is in a solution of the corresponding fixed point equation, although not necessarily in the least (or greatest) solution (see e.g., [10] for an example). Therefore we add extra rules that reflect the least and the greatest solutions, respectively. Since we are in a monotone setting, we can use the pre-fixed point and the post-fixed point as an approach to the least and greatest fixed points. In the following we assume, for simplicity of presentation, that predicates are not mutual-recursively defined. The more general case where mutual recursion is treated can be found in [31].

Let $p\,\bar{x} \triangleq B\,\bar{x}$ be a definition clause and let S be a term of the same type as p. The induction rules for p are

$$\frac{(B\,\bar{x})[S/p] \longrightarrow S\,\bar{x} \quad \Gamma, S\,\bar{t} \longrightarrow C}{\Gamma, p\,\bar{t} \longrightarrow C}\ \mathcal{IL} \qquad \frac{\Gamma \longrightarrow B\,\bar{t}}{\Gamma \longrightarrow p\,\bar{t}}\ \mathcal{IR}$$

The abstraction S is an invariant of the induction. The variables $\bar{x}$ are new eigenvariables. An informal reading of $\mathcal{IL}$ is to consider S as denoting a set (i.e., $\bar{t} \in S$ iff $S\,\bar{t}$ holds), B as denoting a fixed point operator and S as a pre-fixed point of B, i.e., $B[S/p] \subseteq S$. Notice that the right-rule for induction is *def*$\mathcal{R}$. The co-induction rules are defined dually.

$$\frac{B\,\bar{t}, \Gamma \longrightarrow C}{p\,\bar{t}, \Gamma \longrightarrow C}\ \mathcal{CIL} \qquad \frac{\Gamma \longrightarrow S\,\bar{t} \quad S\,\bar{x} \longrightarrow (B\,\bar{x})[S/p]}{\Gamma \longrightarrow p\,\bar{t}}\ \mathcal{CIR},\ \text{where } \mathrm{lvl}(S) \leq \mathrm{lvl}(p)$$

S can be seen as denoting a *post-fixed point*, i.e., $S \subseteq B[S/p]$. The $\mathcal{CIL}$ rule is the *def*$\mathcal{L}$ rule. The proviso in $\mathcal{CIR}$, although mainly technical, is satisfied by every example we have examined, since it requires the given predicate to be used "monotonically" in the simulation.

To avoid inconsistency, some care must be taken in applying induction or co-induction in a proof. One obvious pitfall is when the fixed point equation corresponding to a definition clause has different least and greatest solutions. In such case, mixing induction and co-induction on the same definition clause can lead to inconsistency. For example, let $p \stackrel{\triangle}{=} p$ be a definition clause. Given the scheme of rules above without any further restriction, we can construct the following derivation

$$\dfrac{\dfrac{\dfrac{}{\longrightarrow \top}\ \top\mathcal{R} \quad \dfrac{}{\top \longrightarrow \top}\ \top\mathcal{R}}{\longrightarrow p}\ \mathcal{CIR} \qquad \dfrac{\dfrac{}{\bot \longrightarrow \bot}\ \bot\mathcal{L} \quad \dfrac{}{\bot \longrightarrow \bot}\ \bot\mathcal{L}}{p \longrightarrow \bot}\ \mathcal{IL}}{\longrightarrow \bot}\ cut$$

In the above derivation we use $\top$ and $\bot$ as the invariant and the simulation in the instance of $\mathcal{CIR}$ and $\mathcal{IL}$ rules. This example suggests that we have to use a definition clause consistently through out the proof, either inductively or co-inductively, but not both. To avoid this problem, we introduce markings into a definition, whose role is to indicate which rules are applicable to the corresponding defined atoms.

Definition 3. *An* extended definition *is a stratified definition $\mathcal{D}$ together with a label, that indicates whether the clause is either* inductive, co-inductive, *or* regular. *An inductive clause is written as $p\,\bar{x} \stackrel{\mu}{=} B\,\bar{x}$, a co-inductive clause is written as $p\,\bar{x} \stackrel{\nu}{=} B\,\bar{x}$ and a regular clause is written as $p\,\bar{x} \stackrel{\triangle}{=} B\,\bar{x}$.*

Since we shall only be concerned with extended definitions from now on, we shall refer those simply as definitions. The induction and co-induction rules need additional provisos. The $\mathcal{IL}$ and $\mathcal{IR}$ rules can be applied only to an inductively defined atom. Dually, the $\mathcal{CIL}$ and $\mathcal{CIR}$ rules can only be applied to a co-inductively defined atom. The *def*$\mathcal{L}$ and *def*$\mathcal{R}$ rules apply only to regular atoms. However, we can show that *def*$\mathcal{L}$ and *def*$\mathcal{R}$ are derived rules for (co-)inductively defined atoms.

Proposition 1. *The def$\mathcal{L}$ and def$\mathcal{R}$ are admissible rules in the core* Linc *system with the induction and/or the co-induction rules.*

Proof. We show here how to infer *def*$\mathcal{L}$ using core Linc and induction rules. The other case with co-induction is dual. Let $p\,\bar{x} \stackrel{\triangle}{=} B\,\bar{x}$ be the definition under consideration: *def*$\mathcal{L}$ can be inferred from $\mathcal{IL}$ using the body B as the invariant.

$$\dfrac{\begin{array}{c}\Pi \\ B[B/p]\,\bar{x} \longrightarrow B\,\bar{x}\end{array} \quad B\,\bar{t}, \Gamma \longrightarrow C}{p\,\bar{t}, \Gamma \longrightarrow C}\ \mathcal{IL}$$

We construct the derivation Π by induction on the size of B, i.e., the number of logical constants in B. In the inductive cases, the derivation is constructed by applying the rules for the logical connectives in B, coordinated between left and right rules. Since p occurs strictly positively in B by stratification, the only non-trivial base case we need to consider is when we reach the sub-formula $p\,\bar{t}$ of $B\,\bar{x}$ in which case we just apply the $\mathcal{IR}$ rule

$$\dfrac{\dfrac{}{B\,\bar{t} \longrightarrow B\,\bar{t}}\ init}{B\,\bar{t} \longrightarrow p\,\bar{t}}\ \mathcal{IR}$$

3 Examples

We now give some examples, starting with some that make essential use of HOAS.

3.1 Lazy λ-Calculus

We consider an untyped version of the pure λ-calculus with lazy evaluation, following the usual HOAS style, i.e., object-level λ-operator and application are encoded as constants $\mathrm{lam} : (tm \to tm) \to tm$ and $@ : tm \to tm \to tm$, where tm is the syntactic category of object-level λ-terms. The evaluation relation is encoded as the following inductive definition

$$\begin{aligned} M \Downarrow N \stackrel{\mu}{=} & (\exists M'.[M = \mathrm{lam}\, M'] \wedge [M = N]) \vee \\ & (\exists M_1 \exists M_2 \exists P.[M = M_1 \,@\, M_2] \wedge M_1 \Downarrow \mathrm{lam}\, P \wedge (P\, M_2) \Downarrow N) \end{aligned}$$

Notice that object-level substitution is realized via β-reduction in the meta-logic.

The notion of *applicative simulation* of λ-expressions can be encoded as the (stratified) co-inductive definition

$$\mathit{sim}\; R\; S \stackrel{\nu}{=} \forall T.R \Downarrow \mathrm{lam}\, T \supset \exists U.S \Downarrow \mathrm{lam}\, U \wedge \forall P.\mathit{sim}\; (T\, P)\; (U\, P).$$

Given this encoding, we can prove the reflexivity property of simulation, i.e., $\forall s.\mathit{sim}\; s\; s$. This is proved co-inductively by using the simulation $\lambda x \lambda y.x = y$. After applying $\forall\mathcal{R}$ and $\mathcal{CIR}$, it remains to prove the sequents $\longrightarrow s = s$, and

$$x = y \longrightarrow \forall x_1.x \Downarrow \mathrm{lam}\, x_1 \supset (\exists x_2.y \Downarrow \mathrm{lam}\, x_2 \wedge \forall x_3.(x_1\, x_3) = (x_2\, x_3))$$

The first sequent is provable by an application of $\mathrm{eq}\mathcal{R}$ rule. The second sequent is proved as follows.

$$\dfrac{\dfrac{\dfrac{\dfrac{\dfrac{\dfrac{}{z \Downarrow \mathrm{lam}\, x_1 \longrightarrow z \Downarrow \mathrm{lam}\, x_1}\,\mathit{init} \qquad \dfrac{\dfrac{}{z \Downarrow \mathrm{lam}\, x_1 \longrightarrow (x_1\, x_3) = (x_1\, x_3)}\,\mathrm{eq}\mathcal{R}}{z \Downarrow \mathrm{lam}\, x_1 \longrightarrow \forall x_3.(x_1\, x_3) = (x_1\, x_3)}\,\forall\mathcal{R}}{z \Downarrow \mathrm{lam}\, x_1 \longrightarrow (z \Downarrow \mathrm{lam}\, x_1 \wedge \forall x_3.(x_1\, x_3) = (x_1\, x_3))}\,\wedge\mathcal{R}}{z \Downarrow \mathrm{lam}\, x_1 \longrightarrow (\exists x_2.z \Downarrow \mathrm{lam}\, x_2 \wedge \forall x_3.(x_1\, x_3) = (x_2\, x_3))}\,\exists\mathcal{R}}{x = y, x \Downarrow \mathrm{lam}\, x_1 \longrightarrow (\exists x_2.y \Downarrow \mathrm{lam}\, x_2 \wedge \forall x_3.(x_1\, x_3) = (x_2\, x_3))}\,\mathrm{eq}\mathcal{L}}{x = y \longrightarrow x \Downarrow \mathrm{lam}\, x_1 \supset (\exists x_2.y \Downarrow \mathrm{lam}\, x_2 \wedge \forall x_3.(x_1\, x_3) = (x_2\, x_3))}\,\supset\mathcal{R}}{x = y \longrightarrow \forall x_1.x \Downarrow \mathrm{lam}\, x_1 \supset (\exists x_2.y \Downarrow \mathrm{lam}\, x_2 \wedge \forall x_3.(x_1\, x_3) = (x_2\, x_3))}\,\forall\mathcal{R}$$

The transitivity property is expressed as $\forall r \forall s \forall t.\mathit{sim}\; r\; s \wedge \mathit{sim}\; s\; t \supset \mathit{sim}\; r\; t$. Its proof involves co-induction on $\mathit{sim}\; r\; t$ with the simulation $\lambda u \lambda v.\exists w.\mathit{sim}\; u\; w \wedge \mathit{sim}\; w\; v$, followed by case analyses (i.e., $\mathit{def}\mathcal{L}$ and $\mathrm{eq}\mathcal{L}$ rules) on $\mathit{sim}\; r\; s$ and $\mathit{sim}\; s\; t$. The rest of the proof is basically a series of manipulations of logical connectives.

We can also show the existence of divergent terms. Divergence is encoded as follows.

$$\begin{aligned} \mathrm{divrg}\; T \stackrel{\nu}{=} & (\exists T_1 \exists T_2.T = (T_1 @ T_2) \wedge \mathrm{divrg}\; T_1) \vee \\ & (\exists T_1 \exists T_2.T = (T_1 @ T_2) \wedge \exists E.T_1 \Downarrow \mathrm{lam}\, E \wedge \mathrm{divrg}\; (E\, T_2)). \end{aligned}$$

Let Ω be the term $(\text{lam}\, x.(x \mathbin{@} x)) \mathbin{@} (\text{lam}\, x.(x \mathbin{@} x))$. We show that divrg Ω holds. The proof is straightforward by co-induction using the simulation $S := \lambda s.s = \Omega$. Applying the $\mathcal{CIR}$ produces the sequents $\longrightarrow \Omega = \Omega$ and $T = \Omega \longrightarrow S_1 \lor S_2$ where

$$S_1 := \exists T_1 \exists T_2 . T = (T_1 @ T_2) \land (S\, T_1), \text{ and}$$

$$S_2 := \exists T_1 \exists T_2 . T = (T_1 @ T_2) \land \exists E . T_1 \Downarrow \text{lam}\, E \land S\, (E\, T_2).$$

Clearly, only the second disjunct is provable, i.e., by instantiating T_1 and T_2 with the same term $\text{lam}\, x.(x \mathbin{@} x)$, and E with the function $\lambda x.(x \mathbin{@} x)$.

3.2 Lists

Lists over some fixed type α are encoded as the type *lst*, with the usual constructor nil : *lst* for empty list and :: of type $\alpha \to lst \to lst$. We consider here the append predicate for both the finite and infinite case.

Finite lists The usual append predicate on finite lists can be encoded as the inductive definition

$$\begin{aligned} \text{app}\, L_1\, L_2\, L_3 \stackrel{\mu}{=} & (L_1 = \text{nil} \land L_2 = L_3) \lor \\ & \exists x \exists L_1' \exists L_3' . L_1 = x :: L_1' \land L_3 = x :: L_3' \land \text{app}\, L_1'\, L_2\, L_3'. \end{aligned}$$

Associativity of append is stated formally as

$$\forall l_1 \forall l_2 \forall l_{12} \forall l_3 \forall l_4 . (\text{app}\, l_1\, l_2\, l_{12} \land \text{app}\, l_{12}\, l_3\, l_4) \supset \forall l_{23} . \text{app}\, l_2\, l_3\, l_{23} \supset \text{app}\, l_1\, l_{23}\, l_4.$$

Proving this formula requires us to prove first that the definition of append is functional, that is,

$$\forall l_1 \forall l_2 \forall l_3 \forall l_4 . \text{app}\, l_1\, l_2\, l_3 \land \text{app}\, l_1\, l_2\, l_4 \supset l_3 = l_4.$$

This is done by induction on l_1, i.e., we apply the $\mathcal{IL}$ rule on app $l_1\, l_2\, l_3$, after the introduction rules for $\forall$ and $\supset$, of course. The invariant in this case is

$$S := \lambda r_1 \lambda r_2 \lambda r_3 . \forall r . \text{app}\, r_1\, r_2\, r \supset r = r_3.$$

It is a simple case analysis to check that this is the right invariant. Back to our original problem: after applying the introduction rules for the logical connectives in the formula, the problem of associativity is reduced to the following sequent

$$\text{app}\, l_1\, l_2\, l_{12},\ \text{app}\, l_{12}\, l_3\, l_4,\ \text{app}\, l_2\, l_3\, l_{23} \longrightarrow \text{app}\, l_1\, l_{23}\, l_4. \tag{1}$$

We then proceed by induction on the list l_1, that is, we apply the $\mathcal{IL}$ rule to the hypothesis app $l_1\, l_2\, l_{12}$. The invariant is simply

$$S := \lambda l_1 \lambda l_2 \lambda l_{12} . \forall l_3 \forall l_4 . \text{app}\, l_{12}\, l_3\, l_4 \supset \forall l_{23} . \text{app}\, l_2\, l_3\, l_{23} \supset \text{app}\, l_1\, l_{23}\, l_4.$$

Applying the $\mathcal{IL}$ rule, followed by $\lor\mathcal{L}$, to sequent (1) reduces the sequent to the following sub-goals

$(i)\ S\,l_1\,l_2\,l_{12},\ \text{app}\,l_{12}\,l_3\,l_4,\ \text{app}\,l_2\,l_3\,l_{23} \longrightarrow \text{app}\,l_1\,l_{23}\,l_4,$
$(ii)\ (l_1 = \text{nil} \wedge l_2 = l_3) \longrightarrow S\,l_1\,l_2\,l_3,$
$(iii)\ \exists x, l_1', l_3'.l_1 = x :: l_1' \wedge l_3 = x :: l_3' \wedge S\,l_1'\,l_2\,l_3' \longrightarrow S\,l_1\,l_2\,l_3$

The proof for the second sequent is straightforward. The first sequent reduces to

$$\text{app}\,l_{12}\,l_3\,l_4, \text{app}\,l_{12}\,l_3\,l_{23} \longrightarrow \text{app nil}\,l_{23}\,l_4.$$

This follows from the functionality of append and $\mathcal{IR}$. The third sequent is basically done by a series of case analysis. Of course, these proofs could have been simplified by using a *derived* principle of *structural* induction. While this is easy to do, we have preferred here to use the primitive $\mathcal{IL}$ rule.

Infinite lists The append predicate on infinite lists is defined via co-recursion, that is, we define the behaviour of *destructor operations* on lists (i.e., taking the head and the tail of the list). In this case we never construct explicitly the result of appending two lists, rather the head and the tail of the resulting lists are computed as needed. The co-recursive append requires case analysis on all arguments.

$$\begin{aligned}\text{coapp}\ L_1\ L_2\ L_3 \stackrel{\nu}{=} &(L_1 = \text{nil} \wedge L_2 = \text{nil} \wedge L_3 = \text{nil}) \vee \\ &(L_1 = \text{nil} \wedge \exists x \exists L_2' \exists L_3'.L_2 = x :: L_2' \wedge L3 = x :: L_3' \ \wedge\ \text{coapp nil}\ L_2'\ L_3') \\ &\vee\ (\exists x \exists L_1' \exists L_3'.L_1 = x :: L_1' \wedge L_3 = x :: L_3' \ \wedge\ \text{coapp}\ L_1'\ L_2\ L_3').\end{aligned}$$

The corresponding associativity property is stated analogously to the inductive one and the main statement reduces to proving the sequent

$$\text{coapp}\ l_1\ l_2\ l_{12},\ \text{coapp}\ l_{12}\ l_3\ l_4,\ \text{coapp}\ l_2\ l_3\ l_{23} \longrightarrow \text{coapp}\ l_1\ l_{23}\ l_4.$$

We apply the $\mathcal{CIR}$ rule to coapp $l_1\ l_{23}\ l_4$, using the simulation

$$S := \lambda l_1 \lambda l_2 \lambda l_{12}.\exists l_{23} \exists l_3 \exists l_4.\text{coapp}\ l_{12}\ l_3\ l_4 \wedge\ \text{coapp}\ l_2\ l_3\ l_{23} \wedge\ \text{coapp}\ l_1\ l_{23}\ l_4.$$

Subsequent steps of the proof involve mainly case analysis on coapp $l_{12}\ l_3\ l_4$. As in the inductive case, we have to prove the sub-cases when l_{12} is nil. However, unlike in the former case, case analyses on the arguments of coapp suffices.

4 Cut-Elimination

A central result of our work is cut-elimination, from which consistency of the logic follows. Gentzen's classic proof of cut-elimination for first-order logic uses an induction on the size of the cut formula, i.e., the number of logical connectives in the formula. The cut-elimination procedure consists of a set of reduction rules that reduce a cut of a compound formula to cuts on its sub-formulae of smaller size. In the case of Linc, the use of induction/co-induction complicates the reduction of cuts. Consider for example a cut involving the induction rules

$$\dfrac{\dfrac{\dfrac{\Pi_1}{\Delta \longrightarrow B\,t}}{\Delta \longrightarrow p\,t}\,\mathcal{IR} \qquad \dfrac{\dfrac{\Pi_B}{B[S/p]\,y \longrightarrow S\,y} \quad \dfrac{\Pi}{S\,t, \Gamma \longrightarrow C}}{p\,t, \Gamma \longrightarrow C}\,\mathcal{IL}}{\Delta, \Gamma \longrightarrow C}\,mc$$

There are at least two problems in reducing this cut. First, any permutation upwards of the cut will necessarily involve a cut with S that can be of larger size than p, and hence a simple induction on the size of cut formula will not work. Second, the invariant S does not appear in the conclusion of the left premise of the cut. The latter means that we need to transform the left premise so that its end sequent will agree with the right premise. Any such transformation will most likely be *global*, and hence simple induction on the height of derivations will not work either. We define a proof transformation that we call *unfolding* to deal with the cut involving $\mathcal{IL}/\mathcal{IR}$ and $\mathcal{CIR}/\mathcal{CIL}$ pairs.

In the following definition, we refer to a premise of a rule as a *minor premise* if it is the left-premise of $\supset\mathcal{L}$ or $\mathcal{IL}$, or the right-premise of $\mathcal{CIR}$ or *mc*, otherwise it is a *major premise*. A derivation of a minor [major] premise is a *minor [major] premise derivation.* To simplify the definitions of unfolding, we restrict the *init*-rule to the atomic form. Non-atomic *init*-rule can easily be shown to be derivable using only structural rules, logical rules and atomic *init*. We shall refer to this non-atomic *init* derivation as Π^{Id}. We use the notation $\Pi\theta$ to denote the application of the substitution θ to Π, which amounts to applying the substitution to every sequent in Π.

Definition 4. Inductive unfolding. *Let $p\,\bar{x} \stackrel{\mu}{=} B\,\bar{x}$ be an inductive definition. Suppose we are given a derivation Π of $\Gamma \longrightarrow C$ where each occurrence of p in C is strictly positive, and a derivation Π_S of $B[S/p]\,\bar{x} \longrightarrow S\,\bar{x}$, for some closed term S. We define the derivation $\mu(\Pi,\Pi_S)$ of $\Gamma \longrightarrow C[S/p]$ as follows. If $C[S/p] = C$, then $\mu(\Pi,\Pi_S) = \Pi$. Otherwise, we define $\mu(\Pi,\Pi_S)$ based on the last rule in Π.*

1. *If Π ends with init on atom $p\,\bar{t}$, then $\mu(\Pi,\Pi_S)$ is the derivation*

$$\frac{\begin{array}{cc}\Pi_S & \Pi^{Id}\\ B[S/p]\,\bar{x} \longrightarrow S\bar{x} & S\,\bar{t} \longrightarrow S\,\bar{t}\end{array}}{p\,\bar{t} \longrightarrow S\,\bar{t}}\ \mathcal{IL}$$

2. *If Π ends with $\supset\mathcal{R}$*

$$\frac{\begin{array}{c}\Pi'\\ \Gamma, C_1 \longrightarrow C_2\end{array}}{\Gamma \longrightarrow C_1 \supset C_2}\supset\mathcal{R} \quad \textit{then } \mu(\Pi,\Pi_S) \textit{ is } \quad \frac{\begin{array}{c}\mu(\Pi',\Pi_S)\\ \Gamma, C_1 \longrightarrow C_2[S/p]\end{array}}{\Gamma \longrightarrow C_1 \supset C_2[S/p]}\supset\mathcal{R}$$

   Note that the restriction on the occurrence of p in C implies that $(C_1 \supset C_2)[S/p] = C_1 \supset C_2[S/p]$.

3. *If Π ends with $\mathcal{IR}$ on $p\,\bar{u}$, for some terms $\bar{u}$,*

$$\frac{\begin{array}{c}\Pi'\\ \Gamma \longrightarrow B\,\bar{u}\end{array}}{\Gamma \longrightarrow p\,\bar{u}}\ \mathcal{IR} \quad \textit{then } \mu(\Pi,\Pi_S) \textit{ is } \quad \frac{\begin{array}{cc}\mu(\Pi',\Pi_S) & \Pi_S[\bar{u}/\bar{x}]\\ \Gamma \longrightarrow B[S/p]\,\bar{u} & B[S/p]\,\bar{u} \longrightarrow S\,\bar{u}\end{array}}{\Gamma \longrightarrow S\,\bar{u}}\ mc$$

4. *Otherwise, if Π ends with any other rule, with the minor premise derivations $\Xi_1,\ldots,$ Ξ_m for some $m \geq 0$ and the major premise derivations $\{\Pi_i\}_{i\in\mathcal{I}}$ for some index set $\mathcal{I}$, then $\mu(\Pi,\Pi_S)$ ends with the same rule, with the same minor premises and the major premises $\{\mu(\Pi_i,\Pi_S)\}_{i\in\mathcal{I}}$.*

Definition 5. Co-inductive unfolding. *Let* $p\,\bar{x} \stackrel{\nu}{=} B\,\bar{x}$ *be a co-inductive definition. Let* C *be a formula in which every occurrence of* p *is strictly positive. Suppose we are given a derivation* Π *of* $\Gamma \longrightarrow C[S/p]$ *and a derivation* Π_S *of* $S\,\bar{x} \longrightarrow B[S/p]\,\bar{x}$*, for some closed term* S*. We define the derivation* $\nu(\Pi, \Pi_S)$ *of* $\Gamma \longrightarrow C$ *as follows. If* $C[S/p] = C$*, then* $\nu(\Pi, \Pi_S) = \Pi$*. If* $C = p\,\bar{t}$ *for some terms* $\bar{t}$*, then* $C[S/p]\,\bar{t} = S\,\bar{t}$ *and* $\nu(\Pi, \Pi_S)$ *is the derivation*

$$\cfrac{\begin{matrix}\Pi \\ \Gamma \longrightarrow S\,\bar{t}\end{matrix} \quad \begin{matrix}\Pi_S \\ S\,\bar{x} \longrightarrow B\,\bar{x}\end{matrix}}{\Gamma \longrightarrow p\,\bar{t}}\ \mathcal{CIR}$$

Otherwise, we define $\nu(\Pi, \Pi_S)$ *based on the last rule in* Π*. If* Π *ends with* $\supset \mathcal{R}$

$$\cfrac{\begin{matrix}\Pi' \\ \Gamma, C_1 \longrightarrow C_2[S/p]\end{matrix}}{\Gamma \longrightarrow C_1 \supset C_2[S/p]}\ \supset\mathcal{R} \qquad \text{then } \mu(\Pi, \Pi_S) \text{ is} \qquad \cfrac{\begin{matrix}\nu(\Pi', \Pi_S) \\ \Gamma, C_1 \longrightarrow C_2\end{matrix}}{\Gamma \longrightarrow C_1 \supset C_2}\ \supset\mathcal{R}.$$

If Π *ends with any other rule, with the minor premise derivations* $\Xi_1, \ldots, \Xi_m$ *for some* $m \geq 0$ *and the major premise derivations* $\{\Pi_i\}_{i \in \mathcal{I}}$ *for some index set* $\mathcal{I}$*, then* $\mu(\Pi, \Pi_S)$ *also ends with the same rule, with the same minor premises and the major premises* $\{\mu(\Pi_i, \Pi_S)\}_{i \in \mathcal{I}}$*.*

Our proof of cut-elimination uses the technique of reducibility originally due to Tait. The method was applied by Martin-Löf [13] to the setting of natural deduction, and to sequent calculus by McDowell and Miller for the logic $FO\lambda^{\Delta\mathbb{N}}$ [14]. The original idea of Martin-Löf was to use derivations directly as a measure by defining a well-founded ordering on them. The basis for the latter relation is a set of reduction rules that are used to eliminate the applications of cut rule. For the cases involving logical connectives, the cut-reduction rules used to prove the cut-elimination for Linc are the same to those of $FO\lambda^{\Delta\mathbb{N}}$. The crucial cases involving (co)-induction are given in the following definition. For simplicity of presentation, we assume the reduction involves the leftmost and the rightmost premise derivations of *mc*.

Definition 6. Cut-reduction. *Let* Ξ *be the derivation*

$$\cfrac{\begin{matrix}\Pi_1 \\ \Delta_1 \longrightarrow D_1\end{matrix} \quad \cdots \quad \begin{matrix}\Pi_n \\ \Delta_n \longrightarrow D_n\end{matrix} \quad \begin{matrix}\Pi \\ D_1, \ldots, D_n, \Gamma \longrightarrow C\end{matrix}}{\Delta_1, \ldots, \Delta_n, \Gamma \longrightarrow}\ mc.$$

Case $*/\mathcal{IL}$**:** *If* $D_1 = p\,\bar{t}$*, where* $p\,\bar{x} \stackrel{\mu}{=} B\,\bar{x}$*, and* Π *ends with* $\mathcal{IL}$ *on the cut formula* $p\,\bar{t}$

$$\cfrac{\begin{matrix}\Pi_S \\ B[S/p]\,\bar{x} \longrightarrow S\,\bar{x}\end{matrix} \quad \begin{matrix}\Pi' \\ S\,\bar{t}, D_2, \ldots, D_n, \Gamma \longrightarrow C\end{matrix}}{p\,\bar{t}, D_2, \ldots, D_n, \Gamma \longrightarrow C}\ \mathcal{IL}$$

then Ξ *reduces to*

$$\cfrac{\begin{matrix}\mu(\Pi_1, \Pi_S) \\ \Delta_1 \longrightarrow S\,\bar{t}\end{matrix} \quad \begin{matrix}\Pi_2 \\ \Delta_2 \longrightarrow D_2\end{matrix} \quad \cdots \quad \begin{matrix}\Pi_n \\ \Delta_n \longrightarrow D_n\end{matrix} \quad \begin{matrix}\Pi' \\ S\,\bar{t}, D_2, \ldots, D_n, \Gamma \longrightarrow C\end{matrix}}{\Delta_1, \ldots, \Delta_n, \Gamma \longrightarrow C}\ mc$$

Case $\mathcal{CIR}/\mathcal{CIL}$**:** *If* $D_1 = p\,\bar{t}$*, where* $p\,\bar{x} \stackrel{\nu}{=} B\,\bar{x}$*, and* Π_1 *and* Π *are*

$$\dfrac{\begin{matrix}\Pi_1' \\ \Delta_1 \longrightarrow S\,\bar{t}\end{matrix} \quad \begin{matrix}\Pi_S \\ S\,\bar{x} \longrightarrow B[S/p]\,\bar{x}\end{matrix}}{\Delta_1 \longrightarrow p\,\bar{t}}\ \mathcal{CIR} \qquad \dfrac{\begin{matrix}\Pi' \\ B\,\bar{t}, D_2, \ldots, D_n, \Gamma \longrightarrow C\end{matrix}}{p\,\bar{t}, D_2, \ldots, D_n, \Gamma \longrightarrow C}\ \mathcal{CIL}$$

then Ξ *reduces to*

$$\dfrac{\dfrac{\begin{matrix}\Pi_1' \\ \Delta_1 \longrightarrow S\,\bar{t}\end{matrix} \quad \begin{matrix}\Xi_1 \\ S\,\bar{t} \longrightarrow B\,\bar{t}\end{matrix}}{\Delta_1 \longrightarrow B\,\bar{t}}\ mc \quad \cdots \quad \begin{matrix}\Pi_n \\ \Delta_n \longrightarrow D_n\end{matrix} \quad \begin{matrix}\Pi' \\ B\,\bar{t}, \ldots, D_n, \Gamma \longrightarrow C\end{matrix}}{\Delta_1, \ldots, \Delta_n, \Gamma \longrightarrow C}\ mc$$

where $\Xi_1 = \nu(\Pi_S, \Pi_S)[\bar{t}/\bar{x}]$.

Notice that these two reductions are not symmetric. This is because we use an asymmetric measure to show the termination of cut-reduction, that is, the complexity of cut is always reduced on the right premise. The difficulty in getting a symmetric measure, in the presence of contraction and implication (in the body of definition), is already observed in [25].

To show the termination of cut-reduction, we define two orderings on derivations: *normalizability* and *reducibility* (called computability in [13]). The well-foundedness of the normalizability ordering immediately implies that the cut-elimination process terminates. Reducibility is a superset of normalizability and hence its well-foundedness implies the well-foundedness of normalizability. The main part of the proof lies in showing that all derivations in Linc are reducible, and hence normalizable. This is stated in the Lemma 1, of which cut-elimination is a simple corollary.

Lemma 1. *For any derivation* Π *of* $B_1, \ldots, B_n, \Gamma \longrightarrow C$*, reducible derivations* $\Pi_1, \ldots, \Pi_n$ *of* $\Delta_1 \longrightarrow B_1, \ldots, \Delta_n \longrightarrow B_n$ *(*$n \geq 0$*), and substitutions* $\delta_1, \ldots, \delta_n, \gamma$ *such that* $B_i\delta_i = B_i\gamma$*, for every* $i \in \{1, \ldots, n\}$*, the following derivation* Ξ *is reducible.*

$$\dfrac{\begin{matrix}\Pi_1\delta_1 \\ \Delta_1\delta_1 \longrightarrow B_1\delta_1\end{matrix} \quad \cdots \quad \begin{matrix}\Pi_n\delta_n \\ \Delta_n\delta_n \longrightarrow B_n\delta_n\end{matrix} \quad \begin{matrix}\Pi\gamma \\ B_1\gamma, \ldots, B_n\gamma, \Gamma\gamma \longrightarrow C\gamma\end{matrix}}{\Delta_1\delta_1, \ldots, \Delta_n\delta_n, \Gamma\gamma \longrightarrow C\gamma}\ mc$$

The proof proceeds by induction on the height of Π with subordinate inductions on n and on the (well-founded) reduction tree of $\Pi_1, \ldots, \Pi_n$. We give a general idea of the proof for the cases $*/\mathcal{IL}$ and $\mathcal{CIR}/\mathcal{CIL}$ in Definition 6, and refer to [31] for full details. In the following description, we refer to Definition 6 for the particular shapes of the derivations Π_1 and Π. In the $*/\mathcal{IL}$ case, it is sufficient to show that given the reducibility of Π_1, the unfolding derivation $\mu(\Pi_1, \Pi_S)$ is still reducible. This is done by induction on the construction of $\mu(\Pi_1, \Pi_S)$. The non-trivial case is when new cuts (*mc*) is introduced. But here we see that this instance of *mc* is always cutting with Π_S, and hence by the outer induction hypothesis (Π_S is of smaller height than Π) this instance of *mc* is reducible. The $\mathcal{CIR}/\mathcal{CIL}$ case is more complicated. In addition to showing that the co-inductive unfolding preserves reducibility, we also need to show that the unfolded derivation $\nu(\Pi_S, \Pi_S)$ is "closed" with respect to cut, that is, for every reducible derivation Ψ of $\Delta' \longrightarrow S\,\bar{u}$, the resulting derivation obtained by cutting Ψ with $\nu(\Pi_S, \Pi_S)[\bar{u}/\bar{x}]$ is reducible. This case is dealt with by building into the notion of reducibility this closure condition.

5 Related Work

Linc has been designed as an *intentionally* weak logical framework [6] to be used as a meta-language for reasoning over deductive systems encoded via HOAS. In particular, it can be seen as the meta-theory of the simply typed λ-calculus, in the same sense in which Schürmann's $\mathcal{M}_\omega$ [28] is the meta-theory of LF [11]. $\mathcal{M}_\omega$ is a constructive first-order logic, whose quantifiers range over possibly open LF objects over a signature. In the meta-logic it is possible to express and inductively prove meta-logical properties of an object logic. By the adequacy of the encoding, the proof of the existence of the appropriate LF object(s) guarantees the proof of the corresponding object-level property. It must be remarked that $\mathcal{M}_\omega$ does not support co-induction yet. However, LF can be used directly to specify an inductive meta-theorem as a relation between judgements, with a logic programming interpretation providing the operational semantics.

Of course, there is a long association between mathematical logic and inductive definitions [2] and in particular with proof-theory, possibly the earliest relevant entry being Martin-Löf's original formulation of the theory of *iterated inductive definitions* [13]. From the impredicative encoding of inductive types [4] and the introduction of (co)recursion [8] in system F, (co)inductive types became common [17] and made it into type-theoretic proof assistants such as Coq [20], first via a primitive recursive operator, but eventually in the let-rec style of functional programming languages, as in Gimenez's *Calculus of Infinite Constructions* [9]; here termination (resp. guardedness) is ensured by a syntactic check (see also [1]). Note that this has severe limitations (e.g., in the possibility of using lemmas in the body of a guarded proof) that do not applies to our approach. Circular proofs are also connected with the emerging proof-theory of *fixed point logics* and *process calculi* [24,29,30], in particular w.r.t. the relation between systems with local and global induction, that is, between fixed point vs. well-founded and guarded induction (i.e. circular proofs).

In higher order logic (co)inductive definitions are obtained via the usual Tarski fixed point constructions, as realized for example in Isabelle/HOL [21]. As we mentioned before, those approaches are at odd with HOAS even at the level of the syntax. Several compromises have been proposed: the *Theory of Contexts* [12] (ToC) marries *Weak* HOAS with an axiomatic approach encoding basic properties of names. *Hybrid* [3] is a λ-calculus on top of Isabelle/HOL which provides the user a *Full* HOAS syntax, compatible with a classical (co)-inductive setting. Linc improves on the latter on several counts. First it disposes of Hybrid notion of *abstraction*, which is used to carve out the "parametric" function space from the full HOL space. Moreover it is not restricted to second-order abstract syntax, as the current Hybrid version is (and as ToC cannot escape from being). Finally, at higher types, reasoning via $def\mathcal{L}$ is more powerful than inversion: for example $\forall y.\lambda x.y \neq \lambda x.0$ is provable in Linc, but fails both in Isabelle/HOL and Coq – the latter for extensionality reasons.

6 Conclusion and Future Work

We have presented a proof theoretical treatment of both induction and co-induction in a sequent calculus compatible with HOAS encodings. The proof principle underlying the explicit proof rules is basically fixed point (co)induction. Our proof system is, as far as we know, the first which incorporates a co-induction proof rule and still preserves cut-elimination. We have shown several examples where informal (co)inductive proofs using invariants and simulations are reproduced formally in Linc. Consistency of the logic is an easy consequence of cut-elimination.

We currently have two prototype implementations of Linc. The one in the Hybrid system [3,19] is better characterized as an approximation: definitional reflection is mimicked by the elimination rules of (co)inductive definitions, which also provides (co)induction principles, while the Hybrid λ-calculus takes care of the freeness properties: notwithstanding the limitations mentioned in Section 5, the implementation has the benefit of inheriting all the automation of Isabelle/HOL on whose top Hybrid is realized. The second is a direct implementation of Linc rules in λProlog, with a Java graphical user interface (available on the web at `http://www.lix.polytechnique.fr/ tiu`). This prototype is currently limited to be a proof-checker. A serious implementation would require more study on the proof search properties of Linc. It is true that with induction and co-induction there is no hope of automation in general. Nevertheless, a large subset of the logic may still admit some uniformity in proof search.

On the theoretical level, we conjecture that the proviso in the $\mathcal{CIR}$ rule can be eliminated. Similarly, we can loosen the stratification condition for example in the sense of *local* stratification and of terminating higher-order logic programs [23], possibly allowing to encode proofs such as type preservation in operational semantics directly in Linc rather than with the 2-level approach [15,19].

Another interesting problem to investigate is the connection with *circular proofs* which is particularly attractive from the viewpoint of proof search, both inductively and co-inductively. This could be realized by directly proving a cut-elimination result for a logic where circular proofs, under termination and guardedness conditions completely replace (co)inductive rules. Alternatively, we could reduce "global" proofs in such a system to "local" proofs in Linc, similarly to [30]. Finally, extensions of Linc, for example in the direction of $FO\lambda^{\nabla}$ [18] or the regular world assumption [28] are worth investigating.

Acknowledgements. The Linc logic was developed in collaboration with Dale Miller. Alberto Momigliano has been supported by EPSRC grant GR/M98555 and partly by the MRG project (IST-2001-33149), funded by the EC under the FET proactive initiative on Global Computing. Alwen Tiu has been supported in part by NSF grants CCR-9912387, INT-9815645, and INT-9815731 and LIX at École polytechnique.

References

[1] A. Abel and T. Altenkirch. A predicative strong normalisation proof for a λ-calculus with interleaving inductive types. In T. Coquand, P. Dybjer, B. Nordström, and J. Smith, editors, *Types for Proof and Programs, International Workshop, TYPES '99*, vol 1956 of *Lecture Notes in Computer Science*, pp 21–40. Springer-Verlag, 2000.

[2] P. Aczel. An introduction to inductive definitions. In J. Barwise, editor, *Handbook of Mathematical Logic*, vol 90 of *Studies in Logic and the Foundations of Mathematics*, pp 739–782. North-Holland, Amsterdam, 1977.

[3] S. Ambler, R. Crole, and A. Momigliano. Combining higher order abstract syntax with tactical theorem proving and (co)induction. In V. A. Carreño, editor, *Proceedings of the 15th International Conference on Theorem Proving in Higher Order Logics, Hampton, VA, 1-3 August 2002*, vol 2342 of *LNCS*. Springer Verlag, 2002.

[4] C. Bohm and A. Berarducci. Automatic synthesis of typed lambda programs on term algebras. *Theoretical Computer Science*, 39(2-3):135–153, Aug. 1985.

[5] R. L. Crole. Lectures on [Co]Induction and [Co]Algebras. Technical Report 1998/12, Department of Mathematics and Computer Science, University of Leicester, 1998.

[6] N. de Bruijn. A plea for weaker frameworks. In G. Huet and G. Plotkin, editors, *Logical Frameworks*, pp 40–67. Cambridge University Press, 1991.

[7] J. Despeyroux and A. Hirschowitz. Higher-order abstract syntax with induction in Coq. In *Fifth Conference on Logic Programming and Automated Reasoning*, pp 159–173, 1994.

[8] H. Geuvers. Inductive and coinductive types with iteration and recursion. In B. Nordström, K. Pettersson, and G. Plotkin, editors, *Informal Proceedings Workshop on Types for Proofs and Programs, Båstad, Sweden, 8–12 June 1992*, pp 193–217. Dept. of Computing Science, Chalmers Univ. of Technology and Göteborg Univ., 1992.

[9] E. Giménez. *Un Calcul de Constructions Infinies et son Application a la Verification des Systemes Communicants*. PhD thesis PhD 96-11, Laboratoire de l'Informatique du Parallélisme, Ecole Normale Supérieure de Lyon, Dec. 1996.

[10] J.-Y. Girard. A fixpoint theorem in linear logic. Email to the linear@cs.stanford.edu mailing list, February 1992.

[11] R. Harper, F. Honsell, and G. Plotkin. A framework for defining logics. *Journal of the ACM*, 40(1):143–184, 1993.

[12] F. Honsell, M. Miculan, and I. Scagnetto. An axiomatic approach to metareasoning on systems in higher-order abstract syntax. In *Proc. ICALP'01*, number 2076 in LNCS, pp 963–978. Springer-Verlag, 2001.

[13] P. Martin-Löf. Hauptsatz for the intuitionistic theory of iterated inductive definitions. In J. Fenstad, editor, *Proceedings of the Second Scandinavian Logic Symposium*, vol 63 of *Studies in Logic and the Foundations of Mathematics*, pp 179–216. North-Holland, 1971.

[14] R. McDowell and D. Miller. Cut-elimination for a logic with definitions and induction. *Theoretical Computer Science*, 232:91–119, 2000.

[15] R. McDowell and D. Miller. Reasoning with higher-order abstract syntax in a logical framework. *ACM Transactions on Computational Logic*, 3(1):80–136, January 2002.

[16] R. McDowell, D. Miller, and C. Palamidessi. Encoding transition systems in sequent calculus. *TCS*, 294(3):411–437, 2003.

[17] N. P. Mendler. Inductive types and type constraints in the second order lambda calculus. *Annals of Pure and Applied Logic*, 51(1):159–172, 1991.

[18] D. Miller and A. Tiu. A proof theory for generic judgments: An extended abstract. Proceedings of LICS'03, January 2003.

[19] A. Momigliano and S. Ambler. Multi-level meta-reasoning with higher order abstract syntax. In A. Gordon, editor, *FOSSACS'03*, vol 2620 of *LNCS*, pp 375–392. Springer, 2003.

[20] C. Paulin-Mohring. Inductive definitions in the system Coq: Rules and properties. In M. Bezem and J. Groote, editors, *Proc. of the International Conference on Typed Lambda Calculi and Applications*, pp 328–345, Utrecht, Mar. 1993. Springer-Verlag LNCS 664.

[21] L. C. Paulson. Mechanizing coinduction and corecursion in higher-order logic. *Journal of Logic and Computation*, 7(2):175–204, Mar. 1997.

[22] F. Pfenning. Logical frameworks. In *Handbook of Automated Reasoning*, pp 1063–1147. MIT Press, 2001.

[23] E. Rohwedder and F. Pfenning. Mode and termination analysis for higher-order logic programs. In *Proc. of the European Symposium on Programming*, pp 296–310, April 1996.

[24] L. Santocanale. A calculus of circular proofs and its categorical semantics. In M. Nielsen and U. Engberg editors, *Proc. of 5th Int. Conf. on Foundations of Software Science and Computation Structures, FoSSaCS 2002*, pp 357–371, Grenoble, Apr. 2002, Springer-Verlag LNCS 2303.

[25] P. Schroeder-Heister. Cut-elimination in logics with definitional reflection. In D. Pearce and H. Wansing, editors, *Nonclassical Logics and Information Processing*, vol 619 of *LNCS*, pp 146–171. Springer, 1992.

[26] P. Schroeder-Heister. Definitional reflection and the completion. In R. Dyckhoff, editor, *Proceedings of the 4th International Workshop on Extensions of Logic Programming*, pp 333–347. Springer-Verlag LNAI 798, 1993.

[27] P. Schroeder-Heister. Rules of definitional reflection. In M. Vardi, editor, *Eighth Annual Symposium on Logic in Computer Science*, pp 222–232. IEEE Press, June 1993.

[28] C. Schürmann. *Automating the Meta-Theory of Deductive Systems*. PhD thesis, Carnegie-Mellon University, 2000. CMU-CS-00-146.

[29] A. K. Simpson. Compositionality via cut-elimination: Hennessy-Milner logic for an arbitrary GSOS. In D. Kozen, editor, *Proceedings of LICS'95*, pp 420–430, San Diego, California, June 1995. IEEE Computer Society Press.

[30] C. Spenger and M. Dams. On the structure of inductive reasoning: Circular and tree-shaped proofs in the μ-calculus. In A. Gordon, editor, *FOSSACS'03*, vol 2620 of *LNCS*, pp 425–440,. Springer Verlag, 2003.

[31] A. Tiu. Cut-elimination for a logic with induction and co-induction. Draft, available via `http://www.cse.psu.edu/ tiu/lce.pdf`, Sept. 2003.

QArith: Coq Formalisation of Lazy Rational Arithmetic

Milad Niqui[1] and Yves Bertot[2]

[1] University of Nijmegen
milad@cs.kun.nl
[2] INRIA Sophia Antipolis
Yves.Bertot@sophia.inria.fr

Abstract. In this paper we present the *Coq* formalisation of the *QArith* library which is an implementation of rational numbers as binary sequences for both lazy and strict computation. We use the representation also known as the Stern-Brocot representation for rational numbers. This formalisation uses advanced machinery of the *Coq* theorem prover and applies recent developments in formalising general recursive functions. This formalisation highlights the rôle of type theory both as a tool to verify hand-written programs and as a tool to generate verified programs.

1 Introduction

The present work is the continuation of two earlier parallel works of the authors [3,13] with two principal objectives:

1. To present a library of rational numbers for *Coq* [6] based on a canonical representation for rational numbers also known as Stern-Brocot representation[1].
2. To verify in *Coq* the correctness of a family of lazy algorithms for exact rational arithmetic.

In the present paper we do not detail the lazy algorithms that are described in [13]. For the complete formal development, we refer the reader to [14].

In Sect. 2 we present the set of rational numbers as an inductively defined set of signed binary sequences. In Sect. 3 we describe strict algorithms for the field operations. In Sect. 4 we describe lazy algorithms for these operations, based on homographic and quadratic transformations. In Sect. 5 we discuss the proof of correctness for these algorithms. In Sect. 6 we discuss the question of program extraction as it is provided in the *Coq* type theory and the impact this question had on our formal work. Possible further work is mentioned in Sect. 7.

[1] A presentation of the Stern-Brocot trees and related publications is given in [13].

S. Berardi, M. Coppo, and F. Damiani (Eds.): TYPES 2003, LNCS 3085, pp. 309–323, 2004.

2 Rational Numbers as Binary Sequences

Given a positive fraction $\frac{p}{q}$, its Stern–Brocot representation is a finite binary sequence, consisting of the letters **L** and **R** and is characterised by the following encoding (left) and decoding (right) functions ([] denotes the empty sequence):

$$\ulcorner\tfrac{m}{n}\urcorner := \begin{cases} [] & m = n, \\ \mathbf{L}\ulcorner\frac{m}{n-m}\urcorner & m < n, \\ \mathbf{R}\ulcorner\frac{m-n}{n}\urcorner & m > n\ . \end{cases} \qquad \begin{cases} [\![[]]\!] & := 1, \\ [\![\mathbf{L}\sigma]\!] & := \frac{[\![\sigma]\!]}{[\![\sigma]\!]+1}, \\ [\![\mathbf{R}\sigma]\!] & := [\![\sigma]\!] + 1\ . \end{cases}$$

One can formalise this in *Coq* by first defining the set of positive rational numbers and then the entire set of rational numbers, inductively as:

```
Inductive Q+ : Set := nR: Q+→Q+ | dL: Q+→Q+ | One: Q+.

Inductive Q  : Set := Zero: Q | Qpos: Q+→Q | Qneg: Q+→Q.
```

We formalise the above encoding function that maps pairs of natural numbers p and q to the binary sequence representing $\frac{p}{q}$. The recursion in this function is bounded by an extra measure argument.

```
Fixpoint Q+c (p q n : nat) {struct n} : Q+ :=
  match n with
  | O ⇒ One
  | S n' ⇒ match p - q with
           | O ⇒ match q - p with | O ⇒ One | v ⇒ dL (Q+c p v n') end
           | v ⇒ nR (Q+c v q n')
           end
  end.
```

If either of p or q is zero, the outcome of this function is irrelevant. The encoding function for arbitrary rational numbers always calls $\mathtt{Q}_c^+$ with positive input.

```
Definition makeQ (m n : Z):=
  match m, n with
  | Zpos _, Zpos _ ⇒ Qpos (Q+c (abs m) (abs n) (abs m)+(abs n))
  | Zneg _, Zneg _ ⇒ Qpos (Q+c (abs m) (abs n) (abs m)+(abs n))
  | ZO    , _      ⇒ Zero
  | _     , ZO     ⇒ Zero
  | _     , _      ⇒ Qneg (Q+c (abs m) (abs n) (abs m)+(abs n))
  end.
```

Here the function `abs` is the forgetful projection from `Z` onto `nat` (*Coq* natural numbers). Thus for p and q two integers, *makeQ* `p q` produces the signed binary sequence corresponding to $\frac{p}{q}$. For example:

```
Eval compute in makeQ 9 14.
= Qpos (dL (nR (dL (nR (nR (nR One)))))) : Q
```

Decoding functions have a similar structure, with a main decoding function for arbitrary rational numbers and a recursive function for positive rational numbers. Here the function `Z_of_nat` is the trivial injection of `nat` into `Z`.

```
Fixpoint Q_i^+ (w : Q+) : nat * nat :=
  match w with
  | One ⇒ (1, 1)
  | nR w' ⇒ match Q_i^+ w' with (p,q)⇒ (p + q, q)
  | dL w' ⇒ match Q_i^+ w' with (p,q)⇒ (p, p + q)
  end.

Definition decodeQ(q : Q):=
  match q with
  | Qpos p ⇒ (Z_of_nat (fst (Q_i^+ p)), Z_of_nat (snd (Q_i^+ p)))
  | Qneg p ⇒ ((- Z_of_nat (fst (Q_i^+ p))), Z_of_nat (snd (Q_i^+ p)))
  | Zero ⇒ (0, 1)
  end.
```

We also proved that encoding and decoding are inverse operations.

```
Lemma makeQdecodeQ:∀q:Q, makeQ (fst (decodeQ q)) (snd (decodeQ q))=q.
```

Note that this equality between the resulting signed binary sequence and the original sequence is syntactical (Leibniz equality). For the converse direction we can prove the following lemma:

```
Lemma decodeQmakeQ:∀m n:Z, let (p,q):=(decodeQ (makeQ m n)) in n≠0→m*q=n*p.
```

Here the equality is not syntactical, rather it is the definitional equality on positive fractions. These lemmata show the advantage of our binary representation for rational numbers. In a system like *Coq*, reasoning with data types is considerably easier when we are dealing with the corresponding syntactical equality; we can use the rewriting machinery of the theorem prover to ease the equational reasoning. But the benefits of this canonical representation are not restricted to machinery of the theorem provers. For a more detailed discussion and examples of simplified mathematical proofs see [3].

The lemmata *makeQdecodeQ* and *decodeQmakeQ* demonstrate that the inductively defined set Q is a representation for rational numbers. In the rest of this paper we will show how we can equip the set Q with the usual algebraic operations and prove the correctness of these operations.

3 Field Structure: A Strict Implementation

In this section, we present the formalisation of algebraic operations on Q in the natural mathematical way. When computing an operation with rational numbers, mathematicians usually perform regular natural number computations with the numerators and denominators and then simplify the result to a reduced fraction, using a greatest common divisor computation. For this reason, we shall use the term *fraction* to denote the pair of a numerator and denominator.

In our case, we start with values in the type Q and we use the function *decodeQ* to obtain fractions for each operand and then perform the usual natural number computations. At the end of the computation, the resulting fraction is directly encoded using the function $\mathtt{Q}_c^+$, because this function already integrates the greatest common divisor computation, as was shown in [3].

We only provide operations to manipulate positive fractions. The encapsulating functions which take care of conversions between the type Q take care of sign problems. This means that we need to provide three basic operations for fractions: addition, multiplication, and subtraction. Both addition and subtraction on fractions with positive components are needed for the addition on rational numbers, because adding two numbers with opposite signs tantamounts to a subtraction. Computing the result sign for an addition when the two numbers have opposite sign also requires a function to compare two rational numbers. We do not implement this comparison function at the level of fractions but rather at the level of the type $\mathtt{Q}^+$. For multiplication, the situation is simpler, multiplying rational numbers reduces to multiplying the absolute values and then computing the sign of the result.

Comparing two numbers in the type $\mathtt{Q}^+$ is simple. The constructors nR and dL can actually be interpreted as monotonically increasing functions; the former always returns a result greater than 1 while the second one always returns a result less than 1. Thus, it suffices to compare the two bits bitwise from left to right.

```
Fixpoint Q+_le_bool (w w' : Q+) {struct w'} : bool :=
  match w with
  | One  ⇒ match w' with | dL y ⇒ false | _ ⇒ true end
  | dL y ⇒ match w' with | dL y' ⇒ Q+_le_bool y y' | _ ⇒ true end
  | nR y ⇒ match w' with | nR y' ⇒ Q+_le_bool y y' | _ ⇒ false end
  end.
```

This function is used to define a two argument predicate Q+_le and a strongly specified test function Q+_le_dec which plays the key rôle in the operations' implementations, because the subtraction operation is only meaningful when the first argument is greater than the second argument.

```
Definition Qplus (x y:Q):=
     match x, y with | Qpos x', Qpos y' ⇒ Qpos (Q+_plus x' y')
                     | Qpos x', Qneg y' ⇒
                        match Q+_le_dec x' y' with
                        | left h =>
                            match Q+_eq_dec x' y' with
                            | left h => Zero
                            | right h => Qneg (Q+_sub y' x')
                            end
                        | right h => Qpos (Q+_sub x' y')
                        end
                     | Qneg x', Qneg y' => Qneg (Q+_plus x' y')
                     ...
```

The unary operation of computing the opposite of a rational number is a trivial matter. To compute the inverse, we need to compute the inverse of a positive integer in $\mathtt{Q}^+$. It actually is a very simple function, where we do not need to convert to a fraction of natural numbers and back.

```
Fixpoint Q+_inv (w:Q+):Q+:=
  match w with | One ⇒ One
               | nR w' ⇒ dL (Q+_inv w')
               | dL w' ⇒ nR (Q+_inv w')
  end.
```

With all these operations, it is then quite easy to show that the type Q with comparison, addition, subtraction, multiplication, and inversion is an Archimedean ordered field. We use this 'natural' implementation as a reference implementation (but not a very efficient one) of the field operations (see Sect. 5.1).

Most of these algorithms for the basic operations are strict; in the sense that we need to process the entire bit strings of both arguments to obtain the numerators and denominators and start computing the result. Only the inverse and comparison function can start to return results without having processed their entire input.

4 Field Structure: A Lazy Implementation

4.1 Laziness

Lazy computation is a constructive interpretation of continuity[2]. The idea is that if we are computing continuous functions on sequences, it is possible to do this computation in a lazy manner, outputting partial information about the final result after having processed only initial segments of the input. If we consider streams (infinite sequences) instead of finite sequences, we can make this notion more precise by calling a function on streams *lazy* if it is continuous with respect to the Cantor space topology on the set of streams. In our case the operations addition, multiplication, division and subtraction are all continuous both on $\mathbb{R}$ and on $\mathbb{Q}$ with the subspace topology, and we can devise lazy algorithms for these operations. However, the inputs we consider are finite and this explains why we could provide a strict implementation.

A lazy algorithm on sequences usually consists of two steps: (1) looking at initial segments of the input, the *absorption* step; (2) outputting an initial segment of the output, the *emission* step. An algorithm terminates when it emits the empty sequence. When there are several inputs, the algorithm also contains an *absorption strategy* to decide which input initial segment to absorb next. Classical examples of lazy algorithms are those given by Gosper [8] for adding and multiplying regular continued fractions. The work by Gosper was later generalised for exact real arithmetic [18,12,17,9].

We devised lazy algorithms to compute directly on the $\mathtt{Q}^+$ and Q structures without going through computations on fractions; we then showed their equivalence with the strict algorithms from Sect. 3. One can show that the lazy

[2] There are other aspects of laziness (e.g. laziness in the sense of sharing the reduction) which we do not consider in this paper.

approach should have a lower computational complexity, especially when partial answers are useful (for instance in the case of dealing with the fractions with large denominators). But we discover in this work that the proof complexity has an impact on the usability of the algorithms and the strict approach is still the most efficient one for some purposes (see Sect. 6.3).

4.2 Homographic and Quadratic Algorithms

In this section we briefly discuss the homographic and quadratic algorithms for computations on signed binary sequences. The algorithms that we use are explained in detail in [13] and are available on-line as part of the *Coq* contribution package *QArith* [14]. Following [8], to devise the basic field operations, we consider a larger class of unary and binary operations. The basic operations are then simultaneously obtained from the general algorithms.

A *homographic transformation* of matrix M is a function of the form

$$h_M(x) = \frac{ax+b}{cx+d} \qquad a,b,c,d \in \mathbb{Z}; \qquad M = \begin{bmatrix} a & b \\ c & d \end{bmatrix} .$$

A *quadratic transformation* of matrix T is a binary function of the form

$$q_T(x,y) = \frac{axy+bx+cy+d}{exy+fx+gy+h} \qquad a,b,c,d,e,f,g,h \in \mathbb{Z} \qquad \text{and } T = \begin{bmatrix} a & b & c & d \\ e & f & g & h \end{bmatrix} .$$

By taking the following special values for T we obtain the algorithms for basic arithmetic operations:

$$T_\oplus = \begin{bmatrix} 0 & 1 & 1 & 0 \\ 0 & 0 & 0 & 1 \end{bmatrix}, T_\otimes = \begin{bmatrix} 1 & 0 & 0 & 0 \\ 0 & 0 & 0 & 1 \end{bmatrix}, T_\ominus = \begin{bmatrix} 0 & 1 & -1 & 0 \\ 0 & 0 & 0 & 1 \end{bmatrix}, T_\oslash = \begin{bmatrix} 0 & 1 & 0 & 0 \\ 0 & 0 & 1 & 0 \end{bmatrix} .$$

In [13] the homographic algorithm is presented using two auxiliary algorithms: *the sign algorithm* and *the output-bit algorithm.* The sign algorithm is a function $\mathcal{S}\colon M_{2\times 2}(\mathbb{Z})\times \mathtt{Q}^+ \longrightarrow \{0,+1,-1\}\times M_{2\times 2}(\mathbb{Z})\times \mathtt{Q}^+$ (here $M_{2\times 2}(\mathbb{Z})$ denotes the type of 2×2 matrices over $\mathbb{Z}$). This means that the outcome of the sign algorithm is a triple consisting of the sign, a matrix of coefficients, and the unused part of the input sequence. The output-bit algorithm is a function $\mathcal{B}\colon M_{2\times 2}(\mathbb{Z})\times \mathtt{Q}^+ \longrightarrow \mathtt{Q}^+$ which outputs an unsigned binary sequence. Finally the homographic algorithm is a function $\mathcal{H}\colon M_{2\times 2}(\mathbb{Z})\times \mathtt{Q}^+ \longrightarrow \mathtt{Q}$ which combines the two functions $\mathcal{S}$ and $\mathcal{B}$. Both functions $\mathcal{S}$ and $\mathcal{B}$ are recursive. In the case of $\mathcal{S}$ we are dealing with a simple structural recursion on the binary sequence. The recursion in $\mathcal{B}$ is more complex. If the recursion was structural, then all recursive calls would be absorption steps. In our case, some recursive calls are only emission steps, but the total sum of the matrix coefficients decreases while remaining positive. This is one of the main difficulties of the verification process; in *Coq*, formalising non-structural yet terminating recursion is possible in various ways. But all of the methods either require *a priori* knowledge of the algorithm complexity (for example the Balaa and Bertot's method [1]) or lead to very large proof terms by changing the representation of the function's domain (for example the Bove and Capretta's method [5]). In Sect. 4.4 we explain how we used a variant of Bove and Capretta's method in our formalisation to formalise the non-structural recursion.

Similarly in the case of the quadratic algorithm, the sign algorithm is a function $\mathcal{S}_2\colon T_{2\times 4}(\mathbb{Z})\times\mathtt{Q}^+\times\mathtt{Q}^+\longrightarrow\{0,+1,-1\}\times T_{2\times 4}(\mathbb{Z})\times\mathtt{Q}^+\times\mathtt{Q}^+$ in which $T_{2\times 4}(\mathbb{Z})$ is the type of 2×4 integer matrices. The output-bit algorithm is a function $\mathcal{B}_2\colon T_{2\times 4}(\mathbb{Z})\times\mathtt{Q}^+\times\mathtt{Q}^+\longrightarrow\mathtt{Q}^+$; consequently, the quadratic algorithm will be formalised as a function $\mathcal{Q}\colon T_{2\times 4}(\mathbb{Z})\times\mathtt{Q}^+\times\mathtt{Q}^+\longrightarrow\mathtt{Q}$ which combines the two functions $\mathcal{S}_2$ and $\mathcal{B}_2$. The function $\mathcal{S}_2$ is a structurally recursive function with respect to the binary structure of both inputs while the function $\mathcal{B}_2$ is not.

4.3 Lazy Proof Obligation

In [13] we implicitly assumed that the denominators of all transformations involved are nonzero. This imposes a restriction on the formalisation because it makes the algorithms partial. A standard way to formalise partial functions in type theory is to add a proof obligation to the function's arguments, using a predicate to specify the function's domain. For the homographic algorithm $\mathcal{H}$, the domain predicate has the form

$$\lambda a,b,c,d\colon \mathbb{Z}\;; q\colon \mathtt{Q}.\ \Phi_{\mathcal{H}}(c,d,q)\ .$$

The predicate $\Phi_{\mathcal{H}}\colon Z^2\times\mathtt{Q}\rightarrow\mathtt{Prop}$ *means* $c{*}q{+}d{\neq}0$, but we want to avoid using the strict operations to define the predicate. We first define a domain predicate for the sign algorithm as an inductive property of triples $(c,d,p)\colon \mathbb{Z}\times\mathbb{Z}\times\mathtt{Q}^+$, using only operations on integers and pattern matching on the first bit:

```
Inductive ΦS:Z→Z→Q+→Prop:=
| ΦS0:∀ (c d : Z) (p:Q+), p = One→c+d≠0→ ΦS c d p          (* p=One *)
| ΦS1:∀ (c d : Z) (xs:Q+), ΦS c c+d xs→ ΦS c d (nR xs)     (* p=(nR xs) *)
| ΦS2:∀ (c d : Z) (xs:Q+), ΦS c+d d xs→ ΦS c d (dL xs).    (* p=(dL xs) *)
```

The domain predicate for $\mathcal{H}$ is obtained by adapting $\Phi_{\mathcal{S}}$ according to the sign bit of each rational number:

```
Inductive ΦH (c d : Z) (q:Q):Prop:=
| ΦH0: q = Zero→d≠0→ ΦH c d q
| ΦH1:∀ p:Q+, q = Qpos p→ ΦS c d p→ ΦH c d q
| ΦH2:∀ p:Q+, q = Qneg p→ ΦS -c d p→ ΦH c d q.
```

There is also a domain predicate for the output-bit algorithm, but that one is a consequence of the accessibility predicate (Sect. 4.4).

The precise type of the *Coq* formalisation of the homographic algorithm becomes $\mathcal{H}$:∀ `(a b c d:Z) (q:Q)`,$\Phi_{\mathcal{H}}$ `c d q→ Q`. Since the type of ($\Phi_{\mathcal{H}}$ `c d q`) is `Prop`, the proof obligation is removed during the extraction (Sect. 6.1), and the extracted programs is close to those given in [13]. The same technique is used for the quadratic algorithm and the *Coq* formalisation of the function has the type $\mathcal{Q}$:∀ `(a b c d e f g h:Z) (q1 q2:Q)`,$\Phi_{\mathcal{Q}}$ `e f g h q1 q2→ Q`.

We need only one lemma to prove that the usual field operations satisfy the proof obligations:

```
Lemma addmultPrf:∀ (x y:Q), Φ_Q 0 0 0 1 x y.
Definition QplusLazy (x y:Q):= Q 0 1 1 0 0 0 0 1 x y (addmultPrf x y).
Definition QmultLazy (x y:Q):= Q 1 0 0 0 0 0 0 1 x y (addmultPrf x y).
```

4.4 Accessibility

The mathematical argument to ensure that the output-bit algorithm terminates, is that the length of the input sequence decreases in absorption steps and that the total sum of matrix coefficients decrease in emission steps. Checking that the total sum is decreasing is not syntactically possible impromptu. We follow Bove and Capretta's method of formalising general recursive functions and define the function's domain as an inductive predicate, so that the algorithm can be described as a structural recursive function with respect to this predicate. This method is also known as recursion on an *ad hoc predicate*. For the reasons that we discuss in Sect. 6.2, we use a variant of the method that was suggested by Paulin [15] and further explored in detail in [4]. The domain of the function $\mathcal{B}$ will be quotiented by $\Psi_{\mathcal{H}}(a, b, c, d, p)$, which is an inductively defined predicate that determines which of the 5-tuples (a, b, c, d, p) are accessible for the recursive branches of the output-bit algorithm (cf. [13, Def. 4.3]):

```
Definition isAbove (a b c d:Z):=(c≤a∧d<b)∨(c<a∧d≤b).
Inductive Ψ_H:Z→Z→Z→Z→Q⁺→Prop:=
|  Ψ_H0:∀ (a b c d : Z) (p : Q⁺), p=One→0<a+b→0<c+d→ Ψ_H a b c d p
| Ψ_H1:∀ (a b c d : Z) (p : Q⁺), p≠One→ isAbove a b c d→
     Ψ_H (a-c) (b-d) c d p→ Ψ_H a b c d p
| Ψ_H2:∀ (a b c d : Z) (p : Q⁺), p≠One→¬ isAbove a b c d→
     isAbove c d a b→ Ψ_H a b c-a d-b p→ Ψ_H a b c d p
| Ψ_H3:∀ (a b c d : Z) (xs : Q⁺), ¬ isAbove a b c d→¬ isAbove c d a b→
     Ψ_H a a+b c c+d xs→ Ψ_H a b c d (nR xs)
| Ψ_H3':∀ (a b c d : Z) (xs : Q⁺), ¬ isAbove a b c d→¬ isAbove c d a b→
     Ψ_H a+b b c+d d xs→ Ψ_H a b c d (dL xs).
```

We use this accessibility predicate to formalise the homographic output-bit algorithm. This function's type becomes

```
H_Q⁺_to_Q⁺: ∀ (a b c d : Z) (p : Q⁺), Ψ_H a b c d p → Q⁺.
```

After defining this function in *Coq*, each time we want to use it we should supply a term `H_acc:(Ψ_H a b c d p)`. But we know that all the positive values of a, b, c and d are in the function's domain:

```
Lemma Ψ_H_Wf:∀ (a b c d:Z) (p:Q⁺),
                 0<a+b→0<c+d→0≤a→0≤b→0≤c→0≤d→ Ψ_H a b c d p.
```

We prove this lemma by well-founded induction on the intrinsic order of the accessibility predicate. We denote this order by $<_5$ and we define it as follows.

$$(a_1, a_2, a_3, a_4, p) <_5 (a_1', a_2', a_3', a_4', q) \text{ iff } \mathsf{len}(p) < \mathsf{len}(q) \lor (p{=}q \land \sum_{i=1}^{4} a_i < \sum_{i=1}^{4} a_i') \ .$$

We prove that this order is well-founded on the set $\mathbb{Z}^{+4} \times \mathtt{Q}^{+}$ (where $\mathbb{Z}^{+}$ is the set of nonnegative integers); the lemma $\Psi_{\mathcal{H}}$*_Wf* is a direct consequence.

We take the similar approach for the formalisation of the output-bit algorithm for the quadratic function. There we have an accessibility predicate $\Psi_{\mathcal{Q}}$ on the set $\mathbb{Z}^8 \times \mathtt{Q}^{+2}$. The well-founded order corresponding to this accessibility predicate is an order on 10-tuples which is well founded on the set $\mathbb{Z}^{+8} \times \mathtt{Q}^{+2}$. Consequently we use well-founded induction to prove the following lemma:

```
Lemma ΨQ_Wf:∀ (a b c d e f g h:Z) (p1 p2:Q+),
          0<a+b+c+d→0<e+f+g+h→ 0≤a→0≤b→0≤c→0≤d→
          0≤e→0≤f→0≤g→0≤h→ ΨQ a b c d e f g h p1 p2.
```

This lemma shows that we can use the output-bit algorithm (the function $\mathcal{B}_2$) to compute the quadratic transformations with nonnegative coefficients and with at least one positive coefficient in the numerator and one positive coefficient in the denominator. In order to compute the quadratic transformations with negative coefficients and on negative inputs we use the quadratic algorithm (the function $\mathcal{Q}$) to modify the coefficients with respect to the sign bit and call the output-bit algorithm with nonnegative coefficients.

5 Correctness Proofs

5.1 Using Strict Implementations

In Sects. 3 and 4 we showed how we formalised strict and lazy arithmetic operations on the data type Q. In this section we discuss how the lazy algorithms were formally proven to be correct. One possible approach is similar to what we did for strict operations: to prove that the lazy operations satisfy all the axioms of a field. The second possibility is to use the strict algorithms as a *specification* for the lazy ones, with lemmata of the following form:

```
Lemma QplusLazy_Qplus:∀ (x y:Q), QplusLazy x y = Qplus x y.
```

In our development we took this approach but we proved more general results. The one for the quadratic algorithm has the following form, momentarily using $\oplus$ and $\otimes$ do denote the strict operations.

```
Theorem Q_Correctness:∀ (a b c d e f g h:Z) (q1 q2:Q)
                   (hyp:(e⊗q1⊗q2)⊕(f⊗q1)⊕(g⊗q2)⊕ h ≠ Zero),
  Q a b c d e f g h q1 q2 (Q_nonzeroCorrect e f g h q1 q2 hyp)=
      ((a⊗q1⊗q2)⊕(b⊗q1)⊕(c⊗q2)⊕d)⊗(Qinv ((e⊗q1⊗q2)⊕(f⊗q1)⊕(g⊗q2)⊕h)).
```

The correctness of field operations is just a special instance of this general theorem. In the statement of the above theorem, the term *Q_nonzeroCorrect* corresponds to the correctness of the lazy proof obligations that we defined in Sect. 4.3.

5.2 Using the `field` Tactic

The `field` tactic was devised by Delahaye and Mayero [7] to ease the equational reasoning on field structures in *Coq*. It is a decision procedure for simple equations that generates proof obligations for each occurrence of the division.

We could use this tactic directly after proving that the strict operations of Sect. 3 satisfy the field axioms. It was of great help in the correctness proof; however, there were instances where we had to fine-tune the reduction behaviour of the `field` tactic to prevent unnecessary reduction that slows down the tactic behaviour to an unacceptable level. The default reduction behaviour is based on the eager reduction, probably because the original design was based on an axiomatic field structure. Our experience shows that the `field` tactic will be more useful for equational reasoning on concrete fields (as opposed to abstract axiomatic fields), if this reduction behaviour is less eager. Note that the `Ring` tactic, which is the *Coq* tactic for equational reasoning on rings, does not have this problem with eager reduction; hence it is very useful in reasoning about concrete rings such as the ring of integers.

After proving the correctness of the lazy algorithms, we could define a *second* field structure based on lazy operations. Therefore we have a single data type with two different field structures on it. This is an interesting situation; it deserves a deeper investigation to see whether it is useful — from the theorem proving point of view — to have two underlying fields on the same carrier type, or whether it adds to the complexity of the proofs.

5.3 Functional Induction

As it is obvious from the quadratic and homographic algorithms given in [13] and the formalisation we discussed in Sect. 4, we are dealing with functions of up to 11 arguments (in quadratic algorithms) which are defined by case distinctions of up to 43 cases (in homographic and quadratic sign algorithms). The case distinctions in the definition of functions gets in the way when we want to prove these functions' properties. This means that if we want to prove the correctness of the homographic sign algorithm, we should consider 43 different cases. During the proof of the correctness many of these cases should be handled in a similar way; they can be solved by automatic tactics or are degenerate cases. The tactic `functional induction` is designed by Barthe and Courtieu [2] to assist the user in dealing with these situations by providing some automation. When given a *Coq* function, the tactic `functional induction` tries to automatically generate an elimination principle which is tailored to the shape of that function. It then applies this elimination principle on the current goal generating all the possible different cases based on the case distinctions in the definition of the function. This will generate one subgoal for each case; the tactic then applies some heuristics to solve as many subgoals as possible. In our project, in proving the correctness of the lazy operations, we benefited immensely from the beta version of this tactic. Our usage also contributed in making this tactic more efficient by exposing some of the bugs of that version. Our experience shows that this tactic can make *Coq* a better framework for reasoning about realistic algorithms which are often based on heavy case analysis on a multitude of arguments.

6 Programs versus Proofs

The algorithms for lazy arithmetic on $\mathtt{Q}^+$ were first implemented in *Haskell*. The original *Haskell* implementation was about 16 kilobytes of code. The *Coq* formalisation of the lazy algorithms led to fixing some exception handling bugs in the original *Haskell* code. Moreover the *Coq* formalisation highlighted the symmetries between fractions, homographic transformations and quadratic transformations as members of the larger family of *multilinear functions*. This resulted in generalising the algorithms for multilinear forms in n variables [13]. Such improvements show some advantages of formalising functions in type theory. There is however, the disadvantage that formalising the programs in type theory is a time consuming process; the amount of automation and heuristics available in present day theorem provers is far from being satisfactory.

Table 1 shows the relative size (in kilobytes) of the various phases of formalisation. During this project we used the most novel facilities of *Coq*. The statistics in Table 1 might thus discourage people from using type theoretical tools for verification purposes. Our answer is that, without the existing automation tools in recent versions of *Coq*, and without the recent theoretical advances, such a project seemed impossible only a couple of years ago. This makes us confident that in the coming years, similar projects will help in improving theorem provers and making them more programmer-oriented and will alleviate the task of formalising and verification of the algorithms in theorem provers based on type theory. Our second argument is that such formalisations have a generic nature which can be applied to similar algorithms. The lazy algorithms of *QArith*, are inspired by, and very similar to the existing algorithms for arithmetic on continued fractions [8,18,12]. We believe that a verification of the continued fraction arithmetic is possible based on our *QArith* project (see Sect. 7).

6.1 Extraction

One important aspect of type theory of *Coq* is the distinction between informative and non-informative objects. The informative objects are terms of type `Set`, and consist of those whose computational content is important for the programmer. The non-informative objects are terms of type `Prop` which bear solely a logical and not computational importance. Inside the type theory of *Coq*, however, these non-informative objects are first class citizens and they should be type checked and evaluated when necessary.

In order to recapture the computational content of the formalised programs, *Coq* has *the program extraction mechanism.* This is a tool to extract the underlying program of an object in type theory into a program in a conventional programming language [16,10].

In our case, after finishing the formalisation of the lazy algorithms, we used the program extraction into *Haskell*, to obtain the verified version of the algorithms. It is interesting to compare the *Coq*-generated *Haskell* code (*postverification code*) with the original hand-written *Haskell* code (*preverification code*). Not surprisingly the basic algorithms have the same time and space complexity. The main difference is that in the postverification code all the usual data types such as natural numbers, booleans and integers are reimplemented as new algebraic data types in *Haskell*; while in the preverification code we use the data types already defined in the standard prelude of *Haskell* (and sometimes even built-in as primitive data types). This makes the preverification code much faster; it is also the main cause of the difference in the size of the pre- and postverification code (see Table 1).

Table 1. Comparison of the ASCII size of programs and proofs.

development	*Coq* code
strict operations	112 KB
lazy operations	748 KB
correctness	304 KB
total project	1164 KB

function	preverification	*Coq* code	postverification[3]
homographic	8 KB	200 KB	20 KB (8 KB)
quadratic	8 KB	476 KB	60 KB (20 KB)
total lazy	16 KB	748 KB	88 KB (32 KB)

There is another difference between the pre- and postverification codes. Recall that in *Coq* we had to add the lazy proof obligations and the accessibility predicates to the definition of the functions. Those terms were non-informative objects from the programmer's point of view; hence they had the type `Prop`. During the extraction all the terms of type `Prop` will be replaced by the sole constructor of the unit data type, which is merely a dummy term in *Haskell*. Thus for example the homographic function in the postverification code has 6 arguments; whereas in the preverification code it has 5 arguments. This difference is practically negligible and does not affect the performance of the postverification code.

6.2 `Prop`-Sorted Accessibility

In the *Coq* formalisation of function $\mathcal{B}$ of Sect. 4.2, in every recursive branch once the value of the function (based on the input sequence and four coefficients which are carried around) and once the new subdomain of the new recursive call will be evaluated. Recall that if we extract this term from *Coq* to a *Haskell* program, all the terms of type `Set` will be extracted. Originally, in Bove and Capretta's method, the inductive domain of a non-structurally recursive function is a term of type `Set`. This is because Bove and Capretta work in Martin-Löf type theory

[3] The number in brackets denotes the size of the extracted code disregarding the extraction of the basic libraries.

where there is no distinction between `Set` and `Prop`. This means that if we follow Bove and Capretta's method and take the domain of the function $\mathcal{B}$ to be an inductively defined set rather than a predicate, in the *Haskell* extraction of the function, the inductively defined accessible domain is also extracted; this will considerably decrease the efficiency.

Incidentally that is the approach we took in the beginning. Later we modified the whole formalisation and we used the `Prop`-sorted accessibility. Our tests showed a 25% to 30% decrease in both time and memory usage of the extracted algorithms. However for evaluation inside *Coq* the time and memory complexity of the proof objects do not change. This emphasises the importance of program extraction as one of the basic philosophies behind the design of the type system of *Coq* compared to Martin-Löf type theory.

We mentioned that our first approach was to follow Bove and Capretta's original method and use `Set`-sorted accessibility. This is because unfortunately the second approach is more technical and requires an advanced knowledge of the internals of *Coq* [4]. The first author initially applied the original Bove and Capretta's method; the second author showed how it is possible to modify the proofs to suit the `Prop`-sorted variant. During this modification a detailed study of the proof terms of *Coq* was necessary.

6.3 Computations Inside *Coq*

One of the main objectives of the project was to provide *Coq* with a library of arithmetic on rational numbers. This library had to be similar to the existing libraries for natural numbers and integers. This means that we should at least be able to perform easy computations in the language of *Coq*. The *QArith* library fulfills this requirement. After defining the strict operations, one can add pretty printer and parser for expressions involving rational numbers. This is especially facilitated in recent versions of *Coq*, where user can easily extend the grammar of *Coq*.

In Sect. 4.1 we argued that the lazy functions on sequences are more efficient. This is true in a programming language like *Haskell* where we do not bother with termination checking. But could we use the lazy operations in order to do arithmetic *inside Coq*? The answer is negative. The reason is that inside *Coq* all the proof obligations and accessibility predicates, albeit computationally irrelevant, should be type-checked and evaluated. Consequently a full evaluation of the quadratic function inside *Coq* results in an explosion of proof terms and with current computational power is impractical. However as we discussed in Sect. 6.1, the program extraction will obviate all the non-informative terms and one ends up with an efficient program. Therefore for computations inside *Coq* we use the strict version of field operations.

7 Conclusion and Further Work

The experience with formalisation of *QArith* library shows that the *Coq* theorem prover, in its current state, not only is a good framework for formalisation of mathematical structures and their purely algebraic properties, but also is capable of being used to verify nontrivial algorithms. The algorithms that we formalised have the same underlying complexity as the state of the art algorithms in the field of exact arithmetic [17]. We also contrasted the preverification code versus postverification code. This consists of starting from a hand-written code; formalising it in a theorem prover which offers the possibility of program extraction; finally extracting into the programming language of the origin obtaining the verified executable code. We believe that a more careful investigation of the difference between pre- and postverification codes gives the designers of programming languages (resp. theorem provers) valuable insight into logical (resp. computational) power of their products.

We discuss two possible extensions of our work. First is to consider another important non-redundant representations for rational numbers, namely the continued fractions representation. The algorithms for continued fraction representation are more complicated than the algorithms we formalised in *QArith* project. Nevertheless, extending the present work one could use the intrinsic similarity between our algorithms and the algorithms of continued fraction arithmetic in order to verify the correctness of those ubiquitous algorithms. This requires a clever reuse of the proof objects that we supplied during the present work, in order to minimise the amount of additional effort. The recent work by Magaud [11] seems to provide a useful theoretical background for this approach.

The second possible improvement on our work is to extend the inductive data types and the lazy algorithms on them to coinductive data types and corecursive functions on them, in order to obtain a verified exact arithmetic on real numbers. In *Haskell* there is no distinction between inductive types (data) and coinductive types (codata); therefore, all our algorithms written in *Haskell* are valid for potentially infinite sequences. But in *Coq* there is a clear distinction between infinite and finite objects and one has to use coinductive types in order to formalise algorithms that work on streams; even though the extracted algorithms into *Haskell* will be identical to those for the finite sequences. In an upcoming work the first author will describe the admissible representations — those which come with an intuitive notion of computability induced by the Cantor space topology — based on the Stern-Brocot tree and formalisable by means of coinductive types. A problem to tackle is the syntactic constraints that *Coq* puts on the corecursive functions. These constraints are the dual of the constraints for the structural recursion; they require similar approaches to the ones we discussed in Sects. 4.4, 6.2.

Acknowledgements. The authors wish to thank Pierre Courtieu for his help on the use of `functional induction` tactic, and the anonymous referees for their useful comments. This work was completed during the first author's visit to INRIA Sophia Antipolis, made possible by a grant from the Dutch Organization for Scientific Research (NWO).

References

[1] A. Balaa and Y. Bertot. Fonctions récursives générales par itération en théorie des types. In *Proceedings of JFLA'2002*. INRIA, 2002.

[2] G. Barthe and P. Courtieu. Efficient Reasoning about Executable Specifications in Coq. In V. Carreño, C. Muñoz, and S. Tashar, editors, *Theorem Proving in Higher Order Logics, TPHOLs'02*, volume 2410 of *LNCS*, pages 31–46. Springer-Verlag, 2002.

[3] Y. Bertot. Simple canonical representation of rational numbers. In H. Geuvers and F. Kamareddine, editors, *Electronic Notes in Theoretical Computer Science*, volume 85(7). Elsevier, 2003.

[4] Y. Bertot and P. Castéran. *Coq'Art*. To be published by Springer-Verlag, 2004.

[5] A. Bove and V. Capretta. Nested general recursion and partiality in type theory. In R. J. Boulton and P. B. Jackson, editors, *Theorem Proving in Higher Order Logics, TPHOLs'01*, volume 2152 of *LNCS*, pages 121–135. Springer-Verlag, 2001.

[6] The Coq Development Team. *The Coq Proof Assistant Reference Manual, Version 7.4*. INRIA, `http://coq.inria.fr/doc/main.html`, Feb. 2003.

[7] D. Delahaye and M. Mayero. Field: une procédure de décision pour les nombres réels en Coq. In *Proceedings of JFLA'2001*. INRIA, 2001.

[8] R. W. Gosper. HAKMEM, Item 101 B. `http://www.inwap.com/pdp10/hbaker/hakmem/cf.html\#item101b`, Feb. 1972. MIT AI Laboratory Memo No.239.

[9] M. Konečný. *Many-Valued Real Functions Computable by Finite Transducers using IFS-Representations*. PhD thesis, The University of Birmingham, Oct. 2000.

[10] P. Letouzey. A New Extraction for Coq. In H. Geuvers and F. Wiedijk, editors, *Types for Proofs and Programs, TYPES 2002*, volume 2646 of *LNCS*, pages 388–405. Springer-Verlag, 2003.

[11] N. Magaud. Changing Data Representation within the Coq System. In D. Basin and B. Wolff, editors, *Theorem Proving in Higher Order Logics, TPHOLs'03*, volume 2758 of *LNCS*, pages 87–102. Springer-Verlag, 2003.

[12] V. Ménissier-Morain. *Arithmétique exacte, conception, algorithmique et performances d'une implémentation informatique en précision arbitraire*. Thèse, Université Paris 7, Dec. 1994.

[13] M. Niqui. Exact Arithmetic on Stern–Brocot Tree. Technical Report NIII-R0325, Nijmegen Institute for Computer and Information Sciences, Nov. 2003.

[14] M. Niqui and Y. Bertot. `http://coqcvs.inria.fr/cgi-bin/cvswebcoq.cgi/contrib/Nijmegen/QArith/`, May 2003. Coq contribution.

[15] Ch. Paulin. Coq club mailing list correspondence, Aug. 2002.

[16] Ch. Paulin-Mohring. Extracting F_ω's programs from proofs in the Calculus of Constructions. In *Proceedings of POPL 1989*, pages 89–104. ACM, Jan. 1989.

[17] P. J. Potts. *Exact Real Arithmetic using Möbius Transformations*. PhD thesis, University of London, Imperial College, July 1998.

[18] J. E. Vuillemin. Exact real computer arithmetic with continued fractions. *IEEE Transactions on Computers*, 39(8):1087–1105, Aug. 1990.

Mobility Types in Coq

Furio Honsell and Ivan Scagnetto

Dipartimento di Matematica e Informatica,
Università degli Studi di Udine
Via delle Scienze 206, I-33100 Udine, Italy.
{honsell,scagnett}@dimi.uniud.it

Abstract. The need for formal methods for certifying the *good behaviour* of computer software is dramatically increasing with the growing complexity of the latter. Moreover, in the global computing framework one must face the additional issues of concurrency and mobility. In the recent years many new process algebras have been introduced in order to reason formally about these problems; the common pattern is to specify a type system which allows one to discriminate between "good" and "bad" processes. In this paper we focus on an incremental type system for a variation of the Ambient Calculus called M^3, i.e., Mobility types for Mobile processes in Mobile ambients and we formally prove its soundness in the proof assistant Coq.

1 Introduction

Recently, due to the widespread use of the Internet and to the appearance of new mobile devices (PDAs, smart phones etc.), the traditional notion of computing is quickly fading away, giving birth to new paradigms. Indeed, the need of exchanging data and cooperatively working towards a common goal between entities moving from one location to another gives rise to new non-trivial problems. In order to formally describe and reason about this new computing paradigms, a plethora of calculi have been proposed. Among them, the Ambient Calculus [1] is a process algebra specifically designed in order to model mobility of agents in a dynamic hierarchy of domains (ambients) with local communications. The interest towards this calculus is witnessed by the growing number of variants recently proposed in the literature.

Since the original formulation of the Ambient Calculus, many studies have been carried out in order to find satisfactory alternatives to the open primitive, i.e, the capability allowing to dissolve an ambient revealing its internal structure. Indeed, this is considered a potentially dangerous operation since an agent could maliciously destroy from the outside a domain containing processes operating on sensitive data.

In this paper we focus on a variant of the Ambient Calculus (originally introduced in [3]) which allows inter-ambient communication replacing the open primitive with a "to" instruction which can move *lightweight* processes (i.e., lists of capabilities) without the need of enclosing them into an ambient. On top of

S. Berardi, M. Coppo, and F. Damiani (Eds.): TYPES 2003, LNCS 3085, pp. 324–337, 2004.

the language there is also a type system which regulates the behaviour of processes. Indeed, type systems are essential components in many ambient calculi because they allow to discriminate between "good" processes and "bad" ones; this is extremely important when one wants to model security properties in the global computing framework. A very good feature of the type system introduced in [3] is that it allows to type components in incomplete environments, i.e., it is incremental. Moreover, there is a type inference algorithm which can be used on a "raw" term in order to derive the minimum requirements for accepting it as a good process, which provides also a notion of principal type.

The ultimate result of this paper is the formally certified correctness proof of the type inference algorithm. This formal proof was carried out in the Coq system (developed at the INRIA research institute [8]) incrementally with the definition of the type inference rules introduced in [3] and in few occasions it actually suggested the correct formulation of the inference rules themselves. Completeness will be addressed in a future work.

We capitalize on the Higher-Order Type Theory featured by Coq approach [2,5,9,7]. In particular,we use Higher-Order Abstract Syntax (HOAS) and we represent binders by means of higher-order (i.e., functional) constants. We encode the typing and inference rules in natural deduction style. Thus, we avoid an explicit encoding of many tedious mechanisms like, e.g., alpha-conversion, schemata instantiation, side conditions about the freshness of bound variables and the treatment of typing environments by means of lists.

We capitalize also on some interesting features of Coq such as the Leibniz equality and the associated `Rewrite` tactic in order to deal with unification.

Synopsis. In Section 2 we introduce the M^3 calculus, the typing system and the related type inference mechanism presented in [3]. Each notion of the object language is followed by the description of the corresponding representation in Coq. Section 3 is devoted to the formal derivation in Coq of the soundness of the type inference algorithm. Finally, in Section 4 we draw some conclusions.

2 M^3

In this section we briefly recall the syntax of the M^3 calculus together with the corresponding higher-order encoding in Coq; for further details and application examples about the object language, the interested reader is referred to [3]. We will skip the notion of structural equivalence and the reduction semantics of the calculus since they are not relevant for our purposes.

2.1 The Object Language and Its Encoding

There are four basic syntactic categories, i.e., ambient names, groups, capabilities and processes which are annotated with types (see Section 2.2). Capabilities (messages) are defined by the following grammar:

$M, N, L ::=$

$m, n, \ldots, x, y, \ldots$	ambient names, variables
$in\ M$	moves the containing ambient into ambient M
$out\ M$	moves the containing ambient out of ambient M
$to\ M$	goes out from its ambient into a sibling ambient M
$M.M'$	path

For what concerns processes, the reader should notice that the restriction operator on groups is polyadic, i.e., it binds several groups at once. According to the authors of [3], this is needed since groups can have mutually dependent group types. The grammar defining processes is the following:

$P, Q, R ::=$

0	null
$M.P$	prefixed
$\langle M \rangle.P$	synchronous output
$(x{:}W).P$	typed input
$P \mid Q$	parallel composition
$M[P]$	ambient
$!P$	replication
$(\nu n{:}amb(g))P$	name restriction
$(\nu \{\boldsymbol{g}{:}\boldsymbol{G}\}_{(k)})P$	group restriction

In order to "reconcile" the inductive features of Coq with the HOAS-approach, we represent the syntactic categories of names and groups by means of two parametric types:

```
Parameter name: Set.
Parameter group: Set.
```

Thus, there is no risk of deriving *exotic* terms (i.e., legal terms which do not correspond to an entity of the object language [4]). Specific names and groups are rendered by means of Coq metavariables of type `name` and `group`, respectively.

The encoding of capabilities is straightforward:

```
Inductive cap: Set :=
    name2cap : name -> cap
  | In : cap -> cap
  | Out : cap -> cap
  | to : cap -> cap
  | path : cap -> cap -> cap.
```

For what concerns processes, there is a small issue to overcome if we want to stick to the HOAS-approach. Indeed, we said that the restriction operator on groups is polyadic; hence, since the λ-abstraction operator of the type theory underlying the Coq system is monadic, we have to use a mutual inductive type in order to "mimick" a simultaneous group restriction:

```
Mutual Inductive proc: Set :=
    nil : proc
  | action : cap -> proc -> proc
  | output : cap -> proc -> proc
  | input : (name -> proc) -> msgType -> proc
  | par : proc -> proc -> proc
  | ambient : cap -> proc -> proc
  | bang : proc -> proc
  | nu : group -> (name -> proc) -> proc
  | nuG : res -> proc
with res: Set :=
    proc2res : proc -> res
  | resG : groupType -> (group -> res) -> res.
```

The rôle of terms of type `res` is to encode group restrictions by grouping together several monadic abstractions. For instance, the M^3 process $(\nu g_1 : G_1, g_2 : G_2)0$ is encoded by `(nuG (resG G1 [g1:group](resG G2 [g2:group](proc2res nil))))`.

Since `cap` and `proc` are inductive types, the Coq system automatically provides for free inductive and recursive principles, which are very useful in order to speed up the activity of the formal development of the metatheory.

Notice how the encoding of the calculus, following the principles for encoding syntax in LF (originally proposed in [5]) and the standard specification language provided by type theory, enhance the readability of the original presentation of the calculus. It is often the case that LF encodings enhance the syntax and allow to eliminate unnecessary idiosyncrasies.

In this paper we are only interested in the type inference algorithm; hence, we do not recall the notions of structural congruence and of the reduction system. The interested reader is referred to [3] for more details.

2.2 Mobility Types and Their Encoding

In order to avoid dependent types, in [3] the authors adopt an approach based on groups; hence, there are basically three categories of types: ambient types, capability types and process types. Groups are denoted by the letters $g, h, \ldots$, sets of groups are denoted by $\mathcal{S}, \mathcal{C}, \mathcal{E}, \ldots$ and the syntax for the M^3 types is defined as follows:

Amb	$::= amb(g)$		ambient type: ambients of group g
Pro	$::= proc(g)$		process type: processes that can stay in ambients of group g
Cap	$::= Pro_1 \rightarrow Pro_2$		capability type: capabilities that, prefixed to a process of type Pro_1 turn it into a process of type Pro_2
W	$::=$		message type
		Amb	ambient type
		Cap	capability type
T	$::=$		communication type
		shh	no communication
		W	communication of messages of type W
G	$::= gr(\mathcal{S}, \mathcal{C}, \mathcal{E}, T)$		group type

We recall from [3] that the meaning of the statement $g : gr(\mathcal{S}, \mathcal{C}, \mathcal{E}, T)$ is the following:

- $\mathcal{S}$ is the set of ambient groups where the ambients of group g can stay;
- $\mathcal{C}$ is the set of ambient groups that the ambients of group g can cross;
- $\mathcal{E}$ is the set of ambient groups that lightweight g-processes can enter;
- T is the communication type of g-ambients.

If $G \triangleq gr(\mathcal{S}, \mathcal{C}, \mathcal{E}, T)$, the notation $\mathcal{S}(G)$, $\mathcal{C}(G)$, $\mathcal{E}(G)$ stands for the components $\mathcal{S}$, $\mathcal{C}$, $\mathcal{E}$ of G. Following the notational remark at page 7 in [3], saying that we can simply write g both for $amb(g)$ and for $proc(g)$ since the distinction is always clear from the context, the encoding in Coq of message and communication types is straightforward:

```
Inductive msgType : Set :=
    amb_type : group -> msgType
  | cap_type : group -> group -> msgType.

Inductive comType : Set :=
    Shh : comType
  | msg : msgType -> comType.
```

Group types are encoded by the following predicate, featuring only one constructor:

```
Inductive groupType: Set :=
  gr: Glist -> Glist -> Glist -> comType -> groupType.
```

For the sake of simplicity we chose to render in Coq the sets of group names $\mathcal{S}, \mathcal{C}, \mathcal{E}$, occurring in a group type, by means of lists of elements of type `group`:

```
Inductive Glist : Set :=
   emptyG : Glist
 | consG  : group -> Glist -> Glist.
```

In order to avoid an explicit treatment of typing environments as lists of typing statements, we render them by means of two parametric judgments:

```
Parameter type_group: group -> groupType -> Prop.
Parameter type_name: name -> group -> Prop.
```

such that `(type_group g G)` holds iff `g` has group type `G` and `(type_name n g)` holds iff the name `n` has type `g` in the current environment. For instance, the environment $\{g : G, n : g\}$ is rendered in Coq by declaring the following:

```
Parameter dg: (type_group g G).
Parameter dn: (type_name n g).
```

This choice, followed by the rephrasing of the sequent style rules of the typing system (see Figure 1) in natural deduction, completely delegates to the Coq's metalanguage the treatment of environments. As an example of the mapping from sequent style typing rules to natural deduction style ones, let us consider the case of (AMB RES) in Figure 1:

$$\frac{\Gamma, m{:}g' \vdash P{:}g}{\Gamma \vdash (\nu m{:}g')P{:}g}$$

the corresponding Coq encoding is the following:

```
good_proc_res : (P:name->proc)(g,g':group)
                ((m:name)(type_name m g') -> (good_proc (P m) g))->
                (good_proc (nu g' P) g)
```

Notice how the premise $\Gamma, m{:}g' \vdash P{:}g$ is represented by the *hypothetical judgment* `((m:name)(type_name m g') -> (good_proc (P m) g))`,
where `(type_name m g')` corresponds in Natural Deduction to the discharged hypothesis in the following rule:

$$\begin{array}{c} (m{:}g', m \text{ fresh}) \\ \vdots \\ \dfrac{P{:}g}{(\nu m{:}g')P{:}g} \end{array}$$

Following this approach, the whole type system is encoded by means of the following inductive predicates (the first for capabilities and the second for processes):

```
Inductive good_msg  : cap  -> msgType -> Prop := ...
Inductive good_proc : proc -> group   -> Prop  := ...
```

Due to lack of space we do not report the complete definitions of these predicates which are available at `www.dimi.uniud.it/ scagnett/Coq-Sources/m3coq.v`. Intuitively, `(good_msg M W)` holds iff `M` has type `W` and `(good_proc P g)` holds iff `P` has type `g` in the current environment.

$$\frac{\xi{:}A \in \Gamma}{\Gamma \vdash \xi{:}A}\text{(ENV)} \qquad \frac{\Gamma \vdash g_2{:}G_2 \quad \Gamma M{:}g_1 \quad g_1 \in \mathcal{C}(G_2)}{\Gamma \vdash in\ M{:}g_2 \to g_2}\text{(IN)}$$

$$\frac{\Gamma \vdash g_1{:}G_1 \quad \Gamma \vdash g_2{:}G_2 \quad \Gamma \vdash M{:}g_1 \quad g_1 \in \mathcal{C}(G_2) \quad \mathcal{S}(G_1) \subseteq \mathcal{S}(G_2)}{\Gamma \vdash out\ M{:}g_2 \to g_2}\text{(OUT)}$$

$$\frac{\Gamma \vdash g_2{:}G_2 \quad \Gamma \vdash M{:}g_1 \quad g_1 \in \mathcal{E}(G_2)}{\Gamma \vdash to\ M{:}g_1 \to g_2}\text{(TO)} \qquad \frac{\Gamma \vdash M{:}g_3 \to g_2 \quad \Gamma \vdash N{:}g_1 \to g_3}{\Gamma \vdash M.N{:}g_1 \to g_2}\text{(PATH)}$$

$$\frac{-}{\Gamma \vdash 0{:}g}\text{(NULL)} \qquad \frac{\Gamma \vdash P{:}g \quad \Gamma \vdash Q{:}g}{\Gamma \vdash P|Q{:}g}\text{(PAR)} \qquad \frac{\Gamma \vdash P{:}g}{\Gamma \vdash !P{:}g}\text{(REPL)}$$

$$\frac{\Gamma \vdash M{:}g_1 \to g_2 \quad \Gamma \vdash P{:}g_1}{\Gamma \vdash M.P{:}g_2}\text{(PREFIX)} \qquad \frac{\Gamma, x{:}W \vdash P{:}g \quad \Gamma \vdash g{:}gr(\mathcal{S},\mathcal{C},\mathcal{E},W)}{\Gamma \vdash (x{:}W).P{:}g}\text{(INPUT)}$$

$$\frac{\Gamma \vdash P{:}g \quad \Gamma \vdash M{:}W \quad \Gamma \vdash g{:}gr(\mathcal{S},\mathcal{C},\mathcal{E},W)}{\Gamma \vdash \langle M \rangle.P{:}g}\text{(OUTPUT)}$$

$$\frac{\Gamma \vdash P{:}g \quad \Gamma \vdash M{:}g \quad \Gamma \vdash g{:}G \quad g' \in \mathcal{S}(G)}{\Gamma \vdash M[P]{:}g'}\text{(AMB)} \qquad \frac{\Gamma, m{:}g' \vdash P{:}g}{\Gamma \vdash (\nu m{:}g')P{:}g}\text{(AMB RES)}$$

$$\frac{\Gamma, g_1{:}G_1, \ldots, g_k{:}G_k \vdash P{:}g \quad g_i \notin GN(\Gamma) \quad g_i \neq g (1 \leq i \leq k)}{\Gamma \vdash (\nu\{g_1{:}G_1, \ldots, g_k{:}G_k\})P{:}g}\text{(GRP RES)}$$

Fig. 1. M^3 typing rules

2.3 Type Inference Rules

It is important to notice that we do not provide an implementation in Coq of the inference algorithm introduced in [3]. The purpose of our work is to check that the type inference rules in Figures 12 and 13 of [3] are sound with respect to the typing rules of M^3. Hence, we work at a logical level showing that for every judgment derived using the type inference rules there is a corresponding typing judgment obtained by means of the rules in Figure 1. For instance, while in [3] in Definition 3 the authors deal with the notion of completion-unifiers and the effective way to compute them, we focus on the unification contraints generated by the previously mentioned computation process. Indeed, at a logical level we can forget about the “real shape” of the generated substitution. In this section we illustrate the main ideas behind our encoding.

The type inference algorithm introduced in [3] starts computing a type from a “raw” process, i.e., a well formed process without type annotations and group restrictions (since the latter can always be “pulled out” in front of the process using structural congruence rules):

$$P, Q, R ::= 0 \mid M.P \mid \langle M \rangle.P \mid (x).P \mid P|Q \mid M[P] \mid !P \mid (\nu n)P$$

Thus in Coq we introduce a suitable type `raw_proc` representing raw processes:

```
Inductive raw_proc: Set :=
```

```
   raw_nil     : raw_proc
 | raw_action  : cap -> raw_proc -> raw_proc
 | raw_output  : cap -> raw_proc -> raw_proc
 | raw_input   : (name -> raw_proc) -> raw_proc
 | raw_par     : raw_proc -> raw_proc -> raw_proc
 | raw_ambient : cap -> raw_proc -> raw_proc
 | raw_bang    : raw_proc -> raw_proc
 | raw_nu      : (name -> raw_proc) -> raw_proc.
```

Each constructor corresponds directly to a constructor of type `proc`, if we do not consider the group restriction operator.

Moreover, since during the type inference process of capabilities some occurrences of group names into the $\mathcal{S}$ component of group types are marked with a $*$ in order to be able to infer later the correct set of group names where an ambient can stay, we need to reflect this fact into our encoding. Hence, we introduce the type `star_group` which admits "starred" group names beside "normal" ones:

```
Inductive star_group : Set :=
   simple : group -> star_group
 | star   : group -> star_group.
```

So, `(simple g)` encodes a "normal" group name g, while `(star g)` represents a "starred" group name g^*. It follows that the first component $\mathcal{S}$ of group types must be a list of elements of type `star_group` (instead of elements of type `Glist`):

```
Inductive starGlist : Set :=
   starEmptyG : starGlist
 | starConsG  : star_group -> starGlist -> starGlist.
```

Thus, group types (with "starred" elements in the first component $\mathcal{S}$) are recorded by means of a new inductive judgment:

```
Inductive starGroupType: Set :=
 gr_star: starGlist -> Glist -> Glist -> comType -> starGroupType.
```

where the only difference w.r.t. the previous predicate `groupType` is the fact that the first argument of the constructor `gr_star` is a term of type `starGlist` instead of type `Glist`.

Since we want to reason about the type environment synthesized by the algorithm proposed in [3], we need to introduce a suitable type `env` in order to "manipulate" environments at the object level:

```
Inductive env: Set :=
   emptyE     : env
 | consEgroup : group -> starGroupType -> env -> env
 | consEname  : name  -> msgType -> env -> env.
```

There are three constructors: one for the empty environment (`emptyE`), another for recording statements like $g : gr(\mathcal{S}, \mathcal{C}, \mathcal{E}, T)$ (`consEgroup`) and the last one for statements like $n : g$ or $x : W$ (`consEname`).

The next step consists in the encoding of the operations performed on the environments during the type inference process. More precisely, we have to represent completion-unifiers, compressions and closures.

For what concerns unifications, we prefer to not deal explicitly with them in order to avoid to get lost into syntactical details. Hence, we represent them in form of identity constraints between terms. These constraints are rendered by means of Leibniz equalities in higher-order schematic judgments in order to be able to use the tactic `Rewrite` to effectively unify the terms when needed. For instance, in the rule (I-Path) of Figure 12 in [3] the unification $\phi(\{(W, g_1 \to g_2), (W', g_3 \to g_1)\})$ is rendered by requiring the validity of the Leibniz equalities `W=(cap_type g1 g2)` and `W'=(cap_type g3 g1)`. Moreover, when there is the need of unifying two environments `e1` and `e2`, we render the completion-unifier constraints by means of the judgment `(unify_env e1 e2)` where `unify_env` is defined as follows:

```
Definition unify_env : env -> env -> Prop := [e1:env][e2:env]
((n:name)(W1,W2:msgType)(name_in_env n W1 e1) ->
 (name_in_env n W2 e2) -> W1=W2) /\
((g:group)(S1,S2:starGlist)(C1,C2,E1,E2:Glist)(t1,t2:comType)
 (group_in_env g (gr_star S1 C1 E1 t1) e1) ->
 (group_in_env g (gr_star S2 C2 E2 t2) e2) -> t1=t2).
```

where `(name_in_env n W e)` holds iff the association between the name `n` and the message type `W` occurs in the environment `e`. Similarly `(group_in_env g t e)` holds iff the association between the group name `g` and the group type `t` occurs into `e`. Hence, `(unify_env e1 e2)` means that `e1` and `e2` must agree for what concerns the types of names and the communication types inside group types referred to the same element.

The operation of "merging" two (unified) environments is rendered by the following predicate:

```
Inductive union_env: env -> env -> env -> Prop :=
  trivial_union : (e:env)(union_env emptyE e e)
| group_union   : (e,e',e'',e''':env)(g:group)(S,S':starGlist)
                  (C,C',E,E':Glist)(t:comType)
                  (remove_group e' g e''') ->
                  (union_env e e''' e'') ->
                  (add_S g S e' S') ->
                  (add_C g C e' C') ->
                  (add_E g E e' E') ->
                  (union_env (consEgroup g (gr_star S C E t) e)
                    e' (consEgroup g (gr_star S' C' E' t) e''))
| name_union    : (e,e',e'':env)(n:name)(W:msgType)
                  (union_env e e' e'') ->
```

```
(union_env (consEname n W e)
  e' (consEname n W e'')).
```

In order to check if (union_env e1 e2 e) holds, we proceed by structural induction on e1. The case where the e1 is empty (trivial_union) is straightforward. When the head constructor of e1 is consEname, we simply "copy" the association between the name n and the message type W in the merged environment e. The only interesting case is when the head constructor of e1 is consEgroup, since we must search through e2 the occurrence of g adding the components of the relative group type to those of the occurrence of e1 (using the predicates add_S, add_C and add_E). Then we remove g from e2 (predicate remove_group) and we continue inductively. The definitions of all the previous auxiliary predicates can be found at www.dimi.uniud.it/ scagnett/Coq-Sources/m3coq.v.

Finally the closure operation which computes the correct components $\mathcal{S}$ of group types contained in an environment (eliminating all the occurrences of the marker $*$) is defined as follows:

```
Inductive closure: starGlist -> Glist -> env -> Prop :=
    elim_star : (l:starGlist)(e:env)
                ((g:group)(S:starGlist)(C,E:Glist)(t:comType)
                 (starGlist_isin (star g) l) /\
                 (group_in_env g (gr_star S C E t) e) ->
                 (inc_starGlist S l)
                ) -> (closure l (star_clear l) e)
  | add_grp   : (l,S:starGlist)(C,E,l':Glist)(t:comType)
                (g:group)(e:env)(starGlist_isin (star g) l) ->
                (group_in_env g (gr_star S C E t) e) ->
                 (inc_starGlist S l) ->
                (closure (append_starGlist l S) l' e) ->
                (closure l l' e).
```

where star_clear is the function which erases all the occurrences of the marker $*$ into the list passed as argument:

```
Fixpoint star_clear[l:starGlist]: Glist :=
  Cases l of
      starEmptyG => emptyG
    | (starConsG (simple g) l') => (consG g (star_clear l'))
    | (starConsG (star g) l') => (consG g (star_clear l'))
  end.
```

The two constructors elim_star and add_grp correspond to the computation rules specified in point 1 of Definition 8 in [3]. Indeed, in order to compute the closure of an environment Γ, one has to replace $\mathcal{S}(G)$ with $\mathcal{S}(G) \cup \mathcal{S}(G')$ for every $g^* \in \mathcal{S}(G)$ such that $g : G' \in \Gamma$ and $\mathcal{S}(G') \not\subset \mathcal{S}(G)$ (constructor add_grp). Then, when there are no more g^* satisfying the previous condition, one can erase all the $*$ markers (constructor elim_star).

Now we are ready to introduce the inductive predicates which encode the type inference rules in Figures 12 and 26 of [3]:

```
Inductive msg_inf: cap -> msgType -> env -> Prop := ...

Inductive proc_inf: raw_proc -> proc -> group -> env -> Prop := ...
```

Due to lack of space, we cannot report the complete definitions of these predicates which are available at `www.dimi.uniud.it/ scagnett/Coq-Sources/m3coq.v`.

3 The Formal Development

In this section we describe the formal development carried out in Coq. The ultimate result is the certification of the correctness of the type inference algorithm; however, in order to achieve this goal, there are many subtleties to deal with. In Section 3.1, we introduce the auxiliary notions and properties we have to supply in order to prove the main goal, which we illustrate in Section 3.1.

3.1 Basic Notions and Properties

In order to prove the correctness of the type inference algorithm, we need some basic properties about environments and the related operations (see Section 2.3).

The first two must be stated as axioms and allow to infer from the environment computed by the type inference algorithm the needed hypotheses in the current proof context in order to be able to derive the appropriate typing judgments (recall from Section 2.2 that `type_name` and `type_group` are parametric predicates allowing one to record the current associations between names, groups and their respective types):

```
Axiom TYPE_NAME: (n:name)(g:group)(e:env)
                 (name_in_env n (amb_type g) e) ->
                 (type_name n (amb_type g)).

Axiom TYPE_GROUP: (g:group)(S:starGlist)(C,E:Glist)(t:comType)
                  (e:env)(group_in_env g (gr_star S C E t) e) ->
                  (S':Glist)(closure S S' e) ->
                  (type_group g (gr S' C E t)).
```

Then we need some basic properties ensuring that if a given entity (a group name or a typing association $g : gr(\mathcal{S}, \mathcal{C}, \mathcal{E}, T)$ occurs into an environment, then it also occurs into the result of a merge with another environment or of its closure:

```
Lemma UNION_IN: (e1,e2,e:env)(g:group)(S:starGlist)(C,E:Glist)
                (t:comType)(unify_env e1 e2) ->
                (union_env e1 e2 e) ->
                (group_in_env g (gr_star S C E t) e2) ->
                (Ex [S':starGlist](Ex [C':Glist](Ex [E':Glist]

Lemma GROUP_IN_CLOSURE: (S:starGlist)(S':Glist)(e:env)(g:group)
                        (starGlist_isin (simple g) S) ->
                        (closure S S' e) -> (Glist_isin g S').
```

The previous lemmata depend on some minor results about the decidability of equality over group lists, group types (eventually with "starred" groups), message and communication types:

```
Lemma GLIST_DEC: (l,l':Glist)l=l' \/  l=l'.
Lemma STAR_GROUP_DEC: (s,s':star_group)s=s' \/  s=s'.
Lemma STAR_GLIST_DEC: (l,l':starGlist)l=l' \/  l=l'.
Lemma MSG_TYPE_DEC: (W,W':msgType)W=W' \/  W=W'.
Lemma COM_TYPE_DEC: (c,c':comType)c=c' \/  c=c'.
Lemma STAR_GROUP_TYPE_DEC: (s,t:starGroupType)s=t \/  s=t.
```

All those results are derivable assuming two axioms of the Theory of Contexts [6] about the decidability of equality over names and groups respectively:

```
Axiom dec_name: (n,m:name)n=m \/  n=m.
Axiom dec_group: (g,h:group)g=h \/  g=h
```

The latter axioms allow to render in Coq a common assumption about process algebras (like the Ambient Calculus and its variant M^3), namely that we can always decide whether two names or two groups are equal or not. Indeed, many proofs in the literature are carried out by cases on equalities over names.

Soundness of the type inference algorithm. Since the type inference rules are split in two sets: the first for capabilities and the second for raw processes, we proved two soundness lemmata:

```
Lemma MSG_INF_SOUND   : (M:cap)(W:msgType)(e:env)
                        (msg_inf M W e) -> (good_msg M W).

Lemma PROC_INF_SOUND  : (R:raw_proc)(P:proc)(g:group)(e:env)
                        (proc_inf R P g e) -> (good_proc P g).
```

They are proved by structural induction on M and R, respectively. Obviously, the former result is needed in order to prove the second one, since processes are built on top of capabilities. These two lemmata are the formal equivalent of Theorem 6 of [3]. The complete Coq code is available at the URL `http://www.dimi.uniud.it/ scagnett/Coq-Sources/m3coq.v`.

During the proof development of `MSG_INF_SOUND` we spotted a minor error in the original definition of rule (I-Out) in [3]; indeed, it is stated as follows:

$$\vdash_I \mathit{out}\ \chi{:}\langle g_2 \rightarrow g_2; \{\chi{:}g_1, g_2{:}gr(\{g_1^*\},\{g_1\},\emptyset,t)\}\rangle$$

while it should be

$$\vdash_I \mathit{out}\ \chi{:}\langle g_2 \rightarrow g_2; \{\chi{:}g_1{:}gr(\emptyset,\emptyset,\emptyset,t), g_2{:}gr(\{g_1^*\},\{g_1\},\emptyset,t)\}\rangle$$

otherwise, the clause $\mathcal{S}(G_1) \subseteq \mathcal{S}(G_2)$ of rule (OUT) in Figure 1 cannot be satisfied, since no group types will be associated to g_1.

4 Conclusions

In this paper we encoded the syntax and the type system of a variant of the original Ambient Calculus which replaces the potentially dangerous *open* primitive with a new instruction *to*, moving lightweight processes without enclosing them into an ambient. Moreover, we provided a formal representation of the type inference rules introduced in [3], proving that they are sound w.r.t. the original type system.

The novelty of the approach used in this paper is the treatment of unifications by means of schematic judgments involving Leibniz equalities, since this approach allows us to avoid an explicit implementation of the machinery underlying the theory of most general unifiers. Indeed, Leibniz equality corresponds to $\beta\delta\iota$-equality in Coq and this fact allows to rewrite the terms involved in the unifying constraints as needed during the proof development.

Future work. The material reported in the present paper is part of a larger work in progress about the encoding and formal development of the metatheory of the Ambient Calculus both in the original typeless form and in other typed versions and variants. As a consequence we are still involved in the activity of proof development, since some minor technical results are still to be proved. However, we are confident to finish the whole formal development soon, since, according to our experience, the higher-order approach has proved to be very fruitful when applied to the formal representation of process algebras [7, 10].

An interesting issue to take into consideration in the near future is to formally address the completeness of the type inference procedure introduced in [3].

References

1. L. Cardelli and A. D. Gordon. Mobile ambients. In *Foundations of Software Science and Computation Structures: First International Conference, FOSSACS '98*, pages 140–155. Springer-Verlag, Berlin Germany, 1998.
2. A. Church. A formulation of the simple theory of types. *Journal of Symbolic Logic*, 5:56–68, 1940.
3. M. Coppo, M. Dezani-Ciancaglini, E. Giovannetti, and I. Salvo. M3: Mobility types for mobile processes in mobile ambients. In *Proceedings of CATS'2003*, volume 78 of *ENTCS*. Springer-Verlag, 2003.
4. J. Despeyroux, A. Felty, and A. Hirschowitz. Higher-order syntax in Coq. In *Proceedings of TLCA'95*, volume 905 of *Lecture Notes in Computer Science*, Edinburgh, 1995. Springer-Verlag. Also appears as INRIA research report RR-2556, April 1995.
5. R. Harper, F. Honsell, and G. Plotkin. A framework for defining logics. *J. ACM*, 40(1):143–184, January 1993.
6. F. Honsell, M. Miculan, and I. Scagnetto. An axiomatic approach to metareasoning on systems in higher-order abstract syntax. In *Proceedings of ICALP'01*, volume 2076 of *Lecture Notes in Computer Science*, pages 963–978. Springer-Verlag, 2001. Also available at `http://www.dimi.uniud.it/ miculan/Papers/`.

7. F. Honsell, M. Miculan, and I. Scagnetto. π-calculus in (co)inductive type theory. *Theoretical computer science*, 239–285(2):239–285, 2001. First appeared as a talk at TYPES'98 annual workshop.
8. INRIA. *The Coq Proof Assistant Reference Manual - Version 7.4*. INRIA, Rocquencourt, France, February 2003. Available at `ftp://ftp.inria.fr/INRIA/coq/V7.4/doc`.
9. P. Martin-Löf. On the meaning of the logical constants and the justifications of the logic laws. Technical Report 2, Dipartimento di Matematica, Universit'a di Siena, 1985.
10. M. Miculan and I. Scagnetto. Ambient calculus and its logic in the calculus of inductive constructions. In *In Proceedings of LFM 2002*, volume 70.2 of *ENTCS*. Elsevier, 2002.

Some Algebraic Structures in Lambda-Calculus with Inductive Types*

Sergej Soloviev and David Chemouil

IRIT – Université Paul Sabatier
118, route de Narbonne
31062 Toulouse cedex 4
soloviev@irit.fr

Abstract. This paper is part of a research project where we are exploring methods to extend the *computational content* of various systems of typed λ-calculus adding new reductions. Our previous study had its focus on isomorphisms of simple inductive types and related extensions of term rewriting. In this paper we present some new results concerning representation of finite sets as inductive types and related algebraic structures.

1 Introduction

It is routine to mention user-defined computation rules when the question of specifying type theories for proof development and verification is considered. At the same time the requirements concerning the general form and properies of these rules are never, to our knowledge, described precisely. All concrete examples usually belong to relatively narrow well studied set.

This paper is part of a research project where we are exploring methods to extend the *computational content* of various systems of typed λ-calculus adding new reductions. Our project may be regarded as one of the approaches motivated by the convergence between computer-assisted reasoning and symbolic computation (cf.[1]). Clearly, it would be more important to develop this approach in case of higher order and dependent type systems, but many interesting aspects are already present on the level of simply typed calculus with inductive types, while technical difficulties are considerably lesser.

Our previous study focused on isomorphisms of simple inductive types and related extensions of term rewriting. In this paper we present some new results concerning representation of finite sets as inductive types and related categorical and group-theoretical algebraic structures, but the example of isomorphism is still useful to make some general observations. Consider the following (standard) definition.

* The work was supported partly by the grant N 01-05 of the French-Russian Liapunov Institute

S. Berardi, M. Coppo, and F. Damiani (Eds.): TYPES 2003, LNCS 3085, pp. 338–354, 2004.

Definition 1. *Two types* ρ *and* τ *are isomorphic if there exist* $f : \rho \to \tau$ *and* $g : \tau \to \rho$ *such that* $f \circ g \sim id_\tau, g \circ f \sim id_\rho$. *Then,* g *is denoted* f^{-1} *and called the inverse of* f *and one writes* $f : \tau \cong \rho : f'$.

To apply it in case of typed λ-calculus we need:

- a composition operator $\circ : (\tau \to \nu) \times (\rho \to \tau) \to (\rho \to \nu)$ (with τ, ν, ρ types);
- a term id_τ representing identity;
- and equivalence relation $\sim$ on terms.

Usually these data are subject to certain assumptions:

- The operator $\circ$ is defined for all types τ, ν, ρ and terms $s : \tau \to \nu, t : \nu \to \rho$. This assumption seems natural if the whole λ-calculus is turned into category but it is not if we want to consider categorical (or other algebraic) structure on some part of it, cf. our section 4.

- $\circ$ is associative up to $\sim$. This condition is closely connected with transitivity of isomorphism relation. Thus it seems less natural to omit it completely but it may be restricted to some subset of all types.

- The term id_τ exists for every τ. Same remark as above will apply.

- For any $f : \rho \to \tau$ one has $f \circ id_\rho \sim f$ and $id_\tau \circ f \sim f$. Same remark. In particular, if some subset of the whole λ-calculus is considered then id_τ needs not to be $\lambda x^\tau.x$.

As to the relation $\sim$, usually —though not necessarily— $id_\tau \equiv \lambda x^\tau.x$ and $\sim$ is based on an underlying reduction: for instance, $f \sim g$ means that f and g have the same normal form w.r.t. certain system of reductions (cf. [2,4]).

In previous works, we studied isomorphisms of inductive types (i.e., recursive types satisfying a condition of strict-positivity) in an extensional simply-typed λ-calculus with product and unit types. The $\circ$ and id_τ were defined in ordinary way as $g \circ f \equiv \lambda x^\tau(g(fx))$ and $id_\tau \equiv \lambda x^\tau.x$. It was shown that the calculus enjoys strong normalization and confluence. Note that if $\sim$ means the corresponding equivalence relation, the provability of the equivalences $\forall x^\rho.g(f(x)) \sim x$ and $\forall y^\tau.f(g(y)) \sim y$ doesn't imply in general $f \circ g \sim id_\tau, g \circ f \sim id_\rho$.

At this point we extended the calculus with new conversion rules ensuring that all inductive representations of the product and unit types become isomorphic, and the extended reduction relation remains convergent. Finally we defined a notion of faithful copy of an inductive type (called isomorphic copy in [6]) and a corresponding reduction relation which also preserves the good properties of the calculus.

In this paper, we study some other kinds of extensions of reduction systems. It may be regarded as a first step towards a more efficient treatment of representations of categories and other algebraic structures (groups, G-sets, semi-groups, monoids etc) within typed λ-calculi including inductive types. Our first inspiration was the consideration of a group action on differential equations of certain types (in order to carry out a formal development in a proof-assistant). The equations were represented by vectors of parameters (regarded as elements of some inductive type) and the group itself by operators (symmetries) acting on coefficients. (See [3].)

In this paper we consider "finite types", i.e., inductive types of the form $\omega_n = \mu\alpha(c_1 : \alpha, ..., c_n : \alpha)$ and functions between these types. The principal new reduction is $\overline{f} \circ \overline{g} \to \overline{f \circ g}$ ("lifting" of composition to inductive types). Here $f : \{1,.,n\} \to \{1,..,m\}$ and $\overline{f} : \mu\alpha(c_1 : \alpha, ..., c_n : \alpha) \to \mu\alpha(c'_1 : \alpha, ..., c'_m : \alpha)$ $\overline{f} \equiv (\!| c'_{f(1)}, ..., c'_{f(n)} |\!)$. The particular case of $f, g : \omega_n \to \omega_n$ corresponds to the group of permutations S_n. We show that the extended calculus is convergent, consider other possible reductions and the consequences of this fact in the context of faithful copies of inductive types.

We conclude by a brief outline of future work. The incorporation of reductions that will support the functoriality of the inductive type construction w.r.t. parameters will open the way to a more efficient treatment (based on term rewriting) of group representations in proof assistants. One may notice that isomorphisms correspond already to the representation of inverse elements. Functoriality will be necessary to have associativity of composition. The reductions related to the form of presentation of a group based upon generators and relations, and the properties of corresponding term rewriting systems, will be the task to be studied in a near future.

2 The Simply-Typed Lambda-Calculus with Inductive Types

In this section, we define $\lambda^1\beta\eta\iota$, a simply-typed λ-calculus with inductive types and structural-recursion operators over them, taking most of our inspiration in [7] and in [8].

We will consider given infinite sets of constructor names (Const), term variables (Var) and type variables (TVar), with $\mathsf{Const} \cap \mathsf{Var} = \mathsf{Const} \cap \mathsf{TVar} = \mathsf{Var} \cap \mathsf{TVar} = \varnothing$. We will reserve the letters x, y and z for term variables, α and β for type variables, r, s, t, u and v for arbitraty terms, ρ and τ for arbitrary types, and κ for constructor schemas. The letters i, j, k, l will only be used for indexes and, respectively, n, m, p, q for their upper bound. Finally, constructor names will be denoted either by $c_1, c_2, \ldots, c'_1, c'_2, \ldots$ or by the generic name in. Definitions will be introduced by the symbol $\widehat{=}$, as in $\mathsf{id} \mathrel{\widehat{=}} \lambda x^\tau x$. Terms and types will be considered up to α-congruence (that is, names of bound variables are meaningless), and this last relation will be denoted $\equiv$, thus one has $\lambda x^\tau \cdot x \equiv \lambda y^\tau \cdot y$. Sequences of types or terms $(t_i)_{i=1,n}$ will be written with the usual vectorial notation $\overrightarrow{t_i}$ (or $\overrightarrow{t}$ if the index is not important), and their length will be written $|\overrightarrow{t_i}|$. Using this notation, we will sometimes write $\overrightarrow{\rho} \to \tau$ to mean $\rho_1 \to \ldots \to \rho_n \to \tau$, associated to the right. Furthermore, $s \in \overrightarrow{t_i}$ will mean that there is an i such that $s \equiv t_i$, and $\overrightarrow{t_i} \in S$ will mean that all the t_i's belong to the set S. We shall sometimes write vectors such as $\overrightarrow{t_{i,j}}$, meaning thus that we have a sequence of sequences, that is terms (or types) $t_{1,1}, \ldots, t_{1,m_1}, \ldots, t_{n,1}, \ldots, t_{n,m_n}$. Finally, if some indexes depend on other ones, the former will be themselves indexed by the latter, as in $\overrightarrow{t_{j_i}}$ which stands for $t_{j_1}, \ldots, t_{j_n}$, with $1 \leqslant i \leqslant n$. We will also need a notion of "curried" composition: for given λ-terms $f : \overrightarrow{\rho_i} \to \tau$ and $g : \tau \to \upsilon$, $g \circ f$ will be defined as

$\lambda \overrightarrow{z_i^{\rho_i}}\ g\ (f\ \overrightarrow{z_i})$, with $\overrightarrow{z} \notin \mathsf{FV}(g)$ and $\overrightarrow{z} \notin \mathsf{FV}(f)$. We shall also use the following notation, provided of course that g and f are of suitable types:

$$g \bullet f \equiv \begin{cases} g \circ f & \text{if } g \text{ and } f \text{ are composable,} \\ g\ f & \text{otherwise, and } g \text{ can be applied to } f. \end{cases}$$

Definition 2 (Prototypes). *The grammar of* prototypes *is defined as follows:* $\tau ::= \alpha \mid 1 \mid \tau \times \tau \mid \tau \to \tau \mid \mu \overrightarrow{\alpha}\, (\overrightarrow{c} : \overrightarrow{\tau})$, *with* $\overrightarrow{\alpha} \in \mathsf{TVar}$.

Definition 3 (Types). *We define simultaneously:*

– *the set* Ty *of* types*:*

$$\frac{}{1 \in \mathsf{Ty}} \qquad \frac{\rho, \tau \in \mathsf{Ty}}{\rho \times \tau \in \mathsf{Ty}} \qquad \frac{\rho, \tau \in \mathsf{Ty}}{\rho \to \tau \in \mathsf{Ty}}$$

$$\frac{\overrightarrow{c} \in \mathsf{Const} \qquad \overrightarrow{\alpha} \in \mathsf{TVar} \qquad \overrightarrow{\kappa} \in \mathsf{Sch}(\overrightarrow{\alpha})}{\mu \overrightarrow{\alpha}\, (\overrightarrow{c} : \overrightarrow{\kappa}) \in \mathsf{Ty}}$$

– *and the set* $\mathsf{Sch}(\alpha)$ *of* constructor schemas over *type variable* α*:*

$$\frac{0 \leqslant i \leqslant n \qquad \overrightarrow{\rho}, \overrightarrow{\sigma_{j_1}}, \ldots, \overrightarrow{\sigma_{j_n}} \in \mathsf{Ty}}{\overrightarrow{\rho} \to (\overrightarrow{\sigma_{j_1}} \to \alpha) \to \ldots \to (\overrightarrow{\sigma_{j_n}} \to \alpha) \to \alpha \in \mathsf{Sch}(\alpha)}$$

As usual, constructor names can only belong to one inductive type. Thus, an inductive type is also defined by the names of its constructors.

For the sake of readability, all constructors and constructor types will be indexed by $1 \leqslant k \leqslant p$, and all operators by $0 \leqslant i \leqslant n$ and $0 \leqslant j \leqslant m_i$. Remarks:

– An inductive type is a recursive type built from a sequence of (constructor) schemas.
– Every schema κ_k over α is of the form $\overrightarrow{\rho} \to (\overrightarrow{\sigma_{j_1}} \to \alpha) \to \ldots \to (\overrightarrow{\sigma_{j_n}} \to \alpha) \to \alpha$, and each premise is called an *operator* over α. The number of operators in a schema (/constructor type/constructor) is denoted $\mathsf{ar}(\kappa_k)$ (arity). We write $\mathsf{nb}^P(\kappa_k)$ for the number of ρ's and $\mathsf{nb}^R(\kappa_k)$ for the number of operators $\overrightarrow{\sigma_{j_i}} \to \alpha$, thus we have $\mathsf{ar}(\kappa_k) = \mathsf{nb}^P(\kappa_k) + \mathsf{nb}^R(\kappa_k)$ (since $1 \leqslant i \leqslant n$ we have $\mathsf{nb}^R(\kappa_k) = n$).
  - The ρ's are in Ty, which implies they don't contain any free type variable. They are called *parameter types.* By definition of schemas, parameter types can only occur at the beginning of a schema: this restriction is useful for technical reasons, most notably for the typing of recursors and the definition of their computation rules. It will be clear to the reader that this is a minor restriction which does not impair the system at all.
  - In every operator of the form $\overrightarrow{\sigma_{j_i}} \to \alpha$, the σ_{j_i} are in Ty (for all i and j_i), which enforces the α's to occur only *strictly positively* in the schema. This sort of operator is *recursive*: more precisely, it is a *0-recursive operator* if $|\overrightarrow{\sigma_{j_i}}| = 0$, and a *1-recursive operator* otherwise (by analogy with functionals of types 0 and 1 in Gödel's system T).

- In order to enhance the readability, we will often denote inductive types $\mu\alpha\,\overrightarrow{\kappa}$ *by* μ.

Definition 4 (Terms). *The set of* terms *is generated by the following grammar (with* $x \in \mathsf{Var}$, $k \in \mathbb{N} \setminus \{0\}$ *and* $\tau, \mu \in \mathsf{Ty}$*):*

$$t ::= x \mid \star \mid \langle t, t\rangle^{\rho\times\tau} \mid \mathsf{p}_1^{\rho\times\tau} \mid \mathsf{p}_2^{\rho\times\tau} \mid \lambda x^{\tau} t \mid (t\ t) \mid \mathsf{in}_k^{\mu} \mid (\!|\, \overrightarrow{t}\, |\!)^{\mu,\tau} \ ,$$

Here in_k^{μ} is the k'th constructor of the inductive type μ (in practice, we actually have *constructor names* $\mathsf{c} \in \mathsf{Const}$), and $(\!|\, \overrightarrow{t}\, |\!)^{\mu,\tau}$ is a *recursor* (or *structural-recursion operator*) from μ to another type τ.

Definition 5 (Step Type). *Given inductive type(s)* $\mu \equiv \mu\alpha\,\overrightarrow{\kappa}$ *and a result type* τ*, we define for every* $\kappa_k \equiv \overrightarrow{\rho} \to (\overrightarrow{\sigma_{j_1}} \to \alpha) \to \ldots \to (\overrightarrow{\sigma_{j_n}} \to \alpha) \to \alpha$ *in* $\mathsf{Sch}(\alpha)$ *the* step type

$$\delta^{\mu,\tau} \equiv \overrightarrow{\rho} \to (\overrightarrow{\sigma_{j_1}} \to \mu) \to \ldots \to (\overrightarrow{\sigma_{j_n}} \to \mu) \to (\overrightarrow{\sigma_{j_1}} \to \tau) \to \ldots \to (\overrightarrow{\sigma_{j_n}} \to \tau) \to \tau$$

Definition 6 (Typing). *We define by induction the typing rules of the calculus:*

$$\textsc{Var}\ \frac{}{\Gamma, x:\tau \vdash x:\tau} \qquad \textsc{Nop}\ \frac{}{\Gamma \vdash \star : 1}$$

$$\textsc{Pair}\ \frac{\Gamma \vdash t:\rho \qquad \Gamma \vdash u:\tau}{\Gamma \vdash \langle t, u\rangle^{\rho\times\tau} : \rho\times\tau} \qquad \textsc{Fst}\ \frac{\Gamma \vdash t:\rho\times\tau}{\Gamma \vdash \mathsf{p}_1^{\rho\times\tau}\ t:\rho} \qquad \textsc{Snd}\ \frac{\Gamma \vdash t:\rho\times\tau}{\Gamma \vdash \mathsf{p}_2^{\rho\times\tau}\ t:\tau}$$

$$\textsc{Lambda}\ \frac{\Gamma, x:\rho \vdash t:\tau}{\Gamma \vdash \lambda x^{\rho}\cdot t : \rho\to\tau} \qquad \textsc{App}\ \frac{\Gamma \vdash t:\rho\to\tau \qquad \Gamma \vdash u:\rho}{\Gamma \vdash (t\ u):\tau}$$

$$\textsc{In}\ \frac{c \in \mathsf{Const}}{\Gamma \vdash c_k : \kappa_k[\mu]} \qquad \textsc{Rec}\ \frac{\Gamma \vdash t_k : \delta_k^{\mu,\tau}}{\Gamma \vdash (\!|\, \overrightarrow{t}\, |\!)^{\mu,\tau} : \mu\to\tau}$$

Reduction. We take most of our terminology and notation in [9]. Given a binary relation R on a set A, we will denote the induced *rewrite relation* $\longrightarrow_R$, but shall be a bit loose and will often write R for $\longrightarrow_R$ and vice-versa. We will respectively write $\xrightarrow{+}_R$, $\xrightarrow{*}_R$, and $=_R$ for its transitive, reflexive-transitive, and reflexive-symmetric-transitive closures. We say that a term t *rewrites to* u if there is a term u such that $t \longrightarrow_R u$, and that it *reduces to* u if there is a derivation $t \xrightarrow{+}_R u$. The union $R \cup S$ of binary relations on a same set will be denoted RS. We also write $R; S$ for the set $\{(r, s) \mid \exists t \cdot r\,R\,t \wedge t\,S\,s\}$. A term is in *normal form* if it not rewriteable. A rewrite relation R is *strongly normalising* (*terminating*) if there is no infinite derivation $t_1 \longrightarrow_R t_2 \longrightarrow_R \ldots$, for any term t_1.

Given two rewrite relations R and S: R *commutes* with S if $\xleftarrow{*}_S; \xrightarrow{*}_R \subseteq \xrightarrow{*}_R; \xleftarrow{*}_S$; R *commutes locally* with S if $\longleftarrow_S; \longrightarrow_R \subseteq \xrightarrow{*}_R; \xleftarrow{*}_S$; R *commutes strictly locally over* S if $\longleftarrow_S; \longrightarrow_R \subseteq \xrightarrow{+}_R; \xleftarrow{*}_S$.

This definition is made in [10], and by R. Di Cosmo in [11] to state Akama-Di Cosmo's Lemma under the name of (DPG) condition (see Lemma 1 on the following page).

A relation R is confluent (resp. locally confluent) if it commutes (resp. commutes locally) with itself. A strongly normalising and confluent relation is said *convergent*. We will also write R/S to represent th quotient of a relation R by the reflexive-symmetric-transitive closure of S.

The usual notion of *substitution* will be written $t\{^u/_x\}$, to mean that u replaces every free occurrence of x in t, avoiding capture. Finally, as usual in this kind or work, we will consider *contexts*, written $C[])$, that is terms with a "hole" inside them which can be filled (giving for example $C[(\lambda x^\tau \cdot p)\ q]$.

Definition 7 (β-conversion). *We define the relation of β-*conversion *by the following rule:* $(\beta_\to)$ $(\lambda x^\tau \cdot t)\ u \longrightarrow_{\beta_\to} t\{^u/_x\}$; $(\beta_{\times_1})$ $\mathsf{p}_1^{\rho\times\tau}\ \langle t, u\rangle^{\rho\times\tau} \longrightarrow_{\beta_{\times_1}} t$; $(\beta_{\times_2})$ $\mathsf{p}_2^{\rho\times\tau}\ \langle t, u\rangle^{\rho\times\tau} \longrightarrow_{\beta_{\times_2}} u$, *and we write* $\beta_{\times_{1,2}}$ *for* $\beta_{\times_1} \cup \beta_{\times_2}$, *and* β *for* $\beta_\to \cup \beta_{\times_{1,2}}$.

Definition 8 (η-conversion). *We define the relation of η-*conversion *by the following set of rules:* $(\eta_\to)$ $t \longrightarrow_{\eta_\to} \lambda x^\tau \cdot t\ x$ *if* $t : \tau \to \upsilon$, t *is not in applicative position,* $x \notin \mathsf{FV}(t)$; $(\eta_\times)$ $t \longrightarrow_{\eta_\times} \langle \mathsf{p}_1^{\tau\times\rho} t, \mathsf{p}_2^{\tau\times\rho} t\rangle^{\tau\times\rho}$ *if* $t : \tau \times \rho$ t *is not a pair* t *is not projected;* (η_1) $t \longrightarrow_{\eta_1} \star$ *if* $t : 1 t \not\equiv \star$ *We'll write* $\eta_{\to,\times}$ *for* $\eta_\to \cup \eta_\times$, *and* η *for* $\eta_{\to,\times} \cup \eta_1$.

Definition 9 (ι-conversion). *Let* $\mu \equiv \mu\alpha\,\overrightarrow{\kappa}$, *and* $\kappa_k \equiv \overrightarrow{\rho} \to (\overrightarrow{\sigma_{j_1}} \to \alpha) \to \ldots \to (\overrightarrow{\sigma_{j_n}} \to \alpha) \to \alpha$ *over* α *in* μ. *Given a term* $\mathsf{in}_k^\mu \overrightarrow{u}$, *we write* $\overrightarrow{u_i^R}$ *for the* $n = \mathsf{nb}^R(\kappa_k)$ recursive arguments *it contains. The reader will recall that we have* $u_i^R : \overrightarrow{\sigma_{j_i}} \to \mu$ *for any* $1 \leqslant i \leqslant n$. *Then, we define ι-*conversion *by the rule* (ι) $(\!|\overrightarrow{t}|\!)^{\mu,\tau}(\mathsf{in}_k^\mu \overrightarrow{u}) \longrightarrow_\iota t_k\ \overrightarrow{u}\ \overrightarrow{((\!|\overrightarrow{t}|\!)^{\mu,\tau} \bullet u_i^R)}$.

Remark 1. Recall that $g \bullet f$ is just an abbreviation. Hence, we could describe ι-reduction as $(\!|\overrightarrow{t}|\!)^{\mu,\tau}(\mathsf{in}_k^\mu \overrightarrow{u}) \longrightarrow_\iota t_k\ \overrightarrow{u}\ \overrightarrow{\Delta(u_i^R)}$. where

$$\Delta(u_i^R) \equiv \begin{cases} (\!|\overrightarrow{t}|\!)_{\ell_i}^{\overrightarrow{\mu},\overrightarrow{\tau}}\ u_i^R & \text{if } u_i^R : \mu_{\ell_i} \ (i.e,\ u_i^R \text{ is 0-recursive}) \\ (\!|\overrightarrow{t}|\!)_{\ell_i}^{\overrightarrow{\mu},\overrightarrow{\tau}} \circ u_i^R & \text{if } u_i^R : \overrightarrow{\sigma_{j_i}} \to \mu_{\ell_i} \ (i.e,\ u_i^R \text{ is 1-recursive}) \end{cases}.$$

Often we will write just $(\!|\overrightarrow{t}|\!)\ (\mathsf{in}_k \overrightarrow{u}) \longrightarrow_\iota t_k\ \overrightarrow{u}\ \overrightarrow{((\!|\overrightarrow{t}|\!) \bullet u_i^R)}$.

The λ-calculus thus defined, together with $\beta\eta\iota$-conversion is called $\lambda^1\beta\eta\iota$.

In the rest of the paper, we will often omit type indications, except for abstracted variables, to lighten the notation.

3 Earlier Results

Detailed proofs of our results presented in this section can be found in [5]

Convergence of $\beta\eta\iota$-conversion The following lemma due to Y. Akama (further simplified by R. Di Cosmo) is of great use when one wishes to consider adding expansional rules to a rewrite system.

Lemma 1 (Akama-Di Cosmo's Lemma). *Let R and S be two convergent relations, such that R preserves S-normal forms. Then RS is convergent if R commutes strictly locally over S ([12], [11]).*

The *simulation* technique devised by [13] (which consists in finding a translation, between rewriting systems lifting certain properties) is also very useful.

Theorem 1. *$\beta_{\rightarrow}\iota$-conversion is convergent.*

This is a well-known result: strong normalisation is generally proved (often on stronger calculi, such as extensions of Girard's system F) using (variants of) reducibility candidates, see [14,7,15,16]. Confluence follows from the fact that $\beta_{\rightarrow}\iota$-conversion is an orthogonal higher-order system, see for example chapter 8 of [15] and [17]. Using simulation technique and theorem 1 one obtains

Theorem 2. *$\beta\iota$-conversion is convergent.*

With help of the following proposition several useful results may be obtained.

Proposition 1. *(cf. Prop. 21 from [18]) Let R be a strongly normalising left-linear rewrite relation, generated by rules that do not contain the term $\star$ in their left-hand side. Then $R \cup \eta_1$ is strongly normalising.*

Lemma 2. *$\beta\eta_1\iota$-conversion is strongly normalising.*

Lemma 3. *$\beta\eta_1\iota$-conversion is confluent.*

Theorem 3. *$\beta\eta\iota$-conversion is convergent.*

Our term system is slightly different from Di Cosmo's and some effort is necessary to reuse his proof in [11]. Our proof in [5] uses lemmas 2 and 3, Akama-Di Cosmo's Lemma and case analysis (to show that $\beta\eta_1\iota$-conversion commutes strictly locally over $\eta_{\rightarrow,\times}$-conversion).

Inductive representation of product and unit types. An interesting question is to know whether we may have $\rho\times\tau \cong \Pi(\rho,\tau)$ (for any types ρ and τ) and $1 \cong \mathbf{U}$. Unfortunately, it is not immediately the case: for the product, we would have functions $f : (\rho\times\tau) \rightarrow \Pi(\rho,\tau)$ and $g : \Pi(\rho,\tau) \rightarrow (\rho\times\tau)$ defined as

$$f \mathrel{\hat{=}} \lambda p^{\rho\times\tau} \cdot \mathsf{pair}^{\rho,\tau}\ (\mathsf{p}_1\ p)\ (\mathsf{p}_2\ p) \quad \text{and} \quad g \mathrel{\hat{=}} (\!| \lambda a^{\rho}\lambda b^{\tau} \cdot \langle a, b\rangle |\!)^{\Pi(\rho,\tau),\rho\times\tau} \ ,$$

and then $g \circ f =_{\eta_{\rightarrow}} \mathsf{id}_{\rho\times\tau}$ but

$$f \circ g \equiv \lambda z^{\Pi(\rho,\tau)} \cdot f\ (g\ z) =_{\beta_{\rightarrow}} \lambda z^{\Pi(\rho,\tau)} \cdot \mathsf{pair}^{\rho,\tau}\ (\mathsf{p}_1\ (g\ z))\ (\mathsf{p}_2\ (g\ z)) \neq_{\beta\eta\iota} \mathsf{id}_{\Pi(\rho,\tau)}$$

because the calculus lacks an analog of $\eta_\times$ for $\Pi(\rho,\tau)$. The same situation arises for 1 and **U**.

One solution is to add such an η rule for any inductive representation of the product or of the unit type. Recall now that our calculus features the possibility (though unused in the paper until now) to name the constructors of an inductive type. As a consequence, we should add such an η rule for all representations of the product and the unit types (all these representations shall become isomorphic).

Definition 10. *For any types $\Pi(\rho,\tau) \equiv \mu\alpha\,(\mathsf{pair}^{\rho,\tau} : \rho \rightarrow \tau \rightarrow \alpha)$ and $\mathbf{U} \equiv \mu\alpha\,(\mathsf{nop} : \alpha)$, we define the following conversion rules:*

($\nu_\times$) $t \longrightarrow_{\nu_\times} \mathsf{pair}^{\rho,\tau}\ (\mathsf{proj}_1^{\rho\times\tau}\ t)\ (\mathsf{proj}_2^{\rho\times\tau}\ t)$ if $t : \Pi(\rho,\tau)$, $t \not\equiv \mathsf{pair}^{\rho,\tau} s_1 s_2$, $t \not\equiv \mathsf{proj}_i^{\rho\times\tau} s$;

(ν_1) $t \longrightarrow_{\nu_1} \mathsf{nop}$ if $t : \mathbf{U}$, $t \not\equiv \mathsf{nop}$, where $\mathsf{proj}_i^{\rho_1\times\rho_2} \widehat{=} (\!|\lambda x_1^{\rho_1}\lambda x_2^{\rho_2} \cdot x_i|\!)^{\Pi(\rho_1,\rho_2),\rho_i}$; and we write ν for $\nu_\times \cup \nu_1$.

We consider the properties of strong normalisation and confluence for the calculus with $\beta\eta\iota\nu$-conversion, which we will call $\lambda^1\beta\eta\iota\nu$.

To prove convergence for this set of conversions, we roughly follow the same procedure used to prove this property for $\lambda^1\beta\eta\iota$. It is quite natural as $\nu_\times$- and ν_1-conversions are very similar to $\eta_\times$- and η_1-conversions.

Lemma 4. *$\beta\eta_1\iota\nu_1$-conversion is strongly normalising.*

Lemma 5. *$\beta\eta_1\iota\nu_1$-conversion is confluent.*

Theorem 4. *$\beta\eta\iota\nu$-conversion is convergent.*

As we wrote earlier, in an "actual" setting, many different instances (with different names of types and constructors) of inductive representations of the product and unit types may occur. In this case, as many forms of ν-conversions must be added, let us call them ν^2, ν^3, etc.

We prove, by a simple inductive argument, that adding these conversions to $\beta\eta\iota$-conversion will keep the convergence property.

Recall that, in $\lambda^1\beta\eta$, any isomorphism is obtained by finite composition of the following base of 7 isomorphisms ([4]):

$$\rho\times\tau \cong \tau\times\rho \qquad \rho\times(\tau\times\upsilon) \cong (\rho\times\tau)\times\upsilon \qquad (\rho\times\tau)\rightarrow\upsilon \cong \rho\rightarrow(\tau\rightarrow\upsilon)$$

$$\rho\rightarrow(\tau\times\upsilon) \cong (\rho\rightarrow\tau)\times(\rho\rightarrow\upsilon) \qquad \rho\times 1 \cong \rho \qquad \rho\rightarrow 1 \cong 1 \qquad 1\rightarrow\rho \cong \rho$$

As $\lambda^1\beta\eta\iota$ and $\lambda^1\beta\eta\iota\nu$ contain $\lambda^1\beta\eta$, the 7 isomorphisms still hold, though these are not anymore —of course— the only ones. However, note that this is an interesting result, as isomorphic types may occur in any inductive type (see the next section).

Furthermore, every inductive type similar (with different constructor names) with $\Pi(\rho, \tau)$ and **U** is now (respectively) isomorphic to $\rho \times \tau$ and 1, and thus inherits all CCC-isomorphisms.

Copies. The CCC-isomorphisms holding on inductive representations of the product and unit types are rather "structural". One may then wonder whether less structural isomorphisms (corresponding for example to set-theoretic bijections) may hold computationally between inductive types.

Unfortunately, many isomorphisms of inductive types can't be "internalised" through a conversion relation. For instance, one may wish to have $\tau \cong \mu\alpha\,(\tau \to \alpha)$ for any type τ. This doesn't seem to be easily feasible: various new conversion rules that seem appropriate, combined with $\beta\eta\iota$-conversion yield a non-confluent rewrite system.

Similarly, adding computational rules to have $\Pi(\mathbf{N}, \mathbf{N}) \cong \mathbf{N}$ or $\Sigma(\mathbf{N}, \mathbf{N}) \cong \mathbf{N}$ creates serious problems. Therefore, the best we can do is add specific rules giving us as many isomorphisms as possible. Here comes into play the notion of *faithful copy* [1]

Definition 11. *Let be given types π and π', with $f : \pi \to \pi'$, $f' : \pi' \to \pi$, and inductive types $\varphi \mathrel{\widehat{=}} \mu\alpha\,(\overrightarrow{c} : \overrightarrow{\kappa})$ and $\varphi' \mathrel{\widehat{=}} \mu\alpha\,(\overrightarrow{c'} : \overrightarrow{\kappa'})$. Then φ' is called a* copy *of φ if it differs from φ only by the names of its constructors, and by the fact that* zero or more *occurrences of π in φ are replaced by π' in φ', where π and π' may only appear as parameters or no deeper than the whole domain of 1-recursive operators.*

In [5] we consider only the case when $f : \pi \cong \pi' : f'$ i.e., f, f' are mutually inverse intensional isomorphisms. The copy is then dubbed *faithful.*

Remark 2. We don't consider here the possible task of reordering constructors so that c_i matches c'_i for all $1 \leqslant i \leqslant n$.

For ease of reading, we will fix the symbols π, π', φ, φ', $\overrightarrow{c}$, $\overrightarrow{c'}$, $\overrightarrow{\kappa}$, $\overrightarrow{\kappa'}$, f and f' appearing in the previous definition, and will consistently use them till the end of this section.

If $f : \pi \cong \pi' : f'$, faithful copy is just a special case of isomorphism, which is provable but not computable. In [5] was shown that it is possible to add a new corresponding χ-conversion rule making the isomorphism intensional, and such that the underlying conversion relation of the resulting calculus $\lambda^1\beta\eta\iota\nu\chi$ remains convergent.

To describe this notion of choice, we will write $(f^? \; x)$ to denote $(f \; x)$ if $x : \pi$ *and* x corresponds to an occurrence to be replaced, and just x otherwise. Similarly, $g \circ^? f^?$ will mean $g \circ f$ if the domain of g is to be replaced, and just g otherwise.

[1] We first introduced this notion in [6] under the name of *isomorphic copy.*

Let us now define the function $\mathsf{fc} : \varphi \to \varphi'$ ($\mathsf{fc}' : \varphi' \to \varphi$ can obviously be defined conversely). The reader will notice that this procedure can be automatised. Unformally, we have $\mathsf{fc}\ (c_k\ \overrightarrow{p_s}\ \overrightarrow{r_i}) = c'_k\ \overrightarrow{p'_s}\ \overrightarrow{r'_i}$ where $p'_s = f^?\ p_s$ and $r'_i = (\mathsf{fc} \bullet r_i) \circ^? f'^?$. (We make a difference between parameters $p_s : \rho_s$, for $1 \leqslant s \leqslant \mathsf{nb}^P(\kappa_k)$, and recursive arguments $r_i : \overrightarrow{\sigma_{j_i}} \to \varphi_{\ell_i}$, with $1 \leqslant i \leqslant n$.)

Example 1. Take $f : \mathbf{N} \cong \mathbf{P} : f'$ (what type is $\mathbf{P}$ is of no importance) with $\varphi \mathrel{\widehat{=}} \mu\alpha\,(c_1 : \alpha, c_2 : (\mathbf{N} \to \mathbf{N}) \to \alpha, c_3 : \mathbf{N} \to \alpha \to \alpha, c_4 : (\mathbf{N} \to \alpha) \to \alpha)$ and $\varphi' \mathrel{\widehat{=}} \mu\alpha\,(c'_1 : \alpha, c'_2 : (\mathbf{N} \to \mathbf{N}) \to \alpha, c'_3 : \mathbf{P} \to \alpha \to \alpha, c'_4 : (\mathbf{P} \to \alpha) \to \alpha)$.
Then the definition of $\mathsf{fc} : \varphi \to \varphi'$ is:

$$\begin{array}{llll} \mathsf{fc}\ c_1 & = c'_1 & \mathsf{fc}\ (c_3\ h\ t) & = c'_3\ (f\ h)\ (\mathsf{fc}\ t) \\ \mathsf{fc}\ (c_2\ k) & = c'_2\ k & \mathsf{fc}\ (c_4\ k) & = c'_4\ (\mathsf{fc} \circ k \circ f')\ . \end{array}$$

Definition 12. *(Formal definition of* $\mathsf{fc}\varphi \to \varphi'$*.) We have* $\mathsf{fc} \mathrel{\widehat{=}} (\!|\, \overrightarrow{t}\, |\!)^{\varphi,\varphi'}$ *with* t_k *being the normal form of* $\lambda\overrightarrow{p^\rho}\,\lambda\overrightarrow{r^{\overrightarrow{\sigma_{j_i}} \to \varphi}}\,\lambda\overrightarrow{s^{\overrightarrow{\sigma_{j_i}} \to \varphi'}} \cdot c'_k\ \overrightarrow{(f^?\ p)}\ \overrightarrow{(s \circ^?\ f'^?)}$.

Proposition 2. *If* $f : \pi \cong \pi' : f'$ *then* $\mathsf{fc} : \varphi \cong \varphi' : \mathsf{fc}'$ *is a provable isomorphism.*

The principal result (in case when $f : \pi \cong \pi' : f'$) is that the calculus extended by two conversion rules $\mathsf{fc}'\ (\mathsf{fc}\ x) \longrightarrow_\chi x$ and $\mathsf{fc}\ (\mathsf{fc}'\ x) \longrightarrow_\chi x$ (we shall call them χ-conversion rules) is convergent.

Observe that χ-conversion is convergent. We show that $\beta\eta\iota\nu\chi$-conversion is strongly normalising, and then prove that it is confluent using Newman's Lemma. (It doesn't seem possible to make use of Akama-Di Cosmo's Lemma.)

In order to show strong normalisation, we used the following property which we already used in [6] under the name "deferment" (the better name "adjournment" is due to D. Kesner).

Definition 13 (Adjournment). *Given two binary relations* R *and* S, S *is* adjournable w.r.t R *if* $S; R \subseteq R; (RS)^*$.

Lemma 6 (Adjournment Lemma). *Given two strongly normalising relations* R *and* S, RS *is strongly normalising if* S *is adjournable w.r.t* R.

Proofs of (variations of) this lemma can be found in [19,10,20,6].

A subtle point of the proof of SN is that there are cases when the adjournement lemma can be used only on condition that certain 1-recursive arguments of ι-redex are $\eta_\to$-expanded. The idea is therefore to "insert" suitable $\eta_\to$-expansions in a term before χ-conversion, so that the adjournement remains possible.

Lemma 7. *Let* R *be some rewrite relation such that* η^- *(*η*-reduction* opposite *to* $\eta_\to$*) can be postponed w.r.t. every reduction in* R *(except* $\eta_\to$ *if* $\eta_\to \in R$*). Suppose there is an infinite derivation* $B \xrightarrow{*}_R C[t] \xrightarrow{\infty}_R \ldots$ *where the occurrence of* t *may be* $\eta_\to$*-expanded. Then, there exists another derivation* $B \xrightarrow{*}_R C[t] \longrightarrow_{\eta_\to} C[\underline{t}] \xrightarrow{\infty}_R \ldots$ *which is also infinite.*

We can now state a new lemma, based upon a "conditional" adjournment.

Definition 14 (Adjournment Modulo $\eta_{\rightarrow}$). *Given two binary relations R and S, with R satisfying the assumption of previous lemma and $\eta_{\rightarrow} \subseteq R$, the relation S is* adjournable w.r.t R modulo $\eta_{\rightarrow}$ *if $(S;R)/\eta_{\rightarrow} \subseteq (R;(RS)^*)/\eta_{\rightarrow}$.*

Lemma 8. *Given two strongly normalising relations R and S, with $\eta_{\rightarrow} \subseteq R$, RS is strongly normalising if S is adjournable w.r.t R modulo $\eta_{\rightarrow}$.*

Lemma 9. *$\beta\eta\iota\nu^{\overset{m}{\cup}}\chi$-conversion is strongly normalising.*

In its proof we verify the possibility to apply previous lemmas.

Lemma 10. *$\beta\eta\iota\nu\chi$-conversion is confluent.*

As $\beta\eta\iota\nu\chi$-conversion is strongly normalising, it is enough to show that $\beta\eta\iota\nu\chi$-conversion is locally confluent. As $\beta\eta\iota\nu$- and χ-conversions are both confluent, we are left with showing that $\longleftarrow_{\chi};\longrightarrow_{\beta\eta\iota\nu} \subseteq \overset{*}{\longleftarrow}_{\beta\eta\iota\nu\chi};\overset{*}{\longrightarrow}_{\beta\eta\iota\nu\chi}$. This is done by careful case analysis.

Until now, we only considered adding one couple of χ-rules, which entail the existence of an intensional isomorphism between an inductive type and its faithful copy. This result can be extended to several other χ-rules (call them χ^2, χ^3, etc), in order to get a whole "architecture" of isomorphic inductive types.

It is easy to see that adding these conversions to $\beta\eta\iota\nu^{\overset{m}{\cup}}$-conversion will keep the strong normalisation and local confluence properties. Indeed, writing $\chi^{\overset{n}{\cup}}$ for $\bigcup_{i=1}^{n} \chi^i$, we have the following:

Theorem 5. *$\beta\eta\iota\nu^{\overset{m}{\cup}}\chi^{\overset{n}{\cup}}$-conversion is convergent.*

4 Algebraic Constructions Using Finite Inductive Types

Category of finite types. Let us consider the type $\omega_n = \mu\alpha\,(c_1 : \alpha, ..., c_n : \alpha)$. Constructors c_i have the type ω_n. Recursors have the form $(\!|t_1, ..., t_n|\!)^{\omega_n,\tau}$ where $t_1 : \tau, ..., t_n : \tau$.

Obviously the type ω_n as a representation of a set of n elements is not unique. For example, the names of constructors may be changed. To avoid confusion we use different constructor names in different types. We shall not consider here more complex cases, such as finite types as part of an *inductive family*.

Let $[n]$ denote the set of natural numbers $\{1, ..., n\}$. Let some types $\omega_n = \mu\alpha\,(c_1 : \alpha, ..., c_n : \alpha)$ and $\omega_m = \mu\alpha\,(c'_1 : \alpha, ..., c'_m : \alpha)$ be fixed. To every function $f : [n] \rightarrow [m]$ corresponds the function $(\!|c'_{f(1)}, ..., c'_{f(n)}|\!)^{\omega_n,\omega_m}$. Let us denote it by $\overline{f}$. Note that in this approach f itself remains outside the formal system, it is just some function defined on the set $[n]$.

Let $f : [n] \rightarrow [m], g : [m] \rightarrow [l]$ and the types $\omega_n, \omega_m, \omega_l$ be fixed. If only standard reductions are considered then $\overline{(g \circ f)}t \neq \overline{f}(\overline{g}t)$. Indeed, the terms

$(\!|c^l_{g(1)},...,c^l_{g(m)}|\!)((\!|c^m_{f(1)},...,c^m_{f(n)}|\!)x)$ and $(\!|c^l_{g(f(1))},...,c^l_{g(f(n))}|\!)x$ are already normal.

The first question that arises is whether the calculus extended by new reductions $\overline{f}(\overline{g}t) \to_\theta \overline{(f \circ g)}t$ is convergent. The following lemma is obvious.

Lemma 11. *θ-conversion is convergent.*

Let us take $\beta\eta\iota\nu$-conversion as R and θ-conversion as S.

Lemma 12. *$\beta\eta\iota\nu\theta$-conversion is strongly normalising.*

Proof. . It is easily verified that θ-reduction is adjournable. E.g., if θ-reduction is followed by ι-reduction $C \equiv C[\overline{g}(\overline{f}c_i)] \to_\theta C[\overline{(g \circ f)}c_i] \to_\iota C[c''_{g(f(i))}]$ then it may be replaced by 2 ι-reductions. In other cases θ-reduction can just be postponed.

Lemma 13. *$\beta\eta\iota\nu\theta$-conversion is confluent.*

Proof. By lemma 12 and Newman's lemma it is enough to show that $\beta\eta\iota\nu\theta$-conversion is locally confluent. Since θ-conversion and $\beta\eta\iota\nu$-conversion are convergent we have to check only the cases $\leftarrow_\theta;\to_\iota$, $\leftarrow_\theta;\to_\beta$, $\leftarrow_\theta;\to_\eta$, $\leftarrow_\theta;\to_\nu$. Let us consider for example the case $\leftarrow_\theta;\to_\iota$. In fact only the case of overlapping redexes is of interest: $C[\overline{(g \circ f)}c_i] \leftarrow_\theta C[\overline{g}(\overline{f}c_i)] \to_\iota C[(\overline{g}c'_{f(i)}]$.

The fork is closed by one application of ι at each side. Other three cases are even simpler.

Theorem 6. *$\beta\eta\iota\nu\theta$-conversion is convergent.*

With θ-conversion (and corresponding equivalence relation on terms) we have a possibility to introduce categorical structure on finite types, that is, to define a category with the types ω_n as objects (due to renaming of constructors it may be many for each n) and $\overline{f}$ for all ω_n, ω_m and $f : [n] \to [m]$ as morphisms. For this we don't need the reduction $\overline{id_n} \to id_{\omega_n}$ where $id_n : [n] \to [n]$ is identity map and $id_{\omega_n} \equiv \lambda x^{\omega_n}.x$. Indeed, the property $\overline{f} \circ \overline{id} =_\theta \overline{f} =_\theta \overline{id} \circ \overline{f}$ does hold and more strong property $\overline{id} \circ h = h$ for all $h : \omega_n \to \tau$ and $h \circ \overline{id} = h$ for all $h : \tau \to \omega_n$ is not needed.

Remark 3. This is the case where one may take $\overline{id_n}$ as id_{ω_n} instead of standard term $\lambda x^{\omega_n}.x$. It is due to consideration of a part of the whole calculus as the support of corresponding category. Note that the term $id_{\omega_n} \equiv \lambda x^{\omega_n}.x$ has not the form $\overline{f}$ and doesn't belong to the categorical structure in question.

Groups of permutations. Similar considerations apply to the case when we consider only the functions $\overline{f}$ with $f : [n] \to [n]$ and the same type ω_n fixed as the domain and codomain of $\overline{f}$. This case is of interest for representations of the group of permutations S_n within type theory.

With θ-reduction we may introduce the group with terms $\overline{f}$ as elements. The term $\overline{id_n}$ will play the role of unit and the inverse of $\overline{f}$ is represented by $\overline{f^{-1}}$.

Often in group theory, groups are defined using generators and relations and elements are represented as products of generators. When elements of a group are represented by terms $t : \tau \to \tau$ in type theory, it may be more interesting to consider conversions going the opposite way (w.r.t. the case considered above), i.e., "splitting" t into composition.

We shall consider here one case related to the group of permutations.

It is well known that every permutation $f : [n] \to [n]$ can be represented as a product of disjoint cycles.

More precisely, f is called cycle if there exists some subset $\{i_1, ..., i_k\} \in \{1, ..., n\}$ such that $f(i_1) = i_2, ..., f(i_{k-1}) = i_k, f(i_k) = i_1$ and $f(i) = i$ if i is not in $\{i_1, ..., i_k\}$.

Two cycles are disjoint if the corresponding sets $\{i_1, ..., i_k\}, \{j_1, ..., j_l\}$ have no common elements.

Product in S_n is represented by functional composition of permutations.

If $f : [n] \to [n]$ then $f = f_1 \circ ... \circ f_m$ where $f_1, ..., f_m$ are disjoint cycles and the cycles that appear in the product are unique.

Product (composition) of disjoint cycles is commutative but it is possible to order cycles (for example, lexicographically) and to have for every f unique decomposition $f = f_1 \circ ... \circ f_m$ with $f_1 \leqslant ... \leqslant f_m$.

This suggests to study the conversions $\overline{f}t \to_{\theta'} \overline{f_1}(...(\overline{f_m}t)...)$ instead of $\to_\theta$ where $f : [n] \to [n]$ and $f_1, ..., f_m$ are disjoint cycles of the unique decomposition of f.

Lemma 14. *The $\beta\eta\iota\nu\theta'$-conversion is strongly normalising.*

Proof. . Obviously θ'-conversion is SN. Assume that there exists an infinite reduction sequence consisting of $\beta\eta\iota\nu\theta'$-reductions. It is enough to obtain a contradiction with SN for $\beta\eta\iota\nu$-conversion.

Since $\beta\eta\iota\nu$-conversion and θ'-conversion are SN, this sequence consists of alternating finite intervals of $\beta\eta\iota\nu$- and θ'-conversions. Let us consider the end of first interval consisting of θ'-conversions. If last θ'-conversion of this interval is followed by any of β, η, ν-conversions then it can always be postponed.

The only case that poses problems is $C[\overline{f}c_i] \to_{\theta'} C[\overline{f_1}(...(\overline{f_m}c_i)...)]$
$\to_\iota C[\overline{f_1}(...(\overline{f_{m-1}}c_{f_m(i)}))] \to_{\beta\eta\iota\nu\theta'} ...$

Lemma 15 (Auxilliary). *Assume there is an infinite reduction sequence of the form $C \to_{\beta\eta\iota\nu\theta'} ...$ and the term C is of the form $C[\overline{h}c_i]$. Then there exists an infinite reduction sequence beginning with the reduction $C[\overline{h}c_i] \to_\iota C[c_{h(i)}]$.*

The algorithm modifying initial sequence may be defined explicitely. It is first defined for finite reduction sequences in such a way that it is hereditary w.r.t. initial fragments and this permits to extend it to infinite sequences. Then it is shown that infinite sequences remain infinite.

Thus, we insert the conversions $C[\overline{f_1}(...(\overline{f_{m-1}}c_{f_m(i)}))] \to_\iota^{m-1} C[c_{f_1(...f_m(i)...)}]$ The reduction sequence remains infinite. Then θ'-conversion can be postponed w.r.t. the whole 'block' consisting of m ι-conversions.

As result, we will be able to show that there exists an infinite sequence of $\beta\eta\iota\nu$-conversions. Contradiction.

Lemma 16. *The $\beta\eta\iota\nu\theta'$-conversion is confluent.*

Proof. Verification of local confluence similar to lemma 13.

Thus, we have

Theorem 7. *The $\beta\eta\iota\nu\theta'$-conversion is convergent.*

Faithful copy maps. We studied elsewhere [6] the *isomorphism* reductions, i.e., the calculus with additional reductions of the form $f'(f(x)) \rightarrow_\sigma x$ where f and f' are mutually inverse w.r.t. standard conversions only extensionally (on canonical elements of an inductive type). This is the case for $\overline{f}$ and $\overline{f^{-1}}$ where $f, f^{-1} : [n] \rightarrow [n]$ are mutually inverse permutations. If θ-conversion is already added it seems more natural instead of adding isomorphism reductions $\overline{f}(\overline{f^{-1}}t) \rightarrow t$ to add one reduction $\overline{id_n}t \rightarrow_\omega t$ for each ω_n.

Note that $\overline{id_n} \rightarrow_\eta \lambda x : \omega_n.(\overline{id_n}x) \rightarrow_\omega \lambda x : \omega_n.x \equiv id_{\omega_n}$. If we take mutually inverse functions $f, f^{-1} : [n] \rightarrow [n]$ and $\overline{f} : \omega_n \rightarrow \omega'_n, \overline{f^{-1}} : \omega'_n \rightarrow \omega_n$ then $\lambda x : \omega_n.(\overline{f^{-1}}(\overline{f}x)) \rightarrow_\theta \lambda x : \omega_n.(\overline{id_n}x) \rightarrow_\omega \lambda x : \omega_n.x \equiv id_{\omega_n}$.

Obviously ω-conversion is convergent.

Theorem 8. *The $\beta\eta\iota\nu\theta\omega$-conversion is convergent.*

Now the interesting part is to consider the isomorphisms issued from the mariage of this extension with faithful copy and related reductions.

Theorem 9. *The $\beta\eta\iota\nu\theta\omega\chi$-conversion is convergent.*

Proof. It uses essentially the schema of the proof of theorem 5. We have to check in addition the cases of χ-conversion combined with θ- and ω-conversion (both for adjournement/strong normalisation and confluence). They do not pose problems due to very 'basic' structure of terms $\overline{f}$.

Note that using χ-conversion one may obtain $\overline{id_n} \circ \overline{id_n} \rightarrow id_{\omega_n}$ but it doesn't include ω-conversion since we don't have $\overline{id_n} \rightarrow \overline{id_n} \circ \overline{id_n}$ which is not SN.

5 Conclusion

Our purpose was to explore the possibilities to extend the computational content of various systems of λ-calculus via the extention of reduction systems preserving convergence. In this paper we concentrated on the study of finite inductive types and reductions related to categorical and group-theoretical properties, but the impact of introduction of new reductions is better understood in the context of previous work where the isomorphism reductions, reductions related to representation of Cartesian Closed Structure and the notion of faithful copy were studied.

It should be noted that most of the results were proved using abstract techniques —most of them being due to R. Di Cosmo— instead of more usual ones such as reducibility candidates or critical pairs.

The notion of faithful copy of an inductive type, that is, another inductive type which differs from the former only by the name of its constructors and by the fact that a parameter type may have been replaced by another isomorphic type admits generalisation with parameter change along an arbitrary arrow $f : A \to B$. This has obvious categorical repercussions.

One of next tasks in our project would be naturally to study categorical aspects of these operations. More precisely, the extensions of reduction systems that would support functoriality of inductive type definitions w.r.t. parameter types will be studied.

We would like to extend our inductive types by allowing any *positive* operator in constructor schemas, as these are currently restricted to strictly-positive operators.

Together with this enhancement, we would like to consider an upgrade to system F, giving thus a system with polymorphic and positive recursive types as considered in [15]. We think it is necessary to extend widely our notion of copy and parameter change because it can't handle currently with "deep" parameter types. Furthermore, it would enable to get "generic" terms the transformations.

On the other hand, though desirable, getting intensional isomorphisms for calculi with dependent types may represent a serious increase in difficulty, because of the existence of terms in types. Some preliminary work was carried out in [21] without taking dependent inductive types into account. However, these are most used in proof assistants so much more needs to be done. This might be brought closer with current work aimed at improving computational capabilities of proof assistants such as Coq [22,8,23] by adding higher-order rewrite rules while retaining strong normalisation and confluence.

Another subject of interest lies in giving a semantical account of our syntactical studies.

One interesting topic is for instance to consider isomorphisms of types in a CCC with initial algebras which may be understood as the companion piece of our calculus $\lambda^1\beta\eta\iota$ (extended perhaps with positive inductive types).

However, one of our prime objectives is to study and perhaps extend Fiore's normalisation by evaluation to get a normalisation proof for a calculus involving not only inductive, product and unit types but also sum and zero types, all (but inductive types) equipped with rewrite rules ensuring their uniqueness. Some important work has already been carried out by M. Fiore, R. Di Cosmo and V. Balat and notably appears in [24,25].

References

1. Barendregt, H., Barnedsen, E. Autarkic computations in formal proofs. Journal of Automated Reasoning 28(2002), 321-336.
2. Di Cosmo, R.: Isomorphisms of Types: From λ-Calculus to Information Retrieval and Language Design. Progress in Theoretical Computer Science. Birkhäuser, Boston, MA (1995)

3. Flegontov, A., Soloviev, S.: Type theory in differential equations. In: VIII International Workshop on Advenced Computing and Analysis Techniques in Physics Research (ACA'2002), Moscow, 2002. Abstract.
4. Soloviev, S.: The category of finite sets and Cartesian closed categories. In: Theoretical Applications of Methods of Mathematical Logic III. Volume 105 of Zapiski Nauchnykh Seminarov LOMI. Nauka, Leningrad (1981) 174–194 English translation in *Journal of Soviet Mathematics*, 22(3) (1983), 1387–1400.
5. Chemouil, D.: Isomorphisms of Simple Inductive Types through Extensional Rewriting. Accepted for publication in Mathematical Structures in Computer Science, 42 pp.
6. Chemouil, D., Soloviev, S.: Remarks on isomorphisms of simple inductive types. In Geuvers, H., Kamareddine, F., eds.: Electronic Notes in Theoretical Computer Science. Volume 85., Elsevier (2003)
7. Schwichtenberg, H.: Minimal Logic for Computable Functionals. Mathematisches Institut der Universität München. (2003) Available on `http://www.minlog-system.de`.
8. Blanqui, F., Jouannaud, J.P., Okada, M.: Inductive-data-type systems. Theoretical Computer Science **272** (2002) 41–68
9. Baader, F., Nipkow, T.: Term Rewriting and All That. Cambridge University Press, New York (1998)
10. Geser, A.: Relative Termination. PhD thesis, Universität Passau, Passau, Germany (1990)
11. Di Cosmo, R.: On the power of simple diagrams. In Ganzinger, H., ed.: Proceedings of the 7th International Conference on Rewriting Techniques and Applications (RTA-96). Volume 1103 of LNCS., New Brunswick, NJ, USA, Springer-Verlag (1996) 200–214

Di Cosmo and Kesner, 1996a. Di Cosmo, R. and Kesner, D. (1996a). Combining algebraic rewriting, extensional lambda calculi, and fixpoints. *Theoretical Computer Science*, 169(2):201–220.

12. Akama, Y.: On Mints' reductions for ccc-calculus. In: Proceedings of the International Conference on Typed Lambda Calculi and Applications. Volume 664 of Lecture Notes in Computer Science., Berlin, Springer-Verlag (1993) 1–12
13. Di Cosmo, R., Kesner, D.: Combining algebraic rewriting, extensional lambda calculi, and fixpoints. Theoretical Computer Science **169** (1996) 201–220
14. Girard, J.Y., Lafont, Y., Taylor, P.: Proofs and Types. Cambridge Tracts in Theoretical Computer Science 7. Cambridge University Press (1988)
15. Matthes, R.: Extensions of System F by Iteration and Primitive Recursion on Monotone Inductive Types. PhD thesis, Fachbereich Mathematik, Ludwig-Maximilians-Universität München (1998)
16. Paulin-Mohring, C.: Inductive definitions in the system Coq. Rules and properties. In Bezem, M., Groote, J.F., eds.: Proceedings of the 1st International Conference on Typed Lambda Calculi and Applications, TCLA'93, Utrecht, The Netherlands. Volume 664 of Lecture Notes in Computer Science., Springer-Verlag (1993) 328–345
17. Mayr, R., Nipkow, T.: Higher-order rewrite systems and their confluence. Technical Report Sep26-1, Technical University of Munich (1995)
18. Di Cosmo, R., Kesner, D.: Rewriting with extensional polymorphic lambda-calculus. Lecture Notes in Computer Science (**1092**)
19. Bachmair, L., Dershowitz, N.: Commutation, transformation, and termination. In Siekmann, J.H., ed.: Proceedings of the Eighth International Conference on Automated Deduction (Oxford, England). Volume 230 of Lecture Notes in Computer Science., Berlin, Springer-Verlag (1986) 5–20

20. Doornbos, H., von Karger, B.: On the union of well-founded relations. Logic Journal of the IGPL **6** (1998) 195–201
21. Delahaye, D.: Information Retrieval in a Coq Proof Library using Type Isomorphisms. In: Proceedings of TYPES'99, Lökeberg, Springer-Verlag LNCS (1999)
22. Blanqui, F., Jouannaud, J.P., Okada, M.: The calculus of algebraic constructions. In Narendran, P., Rusinowitch, M., eds.: Proceedings of the 10th International Conference on Rewriting Techniques and Applications (RTA-99), Trento, Italy, Springer-Verlag LNCS 1631 (1999) 301–316
23. Blanqui, F.: Théorie des types et récriture. PhD thesis, Université Paris XI (2001)
24. Fiore, M., Cosmo, R.D., Balat, V.: Remarks on isomorphisms in typed lambda calculi with empty and sum types. In: Logic in Computer Science, Los Alamitos, CA, USA, IEEE Computer Society (2002) 147–156
25. Balat, V.: Une étude des sommes fortes : isomorphismes et formes normales. PhD thesis, Université Paris 7 (2002)

A Concurrent Logical Framework: The Propositional Fragment*

Kevin Watkins[1], Iliano Cervesato[2], Frank Pfenning[1], and David Walker[3]

[1] Department of Computer Science, Carnegie Mellon University
{kw,fp}@cs.cmu.edu
[2] ITT Industries, AES Division iliano@itd.nrl.navy.mil
[3] Department of Computer Science, Princeton University
dpw@cs.princeton.edu

Abstract. We present the propositional fragment CLF_0 of the Concurrent Logical Framework (CLF). CLF extends the Linear Logical Framework to allow the natural representation of concurrent computations in an object language. The underlying type theory uses monadic types to segregate values from computations. This separation leads to a tractable notion of definitional equality that identifies computations differing only in the order of execution of independent steps. From a logical point of view our type theory can be seen as a novel combination of lax logic and dual intuitionistic linear logic. An encoding of a small Petri net exemplifies the representation methodology, which can be summarized as "*concurrent computations as monadic expressions*".

1 Introduction

A logical framework is a meta-language for deductive systems. It is usually defined as a formal meta-logic or type theory together with a representation methodology. A single implementation of a logical framework can then be used to study a variety of deductive systems, thereby factoring the effort that would be required to implement each deductive system separately. Applications of logical frameworks lie mostly in logic and programming languages, where deductive systems have become a common conceptual tool and presentation device. Examples are rules of logical inference, typing rules, and rules specifying the operational semantics of a programming language. Tasks carried out with the help of logical frameworks include proof checking, proof search, and establishing meta-theoretic properties of deductive systems. For an overview and introduction to logical frameworks, their applications, and further pointers to the literature see [6,35,32].

The language features provided by a logical framework have a major impact on each task it supports. The right features can help make representation of

* This research was sponsored in part by the NSF under grants CCR-9988281, CCR-0208601, CCR-0238328, and CCR-0306313, and by NRL under grant N00173-00-C-2086.

S. Berardi, M. Coppo, and F. Damiani (Eds.): TYPES 2003, LNCS 3085, pp. 355–377, 2004.

deductive systems clear, direct, concise, and therefore easy to read and understand. Such elegance can, in turn, make an enormous difference when it comes to proof checking, proof search, and constructing meta-theoretic proofs. Still, each feature we add to a logical framework must be well justified as the design effort is significant and a robust framework must satisfy many subtle properties. Hence, to design an effective framework, we should identify features that most effectively support recurring idioms in the definition and manipulation of deductive systems.

Some of the most commonly recurring concepts in deductive systems are *parameterization* and *variable binding*: quantified formulas are pervasive in logic; programming languages contain parameterized expressions such as functions, objects, modules, and others; and inference rules and deductions themselves are often parameterized. LF [20] and other frameworks provide intrinsic support for parameterized objects through dependent functions. Common tasks such as renaming variables and substitution need not be coded up explicitly, as they are handled automatically by the framework when the appropriate representation strategy is chosen. With this support, simple phenomena such as α-convertibility and syntactic substitution have simple representations in the framework, so users of the framework can focus their efforts on truly complex phenomena of the system under investigation.

With dependent functions alone, however, representation of *stateful* programming languages can be clumsy and complex. In order to better accommodate reasoning with state, LF has been extended with selected constructs from linear logic, giving rise to the logical frameworks LLF [14] and RLF [23]. In these frameworks, users can represent state as linear hypotheses and imperative computations as linear functions, yielding more concise representations than are possible in LF. Since the state concept pervades deductive systems of many different kinds, we judge this extension to be justified, though at present there is much less practical experience with such linear frameworks.

Unfortunately, LF, as well as LLF and RLF, lack effective support for representing or manipulating systems involving *concurrency*, which has come to be nearly as pervasive as state. The obvious encodings of concurrent programming languages in LLF force a transformation of the operational semantics into continuation-passing style (see the example in Section 2.1), thereby fixing the order of all steps in a concurrent computation. This amounts to an interleaving semantics for concurrency rather than a truly concurrent one. While it is possible to develop, within the framework, explicit judgments specifying which computations should be considered equivalent, reasoning with or about such a specification can be exceedingly cumbersome.

Concurrent LF (CLF), the topic of this paper, is a new logical framework that extends LLF with additional linear constructs ($A_1 \otimes A_2$, 1, $\exists x : A_1 . A_2$, and $!A$) that make it possible to represent concurrent computations in a natural and convenient fashion. However, if they were added freely, these new connectives would interfere with standard representation techniques and would destroy one of the most fundamental properties of an LF-style framework: namely, that the structure of a canonical form is essentially determined by its type. To avoid these problems, we take the further step of *encapsulating* these new primitives by means of a *monad* that protects the conventional LF and LLF fragments of the framework. Within the monad, the natural equational theory of our additional operators gives rise to a notion of definitional equality that makes representations of concurrency adequate by ensuring that different interleavings of independent concurrent steps are indistinguishable. Although monads have been used to separate pure and effectful computations in functional programming languages, to the authors' knowledge this is their first use in a logical framework or theorem-proving environment to separate one logic from another.

Developing a logical framework goes beyond assembling a toolkit of useful representation mechanisms. The bulk of the effort consists of proving that the resulting language is well behaved for the purposes of both representation and computation. For example, it is highly desirable that type checking be decidable in a logical framework based on type theory. As the language expands, going from LF to LLF to CLF, the difficulty of this meta-theoretic investigation grows at an alarming rate, even for experienced researchers. In order to offset this increasing complexity the present paper also introduces a new methodology for developing the meta-theory of LF-style logical frameworks. It is based on the observation that, since LF-style representations rely exclusively on canonical forms, there is no need for the framework to define—or the meta-theory to investigate—anything but canonical forms. This is accomplished using an inductive notion of *instantiation*, replacing normalization with respect to β-reduction used in traditional presentations.

The present paper concentrates on CLF_0, the propositional sublanguage of CLF, which already exhibits the principal phenomena concerning concurrency. The use of the framework is illustrated by an encoding of Petri-net computations, a simple but fundamental model of concurrency. The interested reader is referred to the accompanying technical reports [39,15] for the definition of full CLF, the development of its meta-theory [39], and a number of larger examples [15]. These examples include an encoding of a version of ML that supports suspensions with memoization, mutable references, futures in the style of Multilisp [19], concurrency in the style of CML [38], and more. They also include a language for the representation of security protocols based on multiset rewriting [13], and representations of the synchronous and asynchronous π-calculus [29].

The remainder of this paper is organized as follows. In Section 2 we define CLF_0, including its syntax, typing rules, and definitional equality. Section 3 develops the meta-theory of CLF_0, proving decidability of typing and definitional equality. This is followed by a discussion of related work in Section 4 and a conclusion (Section 5) with some comments on future work.

2 Propositional CLF

We introduce the propositional fragment of the concurrent logical framework in stages. In the first stage, we briefly review the linear logical framework (LLF), its properties, and its shortcomings with respect to concurrency. The following stages describe the extensions yielding CLF, which aim to address these shortcomings.

2.1 The Linear Fragment

The propositional fragment LLF_0 of the linear logical framework [14] is based on unrestricted and linear hypothetical judgments $\Gamma; \Delta \vdash_\Sigma M : A$ where Γ is a context of unrestricted hypotheses $u{:}A$ (subject to exchange, weakening, and contraction), Δ is a context of linear hypotheses $x\hat{:}A$ (subject only to exchange), M is an object and A is a type. The signature Σ declares the base types and constants from which objects are constructed. Under the Curry-Howard isomorphism, M can also be read as a proof term, and A as a proposition of intuitionistic linear logic in its formulation as DILL [5].

Since the signature is fixed for a given typing derivation, we henceforth suppress it for the sake of brevity. In addition, syntactic objects are considered only up to α-equivalence of their bound variables. Exchange is not noted explicitly in the typing rules, and only instances of the typing rules for which all variables in the contexts have unique names are allowed.

The LF representation methodology establishes a bijection between *canonical objects* of appropriate type and the terms and deductions of an object language to be represented. The appropriate notion of "canonical" turns out to be long $\beta\eta$-normal form. In order to define these inductively, the single typing judgment $\Gamma; \Delta \vdash M : A$ is refined into two judgments:

$\Gamma; \Delta \vdash N \Leftarrow A$	N is a canonical object of type A
$\Gamma; \Delta \vdash R \Rightarrow A$	R is an atomic object of type A

A canonical object N is an introduction form or is an atomic object of base type. An atomic object R is a sequence of elimination forms applied to a variable or constant. Further judgments check that types, contexts, and signatures are well-formed; they are omitted, being entirely straightforward for the propositional fragment.

The types of LLF_0 are freely generated from the constructors $\multimap$, $\rightarrow$, & and $\top$ and base types. These comprise the largest fragment of intuitionistic linear logic with traditional connectives for which unique canonical forms exist. This property is essential for the use of LLF_0 as a logical framework, because of the central role of canonical forms in its representation methodology. The syntax and the typing rules for the canonical variant of LLF_0 are shown in Figure 1. It is worth noting that since weakening and contraction are not allowed for the linear context, certain of the rules are more restrictive than their intuitionistic logic counterparts would be. In particular, in the conclusions of rules c and u the linear context is empty; otherwise, weakening would be admissible. Also, the linear context in the conclusion of rule $\multimap$**E** is the *disjoint* union of the linear contexts in the premises; otherwise, contraction would be admissible. Finally, in the second premise of rule $\rightarrow$**E** the linear context must be empty; otherwise, the substitution theorem would require weakening and contraction.

$$
\begin{array}{rll}
A, B, C & ::= a \mid A \multimap B \mid A \rightarrow B \mid A \mathbin{\&} B \mid \top & \text{Types} \\
\Sigma & ::= \Sigma, a{:}\mathsf{type} \mid \Sigma, c{:}A \mid \cdot & \text{Signatures} \\
\Gamma & ::= \Gamma, u{:}A \mid \cdot & \text{Unrestricted context} \\
\Delta & ::= \Delta, x\hat{:}A \mid \cdot & \text{Linear context} \\
N & ::= \hat{\lambda} x.\, N \mid \lambda u.\, N \mid \langle N_1, N_2 \rangle \mid \langle\rangle \mid R & \text{Canonical objects} \\
R & ::= c \mid u \mid x \mid R\,\hat{}\,N \mid R\,N \mid \pi_1 R \mid \pi_2 R & \text{Atomic objects}
\end{array}
$$

$$
\frac{\Gamma; \Delta, x\hat{:}A \vdash N \Leftarrow B}{\Gamma; \Delta \vdash \hat{\lambda} x.\, N \Leftarrow A \multimap B}\,{\multimap}\mathbf{I}
\qquad
\frac{\Gamma, u{:}A; \Delta \vdash N \Leftarrow B}{\Gamma; \Delta \vdash \lambda u.\, N \Leftarrow A \rightarrow B}\,{\rightarrow}\mathbf{I}
$$

$$
\frac{\Gamma; \Delta \vdash N_1 \Leftarrow A \quad \Gamma; \Delta \vdash N_2 \Leftarrow B}{\Gamma; \Delta \vdash \langle N_1, N_2 \rangle \Leftarrow A \mathbin{\&} B}\,\mathbf{\&I}
\qquad
\frac{}{\Gamma; \Delta \vdash \langle\rangle \Leftarrow \top}\,\top\mathbf{I}
\qquad
\frac{\Gamma; \Delta \vdash R \Rightarrow a}{\Gamma; \Delta \vdash R \Leftarrow a}\,{\Rightarrow}{\Leftarrow}
$$

$$
\frac{}{\Gamma; \cdot \vdash c \Rightarrow \Sigma(c)}\,c
\qquad
\frac{}{\Gamma; \cdot \vdash u \Rightarrow \Gamma(u)}\,u
\qquad
\frac{}{\Gamma; x\hat{:}A \vdash x \Rightarrow A}\,x
$$

$$
\frac{\Gamma; \Delta_1 \vdash R \Rightarrow A \multimap B \quad \Gamma; \Delta_2 \vdash N \Leftarrow A}{\Gamma; \Delta_1, \Delta_2 \vdash R\,\hat{}\,N \Rightarrow B}\,{\multimap}\mathbf{E}
\qquad
\frac{\Gamma; \Delta \vdash R \Rightarrow A \mathbin{\&} B}{\Gamma; \Delta \vdash \pi_1 R \Rightarrow A}\,\mathbf{\&E}_1
$$

$$
\frac{\Gamma; \Delta \vdash R \Rightarrow A \rightarrow B \quad \Gamma; \cdot \vdash N \Leftarrow A}{\Gamma; \Delta \vdash R\,N \Rightarrow B}\,{\rightarrow}\mathbf{E}
\qquad
\frac{\Gamma; \Delta \vdash R \Rightarrow A \mathbin{\&} B}{\Gamma; \Delta \vdash \pi_2 R \Rightarrow B}\,\mathbf{\&E}_2
$$

Fig. 1. The LLF_0 Language

Example. The Petri net in Figure 2 will serve as a running example of the various encoding techniques used in this paper. The representation of Petri nets in linear logic goes back to Asperti [3] and has been treated several times in the literature (*e.g.*, [4,11,26]). Familiarity with Petri nets is assumed, and their encoding is only given by example. We shall however stress that we are adopting the "individual token philosophy" [10] by which the tokens within a place are not interchangeable. A planned extension of CLF with the notion of proof irrelevance [34,37] would allow a direct encoding of the more mainstream "collective token philosophy". Further details may be found in the companion technical report [15].

Each place in a Petri net is represented by a type constant p. The state of the net is encoded as a collection of linear hypotheses: there is an assumption $x\hat{:}p$ for every token in place p. There is also a separate type constant X representing an (unspecific) goal state.

For each transition t there is an object constant[1]

$$t : (q_1 \multimap \ldots \multimap q_n \multimap \mathsf{X}) \multimap (p_1 \multimap \ldots \multimap p_m \multimap \mathsf{X})$$

expressing that the goal state X can be reached from a state with tokens in places $p_1, \ldots, p_m$ if the goal can be reached from the state with tokens in places

[1] We adopt the convention that the connective $\multimap$ is right associative.

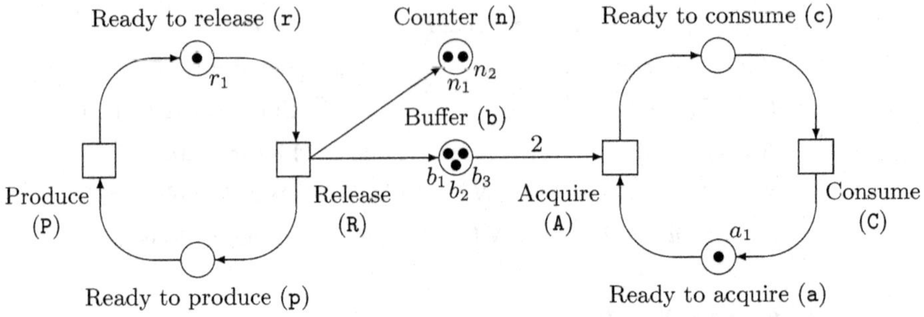

Fig. 2. A Producer/Consumer Petri Net with Labeled Marking

$q_1, \ldots, q_n$ instead. Such a rule can be read as removing tokens from $p_1, \ldots, p_m$ and placing them on $q_1, \ldots, q_n$.

The initial state of the net in Figure 2 is represented by

$$\Delta_0 = r_1 \hat{:} \mathsf{r},\ n_1 \hat{:} \mathsf{n},\ n_2 \hat{:} \mathsf{n},\ b_1 \hat{:} \mathsf{b},\ b_2 \hat{:} \mathsf{b},\ b_3 \hat{:} \mathsf{b},\ a_1 \hat{:} \mathsf{a}$$

and the transitions are represented by the following signature.

$$\begin{array}{ll} \mathsf{P} : (\mathsf{r} \multimap \mathsf{X}) \multimap (\mathsf{p} \multimap \mathsf{X}) & \mathsf{A} : (\mathsf{c} \multimap \mathsf{X}) \multimap (\mathsf{b} \multimap \mathsf{b} \multimap \mathsf{a} \multimap \mathsf{X}) \\ \mathsf{R} : (\mathsf{p} \multimap \mathsf{n} \multimap \mathsf{b} \multimap \mathsf{X}) \multimap (\mathsf{r} \multimap \mathsf{X}) & \mathsf{C} : (\mathsf{a} \multimap \mathsf{X}) \multimap (\mathsf{c} \multimap \mathsf{X}) \end{array}$$

The adequacy theorem for this representation states that:

> *Final state $q_1, \ldots, q_n$ can be reached from initial state $p_1, \ldots, p_m$ iff there is a canonical object N such that*
>
> $$\cdot; \cdot \vdash N \Leftarrow (q_1 \multimap \ldots \multimap q_n \multimap \mathsf{X}) \multimap (p_1 \multimap \ldots \multimap p_m \multimap \mathsf{X})$$
>
> *Moreover, there is a bijection between* sequences of firings *of the transition rules of the Petri net (according to the individual token philosophy) and such canonical objects.*

While a firing is atomic, its LLF_0 emulation occurs in stages, which implies that intermediate sequents do not always have a counterpart in the Petri net world. The risk, first pointed out in [4], that "unfinished transitions" may pollute the final state is prevented here by requiring that it only contains atomic formulas $(q_1, \ldots, q_n)$.

By forcibly distinguishing sequences of firings, the LLF_0 representation fails to capture the inherent concurrency of a Petri net. For example, in the state in Figure 2, the R and A transitions can both fire, and do not interfere with each other. However, our current representation yields different terms for the two interleavings:

$$
\begin{array}{l}
\cdot; \Delta_0, f \mathrel{\hat{:}} (\mathsf{c} \multimap \mathsf{b} \multimap \mathsf{b} \multimap \mathsf{n} \multimap \mathsf{n} \multimap \mathsf{n} \multimap \mathsf{p} \multimap \mathsf{X}) \\
\quad \vdash \mathsf{R}\,\hat{}\,(\hat{\lambda} p_1.\, \hat{\lambda} n_3.\, \hat{\lambda} b_4.\, \mathsf{A}\,\hat{}\,(\hat{\lambda} c_1.\, f\,\hat{}\,c_1\,\hat{}\,b_3\,\hat{}\,b_4\,\hat{}\,n_1\,\hat{}\,n_2\,\hat{}\,n_3\,\hat{}\,p_1)\,\hat{}\,b_1\,\hat{}\,b_2\,\hat{}\,a_1)\,\hat{}\,r_1 \Leftarrow \mathsf{X} \\
\cdot; \Delta_0, f \mathrel{\hat{:}} (\mathsf{c} \multimap \mathsf{b} \multimap \mathsf{b} \multimap \mathsf{n} \multimap \mathsf{n} \multimap \mathsf{n} \multimap \mathsf{p} \multimap \mathsf{X}) \\
\quad \vdash \mathsf{A}\,\hat{}\,(\hat{\lambda} c_1.\, \mathsf{R}\,\hat{}\,(\hat{\lambda} p_1.\, \hat{\lambda} n_3.\, \hat{\lambda} b_4.\, f\,\hat{}\,c_1\,\hat{}\,b_3\,\hat{}\,b_4\,\hat{}\,n_1\,\hat{}\,n_2\,\hat{}\,n_3\,\hat{}\,p_1)\,\hat{}\,r_1)\,\hat{}\,b_1\,\hat{}\,b_2\,\hat{}\,a_1 \Leftarrow \mathsf{X}
\end{array}
$$

The only way to identify these executions in LLF is to write higher-level judgments explicitly relating the representations of admissible interleavings of the same trace. This is undesirable for two reasons: first these declarations are complicated even for simple nets; second, we would need to rewrite them from scratch for every new net we consider. Note that this also forces us to abandon the propositional language LLF_0 for the dependently typed LLF.

Given how pervasive this problem is when analyzing concurrent systems, we devised an extension of LLF_0 that views executions such as the above as partial orders, identifying all of their admissible interleavings. We will describe this language, CLF_0, in the next two sections: we first introduce sufficient infrastructure to provide an alternative to the continuation-passing style of representation forced by LLF (as witnessed by the spurious goal state X). We then adjust the notion of definitional equality so that independent steps can commute.

2.2 The Monadic Fragment

A simple attempt to represent Petri nets without the continuation-passing transformation would introduce the linear logic connective $\otimes$ and its unit 1 to the framework [11]. The LLF_0 transition

$$t : (q_1 \multimap \ldots \multimap q_n \multimap \mathsf{X}) \multimap (p_1 \multimap \ldots \multimap p_m \multimap \mathsf{X})$$

would then be replaced with the more straightforward

$$t' : p_1 \otimes \ldots \otimes p_m \multimap q_1 \otimes \ldots \otimes q_n$$

However, this language does not meet the criteria we require of a *logical framework*. Modeling reachability is not enough: we also want to establish a bijection between Petri net computations and appropriately typed objects in the framework. If LLF_0 is extended with all (or even some) additional connectives of dual intuitionistic linear logic a number of problems establishing adequate encodings arise. The most immediate is that adding an object with any of these types can destroy the adequacy of completely unrelated encodings in the framework.

Observing the declarations

$$
\begin{array}{rlcrl}
\mathsf{c} & : 1 & \qquad\qquad & \mathsf{z} & : \mathsf{nat} \\
\mathsf{nat} & : \mathsf{type} & & \mathsf{s} & : \mathsf{nat} \to \mathsf{nat}
\end{array}
$$

we see that nat contains not only terms such as z and s z but also (let $1 = \mathsf{c}$ in z). There is no longer a bijective correspondence of the type nat with the set of natural numbers.[2] Similar examples would arise in the presence of a constant of

[2] Examples such as $(\hat{\lambda} x.\, \mathsf{let}\ 1 = x\ \mathsf{in}\ \mathsf{z} : 1 \multimap \mathsf{nat})$ show that the term above cannot simply be equal to z since doing so would violate the linearity condition.

type $A \otimes B$ or $!A$. While such a language might technically be conservative over LLF_0, it would be impossible to embed an LLF_0 encoding in a larger signature using the new types—the adequacy of the LLF_0 encoding would be destroyed.

The underlying issue here is difficult to characterize formally, but it can be stated informally as follows: the structure of canonical forms should be *type-directed.* This leads to the inversion principles necessary to prove the adequacy of encodings. For example, we would like to know that every term of type nat is of the form z or $\mathsf{s}\ t$ where $t : \mathsf{nat}$. It is easy to see that the unrestricted use of elimination forms such as $(\mathsf{let}\ 1 = t\ \mathsf{in}\ t')$ subverts this principle, because the subterm t is not constrained by the type of the overall term.

In order to obtain a tractable, yet sufficiently expressive type theory we employ a technique familiar from functional programming, which does not appear to have been used in logical frameworks or theorem provers: use a monad [30] to encapsulate the effects of concurrency. This encapsulation protects the equational theory of LLF_0. Moreover, the notion of canonical form outside the monad extends the prior notions *conservatively.* This property of the method should not be underestimated, because it means that all encodings already devised for LF or LLF remain adequate, and their adequacy proofs can remain exactly the same!

We write $\{A\}$ for the monad type, which in lax logic would be written $\bigcirc A$ [36]. But which types should be available inside the monad? They must be expressive enough to represent the state after a computation step in the concurrent object language. This is most naturally represented by the multiplicative conjunction $\otimes$. Then our transition rule can be written

$$t'' : p_1 \multimap \ldots \multimap p_m \multimap \{q_1 \otimes \ldots \otimes q_n\}$$

where currying eliminates the use of $\otimes$ on the left-hand side. In order to cover the case $n = 0$ the multiplicative unit 1 is included. Though it does not arise in this example, a transition could also generate an element of persistent (unrestricted) type, so we also allow types $!A$. We call the new types *synchronous*, borrowing terminology from Andreoli [2], and denote them by S. We qualify the old types as *asynchronous.* The resulting extension to the language of types is shown in Figure 3. (The complete language is summarized in Appendix A.)

The language of objects is extended accordingly. The synchronous types S type *monadic expressions* E. The introduction forms M are constructors for multiplicative pairs, the multiplicative unit, and the unrestricted modality (!). The elimination form is a let binding eliminating the monad and matching the synchronous constructors against a pattern p. To our knowledge, this canonical formulation of the proof term assignment for lax logic is novel. Patterns are classified by synchronous types S and are collected into a context Ψ.

There are three typing judgments in addition to the judgments already noted for LLF_0:

$\Gamma; \Delta \vdash_\Sigma E \leftarrow S$	E is an expression of type S
$\Gamma; \Delta; \Psi \vdash_\Sigma E \leftarrow S$	E is an expression of type S w.r.t. patterns Ψ
$\Gamma; \Delta \vdash_\Sigma M \Leftarrow S$	M is a monadic object of type S

$\ldots$	*Signatures, contexts, atomic objects*
$A, B, C ::= \ldots \mid \{S\}$	Asynchronous types
$S ::= S_1 \otimes S_2 \mid 1 \mid !A \mid A$	Synchronous types
$\Psi ::= p \hat{:} S, \Psi \mid \cdot$	Pattern contexts
$N ::= \ldots \mid \{E\}$	Canonical objects
$E ::= \mathsf{let}\ \{p\} = R\ \mathsf{in}\ E \mid M$	Expressions
$p ::= p_1 \otimes p_2 \mid 1 \mid !u \mid x$	Patterns
$M ::= M_1 \otimes M_2 \mid 1 \mid !N \mid N$	Monadic objects

$$\ldots \qquad \frac{\Gamma; \Delta \vdash E \leftarrow S}{\Gamma; \Delta \vdash \{E\} \Leftarrow \{S\}}\ \{\}\mathbf{I} \qquad \frac{\Gamma; \Delta_1 \vdash R \Rightarrow \{S_0\} \quad \Gamma; \Delta_2; p \hat{:} S_0 \vdash E \leftarrow S}{\Gamma; \Delta_1, \Delta_2 \vdash (\mathsf{let}\ \{p\} = R\ \mathsf{in}\ E) \leftarrow S}\ \{\}\mathbf{E}$$

$$\frac{\Gamma; \Delta \vdash M \Leftarrow S}{\Gamma; \Delta \vdash M \leftarrow S} \Leftarrow\leftarrow \qquad \frac{\Gamma; \Delta \vdash E \leftarrow S}{\Gamma; \Delta; \cdot \vdash E \leftarrow S} \leftarrow\leftarrow$$

$$\frac{\Gamma; \Delta; p_1 \hat{:} S_1, p_2 \hat{:} S_2, \Psi \vdash E \leftarrow S}{\Gamma; \Delta; p_1 \otimes p_2 \hat{:} S_1 \otimes S_2, \Psi \vdash E \leftarrow S}\ \otimes\mathbf{L} \qquad \frac{\Gamma; \Delta; \Psi \vdash E \leftarrow S}{\Gamma; \Delta; 1 \hat{:} 1, \Psi \vdash E \leftarrow S}\ 1\mathbf{L}$$

$$\frac{\Gamma, u{:}A; \Delta; \Psi \vdash E \leftarrow S}{\Gamma; \Delta; !u \hat{:} !A, \Psi \vdash E \leftarrow S}\ !\mathbf{L} \qquad \frac{\Gamma; \Delta, x \hat{:} A; \Psi \vdash E \leftarrow S}{\Gamma; \Delta; x \hat{:} A, \Psi \vdash E \leftarrow S}\ \mathbf{AL}$$

$$\frac{\Gamma; \Delta_1 \vdash M_1 \Leftarrow S_1 \quad \Gamma; \Delta_2 \vdash M_2 \Leftarrow S_2}{\Gamma; \Delta_1, \Delta_2 \vdash M_1 \otimes M_2 \Leftarrow S_1 \otimes S_2}\ \otimes\mathbf{I} \qquad \frac{}{\Gamma; \cdot \vdash 1 \Leftarrow 1}\ 1\mathbf{I} \qquad \frac{\Gamma; \cdot \vdash N \Leftarrow A}{\Gamma; \cdot \vdash !N \Leftarrow !A}\ !\mathbf{I}$$

Fig. 3. The CLF_0 Extensions to LLF_0

The extended language CLF_0 inherits all the typing rules already presented for LLF_0. The additional typing rules are shown in Figure 3. First, there are introduction and elimination rules for {} ({}**I** {}**E**). We can see that a monadic expression is a sequence of let forms, ending in a monadic object. Immediately after each let the pattern is decomposed into assumptions of the form $x \hat{:} A$ or $u{:}A$ and the body of the let is checked. This is the purpose of the judgment $\Gamma; \Delta; \Psi \vdash E \leftarrow S$, defined by the next group of rules (⊗**L** 1**L** !**L** **AL**). These correspond to left rules in a sequent calculus. Finally, there are rules to introduce the monadic objects at the end of a sequence of {}**E** eliminations (⊗**I** 1**I** !**I**).

Example revisited. The Petri net in Figure 2 is now represented almost as in dual intuitionistic linear logic [5], except that the right-hand sides of the linear implications use the monad.

$$\mathsf{P} : \mathsf{p} \multimap \{\mathsf{r}\} \qquad \mathsf{A} : \mathsf{b} \multimap \mathsf{b} \multimap \mathsf{a} \multimap \{\mathsf{c}\}$$
$$\mathsf{R} : \mathsf{r} \multimap \{\mathsf{p} \otimes \mathsf{n} \otimes \mathsf{b}\} \qquad \mathsf{C} : \mathsf{c} \multimap \{\mathsf{a}\}$$

The monadic encapsulation and the canonical forms of monadic expressions tightly constrain the form of objects constructed from this signature. Adopting α-equivalence—for the moment—as the framework's definitional equality, there is an analog of the earlier adequacy theorem.

$$\epsilon ::= [] \mid \mathsf{let}\ \{p\} = R\ \mathsf{in}\ \epsilon \qquad \text{Concurrent contexts}$$

$$\frac{M_1 = M_2}{M_1 =_c M_2} \qquad \frac{R_1 = R_2 \quad E_1 =_c \epsilon[E_2]}{(\mathsf{let}\ \{p\} = R_1\ \mathsf{in}\ E_1) =_c \epsilon[\mathsf{let}\ \{p\} = R_2\ \mathsf{in}\ E_2]} * \qquad \frac{E_1 =_c E_2}{E_1 = E_2}$$

(*) No variable bound by p is free in the conclusion or bound by the context ϵ, and no variable free in R_2 is bound by the context ϵ.

Fig. 4. Concurrent Equality

The example firings are rewritten as follows.

$$\begin{aligned}
\cdot; \Delta_0 \vdash \{&\mathsf{let}\ \{p_1 \otimes n_3 \otimes b_4\} = \mathsf{R}\hat{\ } r_1\ \mathsf{in}\\
&\quad \mathsf{let}\ \{c_1\} = \mathsf{A}\hat{\ } b_1 \hat{\ } b_2 \hat{\ } a_1\ \mathsf{in}\\
&\qquad c_1 \otimes b_3 \otimes b_4 \otimes n_1 \otimes n_2 \otimes n_3 \otimes p_1\} \Leftarrow \{\mathsf{c} \otimes \mathsf{b} \otimes \mathsf{b} \otimes \mathsf{n} \otimes \mathsf{n} \otimes \mathsf{n} \otimes \mathsf{p}\}\\
\cdot; \Delta_0 \vdash \{&\mathsf{let}\ \{c_1\} = \mathsf{A}\hat{\ } b_1 \hat{\ } b_2 \hat{\ } a_1\ \mathsf{in}\\
&\quad \mathsf{let}\ \{p_1 \otimes n_3 \otimes b_4\} = \mathsf{R}\hat{\ } r_1\ \mathsf{in}\\
&\qquad c_1 \otimes b_3 \otimes b_4 \otimes n_1 \otimes n_2 \otimes n_3 \otimes p_1\} \Leftarrow \{\mathsf{c} \otimes \mathsf{b} \otimes \mathsf{b} \otimes \mathsf{n} \otimes \mathsf{n} \otimes \mathsf{n} \otimes \mathsf{p}\}
\end{aligned}$$

With the introduction of synchronous connectives, and their encapsulation within the monadic construction, we have achieved a simple encoding of Petri nets and provided a syntax for executions that is separate from the traditional LLF_0 terms. However, α-equivalence still distinguishes the two executions above despite the fact that their R and A transitions are independent. Since the two lets bind and use different variables, we *should* be able to identify their permutations, with the sandboxing effect of the monad protecting the surrounding LLF_0 terms. We will now formalize this intuition.

2.3 Concurrent Equality

In essence, our objective is to identify all the usual commuting conversions between synchronous operators, but have them stop at the monadic membrane. In keeping with the philosophy espoused here of presenting the core concepts of the framework computationally, we give a direct definition of this *concurrent equality* as a decision procedure. Figure 4 shows the new syntax and inference rules associated with the definition.

The definition relies on the subsidiary concept of a *concurrent context*. As usual, the notation $\epsilon[E]$ stands for the expression constructed by replacing the hole [] in ϵ with E.

The judgment $E_1 =_c E_2$ holds when E_1 and E_2 represent the same underlying concurrent computation even though their syntactic representations may differ. The rule marked (*) is subject to the side condition that no variable bound by p be free in the conclusion or bound by the context ϵ, and that no variable free in R_2 be bound by the context ϵ. Intuitively, this rule expresses that we have to find a subcomputation R_2 of the right-hand side that starts with the same step R_1 as the left-hand side. Furthermore, the remaining computation E_1 on the left-hand side must equal the remaining computation on the right-hand side, which consists of the steps preceding R_2 (in ϵ) and those following R_2 (in E_2) composed in $\epsilon[E_2]$.

There are also unmarked equality judgments $N_1 = N_2$, $R_1 = R_2$, and $M_1 = M_2$ and congruences for them (not shown). An equality judgment is not taken to mean anything in particular unless the subjects of the judgment are well typed. A typed equality judgment $\Gamma; \Delta \vdash N_1 = N_2 \Leftarrow A$ can then be defined by $(\Gamma; \Delta \vdash N_1 \Leftarrow A) \wedge (\Gamma; \Delta \vdash N_2 \Leftarrow A) \wedge (N_1 = N_2)$.

Returning to the Petri-net example developed in Section 2.2, it is easy to show that the two CLF$_0$ objects corresponding to the two different interleavings of the example Petri net execution are concurrently equal. This is crystallized as a better adequacy theorem:

> *Final state $q_1, \ldots, q_n$ can be reached from initial state $p_1, \ldots, p_m$ iff there is a canonical object N such that*
>
> $$\cdot; \cdot \vdash N \Leftarrow p_1 \multimap \ldots \multimap p_m \multimap \{q_1 \otimes \ldots \otimes q_n\}$$
>
> *Moreover, there is a bijection between* concurrent executions *(*traces*) of the transition rules of the Petri net (according to the individual token philosophy) and equivalence classes of such canonical objects modulo $=$.*

Again, the strict accounting of the final state as atomic formulas $q_1, \ldots, q_n$ does not leave space for the "unfinished transitions" of [4].

3 Meta-theory

This section sketches the meta-theory of the canonical formulation of CLF$_0$. Additional details and a development of the dependent case may be found in the companion theory technical report [39].

3.1 Identity and Substitution Properties

As discussed in Section 2, the CLF$_0$ framework (as well as full CLF) syntactically restrict the form of objects so that they will always be canonical. This is a good design choice in the logical frameworks context, but it carries with it the obligation to ensure that the underlying logic (via the Curry-Howard isomorphism, if you like) is sensible. In particular, the principles of *identity* and *substitution* must hold.

> **Identity.** *Unrestricted case*: For any Γ and A, $\Gamma, u{:}A; \cdot \vdash N \Leftarrow A$ for some N. *Linear case*: For any Γ and A, $\Gamma; x{\hat{:}}A \vdash N \Leftarrow A$ for some N.

> **Substitution.** *Unrestricted case*: if $\Gamma; \cdot \vdash N_0 \Leftarrow A$ and $\Gamma, u{:}A; \Delta \vdash N \Leftarrow C$ then $\Gamma; \Delta \vdash N' \Leftarrow C$ for some N'. *Linear case*: if $\Gamma; \Delta_1 \vdash N_0 \Leftarrow A$ and $\Gamma; \Delta_2, x{\hat{:}}A \vdash N \Leftarrow C$ then $\Gamma; \Delta_1, \Delta_2 \vdash N' \Leftarrow C$ for some N'.

In the standard reduction-oriented treatment of proofs, these are fairly trivial, because variables and general terms are in the same syntactic category. Substitution simply syntactically replaces the target variable with the substituend—possibly creating redices. Here, redices are not syntactially allowed, and variables are syntactically *atomic* while general terms are syntactically *normal*, so it is not possible to directly replace a variable with a substituend. By the same token, a variable of higher type cannot stand by itself as a canonical object—canonical objects of higher type must be introduction forms—so the identity principle cannot be witnessed by a bare variable.

Instead, the meta-theory of CLF relies on *algorithms* that *compute* witnesses to the identity and substitution principles. These are, respectively, the *expansion algorithm* and the *instantiation algorithm.*[3]

Principle	**Algorithm**	**Supersedes**	**Notation**
Substitution	Instantiation	β-normalization	$\mathsf{inst\_n}_A(x.\,N, N_0) \equiv N'$
Identity	Expansion	η-normalization	$\mathsf{expand}_A(R) \equiv N$

Think of the instantiation operator $\mathsf{inst\_n}_A(x.\,N, N_0)$ as an algorithm for computing the canonical form of the result of instantiating the variable x in the object N with the object N_0. The instantiation operator is indexed by the type A of the substituend N_0. If A is a base type, we have $\mathsf{inst\_n}_A(x.\,N, N_0) = [N_0/x]N$; that is, instantiation reduces to ordinary syntactic substitution. At higher type more complex situations arise.

Dually, we think of the expansion operator $\mathsf{expand}_A(R)$ as computing the canonical form of the atomic object R of putative type A. This is analogous to η-expansion, except that the term R and its expansion inhabit different syntactic categories if A is a higher type.

These algorithms must be (and are) effectively presented, because the typing judgment of the full dependent type theory appeals to instantiation, and effective typing is central to the logical framework concept. The use of the instantiation algorithm in dependent typing has a further important ramification: the instantiation algorithm must be *effective on ill-typed terms.* Otherwise, there is a circularity between instantiation and typing, leading to a very complex meta-theory.[4] Since the substitution principle does not hold for ill-typed terms, we allow the witnessing instantiation algorithm to report failure or yield garbage on ill-typed input; e.g., $\mathsf{inst\_n}_A(x.\,x\ x, \lambda x.\,x\ x) \equiv \mathsf{fail}$. Garbage in, garbage out, but at least we get our garbage out in finite time!

[3] Here and in the reminder we use x generically for either a linear or unrestricted variable.

[4] This circularity, which the present treatment of CLF avoids, is analogous to the difficulties encountered in the early reduction-oriented treatments of LF, where typing refers to equality, which is decided by normalization, but normalization is only effective for well-typed terms.

$\mathsf{treduce}_A(x.\,R) \equiv B$ [Type reduction]

$$\mathsf{treduce}_A(x.\,x) \equiv A$$
$$\mathsf{treduce}_A(x.\,R\;N) \equiv C \quad \text{if } \mathsf{treduce}_A(x.\,R) \equiv B \rightarrow C$$

$\mathsf{reduce}_A(x.\,R, N_0) \equiv N'$ [Reduction]

$$\mathsf{reduce}_A(x.\,x, N_0) \equiv N_0$$
$$\mathsf{reduce}_A(x.\,R\;N, N_0) \equiv \mathsf{inst\_n}_B(y.\,N', \mathsf{inst\_n}_A(x.\,N, N_0))$$
$$\text{if } \mathsf{treduce}_A(x.\,R) \equiv B \rightarrow C \text{ and } \mathsf{reduce}_A(x.\,R, N_0) \equiv \lambda y.\,N'$$

$\mathsf{inst\_r}_A(x.\,R, N_0) \equiv R'$ [Atomic object instantiation]

$$\mathsf{inst\_r}_A(x.\,c, N_0) \equiv c$$
$$\mathsf{inst\_r}_A(x.\,y, N_0) \equiv y \quad \text{if } y \text{ is not } x$$
$$\mathsf{inst\_r}_A(x.\,R\;N, N_0) \equiv (\mathsf{inst\_r}_A(x.\,R, N_0))\;(\mathsf{inst\_n}_A(x.\,N, N_0))$$

$\mathsf{inst\_n}_A(x.\,N, N_0) \equiv N'$ [Normal object instantiation]

$$\mathsf{inst\_n}_A(x.\,\lambda y.\,N, N_0) \equiv \lambda y.\,\mathsf{inst\_n}_A(x.\,N, N_0) \quad \text{if } y \notin \mathrm{FV}(N_0)$$
$$\mathsf{inst\_n}_A(x.\,R, N_0) \equiv \mathsf{inst\_r}_A(x.\,R, N_0) \quad \text{if } \mathrm{head}(R) \text{ is not } x$$
$$\mathsf{inst\_n}_A(x.\,R, N_0) \equiv \mathsf{reduce}_A(x.\,R, N_0) \quad \text{if } \mathsf{treduce}_A(x.\,R) \equiv a$$

Fig. 5. Instantiation, LF_0

3.2 Instantiation

Space constraints preclude the incorporation of all the cases of the definitions of these operators. Full details are available, of course, in our technical report [39].

We begin by examining the cases for the LF_0 fragment of instantiation, shown in Figure 5. The recurrence defining instantiation is based on the observation, exploited in cut elimination proofs on the logical side [33], but not so well known on the type theoretic side, that the canonical result of substituting one canonical term into another can be defined by induction on the type of the term being substituted. Accordingly, the instantiation operators are defined as a family parameterized over the type of the object being substituted. In the notation $\mathsf{inst\_c}_A(x.\mathsf{X}, N)$ this type A appears as a subscript. Here c is replaced by a mnemonic for the particular syntactic category to which the instantiation operator applies. The variable x is to be considered bound within the term X (of whatever category) being substituted into. The operators defined in this section should be thought of as applying to equivalence classes of concrete terms modulo α-equivalence on bound variables.

Together with the instantiation operators, and defined by mutual recursion with them, is a *reduction operator* $\mathsf{reduce}_A(x.\,R, N)$ that computes the canonical object resulting from the instantiation of x with N in the case that the *head variable* $\mathrm{head}(R)$ of the atomic object R is x. Thus, roughly speaking, it corresponds to the idea of weak head reduction for systems with β-reduction. The instantiation operator $\mathsf{inst\_r}_A(x.\,R, N)$, by contrast, is only defined if the head of R is *not* x. Another distinguishing feature is that reduction on an atomic object yields a normal object, while instantiation on an atomic object yields an atomic object.

Finally, there is a *type reduction operator* $\mathsf{treduce}_A(x.\,R)$ that computes the putative type of R given that the head of R is x and the type of x is A. Type reduction is used in side conditions that ensure that the recurrence defining instantiation is well-founded.

The recurrence defining these operators is based on a structural induction. There is an outer induction on the type subscripting the operators, and an inner simultaneous induction on the two arguments. Noting first that if $\mathsf{treduce}_A(x.\,R)$ is defined, it is a subterm of A, the fact that the recurrence relations respect this induction order can be verified almost by inspection. The only slightly subtle case is the equation for $\mathsf{reduce}_A(x.\,R\ N, N_0)$, which is the only case in which the subscripting type changes. Here the side condition $\mathsf{treduce}_A(x.\,R) \equiv B \rightarrow C$ ensures that B must be a strict subterm of A for the reduction to be defined. An instantiation such as $\mathsf{inst\_n}_A(x.\,x\ x, \lambda x.\,x\ x)$ is guaranteed to fail the side condition after only finitely many expansions of the recurrence.

Another way in which an instance of the instantiation operators might fail to be defined would be if the recursive instantiation $\mathsf{inst\_r}_A(x.\,R, N_0)$ in the same equation failed to result in a manifest lambda abstraction $\lambda y.\,N'$. In fact, this could only happen if the term N_0 failed to have the ascribed type A. So instantiation always terminates, regardless of whether its arguments are well typed, but it is not defined in all cases. After the meta-theory is further developed, it can be shown that instantiation is always defined on well-typed terms when the types match in the appropriate way.

The cases of instantiation involving the monad, shown in Figure 6, are not without interest. These lean heavily on prior work on proof term assignments for modal logics [36].

In order to extend instantiation to the full CLF_0 language, with its pattern-oriented destructor for the monadic type, it is necessary to introduce *matching operators* $\mathsf{match\_c}_S(p.\,E, \mathsf{X})$, where X is either an expression or a monadic object. The matching operator computes the result of instantiating E according to the substitution on the variables of p generated by matching p against X. (The variables in p should be considered bound in E.) In the case that X is a monadic object M_0, this is straightforward: the syntax of monadic objects corresponds precisely to that of patterns. But in the case that X is a let binding, an interesting issue arises:

$$\mathsf{match\_e}_S(p.\,\mathsf{let}\ \{p_1\} = R_1\ \mathsf{in}\ E_1, \mathsf{let}\ \{p_2\} = R_2\ \mathsf{in}\ E_2) \equiv ?$$

The key is found in Pfenning and Davies' non-standard substitutions for the proof terms of the modal logics of possibility and laxity [36]. These analyze the structure of the object being substituted, not, as in the usual case, the term

$\mathsf{inst\_n}_A(x.\,N, N_0) \equiv N'$ [Normal object instantiation, extended]

$$\mathsf{inst\_n}_A(x.\,\{E\}, N_0) \equiv \{\mathsf{inst\_e}_A(x.\,E, N_0)\}$$

$\mathsf{inst\_m}_A(x.\,M, N_0) \equiv M'$ [Monadic object instantiation]

$$\begin{aligned}
&\mathsf{inst_m}_A(x.\,M_1 \otimes M_2, N_0) \equiv \mathsf{inst_m}_A(x.\,M_1, N_0) \otimes \mathsf{inst_m}_A(x.\,M_2, N_0)\\
&\mathsf{inst_m}_A(x.\,1, N_0) \equiv 1\\
&\mathsf{inst_m}_A(x.\,!N, N_0) \equiv !(\mathsf{inst_n}_A(x.\,N, N_0))\\
&\mathsf{inst_m}_A(x.\,N, N_0) \equiv \mathsf{inst_n}_A(x.\,N, N_0)
\end{aligned}$$

$\mathsf{inst\_e}_A(x.\,E, N_0) \equiv E'$ [Expression instantiation]

$$\begin{aligned}
&\mathsf{inst_e}_A(x.\,\mathsf{let}\ \{p\} = R\ \mathsf{in}\ E, N_0) \equiv (\mathsf{let}\ \{p\} = \mathsf{inst_r}_A(x.\,R, N_0)\ \mathsf{in}\ \mathsf{inst_e}_A(x.\,E, N_0))\\
&\qquad \text{if head}(R) \text{ is not } x,\\
&\qquad \text{and FV}(p) \cap \text{FV}(N_0) \text{ is empty}\\
&\mathsf{inst_e}_A(x.\,\mathsf{let}\ \{p\} = R\ \mathsf{in}\ E, N_0) \equiv \mathsf{match_e}_S(p.\,\mathsf{inst_e}_A(x.\,E, N_0), E')\\
&\qquad \text{if } \mathsf{treduce}_A(x.\,R) \equiv \{S\},\ \mathsf{reduce}_A(x.\,R, N_0) \equiv \{E'\},\\
&\qquad \text{and FV}(p) \cap \text{FV}(N_0) \text{ is empty}\\
&\mathsf{inst_e}_A(x.\,M, N_0) \equiv \mathsf{inst_m}_A(x.\,M, N_0)
\end{aligned}$$

$\mathsf{match\_m}_S(p.\,E, M_0) \equiv E'$ [Match monadic object]

$$\begin{aligned}
&\mathsf{match_m}_{S_1 \otimes S_2}(p_1 \otimes p_2.\,E, M_1 \otimes M_2) \equiv \mathsf{match_m}_{S_2}(p_2.\,\mathsf{match_m}_{S_1}(p_1.\,E, M_1), M_2)\\
&\qquad \text{if FV}(p_2) \cap \text{FV}(M_1) \text{ is empty}\\
&\mathsf{match_m}_1(1.\,E, 1) \equiv E\\
&\mathsf{match_m}_{!A}(!x.\,E, !N) \equiv \mathsf{inst_e}_A(x.\,E, N)\\
&\mathsf{match_m}_A(x.\,E, N) \equiv \mathsf{inst_e}_A(x.\,E, N)
\end{aligned}$$

$\mathsf{match\_e}_S(p.\,E, E_0) \equiv E'$ [Match expression]

$$\begin{aligned}
&\mathsf{match_e}_S(p.\,E, \mathsf{let}\ \{p_0\} = R_0\ \mathsf{in}\ E_0) \equiv \mathsf{let}\ \{p_0\} = R_0\ \mathsf{in}\ \mathsf{match_e}_S(p.\,E, E_0)\\
&\qquad \text{if FV}(p_0) \cap \text{FV}(E) \text{ and FV}(p) \cap \text{FV}(E_0) \text{ are empty}\\
&\mathsf{match_e}_S(p.\,E, M_0) \equiv \mathsf{match_m}_S(p.\,E, M_0)
\end{aligned}$$

Fig. 6. Instantiation, extended

being substituted into. The effect is similar to a commuting conversion:

$$\begin{aligned}
&\mathsf{match_e}_S(p.\,\mathsf{let}\ \{p_1\} = R_1\ \mathsf{in}\ E_1, \mathsf{let}\ \{p_2\} = R_2\ \mathsf{in}\ E_2) \equiv\\
&\qquad (\mathsf{let}\ \{p_2\} = R_2\ \mathsf{in}\ \mathsf{match_e}_S(p.\,\mathsf{let}\ \{p_1\} = R_1\ \mathsf{in}\ E_1, E_2))
\end{aligned}$$

It is interesting that both non-standard substitution and pattern matching—the latter not present in Pfenning and Davies' system—rely in this way on an analysis of the object being substituted rather than the term being substituted

$\mathsf{expand}_A(R) \equiv N$ [Expansion]

$$\mathsf{expand}_a(R) \equiv R$$
$$\mathsf{expand}_{A \multimap B}(R) \equiv \hat{\lambda} x.\,\mathsf{expand}_B(R\,\hat{}\,(\mathsf{expand}_A(x))) \quad \text{if } x \notin \mathrm{FV}(R)$$
$$\mathsf{expand}_{A \to B}(R) \equiv \lambda x.\,\mathsf{expand}_B(R\ (\mathsf{expand}_A(x))) \quad \text{if } x \notin \mathrm{FV}(R)$$
$$\mathsf{expand}_{A \& B}(R) \equiv \langle \mathsf{expand}_A(\pi_1 R), \mathsf{expand}_B(\pi_2 R)\rangle$$
$$\mathsf{expand}_{\top}(R) \equiv \langle\rangle$$
$$\mathsf{expand}_{\{S\}}(R) \equiv (\mathsf{let}\ \{p\} = R\ \mathsf{in}\ \mathsf{pexpand}_S(p))$$

$\mathsf{pexpand}_S(p) \equiv M$ [Pattern expansion]

$$\mathsf{pexpand}_{S_1 \otimes S_2}(p_1 \otimes p_2) \equiv \mathsf{pexpand}_{S_1}(p_1) \otimes \mathsf{pexpand}_{S_2}(p_2)$$
$$\mathsf{pexpand}_1(1) \equiv 1$$
$$\mathsf{pexpand}_{!A}(!x) \equiv !(\mathsf{expand}_A(x))$$
$$\mathsf{pexpand}_A(x) \equiv \mathsf{expand}_A(x)$$

Fig. 7. Expansion

into. In a sense, this commonality is what makes the harmonious interaction between CLF's modality and its synchronous types possible.

The induction order mentioned above leads immediately to the following theorem.

Theorem 1 (Definability of instantiation). *The recurrence for the reduction, instantiation, and matching operators uniquely determines the least partial functions (up to α-equivalence) solving them.*

Proof. The proof is by an outer structural induction on the type subscript, and an inner simultaneous structural induction on the two arguments. □

3.3 Expansion

The definition of expansion is shown in Figure 7. In some cases, new bound variables are introduced on the right-hand side of an equation. Any new variables in an instance of such an equation are required to be distinct from one another and from any other variables in the equation instance.

Again there is a definability theorem based on the induction order implicit in the equations.

Theorem 2 (Definability of expansion).

1. *If* $\mathsf{pexpand}_S(p_1)$ *and* $\mathsf{pexpand}_S(p_2)$ *are both defined then* p_1 *and* p_2 *are the same up to variable renaming.*
2. *Given* S*, there is a pattern* p*, fresh with respect to any given set of variables, such that* $\mathsf{pexpand}_S(p)$ *is defined.*

3. *The recurrence for expansion uniquely determines it as a total function up to α-equivalence.*

Proof. The first part is by induction on S. The second and third parts are by induction on the type subscript, using the first part to ensure that the result of $\mathsf{expand}_{\{S\}}(R)$ is unique up to α-equivalence. □

3.4 Further Results

The following theorem is proved in the full generality of the dependent case in the technical report [39]. The identity and substitution principles follow immediately.

Theorem 3 (Identity and substitution principles). *The following rules are admissible.*

$$\frac{\Gamma; \Delta \vdash R \Rightarrow A}{\Gamma; \Delta \vdash \mathsf{expand}_A(R) \Leftarrow A}$$

$$\frac{\Gamma; \cdot \vdash N_0 \Leftarrow A \quad \Gamma, x{:}A; \Delta \vdash N \Leftarrow C}{\Gamma; \Delta \vdash \mathsf{inst\_n}_A(x.\,N, N_0) \Leftarrow C} \qquad \frac{\Gamma; \Delta_1 \vdash N_0 \Leftarrow A \quad \Gamma; \Delta_2, x \hat{:} A \vdash N \Leftarrow C}{\Gamma; \Delta_1, \Delta_2 \vdash \mathsf{inst\_n}_A(x.\,N, N_0) \Leftarrow C}$$

Proof. By straightforward inductions. □

In the dependently-typed case, lemmas concerning the algebraic laws satisfied by expansion and instantiation (roughly analogous to confluence results) and concerning the interaction of equality and instantiation are required. Other notable theorems (which, in the dependently-typed case, are actually needed to prove the theorem above) include the following.

Theorem 4 (Decidability of equality). *Given N_1 and N_2, it is decidable whether $N_1 = N_2$.*

Proof. The formulation of the equality rules is nearly syntax-directed, so a simultaneous structural induction on the subjects of the judgment suffices. It remains only to observe that an expression can be decomposed into a concurrent context and subexpression in finitely many ways. □

Theorem 5 (Decidability of instantiation and expansion). *It is decidable whether any instance of the instantiation and expansion operators is defined, and if so, it can be effectively computed.*

Proof. For instantiation, this is proved by a simultaneous structural induction on the substituend, the term substituted into, and the putative type of the substituend. For expansion, the induction is over the structure of the type. □

Theorem 6 (Decidability of typing). *It is decidable whether any instance of the typing judgments is derivable.*

Proof. By structural induction on the subject of the judgments. □

In the dependently-typed case, the inference rules for typing are also structured in a syntax-directed manner, leading to a very simple proof of decidability [39]. This is a substantial technical improvement over prior presentations of even the LF sublanguage alone.

The interaction of equality and substitution is particularly important, since CLF's equality is where concurrency enters. Thus, the following theorems describe, in essence, how concurrent computations modeled in our framework compose.

Theorem 7. *Concurrent equality $N_1 = N_2$ is an equivalence relation.*

Proof. Reflexivity, symmetry, and transitivity can each be proved by structural inductions (with appropriate lemmas, also proved by structural induction) [39]. □

Theorem 8. *If $N = N'$ and $N_0 = N_0'$ then*

$$\mathsf{inst\_n}_A(x.\,N, N_0) = \mathsf{inst\_n}_A(x.\,N', N_0'),$$

assuming one side or the other is defined.

Proof. The proof appeals to composition laws for instantiation and a number of other technical lemmas. The inductive proofs of these lemmas and the main theorem follow the same induction order as for the decidability result [39]. □

Theorem 9. *If $R = R'$ then* $\mathsf{expand}_A(R) = \mathsf{expand}_A(R')$.

Proof. This follows by structural induction on A. □

4 Related Work

Past research has identified two main approaches to encoding concurrent computations in linear logic. Abramsky's *proofs-as-processes* [8] assumes a functional perspective where process interaction is captured by cut-elimination (normalization) steps over linear logic derivations. A second direction, which may be identified with the slogan *proofs-as-traces* (and *formulas-as-processes*), models dynamic process behaviors as proof-search, generally in the style of (linear) logic programming [27,2,28,24,16,11].

CLF follows this second path, stressing a one-to-one correspondence between CLF proof-terms and process executions (traces) [15]. CLF differs from most of these proposals in two respects: first, it is a fully dependent logical framework, which means that it expresses not only the constructs of an object process calculus and their behavior, but also executions themselves and meta-reasoning about them. Second, the concurrent equality intrinsically supports true concurrency.

To the authors' knowledge, Honsell et. al. [22] describe the most significant application of a logical framework in the sphere of concurrency. They elegantly encode the π-calculus with substantial meta-theory in the calculus of constructions with inductive/coinductive types ($CC^{(Co)Ind}$). However, since the notion of equality of $CC^{(Co)Ind}$ does not identify permutable computations, more advanced meta-theoretic investigations would require tedious coding of an equivalence similar to CLF's concurrent equality.

The idea of monadic encapsulation goes back to Moggi's monadic meta-language [30,31] and is used heavily in functional programming. Our formulation follows the judgmental presentation of Pfenning and Davies [36], which completely avoids the need for commuting conversions, but the latter treats neither linearity nor the existence of normal forms. The exploration of monads in logic programming by Bekkers and Tarau [7] concentrates on the use of monads for data structures and all-solution predicate. This is quite different from our application and concerned neither with additional logical connectives nor a true extension of the operational semantics. Benton and Wadler [9] explore the relationship of Moggi's monadic meta-language and term calculi for linear logic with Benton's adjoint calculus, which bears some intriguing similarities with CLF. However, it is not a type theory, and the logical connectives (such as implication) common to lax logic and linear logic retain separate identities, rather than being combined, as in CLF.

The method of defining a type theory by a typed operational semantics goes back to the Automath languages [17] and has been applied to LF by Felty [18]. Our canonical formulation significantly extends and streamlines the ideas behind Felty's *canonical LF* and its extension to LLF [14]; the need for confluence and β-normalization results is eliminated. A similar philosophical outlook, but different technical realizations underly PAL+ [25] and work by Adams [1], who also consider frameworks restricted to normal forms.

5 Conclusion

In this paper, we have presented the basic design of a logical framework that internalizes parametric and hypothetical judgments, linear hypothetical judgments, and true concurrency. This supports representation of a wide variety of concepts related to logic and computation in a natural and concise manner. It also poses a host of new questions.

One of the practically important features of the linear logical framework is its operational interpretation as a logic programming language using goal-directed proof search [21,12]. We conjecture that CLF supports a conservative extension of this operational semantics. We have already constructed a representation of Mini-ML with concurrency and parallelism anticipating such an interpretation [15].

Concurrent computations in an object language are internalized as monadic expressions in CLF. The framework allows type families indexed by objects containing such expressions, which means it is possible to formulate properties of concurrent computations and relations between them. Examples are safety and possibly liveness properties, bisimulations, and other translations between models of computations.

Petri nets and other case studies have shown that, in many cases, computations should be indistinguishable also when threads interact over isomorphic objects. It appears that this can be achieved by integrating the notion of proof irrelevance [34,37] within CLF. Once this extension has been fully worked out, CLF would be able to provide an adequate representation to Petri nets under the collective token philosophy, for example.

References

1. Robin Adams. A modular hierarchy of logical frameworks. In *Proceedings of the International Workshop on Types for Proofs and Programs*, Torino, Italy, April 2003. Springer-Verlag LNCS.
2. Jean-Marc Andreoli. Logic programming with focusing proofs in linear logic. *Journal of Logic and Computation*, 2(3):197–347, 1992.
3. Andrea Asperti. A logic for concurrency. Technical report, Department of Computer Science, University of Pisa, 1987.
4. Andrea Asperti, Gianluigi Ferrari, and Roberto Gorrieri. Implicative formulae in the 'proofs as computations' analogy. In *Proceedings of the seventeenth Symposium on Principles of Programming Languages, San Francisco*, pages 59–71. ACM Press, January 1990.
5. Andrew Barber. Dual intuitionistic linear logic. Technical Report ECS-LFCS-96-347, Department of Computer Science, University of Edinburgh, September 1996.
6. David Basin and Seán Matthews. Logical frameworks. In Dov Gabbay and Franz Guenthner, editors, *Handbook of Philosophical Logic.* Kluwer Academic Publishers, 2nd edition, 2001.
7. Yves Bekkers and Paul Tarau. Monadic constructs for logic programming. In J. Lloyd, editor, *Proceedings of the International Logic Programming Symposium (ILPS'95)*, pages 51–65, Portland, Oregon, December 1995. MIT Press.
8. G. Bellin and P. J. Scott. On the π-calculus and linear logic. *Theoretical Computer Science*, 135:11–65, 1994.
9. P. N. Benton and Philip Wadler. Linear logic, monads, and the lambda calculus. In E. Clarke, editor, *Proceedings of the 11th Annual Symposium on Logic in Computer Science*, pages 420–431, New Brunswick, New Jersey, July 1996. IEEE Computer Society Press.
10. Roberto Bruni and Ugo Montanari. Zero-safe nets: Comparing the collective and individual token approaches. *Information and Computation*, 156(1–2):46–89, 2000.
11. Iliano Cervesato. Petri nets and linear logic: a case study for logic programming. In M. Alpuente and M. I. Sessa, editors, *Proceedings of the 1995 Joint Conference on Declarative Programming — GULP-PRODE'95*, pages 313–318, Marina di Vietri, Italy, 1995.
12. Iliano Cervesato. *A Linear Logical Framework.* PhD thesis, Dipartimento di Informatica, Università di Torino, February 1996.
13. Iliano Cervesato. Typed MSR: Syntax and examples. In V.I. Gorodetski, V.A. Skormin, and L.J. Popyack, editors, *Proceedings of the First International Workshop on Mathematical Methods, Models and Architectures for Computer Network*

Security — MMM'01, pages 159–177, St. Petersburg, Russia, 21–23 May 2001. Springer-Verlag LNCS 2052.

14. Iliano Cervesato and Frank Pfenning. A linear logical framework. *Information & Computation*, 179(1):19–75, November 2002.
15. Iliano Cervesato, Frank Pfenning, David Walker, and Kevin Watkins. A concurrent logical framework II: Examples and applications. Technical Report CMU-CS-02-102, Department of Computer Science, Carnegie Mellon University, 2002.
16. Jawahar Lal Chirimar. *Proof Theoretic Approach to Specification Languages*. PhD thesis, University of Pennsylvania, May 1995.
17. N.G. de Bruijn. Algorithmic definition of lambda-typed lambda calculus. In G. Huet and G. Plotkin, editors, *Logical Environment*, pages 131–145. Cambridge University Press, 1993.
18. Amy Felty. Encoding dependent types in an intuitionistic logic. In Gérard Huet and Gordon D. Plotkin, editors, *Logical Frameworks*, pages 214–251. Cambridge University Press, 1991.
19. Robert H. Halstead. Multilisp: A language for parallel symbolic computation. *ACM Transactions on Programming Languages and Systems*, 7(4):501–539, October 1985.
20. Robert Harper, Furio Honsell, and Gordon Plotkin. A framework for defining logics. *Journal of the Association for Computing Machinery*, 40(1):143–184, January 1993.
21. Joshua Hodas and Dale Miller. Logic programming in a fragment of intuitionistic linear logic. *Information and Computation*, 110(2):327–365, 1994. A preliminary version appeared in the Proceedings of the Sixth Annual IEEE Symposium on Logic in Computer Science, pages 32–42, Amsterdam, The Netherlands, July 1991.
22. Furio Honsell, Marino Miculan, and Ivan Scagnetto. Pi-calculus in (co)inductive type theories. *Theoretical Computer Science*, 253(2):239–285, 2001.
23. Samin Ishtiaq and David Pym. A relevant analysis of natural deduction. *Journal of Logic and Computation*, 8(6):809–838, 1998.
24. Naoki Kobayashi and Akinori Yonezawa. ACL — A concurrent linear logic programming paradigm. In D. Miller, editor, *Proceedings of the 1993 International Logic Programming Symposium*, pages 279–294, Vancouver, Canada, 1993. MIT Press.
25. Zhaohui Luo. PAL+: A lambda-free logical framework. *Journal of Functional Programming*, 13(2):317–338, 2003.
26. N. Martí-Oliet and J. Meseguer. From Petri nets to linear logic. *Mathematical Structures in Computer Science*, 1:66–101, 1991. Revised version of paper in LNCS 389.
27. N. Martí-Oliet and J. Meseguer. From Petri nets to linear logic through categories: A survey. *Journal on Foundations of Computer Science*, 2(4):297–399, December 1991.
28. Dale Miller. The π-calculus as a theory in linear logic: Preliminary results. In E. Lamma and P. Mello, editors, *Proceedings of the Workshop on Extensions of Logic Programming*, pages 242–265. Springer-Verlag LNCS 660, 1992.
29. Robin Milner. *Communicating and Mobile Systems: the π-Calculus*. Cambridge University Press, 1999.
30. Eugenio Moggi. Computational lambda calculus and monads. In *Proceedings of the Fourth Symposium on Logic in Computer Science*, pages 14–23, Asilomar, California, June 1989. IEEE Computer Society Press.
31. Eugenio Moggi. Notions of computation and monads. *Information and Computation*, 93(1):55–92, 1991.

32. Frank Pfenning. The practice of logical frameworks. In Hélène Kirchner, editor, *Proceedings of the Colloquium on Trees in Algebra and Programming*, pages 119–134, Linköping, Sweden, April 1996. Springer-Verlag LNCS 1059. Invited talk.
33. Frank Pfenning. Structural cut elimination I. intuitionistic and classical logic. *Information and Computation*, 157(1/2):84–141, March 2000.
34. Frank Pfenning. Intensionality, extensionality, and proof irrelevance in modal type theory. In J. Halpern, editor, *Proceedings of the 16th Annual Symposium on Logic in Computer Science (LICS'01)*, pages 221–230, Boston, MA, June 2001. IEEE Computer Society Press.
35. Frank Pfenning. Logical frameworks. In Alan Robinson and Andrei Voronkov, editors, *Handbook of Automated Reasoning*, chapter 17, pages 1063–1147. Elsevier Science and MIT Press, 2001.
36. Frank Pfenning and Rowan Davies. A judgmental reconstruction of modal logic. *Mathematical Structures in Computer Science*, 11:511–540, 2001. Notes to an invited talk at the *Workshop on Intuitionistic Modal Logics and Applications* (IMLA'99), Trento, Italy, July 1999.
37. Jason Reed. Proof irrelevance and strict definitions in a logical framework. Technical Report CMU-CS-02-153, Computer Science Department, Carnegie Mellon University, 2002.
38. John H. Reppy. *Concurrent Programming in ML*. Cambridge University Press, 1999.
39. Kevin Watkins, Iliano Cervesato, Frank Pfenning, and David Walker. A concurrent logical framework I: Judgments and properties. Technical Report CMU-CS-02-101, Department of Computer Science, Carnegie Mellon University, 2002.

A Syntax and Judgments of Propositional CLF

$A, B, C ::= a \mid A \multimap B \mid A \rightarrow B \mid A \,\&\, B \mid \top \mid \{S\}$		Asynchronous types
$S ::= S_1 \otimes S_2 \mid 1 \mid\, !A \mid A$		Synchronous types
$\Sigma ::= \Sigma, a{:}\mathsf{type} \mid \Sigma, c{:}A \mid \cdot$		Signatures
$\Gamma ::= \Gamma, u{:}A \mid \cdot$		Unrestricted context
$\Delta ::= \Delta, x \hat{:} A \mid \cdot$		Linear context
$\Psi ::= p \hat{:} S, \Psi \mid \cdot$		Pattern context
$N ::= \hat{\lambda} x.\, N \mid \lambda u.\, N \mid \langle N_1, N_2\rangle \mid \langle\rangle \mid \{E\} \mid R$		Canonical objects
$R ::= c \mid u \mid x \mid R \,\hat{}\, N \mid R\, N \mid \pi_1 R \mid \pi_2 R$		Atomic objects
$E ::= \mathsf{let}\ \{p\} = R\ \mathsf{in}\ E \mid M$		Expressions
$p ::= p_1 \otimes p_2 \mid 1 \mid\, !u \mid x$		Patterns
$M ::= M_1 \otimes M_2 \mid 1 \mid\, !N \mid N$		Monadic objects

$$\frac{\Gamma; \Delta, x \hat{:} A \vdash N \Leftarrow B}{\Gamma; \Delta \vdash \hat{\lambda} x.\, N \Leftarrow A \multimap B} \multimap\mathbf{I} \qquad \frac{\Gamma, u{:}A; \Delta \vdash N \Leftarrow B}{\Gamma; \Delta \vdash \lambda u.\, N \Leftarrow A \rightarrow B} \rightarrow\mathbf{I}$$

$$\frac{\Gamma; \Delta \vdash N_1 \Leftarrow A \quad \Gamma; \Delta \vdash N_2 \Leftarrow B}{\Gamma; \Delta \vdash \langle N_1, N_2\rangle \Leftarrow A \,\&\, B} \&\mathbf{I} \qquad \frac{}{\Gamma; \Delta \vdash \langle\rangle \Leftarrow \top} \top\mathbf{I}$$

$$\frac{\Gamma; \Delta \vdash E \leftarrow S}{\Gamma; \Delta \vdash \{E\} \Leftarrow \{S\}} \{\}\mathbf{I} \qquad \frac{\Gamma; \Delta \vdash R \Rightarrow a}{\Gamma; \Delta \vdash R \Leftarrow a} \Rightarrow\Leftarrow$$

$$\frac{}{\Gamma; \cdot \vdash c \Rightarrow \Sigma(c)} c \qquad \frac{}{\Gamma; \cdot \vdash u \Rightarrow \Gamma(u)} u \qquad \frac{}{\Gamma; x \hat{:} A \vdash x \Rightarrow A} x$$

$$\frac{\Gamma; \Delta_1 \vdash R \Rightarrow A \multimap B \quad \Gamma; \Delta_2 \vdash N \Leftarrow A}{\Gamma; \Delta_1, \Delta_2 \vdash R \,\hat{}\, N \Rightarrow B} \multimap\mathbf{E} \qquad \frac{\Gamma; \Delta \vdash R \Rightarrow A \,\&\, B}{\Gamma; \Delta \vdash \pi_1 R \Rightarrow A} \&\mathbf{E}_1$$

$$\frac{\Gamma; \Delta \vdash R \Rightarrow A \rightarrow B \quad \Gamma; \cdot \vdash N \Leftarrow A}{\Gamma; \Delta \vdash R\, N \Rightarrow B} \rightarrow\mathbf{E} \qquad \frac{\Gamma; \Delta \vdash R \Rightarrow A \,\&\, B}{\Gamma; \Delta \vdash \pi_2 R \Rightarrow B} \&\mathbf{E}_2$$

$$\frac{\Gamma; \Delta_1 \vdash R \Rightarrow \{S_0\} \quad \Gamma; \Delta_2; p \hat{:} S_0 \vdash E \leftarrow S}{\Gamma; \Delta_1, \Delta_2 \vdash (\mathsf{let}\ \{p\} = R\ \mathsf{in}\ E) \leftarrow S} \{\}\mathbf{E}$$

$$\frac{\Gamma; \Delta \vdash M \Leftarrow S}{\Gamma; \Delta \vdash M \leftarrow S} \Leftarrow\leftarrow \qquad \frac{\Gamma; \Delta \vdash E \leftarrow S}{\Gamma; \Delta; \cdot \vdash E \leftarrow S} \leftarrow\leftarrow$$

$$\frac{\Gamma; \Delta; p_1 \hat{:} S_1, p_2 \hat{:} S_2, \Psi \vdash E \leftarrow S}{\Gamma; \Delta; p_1 \otimes p_2 \hat{:} S_1 \otimes S_2, \Psi \vdash E \leftarrow S} \otimes\mathbf{L} \qquad \frac{\Gamma; \Delta; \Psi \vdash E \leftarrow S}{\Gamma; \Delta; 1 \hat{:} 1, \Psi \vdash E \leftarrow S} 1\mathbf{L}$$

$$\frac{\Gamma, u{:}A; \Delta; \Psi \vdash E \leftarrow S}{\Gamma; \Delta; !u \hat{:} !A, \Psi \vdash E \leftarrow S} !\mathbf{L} \qquad \frac{\Gamma; \Delta, x \hat{:} A; \Psi \vdash E \leftarrow S}{\Gamma; \Delta; x \hat{:} A, \Psi \vdash E \leftarrow S} A\mathbf{L}$$

$$\frac{\Gamma; \Delta_1 \vdash M_1 \Leftarrow S_1 \quad \Gamma; \Delta_2 \vdash M_2 \Leftarrow S_2}{\Gamma; \Delta_1, \Delta_2 \vdash M_1 \otimes M_2 \Leftarrow S_1 \otimes S_2} \otimes\mathbf{I} \qquad \frac{}{\Gamma; \cdot \vdash 1 \Leftarrow 1} 1\mathbf{I} \qquad \frac{\Gamma; \cdot \vdash N \Leftarrow A}{\Gamma; \cdot \vdash !N \Leftarrow !A} !\mathbf{I}$$

Formal Proof Sketches

Freek Wiedijk

Department of Computer Science, University of Nijmegen
Toernooiveld 1, 6525 ED Nijmegen, The Netherlands

Abstract. Formalized mathematics currently does not look much like informal mathematics. Also, formalizing mathematics currently seems far too much work to be worth the time of the working mathematician. To address both of these problems we introduce the notion of a *formal proof sketch*. This is a proof representation that is in between a fully checkable formal proof and a statement without any proof at all. Although a formal proof sketch is too high level to be checkable by computer, it has a precise notion of correctness (hence the adjective *formal*).
We will show through examples that formal proof sketches can closely mimic already existing mathematical proofs. Therefore, although a formal proof sketch contains gaps in the reasoning from a formal point of view (which is why we call it a *sketch*), a mathematician probably would call such a text just a 'proof'.

1 Introduction

1.1 Problem

This paper is about formalization of mathematics: the encoding of mathematics in a formal language in sufficient detail that a computer program can verify the correctness. The systems that are currently most suitable for this are Coq, NuPRL/MetaPRL, Mizar, Isabelle/Isar, HOL and PVS. Of these systems Mizar and Isabelle/Isar are *declarative*, which means that the input language of the system is designed to be similar to the language of the informal proofs that one finds in mathematical papers and textbooks.

Two main applications of formalized mathematics are:

1. *representation*, and from this *presentation*, of the mathematics
2. verification of the mathematical *correctness* of the mathematics

However, if one looks at the current state of the art in formal mathematics, then both seem to have difficulties:

- A mathematical formalization currently almost always is a big tar file on an ftp server. Inside such a tar file one finds a number of 'proof script' files, which mostly resemble program source code. Even with the declarative systems Mizar and Isabelle/Isar these files are not readable as ordinary mathematical text. At best one can read them like one might study a computer program.

S. Berardi, M. Coppo, and F. Damiani (Eds.): TYPES 2003, LNCS 3085, pp. 378–393, 2004.

This means that the files of a formalization by themselves are useless to communicate the mathematics that is in them.

For this reason several people have developed tools that produce natural language versions of formalized proofs. However, we have never seen a convincing demo of such a system where we were able to follow a non-trivial proof by reading the generated text. The output of such a tool generally is an order of magnitude larger than the proof scripts that were the input, and also it is rather monotone, as it is automatically generated by a computer program. For these reasons, we consider current formalizations not well suited for the communication of mathematics: the proof script files are unreadable, while the generated natural language presentation is generally too verbose and too monotone to keep the reader's attention needed to understand the mathematics.

In practice, to find out what is in a formalization people almost exclusively look at the statements of the lemmas and ignore the proofs (which generally are not in the files that they look at anyway). They only use the proofs for *proof engineering*, like modifying a copy of a proof to prove a similar lemma, or changing a proof to make it check faster or extract to a better program.

- Formalization of mathematics is a very labor-intensive activity. A rough estimate of the amount of work needed for the formalization of mathematics is that with the current state of the art it takes about one work-week (five days from nine to five) to formalize one page from an undergraduate mathematics textbook.

  Eventually, we would like the mathematicians to start using our systems for routine formalization of mathematics. However, currently it will be unrealistic to expect working mathematicians to go to the trouble of doing full formalizations. Even with a proper mathematical library (which currently is not available for any of the existing systems) the cost of doing a full formalization is prohibitive in comparison to the benefit.

  At the TYPES workshop of 2002 in Nijmegen, Peter Aczel claimed that in order to get mathematicians involved with the formalization of mathematics, technology is needed for *reasoning with gaps*, where one can leave out the details of a formalization that one considers to be obvious or well-known, and one only needs to formalize the interesting parts. This vision is the focus of this paper.

1.2 Approach

We will define the notion of a *formal proof sketch* for the declarative proof language of the Mizar system [6,12]. A formal proof sketch is an incomplete Mizar text that only has one kind of error – that justifications do not necessarily justify the steps, the famous *4 error of the Mizar system – such that it can be completed into a correct Mizar text by adding steps, and references between the steps, to the proofs.

Although this paper uses Mizar as the declarative proof language, the notion of formal proof sketch makes sense for any declarative language. For instance one can have formal proof sketches for Markus Wenzel's Isar language for the Isabelle system [11], or for the proof language of Don Syme's Declare system [9].

1.3 Contribution

'An unfinished Mizar article that has only *4 errors left in it' is a well-known concept to every Mizar user. However, we think it is new to consider such a text to be more important than just being an intermediate stage during formalization. In fact, we would like to claim that that kind of text might be *more* interesting and useful than a completed Mizar formalization. Also, it is new to use this kind as text as a *presentation* of the contents of a finished formalization.

New also is the observation that many informal mathematical proofs from the literature can be mimicked closely by formal proof sketches. (This is a primarily an observation on the syntax of the Mizar language.) See for examples Sections 2 and 8 below. Finally it is new to consider the incomplete justifications of a formal proof sketch to be natural targets for automated theorem proving, as discussed in Section 7.

As far as we know no system exists yet that uses the same declarative language both on the formal proof sketch level and on the formalization level. The main contribution of this paper is the proposal of building such a system.

1.4 Outline

In Section 2 we give a detailed example of a formal proof sketch. In Sections 3 and 4 we discuss the notion of formal proof sketch. In Sections 5 and 6 we compare formal proof sketches with other approaches to proof presentation. In Section 7 we point out the relation between formal proof sketches and automated theorem proving. In Section 8 we present two more examples.

2 An Example: Four Versions of the Irrationality of $\sqrt{2}$

On pages 39 and 40 of the fourth edition of Hardy and Wright's *An Introduction to the Theory of Numbers* [3], we find the following proof:

THEOREM 43 (PYTHAGORAS' THEOREM). *$\sqrt{2}$ is irrational.*

The traditional proof ascribed to Pythagoras runs as follows. If $\sqrt{2}$ is rational, then the equation

$$a^2 = 2b^2 \tag{4.3.1}$$

is soluble in integers a, b with $(a, b) = 1$. Hence a^2 is even, and therefore a is even. If $a = 2c$, then $4c^2 = 2b^2$, $2c^2 = b^2$, and b is also even, contrary to the hypothesis that $(a, b) = 1$. □

If we mimic this text in Mizar syntax, it turns out that we get surprisingly close:

THEOREM Th43: sqrt 2 *is irrational* :: PYTHAGORAS' THEOREM

PROOF assume sqrt 2 is rational; consider a, b such that

4_3_1: $$a\hat{\ }2 = 2 * b\hat{\ }2$$

and a, b are_relative_prime; $a\hat{\ }2$ is even; then a is even; consider c such that $a = 2 * c$; $4 * c\hat{\ }2 = 2 * b\hat{\ }2$; then $2 * c\hat{\ }2 = b\hat{\ }2$; b is even; thus contradiction; END;

This is *almost* a correct Mizar text, because the reasoning is too high level for the system to know why the steps in this proof are allowed (to turn it into a correct Mizar formalization one needs to add intermediate steps and labels, as shown below). However, this text is *syntactically* completely correct according to the Mizar grammar. To stress this, we repeat it in conventional Mizar layout:

```
theorem Th43: sqrt 2 is irrational
proof
 assume sqrt 2 is rational;
 consider a,b such that
4_3_1: a 2 = 2*b 2 and
  a,b are_relative_prime;                                  ←1
 a 2 is even;                                              ←2
 a is even;                                                ←3
 consider c such that a = 2*c;                             ←4
 4*c 2 = 2*b 2;                                            ←5
 2*c 2 = b 2;                                              ←6
 b is even;                                                ←7
 thus contradiction;                                       ←8
end;
```

If one runs this through the Mizar system, one gets eight times the error '*this inference is not accepted*' (as indicated by the arrows in the right margin).

The following text is a completed Mizar formalization of the same proof, where the errors have been eliminated. The parts that correspond to the previous text have been underlined:

```
theorem Th43: sqrt 2 is irrational
proof
 assume sqrt 2 is rational;
 then consider a,b such that
A1: b <> 0 and
A2: sqrt 2 = a/b and
A3: a,b are_relative_prime by Def1;
A4: b 2 <> 0 by A1,SQUARE_1:73;
```

```
   2 = (a/b) 2 by A2,SQUARE_1:def 4
    .= a 2/b 2 by SQUARE_1:69;
   then
  4_3_1: a 2 = 2*b 2 by A4,XCMPLX_1:88;
   a 2 is even by 4_3_1,ABIAN:def 1;
   then
  A5: a is even by PYTHTRIP:2;
   then consider c such that
  A6: a = 2*c by ABIAN:def 1;
  A7: 4*c 2 = (2*2)*c 2
    .= 2 2*c 2 by SQUARE_1:def 3
    .= 2*b 2 by A6,4_3_1,SQUARE_1:68;
   2*(2*c 2) = (2*2)*c 2 by XCMPLX_1:4
    .= 2*b 2 by A7;
   then 2*c 2 = b 2 by XCMPLX_1:5;
   then b 2 is even by ABIAN:def 1;
   then b is even by PYTHTRIP:2;
   then 2 divides a & 2 divides b by A5,Def2;
   then
  A8: 2 divides a gcd b by INT_2:33;
   a gcd b = 1 by A3,INT_2:def 4;
   hence contradiction by A8,INT_2:17;
  end;
```

Note that this formalization does not much resemble the Hardy and Wright proof anymore but looks like the kind of 'code' that is customary in proof assistants.

This example shows the three kinds of proof texts that we will consider in this paper:

- the first text fragment is an *informal English proof*
- the second and third are a *formal proof sketch* (in two different layouts)
- the fourth is a *full formalization*

We imagine a prover interface in which all these variant texts are present next to each other, connected by hyperlinks.

Note that the informal English proof and the formal proof sketch are very similar. Also note that the formal proof sketch and the full formalization are both written in the same formal language. Finally note that the formal proof sketch occurs as a 'skeleton' in the text of the full formalization.

This paper proposes to take these formal proof sketches seriously. We claim that a formal proof sketch can be used to precisely communicate mathematics (although the computer cannot check the correctness, a human can, cf. the proposition on page 385). We also claim that a formal proof sketch is the best way to present a formalization, as a 'road map' to the full text of the formalization.

For two more examples of an informal English proof together with a formal proof sketch version, see Section 8 at the end of this paper.

3 Formal Proof Sketches

We now give the informal definition of a formal proof sketch. This definition can be made rigorous but we will not do that here.

Definition. A *formal proof sketch* is a text in the syntax of a declarative proof language that was obtained from a full formalization in that language by removing some proof steps and references between proof steps. The only errors (according to the definition of the proof language) in such a stripped formalization should be *justification errors*: the errors that say that a step is not sufficiently justified by the references to previous steps.

Some people might object to the name 'formal proof *sketch*', claiming that these formal proof sketches are designed to closely follow the informal proofs of mathematics, and that mathematicians consider those to be *proofs*, and not sketches. However, we would like to take the formalizer's point of view that formal proof sketches leave parts of the mathematics implicit, and that therefore we can use the word 'sketch'.

If we specialize the notion of a formal proof sketch to the Mizar proof language, we have the following *formal proof sketch grammar*:

$$
\begin{array}{rcl}
\text{statement} & = & \text{proposition justification} \\
 & | & [\,\textit{label}\ \textbf{:}\,]\ \textit{term} = \textit{term}\ \text{justification} \\
 & & \quad \{\textbf{.=}\ \textit{term}\ \text{justification}\} \\
\text{proposition} & = & [\,\textit{label}\ \textbf{:}\,]\ \text{formula} \\
\text{formula} & = & \textit{formula} \\
 & | & \textbf{thesis} \\
\text{justification} & = & [\,\textbf{by}\ \textit{label}\ \{,\ \textit{label}\}\,] \\
 & | & \textbf{proof}\ \{\text{step}\ ;\}\ [\,\text{cases}\,]\ \textbf{end} \\
\text{step} & = & [\,\textbf{then}\,]\ \text{statement} \\
 & | & \textbf{assume}\ \text{proposition} \\
 & | & \textbf{let}\ \textit{variable}\ \{,\ \textit{variable}\} \\
 & | & (\,\textbf{thus}\ |\ \textbf{hence}\,)\ \text{statement} \\
 & | & [\,\textbf{then}\,]\ \textbf{consider}\ \textit{variable}\ \{,\ \textit{variable}\} \\
 & & \quad \textbf{such that}\ \text{proposition justification} \\
 & | & \textbf{take}\ \textit{term}\ \{,\ \textit{term}\} \\
 & | & \textbf{set}\ \textit{variable} = \textit{term} \\
\text{cases} & = & \textbf{per cases}\ \text{justification}\ ; \\
 & & \quad \{\textbf{suppose}\ \text{proposition}\ ;\ \{\text{step}\ ;\}\}
\end{array}
$$

Note that we do not propose our own proof language here. We use the Mizar system to experiment with formal proof sketches and therefore we do not want to depart from the Mizar syntax. Also note that this grammar is small. Often people seem to have the impression that Mizar has a complex syntax, but the proof part of the language is really not much larger than this.

We can graphically represent the process of removing steps and references from a formalization to obtain a formal proof sketch:

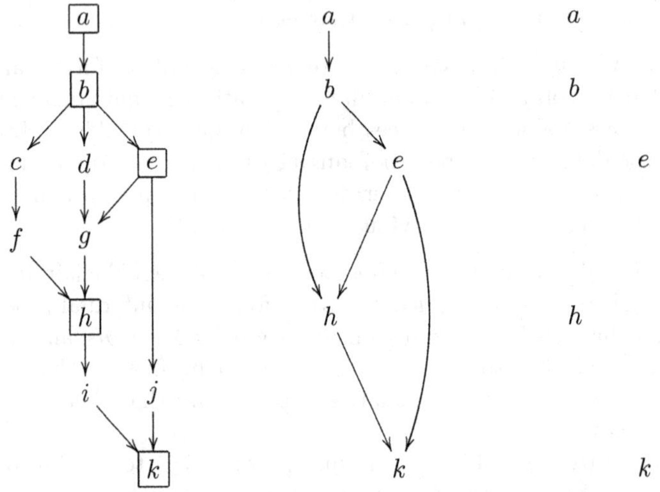

The first diagram corresponds to the full formalization. There are eleven proof steps which are labeled a–k. The justifications in the proof are represented by the arrows. For instance step h is justified by references to f and g. In Mizar syntax it would be written as 'h : ... **by** f, g;'. In the second diagram six of the steps have been removed, but the references between the steps are still present. The third diagram corresponds to the formal proof sketch. Now there are no labels and references to labels left. This is generally what happens in a formal proof sketch that mimics an informal mathematical text.

Two extreme formal proof sketches of a given formalization are those in which all proof steps have been removed,[1] and those in which no proof steps have been removed. These are the end points of a spectrum:

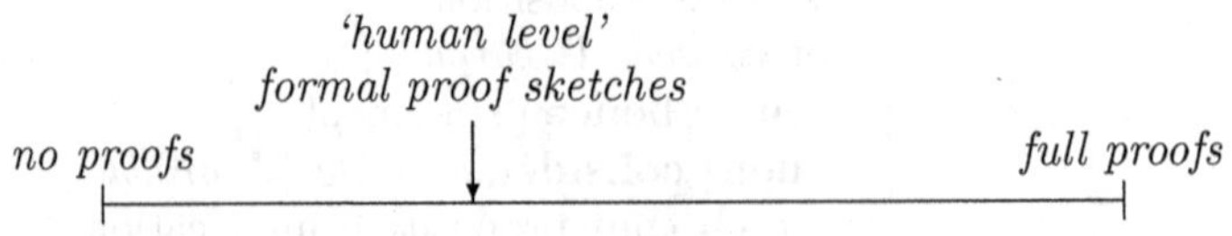

FORMAL PROOF SKETCH SPECTRUM

Most systems have files that correspond to the end points. For instance in the Coq system there are the `.g` and `.v` files, and in the Mizar system there are the `.abs` and `.miz` files. Formal proof sketches give one intermediate levels of proof representation in between these two extremes.

[1] It might seem strange to call such an empty proof a 'proof sketch'. However we think it is natural to include this case in the notion of formal proof sketch, just like 0 is generally considered to be a natural number, and the empty set is considered to be a set.

When we show formal proof sketches to people, we sometimes get the reaction 'we should build systems that can check them!' We think it is overtly optimistic to expect that this will be possible soon. However, as proof checking technology improves we can expect the endpoint of 'full proofs' to get closer to the formal proof sketches at the 'human level':

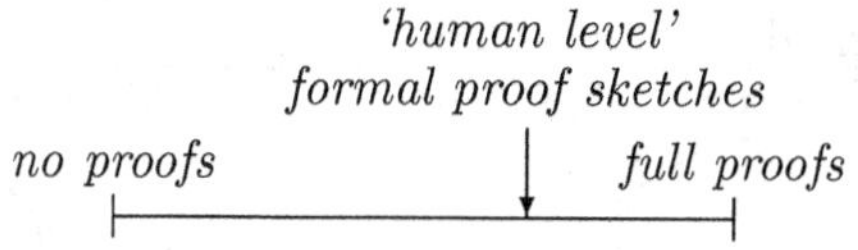

FORMAL PROOF SKETCH SPECTRUM IN 2048

So formal proof sketches are too high level to be checked automatically for mathematical correctness (else they would be 'full formalizations'). However, the notion of being a formal proof sketch is *not* an informal notion. If someone presents you with a formal proof sketch, it is meaningful to say that 'it is correct' or 'it is not correct'.

This is related to the proposition:

Proposition. *It is semi-decidable whether a text is a correct formal proof sketch.*

Proof. If a text is a correct formal proof sketch, this can be shown by showing the full formalization from which it was derived. However, as in general it is not decidable whether a given statement is provable in a given context, it can in general not be decided whether a given statement with an empty justification is a formal proof sketch. □

4 The Proof Development Cycle

The development of a mathematical formalization follows the following pattern:

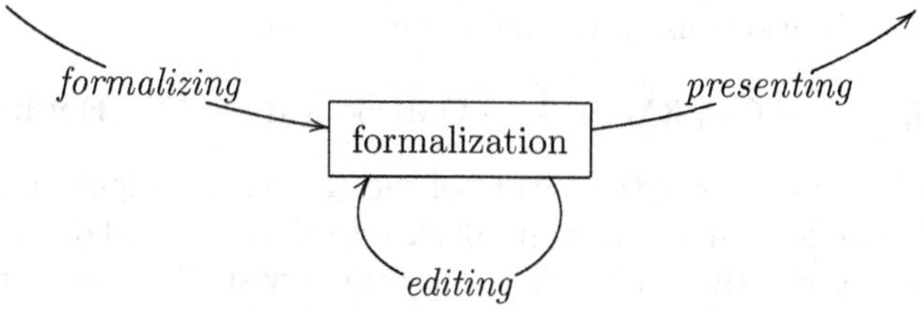

It is important not to forget the activity of editing a formalization. Having a great presentation mode is not very helpful if one needs to deal with the underlying formalization (which often is an unclear tactic script).

If we use formal proof sketches, we can give a more detailed structure to this development diagram:

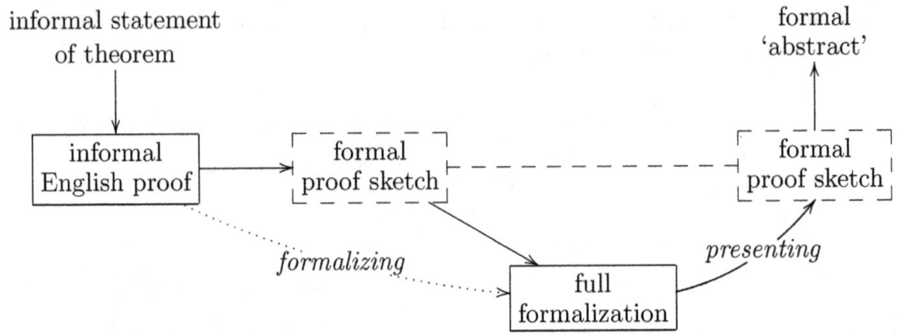

Here we present development of a formalization from an existing informal mathematical text (as in the example from Section 2). The process consists of two phases. First, one mimics the informal English proof in the formal proof sketch language. This is easy and fast. Second, one 'fleshes out' this formal proof sketch to a full formalization. This generally takes much longer. During this second phase one often discovers that the original formal proof sketch was not correct, and so it will change. At the end one has a matched pair of a formal proof sketch and a full formalization. The full formalization then guarantees the correctness of the mathematics, while the formal proof sketch presents it in an understandable way.

Note that the three levels in this second diagram correspond to the three positions on the formal proof sketch spectrum: the top level corresponds to no proofs, the middle level to 'human level' formal proof sketches, and the bottom level to full proofs.

5 Generated Natural Language Proof

There are many systems to generate proofs in natural language from formalized mathematics. An example of such a system is the MoWGLI system from the University of Bologna [1]. It generates web pages with proofs in natural language from Coq formalizations using the following pipeline:

$$\textbf{Coq script} \xrightarrow{\textsf{Coq}} \text{Coq XML} \xrightarrow{\textsf{XSLT}} \text{OMDoc XML} \xrightarrow{\textsf{XSLT}} \textbf{English}\ \text{HTML}$$

If one looks at the syntax of the output of such a system, it looks very similar to the text that one finds in a formal proof sketch. However, although superficially the two ways of presenting a formalization seem very similar, there are important differences:

- The systems that generate proofs in natural language *automatically* convert a formalization to a presentation. We do not have a method to generate a (reasonable) formal proof sketch from a full declarative formalization without human help. However, one can reduce a full formalization *manually* to a good formal proof sketch, in two stages:

1. The first stage is automatic: one just removes all labels and references to labels.[2] This is the most important phase. It is surprising how much more readable a Mizar text becomes without this 'visual noise'.[3]
2. The second stage consists of removing intermediate steps, just keeping the 'interesting steps' of the proof. The problem is how to decide which steps to drop and which to leave in. We do not know of a good heuristic to decide this from the structure of the proof.[4] Currently it will need manual markup of the full formalization to mark these 'interesting steps'. Inserting that kind of markup will not be much work.

– The size of generated proofs in natural language is an order of magnitude *larger* than the size of the original formalizations, while the size of formal proof sketches is an order of magnitude *smaller* than that of the corresponding full formalizations.
  The accepted opinion seems to be that to deal with this one should *fold* subproofs until one has something of reasonable size. However, we doubt that this will work well. In a procedural prover most of the steps are backward steps, while in a declarative prover most of the steps are forward. In both cases there will be no convenient subproofs to fold. Of course one can write the formalizations to combine forward and backward steps in a way that leads to proofs with a nice folding structure, but that is not very practical. And even if one would do that: our experience with Lamport-style proof (as described in the next section) is that a subproof structure obfuscates the 'narrative' of the proof. If one compares formal proof sketches that mimic existing informal proofs to formal proof sketches that mimic proofs with conveniently foldable subproofs (like Lamport-style proofs), then the former kind has far less subproofs than the latter kind.[5]

6 Lamport's 'How to Write a Proof'

Fleshing out a formal proof sketch along the formal proof sketch spectrum toward a full formalization relates to a proof format described in Leslie Lamport's 'How

[2] Removing *all* labels might be a bit too strong (in long proofs references sometimes can be helpful to understand the proof) but it is a very good first order approximation. The number of references in informal mathematics is a tiny fraction of the number of references in formalized mathematics.

[3] Removing all linkage from a Mizar text means removing the '`then`' keywords as well. But of course this first stage does not need to do so too. In informal mathematics words like *then* are often used to link steps together. We illustrated both styles in the example on page 381: in the informal layout of the formal proof sketch we left two 'then' keywords in, but in the Mizar layout we removed them.

[4] Possibly compiler technology like *basic block analysis* is relevant for this.

[5] When discussing this with Laurent Théry at the TPHOLs 2003 conference, he summarized this opinion by saying 'so you like iteration but you do not like recursion'.

to Write a Proof' [5]. In that paper he describes a hierarchical proof style where each step of the proof recursively is 'clarified' by a subproof until the steps are considered to be obvious. These 'recursive proofs' apparently are very natural and seductive.[6] Note that Lamport's proof format is *not* formal.

An implementation of Lamport-style proof on the web was made in the IMP project of Paul Cairns and Jeremy Gow [2]. They have course notes in topology as a set of web pages. On each of these pages is both an informal proof as well as a Lamport-style proof in which subproofs can be collapsed by clicking on buttons. We compared one of these web pages to our approach: we created formal proof sketches both for the informal proof as well as for the Lamport-style proof. Our experience was that the first formal proof sketch was the more understandable of the two. We had the impression that having many subproofs does obscure the structure of a proof rather than clarify it.

It should be clear that we do not claim that it is bad to have lemmas to isolate important parts of proofs. Subproofs certainly have their place on the lemma level. However, having them on the micro-level of the proofs steps seems not to be very helpful.

Interestingly, when doing this experiment we found that without adding steps the Lamport-style proof was not detailed enough to be accepted by the Mizar system, and when we added that detail it turned out that that it contained some mistakes.

7 Proof Obligations for Automated Theorem Provers

The justifications in a formal proof sketch cannot be checked by the computer because the steps are too large and because there are not enough references. If one does not remove the references (i.e., one takes the formal proof sketch that corresponds to the middle graph on page 384), then one might consider the inferences that need to be justified. For the example from Section 2 all but one inference turn out to be a simple algebraic problem:

$$
\begin{array}{ll}
1\!\rightarrow & b \neq 0 \,\wedge\, \sqrt{2} = a/b \;\vdash\; a^2 = 2b^2 \\
2\!\rightarrow & b \in \mathbb{Z} \,\wedge\, a^2 = 2b^2 \;\vdash\; 2 \,|\, a^2 \\
3\!\rightarrow & a \in \mathbb{Z} \,\wedge\, 2 \,|\, a^2 \;\vdash\; 2 \,|\, a \\
5\!\rightarrow & a^2 = 2b^2 \,\wedge\, a = 2c \;\vdash\; 4c^2 = 2b^2 \\
6\!\rightarrow & 4c^2 = 2b^2 \;\vdash\; 2c^2 = b^2 \\
7\!\rightarrow & b \in \mathbb{Z} \,\wedge\, c \in \mathbb{Z} \,\wedge\, 2c^2 = b^2 \;\vdash\; 2 \,|\, b \\
8\!\rightarrow & (a,b) = 1 \,\wedge\, 2 \,|\, a \,\wedge\, 2 \,|\, b \;\vdash\; \perp
\end{array}
$$

The Mizar notion of inference (called 'obviousness') is rather weak, and therefore it is interesting to give these problems – together with the relevant lemmas – to a complete first order prover (if it runs long enough and with enough memory it

[6] When discussing formalization of mathematics with Hendrik Lenstra, he reinvented exactly this proof format on the spot.

eventually will find a justification, if it exists). As an experiment we gave these problems[7] to the Meson prover of the HOL system [4]. The results were rather disappointing (the table also shows the number of steps that the Meson prover needed to solve the problems that it could solve):

	Mizar	*Meson*		
1→	−	−		
2→	+	+	61	1.49 *s*
3→	+	+	20	0.14 *s*
4→	+	+	142	1.02 *s*
5→	−	−		
6→	−	−		
7→	−	+	18839	4.71 *s*
8→	−	−		

We claim that justification problems taken from formal proof sketches of existing mathematical proofs are a good target for the automated theorem proving community. In contrast, current problem sets for automated theorem provers like TPTP [8] are mathematically mostly not very interesting. Of course we would like our automated theorem provers to be able to solve non-trivial problems, but first they should be able to solve the problems that humans consider to be sufficiently trivial that they do not need any words in an informal proof.

8 Two More Examples

In Section 2 we showed that a formal proof sketch of an informal mathematical proof can closely mimic the original. We think that this is generally the case:

Claim. *Most existing informal proofs can be faithfully mimicked as a Mizar formal proof sketch.*

We have experimented with formal proof sketches of various existing proofs and in our experience this claim seems justified.

In this section we will show two more examples. The first is a proof that was on a slide of the talk 'Formalizing an intuitionistic proof of the Fundamental Theorem of Algebra' by Herman Geuvers at the 7th Dutch Proof Tools Day in Utrecht. The slide called it a 'romantic proof', in contrast to the 'cool proofs' of formalized mathematics. (To highlight the correspondence to the formal proof sketch, we underlined two random phrases of the proof.)

THEOREM There are infinitely many primes:
for every number n there exists a prime $p > n$

PROOF [after Euclid]
Given n. Consider $k = n! + 1$, where $n! = 1 \cdot 2 \cdot 3 \cdot \ldots \cdot n$.

[7] Conversion from Mizar justifications to first order problems in TPTP format was kindly done for us by Josef Urban of Charles University in Prague.

Let p be a prime that divides k.
For this number p we have $p > n$: otherwise $p \leq n$;
but then p divides $n!$,
so p cannot divide $k = n! + 1$,
contradicting the choice of p. QED

And here is the corresponding Mizar formal proof sketch:

THEOREM $\{n : n \text{ is prime}\}$ is infinite PROOF
for n ex p st p is prime & $p > n$

PROOF :: [after Euclid]
let n; set $k = n! + 1$;
consider p such that p is prime & p divides k;
take p; thus p is prime; thus $p > n$ PROOF assume $p <= n$;
then p divides $n!$;
not p divides $n! + 1$;
thus contradiction; END; END; thus thesis; END;

The other example is from Rob Nederpelt's report on Weak Type Theory [7]:

THEOREM. Let G be a set with a binary operation $\cdot$ and left unit element e. Let H be a set with binary operation $*$ and assume that ϕ is a homomorphism of G onto H. Then H has a left unit element as well.

PROOF. Take $e' = \phi(e)$. Let $h \in H$. There is $g \in G$ such that $\phi(g) = h$. Then

$$e' * h = \phi(e) * \phi(g) = \phi(e \cdot g) = \phi(g) = h,$$

hence e' is left unit element of H. □

And here is the corresponding formal proof sketch of this simple proof:

---

let G, H be non empty HGrStr; let e be Element of G such that e is_left_unit_of G; let *phi* be map of G, H such that *phi* is_homomorphism G, H and *phi* is onto; thus ex e' being Element of H st e' is_left_unit_of H

PROOF take $e' = phi.e$; now let h be Element of H; consider g being Element of G such that $phi.g = h$; thus

$$e' * h = phi.e * phi.g \mathrel{.=} phi.(e * g) \mathrel{.=} phi.g \mathrel{.=} h;$$

end; hence e' is_left_unit_of H; END;

---

9 Conclusion

9.1 Discussion

In Section 1.1 we listed two problems with formalization of mathematics:

The first problem was that formalized mathematics does not look much like ordinary mathematical text. We think that the notion of formal proof sketch is a step toward a solution of this problem.

The second problem was that formalization of mathematics is too much work. We think that by not fully formalizing a proof, but just using formal proof sketches for the interesting parts, we have an approach that is between no check at all and full verification of the correctness. In the formal proof sketch we will be able to write the interesting parts of the proof (like in Lamport's approach) and the system will check those parts, while we do not have to spend time on the trivial details that take most of the time.

9.2 Related Work

Rob Nederpelt has a language called *weak type theory* or WTT [7], for writing formal mathematics in a way that is closer to informal mathematics than currently is the case in formal systems. It is basically a formalization language where steps in the proofs are just stated but not checked. WTT texts are similar to formal proof sketches (they might be considered the formal proof sketches of the Automath language), but there are several big differences. Although it is structurally similar to informal mathematics, a WTT text does not at all resemble the way informal mathematics looks. Also, there is no notion of mathematical correctness for a WTT text (there is only a notion of 'weak type correctness'). Finally there is currently no way to relate a WTT text to a full formalization of the same mathematics.

Laurent Théry describes in [10] a proof representation (which he there calls 'proof format') that is similar to what we call a formal proof sketch here.[8] Nevertheless, his approach differs in some important respects from ours:

- In [10] there are three very different proofs languages: the XML file that contains the 'formal proof sketch' inside the machine, the natural language presentation with which this file is shown in the interface, and the Coq file that holds the proof obligations that have to be proved. In our approach we use the Mizar language for both the formal proof sketch and for the full formalization, and therefore in our approach all these three languages coincide, giving a much more integrated whole.
- In [10] there are *two* levels: the XML level and the Coq level. In our approach there is a *spectrum* of related formal proof sketches (see page 384 below).

[8] We both seemed to be unaware of each other's work when we were doing it (a preliminary paper about formal proof sketches [13] was only available to the attendees of the 7th Dutch Proof Tools Day in Utrecht), and we only found out about the similarities in each other's work at the UITP workshop in Rome.

- In our approach it is possible to take a full Mizar formalization and systematically reduce it to a formal proof sketch. In the approach from [10] there is no similar way to turn a Coq formalization into anything similar to a formal proof sketch.
- We 'reuse' the language of a full-fledged system for our formal proof sketches. Therefore we have a much richer language than the system from [10]. Especially we get the full Mizar type system, which is very mathematical. Also we get features in our language like definitions, proof by cases and iterated equalities.
- Finally, the correctness of the natural deduction 'skeleton' steps in our formal proof sketches are checked by Mizar with respect to the structure of the current goal, in contrast with [10] where even that kind of checking is considered a proof obligation to be handled later. (An example of this kind of checking occurs when the goal is of the form $A \to B$ and the step says '*assume* A'.)

9.3 Future Work

Formal proof sketches should be integrated into a proof development environment. The same proof language should be used for the formal proof sketches and for the full formalizations. In that system one should then try to mimic the proofs of a non-trivial existing mathematical text (like for instance a chapter from a textbook) as a sequence of formal proof sketches. This will be a good test for the formal proof sketch approach in practice.

Acknowledgments. Thanks to Henk Barendregt, Herman Geuvers, John Harrison, Joe Hurd, Paul Jackson, Hendrik Lenstra, Rob Nederpelt, Claudio Sacerdoti Coen, Bart de Smit, Bas Spitters, Dan Synek and Laurent Théry for stimulating discussions on the subject of this paper. Thanks also to the anonymous referees for helpful comments.

References

1. A. Asperti and B. Wegner. MOWGLI – A New Approach for the Content Description in Digital Documents. In *Proc. of the 9th Intl. Conference on Electronic Resources and the Social Role of Libraries in the Future*, volume 1, Autonomous Republic of Crimea, Ukraine, 2002.
2. Paul Cairns and Jeremy Gow. A Theoretical Analysis of Hierarchical Proofs. In Andrea Asperti, Bruno Buchberger, and James Davenport, editors, *Mathematical Knowledge Management, Proceedings of MKM 2003*, volume 2594 of *LNCS*, pages 175–187. Springer, 2003.
3. G.H. Hardy and E.M. Wright. *An Introduction to the Theory of Numbers.* Clarendon Press, Oxford, fourth edition, 1960.
4. John Harrison. Optimizing Proof Search in Model Elimination. In M. A. McRobbie and J. K. Slaney, editors, *13th International Conference on Automated Deduction*, volume 1104 of *LNCS*, pages 313–327, New Brunswick, NJ, 1996. Springer-Verlag.

5. Leslie Lamport. How to Write a Proof. *American Mathematical Monthly*, 102(7):600–608, 1995.
6. M. Muzalewski. *An Outline of PC Mizar*. Fondation Philippe le Hodey, Brussels, 1993. `<http://www.cs.kun.nl/ freek/mizar/mizarmanual.ps.gz>`.
7. Rob Nederpelt. Weak Type Theory, a formal language for mathematics. Technical Report 02-05, Eindhoven University of Technology, Department of Math. and Comp. Sc., May 2002.
8. Geoff Sutcliffe, Christian Suttner, and Theodor Yemenis. The TPTP problem library. In Alan Bundy, editor, *Proc. 12th Conference on Automated Deduction CADE, Nancy/France*, pages 252–266. Springer-Verlag, 1994.
9. Don Syme. Three Tactic Theorem Proving. In *Theorem Proving in Higher Order Logics, TPHOLs '99, Nice, France*, volume 1690 of *LNCS*, pages 203–220. Springer, 1999.
10. Laurent Théry. Formal Proof Authoring: an Experiment. In Christoph Lüth and David Aspinall, editors, *UITP 2003, Rome, Technical Report No. 189, Institut für Informatik, Albert-Ludwigs Universität*, pages 143–159, Freiburg, September 2003.
11. M. Wenzel. *Isabelle/Isar — a versatile environment for human-readable formal proof documents*. PhD thesis, Institut für Informatik, Technische Universität München, 2002. `<http://tumb1.biblio.tu-muenchen.de/publ/diss/in/2002/wenzel.html>`.
12. F. Wiedijk. Mizar: An Impression. `<http://www.cs.kun.nl/ freek/mizar/mizarintro.ps.gz>`, 1999.
13. F. Wiedijk. Formal proof sketches. In Wan Fokkink and Jaco van de Pol, editors, *7th Dutch Proof Tools Day, Program + Proceedings*, Amsterdam, 2003. CWI. `<http://www.cs.kun.nl/ freek/notes/sketches.ps.gz>`.

Applied Type System*

Extended Abstract

Hongwei Xi

Boston University

Abstract. The framework Pure Type System ($\mathcal{PTS}$) offers a simple and general approach to designing and formalizing type systems. However, in the presence of dependent types, there often exist some acute problems that make it difficult for $\mathcal{PTS}$ to accommodate many common realistic programming features such as general recursion, recursive types, effects (e.g., exceptions, references, input/output), etc. In this paper, we propose a new framework Applied Type System ($\mathcal{ATS}$) to allow for designing and formalizing type systems that can readily support common realistic programming features. The key salient feature of $\mathcal{ATS}$ lies in a complete separation between statics, in which types are formed and reasoned about, and dynamics, in which programs are constructed and evaluated. With this separation, it is no longer possible for a program to occur in a type as is otherwise allowed in $\mathcal{PTS}$. We present not only a formal development of $\mathcal{ATS}$ but also mention some examples in support of using $\mathcal{ATS}$ as a framework to form type systems for practical programming.

1 Introduction

There is already a framework Pure Type System ($\mathcal{PTS}$) [Bar92] that offers a simple and general approach to designing and formalizing type systems. However, in the presence of dependent types, there often exist some acute problems that make it difficult for $\mathcal{PTS}$ to accommodate many common realistic programming features. In particular, we have learned that some great efforts are required in order to maintain a style of pure reasoning as is advocated in $\mathcal{PTS}$ when programming features such as general recursion [CS87], recursive types [Men87], effects [HMST95], exceptions [HN88] and input/output are present. To address such limitations of $\mathcal{PTS}$, we propose a new framework Applied Type System ($\mathcal{ATS}$) to allow for designing and formalizing type systems that can readily support common realistic programming features. The key salient feature of $\mathcal{ATS}$ lies in a complete separation between statics, in which types are formed and reasoned about, and dynamics, in which programs are constructed and evaluated. This separation, with its origin in a previous study on a restricted form of dependent types developed in Dependent ML (DML) [XP99,Xi98], makes it feasible to support dependent types in the presence of effects such as references

* Partially supported by NSF grants no. CCR-0224244 and no. CCR-0229480

S. Berardi, M. Coppo, and F. Damiani (Eds.): TYPES 2003, LNCS 3085, pp. 394–408, 2004.

$$\frac{}{\vdash \mathcal{S}_\emptyset\ [sig]} \qquad \frac{\vdash \mathcal{S}\ [sig]}{\vdash \mathcal{S}, sc : [\sigma_1, \ldots, \sigma_n] \Rightarrow b\ [sig]}$$

$$\frac{\Sigma(a) = \sigma}{\Sigma \vdash_{\mathcal{S}} a : \sigma} \qquad \frac{\mathcal{S}(sc) = [\sigma_1, \ldots, \sigma_n] \Rightarrow b \quad \Sigma \vdash_{\mathcal{S}} s_i : \sigma_i \text{ for } i = 1, \ldots, n}{\Sigma \vdash_{\mathcal{S}} sc[s_1, \ldots, s_n] : b}$$

$$\frac{\Sigma, a : \sigma_1 \vdash_{\mathcal{S}} s : \sigma_2}{\Sigma \vdash_{\mathcal{S}} \lambda a : \sigma_1.s : \sigma_1 \to \sigma_2} \qquad \frac{\Sigma \vdash_{\mathcal{S}} s_1 : \sigma_1 \to \sigma_2 \quad \Sigma \vdash_{\mathcal{S}} s_2 : \sigma_1}{\Sigma \vdash_{\mathcal{S}} s_1(s_2) : \sigma_2}$$

Fig. 1. The signature formating rules and the sorting rules for statics

and exceptions. Also, with the introduction of two new (and thus unfamiliar) forms of types: *guarded types* and *asserting types*, we argue that $\mathcal{ATS}$ is able to capture program invariants in a more flexible and more effective manner than $\mathcal{PTS}$.

The design and formalization of $\mathcal{ATS}$ constitutes the primary contribution of the paper, which aims at setting a reference point for future work that makes use of similar ideas presented in [Zen97,XP99,XCC03]. With $\mathcal{ATS}$, we can readily form type systems to support many common programming features in the presence of dependent types, overcoming certain inherent deficiencies of $\mathcal{PTS}$. We are currently in the process of designing and implementing a typed functional programming language with its type system based on $\mathcal{ATS}$ that can support not only dependent types (like those developed DML) but also guarded recursive datatypes [XCC03]. With such a design, we seek to support a variety of language extensions by mostly implementing new language constructs in terms of existing ones, following an approach like the one adopted by Scheme. In particular, we have already shown that various programming features such as object-oriented programming [XCC03], meta-programming [XCC03,CX03] and type classes [XCC02] can be handled in such a manner.

We organize the rest of the extended abstract as follows. In Section 2, we present a detailed development of the framework $\mathcal{ATS}$, formalizing a generic applied type system ATS constructed in $\mathcal{ATS}$ and then establishing both subject reduction and progress theorems for ATS. We extend $\mathcal{ATS}$ in Section 3 to accommodate some common realistic programming features such as general recursion, pattern matching and effects, and present some interesting examples of applied type systems in Section 4. Lastly, we mention some related work as well as certain potential development for the future, and then conclude. A completed full paper is availabe on-line [Xi03] in which the missing details in this extended abstract can be found.

2 Applied Type System

We present a formalization of the framework Applied Type System ($\mathcal{ATS}$) in this section. We use the name *applied type system* for a type system formed in the $\mathcal{ATS}$ framework. In the following presentation, let ATS be a generic applied type system, which consists of a static component (statics) and a dynamic component (dynamics). Intuitively, the statics and dynamics are each for handling types and programs, respectively. To simplify the presentation, we assume that the statics is a pure simply typed language and we use the name *sort* to refer to a type in this language. A term in the statics is called a *static term* while a term in the dynamics is called a *dynamic term*, and a static term of a special sort *type* serves as a type in the dynamics.

2.1 Statics

We present a formal description of a static component. We write b for a base sort and assume the existence of two special base sorts *type* and *bool*.

$$\begin{array}{lrl} \text{sorts} & \sigma & ::= b \mid \sigma_1 \rightarrow \sigma_2 \\ \text{static terms} & s & ::= a \mid sc[s_1, \ldots, s_n] \mid \lambda a : \sigma.s \mid s_1(s_2) \\ \text{static var. ctx.} & \Sigma & ::= \emptyset \mid \Sigma, a : \sigma \\ \text{signatures} & \mathcal{S} & ::= \mathcal{S}_\emptyset \mid \mathcal{S}, sc : [\sigma_1, \ldots, \sigma_n] \Rightarrow b \\ \text{static subst.} & \Theta_S & ::= [] \mid \Theta_S[a \mapsto s] \end{array}$$

We use a for static term variables and s for static terms. There may also be some declared static constants sc, which are either static constant constructors scc or static constant functions scf. We use $[\sigma_1, \ldots, \sigma_n] \Rightarrow b$ for sc-sorts, which are assigned to static constants. Given a static constant sc, we can form a term $sc[s_1, \ldots, s_n]$ of sort b if sc is assigned a sc-sort $[\sigma_1, \ldots, \sigma_n] \Rightarrow b$ for some sorts $\sigma_1, \ldots, \sigma_n$ and s_i can be assigned the sorts σ_i for $i = 1, \ldots, n$. We may write sc for $sc[]$ if there is no risk of confusion. Note that a sc-sort is not regarded as a (regular) sort.

We use Θ_S for a static substitution that maps static variables to static terms and $\mathbf{dom}(\Theta_S)$ for the domain of Θ_S. We write $[]$ for the empty mapping and $\Theta_S[a \mapsto s]$, where we assume $a \notin \mathbf{dom}(\Theta_S)$, for the mapping that extends Θ_S with a link from a to s. Also, we write $\bullet[\Theta_S]$ for the result of applying Θ_S to some syntax $\bullet$, which may represent a static term, a sequence of static terms, or a dynamic variable context as is defined later.

A signature is for assigning sc-sorts to declared static constants sc, and the rules for forming signatures are in given Figure 1. We assume that the initial signature $\mathcal{S}_\emptyset$ contains the following declarations,

$$\begin{array}{ccc} \mathbf{1} : [] \Rightarrow type & \top : [] \Rightarrow bool & \bot : [] \Rightarrow bool \\ \rightarrow_{tp} : [type, type] \Rightarrow type & & \supset : [bool, type] \Rightarrow type \\ \wedge : [bool, type] \Rightarrow type & & \leq_{tp} : [type, type] \Rightarrow bool \end{array}$$

that is, the static constants on the left-hand side of : are assigned the corresponding sc-sorts on the right-hand side. Also, for each sort σ, we assume that $\mathcal{S}_\emptyset$ assigns the two static constructors $\forall_\sigma$ and $\exists_\sigma$ the sc-sort $[\sigma \rightarrow_{tp} type] \Rightarrow type$. We may use infix notation for some static constants. For instance, we write $s_1 \rightarrow_{tp} s_2$ for $\rightarrow_{tp} [s_1, s_2]$ and $s_1 \leq_{tp} s_2$ for $\leq_{tp} [s_1, s_2]$. In addition, we may write $\forall a : \sigma.s$ and $\exists a : \sigma.s$ for $\forall_\sigma[\lambda a : \sigma.s]$ and $\exists_\sigma[\lambda a : \sigma.s]$, respectively. The sorting rules for the statics are given in Figure 1, which are mostly standard. For instance, $\forall a : type.a \rightarrow_{tp} a$ is a static term that can be assigned the sort *type* since $\emptyset \vdash_{\mathcal{S}_\emptyset} \forall_{type}[\lambda a : type.a \rightarrow_{tp} a] : type$ is derivable. A static constructor *sc* is a type constructor if it is assigned a sc-sort $[\sigma_1, \ldots, \sigma_n] \Rightarrow type$ for some sorts $\sigma_1, \ldots, \sigma_n$. For instance, $\mathbf{1}$, $\rightarrow_{tp}$, $\supset$, $\wedge$, $\forall_\sigma$ and $\exists_\sigma$ are all type constructors, but $\leq_{tp}$ is not. Intuitively, $\mathbf{1}$ represents the usual unit type and $\rightarrow_{tp}$ forms function types, and $\leq_{tp}$ stands for a subtyping relation on types. The static constructors $\supset$ and $\wedge$ form guarded types and asserting types, respectively, which are to be explained later.

We use Σ for a static variable context that assigns sorts to static variables; $\mathbf{dom}(\Sigma)$ is the set of static variables declared in Σ; $\Sigma(a) = \sigma$ if $a : \sigma$ is declared in Σ. As usual, a static variable a may be declared at most once in Σ. A static term s is called a *proposition* under Σ if $\Sigma \vdash s : bool$ is derivable. We use P for propositions (under some static variable contexts). We use the name *guarded type* for a type of the form $P \supset s$ and the name *asserting type* for a type of the form $P \wedge s$, both of which are involved in the following example.

Example 1. Let *int* be the sort for integers[1] and **list** be a type constructor of the sc-sort $[type, int] \Rightarrow type$. Then the following static term is a type:

$$\forall a : type.\forall n : int.\ n \geq 0 \supset (\mathbf{list}[a, n] \rightarrow_{tp} \mathbf{list}[a, n])$$

Intuitively, if $\mathbf{list}[s, n]$ is the type for lists of length n in which each element is of type s, then the above type is intended for a function from lists to lists that preserves list length. Also, the following type is intended to be assigned to a function that returns the tail of a given list if the list is not empty or simply raises an exception otherwise.

$$\forall a : type.\forall n : int.\ n \geq 0 \supset (\mathbf{list}[a, n] \rightarrow_{tp} n > 0 \wedge \mathbf{list}[a, n-1])$$

The asserting type $n > 0 \wedge \mathbf{list}[a, n-1]$ captures the invariant that $n > 0$ holds and the returned value is a list of length $n - 1$ *if the function returns* after it is applied to a list of length n. This is rather interesting feature and will be further explained later in Example 2. While there are already some traces of asserting types in the studies on Dependent ML [XP99,Xi98], the precise notion of asserting types has not be previously formalized: In DML, one must use subset sorts to simulate what we call asserting types here.

As in the design of $\mathcal{PTS}$, the issue of type equality plays a profound rôle in the design of $\mathcal{ATS}$. However, further study reveals that type equality in $\mathcal{ATS}$ can be defined in terms of a subtyping relation $\leq_{tp}$. Given two types s_1 and s_2, we say that s_1 equals s_2 if both the proposition $s_1 \leq_{tp} s_2$ and the proposition $s_2 \leq_{tp} s_1$ hold. In general, we need to determine whether a given proposition holds (under certain assumptions), and we introduce the following notion of constraint relation for this purpose.

[1] Formally speaking, we need to say that for each integer n, there is a static constructor $\underline{n}$ of the sc-sort $[] \Rightarrow int$ and $\underline{n}[]$ is the static term of the sort *int* that corresponds to n.

$$\frac{}{\Sigma; \boldsymbol{P} \models_{\mathcal{S}} \top}\ \textbf{(reg-true)} \qquad \frac{}{\Sigma; \boldsymbol{P}, \bot \models_{\mathcal{S}} P}\ \textbf{(reg-false)}$$

$$\frac{\Sigma; \boldsymbol{P} \models_{\mathcal{S}} P_0}{\Sigma, a:\sigma; \boldsymbol{P} \models_{\mathcal{S}} P_0}\ \textbf{(reg-var-thin)} \qquad \frac{\Sigma \vdash_{\mathcal{S}} P : bool \quad \Sigma; \boldsymbol{P} \models_{\mathcal{S}} P_0}{\Sigma; \boldsymbol{P}, P \models_{\mathcal{S}} P_0}\ \textbf{(reg-prop-thin)}$$

$$\frac{\Sigma, a:\sigma; \boldsymbol{P} \models_{\mathcal{S}} P \quad \Sigma \vdash_{\mathcal{S}} s : \sigma}{\Sigma; \boldsymbol{P}[a \mapsto s] \models_{\mathcal{S}} P[a \mapsto s]}\ \textbf{(reg-subst)} \qquad \frac{\Sigma; \boldsymbol{P} \models_{\mathcal{S}} P_0 \quad \Sigma; \boldsymbol{P}, P_0 \models_{\mathcal{S}} P}{\Sigma; \boldsymbol{P} \models_{\mathcal{S}} P}\ \textbf{(reg-cut)}$$

$$\frac{\Sigma \vdash_{\mathcal{S}} s : type}{\Sigma; \boldsymbol{P} \models_{\mathcal{S}} s \leq_{tp} s}\ \textbf{(reg-refl)} \qquad \frac{\Sigma; \boldsymbol{P} \models_{\mathcal{S}} s_1 \leq_{tp} s_2 \quad \Sigma; \boldsymbol{P} \models_{\mathcal{S}} s_2 \leq_{tp} s_3}{\Sigma; \boldsymbol{P} \models_{\mathcal{S}} s_1 \leq_{tp} s_3}\ \textbf{(reg-tran)}$$

Fig. 2. Regularity Rules

Definition 1. *Let $\mathcal{S}, \Sigma, \boldsymbol{P}, P_0$ be a static signature, a static variable context, a set of propositions under Σ and a proposition under Σ, respectively. We say a relation $\Sigma; \boldsymbol{P} \models_{\mathcal{S}} P_0$ is a regular constraint relation if the following regularity conditions are satisfied:*

1. *all the regularity rules in Figure 2 are valid; that is, for each regularity rule, the conclusion of the rule holds if the premises of the rule hold, and*
2. *$\Sigma; \boldsymbol{P} \models_{\mathcal{S}} s_1 \rightarrow_{tp} s_2 \leq_{tp} s'_1 \rightarrow_{tp} s'_2$ implies $\Sigma; \boldsymbol{P} \models_{\mathcal{S}} s'_1 \leq_{tp} s_1$ and $\Sigma; \boldsymbol{P} \models_{\mathcal{S}} s_2 \leq_{tp} s'_2$, and*
3. *$\Sigma; \boldsymbol{P} \models_{\mathcal{S}} P \supset s \leq_{tp} P' \supset s'$ implies $\Sigma; \boldsymbol{P}, P' \models_{\mathcal{S}} P$ and $\Sigma; \boldsymbol{P}, P' \models_{\mathcal{S}} s \leq_{tp} s'$, and*
4. *$\Sigma; \boldsymbol{P} \models_{\mathcal{S}} P \wedge s \leq_{tp} P' \wedge s'$ implies $\Sigma; \boldsymbol{P}, P \models_{\mathcal{S}} P'$ and $\Sigma; \boldsymbol{P}, P \models_{\mathcal{S}} s \leq_{tp} s'$, and*
5. *$\Sigma; \boldsymbol{P} \models_{\mathcal{S}} \forall a:\sigma.s \leq_{tp} \forall a:\sigma.s'$ implies $\Sigma, a:\sigma; \boldsymbol{P} \models_{\mathcal{S}} s \leq_{tp} s'$, and*
6. *$\Sigma; \boldsymbol{P} \models_{\mathcal{S}} \exists a:\sigma.s \leq_{tp} \exists a:\sigma.s'$ implies $\Sigma, a:\sigma; \boldsymbol{P} \models_{\mathcal{S}} s \leq_{tp} s'$, and*
7. *$\Sigma; \boldsymbol{P} \models_{\mathcal{S}} scc[s_1, \ldots, s_n] \leq_{tp} scc'[s'_1, \ldots, s'_{n'}]$ implies $scc = scc'$.*

Note that we assume $\Sigma \vdash_{\mathcal{S}} P : bool$ is derivable for each $P \in \boldsymbol{P}, P_0$ whenever we write $\Sigma; \boldsymbol{P} \models_{\mathcal{S}} P_0$.

We are in need of a regular constraint relation when forming the dynamics of ATS. Every single regularity rule as well as every single regularity condition is used later for establishing the subject reduction theorem (Theorem 1) and and the progress theorem (Theorem 2). In general, the framework $\mathcal{ATS}$ is parameterized over regular constraint relations. We need not be concerned with the decidability of a regular constraint relation at this point. For each regular constraint relation $\models_{\mathcal{S}}$, we may simply assume that an oracle is available to determine whether $\Sigma; \boldsymbol{P} \models_{\mathcal{S}} P_0$ holds whenever appropriate $\Sigma, \boldsymbol{P}$ and P_0 are given. Later, we will present some examples of applied type systems where there are practical algorithms for determining the regular constraint relations involved.

It should be emphasized that because of impredicativity, it is in general a rather delicate issue as to how a regular constraint relation $\models_{\mathcal{S}}$ can be properly defined for a given signature $\mathcal{S}$. In [Xi03], we have presented a model-theoretical approach to address this important issue.

2.2 Dynamics

The dynamics of ATS is a typed language and a static term of the sort *type* is a type in the dynamics. There may be some declared dynamic constants, and we are to assign a dc-type of the following form to each dynamic constant dc of arity n,

$$\forall a_1 : \sigma_1 \ldots \forall a_k : \sigma_k . P_1 \supset (\ldots (P_m \supset ([s_1, \ldots, s_n] \Rightarrow_{tp} s)) \ldots)$$

where $s_1, \ldots, s_n, s$ are assumed to be types. In the case where dc is a dynamic constructor dcc, the type s needs to be of the form $scc[\boldsymbol{s}]$ for some type constructor scc, and we say that dcc is associated with scc. Note that we use $\boldsymbol{s}$ for a (possibly empty) sequence of static terms. For instance, we can associate two dynamic constructors $\underline{nil}$ and $\underline{cons}$ with the type constructor **list** as follows by assigning them the following dc-types,

$$\begin{aligned} \underline{nil} &: \forall a : type.\mathbf{list}[a, 0] \\ \underline{cons} &: \forall a : type.\forall n : int.n \geq 0 \supset ([a, \mathbf{list}[a, n]] \Rightarrow_{tp} \mathbf{list}[a, n+1]) \end{aligned}$$

where we use $\mathbf{list}[a, n]$ as the type for lists of length n in which each element is of type a.

dyn. terms	$d ::= x \mid dc[d_1, \ldots, d_n] \mid \mathbf{lam}\ x.d \mid \mathbf{app}(d_1, d_2) \mid$
	$\supset^+(v) \mid \supset^-(d) \mid \wedge(d) \mid \mathbf{let}\ \wedge(x) = d_1\ \mathbf{in}\ d_2 \mid$
	$\forall^+(v) \mid \forall^-(d) \mid \exists(d) \mid \mathbf{let}\ \exists(x) = d_1\ \mathbf{in}\ d_2$
values	$v ::= x \mid dcc[v_1, \ldots, v_n] \mid \mathbf{lam}\ x.d \mid \supset^+(v) \mid \wedge(v) \mid \forall^+(v) \mid \exists(v)$
dyn. var. ctx.	$\Delta ::= \emptyset \mid \Delta, x : s$
dyn. subst.	$\Theta_D ::= [] \mid \Theta_D[x \mapsto d]$

Fig. 3. The syntax for dynamics

$$\frac{\vdash \mathcal{S}\ [sig]}{\Sigma \vdash_{\mathcal{S}} \emptyset\ [dctx]} \qquad \frac{\Sigma \vdash_{\mathcal{S}} \Delta\ [dctx] \quad \Sigma \vdash_{\mathcal{S}} s : type}{\Sigma \vdash_{\mathcal{S}} \Delta, x : s\ [dctx]}$$

Fig. 4. The formation rules for dynamic variable contexts

We use Θ_D for a dynamic substitution that maps dynamic variables to dynamic terms and $\mathbf{dom}(\Theta_D)$ for the domain of Θ_D. We omit presenting the syntax for forming and applying dynamic substitutions, which is similar to that for static substitutions. Given Θ_D^1 and Θ_D^2 such that $\mathbf{dom}(\Theta_D^1) \cap \mathbf{dom}(\Theta_D^2) = \emptyset$, we use $\Theta_D^1 \cup \Theta_D^2$ for the union of Θ_D^1 and Θ_D^2.

For $\Sigma = a_1 : \sigma_1, \ldots, a_k : \sigma_k$, we may write $\forall \Sigma.\bullet$ for $\forall a_1 : \sigma_1 \ldots \forall a_k : \sigma_k.\bullet$, where we simply use $\bullet$ for arbitrary syntax. Similarly, For $\boldsymbol{P} = P_1, \ldots, P_m$, we may use $\boldsymbol{P} \supset \bullet$ for $P_1 \supset (\ldots (P_m \supset \bullet) \ldots)$. For instance, a dc-type is always of the form $\forall \Sigma.\boldsymbol{P} \supset ([s_1, \ldots, s_n] \Rightarrow_{tp} s)$. The definition of signatures needs to be extended as follows to allow that dynamic constants be declared,

$$\text{signatures } \mathcal{S} ::= \ldots \mid \mathcal{S}, dc : \forall \Sigma.\boldsymbol{P} \supset ([s_1, \ldots, s_n] \Rightarrow_{tp} s)$$

and the following additional rule is needed to form signatures.

$$\frac{\vdash \mathcal{S}\ [sig] \quad \Sigma \vdash_{\mathcal{S}} P : bool \text{ for each } P \text{ in } \boldsymbol{P} \qquad \Sigma \vdash_{\mathcal{S}} s_i : type \text{ for each } 1 \leq i \leq n \quad \Sigma \vdash_{\mathcal{S}} s : type}{\vdash \mathcal{S}, dc : \forall \Sigma.\boldsymbol{P} \supset ([s_1, \ldots, s_n] \Rightarrow_{tp} s)\ [sig]}$$

The syntax for the dynamics is given in Figure 3, where we use x for dynamic term variables and d for dynamic terms. Given a dynamic constant dc of arity n, we write $dc[d_1, \ldots, d_n]$ for the application of dc to the arguments $d_1, \ldots, d_n$. In the case where $n = 0$, we may write dc for $dc[]$.

The markers $\supset^+(\cdot), \supset^-(\cdot), \wedge(\cdot), \forall^+(\cdot), \forall^-(\cdot), \exists(\cdot)$ are introduced to establish Lemma 3, which is needed for conducting inductive reasoning on typing derivations. Without these markers, it would be significantly more involved to establish proofs by induction on typing derivations as Lemma 3 can no longer be established as it is stated now.

A judgment of the form $\Sigma \vdash_{\mathcal{S}} \Delta\ [dctx]$ indicates that Δ is a well-formed dynamic variable context under Σ and $\mathcal{S}$. The rules for deriving such judgments are given in Figure 4. We use $\Sigma; \boldsymbol{P}; \Delta$ for a typing context. The following rule is for deriving a judgment of the form $\vdash_{\mathcal{S}} \Sigma; \boldsymbol{P}; \Delta$,

$$\frac{\Sigma \vdash_{\mathcal{S}} P : bool \text{ for each } P \text{ in } \boldsymbol{P} \quad \Sigma \vdash \Delta\ [dctx]}{\vdash_{\mathcal{S}} \Sigma; \boldsymbol{P}; \Delta}$$

which indicates that $\Sigma; \boldsymbol{P}; \Delta$ is well-formed.

A typing judgment is of the form $\Sigma; \boldsymbol{P}; \Delta \vdash_{\mathcal{S}} d : s$, where we assume that $\Sigma; \boldsymbol{P}; \Delta$ is a well-formed typing context and $\Sigma \vdash_{\mathcal{S}} s : type$ is derivable. The typing rules for deriving such judgments are presented in Figure 5, where we assume that the constraint relation $\models_{\mathcal{S}}$ is regular. We write $\Sigma \vdash_{\mathcal{S}} \Theta_{\mathcal{S}} : \Sigma_0$ to mean that $\Sigma \vdash_{\mathcal{S}} \Theta_{\mathcal{S}}(a) : \Sigma(a)$ is derivable for each $a \in \mathbf{dom}(\Theta_{\mathcal{S}}) = \mathbf{dom}(\Sigma)$. Note that we have omitted some obvious side conditions associated with some of the typing rules. For instance, the variable a is not allowed to have free occurrences in $\boldsymbol{P}$, Δ, or s when the rule **(ty-∀-intro)** is applied. Also, we have imposed a form of value restriction on the typing rules **(ty-gua-intro)** and **(ty-∀-intro)**, preparing for introducing effects into ATS later.[2] For a technical reason, we are to replace the rule **(ty-var)** with the following rule,

$$\frac{\vdash_{\mathcal{S}} \Sigma; \boldsymbol{P}; \Delta \quad \Delta(x) = s \quad \Sigma; \boldsymbol{P} \models_{\mathcal{S}} s \leq_{tp} s'}{\Sigma; \boldsymbol{P}; \Delta \vdash_{\mathcal{S}} x : s'} \ \textbf{(ty-var')}$$

which combines **(ty-var)** with **(ty-sub)**. This replacement is needed for establishing Lemma 2.

Before proceeding to the presentation of the rules for evaluating dynamic terms, we now sketch a scenario in which a guarded type and an asserting type play an interesting role in enforcing security, facilitating further understanding of such types.

---

2 Actually, it is already necessary to impose this form of value restriction on the typing rule **(ty-gua-intro)** in order to establish Theorem 2.

Example 2. Assume that $\underline{Secret}$ is a proposition constant and $\underline{password}$ and $\underline{action}$ are two declared functions, which are assigned the following dc-types.

$$\underline{action} : \underline{Secret} \supset [\mathbf{1}] \Rightarrow_{tp} \mathbf{1} \qquad \underline{password} : [\mathbf{1}] \Rightarrow_{tp} \underline{Secret} \wedge \mathbf{1}$$

The function $\underline{password}$ can be implemented in a manner so that some secret information must be verified before a call to $\underline{password}$ returns. On one hand, the proposition $\underline{Secret}$ needs to be established before the function call $\underline{action}[\langle\rangle]$ can be made, where $\langle\rangle$ denotes the value of the unit type $\mathbf{1}$. On the other hand, the proposition $\underline{Secret}$ is established after the function call $\underline{password}[\langle\rangle]$ returns. Therefore, a proper means to calling $\underline{action}$ is through the following program pattern:

$$\mathbf{let}\ \wedge(x) = \underline{password}[\langle\rangle]\ \mathbf{in}\ \ldots \underline{action}[\langle\rangle] \ldots$$

In particular, a call to $\underline{action}$ outside the scope of x is ill-typed since the proposition $\underline{Secret}$ cannot be established.

$$\frac{\Sigma; \boldsymbol{P}; \Delta \vdash_S d : s \quad \Sigma; \boldsymbol{P} \models_S s \leq_{tp} s'}{\Sigma; \boldsymbol{P}; \Delta \vdash_S d : s'} \ \textbf{(ty-sub)}$$

$$\frac{\begin{array}{c}\vdash_S \Sigma; \boldsymbol{P}; \Delta \qquad \mathcal{S}(dc) = \forall \Sigma_0.\boldsymbol{P}_0 \supset [s_1, \ldots, s_n] \Rightarrow_{tp} s \\ \Sigma \vdash_S \Theta_S : \Sigma_0 \qquad \Sigma; \boldsymbol{P} \models_S P[\Theta_S] \ \text{for each } P \in \boldsymbol{P}_0 \\ \Sigma; \boldsymbol{P}; \Delta \vdash_S d_i : s_i[\Theta_S] \ \text{for } i = 1, \ldots, n \qquad \Sigma; \boldsymbol{P} \models_S s[\Theta_S] \leq_{tp} s'\end{array}}{\Sigma; \boldsymbol{P}; \Delta \vdash_S dc[d_1, \ldots, d_n] : s'} \ \textbf{(ty-dc)}$$

$$\frac{\vdash_S \Sigma; \boldsymbol{P}; \Delta \quad \Delta(x) = s \quad \Sigma; \boldsymbol{P} \models_S s \leq_{tp} s'}{\Sigma; \boldsymbol{P}; \Delta \vdash_S x : s'} \ \textbf{(ty-var)}$$

$$\frac{\Sigma; \boldsymbol{P}; \Delta, x : s_1 \vdash_S d : s_2}{\Sigma; \boldsymbol{P}; \Delta \vdash_S \mathbf{lam}\ x.d : s_1 \rightarrow_{tp} s_2} \ \textbf{(ty-fun-intro)}$$

$$\frac{\Sigma; \boldsymbol{P}; \Delta \vdash_S d_1 : s_1 \rightarrow_{tp} s_2 \quad \Sigma; \boldsymbol{P}; \Delta \vdash_S d_2 : s_1}{\Sigma; \boldsymbol{P}; \Delta \vdash_S \mathbf{app}(d_1, d_2) : s_2} \ \textbf{(ty-fun-elim)}$$

$$\frac{\Sigma; \boldsymbol{P}, P; \Delta \vdash_S d : s}{\Sigma; \boldsymbol{P}; \Delta \vdash_S \supset^+(d) : P \supset s} \ \textbf{(ty-gua-intro)}$$

$$\frac{\Sigma; \boldsymbol{P}; \Delta \vdash_S d : P \supset s \quad \Sigma; \boldsymbol{P} \models_S P}{\Sigma; \boldsymbol{P}; \Delta \vdash_S \supset^-(d) : s} \ \textbf{(ty-gua-elim)}$$

$$\frac{\Sigma; \boldsymbol{P} \models_S P \quad \Sigma; \boldsymbol{P}; \Delta \vdash_S d : s}{\Sigma; \boldsymbol{P}; \Delta \vdash_S \wedge(d) : P \wedge s} \ \textbf{(ty-ass-intro)}$$

$$\frac{\Sigma; \boldsymbol{P}; \Delta \vdash_S d_1 : P \wedge s_1 \quad \Sigma; \boldsymbol{P}, P; \Delta, x : s_1 \vdash_S d_2 : s_2}{\Sigma; \boldsymbol{P}; \Delta \vdash_S \mathbf{let}\ \wedge(x) = d_1\ \mathbf{in}\ d_2 : s_2} \ \textbf{(ty-ass-elim)}$$

$$\frac{\Sigma, a : \sigma; \boldsymbol{P}; \Delta \vdash_S v : s}{\Sigma; \boldsymbol{P}; \Delta \vdash_S \forall^+(v) : \forall a : \sigma.s} \ \textbf{(ty-}\forall\textbf{-intro)}$$

$$\frac{\Sigma; \boldsymbol{P}; \Delta \vdash_S d : \forall a : \sigma.s \quad \Sigma \vdash_S s_0 : \sigma}{\Sigma; \boldsymbol{P}; \Delta \vdash_S \forall^-(d) : s[a \mapsto s_0]} \ \textbf{(ty-}\forall\textbf{-elim)}$$

$$\frac{\Sigma \vdash_S s_0 : \sigma \quad \Sigma; \boldsymbol{P}; \Delta \vdash_S d : s[a \mapsto s_0]}{\Sigma; \boldsymbol{P}; \Delta \vdash_S \exists(d) : \exists a : \sigma.s} \ \textbf{(ty-}\exists\textbf{-intro)}$$

$$\frac{\Sigma; \boldsymbol{P}; \Delta \vdash_S d_1 : \exists a : \sigma.s_1 \quad \Sigma, a : \sigma; \boldsymbol{P}; \Delta, x : s_1 \vdash_S d_2 : s_2}{\Sigma; \boldsymbol{P}; \Delta \vdash_S \mathbf{let}\ \exists(x) = d_1\ \mathbf{in}\ d_2 : s_2} \ \textbf{(ty-}\exists\textbf{-elim)}$$

Fig. 5. The typing rules for the dynamics

In order to assign a call-by-value dynamic semantics to dynamic terms, we make use of evaluation contexts, which are defined below:

$$\text{eval. ctx. } E ::= [] \mid dc[v_1, \ldots, v_{i-1}, E, d_{i+1}, \ldots, d_n] \mid \mathbf{app}(E, d) \mid \mathbf{app}(v, E) \mid \supset^-(E) \mid \forall^-(E) \mid \wedge(E) \mid \mathbf{let}\ \wedge(x) = E\ \mathbf{in}\ d \mid \exists(E) \mid \mathbf{let}\ \exists(x) = E\ \mathbf{in}\ d$$

Definition 2. *We define redexes and their reductions as follows.*

- $\mathbf{app}(\mathbf{lam}\ x.d, v)$ *is a redex, and its reduction is* $d[x \mapsto v]$.
- $\supset^-(\supset^+(v))$ *is a redex, and its reduction is* v.
- $\mathbf{let}\ \wedge(x) = \wedge(v)\ \mathbf{in}\ d$ *is a redex, and its reduction is* $d[x \mapsto v]$.
- $\forall^-(\forall^+(v))$ *is a redex, and its reduction is* v.
- $\mathbf{let}\ \exists(x) = \exists(v)\ \mathbf{in}\ d$ *is a redex, and its reduction is* $d[x \mapsto v]$.
- $dcf[v_1, \ldots, v_n]$ *is a redex if* $dcf[v_1, \ldots, v_n]$ *is defined to equal some value* v, *and its reduction is* v.

Given two dynamic terms d_1 *and* d_2 *such that* $d_1 = E[d]$ *and* $d_2 = E[d']$ *for some redex* d *and its reduction* d', *we write* $d_1 \hookrightarrow d_2$ *and say that* d_1 *reduces to* d_2 *in one step. We use* $\hookrightarrow^*$ *for the reflexive and transitive closure of* $\hookrightarrow$.

We assume that the type assgined to each dynamic constant function dcf is appropriate, that is, $\emptyset; \emptyset; \emptyset \vdash_S v : s$ is derivable if $\emptyset; \emptyset; \emptyset \vdash_S dcf[v_1, \ldots, v_n] : s$ is derivable and $dcf[v_1, \ldots, v_n] \hookrightarrow v$ holds.

Given a judgment J, we write $\mathcal{D} :: J$ to indicate that $\mathcal{D}$ is a derivation of J, that is, $\mathcal{D}$ is a derivation whose conclusion is J.

Lemma 1 (Substitution). *We have the following.*

1. *Assume* $\mathcal{D} :: \Sigma, a : \sigma; \boldsymbol{P}; \Delta \vdash_S d : s$ *and* $\mathcal{D}_0 :: \Sigma \vdash_S s_0 : \sigma$. *Then* $\Sigma; \boldsymbol{P}[a \mapsto s_0]; \Delta[a \mapsto s_0] \vdash_S d : s[a \mapsto s_0]$ *is derivable.*
2. *Assume* $\mathcal{D} :: \Sigma; \boldsymbol{P}, P; \Delta \vdash_S d : s$ *and* $\Sigma; \boldsymbol{P} \models_S P$. *Then* $\Sigma; \boldsymbol{P}; \Delta \vdash_S d : s$ *is derivable.*
3. *Assume* $\mathcal{D} :: \Sigma; \boldsymbol{P}; \Delta, x : s_1 \vdash_S d_2 : s_2$ *and* $\Sigma; \boldsymbol{P}; \Delta \vdash_S d_1 : s_1$. *Then* $\Sigma; \boldsymbol{P}; \Delta \vdash_S d_2[x \mapsto d_1] : s_2$ *is derivable.*

Proof. We can readily prove (1), (2) and (3) by structural induction on $\mathcal{D}$. When proving (1) and (2), we need to make use of the regularity rules **(reg-subst)** and **(reg-cut)**, respectively.

Given a derivation $\mathcal{D}$, we use $\mathbf{h}(\mathcal{D})$ for the height of $\mathcal{D}$, which can be defined in a standard manner.

Lemma 2. *Assume* $\mathcal{D} :: \Sigma; \boldsymbol{P}; \Delta, x : s_1 \vdash_S d : s_2$ *and* $\Sigma; \boldsymbol{P} \models_S s_1' \leq_{tp} s_1$. *Then there is a derivation* $\mathcal{D}' :: \Sigma; \boldsymbol{P}; \Delta, x : s_1' \vdash_S d : s_2$ *such that* $\mathbf{h}(\mathcal{D}') = \mathbf{h}(\mathcal{D})$.

Proof. The proof follows from structural induction on $\mathcal{D}$ immediately. The regularity rule **(reg-trans)** is used to handle the case where the last applied rule in $\mathcal{D}$ is **(ty-var')**.

The following inversion is slightly different from a standard one because of the existence of the rule **(tyrule-eq)**.

Lemma 3 (Inversion). *Assume* $\mathcal{D} :: \Sigma; \boldsymbol{P}; \Delta \vdash_{\mathcal{S}} d : s$.

1. *If* $d = \mathbf{lam}\ x.d_1$ *and* $s = s_1 \rightarrow_{tp} s_2$, *then there is a derivation* $\mathcal{D}' :: \Sigma; \boldsymbol{P}; \Delta \vdash_{\mathcal{S}} d : s$ *such that* $\mathbf{h}(\mathcal{D}') \leq \mathbf{h}(\mathcal{D})$ *and the last rule applied in* $\mathcal{D}'$ *is not* **(ty-sub)**.
2. *If* $d = \supset^+(d_1)$ *and* $s = P \supset s_1$, *then there is a derivation* $\mathcal{D}' :: \Sigma; \boldsymbol{P}; \Delta \vdash_{\mathcal{S}} d : s$ *such that* $\mathbf{h}(\mathcal{D}') \leq \mathbf{h}(\mathcal{D})$ *and the last rule applied in* $\mathcal{D}'$ *is not* **(ty-sub)**.
3. *If* $d = \wedge(d_1)$ *and* $s = P \wedge s_1$, *then there is a derivation* $\mathcal{D}' :: \Sigma; \boldsymbol{P}; \Delta \vdash_{\mathcal{S}} d : s$ *such that* $\mathbf{h}(\mathcal{D}') \leq \mathbf{h}(\mathcal{D})$ *and the last rule applied in* $\mathcal{D}'$ *is not* **(ty-sub)**.
4. *If* $d = \forall^+(d_1)$ *and* $s = \forall a : \sigma.s_1$, *then there is a derivation* $\mathcal{D}' :: \Sigma; \boldsymbol{P}; \Delta \vdash_{\mathcal{S}} d : s$ *such that* $\mathbf{h}(\mathcal{D}') \leq \mathbf{h}(\mathcal{D})$ *and the last rule applied in* $\mathcal{D}'$ *is not* **(ty-sub)**.
5. *If* $d = \exists(d_1)$ *and* $s = \exists a : \sigma.s_1$, *then there is a derivation* $\mathcal{D}' :: \Sigma; \boldsymbol{P}; \Delta \vdash_{\mathcal{S}} d : s$ *such that* $\mathbf{h}(\mathcal{D}') \leq \mathbf{h}(\mathcal{D})$ *and the last rule applied in* $\mathcal{D}'$ *is not* **(ty-sub)**.

Proof. By induction by $\mathbf{h}(\mathcal{D})$. In particular, Lemma 2 is needed to establish (1).

The type soundess of ATS rests upon the following two theorems, who proofs are largely standard and thus omitted here.

Theorem 1 (Subject Reduction). *Assume both* $\mathcal{D} :: \Sigma; \boldsymbol{P}; \Delta \vdash_{\mathcal{S}} d : s$ *and* $d \hookrightarrow d'$. *Then* $\Sigma; \boldsymbol{P}; \Delta \vdash_{\mathcal{S}} d : s$ *is derivable.*

Theorem 2 (Progress). *Assume* $\mathcal{D} :: \emptyset; \emptyset; \emptyset \vdash_{\mathcal{S}} d : s$. *Then* d *is a value, or* $d \hookrightarrow d'$ *holds for some dynamic term* d', *or* $d = E[dcf(v_1, \ldots, v_n)]$ *for some dynamic term* $dcf(v_1, \ldots, v_n)$ *that is not a redex.*

2.3 Erasure

We present a function from dynamic terms to untyped λ-expressions that preserves semantics. We use e for the erasures of dynamic terms, which are formally defined as follows:

$$\begin{array}{ll} \text{erasures} & e ::= x \mid dc[e_1, \ldots, e_n] \mid \mathbf{lam}\ x.e \mid \mathbf{app}(e_1, e_2) \mid \mathbf{let}\ x = e_1\ \mathbf{in}\ e_2 \\ \text{erasure values} & w ::= x \mid dcc\,[w_1, \ldots, w_n] \mid \mathbf{lam}\ x.e \end{array}$$

We can then define a function $|\cdot|$ as follows that translates dynamic terms into erasures.

$$\begin{array}{rclrcl} |x| &=& x & |dc[d_1, \ldots, d_n]| &=& dc[|d_1|, \ldots, |d_n|] \\ |\mathbf{lam}\ x.d| &=& \mathbf{lam}\ x.|d| & |\mathbf{app}(d_1, d_2)| &=& \mathbf{app}(|d_1|, |d_2|) \\ |\supset^+(d)| &=& |d| & |\supset^-(d)| &=& |d| \\ |\wedge(d)| &=& |d| & |\mathbf{let}\ \wedge(x) = d_1\ \mathbf{in}\ d_2| &=& \mathbf{let}\ x = |d_1|\ \mathbf{in}\ |d_2| \\ |\forall^+(d)| &=& |d| & |\forall^-(d)| &=& |d| \\ |\exists(d)| &=& |d| & |\mathbf{let}\ \exists(x) = d_1\ \mathbf{in}\ d_2| &=& \mathbf{let}\ x = |d_1|\ \mathbf{in}\ |d_2| \end{array}$$

Similar to assigning dynamic semantics to the dynamic terms, we can readily assign dynamic semantics to the erasures, which are just untyped λ-expressions. We write $e_1 \hookrightarrow e_2$ to mean that e_1 reduces to e_2 in one step, and use $\hookrightarrow^*$ for the reflexive and transitive closure of $\hookrightarrow$.

Theorem 3. *Assume* $\mathcal{D} :: \emptyset; \emptyset; \emptyset \vdash_S d : s$.

1. *If* $d \hookrightarrow^* v$, *then* $|d| \hookrightarrow^* |v|$.
2. *If* $|d| \hookrightarrow^* w$, *then there is a value* v *such that* $d \hookrightarrow^* v$ *and* $|v| = w$.

Proof. (1) is straightforward and (2) follows from structural induction on $\mathcal{D}$.

With Theorem 3, we can evaluate a dynamic term d by simply evaluating the erasure of d.

3 Extensions

We extend $\mathcal{ATS}$ to accommodate some common realistic programming features in this section.

General Recursion. We introduce a fixed-point operator **fix** to support general recursion in $\mathcal{ATS}$. We now call variables x **lam**-variables and introduce **fix**-variables f. We use xf for a variable that is either a **lam**-variable or a **fix**-variable.

$$\begin{array}{lrl} \text{dyn. terms} & d ::= & \ldots \mid f \mid \mathbf{fix}\ f.d \\ \text{dyn. var. ctx.} & \Delta ::= & \ldots \mid \Delta, f : s \\ \text{dyn. subst.} & \Theta_D ::= & \ldots \mid \Theta_D[f \mapsto d] \end{array}$$

The rule **(ty-var)** needs to be modified and the rule **(tyrule-fix)** needs to be added to handle the fixed-point operator:

$$\frac{\vdash_S \Sigma; \boldsymbol{P}; \Delta \quad \Delta(xf) = s}{\Sigma; \boldsymbol{P}; \Delta \vdash_S xf : s'}\ \textbf{(ty-var)} \qquad \frac{\Sigma; \boldsymbol{P}; \Delta, f : s \vdash_S d : s}{\Sigma; \boldsymbol{P}; \Delta \vdash_S \mathbf{fix}\ f.d : s}\ \textbf{(ty-fix)}$$

A dynamic term of the form **fix** $f.d$ is a redex and its reduction is $d[f \mapsto \mathbf{fix}\ f.d]$. It is straightforward to establish both the subject reduction theorem (Theorem 1) and the progress theorem (Theorem 2) for this extension.

Datatypes and Pattern Matching. We present an approach to extending $\mathcal{ATS}$ with support for datatypes and pattern matching and then provide with some simple examples. The following is some additional syntax we need.

$$\begin{array}{lrl} \text{patterns} & p ::= & x \mid dcc\,[p_1, \ldots, p_n] \\ \text{dyn. terms} & d ::= & \ldots \mid \mathbf{case}\ d_0\ \mathbf{of}\ p_1 \Rightarrow d_1 \mid \cdots \mid p_n \Rightarrow d_n \\ \text{eval. ctx.} & E ::= & \ldots \mid \mathbf{case}\ E\ \mathbf{of}\ p_1 \Rightarrow d_1 \mid \cdots \mid p_n \Rightarrow d_n \end{array}$$

As usual, we require that any variable x can occur at most once in a pattern. Given a value v and a pattern p, we use a judgment of the form $v \Downarrow p \Rightarrow \Theta_D$ to indicate $v = p[\Theta_D]$. The rules for deriving such judgments are given as follows,

$$\frac{}{v \Downarrow x \Rightarrow [x \mapsto v]}\ \textbf{(vp-var)} \qquad \frac{v_i \Downarrow p_i \Rightarrow \Theta_D^i \quad \text{for } 1 \leq i \leq n}{dcc\,[v_1, \ldots, v_n] \Downarrow dcc\,[p_1, \ldots, p_n] \Rightarrow \Theta_D^1 \cup \ldots \cup \Theta_D^n}\ \textbf{(vp-dcc)}$$

and we say that v matches p if $v \Downarrow p \Rightarrow \Theta_D$ is derivable for some dynamic substitution Θ_D. Note that in the rule **(vp-dcc)**, the union $\Theta_D^1 \cup \ldots \cup \Theta_D^n$, which becomes the empty dynamic substitution $[]$ when $n = 0$, is well-defined since any variable can occur at most once in a pattern.

A dynamic term of the form **case** v **of** $p_1 \Rightarrow d_1 \mid \cdots \mid p_n \Rightarrow d_n$ is a redex if $v \Downarrow p_i \Rightarrow \Theta_D$ holds for some $1 \leq i \leq n$, and its reduction is $d_i[\Theta_D]$. Note that reducing such a redex may involve nondeterminism if v matches several patterns p_i.

$$\frac{\Sigma \vdash_S s : type}{\Sigma \vdash x \Downarrow s \Rightarrow \emptyset; \emptyset; \emptyset, x : s} \ \textbf{(pat-var)}$$

$$\frac{\begin{array}{c} \mathcal{S}(dcc) = \forall \Sigma_0.\boldsymbol{P}_0 \supset ([s_1, \ldots, s_n] \Rightarrow_{tp} scc[\boldsymbol{s}_0]) \\ \Sigma, \Sigma_0 \vdash p_i \Downarrow s_i \Rightarrow \Sigma_i; \boldsymbol{P}_i; \Delta_i \quad \text{for } 1 \leq i \leq n \\ \Sigma' = \Sigma_1, \ldots, \Sigma_n \quad \boldsymbol{P}' = \boldsymbol{P}_1, \ldots, \boldsymbol{P}_n \quad \Delta' = \Delta_1, \ldots, \Delta_n \end{array}}{\Sigma \vdash dcc[p_1, \ldots, p_n] \Downarrow scc[\boldsymbol{s}] \Rightarrow \Sigma_0, \Sigma'; \boldsymbol{P}_0, scc[\boldsymbol{s}_0] \leq_{tp} scc[\boldsymbol{s}], \boldsymbol{P}'; \Delta'} \ \textbf{(pat-dc)}$$

$$\frac{\Sigma \vdash p \Downarrow s_1 \Rightarrow \Sigma'; \boldsymbol{P}'; \Delta' \quad \Sigma, \Sigma'; \boldsymbol{P}, \boldsymbol{P}'; \Delta, \Delta' \vdash_S d : s_2}{\Sigma; \boldsymbol{P}; \Delta \vdash p \Rightarrow d \Downarrow s_1 \Rightarrow s_2} \ \textbf{(ty-cla)}$$

$$\frac{\Sigma; \boldsymbol{P}; \Delta \vdash_S d_0 : s_1 \quad \Sigma; \boldsymbol{P}; \Delta \vdash p_i \Downarrow d_i : s_1 \Rightarrow s_2 \quad \text{for } 1 \leq i \leq n}{\Sigma; \boldsymbol{P}; \Delta \vdash_S (\textbf{case } d_0 \textbf{ of } p_1 \Rightarrow d_1 \mid \cdots \mid p_n \Rightarrow d_n) : s_2} \ \textbf{(ty-cas)}$$

Fig. 6. The typing rules for pattern matching

The typing rules for pattern matching is given in Figure 6. The meaning of a judgment of the form $\Sigma \vdash p \Downarrow s \Rightarrow \Sigma'; \boldsymbol{P}'; \Delta'$ is formally captured in the following lemma.

Lemma 4. *Assume* $\mathcal{D} :: \emptyset; \emptyset; \emptyset \vdash_S v : s$, $\mathcal{E}_1 :: \emptyset \vdash p \Downarrow s \vdash \Sigma; \boldsymbol{P}; \Delta$ *and* $\mathcal{E}_2 :: v \Downarrow p \Rightarrow \Theta_D$. *Then there exists* $\Theta_S : \Sigma$ *such that* $\emptyset; \emptyset \models_S P[\Theta_S]$ *for each* P *in* $\boldsymbol{P}$ *and* $\emptyset; \emptyset; \emptyset \vdash_S \Theta_D : \Delta$.

Proof. The lemma follows from structural induction on $\mathcal{E}_1$.

As an example, the judgment below is derivable,

$$a' : type, n' : int \vdash \underline{cons}[x_1, x_2] \Downarrow \textbf{list}[a', n'] \Rightarrow \Sigma; \boldsymbol{P}; \Delta$$

where $\underline{cons}$ is assigned the following dc-type,

$$\forall a : type. \forall n : int. n \geq 0 \supset ([a, \textbf{list}[a, n]] \Rightarrow_{tp} \textbf{list}[a, n+1])$$

and $\Sigma = (a : type, n : int)$, $\boldsymbol{P} = (n \geq 0, \textbf{list}[a, n+1] \leq_{tp} \textbf{list}[a', n'])$ and $\Delta = (x_1 : a, x_2 : \textbf{list}[a, n])$.

We can readily prove the subject reduction theorem (Theorem 1) for this extension: Lemma 4 is needed to handle the case where the reduced index is of the following form:

$$\textbf{case } d_0 \textbf{ of } p_1 \Rightarrow d_1 \mid \ldots \mid p_n \Rightarrow d_n$$

Also, we can establish the progress theorem (Theorem 2) for this extension after slightly modifying it to include the possibility that a well-type program d

may be of the following form,

$$E[\textbf{case } v_0 \textbf{ of } p_1 \Rightarrow d_1 \mid \ldots \mid p_n \Rightarrow d_n]$$

where v_0 does not match any p_i for $1 \leq i \leq n$ if d is neither a value nor can be further reduced.

Effects. Unlike $\mathcal{PTS}$, $\mathcal{ATS}$ can be extended in a straightforward manner to accommodate effects such as references and exceptions. For instance, to introduce references into $\mathcal{ATS}$, we can simply declare a type constructor *ref* of the sc-sort $[type] \Rightarrow type$ and then the following dynamic functions of the corresponding assigned dc-types.

$$\begin{aligned} mkref &: \forall a : type.[a] \Rightarrow_{tp} ref(a) \\ deref &: \forall a : type.[ref(a)] \Rightarrow_{tp} a \\ assign &: \forall a : type.[ref(a), a] \Rightarrow_{tp} \mathbf{1} \end{aligned}$$

The intended meaning of these functions should be obvious. We also need to add into Definition 1 the following regularity condition to address the issue of *ref* being an invariant type constructor.

- $\Sigma; \boldsymbol{P} \models_{\mathcal{S}} ref(s) \leq_{tp} ref(s')$ implies $\Sigma; \boldsymbol{P} \models_{\mathcal{S}} s \leq_{tp} s'$ and $\Sigma; \boldsymbol{P} \models_{\mathcal{S}} s' \leq_{tp} s$.

It is a standard procedure to assign dynamic semantics to this extension and then establish both the subject reduction theorem and the progress theorem. Please see [Har94] for some details on such a procedure.

It is straightforward as well to introduce exceptions into $\mathcal{ATS}$, and we omit further details.

4 Examples of Applied Type Systems

Unsurprizingly, it can be readily shown that the systems λ_2 and λ_ω in λ-cube [Bar92] are applied type systems. Also, the language $\lambda_{G\mu}$ [XCC03], which extends λ_2 with guarded recursive datatypes, and Dependent ML [XP99] are applied type systems. Please see [Xi03] for more detailed explanation.

5 Related Work and Conclusion

The framework $\mathcal{ATS}$ is rooted in the work on Dependent ML [XP99,Xi98], where the type system of ML is enriched with a restricted form of dependent datatypes, and the recent work on guarded recursive datatypes [XCC03]. Given the similarity between these two forms of types[3], we are naturally led to seeking a unified presentation for them.

For those who are familiar with qualified types [Jon94], which underlies the type class mechanism in Haskell, we point out that a qualified type can *not* be regarded as a guarded type. The simple reason is that the proof of a guard in an applied type system bears no computational meaning, that is, it cannot affect

[3] Actually, guarded recursive datatypes may be thought of as "dependent types" in which the type indexes are also types.

the run-time behavior of a program, while a dictionary, which is really the proof of some predicate on types in the setting of qualified types, can and is mostly likely to affect the run-time behaviour of a program.

Another line of closely related work is the formation of a type system in support of certified binaries [SSTP02], in which the idea of a complete separation between types and programs is also employed. Basically, the notions of type language and computational language in the type system correspond to the notions of statics and dynamics in $\mathcal{ATS}$, respectively, though the type language is based on the calculus of constructions extended with inductive definitions (CiC) [PPM89,PM93]. However, the notion of a constraint relation in $\mathcal{ATS}$ does not have a counterpart in [SSTP02]. Instead, the equality between two types is determined by comparing the normal forms of these types. It is not difficult to see that an applied type system can also be constructed to certify binaries in the sense of [SSTP02] as long as we have an approach to effectively representing and verifying proofs of the constraint relation associated with the applied type system.

In summary, we have presented a framework $\mathcal{ATS}$ for facilitating the design and formalization of type systems to support practical programming. With a complete separation between statics and dynamics, $\mathcal{ATS}$ works particularly well on supporting dependent types in the presence of effects. Also, the availability of guarded types and asserting types in $\mathcal{ATS}$ makes it both more flexible and more effective to capture program invariants. We also see $\mathcal{ATS}$ as a unification as well as a generalization of the previous work on a restricted form of dependent types [XP99,Xi98] and guarded recursive datatypes [XCC03].

A static component in $\mathcal{ATS}$ is currently based on a simply typed λ-calculus. Therefore, it is natural to study how a static component can be built upon a typed λ-calculus supporting polymorphism and/or dependent types. Also, we are particularly interested in designing and implementing a functional programming language with a type system based on $\mathcal{ATS}$, which can then offer a means to language extension by mostly implementing new language constructs in terms of some existing ones.

Acknowledgments. The author thanks Assaf Kfoury for his comments on a preliminary draft of the paper and also acknowledges some discussions with Chiyan Chen on the subject of the paper.

References

[Bar92] Hendrik Pieter Barendregt. Lambda calculi with types. In S. Abramsky, Dov M. Gabbay, and T.S.E. Maibaum, editors, *Handbook of Logic in Computer Science*, volume II, pages 117–441. Clarendon Press, Oxford, 1992.

[CS87] Robert L. Constable and Scott Fraser Smith. Partial objects in constructive type theory. In *Proceedings of Symposium on Logic in Computer Science*, pages 183–193. Ithaca, New York, June 1987.

[CX03] Chiyan Chen and Hongwei Xi. Meta-Programming through Typeful Code Representation. In *Proceedings of the Eighth ACM SIGPLAN International Conference on Functional Programming*, pages 169–180. Uppsala, Sweden, August 2003.

[Har94] Robert Harper. A simplified account of polymorphic references. *Information Processing Letters*, 51:201–206, 1994.

[HMST95] Furio Honsell, Ian A. Mason, Scott Smith, and Carolyn Talcott. A variable typed logic of effects. *Information and Computation*, 119(1):55–90, 15 May 1995.

[HN88] Susumu Hayashi and Hiroshi Nakano. *PX: A Computational Logic.* The MIT Press, 1988.

[Jon94] Mark P. Jones. *Qualified Types: Theory and Practice.* Cambridge University Press, The Edinburgh Building, Cambridge CB2 2RU, UK, November 1994.

[Men87] N.P. Mendler. Recursive types and type constraints in second-order lambda calculus. In *Proceedings of Symposium on Logic in Computer Science*, pages 30–36. The Computer Society of the IEEE, Ithaca, New York, June 1987.

[PM93] Christine Paulin-Mohring. Inductive Definitions in the System Coq: Rules and Properties. In M. Bezem and J.F. de Groote, editors, *Proceedings of the International Conference on Typed Lambda Calculi and Applications*, volume 664 of *Lecture Notes in Computer Science*, pages 328–345. Utrecht, The Netherlands, 1993.

[PPM89] Frank Pfenning and Christine Paulin-Mohring. Inductively defined types in the Calculus of Constructions. In *Proceedings of fifth International Conference on Mathematical Foundations of Programming Semantics*, volume 442 of *Lecture Notes in Computer Science*, pages 209–228, 1989.

[SSTP02] Zhong Shao, Bratin Saha, Valery Trifonov, and Nikolaos Papaspyrou. A Type System for Certified Binaries. In *Proceedings of 29th Annual ACM SIGPLAN Symposium on Principles of Programming Languages (POPL '02)*, pages 217–232. Portland, OR, January 2002.

[XCC02] Hongwei Xi, Chiyan Chen, and Gang Chen. Guarded Recursive Datatype Constructors, 2002. Available at
`http://www.cs.bu.edu/ hwxi/GRecTypecon/`.

[XCC03] Hongwei Xi, Chiyan Chen, and Gang Chen. Guarded recursive datatype constructors. In *Proceedings of the 30th ACM SIGPLAN Symposium on Principles of Programming Languages*, pages 224–235. New Orleans, January 2003.

[Xi98] Hongwei Xi. *Dependent Types in Practical Programming.* PhD thesis, Carnegie Mellon University, 1998. viii+181 pp. pp. viii+189. Available as `http://www.cs.cmu.edu/ hwxi/DML/thesis.ps`.

[Xi03] Hongwei Xi. Applied Type System, July 2003. Available at:
`http://www.cs.bu.edu/ hwxi/ATS/ATS.ps`.

[XP99] Hongwei Xi and Frank Pfenning. Dependent Types in Practical Programming. In *Proceedings of 26th ACM SIGPLAN Symposium on Principles of Programming Languages*, pages 214–227. San Antonio, Texas, January 1999.

[Zen97] Christoph Zenger. Indexed types. *Theoretical Computer Science*, 187: 147–165, 1997.

Author Index

Adams, Robin 1
Alessi, Fabio 17

Ballarin, Clemens 34
Barbanera, Franco 17
Baro, Sylvain 51
Berghofer, Stefan 66
Bertot, Yves 309
Bettini, Lorenzo 83
Bono, Viviana 83, 99
Brady, Edwin 115

Cervesato, Iliano 355
Chemouil, David 338
Chrząszcz, Jacek 130
Cirstea, Horatiu 147
Corbineau, Pierre 162

Dal Lago, Ugo 178
Dezani-Ciancaglini, Mariangiola 17

Espírito Santo, José 194

Gambino, Nicola 210
Ghilezan, Silvia 226

Honsell, Furio 242, 324
Hyland, Martin 210

Kießling, Robert 259

Lenisa, Marina 242
Lescanne, Pierre 226
Likavec, Silvia 83
Liquori, Luigi 147
Luo, Yong 276
Luo, Zhaohui 259, 276

Martini, Simone 178
McBride, Conor 115
McKinna, James 115
Momigliano, Alberto 293

Niqui, Milad 309

Pfenning, Frank 355
Pinto, Luís 194

Roversi, Luca 178

Scagnetto, Ivan 324
Soloviev, Sergej 338

Tiu, Alwen 293
Tiuryn, Jerzy 99

Urzyczyn, Paweł 99

Wack, Benjamin 147
Walker, David 355
Watkins, Kevin 355
Wiedijk, Freek 378

Xi, Hongwei 394

Lecture Notes in Computer Science

For information about Vols. 1–2985

please contact your bookseller or Springer-Verlag

Vol. 3092: J. Eckstein, H. Baumeister (Eds.), Extreme Programming and Agile Processes in Software Engineering. XVI, 358 pages. 2004.

Vol. 3091: V. van Oostrom (Ed.), Rewriting Techniques and Applications. X, 313 pages. 2004.

Vol. 3089: M. Jakobsson, M. Yung, J. Zhou (Eds.), Applied Cryptography and Network Security. XIV, 510 pages. 2004.

Vol. 3085: S. Berardi, M. Coppo, F. Damiani (Eds.), Types for Proofs and Programs. X, 409 pages. 2004.

Vol. 3084: A. Persson, J. Stirna (Eds.), Advanced Information Systems Engineering. XIV, 596 pages. 2004.

Vol. 3083: W. Emmerich, A.L. Wolf (Eds.), Component Deployment. X, 249 pages. 2004.

Vol. 3078: S. Cotin, D.N. Metaxas (Eds.), Medical Simulation. XVI, 296 pages. 2004.

Vol. 3077: F. Roli, J. Kittler, T. Windeatt (Eds.), Multiple Classifier Systems. XII, 386 pages. 2004.

Vol. 3076: D. Buell (Ed.), Algorithmic Number Theory. XI, 451 pages. 2004.

Vol. 3074: B. Kuijpers, P. Revesz (Eds.), Constraint Databases and Applications. XII, 181 pages. 2004.

Vol. 3073: H. Chen, R. Moore, D.D. Zeng, J. Leavitt (Eds.), Intelligence and Security Informatics. XV, 536 pages. 2004.

Vol. 3070: L. Rutkowski, J. Siekmann, R. Tadeusiewicz, L.A. Zadeh (Eds.), Artificial Intelligence and Soft Computing - ICAISC 2004. XXV, 1208 pages. 2004. (Subseries LNAI).

Vol. 3066: S. Tsumoto, R. S lowiński, J. Komorowski, J.W. Grzymala-Busse (Eds.), Rough Sets and Current Trends in Computing. XX, 853 pages. 2004. (Subseries LNAI).

Vol. 3065: A. Lomuscio, D. Nute (Eds.), Deontic Logic in Computer Science. X, 275 pages. 2004. (Subseries LNAI).

Vol. 3064: D. Bienstock, G. Nemhauser (Eds.), Integer Programming and Combinatorial Optimization. XI, 445 pages. 2004.

Vol. 3063: A. Llamosí, A. Strohmeier (Eds.), Reliable Software Technologies - Ada-Europe 2004. XIII, 333 pages. 2004.

Vol. 3062: J.L. Pfaltz, M. Nagl, B. Böhlen (Eds.), Applications of Graph Transformations with Industrial Relevance. XV, 500 pages. 2004.

Vol. 3060: A.Y. Tawfik, S.D. Goodwin (Eds.), Advances in Artificial Intelligence. XIII, 582 pages. 2004. (Subseries LNAI).

Vol. 3059: C.C. Ribeiro, S.L. Martins (Eds.), Experimental and Efficient Algorithms. X, 586 pages. 2004.

Vol. 3058: N. Sebe, M.S. Lew, T.S. Huang (Eds.), Computer Vision in Human-Computer Interaction. X, 233 pages. 2004.

Vol. 3056: H. Dai, R. Srikant, C. Zhang (Eds.), Advances in Knowledge Discovery and Data Mining. XIX, 713 pages. 2004. (Subseries LNAI).

Vol. 3054: I. Crnkovic, J.A. Stafford, H.W. Schmidt, K. Wallnau (Eds.), Component-Based Software Engineering. XI, 311 pages. 2004.

Vol. 3053: C. Bussler, J. Davies, D. Fensel, R. Studer (Eds.), The Semantic Web: Research and Applications. XIII, 490 pages. 2004.

Vol. 3052: W. Zimmermann, B. Thalheim (Eds.), Abstract State Machines 2004. Advances in Theory and Practice. XII, 235 pages. 2004.

Vol. 3051: R. Berghammer, B. Möller, G. Struth (Eds.), Relational and Kleene-Algebraic Methods in Computer Science. X, 279 pages. 2004.

Vol. 3050: J. Domingo-Ferrer, V. Torra (Eds.), Privacy in Statistical Databases. IX, 367 pages. 2004.

Vol. 3047: F. Oquendo, B. Warboys, R. Morrison (Eds.), Software Architecture. X, 279 pages. 2004.

Vol. 3046: A. Laganà, M.L. Gavrilova, V. Kumar, Y. Mun, C.K. Tan, O. Gervasi (Eds.), Computational Science and Its Applications – ICCSA 2004. LIII, 1016 pages. 2004.

Vol. 3045: A. Laganà, M.L. Gavrilova, V. Kumar, Y. Mun, C.K. Tan, O. Gervasi (Eds.), Computational Science and Its Applications – ICCSA 2004. LIII, 1040 pages. 2004.

Vol. 3044: A. Laganà, M.L. Gavrilova, V. Kumar, Y. Mun, C.K. Tan, O. Gervasi (Eds.), Computational Science and Its Applications – ICCSA 2004. LIII, 1140 pages. 2004.

Vol. 3043: A. Laganà, M.L. Gavrilova, V. Kumar, Y. Mun, C.K. Tan, O. Gervasi (Eds.), Computational Science and Its Applications – ICCSA 2004. LIII, 1180 pages. 2004.

Vol. 3042: N. Mitrou, K. Kontovasilis, G.N. Rouskas, I. Iliadis, L. Merakos (Eds.), NETWORKING 2004, Networking Technologies, Services, and Protocols; Performance of Computer and Communication Networks; Mobile and Wireless Communications. XXXIII, 1519 pages. 2004.

Vol. 3039: M. Bubak, G.D.v. Albada, P.M. Sloot, J.J. Dongarra (Eds.), Computational Science - ICCS 2004. LXVI, 1271 pages. 2004.

Vol. 3038: M. Bubak, G.D.v. Albada, P.M. Sloot, J.J. Dongarra (Eds.), Computational Science - ICCS 2004. LXVI, 1311 pages. 2004.

Vol. 3037: M. Bubak, G.D.v. Albada, P.M. Sloot, J.J. Dongarra (Eds.), Computational Science - ICCS 2004. LXVI, 745 pages. 2004.

Vol. 3036: M. Bubak, G.D.v. Albada, P.M. Sloot, J.J. Dongarra (Eds.), Computational Science - ICCS 2004. LXVI, 713 pages. 2004.

Vol. 3035: M.A. Wimmer (Ed.), Knowledge Management in Electronic Government. XII, 326 pages. 2004. (Subseries LNAI).

Vol. 3034: J. Favela, E. Menasalvas, E. Chávez (Eds.), Advances in Web Intelligence. XIII, 227 pages. 2004. (Subseries LNAI).

Vol. 3033: M. Li, X.-H. Sun, Q. Deng, J. Ni (Eds.), Grid and Cooperative Computing. XXXVIII, 1076 pages. 2004.

Vol. 3032: M. Li, X.-H. Sun, Q. Deng, J. Ni (Eds.), Grid and Cooperative Computing. XXXVII, 1112 pages. 2004.

Vol. 3031: A. Butz, A. Krüger, P. Olivier (Eds.), Smart Graphics. X, 165 pages. 2004.

Vol. 3030: P. Giorgini, B. Henderson-Sellers, M. Winikoff (Eds.), Agent-Oriented Information Systems. XIV, 207 pages. 2004. (Subseries LNAI).

Vol. 3029: B. Orchard, C. Yang, M. Ali (Eds.), Innovations in Applied Artificial Intelligence. XXI, 1272 pages. 2004. (Subseries LNAI).

Vol. 3028: D. Neuenschwander, Probabilistic and Statistical Methods in Cryptology. X, 158 pages. 2004.

Vol. 3027: C. Cachin, J. Camenisch (Eds.), Advances in Cryptology - EUROCRYPT 2004. XI, 628 pages. 2004.

Vol. 3026: C. Ramamoorthy, R. Lee, K.W. Lee (Eds.), Software Engineering Research and Applications. XV, 377 pages. 2004.

Vol. 3025: G.A. Vouros, T. Panayiotopoulos (Eds.), Methods and Applications of Artificial Intelligence. XV, 546 pages. 2004. (Subseries LNAI).

Vol. 3024: T. Pajdla, J. Matas (Eds.), Computer Vision - ECCV 2004. XXVIII, 621 pages. 2004.

Vol. 3023: T. Pajdla, J. Matas (Eds.), Computer Vision - ECCV 2004. XXVIII, 611 pages. 2004.

Vol. 3022: T. Pajdla, J. Matas (Eds.), Computer Vision - ECCV 2004. XXVIII, 621 pages. 2004.

Vol. 3021: T. Pajdla, J. Matas (Eds.), Computer Vision - ECCV 2004. XXVIII, 633 pages. 2004.

Vol. 3019: R. Wyrzykowski, J.J. Dongarra, M. Paprzycki, J. Wasniewski (Eds.), Parallel Processing and Applied Mathematics. XIX, 1174 pages. 2004.

Vol. 3016: C. Lengauer, D. Batory, C. Consel, M. Odersky (Eds.), Domain-Specific Program Generation. XII, 325 pages. 2004.

Vol. 3015: C. Barakat, I. Pratt (Eds.), Passive and Active Network Measurement. XI, 300 pages. 2004.

Vol. 3014: F. van der Linden (Ed.), Software Product-Family Engineering. IX, 486 pages. 2004.

Vol. 3012: K. Kurumatani, S.-H. Chen, A. Ohuchi (Eds.), Multi-Agnets for Mass User Support. X, 217 pages. 2004. (Subseries LNAI).

Vol. 3011: J.-C. Régin, M. Rueher (Eds.), Integration of AI and OR Techniques in Constraint Programming for Combinatorial Optimization Problems. XI, 415 pages. 2004.

Vol. 3010: K.R. Apt, F. Fages, F. Rossi, P. Szeredi, J. Váncza (Eds.), Recent Advances in Constraints. VIII, 285 pages. 2004. (Subseries LNAI).

Vol. 3009: F. Bomarius, H. Iida (Eds.), Product Focused Software Process Improvement. XIV, 584 pages. 2004.

Vol. 3008: S. Heuel, Uncertain Projective Geometry. XVII, 205 pages. 2004.

Vol. 3007: J.X. Yu, X. Lin, H. Lu, Y. Zhang (Eds.), Advanced Web Technologies and Applications. XXII, 936 pages. 2004.

Vol. 3006: M. Matsui, R. Zuccherato (Eds.), Selected Areas in Cryptography. XI, 361 pages. 2004.

Vol. 3005: G.R. Raidl, S. Cagnoni, J. Branke, D.W. Corne, R. Drechsler, Y. Jin, C.G. Johnson, P. Machado, E. Marchiori, F. Rothlauf, G.D. Smith, G. Squillero (Eds.), Applications of Evolutionary Computing. XVII, 562 pages. 2004.

Vol. 3004: J. Gottlieb, G.R. Raidl (Eds.), Evolutionary Computation in Combinatorial Optimization. X, 241 pages. 2004.

Vol. 3003: M. Keijzer, U.-M. O'Reilly, S.M. Lucas, E. Costa, T. Soule (Eds.), Genetic Programming. XI, 410 pages. 2004.

Vol. 3002: D.L. Hicks (Ed.), Metainformatics. X, 213 pages. 2004.

Vol. 3001: A. Ferscha, F. Mattern (Eds.), Pervasive Computing. XVII, 358 pages. 2004.

Vol. 2999: E.A. Boiten, J. Derrick, G. Smith (Eds.), Integrated Formal Methods. XI, 541 pages. 2004.

Vol. 2998: Y. Kameyama, P.J. Stuckey (Eds.), Functional and Logic Programming. X, 307 pages. 2004.

Vol. 2997: S. McDonald, J. Tait (Eds.), Advances in Information Retrieval. XIII, 427 pages. 2004.

Vol. 2996: V. Diekert, M. Habib (Eds.), STACS 2004. XVI, 658 pages. 2004.

Vol. 2995: C. Jensen, S. Poslad, T. Dimitrakos (Eds.), Trust Management. XIII, 377 pages. 2004.

Vol. 2994: E. Rahm (Ed.), Data Integration in the Life Sciences. X, 221 pages. 2004. (Subseries LNBI).

Vol. 2993: R. Alur, G.J. Pappas (Eds.), Hybrid Systems: Computation and Control. XII, 674 pages. 2004.

Vol. 2992: E. Bertino, S. Christodoulakis, D. Plexousakis, V. Christophides, M. Koubarakis, K. Böhm, E. Ferrari (Eds.), Advances in Database Technology - EDBT 2004. XVIII, 877 pages. 2004.

Vol. 2991: R. Alt, A. Frommer, R.B. Kearfott, W. Luther (Eds.), Numerical Software with Result Verification. X, 315 pages. 2004.

Vol. 2990: J. Leite, A. Omicini, L. Sterling, P. Torroni (Eds.), Declarative Agent Languages and Technologies. XII, 281 pages. 2004. (Subseries LNAI).

Vol. 2989: S. Graf, L. Mounier (Eds.), Model Checking Software. X, 309 pages. 2004.

Vol. 2988: K. Jensen, A. Podelski (Eds.), Tools and Algorithms for the Construction and Analysis of Systems. XIV, 608 pages. 2004.

Vol. 2987: I. Walukiewicz (Ed.), Foundations of Software Science and Computation Structures. XIII, 529 pages. 2004.

Vol. 2986: D. Schmidt (Ed.), Programming Languages and Systems. XII, 417 pages. 2004.